Cambridge Studies in Early Modern British History

JOHN LOCKE

Cambridge Studies in Early Modern British History

Series editors

ANTHONY FLETCHER
Professor of Modern History, University of Durham

JOHN GUY
Professor of Modern History,
University of St Andrews

and JOHN MORRILL
Reader in Early Modern History, University of Cambridge, and
Fellow and Tutor of Selwyn College

This is a series of monographs and studies covering many aspects of the history of the British Isles between the late fifteenth century and the early eighteenth century. It includes the work of established scholars and pioneering work by a new generation of scholars. It includes both reviews and revisions of major topics and books which open up new historical terrain or which reveal startling new perspectives on familiar subjects. All the volumes set detailed research into broader perspectives and the books are intended for the use of students as well as of their teachers.

For a list of titles in the series, see end of book

JOHN LOCKE
Resistance,
Religion and Responsibility

JOHN MARSHALL
Assistant Professor of History, University of Denver

CAMBRIDGE
UNIVERSITY PRESS

Published by the Press Syndicate of the University of Cambridge
The Pitt Building, Trumpington Street, Cambridge CB2 1RP
40 West 20th Street, New York, NY 10011-4211 USA
10 Stamford Road, Oakleigh, Melbourne 3166, Australia

© Cambridge University Press 1994

First published 1994
Reprinted 1996

Printed in Great Britain by Athenæum Press Ltd, Gateshead, Tyne & Wear

A catalogue record for this book is available from the British Library

Library of Congress cataloguing in publication data
Marshall, John, 1961–
John Locke: resistance, religion and responsibility / John Marshall.
    p.   cm. – (Cambridge studies in early modern British history)
Includes bibliographical references and index.
ISBN 0 521 44380 6 (hc)
1. Locke, John, 1632–1704 – Political and social views.
2. Locke, John, 1632–1704 – Religion. I. Title. II. Series.
B1297.M34   1994
192–dc20   93-30796 CIP

ISBN 0 521 44380 6 hardback
ISBN 0 521 44687 3 paperback

1002626400

CE

For Nina, Eileen and Walter

CONTENTS

ACKNOWLEDGEMENTS

Many debts have been incurred during the creation of this book. For support during research I would like to thank the History Department of the Johns Hopkins University. For electing me into a Research Fellowship, and thus for supporting the final stages of research, I would like to thank the previous Master of Peterhouse, Cambridge, Lord Dacre, and the present Master and Fellows. Ray Sun, Clive Lambert, Ian Brown, Oonagh Bathgate, Matthew Arcus, Sylvia Carter, Justin Champion, Roy Porter, John Theibault, Lisa Rosner, Jeff and Rosemarie Ostler, Joe Fracchia, Cynthia Brokaw, Richard Stephenson, Randall Macgowen, George Sheridan, Bob Lang, Peter Parshall, Lisa Steinman, Mark Bedau, David Sacks, Ray Kierstead, Chris Lowe and Jacqueline Dirks provided help at moments when I needed it. Sheila and Philip Solomon deserve many thanks for support and friendship. For their enormous emotional help over many years, all of the members of my family, and especially my mother, deserve many more thanks than they have ever received. Fred Conrad taught me the meaning of *amicitia*, and much else besides.

For encouragement and discussions of Locke, or for reading and commenting upon various sections, I am grateful to Michael Ayers, Brendan Bradshaw, Henry Chadwick, Colin Davis, John Dunn, Jack Fruchtman, Robert Iliffe, Richard Kroll, John Rogers, Jonathon Scott, Sandy Stewart, Martyn Thompson, Richard Tuck, Perez Zagorin and the audiences of the many seminars and conferences where materials included in this book were presented. Orest Ranum, Nancy Struever and Jerry Schneewind will recognise elements of this story that were first explored in MA fields that they taught, and I am very grateful to them for many suggestions and much inspiration. The work on Locke of scholars far too numerous to name has influenced me considerably, but it would be unjust not to single out in addition to those noted later the works of John Dunn, Neal Wood, David McNally, Jeremy Waldron, James Tully, and Richard Ashcraft. The arguments that follow are deeply indebted to all of these scholars, even where my disagreements with them are most pronounced.

David Wootton's work on Locke and Justin Champion's studies of late seventeenth-century religion and politics have significantly influenced elements of this book. They have each commented at various stages upon major sections of this book. John Morrill has been an exemplary editor, demonstrating a devotion far beyond the call of duty. All three have given me the kind of friendship, support and encouragement that helps considerably in the bleakest moments of research and writing. As an undergraduate at Churchill College under the supervision of Mark Goldie I became interested in intellectual history, and his suggestions and inspiration have improved almost everything that I have since written, including this book. His own interpretations of Locke's religious contexts have significantly influenced the work that follows. My account of Locke is similarly influenced by the interpretations of Locke's political contexts composed over many years by my Ph.D supervisor, John Pocock. He has inspired me in person and through his writings for many years, has suffered several drafts of this book as an inordinately lengthy thesis, and has made suggestions which have considerably sharpened its final arguments. The mistakes that remain are, unfortunately, my own.

My greatest debt of all is to my wife, Nina. It cannot be put into words.

Elements of the interpretations in this book were originally sketched in 'The Ecclesiology of the Latitude-Men 1660–89: Stillingfleet, Tillotson and "Hobbism"', *The Journal of Ecclesiastical History* 36 (1985), 407–27; 'The Religious, Educational and Moral Thought of John Locke', *Historical Journal* 33: 2 (1990), 997–1007 and 'John Locke and Latitudinarianism' in R. Kroll, R. Ashcraft and P. Zagorin (eds.), *Philosophy, Science and Religion in England 1640–1700* (1992), 253–82. All were published by Cambridge University Press. My thanks are due to the Keeper of Western Manuscripts, Bodleian Library, Oxford for permission to study and quote from the Locke manuscripts.

ABBREVIATIONS

The following abbreviations are used in the notes for works by Locke that are frequently cited.

Correspondence   *The Correspondence of John Locke*, 8 vols. + index, ed. E. S. De Beer, Oxford 1978– . References are to volume and letter

Discourses   John Locke, *Discourses Translated From Nicole's Essais*, ed. T. Hancock, London 1828

Education   John Locke, *Some Thoughts Concerning Education*, ed. J. Axtell, Cambridge 1969

Essay   John Locke, *An Essay Concerning Human Understanding*, ed. P. Nidditch, Oxford 1978

Letter   John Locke, *A Letter Concerning Toleration*, ed. J. Tully, Indianapolis 1983 unless indicated as ed. R. Klibansky and J. Gough, Oxford 1968

Library   *The Library Catalogue of John Locke*, ed. P. Laslett and J. Harrison, Oxford 1965

Paraphrase   John Locke, *A Paraphrase Upon the Epistles of St Paul*, ed. A. Wainwright, Oxford 1989

Reasonableness   *The Reasonableness of Christianity*, in Works, VII (see below)

Tracts   John Locke, *Two Tracts Upon Government*, ed. P. Abrams, Cambridge 1969

Treatises   John Locke, *Two Treatises of Government*, ed. P. Laslett, Cambridge 1963 unless noted as 1987

Works   John Locke, *The Works of John Locke*, 9 vols., London 1794 or 10 vols., London 1801 as indicated

INTRODUCTION: LOCKE'S INTELLECTUAL DEVELOPMENT

At the Restoration of the Stuart monarchy and of the Church of England in 1660–2 John Locke supported almost none of the positions of the *Two Treatises* and the *Essay Concerning Human Understanding* that have made him the subject of continuing study. In the early 1660s Locke appears to have been a believer in innate ideas as the foundation of much of morality and religion. He was an unequivocal opponent of religious toleration and of rights of resistance and was instead a supporter of absolute and arbitrary government in all civil and ecclesiastical 'indifferent' matters – that is, those matters that were not expressly commanded or forbidden in Scripture. He countenanced a consensual source of governmental authority only as a theoretical possibility irrelevant to its extent.

During the following twenty-five years Locke became the strong opponent of innatism that is now famous from the *Essay*; the leading theoretician in England of religious toleration in several *Letters Concerning Toleration*; and the advocate of limited government, of rights of resistance, and of the necessity of individual consent to political society in the *Treatises*. Between the early 1660s and the 1690s he changed from being a trinitarian who very probably held a strong view of the Fall and of original sin – in common with almost all of his contemporaries – to becoming at the least heterodox in his expressions about the Trinity and original sin and very probably in private an unitarian heretic. Although Locke's moral and social thought throughout his life emphasised the need for extensive services towards other men and accepted considerable social subjection, Locke moved from advocacy of this extensive service to others at one's own loss to an hedonic psychology legitimating pursuit of one's own interests and making the pleasures received from service to others and the rewards of God central to the performance of such service.

Many of the best accounts of Locke's thought describe his mature commitments to free intellectual enquiry in religion and morality, to freedom of the press, to religious toleration, and to political liberty. This book will not focus upon the links between these different areas of Locke's mature thought. Instead, it will examine in detail the historical development of

xv

Locke's political, religious, moral and social thought throughout his entire life. The conjunction of support for religious, intellectual and political liberty in Locke's thought in the 1690s will be shown to have been in significant part the result of external influences from the varied political, religious, social and moral causes which Locke supported between the late 1660s and the 1690s, and in significant part of intensive personal reflection, particularly influenced by massive reading and by a series of significant encounters in years spent on the Continent with works by Dutch, French, Polish and Hungarian authors.

The enterprise undertaken in this book is therefore somewhat similar to that of John Dunn's *The Political Thought of John Locke*, although broader in its study of religious and moral thought and more contextually oriented. Dunn's work provides the best available study of the internal development of Locke's political thought, arguing that Locke's politics in the *Two Treatises* are explained by elements of his own thought, particularly by his religious commitments, and by his intensive confrontation with the thought of Sir Robert Filmer in the context of the Exclusion crisis. This analysis will be examined as part of a broad consideration of the extent to which the politics of the *Two Treatises* can plausibly be explained by having been written as a response to the works of Sir Robert Filmer, and by Locke's desire to compose part of a treatise of ethics, on the basis of Locke's preceding commitments. It will be suggested that this analysis does not provide a sufficiently plausible explanation of Locke's composition of the central argument for resistance in the Second Treatise.

This book will endorse the argument of Richard Ashcraft's *Revolutionary Politics and Locke's Two Treatises of Government* that Locke's Second Treatise was in significant part shaped by Locke having been involved in justifying and in actively planning armed resistance to Charles II. In an analysis which has enormously advanced the possibility of an accurate understanding of the text, Ashcraft has argued that the central argument for resistance in the Second Treatise was composed in order to urge resistance in 1681–3. Very much of Ashcraft's case will be supported, but some of Ashcraft's suggestions about dating and about the audience for Locke's arguments will be questioned. This book will suggest that the burden of the Second Treatise was probably very largely written not as early as early 1681, as Ashcraft implies, but instead in 1682 (or even 1683) in order to be published once the resistance which was by then being actively planned had at least already commenced. This book will briefly describe the social implications of the Second Treatise and indicate the limits to the change in the form of the government that Locke's text allowed, suggesting that Locke was primarily attempting to justify to the gentry, yeomanry and merchants a rare and limited resistance to the monarch which would not threaten the social hierarchy and lay the foundations for anarchy or for frequent challenge to the political establishment and which was perfectly compatible with the re-establishment of a mixed monarchy with different personnel.

The provision of this historical explanation of the composition and intended meaning of the Second Treatise is only one of the aims of this book, although it stands physically at the centre of this work. The second major task of this book is to provide a broader historical description of Locke's moral and social thought than is available to readers who concentrate upon the *Two Treatises* because that was a work written to justify resistance and not to describe more than a small part either of the society that Locke saw around him or of the society that he wished to see develop in England. Locke's *Essays on the Law of Nature* of 1663–4 will be shown to have exalted service to other men being undertaken at one's own loss; although Locke amended this notion to include a greater legitimation of individuals' pursuit of their own interests as he developed an hedonic psychology by the mid-1670s, his major ethical response to the development of an hedonic psychology was to place an ever greater stress upon God's rewards for (in his eyes) a still extensive service of others. Locke's shamefully neglected translation of Nicole's *Essais de Morale* in the mid-1670s established this ethos of men serving men as much as they could, and their being motivated to serve God and their fellow men on the basis of God's secure rewards for such service, at almost the same moment that Locke became explicitly and intensely committed to an hedonic psychology. Nicole's work also influenced Locke's definitions of the virtues, particularly of civility. An ethic of service to others continued to be important to Locke throughout the remainder of his life, including the period of composition and publication of the *Two Treatises*. By the end of his life Locke was declaring not merely that Christianity made virtue 'visibly . . . the best bargain' but also that it required service to other men as much as if we were their 'vassals and bondmen'. This ethic, particularly in its elements of liberality and civility, will be connected to Locke's own frequently-avowed social identity as a gentleman who was concerned at many points in his life with emphasising the responsibilities of service to others involved in a 'Gentleman's calling', and with performing these duties himself.

Towards the end of his life John Locke composed chronologies of the lives of two individuals. One was Jesus Christ. The other was Cicero. Locke advocated Cicero's *De Officiis* as the work other than the Bible setting out the principles of morality by which children should be educated. Locke's own recommendations and reading of *De Officiis* will therefore be anatomised, and will allow the reconciliation of the different elements of Locke's politics and ethics; of industriousness and acquisitiveness with service to others and to one's country. For Cicero, it was legitimate to pursue one's own interests as long as one did so with justice, with the recognition that one's friends, family and country 'claimed a share', and with devotion of appropriate amounts of one's wealth and efforts to beneficence. Such pursuit of one's own interests was in fact necessary to provide the means for such beneficence. It was this vision, it will be suggested, that Locke would have placed at the centre of the extended book of ethics that he frequently promised to friends who knew him as author of the *Two Treatises*, and who never for a moment thought that that work set out the majority of Locke's social or ethical vision.

Locke never composed this book of ethics, very probably in large measure because he could not see how to integrate fully his hedonic psychology and his account of men's duties to other men and did not accept contemporary accounts that generated duties to serve others on the basis of terrestrial self-interest. A second very major inhibition to composition of his 'book of offices' was his inability to demonstrate the rewards and punishments attached to natural law. While Locke probably continued to believe – or at the least fervently to hope – that this was a soluble problem, he never succeeded in solving it, and he came to rely increasingly upon revelation. His discussions of the content of ethics at the end of his life were published in a series of religious works, most notably the *Reasonableness of Christianity* and the *Paraphrase Upon the Epistles of St Paul*.

Although most obviously crucial to Locke as he neared death and composed several works of biblical exegesis and commentary, Locke's religious commitments were influential throughout his entire life. Locke's theology has been accurately described by Dunn as the central axiom of his political theory. For Ashcraft, Locke's practical religious commitments and his association with an 'ideology of dissent' were central to the development of his political arguments for resistance. Locke's religious views were alleged to be important to the shaping of the *Essay* within a few years of its publication: the most significant contemporary accusations against Locke's epistemology were prompted by its assault upon innatism and by the belief of critics such as Leibniz and Bishop Edward Stillingfleet that it favoured Socinianism, the heretical denial of the Trinity.

Yet Locke's religious thought has been very little studied. As one commentator observed, a profound study of his theology is 'a striking gap in the literature'.[1] As a result of this paucity of study, contradictory estimates of Locke's religious thought have abounded even in the best works on his

[1] G. Parry, *John Locke*, Manchester (1978), 28. Since Parry's comment, W. Spellman, *Locke and the Problem of Depravity*, Oxford (1988) and A. Wainwright (ed.), John Locke, *A Paraphrase and Notes Upon the Epistles of St Paul*, Oxford (1989), 2 vols., I, introduction have valuably described many of the details of Locke's theology, but each is limited in

thought. Boxing the compass of Protestantism, Locke has been seen as essentially Calvinist, an ideologist of dissent, a Latitudinarian Anglican or Arminian, and an unitarian (or Socinian).[2] The third major task of this book is therefore the description and analysis of the major dimensions of Locke's relatively neglected religious thought, including his own church affiliations, his thought on religious toleration, his analysis of the nature of church and state, his attacks on the powers of 'priests' of all religions, and his increasingly heterodox theological commitments and scriptural methodology in an age of sophisticated biblical hermeneutics.

It will be shown that Locke was a member of the Church of England from its re-establishment in 1662 to the end of his life, and that descriptions of him as effectively an 'ideologist of dissent' because of his support for religious toleration, as in Richard Ashcraft's *Revolutionary Politics*, may obscure as much as they reveal. Locke's initial advocacy of magisterial authority over the church and hostility to the excesses of Interregnum clericalism, sectarianism and enthusiasm will be established. It will be shown that when Locke became an advocate of toleration he remained persistently suspicious of dissenting arguments for toleration, a suspiciousness bred by mid-century puritan intolerance. Locke's support from 1667 for toleration within the established church, or comprehension, as well as support for toleration outside of its boundaries, will be described and linked in part to Locke's friendship with a number of Anglican Latitudinarians in the 1670s. Locke's arguments and especially his venomously anticlerical tolerationism will, however, be contrasted strongly with the arguments of most Latitudinarians as well as with the arguments expressed by contemporary dissenters in debates over toleration. Locke's commitment to comprehension and toleration and his significant distances from the arguments both of the leading Latitudinarians and of leading dissenters will be shown to have continued even in 1681, shortly before – or, in other scholars' accounts, in the period when – he was composing the Second Treatise.

It will be shown that in later years Locke's belief that toleration within

scope and Spellman's work is misleading on some points. See my 'John Locke's Religious, Educational and Moral Thought', *Historical Journal* 33:2 (1990), 997–1007 and below passim.

[2] Among other accounts, the views are respectively set out most clearly by J. Dunn, *The Political Thought of John Locke*, Cambridge (1969); R. Ashcraft, *Revolutionary Politics and Locke's Two Treatises of Government*, Princeton (1986); Spellman, *Locke*; and H. McLachlan, *The Religious Opinions of Milton, Locke and Newton*, Manchester (1941). Dunn was far more concerned with accurate description of Locke as deeply religious and not secular and 'possessive individualist' than with suggesting that Locke was essentially Calvinist rather than Arminian or unitarian, as his account indicated at various points.

the church could be achieved in the foreseeable future declined, but that this nonetheless remained a significant ideal for the English church. The development of Locke's arguments for religious toleration will be traced, with identification of the points at which his early arguments from the separate purposes of church and state were combined with arguments from his developing scriptural methodology, from his firm epistemological distinction of faith and reason, from his belief in the importance of persuasion and civility, and from his theological commitments. It will be suggested that until the early 1680s the driving forces of Locke's religious thought came from his political concerns and his epistemological investigations, both guided by substantial anticlericalism, and that from about 1680, and especially after 1683, under the impact of much reading and of crucial years in France and the Netherlands, Locke became fully integrated into the 'republic of letters' and became much more interested in sophisticated biblical criticism and broader theological investigations.

The paucity of discussions of theology in Locke's early years will prevent more than a number of strong hints about the complexion of Locke's theology before 1683 being validly teased from Locke's manuscripts. It will be indicated, however, that this lack of material was in part the result of conscious reflection on Locke's part: that he was unable to reconcile a number of theological positions, most notably man's free agency and God's omniscient omnipotence, and that he resolved to maintain these very broad commitments without understanding how they could all be true. It will be argued, partly on the basis of Locke's 1676 translation of Pierre Nicole's *Essais de Morale*, that at least until the later 1670s Locke maintained a view of man as having inherited considerable sinful dispositions from the Adamic lapse.

Locke's unitarianism in the mid-1690s has long been alleged by scholars, but never proven. A large number of notes indicating Socinian reading by Locke, never before studied, and a lengthy manuscript, probably by Locke himself, which has been only very briefly and inadequately discussed by two other scholars, will be analysed. It will be suggested that Locke had very probably become unitarian in his view of Christ by the mid-1690s at the latest. Examination of the *Reasonableness of Christianity*, the *Paraphrase Upon the Epistles of St Paul*, and a number of theological manuscripts from the 1690s will show that Locke was similarly broadly unitarian in his denial of inherited original sin in the mid-to-late 1690s. It will be argued, however, that Locke's intellectual commitment to eclecticism throughout his life invalidates any simple description of Locke as Socinian in a systematic, dogmatic sense.

Ending this book with Locke's Unitarianism, tolerationism, credal minimalism and assault upon 'priestcraft' is important in describing the culmination of Locke's intellectual trajectory. Locke's heterodox or heretical religious, political and epistemological views in his works of the late 1680s and 1690s significantly contributed to the enlightened heterodoxy that spread widely over the next century through the thought of such authors as le Clerc, Voltaire and Priestley. As early as the 1690s Locke's friends began to describe his works as crucial in dispelling the priests' 'Empire of darkness'. By the time of his death Locke was friends with free-thinkers and deists such as Anthony Collins and Matthew Tindall. Since Locke's dissemination of religious and epistemological views corrosive of religious orthodoxy and of the political power of the priesthood was perhaps his most important contribution to the thought of the following century, analysis of this dimension of his thought provides an extremely appropriate conclusion to this book.

Part I

RELIGION AND THE POLITICS
OF TOLERATION

1

Against the 'tyranny of a religious rage'

I

John Locke was baptised into the Church of England at Wrington in Somerset in 1632. He was almost certainly brought up as a Calvinist. His family seem to have been Anglican communicants in the 1630s and presbyterians at the time of the establishment of presbyterian classes in Somerset in 1647. Like almost all of those with presbyterian sympathies up to the Restoration, his family very probably did not believe in the significant but still very limited degree of religious toleration that was supported by such sects as Independents as a 'liberty of conscience' – a 'toleration' which excluded at least all those people that these groups defined as 'heretics', 'blasphemers' and 'idolators' and as therefore unable to claim 'conscience'. Locke's family and their friends probably instead believed with most presbyterians that there should be one uniform church in the nation, with the devolution of some disciplinary powers from bishops to presbyters and significant revisions of the liturgy to reduce the similarities to Roman Catholic forms of worship which had been retained during the sixteenth-century English Reformation.

Locke's paternal grandfather Nicholas Locke had bequeathed money for weekly Bible lectures, a form of bequest that was often an indication of Calvinist beliefs. Locke's father, John Locke senior, served on the Parliamentarian side in the Civil War in 1642 and 1643 in the troop of his patron Alexander Popham. He was probably therefore a member of Popham's troop when it attacked windows, organs, fonts and the bishop's seat in Wells Cathedral in 1643. A notebook dating from the 1630s to 1650s, later used by Locke himself, suggests, however, that John Locke senior may well not have made up his mind on disputed issues such as paedobaptism and bowing at the name of Jesus as late as the 1640s and 1650s, and that he was probably a moderate presbyterian: he was apparently very interested in Archbishop Ussher's 1641 attempts to secure compromise between episco-

3

palians and presbyterians, taking several pages of notes on Ussher's plans to 'reduce' episcopacy.[1]

The rest of Locke's family in Somerset seem to have been similarly inclined to Calvinist presbyterianism. The establishment of presbyterian classes in Somerset in 1647 involved a devolution of church power to presbyterian elders and a replacement by the Elders of some Anglican vicars that was unacceptable to many high Anglicans, but which more moderate Anglicans saw as a reasonable compromise, and which was not intended by the presbyterians to be an attack on the need for one uniform church. Edmund Keene, Locke's cousin on his mother's side of the family, was appointed an Elder of Wrington itself. Locke's uncle Peter Locke, his father's deeply pious brother, was similarly appointed an Elder at nearby Chew Magna and helped to evict their Anglican vicar. No evidence survives concerning the theological or ecclesiological commitments of Locke's mother Agnes, but Locke later described her as a 'very pious woman'. It is at least likely that she shared the attitudes of her husband and the rest of their family, particularly because of the influence upon her of the rector of Wrington, Dr Samuel Crook, who was puritanically inclined although not a separatist. Crook was mistrustful of the Book of Common Prayer, frequently the preacher of three sermons a day, and often in trouble with the Laudian bishop of Bath and Wells, William Piers. Puritans had been presented for travelling miles to hear his sermons as early as 1620, and he unsurprisingly continued as rector at Wrington after the 1647 ejections of high Anglicans elsewhere in Somerset.[2] The influence of Alexander Popham surely reinforced still further Locke's familial outlook. In addition to leading his troop in destruction of 'popish' elements of Anglicanism at Wells Cathedral in 1643, Popham was appointed an Elder in Somerset in 1647, and was the leading presbyterian of his Somerset community. He was the patron of Locke senior and then of Locke himself; Locke called Popham his 'god'.[3]

It is difficult to gauge the effect of Westminster School on Locke. Despite parliamentary control from 1646 the school remained under the immediate direction of Dr Richard Busby. When the King was executed at Westminster next to the school in 1649 Busby made all of the students pray for Charles' soul. There is little sign of even a significant Calvinist tinge to the education of Westminster students, and the school retained throughout

[1] M. Cranston, *John Locke*, Oxford (1957), 4n.1, 16; BM Add. MSS 28273, 31, 129v–30, 131–5v.
[2] Cranston, *Locke*, 1–2, 13; *Tracts*, 49; W. A. Shaw, *The History of the English Church during the Civil War* (1900), II, appendix 3, pp. 413–15; *Correspondence*, I, 306; 443; II, 511; 712; 733; 767.
[3] Cranston, *Locke*, 14–17, 27, 29; *Correspondence*, I, 6, 8, 96.

Locke's years there its traditional emphasis upon classical texts and Latin exercises, nurturing its students on a steady diet of Cicero, Livy and Erasmus rather than Luther and Calvin. Busby was a staunch Anglican, proudly declaring in his will that he had always 'lived in the communion of the Church of England', and later boasting of the number of Restoration bishops that he had educated and for whom he had maintained Anglican devotions.[4] In Westminster School Locke may have begun to separate himself intellectually from his Calvinist upbringing. He was certainly old enough to begin to question received views; much older than most Westminster students, he was fifteen when he entered Westminster and twenty when he left it for Oxford. None of Locke's notebooks or letters from these years record any detailed personal theological commitments or any detailed theological reflection at all. It is very tempting in light of Locke's later clear opposition to Calvinism to suggest that this silence involved a deliberate distancing of himself from the theological commitments of so many of his contemporaries, but it may well have involved little more than a concentration of his intellectual energies elsewhere while maintaining his familial Calvinism.[5]

The years following Locke's move to Christ Church, Oxford in 1652, where he was first an undergraduate and then a don, saw Locke once again living in a very highly Calvinist atmosphere, although one that was more Independent than presbyterian, and thus much more inclined to toleration outside of a uniform national church – or within a merely nominal national church – than to the presbyterian ideal of a national church with a uniform liturgy and effective discipline. Locke's reading in these years, about which we know all too little, was not undilutedly Calvinist and Independent, including one of Bishop Hall's devotional tracts, the eirenic Anglican Jeremy Taylor's *Works*, including his plea for toleration, *The Liberty of Prophesying*, and the translation of Joseph Drexel's *Considerations . . . Upon Eternity*, a very popular work in the Interregnum which emphasised very strongly the role of heavenly rewards as a motivation to virtue. There is, remarkably, no evidence of Locke having read in these years any of Calvin's works or even the recently composed *Westminster Confession of Faith*, the high-water mark of Calvinist theology in England, but the theology that poured forth from the Christ Church pulpit was very strongly Calvinist. As head of the college and frequent preacher, John Owen was undoubtedly the dominant figure in college life, and he was the finest expositor of strict Calvinism in both mid-century and Restoration England. Shortly before Locke's time at Christ Church Owen had been a

---

[4] G. F. R. Barker, *Memoir of Busby* (1895), 16, 18, 24, 30, appendix 1.
[5] For an opposing view, Cranston, *Locke*, 19.

leading member of the Westminster Assembly which had drawn up the *Westminster Confession of Faith*. As an undergraduate Locke had to attend at least two sermons a day and give an account of these every Sunday to a person of 'known ability and piety' appointed by Owen. A Calvinist Independent, Thomas Cole, was Locke's tutor, with whom he had to pray every night.[6]

The prevalence of Calvinist theology in Locke's early family and scholarly life is attested most clearly in the comments of Damaris Masham to Jean Le Clerc after Locke's death in 1704. Masham, daughter of the Cambridge Platonist Ralph Cudworth, was at one time Locke's love and the recipient of some truly awful love poetry. She was a very important and close friend, with whom he discussed religious questions from their meeting in 1681, was Locke's hostess for most of the last fourteen years of his life at her house at Oates in Essex, and was reading the Scriptures to him at his bedside when he died. According to Masham, Locke was 'born and had finished his studies at a time when Calvinism was all the fashion in England. But these doctrines had come to be little thought of before I came into the world [1659] and Mr Locke used to speak of the opinions I had been accustomed to at Cambridge, even among the clergy there, as something new and strange to him.' Although Masham did not know Locke until 1681 there is very little reason to doubt this picture of Locke's religious environment in early life.[7]

II

Under Owen Locke may even have become an active supporter of religious toleration in the 1650s, although this seems unlikely. In the mid-1650s Henry Stubbe the younger, a former student at Westminster, recorded that all of the scholars formerly at Westminster School and now at Christ Church were Owen's 'creatures' and noted that they had all promised to support Owen's cause of liberty of conscience. Locke's early notebooks show that Stubbe was recommending to Locke Milton's antipresbyterian *Areopagitica* and the Quaker Anthony Pearson's *Great Question of Tithes Truly Stated*. In 1659 Stubbe published a strong defence of religious toleration, the *Essay in Defence of the Good Old Cause*, which he sent to Locke for comments. According to Stubbe, toleration was necessary because there was no shared infallible interpreter of Scripture. He cited at length Roman

[6] Cranston, *Locke*, 24, 31–2; Locke, *Some Thoughts Concerning Education*, ed. J. Axtell, Cambridge (1969), 28–9; BM Add. MSS 32553 fos. 8–18 cited in *Tracts*, 32; Axtell, *ibid.*, 28–9; MS Locke f11; MS Locke e6.
[7] Amsterdam: Remonstrants' MSS J57A. There is little reason to exhibit the doubt of Spellman, *Locke*, 1 about Locke's familial religiosity.

and especially Hebrew practices of religious toleration and held that these recommended 'the like forbearance'. Stubbe combined his tolerationism with owning 'entirely' the supralapsarian predestinarianism of the puritan William Perkins' 'doctrine of the chain of election', holding that the 'testimony of the private Spirit in the breast of a Saint' guided and obliged the elect, but 'obligeth not others' because to them it was merely tradition and not revelation.[8]

Locke's reply to Stubbe's work was broadly complimentary, with carefully understated criticisms. It is possible to read these comments as indicating a support for toleration of most Protestants, and they do indicate at least a desire for this to be practicable. Locke agreed with Stubbe that it would be 'excellent for men of different persuasions' to 'unite under the same government . . . and march to the same end of peace and mutual society though they take different ways towards heaven'. The only explicit reservation that Locke voiced to Stubbe was that Catholics could not be tolerated since they could not 'obey two different authorities carrying on contrary interests'. Papal claims of infallibility, the power to dispense with oaths, and promise of eternal reward for those who 'did not keep faith with heretics' meant that Roman Catholics could not be tolerated. This early political opposition to toleration for Catholics because they did not need to keep faith with heretics was to be extremely important and to persist throughout Locke's life.[9]

These gently-phrased criticisms of Stubbe's case for toleration and endorsement of the desirability of each going to heaven their own way may not, however, indicate that Locke was a supporter of toleration but rather that one young fellow was giving a slightly more senior fellow of his college comments on the latter's work, particularly since these comments were expressed at a very uncertain moment in the politics of the college and of England, as the leadership of the college quickly changed several times along with the leadership of the nation in the wake of the 1658 death of Oliver Cromwell. Locke's notebooks do not record what Locke thought of the tolerationist works that Stubbe recommended. As Owen's protégé in the cause of toleration, Stubbe was not an unbiassed judge, and Locke was to display a great ability to keep his own opinions secret throughout a college career spent largely in hostile intellectual environments. Locke declared that he wished that Stubbe had made his history of toleration contemporary as well as ancient and surveyed Poland, Holland and

[8] MS Locke f14, 5–9. I am grateful to Dr J. Milton for discussion of this manuscript; H. Stubbe, *An Essay in Defence of the Good Old Cause* (1659), passim, esp. preface; [1–2]; 21; 40; 42; J. Jacob, *Henry Stubbe: Radical Protestantism and the Early Enlightenment*, Cambridge (1983), 9; 18; 31.
[9] Locke, *Two Tracts Upon Government*, ed. P. Abrams, Cambridge (1969), 242–4.

France, a comment that was probably prompted in part because these were contemporary examples of toleration which Stubbe had himself mentioned in passing, but which Locke then significantly contended was necessary to quell the doubts that toleration was 'now practicable'.

It is extreme political anxieties focused upon wars over religion that dominate Locke's writing in these years and underpin this doubt about the practicability of toleration. Locke had been ten when the Civil War broke out, sixteen when the King was executed next to his school, and twenty-six when Oliver Cromwell's death in 1658 plunged England back into political turmoil for two years until the Restoration of Charles II. He had grown up and come to maturity during years when most leaders of Protestant sects claimed the duty to institute a 'thorough' reformation and the right of conscience to resist, and had either been opposed to religious 'toleration' in principle, or attempted to limit religious 'toleration' by arguing that liberty of conscience ought to extend no further than liberty for conscience as they defined this. Religious sectarianism had then created what Locke described as a 'great Bedlam' England, with individuals claiming to be the second Christ or claiming personal inspiration in ways that Locke described to his moderate presbyterian father as 'hot-headed' and 'mad'. It is little wonder that Locke recorded in the *Two Tracts* his frequently-quoted comment that 'I had no sooner found myself in the world than I perceived myself in a storm which hath lasted almost hitherto.' Locke's earliest work in print, published in a 1655 volume of poems to Oliver Cromwell by Oxford fellows, was a poem which celebrated Cromwell almost exclusively as the deliverer of peace and order from chaos. Locke composed a remarkably similar poem to greet Charles' Restoration. His 'Adversaria 1661' indicated that one of the main ends of 'prudentia' was to secure 'Tranquilitas'. Reporting on events to his father in Somerset, Locke's anxiety grew palpably between 1658 and 1660 until in early 1660 he declared that 'I would be quiet and I would be safe.'[10]

Crucially, Locke explicitly identified religious contentions as the major

10 For Locke, see *Tracts*, 51–2; 119; 245; *Correspondence*, I, 30, 43, 54, 59, 82, 91. It is not possible to do more here than point to a few works as starting-points of enquiry into the complex relationships between liberty and authority in 'puritan' demands for liberty of conscience. It is important to stress, however, that the following historians' accounts have shown that Locke had very considerable ground in the structure and purpose of Civil-War and Interregnum religious thought for his understanding of the self-serving and restrictive character of demands for liberty of conscience and for his persistent suspicion that 'puritan' desires for intolerance and authority were generally cloaked under demands for liberty: B. Worden, 'Toleration and the Cromwellian Protectorate' in W. Sheils (ed.), *Persecution and Toleration*, Oxford (1984), 199–233; J. C. Davis, 'Religion and the Struggle for Freedom in the English Revolution', *Historical Journal* 35:3 (1992), 507–30; W. Lamont, *Godly Rule* (1969); M. Walzer, *The Revolution of the Saints*, Cambridge, Mass. (1965).

cause of turmoil. He decried the threats 'of danger and destruction which are soe perremptorily asserted by a sort of men which would perswade us that the cause of God suffers when ever they are disappointed of their ambitious and coviteous ends'. In an extremely important rejection of Civil War religious claims to foster liberty, he discouraged his father from taking up arms again in the politically unsettled years following the death of Oliver Cromwell for 'deceitfull [men] as all religious pretenders are, nor tyrants such as are the promisers of liberty'. Viewing men as untrustworthy and 'ungratefull' and voicing no hope for political stability through their hands, Locke placed his political trust instead in a providentialist God, 'the hand that governs all things, that manages our Chaos and will bring out of it what will be best for us, and what we ought to acquiesce in'. Locke's political thought in 1660–2 was as thoroughly providentialist in its assumptions as that of the vast majority of his contemporaries, who either saw God as vindicating Anglicanism by its restoration or as trying their faith with 'afflictive providences' and advocated political quiescence.[11]

It is possible to read Locke's decision to conform to the Church of England in 1660–2 as essentially the result of thinking amidst the floodtide of Anglican sentiment in Oxford that that was the likeliest way to secure peace in England, and believing that the very fact of its successful reestablishment indicated that this was God's will. This would, however, underestimate the forces pulling Locke towards the Church of England in the period 1658–62, from the death of Cromwell to the reestablishment of the Church. Not merely was Locke to conform; he was also to compose a manuscript defending the Church that significantly expressed many of the views of his close friends in Oxford, who were all either already committed Anglicans or who were to conform very quickly at the Restoration, and several of whom were composing similar works. Prominent among these were James Tyrrell, Robert Boyle, Thomas Barlow, Samuel Tilly, John Parry and Gabriel Towerson.

In about 1658 Locke became acquainted with Tyrrell, grandson of Archbishop Ussher and editor in 1661 of Ussher's suggestively titled work, originally written to teach unequivocal obedience to Charles I, *The Power Communicated by God to the Prince and the Obedience Required by the Subject*. Tyrrell was to be one of Locke's closest friends throughout his life and Locke's frequent host at his house at Shotover near Oxford. He was the author of an attack in 1681 on Sir Robert Filmer parallel at many points to Locke's *Two Treatises of Government*, and Locke's assistant in

---

[11] *Correspondence*, I, 59, 91; 3; B. H. G. Wormald, *Clarendon*, Chicago (1967), 238–9; N. Keeble, *The Literary Culture of Nonconformity*, Leicester (1987), 17.

composition of a lengthy manuscript on ecclesiastical issues in early 1681.[12] By 1660 Locke was eagerly seeking the approbation of Boyle, already a leading Oxford virtuoso. Had Boyle not turned down various offers of clerical positions in order to devote himself to scientific investigation and writing on religious questions as an avowedly disinterested layman, he would surely have risen high in the church. Bishop Gilbert Burnet, who preached his funeral sermon in 1691, noted that 'He had . . . formed . . . a clear judgement of all the eminent' church Fathers and 'had a just idea of the entire body of divinity'. In the early 1660s Boyle had not yet composed most of the important religious works that he was to publish over the next thirty years, but many of his attitudes were already well developed and he had already published his *Considerations on the Style of the Scriptures*. This was one of two works by Boyle that Locke took many notes from in the early 1660s, and which he was to read again in the 1680s.[13]

Locke's most significant friendships in the late 1650s and early 1660s, however, like those of many young fellows at any time in Oxford college life, were with other young fellows. In 1659–60 Locke was one of a group of eligible bachelors that frequented Black Hall near Oxford and competed for the hearts of the young ladies there. He often dined in this company, and was the host of some of their dinners in Christ Church. Among Locke's close friends of this period only one did not become a cleric in the Church of England and that was because he inherited a fortune.[14] In 1660–1 all were actively promoting support of Anglicanism in correspondence with Locke, and their letters are likely to have been only minor elements of a shared celebration of Anglicanism. Tilly wrote to Locke that he could see 'little of truth' in the case of those who opposed imposition of indifferent matters of worship by the Church of England. Parry, the son of a bishop and later himself a bishop, published *A Resolution of a Seasonable Case of Conscience*, with a title page declaring himself 'a Son of the Church of England'. Contending that he was merely following the revered Anglican authorities of Richard Hooker and Robert Sanderson, Parry defended the imposition of matters indifferent in worship by 'lawful authority' on the grounds of 'prudence'. Obedience to the determination of

[12] On Ussher, Cranston, *Locke*, 66; on Tyrrell and Locke, J. Gough, 'James Tyrrell, Whig Historian and Friend of John Locke', *Historical Journal* 19 (1976), 541–60; R. Tuck, *Natural Rights Theories*, Cambridge (1979), 154–5, 169–76; Ashcraft, *Revolutionary Politics*, 183ff.; below, chapter three.
[13] Cranston, *Locke*, 75–7; Burnet, *The Funeral Sermon . . . of Robert Boyle* (1691) cited in L. T. More, *The Life and Works of the Honourable Robert Boyle*, Oxford (1944), 162 and passim; MS Locke f14, 19; 54; 58; 78; 86; 102; 112; *Paraphrase*, I, 17 and n.; *The Library Catalogue of John Locke*, ed. P. Laslett and J. Harrison, Oxford (1965) [henceforward '*Library*']: Boyle.
[14] Cranston, *Locke*, ch. 4.

lawful authority was necessary; the locus of such authority was not discussed at all. Dispute about indifferent things Parry identified as the cause of the 'recent miseries' of the Civil War.

In 1660 Towerson, later author of works defending the catechism of the Church of England, the Trinity and natural law, wrote to Locke recommending John Pearson's 'reply to Dr Burges', probably Pearson's *An Answer to Dr Burges*. This he believed would 'give you [Locke] as much content as his former papers did . . . [probably Pearson's *No Necessity of Reformation*] . . . for the assurance he there gives of a sudden and just reply to all . . . exceptions against the doctrine, discipline, and ceremonies of the church of England'.[15]

If Stubbe still had any influence on Locke after 1660, even that influence would have encouraged Locke's commitment to the Church of England. Even in 1659 it had been liberty of belief, not liberty of ceremonial practice, that was vital to Stubbe. In 1660 Stubbe conformed, and was personally confirmed by his new patron Bishop Morley, not merely on the grounds that the Church of England was 'publickly imposed' but also, he argued in 1665, because it allowed the largest practical liberty of conscience, being 'the least defining, and consequently the most comprehensive and fitting to be national'.[16]

Locke's reading and the sources for copious note-taking in the period 1659–62 included not merely works by Boyle, Stubbe and Bishop Pearson, but also John Hales' *Golden Remains*, a work that defended the magisterial power of imposition in matters indifferent in religious worship, or *adiaphora*, while also in parts pleading for little to be imposed. Locke noted Hales' defence of authority to impose ceremonial forms, recording that Hales was 'clear against' those who urged conscience and the all-sufficiency of Scripture against the powers of imposition. Locke read Falkland's redaction of the central arguments of William Chillingworth's *Religion of Protestants*, the *Discourse on Infallibility* (1661). Locke began, at the very least, Richard Hooker's defence of the Anglican establishment and of imposition in *adiaphora* against puritan opponents, *Of the Laws of Ecclesiastical Polity*, a work then in vogue due to the very recent publication for the first time of its last three books.[17]

Locke also read the other work that Parry had followed in his *Resolution*, Sanderson's *De Obligatione Conscientiae*. *De Obligatione* set out a

[15] *Correspondence*, I, 127; *DNB* S. N. Parry; J. Parry, *A Resolution of a Seasonable Case of Conscience*, Oxford (1660), title page, 1–2, 4, 13–17; Cranston, *Locke*, ch. 4; G. Towerson, *An Explication of the Decalogue* (1676); idem, *An Explication of the Catechism of the Church of England* (1678); *Correspondence*, I, 104.
[16] J. Casa, *The Arts of Grandeur and Submission* (1665), transl. H. Stubbe, dedication, cited in Jacob, *Stubbe*, 44.
[17] MS Locke f14, 16; 32; 52; 62; 66; 84–5; 110; 118; 120; 122; 128; 130.

lengthy defence of natural law and authority, assaulting those who had used the pretext of zeal for the glory of God to cause revolution in church and state. 'Daily experience', he declared showed that 'every wickedness begins with this preamble "In nomine Domini"'. He defended the imposition of the outward circumstances of worship by 'any particular church', that is 'by those invested with public authority in the several churches', 'for decency, order and edification'. For Sanderson there was simply no distinction between religious and civil indifferent acts. He attacked the 'puritan reformers' who turned 'all things into confusion' with their 'classes and conventions'. For Sanderson, the 'right of making ecceslastical laws' in England was 'vested in the bishops and presbyters, and other persons duly elected by the whole body of the clergy of the whole realm ... in a lawful synod', though the canons that they made only became law when issued with the 'authority of the supreme magistrate'. According to Sanderson, liberty of conscience remained even with such imposition, as long as indifferent matters were not imposed as being intrinsically necessary to salvation and therefore as requiring the assent of the understanding as well as the will.[18]

III

It was thus in the context of many friendships with committed Anglicans, themselves composing works defending Anglicanism, and of extensive reading of other defences of Anglicanism that were shared resources in the composition of these arguments, that Locke observed acrimonious religious debates within Christ Church and read the work of Edward Bagshawe the younger, another student (fellow) of Christ Church, attacking Anglican imposition in 1660, *The Great Question Concerning Things Indifferent in Religious Worship*. Bagshawe argued that individuals should be allowed to worship according to 'their inward consciences' and that the civil magistrate did not have the power to impose indifferent matters in religion. The essential nature of Christian religion was to be 'free and unforced'; worship had to be a 'free-will offering'. Variety in worship was 'comely and harmonious' and showed 'the saints' in liberty preserving unity without uniformity. The *Great Question* quickly became a popular work.

In late 1660 Locke composed his first extensive manuscript in detailed reply to Bagshawe. This was the first of Locke's *Two Tracts Upon Government*; he added a more theoretical piece in Latin, probably about a year or so later as an academic piece for a Christ Church audience. Locke circu-

---

[18] R. Sanderson, *De Obligatione Conscientiae* (1660); citations from Bishop Sanderson's *Lectures on Conscience and Human Law*, ed. and transl. C. Wordsworth, Oxford and Cambridge (1877), 46–7, 113, 116–9, 164ff., 183, 187–91, 193, 197ff., 273.

lated the first tract to Towerson and Tilly; Towerson encouraged him to publish and thereby do 'God and the church a piece of seasonable service'. Although Locke eventually decided against publication, he seriously considered thus serving the Church of England in 1660.[19]

Locke's *Two Tracts* rehearsed at length many of the themes that had occupied much of his reading of Anglican works. Equally significantly, however, they combined the hostility to the puritan case for liberty that those works expressed with a formidable anticlericalism that was very much his own personal sentiment, and the *Tracts* did not support Sanderson's vision of clerical re-establishment of the Anglican church. According to Locke's *Two Tracts*, 'almost all' the 'tragical revolutions' in 'Christendom these many years' had 'turned upon' the 'hinge' and 'worn the vizor' of religion. He declared that none had ever gone about to 'ruin the state but with pretence to build the temple'. Civil War in England had been caused by 'overzealous contention about things' in religion 'which they themselves confess to be little and at most are but indifferent'. Following Sanderson and Parry, Locke declared that only a stranger to England could think that trifles such as 'the time and place of worship' were insufficient causes for turmoil. Expanding on the distrust of many preachers' motivations intimated in his comments on 'religious pretenders' to his father, Locke held them most responsible for having fomented the war. They had perverted the 'doctrine of peace and charity' and kindled the flames of conflict 'with coals from the altar . . . too much blown with the breath of those that attend the altar'. Placing the blame for war firmly on the puritan side he declared that ambition had adopted the 'specious outside of reformation and the cause of God' and that the war had been caused by 'a predatory lust under the guise of Christian liberty and religion'. He indicted the 'overheated zeal of those who know how to arm the rash folly of the ignorant and passionate multitude with the authority of conscience'. According to Locke, the claim of 'liberty for tender consciences' against the enforced ceremonial of the Church of England had been 'the first inlet' to all destructive opinions that had spread throughout England. Men who were generally discontented, ambitious and liable to 'zealous mistakes and religious furies' had been 'inspirited' with dangerous doctrines by 'crafty men'.[20]

Locke declared that the only freedom that he desired was 'of the protection of those laws' which had established in pre-war England the 'purest church of the latter age'. In part Locke was here viewing the restoration of

[19] The background to Locke's tracts is discussed in *Tracts*, Introduction; E. Bagshawe, *The Great Question Concerning Things Indifferent In Religious Worship* (1660), 2–4, 6, 14–16; *Correspondence*, I, 115.

[20] *Tracts*, 160–1, 120–1, 211.

these laws as the will of his providentialist God working 'those many miracles that have restored, and we hope will continue his Majesty to us'; the psychological importance of this providential series of miracles to the anxious Locke was undoubtedly considerable. He also, however, very importantly repeated the hostility that he had expressed to his father about the striving for dominion cloaked under claims of religious liberty in the Interregnum. Locke wrote that a general freedom of conscience in religion had caused 'but a general bondage' with the 'popular assertors of public liberty' actually the 'greatest engrossers of it'. If indulged, the claims of liberty in indifferent matters would prove merely a liberty for 'contention, censure and persecution' and the 'tyranny of a religious rage'.[21]

Although not explicitly defining his target, Locke clearly had in mind in part of his assault the anarchic consequences of Calvinist conceptions of the duty of the predestinate elect to reform the world – a duty to be denied throughout the Restoration by almost all nonconformists, but nonetheless ascribed to them with equal consistency by Anglicans. Bagshawe was as firm as any Restoration nonconformist in denial of rights of resistance and duties of reformation, declaring that disobedience was 'a practice he abhors', and condemning even passive 'repining'; Locke was as fierce as any Anglican in nonetheless assaulting opposition to imposition of *adiaphora* as leading inexorably to such doctrines. Liberty did not consist in 'a liberty for men at pleasure to adopt themselves children of God, and from thence assume a title to inheritance here and proclaim themselves heirs of the world'. The claim to unlimited freedom in religion actually involved men declaring it 'religion to destroy all that are not of their profession' and 'make Christ reign and they prepare for his coming by cutting off the wicked'. Ceremonial injunction might be thought wicked by Bagshawe, but the freedom that he desired would make even the use of indifferent matters odious to men with these views, and the 'several bands of Saints' would claim the liberty to do 'the work of the Lord', with further revolution the result. Echoing his comments to Stubbe, and significantly standing aside from many Anglicans' suggestions of the desire of God for a uniform and decorous worship, Locke wrote that it would be excellent if men 'would suffer one another to go to heaven every one his own way'. This was not possible, however, while men concluded 'God dishonoured upon every small deviation from that way of worship which either edu-

21 *Ibid.*, 119–21, cf. Cromwell: 'Every sect saith. Oh! Give me liberty. But give him it, and to his power he will not yield it to anybody else. Where is our ingenuity? Truly thats a thing ought to be very reciprocal' in W. C. Abbott, *The Writings and Speeches of Oliver Cromwell*, Cambridge, Mass. (1937–47), III, 459, 607–16. I am grateful to J. C. Davis for this reference and informative discussions of Interregnum religion.

cation or interest hath made sacred to them' and thought it their duty to take up arms to defend his cause.[22]

The *Two Tracts* were legalist and voluntarist. According to Locke, without law there would be no moral good or evil. Without God there would be no law. Indifferent things were those not commanded by God either through natural law or through Revelation. For Locke, like Sanderson, indifferent things were all of 'the same nature' whether they were in civil or religious matters. If conscience was allowed dominion over religious *adiaphora*, then all things would become identified as religious, with all government and order perishing. It was therefore necessary for any government to exist that the civil magistrate, of whatever form and number, had an 'absolute and arbitrary power' over religious indifferent matters. Taking this as evident if the magistrate ruled by immediate appointment of God, for Locke in 1660 this was also true even if the magistrate derived all his power from the consent of the people, a position that Locke discussed but to which he certainly did not commit himself in the first Tract. This was because if men possessed a right to dispose of their own actions, they could alienate this right in religious *adiaphora* to the magistrate. Since a magistrate who was created by consent 'concentrates in his person the authority and natural right of every individual by a general contract' all indifferent things, 'sacred no less than profane', could be 'entirely subjected to his legislative power and government'. The civil magistrate was to command indifferent matters as he thought best and the people were obligated to obey his commands even if he commanded sinful actions.[23]

Magisterial authority to determine indifferent matters was necessary not merely because without it there could be no government, but also because men's opinions varied so much over time and place that God could not have set up any universal standard in circumstances of worship. Articulating an intense sense of the variations between men's opinions, with one man's beauty another man's 'deformity', Locke ascribed this variation, without giving any clear indication of relative influence, to the powers of education, custom, the passions, ignorance and party. God had therefore, Locke suggested at one point, left it to the 'churches themselves', which apparently meant simply 'to their governors', to establish ceremonies as 'it should seem necessary under this single law and token, namely that dignity decency and order should be sought after'. Where Sanderson identified the church governors as the synod whose canons then needed to be issued by the authority of the civil magistrate, Locke did not explicitly identify the

[22] *Tracts*, 120–1, 159–61; Bagshawe, cited p. 18.
[23] *Ibid.*, 122–6, 153–5, 218–20, 231; cf. 226–7.

church governors but spoke in the bulk of his text with a remarkable
elision as if the church governors meant simply the civil magistrate. God,
he asserted, had 'relinquished these rites to the discretion of the magistrate
and entrusted them to the care of him who holds power and has the right of
governing the church, to be amended, abolished, renewed, or in whatever
way soever enjoined as he should judge best in the light of the times and the
customs of the people, and as the needs of the church should demand'.
Equally importantly for the unequivocal support of magisterial authority,
Locke asserted repeatedly in the *Two Tracts* that the precept 'Let all things
be done decently and in order' 'encompasses the particular laws regarding
the ceremonies of divine worship . . . to be enacted by the governors of the
church'. Unlike Sanderson, who added to decency and order the need for
ceremonies to foster edification, and therefore introduced the notion also
important to many nonconformists, that the efficacy of ceremonies for the
individual worshippers had to be considered, in 1660 Locke's desire to
defend the authority that he felt vital to the maintenance of government
was so great that he did not even mention the need for worship to secure
edification. There is no sense that freely-chosen worship was seen by Locke
in 1660 as a rewarding form of religious experience for anyone.[24]

For Locke, as for other Anglican writers in 1660 such as Parry, Sanderson and Stillingfleet, the authority of the magistrate to command indifferent circumstances in worship did not cancel liberty of conscience, but
instead marked its appropriate boundaries. An 'outward conformity' was
all that was required of members of the Church of England. Indeed, for
Locke in 1660–2, as in his later works defending toleration, the understanding could not be positively influenced by coercion, since it was
beyond the power of the individual to alter his mind at will. If used to plant
beliefs, penalties increased an 'aversion' and made 'enemies rather than
proselytes'. Penalties were only useful in exacting outward conformity. In
his intolerance on issues of worship in 1660–2 Locke did not adopt the
theory to be popular with many Anglicans throughout the Restoration,
that penalties could make men consider and thus change their beliefs,
including coming to a recognition of the objective indifference of worship.
According to Locke, liberty of the judgement existed even under enforcement of worship as long as the ceremonies were not pressed as necessary to
salvation, compelling the understanding to declare an assent to these as
necessary. As Locke put it, the magistrate's laws in religion obliged men
'to act but not to judge; and, providing for both at the same time, unite a
necessity of obedience with a liberty of conscience'. Liberty of conscience
consisted only of liberty of judgement and not of practice, of understand-

---

[24] *Ibid.*, 129; 146; 216; 234; cf. 132; 172.

ing but not of will. This liberty was, however, important to Locke in 1660, and it was what allowed him to present the *Two Tracts* as animated by 'no less a love of liberty' than reverence for authority. For Locke, the understanding was 'the noblest part', and it ought not to be imposed upon. The distinction between imposing as decent and orderly and as necessary allowed Locke to deny Bagshawe's comparison of Anglican imposition and Roman Catholicism.[25]

Focusing almost entirely upon a defence of the authority of the magistrate to impose the circumstances of religious ceremonial, Locke gave very little detailed indication of the ceremonial character of the Church of England that he would have liked to see restored. This was in part in keeping with many of the other works on the issue published in 1660–2, before the Church was reestablished; these works declared the form of the church to be the province of the Civil Magistrate or of the synod of the church, and that they were therefore not to be discussed at length by others. At one point, when Locke came close to stating his preferences, he broke off with the declaration that this would be to 'too forwardly intrude into the council chamber . . . it being our duty not curiously to examine the counsels but cheerfully to obey the commands of the magistrate'. Various hints of Locke's own preferences are, however, scattered throughout the *Two Tracts*. These strongly suggest that in 1660–1 he favoured the enforcement of a significant number of ceremonies, saw magisterial indulgence as something that would be necessary every so often to quiet the multitude's incessant demands but not as a good thing, and that he saw little if anything wrong with the pre-war Church of England.[26]

Locke's description of the pre-war Church of England as having been 'the purest church of the latter age' has already been cited. Although certainly not defending the 'beauty of holiness' in ceremonies as being vital to inculcate reverence, the view that high-church Anglicans such as Herbert Thorndike were expressing, Locke showed very little sympathy for puritan worries over ceremonies that they thought inclined to superstition. Responding to Bagshawe's specific worries, he explicitly said that he saw nothing in bowing at the name of Jesus, using the sign of the cross in baptism, or kneeling at the Lord's Supper, that was more inclined to superstition than the time and place of worship that all agreed were 'trivial'; these were precisely the ceremonial requirements in the Book of Common Prayer that forced many thousands to separate from the Church of England in 1662. Without arguing that there was any particular efficacy in the surplice, Locke suggested that it would 'add but little heat to the body, but I know not why it should chill our devotions'. According to Locke, the

---

[25] *Ibid.*, 127–8; 139; 238.   [26] *Ibid.*, 159.

important thing was that whatever the outward set form of worship the Spirit of God could still enter and 'enliven' the soul of the worshipper.[27]

Showing a lack of sympathy with the arguments and motivation of the 'precyse protestants' in the decade before the Civil War, Locke condemned the 'malicious' men who were of the same profession as the magistrate and brought 'proofs from Scripture that he is not true to his own profession, that he either superstitiously innovates the worship, or is supinely careless of reformation or tyrannically abridges them of . . . liberty . . . and at last will arrive at this, if he will not reform . . . they themselves may'. His conclusion was that the state religion needed to be 'carefully eyed and directed by a strong and steady hand'. Indeed, a degree of magisterial indulgence was far better bestowed on entirely different professions of religion, such as 'Mahometanism', whose professors were 'quiet' because they sought thereby to commend themselves and their religion 'by the strictness and sobriety of their lives'.[28]

According to Locke, the multitude were 'always craving, never satisfied'. Nothing could be set up which they would not endeavour always to pull down. He recommended therefore that

those constitutions in outward things may be erected as the outward fences to secure the more substantial parts of religion which experience tells us they will be sure to be tampering with when these are gone which are therefore fit to be set up, because they may be with least danger assaulted and shaken and that there may be always something in a readiness to be parted with to their importunity when their fury and impatience shall make such an indulgence necessary.[29]

Unless the rather unspecific commendation of the Church of England as the 'purest church of the latter age' was meant to indicate a preference for episcopal church government, which is possible but unlikely, Locke gave no indication in the *Two Tracts* of his preferred form of church government. He did, however, clearly indicate that he thought none *jure divino* and subjected all to the civil magistrate, writing that questions of 'paedo-baptism, church government, and ordination' had not been settled in Apostolic times and were therefore themselves *adiaphora* for the magistrate to command. Indeed, it was Bagshawe and not Locke who proclaimed his own ordination by a bishop and wrote that episcopacy was 'of Apostolical Institution; that is . . . *Jure Divino*'.[30]

Locke's concern in the *Two Tracts* was to show that a civil magistrate possessed an 'absolute and arbitrary power over all the indifferent actions of his people, whatever the origins and whatever the form of that magistrate. He did 'not meddle' with settling 'whether the magistrate's crown

[27] *Tracts*, 127, 162–4; Bagshawe, *Great Question*, 2.   [28] *Tracts*, 169–71.
[29] *Ibid.*, 158–9.
[30] *Ibid.*, 138, 157, 172; Bagshawe, *Great Question*, 1.

drops down on his head immediately from heaven' or was derived from consent, being 'placed there by the hands of his subjects'. He defended this claim largely by a simple appeal to the further argument that 'society, government and order' were simply impossible without such an authority. Locke argued that the possession by the magistrate of an 'absolute and arbitrary Power over all indifferent actions' and the duty of obedience to the magistrate would exist just as much in 'pure commonwealths' (if such were even possible) as in absolute monarchies, with the only difference between them being the 'inconsiderable' power of 'one vote' in the legislature in a commonwealth, something that was about as effective as the power of petition in an absolute monarchy.[31]

Although not explicitly ranking the various accounts of the origin of legitimate authority in the final draft of the *Two Tracts* to indicate whether he thought government had received power immediately from God or mediately from the people, Locke recognised a preference at one point in the Second Tract for the view that the authority to rule came from God, but that men appointed the particular ruler to exercise that power. This was said to solve the problems of generating a right to govern from paternal right, and of establishing the power over life and death from consent. More significantly, the purpose of Locke's argument was to show that government of whatever form had absolute power over the subjects in all indifferent matters in order to show that indifferent matters in religion could be commanded, but not to argue for monarchical absolutism against Parliament. Various of Locke's comments strongly suggest that he meant by 'civil magistrate' in England the legislative body of King in Parliament, and that he saw them governing through the basic fabric of pre-Civil-War laws. He described those who had proclaimed the duty to reform religion throughout Europe and in England as having assaulted 'well-framed constitutions'. Even when declaring that he was 'not considering the form of government or number of persons wherein it is placed' in describing the power of the civil magistrate, he continued by noting that the 'happy return' of our 'ancient freedom and felicity' were 'sure signs' of where magistracy was most advantageously placed in England. He contended that

All the freedom I can wish my country or myself is to enjoy the protection of those laws which the prudence and providence of our ancestors established and the happy return of his Majesty hath restored: a body of laws so well composed, that whilst this nation would be content only to be under them they were always sure to be above their neighbours . . . we were not only the happiest state but the purest church of the latter age.

---

[31] *Tracts*, 121–5.

It was explicitly 'in defence of the laws' as well as the imposition by those laws that Locke wrote his work.[32]

One passage went a stage further towards support for parliamentary jurisdiction, and suggested that men had consented in Parliament to the legislation passed in indifferent matters. In a section added to the 'preface to the Reader' of the first tract, probably in May–June 1661, Locke argued that it was unreasonable for a man to question the obligation of those laws which 'are not ratified nor imposed on him but by his own consent in Parliament'. It is true that the meaning of this last comment is not pellucid. However, since it was the comment with which Locke intended to conclude the 'Preface to the Reader' of the first tract which specifically replied to Bagshawe's arguments against the imposition of indifferent matters in religion, and since Locke added this passage to the introduction at about the time that Parliament began to introduce measures to re-establish by law the uniform Church of England with the 'bill for uniformity of public prayers', it seems very likely indeed that Locke had in mind here Parliamentary legislation on indifferent matters in religion.[33]

The primary shaping fear of the *Two Tracts* was unquestionably that of 'anarchy', and both the political authority over all indifferent actions and the particular impositions in religion that Locke explicitly supported would have appeared 'tyrannous' to some nonconformists. The magistrate was explicitly described as having power over the liberties, fortunes and lives of subjects. Each subject was said to 'hold his life as a tenant at will', and to need to be ready to 'part with his head when it shall be demanded'. It was certainly not desirable that a man had to 'rob' himself of his possessions – indeed, his 'own necessities' – to maintain the 'pomp and pleasure' of 'one that regards him not', but for Locke that was better than the alternative of anarchy. The *Two Tracts* provided nothing in terms of a fabric of rights or liberties against magistracy. Defining magistracy in terms of its powers to impose laws, only the law of nature was said to place legal restraint upon the magistrate. There was not the slightest hint of the notion of the 'harmlessness' of actions and beliefs delegitimating magisterial imposition that was to be central to Locke's support of toleration from 1667.[34]

Locke's somewhat opaque comment on parliamentary legislation being consented to by each individual does, however, suggest that in practice Locke supported parliamentary legislative authority in England. It also suggests that Locke completely accepted the theory of 'virtual' or 'partial' representation that was often used to explain that those without the right

[32] *Ibid.*, 121–5, 231 and passim.   [33] *Ibid.*, 123.
[34] *Ibid.*, 156; 212–13 and passim; Bagshawe denounced imposition of *adiaphora* as 'Tyranny': Bagshawe, *Great Question*, 4.

to vote nonetheless consented to legislation by their 'representation' by others who possessed the franchise; we will later see that this acceptance was to continue until at least 1681 and very probably even after that date. While supporting absolute authority over subjects, Locke professed opposition to 'Tyranny' and declared his 'love' of 'liberty'. He was explicit in arguing that the magistrate was 'entrusted' to secure the good of those that they ruled, to use 'discretion' for the 'care to the people' and as the 'steward' of the 'public good'. He praised the professed 'tenderness' of Charles II. Indeed, in defining the magistrate Locke started by declaring that 'By magistrate we understand one who has responsibility for the care of the community.' The magistrate who did not aim to 'provide for the common good' in his legislation sinned, even though subjects were obliged to an active obedience to laws that the magistrate made with the sole intent of personal benefit. No consideration was given by Locke to the possibility of another clash between the component parts of a composite magistrate of King and Houses of Parliament.[35]

IV

Locke expressed considerable concern in the *Two Tracts* about the manner in which Scripture was interpreted. Without excluding the aid of the Holy Spirit in interpretation of Scripture, Locke struck the note of considerable caution about interpretation that reverberated in many of the Anglican works that he had read, such as Hales' *Golden Remains*, Falkland's *Discourse on Infallibility* and Boyle's *Style of Scripture*. We have already seen that he attacked those who wrested 'proofs from scripture' that the magistrate was failing in his duty to enforce true religion, and it was the political use of scriptural interpretation that was Locke's primary concern in the *Two Tracts*. He also assaulted more generally those who had 'got the right use of Scripture and the knack of applying it with advantage, who can bring God's word in defence of those practices which his soul abhorrs and do already tell us we are returning to Egypt'. Scripture was a perfect rule of the 'inward and necessary worship' but did not descend to specifying all necessary particulars of worship, and thus to forbidding any imposition beyond what was commanded in the express words of Scripture, as some nonconformists including Bagshawe argued, and as many more were said by Anglicans to argue. The 'discourses of Christ and his Apostles seldom' went beyond 'the general doctrines of the Messiah or the duties of the moral law'. Castigating Bagshawe for 'stretching' Scripture in making the imposition of indifferent things the mark of Antichrist, Locke declared that

---

[35] *Tracts*, 119–20, 123, 136, 150, 212; 220–1, 245 and passim.

men should 'content ourselves with those discoveries the Scripture allows us' and 'not grope for Antichrist in the dark prophesies of the revelations, nor found arguments upon our own interpretation wherein the mistakes of eminent men might teach us to be wary and not over-peremptory in our guesses'. He described himself as 'very cautious to be an over-confident interpreter', adding in a sentiment that was to be massively expanded in later years into a full-scale assault upon the interested interpretations of commentators but was already significant in its indication of a mind distancing itself from clerical powers of religious expertise, that he thought it 'too servile wholly to pin my faith upon the not seldom wrested expositions of commentators' and was content 'with that light the Scripture affords itself'.[36]

The political power involved in interpreting Scripture remained on Locke's mind after he had completed the *Two Tracts* and dominated another manuscript that Locke composed in late 1661 or early 1662. This time Locke's main force was directed against the infallibility claimed by Roman Catholics, but he was also importantly concerned to buttress church authority against individual interpretation. The manuscript is scrappy, appears to have been composed hurriedly, and is clearly unfinished in its present state. Indeed, the most important thing that the manuscript conveys is the overall impression of Locke thinking in a quite rudimentary manner about questions of scriptural interpretation. Having assaulted in the *Two Tracts* the crafty preachers who had caused the Civil War, Locke's 'Essay on Infallibility' indicted Catholics firstly for their claims of papal infallibility and secondly for their elevation of traditions 'which grow up continually as the occasion demands'. These were the twin products of 'sharp-sighted priests' who wrenched Scripture in order to 'establish in every way . . . control over the conduct and consciences of men'. The consequence for the individual of accepting Catholic claims was 'Blindness'. Even if liberty of conscience did not mean for Locke in 1660–2 a liberty to practice, liberty of enquiry against priestly control was already important to him. Using arguments that Locke may have taken from Falkland's *Discourse on Infallibility*, he suggested that the disagreements within the Catholic church proved that it was not infallible, and that even if this were not accepted, an infallible interpreter was 'utterly useless' since an infallible interpreter could not infallibly show that he was infallible. Locke thereby dismissed without mention the passages of Scripture that Catholics brought in proof of the infallibility of Peter and his successors, something that he continued to do throughout his life.[37]

---

[36] *Ibid.*, 159–62, 172, 174.
[37] 'John Locke's "Essay on Infallibility": Introduction, Text, and Translation', ed. J. C. Biddle, *Journal of Church and State* 19 (1977), 301–27 at 316–21.

Locke argued that there were many things in Scripture which did not need an interpreter, which could 'exercise petty minds but scarcely detain a sober and pious man'. Scripture also contained mysteries which 'utterly transcend the human intellect'. God had proclaimed these in terms which could not be made clearer. Numbered among these were two propositions that Locke was later at least to doubt, and probably also actually to deny, but which there is no sign whatever of his even having considered the possibility of doubting in 1662: 'the Trinity of persons in the divine nature' and the 'union of divine and human nature in the person of the mediator'. The truth of these two was for Locke 'certain and is to be believed, but the way in which they are true cannot be expressed in discourse nor grasped by the mind'. The 'magnitude of the matters and the weakness of our minds' combined to put any further explanation of these beyond man.[38]

There were other things, Locke asserted, that were so plain that no one could doubt them. Such were the 'principal duties' of a Christian. He specified justice, charity, chastity and benevolence, but did not expand upon the content of these duties. There were, however, also many matters of a 'more general nature' such as the precept 'let all things be done decently and in order'. These needed interpretation; they were therefore to be interpreted by 'the fathers and leaders of every church', by which Locke presumably intended, although he did not indicate this, every national church. It is a measure of Locke's concern in this period about the political consequences of this issue that he then proceeded to suggest strikingly that these 'fathers and leaders' possessed a kind of infallibility in directing their followers. The shepherds, Locke declared, could err in determining, but the duty of obedience was of such importance that 'the sheep' could not err in following their directions.[39]

In concluding the manuscript Locke descended to a level barely above platitude, although one that reveals all too clearly his attempt to balance firstly political authority and secondly reason with the operations of the Holy Spirit in the interpretation of Scripture. In the 'Essay on Infallibility' he suggested that it was very difficult to determine how much was 'to be granted to each individual' in the interpretation of Scripture and how much to 'the authority of the church', how much was to be achieved 'by reason' and how much 'by the illumination of the Holy Spirit'. Man needed to be careful not to rely too much on reason in matters of faith, but equally 'enthusiasm' had to be avoided, lest 'while we await the inspiration of the Holy Spirit, we honour and worship our own dreams'. It was certainly true, he ended, that much was contributed 'by learning, much by reason, and finally much by the Holy Spirit's enlightening the minds of

[38] Ibid., 320–3.   [39] *Ibid.*, 322–7.

men'. In thus still envisioning a considerable individual assistance in interpretation of Scripture by the enlightening Holy Spirit, he was much closer
to the central strands of Calvinism, and to the early and mid-seventeenth-
century Anglican thought that had so far provided the bulk of his reading,
than his thought was later to become.[40]

V

In 1663–4 Locke served as Censor of Moral Philosophy in Christ Church,
an academic position in which he was lecturing mainly to undergraduates
who were destined to be clerics in the re-established Church of England.
He saw his job in part as giving these future 'teacher[s] of the Church'
material for their sermons with extensive discussions of morality. In the
resultant *Essays on the Law of Nature* Locke gave neither a clear account
of the origin of political authority nor of its purposes, although he was
clear that without government and the keeping of promises no society
could be sustained. His comments make it seem extremely unlikely that his
views had changed significantly since writing the *Two Tracts*. He declared
at the start of one essay that 'we' had learned from recent horrors how
erroneous was the view that the 'voice of the people' was 'the voice of
God', and continued with a general comment which was nonetheless
clearly meant to depict recent events in England, speaking of the sins of
defiling of temples and of disobedience to and destruction of government.
He argued at one point that the law of nature was necessary in order to
restrain the supreme power in a community. Rulers 'in whose power it is to
make or remake laws at their will and as masters of others' would have
been able to 'do everything' for their own advantage and dominion were
they not bound by natural law. Without natural law Locke declared that
men would 'unite' into commonwealths only to become the 'prey' of
others. Whether or not an intimation that consent was the origin of political society was intended to be conveyed in the notion of men 'uniting'
into commonwealths, the clear implication of the comment was that once
established in power rulers did not possess their position as trustees subject
to any forms of positive law, to recall, to legitimate deposition, or to armed
resistance. In one passage Locke declared that command was donated to
rulers by God, and then canvassed without showing any preference the
possibilities of donation to the 'first-born', to 'monarchs', or by 'contract'.
As in the *Two Tracts*, even if consent was the basis of rule through contract, such contract for Locke clearly involved alienation. Contractual rule
occurred 'when someone has voluntarily surrendered himself to another

[40] *Ibid.*, 326–7.

and submitted himself to another's will'. Even if such submission was probably Locke's own preference as a theory, as in the *Two Tracts*, it was probably thought by Locke to be given once by an original generation, and not to need renewal in succeeding generations; Locke spoke simply at one point of Kings being 'born to rule', and there was no point in his own thought before the *Treatises* where he advocated or considered the possibility of a contemporary individual consent to the political society. Locke mentioned at various points the duty of obedience to magistrates or princes; he gave it no qualification. The law of nature was said to require obedience to superiors, and he made it clear that magistrates were such superiors to all of their subjects.[41]

VI

As Locke was reading and recommending for his students works that were ecclesiologically supportive of the Church of England and critical of Calvinist conceptions of the duty to reform the world in the period from 1658 to 1662, he was also reading and recommending works theologically divergent from mainstream Calvinist thought either by the degree of their emphasis upon natural theology or because they were written from a perspective closer to the main seventeenth-century Protestant alternative to Calvinism, Arminianism, than they were to Calvinism. Locke read Hales' *Golden Remains* and read and recommended for some of his students the Dutch Remonstrant Hugo Grotius' *De Veritate Religionis Christianae*. Grotius' work stressed a natural theology against atheism, expending much effort in proving that there was a God and avoiding discussion of almost all theological controversies, from predestination to the Trinity itself. Many of the undergraduates placed in Locke's care, like most undergraduates of the day, were only fourteen or fifteen, and the clear and simple elucidation of the basic principles of Christianity by Grotius was an eminently suitable choice for their reading. Locke also set for his students the more overtly Arminian and then very popular *Whole Duty of Man* by Richard Allestree, ejected from Christ Church for his uncompromising Anglicanism during the Interregnum, but reinstalled at the Restoration and elevated to the Professorship of Divinity in 1663. His work, issued with a preface by the broadly Arminian Anglican Henry Hammond, was largely a practical book of moral lessons, but it emphasised repentance in a manner uncharacteristic of Calvinist thought. Christ had purchased salvation for 'all those who truly repent and amend' their lives, involving a 'hearty,

---

[41] Cranston, *Locke*, 76; *Essays*, 118–19; 160–1; 184–7; 196–7. The *Essays on the Law of Nature* were recorded in the same notebook, MS Locke e6, in which Locke had written the second tract upon government.

honest endeavour of obeying the will of God'. The main end of Christ's coming was not satisfaction for man's sins but 'to plant good life among men'. As the Apostle James testified, faith without works was dead. Faith alone could not gain salvation.[42]

Locke read and took similar notes from Hammond's own *Pacific Discourse* (1660). This work, dedicated to 'All our Brethren of the Church of England', assaulted at great length 'an hasty premature persuasion of . . . "being in Christ"' backed by 'a beliefe of irrespective Decrees, and Grace irresistible' as the source of much immorality. Hammond sought to show that Sanderson had completely rejected the Calvinism of his youth in favour of the broadly Arminian belief that grace was resistible and Christ's death of universal intent. According to Hammond, Sanderson had correctly interpreted election as the choice of those who voluntarily received Christ and obeyed him by employing his grace. While his thought was thus closer to Arminianism than to Calvinism, Hammond nonetheless emphasised strongly that the Arminians erred in placing too heavy an emphasis upon free will, asserted that his position made clear that only those who received grace could turn to God, and argued that those who had not heard of the Gospel had received no grace. Sanderson and Hammond both viewed men as significantly corrupted by the Fall. Suggesting interest in Sanderson's attitude towards Calvin and a consideration of Calvin's thought in 1660–2, Locke took several notes from this work on Sanderson's attitudes towards Calvin. One of these notes suggested the reading of Hooker as 'a preparative' if not 'an antidote' to the reading of Calvin; on the following page of his notebook Locke took a note from Hooker on Calvin, suggesting that he was following Sanderson's advice on this point.[43]

There was little theology in the *Two Tracts*. Locke did attack the political consequences of the duty of the elect to remodel the world, important in much Calvinist thought, but by no means essential to Calvinist thought in the Restoration. The *Two Tracts* included no extended theological discussion, and certainly nothing directly antithetical to quietist strains of Calvinist thought. The few theological comments that Locke made in passing indicate little that would not be agreed upon by almost all Protestants, and certainly by all shades of Calvinist and Arminian thought. Locke identified Christ's role as the promulgation of the law of liberty – from the ceremonial yoke of Moses – and the redemption of mankind from the 'slavery of sin' and of Satan. He wrote of Christians as those whom

[42] MS Locke f11, 11–12; R. Allestree, *The Whole Duty of Man* (1659), preface; 1–16; cf. Spellman, *Locke*, 68–9.
[43] H. Hammond, *A Pacifick Discourse of God's Grace and Decrees* (1660), title page, [1], [4], 1–5, 7, 9–17, 19–21, 23–4, 26, 50; MS Locke f14, 19; 40; 42; 56; 116.

Christ had 'purchased with his blood'. Recognition of this 'purchase' by Christ's blood almost certainly indicate that in 1660 Locke believed, like all shades of Calvinists and Arminians, that Christ had satisfied for man's sins in the sense of a payment to God's justice; only very many years later did Locke show any signs of questioning such a view. Locke wrote at several points about the immediate operations of the Holy Spirit upon man, but only in order to argue that these were possible whatever the set form of worship, not in order to explicate their role in salvation. Similarly, he noted that God used both the ordinary course of his Providence and the immediate operations of the Holy Spirit to enlighten men, but gave no indication of the balance between these means, and no indication, for instance, of whether these operations of the Holy Spirit were resistible or not.[44]

A strong view of man's inherited disposition to sin from Adam's Fall may have stood behind Locke's intense concern, repeatedly stated in the *Two Tracts*, with the brutality and unruly passions of the multitude. Locke never explicitly drew this link, however. He spoke briefly of man's 'frail nature or improved corruption' and then continued with the declaration that 'ever since man first threw himself into the pollution of sin, he sullies whatever he takes into his hand, and he that at first could make the best and perfectest nature degenerate cannot fail now to make other things so too'. This probably indicates a belief in a strong inherited disposition to sin, particularly because this was so widely accepted that Locke did not need to spell it out more precisely, and because this was once again the view supported strongly in the works that he had by then read. Examined carefully, however, it is unclear whether man's 'improved corruption' was meant to indicate something caused directly by the Fall or to contrast with his 'frail nature' and indicate the effect of individuals' cumulative voluntary and habitual viciousness. It is also unclear exactly how powerful a force is implied in the notion that man 'cannot fail' to make 'other things' degenerate; or how powerful an effect was involved in the 'sullying' of 'whatever' was taken into man's hand. Locke was interested in contending that man had a great capacity for sin in all areas rather than in showing the degree of necessity of his sinning. In 1666 the high-church Dean of Christ Church, John Fell, his sub-Dean Richard Gardiner and another signed a statement that was presumably meant to help Locke to secure clerical appointment. This declared that Locke was orthodox in theology and obedient to the Church. There is no reason to suppose that either part of this declaration was false at this point in Locke's life.[45]

In addition to his apparent suspicion of all arguments created by clerics,

---

[44] *Tracts*, 138, 129, 133, 141, 143, 162, 233.   [45] *Ibid.*, 155, 246–7; *Education*, 35ff.

however, Locke's thought by 1664 had probably turned far away from several central elements of the religious views of the vast majority of his contemporaries, whether Calvinist or Arminian. In 1659 Locke indirectly betrayed considerable doubt about Calvinist confidence in the predestinate elect who were informed by the irresistible grace of the Holy Spirit. He declared that it was 'Phansye' that ruled the world, and queried 'where is that great Diana of the world Reason'. Given his vituperation of Quakers as 'hot-headed' men in letters to his father, Locke continued strikingly that 'we are all Quakers here and there is not a man but thinks he alone hath this light within and all beside stumble in the darke'. It was men's passions that disposed them and 'every one's Recta ratio is but the traverses of his owne steps'. Men lived not by inspired conscience delivering knowledge but by 'opinion moulded up between custome and Interest, the two great Luminaries of the World'. These were the 'only lights' that men actually followed. The cure for this predicament that Locke sketched for his correspondent gave no role to God's enlightening grace, but instead advocated men harnessing the power of custom by treading in the steps of the bravest men which led to 'virtue and honour' and utilising the influence of interest by making it 'our Interest to honour our Maker and be usefull to our fellows'. Simply stated in a letter in 1659, without any sense that at this stage this notion of interested virtue was the result of any sophisticated or elaborate consideration or deep commitment, it was later to become central to much of Locke's ethical and religious thought.[46]

Locke had thus given essentially sociological and motivational reasons for the failures of men to reason properly, expressing very deep reservations indeed about the extent of their use of reason but not completely denying their capacity to reason. The *Essays* concentrated on description of the problems attached to reasoning but also directly held out the possibility of properly directed reason achieving knowledge of natural law without the aid of revelation. The inhibitions upon reasoning properly that Locke sketched in the *Essays* did little more than rehearse the problems that he had mentioned in the *Two Tracts*. Investigations were restricted by 'a bad way of life, becoming strong by lapse of time' which established 'barbarous habits' if men had been brought up viciously. They were not pursued because of the influence of 'evil customs', and in many cases due to a 'natural defect of mind'. Men were born different in inclinations and appetites and some simply never had the capacity to attain to knowledge themselves. Most men were guided by belief, 'by the example of others, or by traditional customs and the fashion of the country, or finally by the

---

[46] *Correspondence*, I, 81; cf D. Wootton, *John Locke: Political Writings*, Harmondsworth, Middlesex (1993), 26ff.

authority of those whom they consider good and wise' instead of being guided by reasoning for themselves. Most of the precepts of the law of nature were transmitted to children by their parents and teachers; unfortunately, this was as true of evil opinions as it was of good. Either 'corrupted by vice' or 'carelessly indifferent', few attained to knowledge of the natural law.[47]

As in the *Two Tracts*, in the *Essays* Locke neither identified the cause of vice as an inherited disposition to sin nor turned to grace as the cure for man's sinfulness. Instead, he argued that men should attempt to follow the more rational members of society – a point similar to his argument of 1659 that men should attempt to imitate the bravest and most virtuous – that they should reason for themselves, and that they could gain knowledge of natural law by this reasoning. In part the absence of theological discussion or description of original sin was a consequence of the character of the *Essays*. Locke noted that he was not discussing what a man could experience who was 'divinely inspired, or what a man can behold who is illuminated by a light from heaven'; in speaking here of 'a man' Locke probably meant to indicate not merely the immediate inspiration of a prophet but also the operations of the Holy Ghost in regenerate Christians. At another point Locke suggested that the Fall did not concern him in the *Essays* as it 'does not particularly concern philosophers'. In the *Essays* Locke had clearly set himself to lecture on what could be known by a man who had no access to historical revelation, in keeping with his role as a teacher of classical moral philosophy, and it is therefore not possible to tell what Locke thought that a man who had the information of revelation would be able to know. Yet Locke's contention that men could attain to full knowledge of the law of nature by reason and sense-experience alone, and his explicit identification of the content of the law of nature as exactly the same as positive divine law in revelation, set him at considerable distance from the fideism consequent upon a strong, Calvinist view of the Fall. Imbued with a deep sense of the loss of ability caused by man's Fall, Calvinists held that man could attain to full knowledge of the content of natural law only through grace. Indeed, even in Calvin's book in the *Institutes* on the knowledge of God as creator he asserted the need for grace in order for man to properly know God as creator, let alone to know the content of his duties. In later life Locke was explicitly to attack the Calvinist vision of the Fall; as early as the *Essays* he had moved decisively away from some of its central consequences for many of his contemporaries, even if this move involved a stress on men's capacity to attain full knowledge of natural law and on the need for them to pursue such knowledge by

[47] *Essays*, 114–15; 134–5; 140–1; 202–3.

reason and not a declaration that most or even many men would in fact pursue and attain such knowledge.[48]

In the *Essays* Locke also moved decisively away from the views of almost all of his contemporaries by rejecting the major contemporary forms of innatism, dispositional innatism, where ideas were said to be implicit in the soul as their source but only present to the mind when elicited by experience as the stimulus to their recognition, and naive innatism, where God was said to have impressed a number of ideas or precepts on the mind or soul at birth. Locke's shift from innatism apparently occurred during the composition of the *Essays* or during their delivery as lectures to his students. In the *Two Tracts* Locke had noted that there was a natural conscience implanted in men. In his first draft of the first chapter of the *Essays* Locke had still accepted that there were some 'moral principles which the whole of mankind recognizes and which all men in the world accept unanimously'. Quoting Grotius' *De Jure Belli Ac Pacis*, Locke declared that this basis of morality in 'nature' rather than convention or custom allowed it to be a science. When men in 'different times and places affirm one and the same thing as a certain truth, this thing must be related to a universal cause which can be nothing else but a dictate of reason itself and a common nature'. He deleted this entire passage, however, and went on in his third essay to mount a lengthy assault on innatism, arguing that there were simply no universally agreed principles; even the existence of God was denied by many. The ignorant and illiterate, least corrupted from their first nature by a second nature of custom and civilisation, recognised little of natural law. The mind, Locke concluded, was an empty tablet, onto which were inscribed the experiences of the senses, the foundation of all knowledge. Principles that people claimed were innate were either collected by reasoning upon the basis of sense-experience, or they were inculcated at an early age by parents or teachers and then had their origin forgotten.[49]

The source of Locke's rejection of innatism is unclear. It probably was influenced by a growing interest in scientific investigations in collaboration with Boyle and others in Oxford who argued that hypotheses should be generated by the thrust of empirical evidence; participation in experiments moved Boyle from scholasticism to empiricism. One of the major claims of those who argued for the existence of innate moral principles was that

[48] *Ibid.*, 114–15; 122–3; 138–9; 188–9; Calvin, *Institutes*, Bk. 1, chs. 1–2, 3, 5–6. Cf William Perkins, *A Discourse of Conscience* in T. E. Merrill (ed.), *William Perkins: 1558–1602*, Nieuwkoop (1966), 42: 'the law of nature though it affoarde indeede some direction; yet it is corrupt, imperfect, uncerten: and whatsoever is right and good therein, is contained in the written word of God', cited in J. Colman, *John Locke's Moral Philosophy*, Edinburgh (1983), 20.
[49] *Tracts*, 222; 225; *Essays*, 126–7; 136–45; 148–9; 282–3.

there were also innate speculative principles, and that these were largely principles of science. Locke denied in the *Essays* that there were any such innate speculative principles, arguing that these were all empirical generalisations. The assault upon naive innatism in the works of various Cambridge Platonists, and by Boyle, may well have been important to Locke; his reading by the time that he wrote the *Essays* included works in which More and Boyle assaulted naive innatism.[50]

More difficult to explain is Locke's divergence from these thinkers by attacking dispositional innatism. The widespread moral turpitude that Locke documented to show that men did not agree about any moral principles, even to the extent that many denied the existence of God, may itself have convinced him that both forms of innatism were also erroneous. He was already an assiduous note-taker from travel books on the different opinions of foreign peoples in fields of knowledge from religion and morality to medicine and navigation. His position as college teacher of Greek and then rhetoric in 1661 and 1662, the years prior to becoming Censor of Moral Philosophy, had given him ample recent opportunity to study the widespread disagreements about morality and about the existence, nature and number of the gods among classical nations and authors. The steady accretion of this information, much of which he used in the essays to illustrate the ubiquity of immorality, may have convinced Locke almost as soon as he began to reflect seriously upon the doctrine of innatism that it was erroneous. Locke's reading in these years of late sixteenth-century scepticism about the founding of any principles of morality, very significant direct echoes of which are to be found in passages of the *Essays* themselves, was probably extremely influential in demolition of belief in innate principles of morality, as it had been on the thought of Grotius and Hobbes earlier in the century.[51] If the belief that some innate moral principles still existed was not deleted by the time that Locke actually delivered his first lecture, then his audience may have contributed to Locke's rejection of innatism. His students certainly had the academic role of challenging the existence of natural law itself, and they may have done this by pointing out the variation of views of what constituted immorality between societies and times in a way that Locke, with his already acute perception of the variations of belief due to custom and interest, found an unanswerable case against innatism without recourse to a stronger notion of the Fall than he was willing to countenance. Locke's valedictory address to these students at the end of his year as censor

---

[50] *Ibid.*, 144–5; MS Locke f14, passim. On Boyle, *Tracts*, 245.
[51] On Locke's reading and echoing of Pierre Charron in the *Essays* see Wootton, *Locke: Political Writings*, 26ff.

suggests that they had a large degree of success in their academic assault upon natural law.[52]

From the evidence of the deleted passage in his first essay, Locke would seem to have originally believed in what he described as a moderate view of the Fall, one that obliterated many but not all innate principles. It is significant that in coming to believe that widespread immorality indicated that there were no innate ideas Locke had not instead maintained support for innatism by explaining that different views of morality were the result of a considerably intensified view of the effects of the Fall. That would of course have led naturally to grace and fideism as the only hope for knowledge of morality. Against the background of his other writings and the experience of the Civil Wars it seems very likely indeed that it was the political difficulties and religious enthusiasm that Locke feared from such a need for gracious renewal of men's understandings in morality that dictated his turn in the opposite direction, to the view that man's sense-experience and faculty of reason alone were sufficient, if properly employed, to attain knowledge of morality. There is no sense in the *Essays* or evidence from Locke's notebooks that this choice was itself the result of reading of Scripture or of the influence of other theological works.[53]

Whatever the source of Locke's rejection of innatism, it is important that Locke had clearly reflected upon and rejected a major theological teaching, the belief of which had almost certainly been maintained by his family, and which he had himself supported as the basis of natural law in the *Two Tracts*. In so doing, he was willing to commit himself to a rejection of innatism whose extent was shared by very few of his contemporaries; the intellectual independence and eclecticism and the ever greater steps away from Calvinism that we will find marking his later theology and ecclesiology may be said to have been clearly and crucially exhibited even at this early point.

[52] *Tracts*, 162–3; 166–7; 170–3; 190–1.   [53] *Essays*, 138–9.

2

Restoration churchmanship and the 'Essay on Toleration'

I

Setting the agenda for much political and religious conflict throughout the Restoration, when the Church of England was re-established in 1662, shortly after Locke's second tract on government, it was restored as a severely defined episcopalian regime retaining ceremonial forms thought by many to incline to 'popish' superstition. Instead of achieving an uniform religion in the nation, this resulted in severe divisions. Over seventeen hundred of the clergy resigned or were ejected from their parishes. Estimates of those who followed them and worshipped as nonconformists in the Restoration varied, but there were probably at least several hundred thousand – somewhere between 5% and 20% of the population. Most of those who became nonconformists were presbyterians who agreed with Anglicans that they were separated by 'indifferent matters' but thought that these ought to be removed because they limited their 'edification', at least as important a requirement of worship as 'decency and order'. For many other nonconformists, including some of the Independents, the next largest nonconformist group, nothing ought to be commanded as necessary to communion but what was recognised to be expressly commanded in the Scripture, and a devolved rather than hierarchic church authority was required by Christianity.[1]

---

[1] See especially R. Thomas, 'Comprehension and Indulgence' in G. Nuttall and O. Chadwick (eds.), *From Uniformity to Unity 1662–1962* (1962), 191–253; Keeble, *Literary Culture*; R. S. Bosher, *The Making of the Restoration Settlement* (1951); I. M. Green, *The Re-establishment of the Church of England 1660–3*, Oxford (1978). For a good summary of hostility to imposition of 'things indifferent' from an Independent point of view, stressing conscience, see J. Owen, *Indulgence and Toleration Considered* (1667), in J. Owen, *Works*, ed. W. Goold (1967), XIII, 520–1. That Scripture was the perfect rule of life and worship was 'the characteristic principle of the Congregationalists' by 1660: G. Nuttall, *Visible Saints: The Congregational Way 1640–60*, Oxford (1957), ch. 2; *Tracts*, 234. It is very difficult to gain a reliable estimate of the number of nonconformists in England in the Restoration. There were almost certainly considerably more than the 108,000 estimated in the census of 1676 (named the Compton Census after the bishop of London), and almost certainly considerably less than the one million that were occasionally claimed by dissent-

The strict episcopalian settlement was supported by many Anglican clerics for whom the central ecclesiastical message of the Civil War was that 'the same hands . . . took the crown from the king's head and the mitre from the bishops'. Having harboured their episcopalianism through exile or proscription, many churchmen did not intend to see it emasculated in a compromise with the presbyterians who had caused the Civil War.[2] Alone, these churchmen could have achieved little, and many initially expected to need to compromise. Crucially, however, the gentry who sat in the 'Cavalier Parliament' from 1661 until 1679 combined their Cavalier support for the King with equal support for the Church.[3]

Reversing the alignment of pre-Civil-War politics, in the years from 1660 to 1679 it was Parliament that was the Restoration Church's staunchest ally, and the King that wished for ecclesiastical concessions to unite his Protestant subjects. Charles II had long promised from exile a 'liberty to tender consciences' and supported Restoration attempts to obtain toleration both within the church by broadening the terms of communion to allow most Protestants to join, a policy that was alternatively known as toleration or as comprehension, and supported more strongly still toleration outside the church, known as toleration or indulgence, probably because of personal Catholic sympathies. On each occasion it was the strict

ers who wished to demonstrate the need for toleration. There were probably very approximately about half a million dissenters, roughly the number who did not conform to the Church after toleration had finally been provided in 1689. The pattern of licences taken out by dissenters in 1672 and various local censuses suggest that about half of these Protestant dissenters were presbyterians, with most of the remaining half divided between Independents, Quakers, and a lesser number of Baptists. There were up to two-and-a-half million adult conformists to the Church of England recorded in the official census in 1676, but many of these would then have conformed due to the census itself and there were a considerable number who took communion in the Church of England but also worshipped elsewhere. The figures alone indicate two things: that if all presbyterians could have been persuaded to join the church then there would have been relatively few Protestants left outside the church, and that the 'hearty' friends to the narrow and persecuting church of the Restoration were probably at most no more than equal to the numbers of the 'hearty' nonconformists. See especially J. R. Western, *Monarchy and Revolution* (1972), 164; A. O. Whiteman (ed.), *The Compton Census of 1676: A Critical Edition* (1986).

2 R. South, *A Sermon Preached . . . Nov 25 1661*, cited in G. V. Bennett, *The Tory Crisis in Church and State*, Oxford (1975), 5. For the attitudes of these high churchmen see Bosher, *Restoration Settlement*, passim and below. The term 'high church' only came into frequent usage in contrast to 'low church' in the 1690s, and the primary meaning of 'high' in the Restoration was 'extreme', but 'high church' was occasionally used in the Restoration to identify the combination of strong episcopalianism, sacramentarianism and support for persecution that it is used to denote in this chapter, and which indicates its continuity with the 'high churchmanship' of the 1690s. In this sense, Sheldon, Sancroft, Thorndike and Heylyn all deserve the name, as do a number of other Anglicans such as Cosin, Gunning, Laney, Fell, Turner, Lowth and Barne.

3 Green, *Church of England*, passim; Bosher, *Restoration Settlement*, passim; Thomas, 'Comprehension', 192–6; P. Seaward, *The Cavalier Parliament and the Reconstruction of the Old Regime*, Cambridge (1989), ch. 7.

Anglican majority in Parliament that opposed his plans. This alignment was established as early as December 1662 when Charles issued a Declaration of Indulgence suspending the penal laws against dissent. As soon as he became archbishop in 1663 Gilbert Sheldon wrote to encourage a 'resolute execution of the law' so that 'they who will not be governed as men, by reason and persuasion, should be governed as beasts, by power and force; all other courses will be ineffectual, ever have been soe, ever will be'. Charles was forced by Parliament to withdraw his Declaration, and in 1664–5 Parliament added to the Act of Uniformity further penal laws against dissent. For Sheldon, the enforcement of these laws was 'to the glory of God, the welfare of the Church . . . and the happiness of the whole kingdom'.[4]

When Richard Baxter wrote his autobiography he argued that there had been three main types of conforming clergy at the Restoration. There were many former presbyterians who either thought that episcopacy was lawful or had simply conformed out of need. The other two types of conforming churchmen are more important to an understanding of the character of the principles and policy of the Restoration church and particularly to the politics of religious toleration. Each exercised an influence far greater than their numbers, and each will be considered in turn over the next pages. First were those who were 'heartily such [Anglicans] throughout', including those of the 'high and swaying Party' who were 'zealous for the Diocesan party and desirous to extirpate or destroy the nonconformists'. Many were 'high prelatists' who maintained that episcopal church government was 'of Divine Institution, and perpetual usage in the church' and 'necessary to order'.[5]

Building upon the increasing celebration of episcopacy from the late sixteenth century, by the Laudians in the 1630s, and in the Interregnum patristic research of Henry Hammond, a cadre of high church polemicists such as John Pearson, Herbert Thorndike, Peter Heylyn, Henry Dodwell, Francis Turner, Thomas Long, Benjamin Laney, John Fell, Simon Lowth and Miles Barne argued at the very least that episcopacy was the best form of church government, and that it had been handed down in unbroken

---

[4] P. Hardacre, 'Sir Edward Hyde and the Idea of Liberty to Tender Conscience 1641–56', *Journal of Church and State* 13 (1971), 23–42; idem, 'The Genesis of the Declaration of Breda 1657–60', *ibid.* 15 (1973), 65–82; Thomas, 'Comprehension', 192–5; Keeble, *Literary Culture*, 25; G. R. Abernathy, 'Clarendon and the Declaration of Indulgence', *Journal of Ecclesiastical History* 11 (1960), 59–64; Sheldon, cited in Beddard, 'Sheldon', 1016n.; Sheldon cited in G. Cragg, *From Puritanism to the Age of Reason*, Cambridge (1950), 220; V. Sutch, *Gilbert Sheldon*, The Hague (1973), *passim* but cf. Beddard, 'Sheldon', 1012 and n.
[5] R. Baxter, *Reliquiae Baxterianae* (1696), 386–7; cf. M. Tindall, *The Rights of The Christian Church Asserted* (1706), liii–lv.

succession since the Apostles. In some of their works their arguments went further, advancing to the contention that episcopacy was *jure divino*, the only legitimate form of church government, having been established as unalterable by the Apostles. In these latter works episcopacy was coming to be seen as not merely advantageous but even as necessary.

Heylyn, Laud's chaplain, linked elegiac defence of Laudianism to patristic defences of episcopacy. His 1657 *History of Episcopacy*, reprinted in 1681, emphasised the episcopalian Father Cyprian of Carthage; his biography of Laud in 1668, republished in 1671, depicted the Archbishop as a martyr to episcopacy under the revealing title *Cyprianus Anglicus*. Fell, Dean of Christ Church and bishop of Oxford, composed both Hammond's *Life* and an edition of Cyprian's works, *Sancti Caecili Cypriani Opera*. Dodwell, an influential lay theologian, edited another edition of Cyprian's *Opera*, and composed lengthy *Dissertations on Cyprian* in 1682. Dodwell composed various other works in the Restoration condemning nonconformists as schismatics by using the definition of schism as the setting up of altars against the authority of the local bishop. Pearson's 1672 *Vindiciae Epistolarum S. Ignatii* similarly declared illegitimate the administration of the sacraments without a bishop's permission.[6]

Unsurprisingly, these writers opposed any attempts to alter the terms of the Restoration re-establishment of the Church by reducing the powers of the bishop in order to allow dissenters to conform. In his *Promiscuous Ordinations are Destructive to the Safety and Honour of the Church of England* (1668), Pearson opposed those who were willing to accept presbyterian ordination for ministry in the Church of England. Thorndike's *Just Weights and Measures* (1662), republished in 1680, insisted upon the exclusively episcopal power of the keys and thus of ordination and declared that episcopacy was 'part of God's law by the Scriptures'. In his 1667–8 'The plea of Weakness and Tender Consciences Discussed and Answered against plans for comprehension and toleration', and the *True*

---

[6] H. Hammond, *Of the Power of the Keyes* (1647), 215–16 and passim; idem, *Dissertationes Quatuor* (1651), passim; J. Pearson, *Vindiciae Epistolarum S. Ignatii* (1672), passim; Bosher, *Restoration Settlement*, passim; J. W. Packer, *The Transformation of Anglicanism* (1969), ch. 5, esp. 127 on Hammond and Pearson; Beddard, 'Sheldon', 1009; on Ignatius and Cyprian see also H. Chadwick, *The Early Church* (1967), 46–9, 119–21; Baxter, *Reliquiae*, II, 386–7; Bosher, *Restoration Settlement*, passim; P. Heylyn, *History of Episcopacy* in Heylyn, *Historical and Miscellaneous Tracts* (1681), passim; idem, *Cyprianus Anglicus* (1668), passim; H. Dodwell, *S. Caecilii Cypriani Opera*, Amsterdam (1700), passim (this edition includes the earlier editorial work by Fell); idem, *Dissertationes Cyprianicae* (1682), passim; idem, *Dissertationes Irenaeii* (1689), passim; idem, *An Admonitory Discource Concerning the Late English Schism* (1714); idem, *Separation of Churches from Episcopal Government as practised by the Present nonconformists, proved Schismatical* (1679), passim; idem, *A Discourse of the one Alter and the One Priesthood insisted on by the Ancients in their Disputes against Schism* (1683), passim.

Principle of Comprehension he stressed the continuity of the Catholic Church in England and the necessity of episcopal command. In 1670 he added *A Discourse of the Forbearance which a Due Reformation Requires*, which argued that episcopacy was by 'the law of God', that presbyters could at most assist bishops, and that only synods of the church could alter ceremonies, a proposal that would have ensured the failure of a true comprehension by making the Anglican Convocation arbiter of any changes.[7]

Bishop Matthew Wren and others wrote works showing that the liturgy and sacraments of the Church similarly conformed to patristic practices. Again Herbert Thorndike provided the most extreme advocacy of the necessity of 'reverence' due in ceremonial in the Restoration, a direct continuation of the Laudian sentiments on the 'beauty of holiness' that he had voiced in his popular 1642 *Of Religious Assemblies*. His *Forbearance Due* of 1670 declared the Eucharist the 'principal office of religious assemblies'; the best preaching was simply that 'which may fit the people for the eucharist'. For Thorndike it was even necessary to 'abate the sermon to restore the eucharist' to its central place. The 'True Way of Comprehension' defended current Anglican ceremonial as the best for edification. Bishop Peter Gunning of Ely displayed the sentiments appropriate to his beautiful medieval cathedral, whose chapel had recently suffered at the hands of puritans. Gilbert Burnet recorded as early as 1663 that Gunning was 'carrying things so high that I saw latitude and moderation were odious' and Baxter described Gunning as 'vehement for his high opposing principles, and so overzealous . . . for Church pomp'. For Bishop Laney, an aging sacramentarian who had been one of 'Laud's creatures', the church was 'a garden enclosed' which was not to have its 'walls' torn down in order to bring in even the moderate presbyterians. This would gain only faction and dissension and lose the primitive lustre of the church's pure forms of worship and discipline. Comprehension would be what 'The Horse with a Comprehensive Belly' had been to the Trojans. The compromises needed for comprehension of the presbyterians were condemned as 'abolishing all our ceremonies and blending our orders'. For these churchmen, the ceremonial forms surrounding the Lord's Supper had to inculcate due reverence; their stress upon edification in worship equalled the nonconformists' emphasis, but with directly opposed results for the circumstances of worship.[8]

[7] J. Pearson, *Promiscuous Ordinations* (1668), passim; H. Thorndike, *Theological Works* (1844–56), I, 7–97; 399–410; 464; 502–5; 536; 572–3; 585–6; 590; 593; 619; 663–5; 687–95; V, 71–298; 299–344; 358–66; 381–488 esp. 396, 409, 420–6, 440–8, 452–3, 456.
[8] Thorndike, *Works*, I, 99–394; V, 299–344; 364–6; 381–488; F. A. Lacey, *Herbert Thorndike* (1929), 52–8, 78, 99–105; G. Burnet, *A Supplement to the History of My Own Time*, Oxford (1902), 464 cited in J. Gascoigne, 'The Holy Alliance', unpublished Ph.D thesis, Cambridge University 1981, 21–2; on Gunning at Savoy, D. Ogg, *England in the Reign of*

These polemicists did not merely oppose plans for comprehension and toleration for those whom they blamed for the Civil War and depicted as continued subversives; they trumpeted a patristic, theological case for intolerance. Citing in a host of works Augustine's argument for punishment of dissenters during the Donatist schism, based on Luke 14.23, during the Restoration authors such as Thomas Long and William Cave paralleled that schism with contemporary dissent. They declared biblical and patristic authority for the duty to compel dissenters by civil penalties in order to make them consider their religious views; accepting that 'conscience' should not be compelled, they nonetheless insisted that conscience could not be claimed for unexamined views that were simply adopted because of the influence of custom or party, that penalties could counterbalance these influences and make people reflect, and that the dissenters had not examined their views properly. As Laney put it in phraseology frequently echoed by many others, 'fear is the beginning of wisdom'.[9]

As the two archbishops of Canterbury from shortly after the Restoration to shortly after the Revolution of 1688, Sheldon (1663–77) and William Sancroft (1677–91) were both primarily concerned with preserving and extending the powers of the church. Neither wrote the extensive polemic of Thorndike or Heylyn, and both were probably marginally less sacramentarian than their colleagues. Nonetheless, both were committed to a strong episcopacy and to a reverent view of church ceremonial. Sheldon, advocate of episcopacy in the Civil War, had gone to considerable trouble to preserve the *Codex Authenticus* of Laud's Oxford statutes throughout the Interregnum, and in the Restoration he secured publication of Laud's *Diary*, *History* and *Prayers*. He helped Pearson to obtain Chester in 1673, a preferment that was said to please greatly the 'high church party'. Sancroft had been John Cosin's secretary and the amanuensis to the bishops drafting revisions of the Prayer Book in 1661 which would have stressed the role of the priest. He was then Sheldon's chaplain, and in that role he was responsible for publishing Laud's *Diary* and *History*. For Sancroft, close to Gunning and Thorndike, the presbyterians were 'that cursed Puritan faction . . . responsible for the ruin of the most glorious Church upon

Charles II, Oxford (1934), I, 200; Baxter, *Reliquiae* (1931 edn.), 169. See also [H. Croft], *The Naked Truth* (1674), passim; B. Laney, *A Sermon Preached Before the King at Whitehall* (1675), passim; [P. Gunning or P. Fell], *Lex Talionis* (1676), passim; F. Turner, *Animadversions upon a Late Pamphlet entituled the Naked Truth* (1676), passim; E. W. Kirby, 'The Naked Truth: A Plea for Church Unity', *Church History* 7 (1938), 45–61.
9 M. Goldie, 'The Theory of Religions Intolerance in Restoration England' in O. Grell, J. Israel and N. Tyacke (eds.), *From Persecution to Toleration*, Oxford (1991), 331–68.

earth'. Between 1681 and 1685 Sancroft presided over the years of fiercest persecution of the entire Restoration.[10]

Often but not always opposed to this high-church persecution were Baxter's third group of conforming clergy, the Latitudinarians. For Baxter these were 'mostly Cambridge men', and of 'Universal Principles and free'. Largely educated by the Cambridge Platonists, during the Restoration many of these Latitudinarians preached to enormous audiences in large London parishes.[11] The Latitudinarians were never more than a small group within the restored church, and were described by others far more than by themselves as 'Latitudinarians'. They shared a collection of similar but not identical attitudes and emphases, and maintained close personal relationships rather than functioning as an organised party within the church. They also grew more conservative in the later years of the Restoration and when they were elevated to the topmost ranks of its hierarchy after 1689. Much of their work for the Church of England was viewed by men of opposite ecclesiological temperaments, such as Sheldon, as the exercise of different ministries appropriate to different gifts. Several Latitudinarians received promotions at Sheldon's and Sancroft's hands that were appropriate recognitions not merely of their increasing conservatism, but also of the value placed upon the use of these different gifts in service of Christianity. Thus, the many arguments from natural religion against atheism that the Latitudinarians composed in the Restoration were often seen by their high-church colleagues as complementary to their own sacramentarian emphases rather than as directly opposed to their reverence for the priestly office and ceremony. Restoration Latitudinarians and high churchmen largely shared a 'moral theology' that was more or less close to Arminianism and more or less opposed to strict Calvinism.[12]

[10] On Sheldon, Sutch, *Sheldon*, passim; Beddard, 'Sheldon', 1005–17; idem, 'The Privileges of Christchurch, Canterbury: Archbishop Sheldon's Enquiries of 1671', *Archaeologia Cantiana* 87 (1972), 81–100. On Sancroft and the Readership, Bodl. Tanner 155: 76–82 cited in Gasgoigne, 'Holy Alliance', 27; on Sheldon and Pearson, Bodl. Add. C. 305: 66 cited in Gasgoigne, 'Holy Alliance', 24.

[11] Baxter, *Reliquiae*, 386–7; T. Birch, 'Life of Tillotson' in idem (ed.) John Tillotson, *Works* (1752), 28; N. Sykes, 'The Sermons of Archbishop Tillotson', *Theology* 58 (1955), 298; S. Pepys, *The Diary of Samuel Pepys*, ed. R. Latham and W. Matthews (1976), IX, 548, V, 87; J. Gascoigne, 'The Holy Alliance'.

[12] Not merely did high churchmen and Latitudinarians share many soteriological attitudes, but both held works of natural theology such as Grotius' *De Veritate Religionis Christianae* in high regard. Sheldon had been a member of the Tew Circle before the Civil War as well as Falkland and Chillingworth; Chillingworth was Laud's son-in-law. For an argument stressing the areas of agreement between the Latitudinarians and other Restoration Anglicans to the extent of denying the reality of the Latitudinarians as more than a polemic label used by nonconformists see J. Spurr, '"Latitudinarianism" and the Restoration Church', *Historical Journal* 31: 1 (1988), 61–82; also idem, *The Restoration Church*, Yale (1991). That the Latitudinarians did not share a set of identical attitudes and were not a 'party' means that caution should be used in specifying the attitudes of each Lati-

Nonetheless, the Latitudinarians were a very significant force aiming at broadening the church through comprehension throughout the Restoration, which often drew them into conflict with high-church views. Having been conformists to the Cromwellian church, many Latitudinarians maintained links with dissenters. Some – but certainly not all – attempted to soften the impact of persecution in their own parishes and allowed a greater variety of worship in their own churches than was officially required. Surveying the attitudes of the Restoration Latitudinarians, Richard Baxter wrote that they abhorred 'the imposition of . . . little things'. Burnet summed up the sentiments of his fellow Latitudinarians similarly, writing that while they 'loved the constitution of the Church and the liturgy, and could live well under them' they 'did not think it unlawful to live under another form' and 'wished that things might have been carried with more moderation'.[13]

Before the re-establishment of the Church of England, Edward Stillingfleet's *Irenicum* had pleaded for moderation, praised Charles II's promise in his Declaration of Breda of 'liberty for tender consciences' and pointed

tudinarian and their areas of disagreement with others, not that they did not share sufficient attitudes and personal relationships to have constituted a recognised grouping within the church, during the Restoration itself and immediately afterwards when contemporaries such as Burnet described them as 'Latitudinarians'. That Latitudinarianism was a label applied abusively by others in the Restoration more than it was applied by themselves does not mean that they did not support many of the attitudes labelled as 'Latitudinarian' or 'moderate'; that 'high church' was a rarely used term before 1689 does not mean that there were not Restoration high churchmen. Spurr's case is built far too much upon nominalism. For instance, he quotes Barrow on his dislike for application of the name 'Latitudinarian', but fails to quote the rest of Barrow's manuscript from which this quotation is drawn, in which Barrow sets out an extended plea for ecclesiastical moderation and the alteration of some ceremonies in order to allow the nonconformists to conform, and assaults Anglican 'formalists'; in the lines immediately following Barrow's denunciation of the name Latitudinarian, he declared that those who were thus named held the best opinions held by contemporary Anglican churchmen.

13 Baxter, *Reliquiae*, 386–7; G. Burnet, *History of My Own Time*, Oxford (1823), I, 323–4, cited in Cranston, Locke, 127; *DNB* s.n. Stillingfleet, Tillotson, Patrick (the first two maintaining close links with dissenters and the last being far more willing to persecute them); cf. Locke's page list and the pages referred to in his copy of E. Calamy's *An Abridgement of Mr Baxter's History of his Life and Times* (1702) in the Bodleian Library, Oxford for his interest in *c.* 1703 in comprehension and links between Latitudinarians and nonconformists. R. Ashcraft very valuably emphasises that some Latitudinarians were active in persecuting dissenters in his 'Latitudinarianism and Toleration: Historical Myth versus Political History' in R. Ashcraft, R. Kroll and P. Zagorin (eds.), *Philosophy, Religion and Science in England 1640–1700*, Cambridge (1992), 151–77. This is unquestionably true. However, Fowler's brother and father had both been ejected in 1662, Fowler apparently himself smashed a 'popish' window in Gloucester Cathedral in 1671, and he was not one of those persecuting nonconformists. Tillotson thought hard before conforming, and was generally opposed to persecution. These are the two Latitudinarians that Spurr has also identified as the most eirenic. It was – significantly – with these two most eirenic of the Latitudinarians that Locke had the closest relations.

out the incongruity of men being 'tied up to such things which they may do or let alone, and yet be very good Christians still'. He suggested that

> were we so happy but to take off things granted unnecessary by all, and suspected by many, and judged unlawful by some; and to make nothing the bonds of our communion, but what Christ hath done . . . allowing a liberty for matters of indifferency . . . we might indeed be restored to a true, primitive lustre far sooner, than by furnishing up some antiquated ceremonies, which can derive their pedigree no higher than from some ancient custom and tradition.

He also argued that the primitive church had been 'promiscuously' governed by bishops and presbyters without the later distinction between their offices, an argument that presbyterians were repeatedly to cite against him when he later came to find rather more to say in favour of episcopacy and became less sympathetic to dissent.[14]

The most eirenic were John Tillotson, Edward Fowler and John Wilkins. Tillotson had been a presbyterian, was frequently rumoured to allow different postures at the Sacrament due to the major opposition to Anglican requirements of kneeling, and his student John Beardman declared later that he had 'no great liking for the liturgy or ceremonies, or indeed, the government of this church'. Tillotson frequently pleaded for the church 'not to insist upon little things, but to yield them up', writing of the 'plausible exceptions of those, who differ from us'. As Burnet summed up Tillotson's attitude, he thought that 'the less the communion of the church was clogged with disputable opinions or practices, the world would be the happier, consciences the freer, and the church the quieter'. Wilkins, Tillotson's father-in-law, similarly declared in 1668 his opposition to the maintenance of a narrow church by severe penal codes 'which set up the Church as a top on the toe, it will not spin or stand longer than as it is whipped by penal laws; I would have it stand on the broad basis, and then it will stand without whipping'. In his 1670 *Principles and Practices of Certain Moderate Divines*, Fowler declared it 'extremely desirable' that 'the terms of communion with the Church of England and likewise of exercising the ministerial function therein, may be so enlarged, as to take in all that are of any reason, sobriety and moderation'. He would be 'very glad', he wrote in concluding the work, 'if our Church Doors were set wider open'.[15]

[14] E. Stillingfleet, *Irenicum* (1662), title page, preface sig. a2r–sig. a3r, 121, and passim; on Stillingfleet's changing attitudes see my 'The Ecclesiology of the Latitude-Men 1660–89: Stillingfleet, Tillotson and "Hobbism"', *Journal of Ecclesiastical History* 26 (1985), 407–27.

[15] T. Birch, 'Life of Tillotson' in *Works* (1752), xxix, 407; G. Burnet, *A Sermon Preached at the Funeral of . . . John . . . Archbishop of Canterbury* (1695), 31; E. Fowler, *The Principles and Practices of Certain Moderate Divines* (1670), title page, 333–4; *The Memoirs of John Howe*, ed. E. Calamy (1724), 33.

These sentiments led to several attempts in the Restoration by some of the Latitudinarians to secure a comprehension, and at various moments they added to this – although often with considerable reluctance – support for toleration of those few who would still be unable to conform. The first of these attempts at comprehension and toleration came in 1667–8 when Charles dismissed the Anglican Clarendon and turned to a ministry of five leading politicians, known by the first letters of their surnames as the 'Cabal' ministry, who shared few sentiments other than support for religious toleration. A bill for comprehension was drawn up in 1667 by several of Charles' advisers, although it was finally not proposed in Parliament, apparently simply because its sponsor got cold feet. In early 1668 Wilkins discussed with some of the moderate bishops his desire to determine 'what might be yielded without damage to . . . our worship to effect an understanding among all moderate Protestants' and was involved with his close friend Thomas Barlow in conferring with various dissenters to see what they would require to enter the church and then in drawing up proposals for comprehension and toleration; Tillotson and Stillingfleet may also have been involved. Wilkins proposed that the church 'left indifferent or wholly omitted' many disputed ceremonial issues, such as the wearing of surplices and kneeling at receipt of the Lord's Supper, review of the liturgy, and no required reordination for Anglican ministers who had been ordained by Presbyterians, the suggestion which promoted Pearson's hostile *Promiscuous Ordinations*. To this comprehension they added support for toleration outside the church of those who would remain unable to enter, expecting these to be very few in number. There was no suggestion of doctrinal tests for those to be tolerated. Before launching these discussions Wilkins had been closeted with Charles II for two hours and there can be little doubt that Charles' support for both forms of toleration was important to the formation of these plans. Sheldon attacked the Anglican supporters of these plans as 'treacherous divines' and led an energetic campaign against comprehension which therefore foundered on the rocks of parliamentary opposition.[16]

Wilkins and Barlow had discussed their 1667–8 proposals with leading nonconformists, including Baxter, Manton and Bates from the presbyterians, and apparently also John Owen, the leading Independent. Some older presbyterians, such as Baxter, desired comprehension but were uninterested in or disliked toleration outside the church because of their long-standing desire for one uniform Protestant church in the nation and opposition to toleration of Catholics. Independents like Owen and a number of

---

[16] Barlow's manuscript introduction to the Bodleian Library copy of *Several Tracts Relating to the Great Acts for Comprehension* (1680), xiii cited in W. Simon, 'Comprehension in the Age of Charles II', *Church History* (1962), 442 and passim; Thomas, 'Comprehension'.

younger presbyterians desired toleration, but wished to see strict enforcement of morality and doctrine and disliked the moral and doctrinal laxity
involved in the Anglican proposals.[17] On behalf of the Independents Owen
proposed indulgence for all those who were strictly orthodox, excluding
antitrinitarians by specifying the necessity of belief in 'God the Father; and
Jesus Christ His Eternall Sonne, the true God; and in the Holy Ghost, God
co-equal with the Father and the Sonne, God blessed for ever'. For Owen,
liberty of worship was also to be denied to the blasphemous or licentious.
In direct contrast to the Anglican proposals, Owen's proposals were thus
almost entirely concerned with securing doctrinal orthodoxy and moral
discipline.[18]

In two pamphlets of 1667, Owen expressed similar views and concern
with morality and the 'fundamental points of Christianity'. Pointing out
that dissenters embraced all the doctrine of the Church of England, Owen
argued that if their worship and belief did not attack the 'fundamentals of
Christian Religion' or 'public tranquility' then they should not be persecuted. Men should worship according to 'their light'. Owen opposed the
Anglican claim that liberty of judgement was allowed with ceremonial
enforcement; men had to worship as they judged was 'acceptable to God'.
He argued that toleration had been the practice of early Christians except
when used against those 'who differed in great and weighty fundamental
truths', the Arians, or when 'moral honesty' was not realised. It is not
entirely clear what Owen meant by 'moral honesty', but it seems to have
been wider than simply not threatening 'public tranquility' and to have
involved more instances of immorality than those of direct harm to others.

[17] Thomas, 'Comprehension', 197–207; Thorndike, *Works*, V, 302–8. Burnet names Tillotson and Stillingfleet as involved in 1668: Burnet, *History*, I, 259. He may have confused
this with later attempts, or he may have known better than some other
participants, such as Baxter, whose *Reliquiae* falsely magnifies his own awareness of
events: Simon, 'Comprehension', 446–7 n. 15. On Wilkins generally see B. Shapiro, *John
Wilkins*, Berkeley (1969); S. Parker, *History of His Own Time* (1727), 36–7 cited in N.
Sykes, *From Sheldon to Secker*, Cambridge (1959), 81; Tanner MS 44 fo. 37, 196 cited in
Spurr, 'Latitudinarianism', 72 on Sheldon calling Wilkins' elevation 'bad news'; Sheldon
seems to have promoted several other works against comprehension and toleration by his
chaplains, including works by Thomas Tomkyns, and Richard Perrinchief, and he may
have encouraged publication of Herbert Thorndike's pamphlets and John Pearson's
Promiscuous Ordinations, discussed above. Thomas, 'Comprehension', 203–6; Baxter,
Reliquiae, III, i cited in *ibid.*, 205; Lamont, *Baxter*, ch. 4; R. A. Beddard, 'Vincent Alsop
and the Emancipation of Restoration Dissent', *Journal of Ecclesiastical History* 24 (1973),
173–84.
[18] Owen's terms are stated in Thorndike's *Works*, V, 302–8 at 308. Cf. Owen's desire for
defining fifteen doctrinal 'fundamentals' to set clear limits to toleration in 1652. This is
discussed in Worden, *The Rump Parliament*, 284–5; 294–7; P. Toon, *God's Statesman:
The Life and Work of John Owen*, Exeter (1971), 83–6; A. Woolrych, *Commonwealth to
Protectorate*, Oxford (1982), 38; cf. also the works cited in note one of chapter two above.
I am grateful to Dr J. Champion for discussion of this point.

He thus argued that all opinions which 'produce practices contrary to civil society, moral honesty, or the light of nature, ought in all instances of them to be restrained'. Wide as it was, Owen's case was still fundamentally a case for the liberty that was desirable for conscience, the overriding requirement of religion: conscience could be pleaded for differing forms of worship, but no claim of conscience could be made for immorality or for heresy.[19]

Owen made no plea for a comprehension. The Independents had defined their view of worship in the 1640s and 1650s not merely against Anglican episcopalian uniformity but also against presbyterian desire for a uniform national church persecuting those outside of its boundaries. Their ideal was of the gathered church composed only of members who testified publicly to their conversion by God's grace and agreed in their interpretation of the faith. This ideal was expressed well in the 1640s when John Gifford advised his church to admit any new member only 'after you are satisfied in the worke of grace in the party you are to joyne with'. The ideal was that the church was to be a voluntary congregation of worshippers who were moved by the Spirit to join in communion. By the late 1650s John Owen was formulating these congregational principles in the *Declaration of the Faith and Order Owned and Practiced in the Congregational Churches in England*. In this *Declaration*, Owen argued that Christ had established local churches to administer the sacraments. Various such local churches or independent congregations could join together into a synod for advice to each other, but such a synod would have absolutely no power to institute forms of discipline, belief or worship. These principles carried on in the Restoration, and the Independents criticised the Anglican practice of admitting to communion the unregenerate and regenerate alike. Their principles were thus supportive of a toleration defined for and circumscribed by 'conscience' rather than comprehensive. They certainly had no desire to see a comprehension that would leave them persecuted.[20]

Owen recognised, however, that an indulgence would leave the Church established with all 'outward privileges' and 'legal maintenance' continued. At no point in the Interregnum had he proposed that religion should be disestablished; it was the duty of the civil magistrate to see his own religion taught and financially supported. Owen agreed with most Anglicans and presbyterians that it was the duty of the magistrate to seek

[19] J. Owen, *Indulgence* in *Works*, XIII, 519–40; idem, *A Peace Offering in an Apology and Humble Plea for Indulgence and Liberty of Conscience* in *ibid.*, 541–74.
[20] Generally, G. Nuttall, *Visible Saints*, passim; M. Sommerville, 'Independent Thought 1603–49', unpublished Cambridge University Ph.D Thesis 1982; Thomas, 'Comprehension', passim; H. Tibbutt (ed.), *The Minutes of the First Independent Church at Bedford* (1976), 19 cited in Keeble, *Literary Culture*, 9–10.

the spiritual good of his subjects. There was, however, for Owen a vital distinction between support through money and support through persecution. The civil magistrate was to support his own religion, and he was not to tolerate those who were licentious or blasphemous, but he was also not to interfere in the worship of local congregations or to persecute them if they were peaceful and orthodox. In 1667 Owen continued to argue that those indulged would have to pay the maintenance to the established church commanded by the sovereign. He recognised that the Kings in England had long dispensed with penalties against conformity, and asked for similar dispensation. He expressed confidence in the royal declarations by Charles (such as the Declaration of Breda) which had signified Charles' desire to allow liberty of conscience. He did argue that the King should grant this indulgence in Parliament, but this support for a parliamentary role in jursidiction was given little stress, with explicit recognition of recent parliamentary intolerance.[21]

II

There are a few very slight indications that John Locke may have become more sympathetic to toleration – both through comprehension and through indulgence – between composing his *Two Tracts* and the 1667–8 plans for and debates over 'toleration'. The rereading of a work which Locke had initially read as simply defending Anglican imposition may have promoted support for comprehension. In 1665 Locke reread and took notes from Falkland's *Discourse on Infallibility*. Falkland assaulted the Catholic stress upon ritual and declared that the holding of many beliefs, including such important beliefs as the Trinity, did not itself effect moral behaviour and was therefore to be left to the individual's interpretation of Scripture rather than to be enforced by the church. There was a point at which the Anglican enforcement of ceremonial forms as *adiaphora* and its enforcement of even the most central beliefs of Chrsitianity could seem to come close to 'popish' enforcement or at least as undesirable; the Latitudinarians were frequently to claim Falkland as an inspiration for their support for comprehension.

Locke had probably read the 1661 *Discourse on Liberty of Conscience* at about the time of its publication, and therefore before composing the second tract. The *Discourse* argued, in common with most Anglican works of the period, that liberty of conscience was preserved as liberty of belief despite enforced *adiaphora*, but it also pleaded energetically for comprehension in ceremonial. The *Discourse* was by Boyle's friend Peter Pett

---

[21] Owen, *Indulgence in Works*, XIII, 532–7.

and published with his encouragement. Locke was seeking Boyle's friendship and approval in the early 1660s, and his reading of the tract is likely
to have been prompted by this knowledge. Like Boyle's works, the
Discourse also declared that Christianity was focused upon morality and
described its essential matters as agreed upon by almost all Protestants.
While Locke was probably not convinced by the *Discourse*'s plea for comprehension when reading it, since the second of the *Two Tracts* was most
probably composed after reading the *Discourse*, he did thereby gain an
early awareness of 'Latitudinarian' views.[22]

Boyle's personal influence in the years after 1660 was probably pushing
him away from seeing rigid uniformity as necessary to order. It was surely
significant that it was to Boyle that Locke wrote several letters seeking
Boyle's approbation while on a diplomatic mission to Cleves in 1665.
Locke reported to Boyle that in Cleves, which had large Calvinist,
Lutheran and Catholic congregations, uniformity was not necessary to
peace: 'the distance in their churches' did not enter 'into their houses'.
They 'quietly permit one another to choose their way to heaven; for I
cannot observe any quarrels or animosities amongst them upon the
account of religion'. This reiteration, almost word for word, of the
phraseology of both Locke's 1659 objections to Stubbe's proposed toleration and of the ideal held to be impracticable in the *Two Tracts* is
unquestionably significant: the methodically-minded Locke had clearly
himself recognised that he had found practised what he had opposed as
impracticable. According to Locke, this 'good correspondence' of the
people owed much to 'the power of the magistrate' but also much to the
'prudence and good nature of the people' who entertained 'different opinions, without any secret hatred or rancour'.[23]

While in Cleves, Locke attended many different professions' religious
performances. He assiduously documented their absurdities, with personal
experience substituting for travel literature as his source of information on
the bizarre things that people were willing to believe and practise because
of their education and customs. A Lutheran meeting had seemed like a
'theater' performance with people singing merrily 'with their hats on';
Catholic choristers were a 'consort of little pigs'. The letters also communicate at times, however, an important sense of Locke trying to understand

22 MS Locke f27 55b (mispaginated); 57b on reading of Falkland between 1664 and 1666;
    Falkland, *Discourse on Infallibility* (1659), passim; [Pete] R. [Pet] T., *A Discourse Con-
    cerning Liberty of Conscience* (1661), passim; MS Locke f14, 122 (a note recorded before
    Gassendi's *Life of Peiresk*, which was read in 1664): MS Locke f27, 2ff.; cf. PRO 30/24/
    6A/347 and MS Locke f5, Oct. 14, 1681 on Pett and Locke; cf. also PRO 30/24/47/30 on
    Locke and Falkland. MS Film. 79, 35 includes a 1667 note to Chillingworth, probably
    indicating purchase, but not definitely indicating reading; it is possible that Chilling-
    worth's *Religion of Protestants* was influential in softening Locke's attitudes in 1667.
23 Cranston, *Locke*, 79–87; *Correspondence*, I, 175.

and appreciate the religious sentiments of those involved. Locke wrote that 'to be serious' the Catholic religion in Cleves was 'a different thing from what we believe it in England'. He had confronted his 'prejudices' and recognised that he had not met any 'soe good naturd people or soe civill as the Catholick preists'. This softening of Locke's attitudes did not stop him from continuing to see Roman Catholic priests as the essence of priestly domination over their communicants. The Christmas crèche in the Catholic church had had a 'flock of sheepe cut out of cards' standing outside the stable and untended by their shepherds, 'the best emblem I had seene a long time, and me thought represented these poore innocent people, who while their sheepheards pretend soe much to follow Christ . . . are left unregarded in the barren wildernesse'.[24]

Locke went on by arguing that the Catholic communicants had been 'negligent . . . in their service'. Indicating a belief that elaborate outward performance was responsible for this, Locke declared that 'these mummerys in religion, would bring it everywhere to this passe, did not feare and the severity of the Magistrate preserve it, which being taken away here they very easily suffer themselves to slubber over their ceremonys, which in other places are kept up with soe much zeale and exactnesse'. He continued, however, by equating such enforced practice with the 'slubbering negligence' of Cleves' Catholics: 'methinks they [Cleves' Catholics] are not to be blamd, since the one seems to me as much religion as the other'. Locke's own sentiments about worship are not set out clearly in this passage, his comparison is of the equivalent inauthenticity of magisterially enforced ceremonial and Catholic 'mummeries', and his comments may well refer only to differing Catholic practices in different countries. His equation of the different practices in worship as equally inauthentic may just possibly, however, show his first, faint glimmerings of concern about the lack of authenticity in ceremonial performance where the magistrate's force compelled 'zeale and exactnesse', as perhaps in the English church envisioned in the *Two Tracts*.[25]

Locke may, then, have come to see some desirability for authenticity of worship, some possibility for toleration if all were prudent and the magistrate strong, and some desirability for toleration through comprehension through his reading, friendship with Boyle and travel to Cleves, even before meeting in 1666 the anticlerical and tolerationist Lord Ashley. Ashley, later first earl of Shaftesbury, was one of the most important political figures of the late seventeenth century as a leading minister to the King, then as a leading opponent of the King's policies, and ultimately as a

[24] *Correspondence*, I, 177; 180; cf. *Correspondence*, I, 180, 182 for a hostile comparison of English presbyterians with a Clevan Calvinist expressing 'rubish of divinity'.
[25] *Correspondence*, I, 180.

plotter of armed resistance to the King. Locke and Ashley struck up an immediate rapport and at Easter of 1667 Locke went to stay with him at Exeter House in London, and only returned to Oxford occasionally in the next sixteen years.[26] Throughout the Interregnum Ashley had been a supporter of a nationally established church maintained by tithes, with toleration for those who remained outside of its boundaries and worshipped peacefully, but not for 'anabaptist' extremes. This commitment to a very largely tolerationist settlement and an established national church continued into the Restoration, and Ashley supported the King's attempts to provide toleration by suspension of the penal laws against dissenters in his Declaration of Indulgence in December 1662. He supported the monarchical ecclesiastical authority claimed in the Declaration and opposed the later penal measures.[27]

Within a very short time after Locke had entered Ashley's household at Easter 1667 the two had become close friends, not least because Locke performed an operation on Ashley that saved his life. Locke became Ashley's adviser on the many affairs of state and business that occupied him as one of the leading ministers of state from 1667 to 1672, and as the Lord Chancellor from November 1672 to November 1673, by which time he had become the first earl of Shaftesbury. Locke's pupil and Ashley's grandson, the third earl of Shaftesbury, famously recounted that his grandfather had quickly set Locke 'upon the study of the religious and civil affairs of the nation, with whatsoever related to the business of a Minister of State, in which he was so successful that my grandfather soon began to use him as a friend and consult with him on all occasions of that kind'. By becoming adviser to a minister of state Locke had found a position sufficiently challenging for a man of his abilities – and even one that was challenging enough for his own elevated estimate of these abilities. It is important to stress that when Locke became Ashley's friend and adviser in the unforeseen and far-off future lay his role as a leader of political opposition to Charles II for most of the years from 1675 to 1681. Even this political opposition was that of a frustrated courtier desiring a change of policies who accepted office in 1679 and who desired it at all other times, and not that of leader of a permanent party of opposition. Even further in the future and surely in 1667 completely unthinkable to Locke was Ashley's role as one of the leaders of plans for armed resistance to Charles II in about 1682. Locke's continued role as Shaftesbury's adviser during those later events must not obscure the fact that at Easter 1667 Locke was enter-

[26] Cranston, *Locke*, 95–7.
[27] K. H. D. Haley, *The First Earl of Shaftesbury*, Oxford (1978); for the details cited in this paragraph see chs. 3–9 and pp. 49, 66–7; 141; 161; 163–6; 180; 307–8; 740–1; chs. 17–28.

ing the service and household of an important supporter of Charles II, and that by late 1667 that supporter was one of Charles' leading ministers.[28]

III

In 1667 or early 1668 Locke wrote an 'Essay on Toleration'. It is extremely likely that consultations with Ashley were part of the context in which Locke first composed this 'Essay on Toleration'. A discussion of religious toleration would have been exactly the kind of issue that Ashley, with his own firm commitment to ecclesiastical liberty, would have requested of Locke in the period which began with the pleas for comprehension of Bishop Edward Reynolds in a sermon to Parliament in late 1666 and ended with bills and proposals being drawn up for comprehension and toleration. It is possible that in at least its final version the 'Essay on Toleration' was intended to be read by the King; its second half raised a number of prudential issues concerned with the practice of toleration or persecution in England, and spoke then of toleration in 'your' church, the appropriate term for address to the King. The King supported and consulted with Wilkins and almost certainly with Bridgeman and Hale on the various plans for comprehension and indulgence. He probably consulted with Ashley and thus with Locke, particularly because Locke seems to have been involved in composition of several other manuscripts of ecclesiastical advice on behalf of, if not actually for perusal by, the King over the next few years. It is also possible, however, that the 'Essay on Toleration' began simply as some form of discussion document involving a group of friends. It went through four drafts, at least two of which were not in Locke's hand. One version was signed by Locke as 'Atticus', a pseudonym that he used with various of his Oxford friends. The first two *Drafts* of the *Essay Concerning Human Understanding* were the result of a group that met at Exeter House in about 1670 or 1671 which probably included some of Locke's Oxford friends. The influence of such a group might help to explain some of the contradictions and tensions between the four drafts, and even within single drafts, that will become apparent during the discussion that follows.[29]

---

[28] Amsterdam Remonstrants MSS J. 20 cited in Cranston, *Locke*, 114; *ibid.*, 113.

[29] The most readily available version of the 'Essay on Toleration' is in Fox Bourne's *Life*, I, 174–94, and J. Gough, *John Locke's Political Philosophy: Eight Studies*, Oxford (2nd edn., 1973), 197–9 prints the addenda and corrigenda from one of the other two versions. The best currently available version of all four drafts together is edited by K. Inoue, *John Locke, An Essay Concerning Toleration and Toleratio*, Nara Women's University, Nara, Japan (1974). Citations that follow are from Fox Bourne wherever this is possible, as that is the most accessible version, and supplemented by Gough, but in several instances are from Inoue as the only printed source for the other two versions. The original spelling is retained.

All four drafts of the 'Essay on Toleration' declare straightforwardly that all 'speculative opinions and divine worshipp' had a 'clear title to universal toleration', an 'absolute and universall right to toleration', a perfect and 'uncontrollable liberty'. Locke's examples of such 'speculative opinions' covered a wide range, from transubstantiation and the antipodes to Christ's reign on earth, but was most startling in explicitly including 'belief of the Fall' in one of the early drafts and 'belief of the Trinity' in all four drafts. Only atheism was explicitly excluded from the list of speculative opinions. Locke argued that the belief of these speculative opinions did not affect at all one's neighbour 'or civill society'. They contained nothing against peace and nothing to injure one's neighbour. It was not belief of speculative opinions that caused dispute, but men forgetting their fallibility and out of 'a secret conceit' of their own infallibility attempting to compel others to accept their views. While not an explicit denial of strict Calvinism, there is here once again an implicit denial of the necessity of the remodelling of the world to conform to the theological certainties of a regenerated conscience that had been a prominent result of that soteriology in several of its major strains in Civil-War and Interregnum England.[30]

Locke paired the 'time, place and manner' of divine worship with speculative opinions in possessing an absolute right to toleration. These were 'a commerce passing only between God' and the individual. Locke argued that this divine worship also did not affect one's neighbour at all; whether one worshipped, for example, in the 'pompous' manner of the Catholics or in the 'plainer' way of the Calvinists had no effect on any one else. This harmlessness conferred upon worship a right to toleration as a 'private . . . superpolitical concernment', but Locke also alleged the need for worship to be authentic. In worship nothing was indifferent unless it was believed to be indifferent. Worship was 'that homage I pay to that God I adore in the way I judge acceptable'. It could not be a 'forced exterior performance' but had to be a 'voluntary and secret choice of the mind'. As in the *Two Tracts*, men's convictions were declared to be beyond the power of force to change; in the 'Essay on Toleration' this became a ground for toleration of practice and not merely of belief. In an early draft of the 'Essay on Toleration' the need for personal authenticity may have stood behind the argument that 'I ought to have liberty in my religious worship because it is a thing between God and me.' Locke's position had here changed dramatically from the *Two Tracts*.[31]

According to the 'Essay on Toleration', the civil magistrate's whole 'trust, power and authority' was confined to securing man's preservation

---

[30] Fox Bourne, *Life*, 175–6; 178; 186; Gough, *Locke's Political Philosophy*, 197; Inoue, *Locke*, 36.
[31] Fox Bourne, *Life*, 176–7; Inoue, *Locke*, 36.

and the interests of the community. His whole trust was 'but for the good, preservation and peace of men in that society over which he is sett'. This was a largely unexceptional statement, and explicitly declared to be such by Locke; the *Two Tracts* advanced nothing against such a broadly-phrased view. In itself, this says nothing about the origins of, or any practical limitations upon, such authority. What was striking was that men's spiritual good was not included in the good that the magistrate was to seek. The ends of magistracy defined the 'standard and measure' of its jurisdiction, and these ends did not extend beyond the concerns of this life. The magistrate was simply an 'umpire between man and man'. The magistrate was neither entrusted nor empowered to force men to speculative opinions or to a set form of divine worship. For Locke, it was not merely religious issues that exceeded the bounds of magisterial jurisdiction. The magistrate was not to enforce morality except as this was necessary to the preservation of men and society and for the 'good' of the community. It was, indeed, 'injustice' to force men further than the public good required and to 'enjoin men care of their private civil concernments'. The magistrate was merely to prevent men 'invading' others' rights and to secure the 'good of the public', including especially and explicitly the preservation of the society. Government existed only to prevent 'violence' between men and laws were therefore to be made only for the security of government and 'protection of the people in their lives, estates and liberties'.[32]

Locke argued that 'however strange it may seeme . . . the lawmaker hath nothing to doe with morall vertues and vices, nor ought to enjoyn the duties of the second table any otherwise then barely as they are subservient to the good and preservation of mankind under government'. Thus 'ingratitude' was a vice, but since gratitude was not necessary to the preservation of the society or to prevent injury the magistrate was therefore not empowered to enforce it. Locke did not give much indication of how extensive a morality it might be necessary to enforce in order to secure protection from injury, the common good and the preservation of the society itself, although one concluding comment which suggested that this might be considerable will be examined in a few moments. Ironically, the most substantial comment on what might be necessary to preserve society and government came in a suggestion that a very significant part of morality might *not* be enforced. Locke canvassed in one draft of the 'Essay on Toleration' – although he obviously then thought better of it – the view that the preservation of the society was so important that theft itself might be permitted when it was useful for preserving the society. In the *Essays* he had described Sparta as a country whose men were brave but which broke

---

[32] Fox Bourne, *Life*, 176; 180; 185–6.

the law of nature by encouraging theft; in this deleted discussion in the 'Essay on Toleration' he suggested that such theft had been useful in preserving the courage of the men, and that it was legitimate since that courage was necessary to Sparta's preservation. Despite his discussion of laws to protect property, he argued that the magistrate had the power to make rules transferring property from one man to another where this was judged necessary to the preservation of the society.[33]

Locke had shifted from defining the power of the magistrate as an 'absolute and arbitrary' power over all indifferent matters in the *Two Tracts* to a jurisdiction clearly limited to securing the terrestrial 'public good'. This was not primarily a shift on the origins of political authority, but in the 'Essay' Locke also importantly condemned the view that monarchy was *jure divino*, a view which he described as involving belief that a 'sole, supream, arbitrary power . . . is . . . by divine right in a single person'. He cited against this both 'Magna Charta' and 'the laws' under which Englishmen lived. He did not clearly commit himself to the view that government had originated in the 'grant and consent' of the people, although he did alter his initial phraseology of men 'growing into a commonwealth' to that of men 'entering' into a commonwealth. It is significant that Locke was willing to make such a straightforward declaration of the limits of royal authority in a manuscript that was very probably intended at some point to be advice for the King himself.[34]

As importantly, however, Locke was unequivocal in describing passive resistance as the only recourse against rulers who exceeded their authority. If, for instance, the magistrate imposed a religious settlement on every member of the society and thus denied them precisely that 'absolute right' to liberty of worship and belief that was proclaimed in the 'Essay on Toleration', they had no consequent right to resist him. Men were instead 'quietly to submit to the penalty the law inflicts'. The magistrate was 'not accountable to any tribunal here'. Locke roundly condemned as an hypocrite any individual who proclaimed the need for disobedience for the sake of conscience but was unwilling 'to purchase heaven' at the cost of 'estate, liberty', or even 'life itself'.[35]

33 *Ibid.*, 180–3; *Essays*, 169; 175.
34 Fox Bourne, *Life*, 175. Cf. Gough, *Locke's Political Philosophy*, 211 on the amendment from 'growing' to 'entering'. On Magna Carta itself, see J. C. Holt, *Magna Carta*, Cambridge (1965); on Magna Carta in the seventeenth century, J. G. A. Pocock, *The Ancient Constitution and the Feudal Law*, Cambridge (1987); J. Sommerville, *Politics and Ideology in England 1603–40* (1986). In the *Letter From a Person of Quality* in 1675 Magna Carta was discussed again, then explicitly for its protection of property from the King's arbitrary action, with the clergy declared to be opponents to its statement that 'Our Kings may not take our fields, our vineyards, our corn and our sheep': *Letter* in *Works*, X, 246.
35 Fox Bourne, *Life*, 180–1.

Locke's commitment standing behind the illegitimacy of resistance was not spelled out, but all four drafts of the 'Essay on Toleration' were permeated by a sense of the fragility of political society. All of the drafts clearly excluded from the practice of toleration a number of groups which were seen as untrustworthy; the first three drafts also suggested the exclusion of many further groups as these were potentially but not already dangerous. According to all drafts, Roman Catholics of any country other than the papal state were not to be tolerated. Locke declared that men usually took up 'their religion in gross'; Roman Catholics mixed with their religious belief and worship a number of opinions destructive to human society, most notably the view that faith was not to be kept with heretics. The Pope claimed infallibility and absolute obedience, tying his subjects' 'consciences . . . to his girdle'. He proclaimed his ability to dispense with all oaths, promises and obligations to princes. Since these views were mixed with religion they were reverenced as 'fundamentall truths' and were then defended as sacred. At several points in the 'Essay on Toleration' Locke recognised that Catholic worship and belief – however pompous and preposterous – had a 'right' to toleration equal to that of any other form of speculative opinions and worship, but answered that it was 'very hard' to separate this worship and belief from the opinions 'absolutely destructive of all society'. Indeed, shifting from the juristic concerns of the first part of the 'Essay on Toleration', the second half of the 'Essay' focused on prudential issues of toleration in contemporary England and declared the persecution of Catholics a desirable policy. Such persecution convinced Protestants that the King and Church of England were truly separate from and implacably opposed to Roman Catholicism – a comment that was perhaps an oblique recognition of the dissenters' claims that the ceremonial of the Church of England was not fully reformed from 'popery', and was perhaps even Locke's own opinion of the form of the restored church, but not clearly stated as his own opinion.[36]

Proclaiming the right to toleration of forms of divine worship, and therefore implicitly strongly critical of current Anglican persecution, the 'Essay on Toleration' referred nonetheless to 'our church' and argued, as we will see, that the uniting of most Protestants in the Church of England by persuasion and comprehension was desirable. The first three drafts of the 'Essay' were also particularly unsympathetic to nonconformity and permeated by Locke's continued fear of nonconformist sedition. They declared that most men with power attempted to establish only themselves in authority, few men 'forbearing to grasp at dominion' when they had the power to achieve it. Although not specifying its target here, behind this

---

[36] *Ibid.*, 183–4; 186–9.

comment was surely not merely hostility to current Anglican persecution but also the repeated Anglican assertion that the nonconformists had themselves been very intolerant in the Interregnum, a claim that Locke had already voiced in the *Two Tracts*, and which we will later see that he was to reiterate in his 1681 'Critical Notes Upon Edward Stillingfleet's Mischief and Unreasonableness of Separation' and in outline in the *Letter Concerning Toleration*: the current nonconformists' intolerance was obliquely mentioned at one point in the 'Essay on Toleration'.[37]

The political consequence that Locke drew from this desire for dominion *in all of the first three drafts* of the 'Essay' was that when men 'herd themselves' – an interesting choice of verb – into groups 'with distinctions from the public', they were to be suppressed as soon as they seemed dangerous. Size alone seemed to constitute sufficient hazard to demand magisterial suppression. Locke declared that the Quakers were to be watched and suppressed if they grew numerous, their 'bare keeping on their hats' being as much 'dangerous' when numerous as if they had 'a set forme of religion separate from the state'. The Quakers were probably chosen as the explicit target because they were far more clearly antipathetic to the Church of England than were presbyterians or Independents, had been the target of much attack by these groups as well as by Locke himself in the 1650s, and most importantly were refusing a central element of social subordination and thus posed to many a clear danger to 'order' in their refusal to do hat honour – in this period the head of the household wore his hat at home while sons and servants doffed theirs to him, and members of parliament wore their hats in the chamber to emphasise that they alone were masters there. More importantly, while it is not clear what constituted for Locke a 'set form of religion separate from the state', the apparent meaning of his comment is that all separate forms of religious worship with significant support were dangerous and were to be watched and suppressed.[38]

Ranged alongside the Catholic doctrine that faith was not to be kept with heretics were two other doctrines considered by Locke 'absolutely destructive to human society' and therefore not to be tolerated. The first was that if the magistrate did not make a public reformation in religion

---

37 *Ibid.*, 184–5; 189–90; 193–4. The 'Essay' did shift rather awkwardly from talking about 'our' church to 'your' church, most probably because it was intended to be shown to the King. Generally, however, the perspective adopted was that of persuading dissenters as 'them' to come to 'us' in 'our' church, very probably a self-identification of the author with the Church of England.

38 Cf. Wootton, 'Leveller Democracy and the Puritan Revolution' in J. Burns (ed.), *The Cambridge History of Political Thought 1450–1750*, Cambridge (1991), 412–42 at 432–3; C. Hill, *The World Turned Upside Down*, Harmondsworth, Middlesex (1972), 233; 246–7.

then the subject could or should. The target of this attack was again not spelled out, but in writing the *Two Tracts* Locke had himself directed this assault against Civil-War 'puritans'. They were the most notorious proponents of this doctrine in the eyes of most Restoration Anglicans, and the only apparent contemporary target of Locke's attack were any nonconformists who still legitimated the use of force to reform the church and establish the 'true' religion. The other view that Locke vilified was that one was 'bound to teach and propagate publicly' any opinion that one believed. Again the target was not explicitly identified, but again the only apparent contemporary target were those nonconformists who claimed that they had a duty to publicly preach and proselytise into their 'true religion' when this was against the law. Ranging this restriction alongside Locke's 'absolute right' to toleration of worship suggests that when writing the 'Essay on Toleration' Locke may have envisaged toleration of various forms of worship which did not extend to allowing their ministers to proselytise against the established religion, hardly the most generous form of toleration. Such a toleration, not allowing any 'derogation' of the doctrine or discipline of the Church of England, was to be instituted by the King in 1672, with Locke's support.[39]

It was only in the fourth and final version of the 'Essay on Toleration' that Locke dramatically changed his position, this time raising the issue of churches separate from the established religion in order to answer the argument that he had himself used in the first three drafts. He declared that if suppression was necessary for religious differences then it would be necessary for all differences in society to be suppressed, including the meetings of towns or corporations. Large separate churches were to be tolerated. This change was, however, accompanied by the argument that since the minds of men were 'nice and scrupulous' in religious questions dissenters were apt to divide and subdivide. They were – apparently currently – 'crumbled' in England, as separate from each other as from the Church of England. It was therefore said to be in the magistrate's interest to let them subdivide and not to unite them. Force would join them together; toleration would make them try to perpetuate the current regime since they could not hope for better treatment under another power. Here there is a hint – but not really much more than a hint – that Locke's category in the *Two Tracts* of the different professions of religion who sought to recommend themselves by peaceableness and sobriety had come to seem applicable in the fourth draft of 1667 to those dissenters who had separated from the Church of England in 1662, after the *Two Tracts* were written, and

---

[39] Fox Bourne, *Life*, 186 (three of the four versions read 'broach' instead of 'teach'); chapter 3 below on 1672.

who were also expending much effort denying at least the first of the opinions that Locke condemned – the duty to use force to reform religion if the magistrate did not.[40]

Force would unite dissenters. Experience showed that it did not convince men of their errors. This experience was of two kinds. Clearly opposing the behaviour of the pre-war Church of England, Locke identified Laudian force as having abetted rather than suppressed the growth of puritanism (a way of discussing the concerns of pre-war puritans that showed no necessary sympathy for their views). Equally, Locke cited the persecution of Anglicans by puritans in the Civil War as not having convinced them to adopt the views of their puritan persecutors. Locke also declared that the experience of man's 'own bosom' testified that he was 'chary' of preserving the liberty appropriate to men, the liberty of the mind. This was the faculty that raised them above 'beasts'. Force was directly antithetical to man's natural desire for such liberty. These two arguments, that force had generally caused the growth of dissension, and that persuasion was impossible through force since men naturally reacted against force because of their desire for intellectual liberty, were later to be important arguments for Locke, providing much of the evidentiary basis for his proclamations of the inefficacy of force. Without giving it quite the level of obvious emphasis within his argument that he was later to give to it, the ineffectiveness of force was already a significant element of his case for toleration in the 'Essay on Toleration'.[41]

Force was inefficient. According to Locke, other methods could be used to convert men to 'our church'. 'Courtesy, friendship and soft usage' all encouraged conversion. Recognising the power of custom and environment, Locke argued that many men took up their opinions 'upon trust'. Friendly behaviour towards them harnessed this. Men accepted opinions from those who acted well towards them. Even the 'inquisitive' who wished to adopt their religious beliefs from their own studies were more likely to consider the reasons behind the beliefs held by those who treated them well. In a concluding section of the 'Essay' in which Locke enumerated topics to be surveyed later, he condemned those who thought that force was the 'only art of government'. Men could at least be made 'friends to the state' even if they did not become 'sonnes of the church'. This was 'separation', but at least it was not a 'quarrel'.

It was more desirable, however, to 'alter minds and bring them over to your profession' (these last words were a point where Locke shifted awkwardly from speaking of 'our' church to speaking of 'your profession',

---

[40] *Ibid.*, 192; Gough, *Locke's Political Philosophy*, 198–9.
[41] Fox Bourne, *Life*, 189–90; 192–3.

perhaps as a failure of his prose, but more probably as an indication that the King was among the intended audience of the 'Essay', and without any sign at all that he wished to suggest thereby that this was not also his own 'profession'). Locke's hope in 1667 seems to have been that there would be a very broad Anglicanism indeed, with toleration for those few left outside the church and the attempt to persuade even these few to conform, although great care is necessary in interpreting his comments. He declared that his further discussion would show how it was 'that Christian religion had made more factions, wars and disturbances' than any other and whether 'toleration and latitudinism' would prevent these evils. Toleration was described as conducive to the settlement of a government 'noe otherwise . . . than as it makes the majority of one mind and encourages virtue in all, which is done by making and executing strict laws concerning virtue and vice, but making the terms of church communion as large as may be; ie that your articles in speculative opinions be few and large, and ceremonies in worship few and easy, which is latitudinisme'.[42]

Locke clearly meant to support at least temporary toleration outside of the established church in the fourth draft of the 'Essay on Toleration', speaking of a 'separation' that was not a quarrel. The comment just cited, however, is more difficult to interpret. When Locke wrote the 'Essay on Toleration' toleration was often spoken of as something that could occur within the church as well as outside of its boundaries; indeed, it was only in 1668, the year after the 'Essay on Toleration', that the term 'comprehension' gained wide currency to indicate such a system. Locke himself discussed 'toleration' within and without the church, meaning thereby comprehension and toleration by indulgence, as late as 1689. The toleration in the title of the 'Essay on Toleration' was therefore not necessarily meant to indicate toleration by indulgence in contradistinction to comprehension, and it may have been meant to indicate both forms of toleration. In describing toleration as conducing to settlement of government in his comment in the concluding section of themes that were to be discussed in the future, it is not entirely clear whether Locke was using it in contradistinction to comprehension, as his use of 'latitudinism' at the end of the comment might suggest, and as his earlier mention of 'toleration and latitudinism' preventing strife does suggest, or whether his comment was intended to speak of the only form of toleration that could conduce to the settlement of a government, which was comprehension. Whichever Locke meant, he was clearly indicating that for him – the settlement of a government being to him a very important concern – the *best* realisation of toler-

---

[42] *Ibid.*, 189; 192; 194.

ation was through a very wide comprehension. His ideal thus appears to have been the comprehension of almost all Protestants.[43]

It is also not clear, in the light of the proposal of 'large and few' terms, exactly what Locke meant by his suggestion of making men 'all of one mind' in bringing them over to the church. He might have been attempting merely to indicate their mutual concern or sympathy, their willingness to accept the differences of others' opinions in disagreements recognised as insignificant or blurred over. That would make the 'large and few' opinions intended to allow wide interpretation of the meaning of supposedly shared positions, rather as the communiqués issued at economic and political summits nowadays use 'large and few' terms. He might also, however, have been thinking of an agreement in beliefs that would follow from such breadth when it was joined with the persuasion by reason that could flourish under toleration; here the important declaration is the earlier comment that the best way to '*alter their minds*' and thus 'bring them over to your profession' was to persuade 'them'.

Finally, it is not clear what Locke meant by the other declaration in his comment, that 'strict laws' were to be made enforcing morality and 'encouraging virtue in all' if toleration were to conduce to the settlement of government. This would seem at first sight to contradict Locke's own argument earlier in the 'Essay on Toleration' itself that the magistrate was not to enforce morality except as that was necessary to prevent injury and to preserve the society. Certainly there were passages where Locke seemed to take back with one hand what he had just written with the other. He stressed that the magistrate could never be expected to attempt to enforce vice since the practice of virtue was so necessary to the preservation of the government; he indicated several vices against which the magistrate's 'sword' was never drawn; and his concluding comment was couched in terms of the need for virtue to settle government. It is therefore likely that his terse comment meant that the magistrate was to make strict laws concerning virtue only in those parts of morality necessary to preserve society. This was a view that we will see that Locke was to hold until at least the early 1690s, and perhaps thereafter, although in the early 1690s he either began to argue that the magistrate ought to enforce morality even when it was not necessary to the preservation of men and the society or more probably expanded significantly the morality explicitly designated as necessary to secure preservation.[44]

While explicitly aligning himself with the Latitudinarian wing of the Church of England in support for 'latitudinism', and clearly expressing views that were antithetical to the strident and politically powerful high

[43] *Ibid.*, 194.   [44] *Ibid.*, 174–94.

Anglicanism of Sheldon, Locke was going very far beyond even the most eirenic of the clerical Latitudinarians in disallowing the magistrate any role to enforce the true religion, and in his astonishingly capacious freedom for speculative opinions. While his desire for a united comprehensive Church of England was in agreement with the Latitudinarians' broad ideals, on a more practical level his very general advocacy of toleration outside of the church gave this far more overt support than was forthcoming from all of the Latitudinarians. His declaration that nothing was indifferent in worship unless thought indifferent was also not echoed in their writings, which cleaved to the line that had been taken by Locke himself in the *Two Tracts*, that an error of conscience did not alter the objective indifferency of ceremonies.[45]

It might be thought, therefore, that Locke was returning to an earlier commitment to independent ecclesiology nurtured under John Owen and alongside Henry Stubbe at Christ Church. Some of Locke's arguments, particularly his support for religious toleration outside of the church, found very important parallels in independent thought. However, most Independents from the Civil War on shared with Anglicans and presbyterians the view that the promotion and support of true religion by laws was a duty of the magistrate. Most desired gathered congregational churches and not a national church, in large part because they believed that churches should be communions of the elect and that communion with the unregenerate should be avoided as much as possible. Their intention in advocating 'toleration' or liberty of conscience was to create separate congregations of the godly. While they denied the magistrate the power to interfere in the belief and discipline of such churches with true belief and discipline, they generally strongly upheld the magistrate's duty to suppress false worship and false belief, or idolatry and heresy. In contrast to the 'Essay', doctrines such as the Trinity were often explicitly included in their works as among those that had to be enforced. Their demand was for liberty for conscience, not for beliefs so obviously – to them – heretical or immoral that no conscience could be claimed for them.[46]

---

[45] See chapter one above and the beginning of this chapter.
[46] See pp. 42–5 above on Independent ecclesiology, and M. Sommerville, 'Independent Thought 1603–49', unpublished Ph.D dissertation, Cambridge University 1981; see, for instance, *The Ancient Bounds* (1645) in A. S. P. Woodhouse, *Puritanism and Liberty* (1938), 250–1, 253 on punishment of idolatry, heresy, and prevention of antitrinitarianism. For the author, the magistrate was 'custos utriusque tabulae'. Cromwell might bemoan the way in which sects did not allow liberty of conscience to each other, but he was also not a tolerationist and his support was for the liberty of *conscience*, which could not be claimed legitimately by the heretical, as for instance, Socinians, or by the 'licentious', both groups which Cromwell's various religious experiments excluded from toleration. See especially Worden, 'Toleration', 199–233. I am again grateful to Dr J. C. Davis for discussion of this point.

There were a few radical Independents who declared that the magistrate had no duty to enforce true religion, possessing only civil rule for civil ends. In the Interregnum John Goodwin, for instance, was the advocate of extremely wide toleration of doctrinal differences, and in the process came close to denying the existence of heresy. Even Goodwin, however, argued that it was the magistrate's duty to enforce all of morality. Moreover, the arguments for toleration of Goodwin, Roger Williams and, to a slightly lesser extent those of Henry Stubbe before the Restoration, stressed that toleration was a *duty* required by Christianity. Their defences of toleration as a duty were, unsurprisingly, embedded in a welter of scriptural quotations. While later to loom large in Locke's defence of religious toleration, it is evident that the Christian *duty* to tolerate others was entirely absent from the arguments of the 'Essay on Toleration', and that it would have been enormously difficult to combine with the kinds of very substantial denials of toleration countenanced in the first three drafts of the 'Essay'. Not merely was there no indication at all that such a conception was a source of Locke's commitment to toleration, but there was even no attempt to use it as a collateral argument in its favour. Unlike Locke, the Independents generally tied the denial of magisterial power to interfere with religion to an unequivocal statement that the civil magistrate's power and trust were derived from the consent of the people, and then argued that the power to reform religion could not belong to civil magistrates because God could not have given it to all men, since the majority of men were neither good nor even Christian. Their argument, in other words, proceeded from the danger of the people having and delegating this power. Although support for toleration was shared, this argument is located at the opposite end of the spectrum from Locke's argument that if men consented to government – and the 'Essay on Toleration' canvassed this only as a possibility – they could not give away this power because it was 'too great' to give away, a calculation about the potential costs through damnation of giving others the power to make a wrong choice for you.[47]

Locke's argument that the ends of government were only civil and alone legitimated the use of force was closest to the argument of John Owen at his most tolerationist in the Interregnum, the kind of tolerationism expressed in Owen's important sermon before Parliament on 31 January 1649, the day after the execution of the King. For Owen in these most tolerationist moments and for a few radical Independents such as William Walwyn and Roger Williams, the civil magistrate was not allowed to enforce true religion, nor even morality, except as this effected civil peace

---

[47] J. Goodwin, *Independency God's Verity* (1647) in Woodhouse, *Puritanism*, 186; idem, *Innocency and Truth*, 51 cited in Sommerville, 'Independent Thought', 172; *ibid.*, 173–82; R. Williams, *The Bloody Tenent of Persecution* (1644), passim, esp. 137; 202–3.

and the preservation of men. Offences against the second table, or the duties of morality, were only punishable if they were such 'as by a disorderly eruption pervert the course of publicke quiet and society . . . and this is allowed, as to the offences against the first Table, if any of them in their owne Nature . . . are disturbances of publicke peace they also are punishable'. Owen's arguments in this vein relied far less than most Independent arguments on scriptural texts and on the duty of toleration, although they were still heavily reliant upon conscience. Locke must have been very familiar from his time in Christ Church with Owen's arguments, and we have seen that Stubbe identified Locke as one of those who had pledged themselves to support liberty of conscience.[48]

In many moments of his career, however, including much of his time as Dean of Christ Church, Owen advocated the restriction of toleration to those who were of the true religion, and the suppression of heretical 'speculative' beliefs such as antitrinitarianism. Indeed, even in the extremely eirenic sermon just quoted, Owen came close to declaring Socinianism beyond the pale of toleration, and he was the author of the two most viciously antiunitarian works of the entire century. Few Independents, Owen included, would have been happy with the breadth of opinions that Locke desired to be tolerated in 1667. We have seen that Owen's own reaction as leader of the Independents to the bills for comprehension and toleration in 1667 and 1668 was to draft proposals for extending toleration to the strictly orthodox only, and for enforcing morality. While Bishop Wilkins almost certainly did not intend to extend toleration to antitrinitarians, it was in Owen's proposals, not in those of Wilkins, that orthodoxy was made an issue. Very few Independents, Owen included, would have been happy with Locke's vision of a 'latitudinarian' church with 'few and easy' ceremonies and 'large and few' speculative opinions, which carried the clear implication of communion with the profane, and made no mention of the need to devolve church authority to local congregations. Very few Independents, whose ecclesiological commitments were in large measure shaped by desire for an effective parochial discipline to promote morality, would have been entirely happy with Locke's limitations upon magisterial enforcement of morality. They wished for the church to provide the primary discipline for its members who lapsed into immorality, but for many if this failed the magistrate should use his sword to punish immorality. In his 'Critical Notes' of 1681, as we will see later,

---

[48] J. Owen, *A Sermon Preached . . . 31 Jan 1649* (1649) in idem, *Works*, VIII, 164; 168; 197; 205; also cited and discussed in Sommerville, 'Independent Thought', 192–3 (cf., however, Owen, *Works*, VIII, 392–5 for an Interregnum sermon far less clear about not punishing immorality); W. Walwyn, *Toleration Justified* (1646), 8; Williams, *Bloody Tenent*, passim.

Locke condemned Owen's vision of *jure divino* Independent congregations and included Independents among those who would willingly use force to establish their beliefs. The 'Essay on Toleration' itself very importantly declared that the toleration that it was proposing had not been tried in the years of Independent supremacy in the Interregnum.[49]

Locke's 'Essay on Toleration', while almost certainly composed with some awareness of the contemporary debate over comprehension and toleration in 1667–8, and very probably in part provoked by this debate, would thus have satisfied very few of those arguing on any side of the issue in the public arena. Locke was combining elements of the thought of Independents and Latitudinarians, accepting some of the final arguments of each but sharing few of the presuppositions on which these arguments were based, and going beyond both groups in the formulation of the final combination of ideas. The sources of the abrupt and significant transformation in Locke's thought between the *Two Tracts* and the 'Essay on Toleration' are obviously not sufficiently explained by any specific contemporary ecclesiastical allegiance or by commitment to an ideology of dissent; they suggest instead an ecclesiological eclecticism. It is necessary to look elsewhere for the causes of the shift in Locke's thought.[50]

IV

The obscurity of the origins of the 'Essay on Toleration' poses a severe problem for any attempt either to identify the source or sources of Locke's dramatic *volte face* between the *Two Tracts* and the 'Essay on Toleration' or to specify his reasons for selecting the precise range of toleration that he chose to defend in 1667. Although no certainty can be obtained about the causes of the crucial transformation of Locke's arguments between 1660 and 1667, some important suggestions may be made about the plausibility of the various alternatives on the basis of analysis of Locke's developing views before 1667 and of his developing association with Ashley in 1667.

There seem to be several main reasons for which, separately or jointly, Locke could have been impelled to write in support of religious toleration

---

49 Owen, *Works*, VIII, 194; Owen, *Vindiciae Evangelicae*, in *Works*, XII, passim; *A Dissertation on Divine Justice*, in *Works*, X, 498–506; *Truth and Innocency Vindicated* (1669) in *Works*, XIII, 416–26; *The Doctrine of Justification by Faith* (1677) in *Works*, V, passim; and the discussions of Owen's thought in Wallace, *Puritans*, 144–57 esp. 154–5; C. F. Allison, *The Rise of Moralism* (1966) 174–7; Toon, *God's Statesman*, passim, cf. chapter three below on Locke's 'Critical Notes' and Owen's role in 1652 discussed in the works in n. 18 above.

50 Ashcraft, *Revolutionary Politics*, 94–101 does not give sufficient attention to the sources and the purpose of toleration for Independents, the attitudes towards toleration of presbyterians, and Locke's persistent suspicion of dissenting arguments because of their Civil-War antecedents. He ignores the Latitudinarian elements of the 'Essay on Toleration'.

in 1667. Due to a developing conception of men's intellectual duties and epistemological potential in the early 1660s he might have come to believe that an extensive liberty of enquiry and of practice was so vital that he had to find a way that such liberty could be realised, with the drafts being his attempts to reconcile this more extensive liberty with the measures necessary to secure the peace. He might have developed a number of concerns about the practices and beliefs being enforced by the Church of England in such a way that he desired a greater liberty of belief and practice in these specific areas than they were allowing and then sought a theoretical basis for such freedom that would not threaten civil peace in the way that it would be threatened by a simple assertion of liberty of conscience given the Civil-War history of that assertion and his view of the greatest promoters of liberty as the tyrants of religious rage. He might have come to think that toleration was the best way to secure the peace as an adoption of an hedonic psychology which asserted that men could only follow the path that they thought led to spiritual happiness and a general *politique* view that toleration would promote peace, or at least have come to think that the greater degree of toleration that he had thought to be desirable even when writing the *Tracts* was now practicable in England. Or, on the simplest level, he might have come to write the 'Essay' primarily or exclusively because of the designs and desires of Ashley and the King in 1667.

Locke's comments in the *Two Tracts* and in his letter to Stubbe had focused upon the desirability but impracticability of men choosing their own way to heaven, and the *Essays* had focused on men's individual duties of moral enquiry. Although Locke had depicted an absolute power in civil and religious indifferent matters in the *Two Tracts* as preserving liberty of conscience because that consisted simply of a liberty of the mind, he had indicated even in that work that it would have been more desirable if it had been politically viable that each man should go to heaven in his 'own way'. Two elements of his thought may have intensified this desire between the *Tracts* and the 'Essay'. The *Essays* suggest that individual moral enquiry had become more important to Locke during the early 1660s, because of his denial that tradition or custom could be sources of moral knowledge, and particularly because he had come to argue, against his own original view, that innatism was not a possible source of moral knowledge. A more general softening of Locke's theological beliefs may also have made his desire for toleration of various religious practices seem more pressing than it had been in 1660–2. Although the 'Essay on Toleration' itself identified man's 'depraved ambitious human nature' as lying behind desire for dominion over other men and declared that without belief in God men were no more than beasts, this very considerable potential bestiality was not located in the severest of views of the effects of the Fall, which would have suggested it was ineradicable except by particular grace. Man's potential bestiality had come to be at least partly balanced by an overt commitment to the potential rationality of all men that the *Two Tracts* had lacked, with their unqualified description of the vast majority of men as 'beasts'. In the 'Essay on Toleration' Locke described the King as being as fallible as his 'fellow-men'. The shift that this involved was not the recognition that the King was fallible, which was not denied in the *Two Tracts* despite his relationship to subjects being described there as that of a 'God' to 'beasts'. It was the overt elevation of the potential rationality of all men, described in the *Two Tracts* as beasts and in the 'Essay on Infallibility' as 'sheep', but spoken of in the 'Essay on Toleration' as possessing minds, the exercise of whose liberty set them above the beasts. The desirability of a more extensive form of liberty than simply that of the mind *may* thus have come to seem more acute simply as Locke began to recognise explicitly that *all* men were potentially rational.[51]

Alternatively, or additionally, Locke may have come to write the 'Essay' because of developing a series of specific concerns about the practices and beliefs which the Church of England was attempting to enforce in the 1660s. The listing of the Trinity and the Fall among speculative opinions to be tolerated does not indicate that Locke had come by 1667 to disbelieve either of these doctrines. Locke's other examples of beliefs to be tolerated included beliefs about which he never had any doubts: transubstantiation (false) and the existence of the antipodes (true). These views were only 'speculative' with reference to political society, not with respect to faith. The doubts about or actual disbelief in the Trinity with which Locke ended his life were one reason for his support for toleration in the 1690s, but not in the 1660s. However, although he did not disbelieve any of these doctrines, Locke's rereading of works such as Falkland's *Discourse on Infallibility* and especially Grotius' *De Veritate*, with their opposition to precise doctrinal formulations and deliberate silence on the Trinity and predestination, may have been influential in making him oppose the doctrinal requirements of the Church of England. He declared at the end of the 'Essay' that 'the difining and undertaking to prove several doctrines that are confessed to be incomprehensible, and to be no otherwise known but by revelation, and requireing man to assent to them in the termes proposed by the doctors of your several churches, must needs make a great many atheists'. Concerned throughout his life to prove that God existed, the arguments to convince atheists to be religious were always very important to Locke; no mere rhetorical worry was being voiced in opposing such explanations and formulations of doctrine. In the 1661 'Essay on Infalli-

---

[51] Fox Bourne, *Life*, 176–8 and passim; cf. chapter one above.

bility', as we have seen, Locke had voiced a similar protest against hubristic explanations of doctrines that included the Trinity. The hostility to doctrinal formulation expressed in the 'Essay on Infallibility' may have developed by the 'Essay on Toleration' into a feeling that the doctrinal requirements of Anglicanism were too restrictive, that the claim of Anglicanism to doctrinal latitude voiced by Locke himself in the *Two Tracts* was not being adequately realised in its practice, because although it allowed greater freedom than most churches, it had still established a restrictive creed.[52]

Such a change of attitude could have been combined with one or more important alterations in Locke's attitude towards ritual. The ecclesiology of the *Two Tracts* had given very little importance to ritual, except as a fence to protect other parts of religion from the 'beastly' multitude. It is possible that the practice of Anglican rigidity in ceremonial in the early 1660s, however much it fulfilled Locke's own proposals, had pushed Locke towards toleration in ritual, particularly within the church. There is no indication that Locke had personally come to think every detail of worship was prescribed or proscribed in Scripture. Indeed, for him 'for the most parte the matters of controversy and distinction between sects' were still 'no partes, or very inconsiderable ones and but appendixes, of true religion'. This comment and his attitude that peace might be settled through 'few and easy' ceremonies betrayed the Latitudinarian laxity towards ceremonies that many nonconformists found almost as irreligious as they found 'popish' the imposition of ceremonies retained since the Reformation. There was no point in his life where Locke ever came to think ceremonies themselves significant elements of his own religious experience, positively in aiding devotion or negatively in hurting it. Locke had very probably come to feel, however, that by 1667 the Anglican hierarchy were wrongly – popishly – placing too much emphasis upon Anglican ceremonial practices, particularly since he was associating with Anglicans such as Boyle who thought that the Church had imposed too much in the way of ceremonial forms in 1662 and that this was distracting many from the true essence of religion.

There is also a sense in which between 1660 and 1667 Locke had come to recognise the necessity for others of authenticity of practice, with worship following individual beliefs; this sense may have been glimpsed in Locke's correspondence from Cleves. If so, it was no more than glimpsed there, and it was certainly not presented there as necessitating toleration; opposition to ritualistic Anglicanism seems to have been a more powerful influence upon Locke's tolerationism concerning worship than sympathy for non-

[52] *Ibid.*, 176; 194.

conformist views about the importance of ritual. The theme of the necessity of edification in defining the forms of ceremony to be used, absent from the *Two Tracts*, was still absent from the 'Essay on Toleration'. It did not appear in Locke's writings before the 'Critical Notes' of 1681, when it was to assume great importance, and when Locke's tolerationism was correspondingly to place more emphasis on toleration of separate congregations.[53]

For Locke the ability to worship as the individual judged best was declared to be inalienable because it was 'too great . . . if not impossible' to be parted with. Locke's argument suggested, however, that it was too great to be parted with because any attempt at the kind of alienation of decisions about the forms to be used in worship that had been suggested in the *Two Tracts* and in the 'Essay on Infallibility' was doomed to failure since anyone who believed that worshipping (or not worshipping) in certain ways was necessary for salvation would simply disobey the injunctions of terrestrial authority. He argued simply that whatever the magistrate enjoyed in worship 'no consideration could be sufficient to force a man from, or to, that which he was fully persuaded was the way to infinite happiness or infinite misery'. The central issue here would appear to be not the value of worship, nor even the authenticity of worship for the individual worshipper, but the sense in which men would not – indeed, could not – obey any command forbidding that which they thought would lead to infinite happiness. It will be suggested later that Locke may have been the author of a draft sermon of January 1667 among his papers, and that if Locke was not the author of this draft sermon that it is likely that he had been very interested by it. According to this sermon, man 'could not but follow happiness', and good was simply 'what' tended 'to the advancement of . . . happinesse'. This view was to be a significant part of his epistemological writings from the 1670s until 1694, and Locke was later to say that he had accepted it because it was the commonly accepted view. It seems probable that the example of thousands of dissenters in England who were accepting persecution and damage to their civil interests, and the influence of an increasing number of hedonic analyses of men being developed in the Restoration that Locke had encountered if not composed, including this sermon, had led Locke to think that his theory in the *Two Tracts* of the alienation of religious decisions was simply not a sustainable basis for a regime, either in political theory, or in practice.[54]

It is possible, then, that Locke had become convinced by the example of thousands of dissenters of the need for authentic worship by each individual, and of the ineradicable motivation of all men by their perception of

[53] *Ibid.*, 194.   [54] *Ibid.*, 176–7.

the rewards of God, and probable from considerations of Locke's thought both external and internal to the 'Essay' that he had come to think the Church of England too narrow in its doctrinal and ceremonial requirements. It is possible that he had come to a softened picture of the potential rationality of all men that made a more extensive liberty of conscience seem more desirable, and that through epistemological investigations the liberty of individual moral enquiry and *perhaps* from this the liberty of moral practice had come to seem more important to him. It is possible that some or all of these factors had combined together to make Locke attempt to compose a defence of toleration, however many dangers he had initially thought that it would present in England, and however close to omnicompetent he had formerly therefore thought that the magisterial authority had had to be when he had been writing the *Two Tracts*.

These kinds of developments in Locke's thought seem far more plausible as explanations of the impetus leading Locke to write the 'Essay' than that it was solely a result of a shift in Locke's view of what was now practicable, even given that his ideal before and in the *Two Tracts* had been that of men choosing their own way to heaven, or of any more general conversion to the *politique* view that toleration would easily bring civil peace. It is true that a number of factors had probably made toleration seem more viable to Locke than it had in 1660. Toleration in Cleves had certainly shown Locke that uniformity was not absolutely necessary to peace. Boyle had almost certainly conveyed a similar message to Locke in their conversations, and it is just possible that learning of De Ossat's policy in France during the early seventeenth century from rereading of Falkland's *Discourse* had underlined the point; evidence of (near-) contemporary toleration in France, which was exemplified by De Ossat, had been one of Locke's requests of Stubbe. A theological softening of his views of men might also have made toleration seem more viable; it was notably not merely the prudence but also the 'good nature' of Cleves' population that Locke had described to Boyle as allowing toleration there.

That Locke had centrally come to see toleration as viable in England, however, is extremely difficult to believe in the light of his first three drafts, which so awkwardly balanced 'absolute rights' to toleration with the prevention of any significant grouping of dissenters. While the *Essays* may have involved or expressed an important theological softening of Locke's views, they have already been shown to have been very doubtful about the practical rationality of most men in their condemnation of '*vox populi vox dei*'; Locke still declared that men were 'depraved and ambitious' in the 'Essay'; and he still saw the government as needing to make strict laws to enforce virtue and vice, indicating that he still viewed most men as sinful and injurious. As we will see, Locke was in fact never to stop thinking most men very sinful and injurious to other men unless prevented from injury by magisterial force.

A similar objection stands against viewing the 'Essay' as simply the result of the adoption of a more general *politique* view that peace would be secured by toleration. Part of Locke's argument did suggest that he had changed his mind about the effects of the use of force to maintain a uniform church, viewing it as causing rather than preventing civil disturbance. The vicious persecution of the early 1660s may have made Locke feel that its main result, given hedonic motivation, was the uniting of the dissenters in opposition to the church and monarchy, making toleration the best way to secure peace in England. There was certainly a significant *politique* strain to Locke's thought in the 'Essay on Toleration', which argued that there were as many dissenters as 'hearty friends' to the established church. However, while Locke's comment on the 'crumbling' of dissenters who would be united by the use of force was awkwardly phrased, so that it is not entirely clear whether it was of current or future reference, it seems to have been intended to refer to the present. As such it contradicts his own argument that force would unite the dissenters, and suggests that a *politique* response to the Clarendon Code was at least not a major cause of the 'Essay on Toleration'. More importantly, while the considerable fear about any significant combination of religious dissent was maintained in the most tolerationist draft, where it was used as an argument against the use of force since much force was held to unite dissenters, in the first three drafts it had been combined with advocacy of the prevention by force of any significant number of dissenters from joining together. Although the second part of the 'Essay on Toleration' focused on prudential considerations, Locke's argument was not primarily cast in a *politique* manner, but was a singularly uneasy amalgam of juristic absolutes, of 'uncontrollable rights' to liberty of worship, with the expectation of considerable practical limitation of those rights on the ground of civil peace. It is quite easy to conceive of a work which stressed the advantages to peace in England of toleration without declaring absolute rights to toleration. The 'Essay on Toleration' was manifestly not such an account. It seems unlikely that *politique* attitudes were significantly responsible for providing the impetus for the enormous shift in attitude between the *Two Tracts* and the 'Essay on Toleration' or that toleration had simply come to seem much more viable to Locke than it had in 1660–2, although once that shift had been made, and especially after the most extensively tolerationist fourth draft had been written, Locke was to spend the rest of his life both believing and arguing that genuine toleration (always excluding atheists and Catholics) would bring peace and that persecution would cause frequent civil disturbances.[55]

55 Fox Bourne, *Life*, 192 and passim.

The degree of tension within each version of the 'Essay' about the conditions necessary to secure the peace and liberty of conscience, and the very important contradiction between the first three drafts and the final version of the 'Essay', make it seem unlikely that Locke commenced the 'Essay' in the belief that he could easily find a way to successfully reconcile liberty and security of the peace. It is possible that the drafts were the result of Locke attempting to see if he could find a way to convince himself that the kind of toleration that he desired was in fact viable, undertaken solely for some combination of the intellectual reasons just sketched, particularly the move to an hedonic calculation of behaviour. Given the strength of Locke's earlier commitment to security and preservation of the peace, that this commitment and his acute sense of the need to provide for security as well as liberty was to be maintained throughout his life, and given the severe restrictions both directly placed upon liberty in the 'Essay' and indirectly allowed by the assertion of nonresistance, the doubts about the reconciliation of liberty and peace voiced in the initial versions of the 'Essay' make it seem unlikely that these intellectual concerns alone provided the major impetus for undertaking the 'Essay'.

The dating of the 'Essay' as probably composed in Ashley's household, in which Locke spent most of 1667, the apparent intention in the 'Essay' itself of advising the King on toleration, and the form of the 'Essay' together make it seem much more likely that in fact the crucial initial impetus for composition of the 'Essay' came from encouragement or commission by Ashley, long a proponent of religious toleration. While the series of alterations in Locke's particular views of what should be enforced may well have been important predispositions of the 'Essay', and of the range of toleration that he defended – of which more will be said in a moment – Locke's difficulties in constructing a consistent argument seem very likely to indicate that Locke was initially engaged in an attempt to defend toleration at Ashley's request when he himself was still not convinced of its viability, and most certainly while he was very far from convinced by the time that he first undertook to defend toleration of the particular range of liberty for significant separate churches that he was to support by the time that he reached the final version of the 'Essay'. The 'Essay' may well have been Locke's first substantial intellectual contribution as adviser to Ashley, and perhaps his first contribution to Ashley in the latter's new role as minister of the King. The awkward combination of his own deep fear of political instability and the imperative to take a tolerationist position in the advice given in such circumstances would certainly provide a plausible explanation of all of the very considerable awkwardness of the various versions of the 'Essay'.

It is also very likely indeed that the influence of Ashley was responsible for one of the 'Essay on Toleration''s main arguments for toleration. In the *Essays on the Law of Nature* Locke had identified economic goods as relatively static; the gain of one man was the loss of another. Once in Ashley's household, Locke quickly came to value encouragement of trade and development of England's wealth as a very important concern. Ashley was an avid supporter of the generation of wealth through trade, having long engaged in the sugar and slave trades with Barbados. The 'Essay on Toleration' stated very clearly as part of the ends of civil society the securing of riches and wealth for its members; indeed, in one passage the 'welfare of the kingdom' was described straightforwardly as consisting simply of 'riches and power'. One of the concluding arguments of the 'Essay' for future exploration was showing that toleration would encourage 'the power and riches of the Kingdom' which depended upon 'the number and industry of your people'. The 'commonwealth' to which Locke was to be committed was not so much a godly as a rich commonwealth.

Toleration was seen by many in England as singularly propitious for economic development, because of the example of the Dutch who were tolerant and wealthy, and because of the number of dissenters who engaged in trade in England. Although trade was often cited as one reason for toleration, and 1667 saw a trade depression that made this a particularly pressing issue, it is difficult indeed to believe that the primary influence on the 'Essay' here was not that of Ashley himself. Ashley pressed upon the King the legitimation of the Declaration of Indulgence of 1672 by proclaiming it necessary for the encouragement of trade.[56]

These alternative motivations for composition of the 'Essay' provide several separate answers to the question of why Locke argued in the 'Essay' for the toleration of the specific range of actions and beliefs that he supported, and of why he argued for their toleration from their harmlessness. It may very well have been Ashley who first suggested to Locke, because of Ashley's own secular and instrumental conception of political society, the form of the argument that Locke declared to be the 'foundation' of the range of toleration supported in the 'Essay on Toleration', that the magistrate was empowered only to seek civil goods, and neither the spiritual good of his subjects, nor even morality, unless those were separately necessary to secure civil goods and the overall preservation of the society. It may have been Ashley who pushed Locke to attempt to make a substantial range of liberty in religion and morality compatible with security, with the tensions and contradictions between and within the drafts the result of Locke still being deeply fearful of the political consequences of any claim

---

[56] *Ibid.*, 174–6; 186; 194. The point about the practice of virtue leading to greater knowledge of both God's revealed will and men's duties was made explicitly by Locke himself in 1682: *Draft*, 124; and frequently thereafter.

to religious freedom of practice, and without Locke being personally committed to liberty in some of the detailed consequences of the range of liberty that he was to defend, most notably in the case of actions which were harmless but immoral.

Even if Ashley had called for or encouraged Locke to compose a defence of toleration, however, he may well not have specified the exact range of liberty to be defended or the form of argument to be used. Just as much as if he had been impelled to compose the work for his own reasons, Locke's own views may have been what prompted both his form of argument and his desire for toleration for the range of actions and beliefs which were supported in the 'Essay'. Locke may have started from man's hedonic motivations and the desirability of the individual's freedom to search and to act, and decided that unless freedom was harmful to others it was better and more likely to bring peace that men could act immorally and irreligiously but freely unless seditiously, than that they were coerced by the government into religious obedience and moral behaviour even when the government was correct. In religious affairs a major impetus may have been that the magistrate had no greater infallibility than other men. In moral practice freedom may have been supported because he took it as self-evident that men should not be forced to be moral, healthy or wealthy, because he placed a high value upon authenticity of belief, because he thought that unfettered enquiry and practice would lead to a greater ultimate recognition of morality, or because he thought that the government was unlikely to be correct in its choice of morality to be enforced. The first of these possible views on morality seems plausible, but the second, third and fourth seem unlikely, given that there was no reason for Locke to think that authenticity of moral belief required freedom of practice, that practising sin seemed to very few seventeenth-century minds, Locke's included, to be a way to gain greater truth, and that at this stage of his life Locke held that much of morality was plain both to the government and to all men.

Alternatively, Locke's separate concerns with ritual and belief, indicated at the beginning of this chapter as having some degree of evidence outside of the 'Essay on Toleration' itself, may have come together in Locke's thought to specify a significant amount of the range of liberty for which Locke explicitly contended in the 'Essay on Infallibility', with the central argument from harmlessness generated as a way both of allowing liberty in these specific areas such as freedom for 'speculative opinions' even if erroneously sinful, and, equally importantly, as a way of circumscribing the claims to liberty that Locke knew only too well could be made if the claim for toleration was based instead upon an unequivocal assertion of the necessity of liberty of conscience. The argument from harmlessness would thus have been Locke's way of providing for the external practice of liberty of conscience in those particular areas that had come to seem important to him, and simultaneously as allowing Locke to prevent anyone who claimed a right to liberty of conscience from asserting as a consequence of such a liberty the right to act in the very many ways that were injuriously licentious and threatening to civil peace, or which were based upon a religious certitude of 'conscience' that would then require the establishment of their own religious belief and be even more threatening to civil peace. In this kind of pattern of thought the argument that immorality ought to be tolerated when it was harmless could just as easily be simply one result of the form of an argument – harmlessness – that was chosen for other reasons as the expression of an intense desire for men's free enquiry and practice which was a significant part of the cause of Locke's general argument for toleration.

We will see later that in the 1690s Locke was to place considerable limitations upon allowable immorality and these might be thought to suggest that the recognition of the allowable immorality in 1667 was purely a consequence of the form of his argument from harmlessness. By then, however, Locke appears to have changed his mind significantly, and it is therefore unfortunately simply not possible to arbitrate decisively between these various possible – and perhaps cumulative – explanations of the origins of the 'Essay'. Failing this, it is important to emphasise at this point instead that after composition of the fourth draft of the 'Essay' in 1667 Locke was to remain committed to advocating almost exactly the range of toleration in religion and morality that he supported in the 'Essay', and convinced of its advantages to peace and religion, at least up to and including his publication of the *Letter Concerning Toleration* in 1689.

Undermining the temple of worship of priest and prince

I

Locke reiterated many times between 1667 and 1674 as an adviser to Ashley when he was a leading minister of Charles II both the commitments to toleration through indulgence and comprehension and the opposition to Anglican and nonconformist intolerance of the fourth draft of the 'Essay on Toleration'. These were combined with the anticatholicism, anticlericalism, personal lay Anglicanism and support for nonresistance to which he had been committed as early as the *Two Tracts*. He maintained these commitments when Ashley became a leading political opponent of Charles' early moves towards absolutism from 1675 to 1681 and when in 1675–8 he saw at first hand increasing French intolerance, to him a particularly onerous symptom of the generally horrifying character of French absolutism. From 1675, in opposing an oath declaring that it was unlawful upon any pretence to take up arms against the King, he very importantly helped to construct, or at least to transcribe, an argument that English monarchy was bounded, and that the fear of 'breaking the golden chain and contexture between' King and people was useful to making sure that the King maintained the interest that the people 'justly and rightly' claimed. In tandem with that argument, however, it was declared that to take up arms against the King himself was treason, and that any who invaded the King's person or right invaded 'his whole people' who derived from him all 'liberty, property, and safety'. Furthermore, in 1676 Locke privately declared the necessity of every individual obeying 'the magistrate' so 'as not to endanger or disturb the government' under any 'form of government soever he lived'; the magistrate could penalise men 'even to the loss of life' and the subject was still, in Locke's view, 'in conscience obliged' to submit 'patiently to the penalty'.

Locke's tolerationism was quickly expressed after the 1667 *Essay* in a series of manuscripts and it was his most significant political commitment of the late 1660s and early 1670s. In 1668 Locke helped Ashley and the other Lords Proprietors in drawing up a constitution for their colony in the

Carolinas; since others wrote to congratulate him upon the constitution that he had framed he seems to have claimed credit for its content. The *Fundamental Constitutions* provided that any seven or more people 'agreeing in any religion' constituted a church which had a right to toleration and defended this toleration partly by argument about the harmlessness of 'speculative' opinions and worship that Locke had supported in the 'Essay', using very similar phraseology to the 'Essay'. This toleration of different churches was soon combined with the establishment and funding of the Anglican Church in the Carolinas, but Locke's own role in this establishment was probably negligible, and he may have opposed this provision.[1]

The pursuit by the Anglican hierarchy of further penal laws in the wake of the defeat of the 1667–8 plans for toleration placed toleration at the top of Locke's domestic as well as colonial agenda. In 1669 Sheldon's chaplian Samuel Parker asserted the patriarchal and absolute power of political authority and launched an extremely erastian assault upon nonconformity in *A Discourse of Ecclesiastical Polity*. Opposing Calvinist theories of the indwelling spirit, he denied the legitimacy of any claim to freedom of worship based upon conscience, as was indicated by his subtitle: 'Wherein The Authority of the Civil Magistrate Over the Consciences of Subjects in Matters of Religion is Asserted'. The sarcastic responses to Parker of Andrew Marvell elevated the *Discourse* to a *cause célèbre* and even prompted the mirthful interest of Charles II; the more weighty responses of Owen and his Independent colleague Robert Ferguson vilified both Parker's erastianism and his theology. It was partly in response to Parker's work that Fowler published his *Principles and Practices*, importantly signalling the continued commitment of the Latitudinarians to toleration through comprehension.

Locke read Parker's discourse soon after it appeared, and in 1670 he composed a very brief manuscript in response. Parker had identified the first governments of the world as 'established purely upon the natural rights of paternal authority', and declared that 'afterward' these had grown up 'to a kingly power by the increase of posterity'. Locke queried whether a paternal 'right' of government had descended only to the eldest son or to all sons equally; the first would lead to there only being 'one rightful

---

[1] Haley, *Shaftesbury*, 238–46; Locke, *Works*, IX, 175–99 esp. 193–6. Suggestion that Locke was unhappy with this provision derives from one of Locke's amanuenses at a point in life when Locke was more clearly radical in his religious views, but there is a significant possibility that Locke did not wish to see a church established by law in the Carolinas, and the initial draft of the Constitutions suggests that this was probably the case. See Wootton, *Locke: Political Writings*. Cf. PRO 30/24/47/3 for a copy partly in Locke's hand, and partly in another hand similar to that of one of the drafts of Locke's 'Essay on Toleration', perhaps a further suggestion that that 'Essay' was composed in Ashley's household.

monarch over the whole world'. If the latter, Locke declared that 'all government, whether monarchical or other, is only from the consent of the people'. There is thus an important suggestion here, stronger than Locke's cautious comments in the *Two Tracts* and *Essays*, that government originates from consent; Locke's assault a decade later on the republication of Filmer's patriarchalist account of government was to repeat these arguments. It is important to underline that in 1670 patriarchal views of absolute monarchical authority had not yet become the predominant view being heard in royal counsels, and that Locke wrote this manuscript as an adviser to the powerful ministerial supporter of an alternative view, Ashley. As importantly, even if a commitment that government *originated* from consent is present in embryo at this point in Locke's thought, it involved no commitment to the argument of the Second Treatise that government needed the consent of contemporary individuals for them to become its subjects, and in no way implied that there was any right to resist a supreme power which Locke explicitly declared in this manuscript to have an 'uncontrollable right' to ordain whatever it judged necessary.[2]

Parker combined his patriarchalism with argument that 'Religion' was the single most 'important influence upon government' and that the princes therefore had to have the power 'to bind their subjects to that religion that they apprehend most advantageous to public peace and tranquility'. True piety made men 'governable' but 'superstition and wrong notions of God' made them seditious. Locke queried both the unspoken presumption of magisterial rectitude and whether the magistrate could force men to renounce their own opinions 'however quiet and peaceable'. Against Parker's conventional declaration that any commonwealth allowing liberty of conscience was 'overrun with numberless divisions and subdivisions of sects' and thus fragile, Locke responded with the argument of the final version of the 'Essay on Toleration', wondering whether the 'subdivision of opinions into small sects be of such danger to the government'. Again opposing any right of resistance in the people, and again being markedly unspecific about the location of magisterial authority, Locke declared that 'The end of government being public peace 'tis no question that the supreme power must have an uncontrollable right to judge and ordain all things that may conduce to it.' It was only questionable whether 'uniformity established by law' was, as Parker supposed, necessary for peace 'ie whether it be at all dangerous to the magistrate that he believing free will some of his subjects shall believe predestination, or whether it be more

[2] The extracts from Parker's arguments and Locke's responses to them are most conveniently found in Cranston, *Locke*, 131–3; cf. more broadly S. Parker, *A Discourse of Ecclesiastical Polity* (1670), 31–2, 187, 308.

necessary for his government to make laws for wearing surplices than it is for wearing vests'.[3]

That the migistrate was to watch carefully the doctrines taught in his dominions did not mean for Locke that force was necessary in 'speculative opinions in religion or worship'. Suggesting increasing concern over Anglican persecution Locke queried what spirit – perhaps 'fanaticism', but obviously also priestly interest – had led Parker to stir up the magistrate to a persecution of dissenters from 'those opinions and ways of worship the public support whereof is to give him preferment'. There is a very important sense here in which Locke's hostility to interested teachings of puritan preachers in the *Two Tracts*, and to the 'sharp-eyed' priests of Roman Catholicism in the 'Essay on Infallibility', had very clearly become explicitly and equally directed against Anglican clerical champions of persecution, although not therefore necessarily against the eirenic views of Fowler and other Latitudinarians.[4]

For Richard Ashcraft, Locke's turn in 1671 to composition of two *Drafts* later to be massively expanded and turned into the *Essay Concerning Human Understanding* is to be understood as a further element of Locke's response to Parker and of his commitment to the cause of toleration and thus, apparently, to an 'ideology of dissent'. The *Drafts* did indeed expand upon the anticlericalism voiced against Parker. According to Locke, the need for labour and lack of education unavoidably gave a 'great part of mankinde up to invincible ignorance'. Even the wealthy, however, were also generally ignorant and enslaved 'in that which should be the freest part of man, their understandings' because they were 'cooped in' by 'the strict gards of those whose interest it is to keepe them ignorant, lest knowing more they should believe the lesse in them'. It is difficult not to believe that all self-interested clerics were thereby indicted, although only Roman Catholic priests were specified; the Inquisition was a 'great office of ignorance' and so good Catholics had to 'swallow down opinions as silly people doe empiricks pills'. For Locke, religious ignorance was fostered not merely directly by self-interested clerics, but also indirectly because most men had simply resigned themselves up to 'received but false and unproved principles', to 'propositions (espetialy about matters of religion)' received 'from their parents, nurses or those about them'. These were 'riveted there' because they became 'reverence[d] as sacred things'. For

---

[3] Cranston, *Locke*, 131–2.
[4] *Ibid.*, 133. Locke's analysis was hardly original, and may have been influenced by his own earlier reading. Stubbe's *Essay in Defence of the Good Old Cause*, which Locke had read a decade earlier, made very similar points against paternal political authority: Stubbe, *Essay*, 2–9.

Locke, this was the basis of the prevalent absurdities in 'the various religions of mankinde'.[5]

By thus indicting the force of clericalism, custom, and education in
religious matters, as well as by arguments that will be discussed in the next
chapter which set out a firm distinction between faith and knowledge and
indicated a series of limits upon men's knowledge of the world and upon
scriptural interpretations, Locke surely thought that he was providing
reasons why men had to study and why others were to tolerate their extensive enquiry. These were later to be grounds on which the *Essay* raised an
explicit plea for mutual commiseration – and thus for religious toleration.
Locke had started the *Drafts* already committed to religious toleration, and
the discussion of these points was doubtless shaped by that purpose. In the
Drafts, however, no direct plea for toleration was voiced. In fact, the arguments of the *Drafts* would have been quite compatible with arguments for
considerable toleration of belief and enquiry but not of practice; there was
nothing in the *Drafts* which excluded the position Locke had taken in the
Two Tracts, which proclaimed liberty of enquiry but not of practice.

Ashcraft has made it appear that Locke composed both his response to
Parker and the *Drafts* in a circle dominated by nonconformists because of
Ashley's close connections with many leading nonconformist merchants.
Ashley had been an important supporter of toleration of nonconformist
dissent in the 1660s and was to be again in 1672, and he did deal with a
number of leading nonconformist merchants, such as the Baptist William
Kiffin (or Kiffen), and Thomas Papillon, a patron of Owen. It is likely that
Locke came into some contact with these nonconformists. The only one
with whom there is any real sign that Locke was to think himself friendly,
however, is Robert Pawling, an Oxford merchant and later Whig Mayor
who was licensed as a presbyterian teacher in 1672. Locke's *Drafts* did
indeed arise from discussions of religion, but apparently from broad discussion about the principles of revealed religion and morality, not of toleration, in discussions held by a group of Locke's friends at Ashley's house,
including several Anglicans, lay and clerical, and no dissenters. They
expanded upon arguments and investigations which Locke had pursued
many years before reading Parker.[6]

---

[5] *Drafts*, 60–4, 80–1. Locke's comment on the guards who benefit from people accepting
their teachings is capable of applying to the Anglican preachers *by extension*; Ashcraft,
however (*Revolutionary Politics*, 110), cites Locke's discussion of people swallowing the
opinions taught by the Roman Catholic Church as opposing the swallowing of 'opinions
given to us by the church' as though Locke was writing directly against the Church of
England.

[6] R. Ashcraft, *Revolutionary Politics*, ch. 2, errs firstly in treating Parker as if he was representative of all of Anglicanism in 1670. He was not, and Fowler's *Principles and Practices*
both signalled this to contemporaries and marked as important a commitment to treating

The significant ways in which the *Drafts'* arguments on faith and knowledge diverged from those of leading dissenters and paralleled more closely the arguments of the Latitudinarians will be described in the next chapter. Although some important divergence from the arguments of the Latitudinarians will then be noted, and Locke's intellectual independence stressed, in the late 1660s and early 1670s, around the time of his attack upon Parker and the *Drafts*, it was emerging friendships with at least some of the leading London Latitudinarians that were more significant to Locke than his friendships with any dissenters. We will later see that according to Damaris (Cudworth) Masham Locke viewed himself as distant from all clerics before 1683, but his own recognition of these friendships in the 1670s should nonetheless be underlined, because friendship was central to Locke's ethics, to his personal intellectual life of discussion of ideas, and to his description of the centre of the desirable intellectual and moral life of other men.[7]

Locke probably met many Latitudinarians at meetings of the Royal Society and at dinners in London society. Sometime between 1667 and 1675 it is very likely indeed that Locke became at least an occasional member of the congregation at St Lawrence Jewry and clear that he became close friends with several Latitudinarians. There is, to date, no contemporary evidence of Locke's membership of the congregation at St Lawrence Jewry, despite its frequent assertion in the secondary literature. In his *Life . . . of Locke*, published in 1704, however, le Clerc reported on the basis of

---

dissenters as reasonable individuals as did any dissenter work composed against Parker in the following years. Ashcraft errs further in failing to develop any distinction between Locke and the nonconformists who wrote against Parker on the basis of the absence of theology in Locke's comments. There is a substantial difference between arguing against the presumption of rectitude underlying a theological view, as Locke did in his manuscript on Parker, and attacking the theological view itself, which Locke did not but nonconformists prominently did. Neither the suggestion (*Revoutionary Politics*, 110–11) that the drafts of the *Essay* were specifically an attempt by Locke to work out an epistemological basis for his case for toleration, nor the suggestion that their content should be read as essentially a response to Parker's *Discourse* and thus to Anglicanism, fits the description of the genesis of the *Essay* that we have from Locke and from a close friend who was present, Tyrrell. Ashcraft's claim is not substantiated by his few comments on the *Drafts* and declaration of 'belief' that this was the case. See the stout Anglican Tyrrell's comment in his copy of Locke's *Essay* in the British Library and the *Essay*, 7. Other members of Locke's circle of five or six friends discussing the principles of revealed religion and morality (and not toleration) were probably Ashley, Hodges and Stringer, and perhaps Sydenham and Thomas; *all* were Anglicans. Cf. my 'John Locke in Context: Religion, Ethics and Politics', Ph.D diss., The Johns Hopkins University (1990), ch. 3.

[7] On friendship see chapters five and seven. There is an important sense in which many of Locke's commitments and changes of views were very significantly influenced by his friendships with individuals who helped him to question his received views – as, for instance, in theology and ecclesiology where he was friends in turn with Oxford Anglicans, then with London Anglican Latitudinarians and Shaftesbury, then with Dutch Arminians, and finally with continental and English unitarians.

Damaris Masham's testimony that Locke had just read and approved of Benjamin Whichcote's selected sermons, which he said that he had formerly 'heard' Whichcote preach. Whichcote was vicar of St Lawrence Jewry from 1668 to his death in 1683. That Locke attended at least some services at St Lawrence Jewry is clearly suggested not merely by this comment on hearing Whichcote, but also by Locke's close friendship with John Mapletoft. Mapletoft was a friend of many Latitudinarians, and he was to become vicar of St Lawrence Jewry in 1686, three years after Whichcote's death. Through Mapletoft Locke came to know Thomas Firmin, an Unitarian merchant but an Anglican conformist, whom Tillotson left in charge of finding substitute lecturers for St Lawrence Jewry after he became Dean of Canterbury in 1672. Locke's letters to Mapletoft show that Locke knew Firmin well. Firmin played generous host to a circle of intellectuals at his Lombard Street house in the 1670s and 1680s; many of the Latitudinarian preachers, such as Tillotson and Stillingfleet, were members of this group. It is again very likely that Locke was at least occasionally a member of this group; when Locke was in France in the late 1670s he sent his regards back to his 'friends' through Mapletoft, including Whichcote and Firmin by name, and he showed a marked proclivity for joining such groups whenever the opportunity arose throughout his life.[8]

---

[8] J. le Clerc, *An Account of the Life and Writings of Mr John Locke* (1713), 52–3; H. W. Robinson and W. Adams (eds.), *The Diary of Robert Hooke* (1935), 155; Cranston, *Locke*, 124–8; H. Stephenson, 'Thomas Firmin', Oxford D Phil. thesis (1949), 40, 74 and passim; *Correspondence*, I, 417 ('My service to . . . our friends, and amongst them to good Dr Whichcock [sic], Mr Fowler, and Mr Firmin') and Locke's many letters to Mapletoft. Ashcraft (*Revolutionary Politics*, 112–14) places Locke in 'one important nucleus' of an extended circle of sympathisers with and leaders of the community of dissenters. He lists a number of nonconformists whom Locke is supposed to have known – and whom other people that Locke knew are supposed to have known. Of those that Locke is supposed to have known personally, Firmin is misdescribed as a nonconformist when he was an Anglican unitarian, Robert Blaney is cited as a sometime member of Shaftesbury's household and it is not recorded that the evidence for this comes in the form of a note by Haley (*Shaftesbury*, 440) showing that Danby attempted to get one Robert Blaney (sic) to inform against Shaftesbury in 1676; and William Stratton, Locke's friend in *Somerset*, appears extremely unlikely to have been the nonconformist licensed in *Leicestershire*. One of Locke's former students, Edward West, did become a nonconformist – but several others became Anglican clerics, and Locke was not West's only tutor. Robert Ferguson is asserted to enter Shaftesbury's household 'sometime in the 1670s', but no primary evidence is shown for this, it may mean that Ferguson did not enter Shaftesbury's household until the end of 1679, and Locke was never close to Ferguson in religious attitudes – indeed, Ferguson later attacked him for unitarianism. Ashcraft fails to note Locke's friendships with the Latitudinarians, with whom it is more likely that there was a 'network of social interaction'. He does not discuss Locke's friendship with Nathaniel Hodges, Shaftesbury's Anglican chaplain, nor register the significance of Shaftesbury's own preferences reflected in his choice of Hodges and in his attitudes about preachers. See *DNB* s.n. Hodges; H. Prideaux, *The Letters of Humphrey Prideaux to John Ellis*, ed. E. M. Thompson, Camden Society (1875), 159, 161; Cranston, *Locke*, 148; MS Film. 79, 5; 8 (showing Locke and Hodges interacting in London in January 1667 before Locke entered Ashley's household);

Either through this group, or separately, Locke came to know Tillotson by 1672 at the latest, by which date he was either conveying books to Tillotson for Mapletoft or discussing them with him. Tillotson was much later to be described by Locke as one of his closest friends, whom he consulted on all 'doubtful points of divinity'. Tillotson was also a visitor to Exeter House in the early 1670s. Although there is one early reference to him in a letter in the 1650s, Locke probably came to know Edward Fowler personally in the late 1660s or early 1670s. Fowler was another of the 'friends' to whom Locke sent his regards in 1678, and Fowler travelled to visit Locke when he was very ill at the end of his life. In the 1680s Fowler was alleged to have been a frequent dinner guest at Exeter House in the 1670s; he did not deny that, but merely claimed that he had stopped visiting Shaftesbury during the Exclusion Crisis. Among the books that Locke recorded taking 'into the country' for Shaftesbury in 1674 were an unknown number listed simply as 'Latitudinarians', perhaps more likely to have denoted simply Fowler's *Principles and Practices*. The death in 1677 of Isaac Barrow, whose ecclesiological sympathies were clearly Latitudinarian, and whose works Tillotson edited, was described by Locke as robbing him of a 'very considerable friend'.[9]

Finally, Locke also knew very well Thomas Grigg, husband of his cousin Anne, and vicar of St Andrew Undershaft in London. Grigg died very young in 1670, but his support of liberty of conscience was noted by Simon Patrick, the Latitudinarian preacher who preached Grigg's funeral sermon. Although Anne Grigg was personally inclined to high-church views, her correspondence with Locke after 1670 shows that Tillotson and Fowler had been close to her husband and kept in contact with her. Locke attended Grigg in his final illness and recorded in one of his notebooks the comment 'vir optimus' at Grigg's death. Grigg's son later wrote to Locke about his father's sermons in a manner that suggests that he thought that Locke knew of these; Locke bequeathed to the younger Grigg copies of Grotius' religious writings that his father had given to Locke, significantly

---

on Hodges' probable influence upon Locke as personally anti-Calvinist, see *Correspondence*, I, 459; Haley, *Shaftesbury*, 97 notes Ashley Cooper's disdain for the 'grocers' who had become ministers in the Interregnum and declares that his preference was for 'the more learned type of preacher'. Locke was certainly sympathetic to dissenters and certainly knew some dissenters, but in his emphasis on the politics of dissent and the 'ideology of dissent' Ashcraft paints only part of the picture of Locke's thought and associations and obscures as much as he reveals thereby.

[9] On Fowler dining at Exeter House see W. Smythies, *A Reply to a Letter sent by William Newbery and William Edmunds to Dr Fowler*, n.p., n.d. [1685?], 3. I owe this reference to Dr M. Goldie; *Correspondence*, I, 265; 348; 417; V, 1826; Haley, *Shaftesbury*, 292; Cranston, *Locke*, 470.

suggesting an eirenic religious correspondence between Locke and Grigg while he was alive.[10]

Not merely are lay Anglican sympathies suggested by Locke's friendship with so many Latitudinarians, by his 1667 attitudes towards comprehension, and by the opposition to much nonconformist theology and epistemology that will be sketched in the next chapter, but his own Anglicanism in the period from 1672 resulted in two new appointments. In 1672 he was appointed by Shaftesbury, then Lord Chancellor, as his 'Secretary to the Clergy' and was thus in charge of the considerable ecclesiastical patronage in the King's gift. Among those that he preferred was Shaftesbury's Anglican chaplain and Locke's close friend Nathaniel Hodges. Locke corresponded in Shaftesbury's name with many of the bishops, and composed manuscripts on parish reform. Locke then became Secretary to the Council of Trade and Plantations when the Test Act of 1673, which Locke and Shaftesbury supported, required every office holder to take the sacraments of the Church of England and the dissenter Benjamin Worsley was removed from office.[11]

In these years of Ashley's greatest power Locke's support for the policy of religious toleration required him to defend frequently the monarchical and not parliamentary control of religion in England as the King attempted to grant toleration by indulgence. He may even have advised Ashley that the King could appoint a minister to declare heresies and to excommunicate. On 15 March 1672 the King issued his Declaration of Indulgence stating that 'we think ourselves obliged to make use of that supreme power in ecclesiastical matters, which is not only inherent in us, but hath been declared and recognised to be so, by several statutes and acts of Parliament'. The 'forcible courses' employed since the Restoration had not reduced 'erring or dissenting persons'. The Declaration would quiet 'our good subjects' and encourage strangers to come and live in England. It was not intended that the Church of England would be reduced in any way. The church was to remain in its 'doctrine, discipline and government as now it stands established by law', and was to remain 'the basis, rule and stan-

---

[10] S. Patrick, *A Sermon Preached at the Funeral of Thomas Grigg* (1670), 48ff.; Cranston, *Locke*, 134–7; 474. Locke was at Grigg's bedside daily for two weeks.

[11] MS Locke c44 (Adversaria Physica), 1–23; Locke's sixty-odd appointments included Hodges, John Highmore, rector of Wimborne St Giles, John Williams, later Latitudinarian bishop and friend of Tillotson, and John Spencer, later friend of Newton. Cf. PRO 30/24/47/30 fo. 2; 16–17; 24–5; 45 (dated 1668); Haley, *Shaftesbury*, 322–5; Cranston, 153–6; and on Locke's appointments J. A. Venn (ed.), *Alumni Cantabrigienses*, Cambridge (1922) on Shipton, Pettifer, Trappet, Hatton, West, Rednall, Burrough, Ward, Brereton, Bromesgrove, Littleton and Wright; *Alumni Oxonienses* on Criche, Woodforde, Wolley, Littler, Whitford, Lye, Hodges, Frayer, Roberts, Stillingfleet, Jones, Crewes, Clithero, Fenwick, Humphreys, Badger, Pretty, Stoning; *DNB* s.n. Williams, Spencer.

dard of the general and public worship of God'. The 'orthodox conformable clergy' were to continue receiving its revenues and none were to be
exempted from 'tithes or dues'. None 'not exactly conformable' were to be
capable of holding any ecclesiastical dignity or preferment. Penal laws
against dissenters were suspended. Public dissenting meetings were
allowed, but only with a licence obtained from the King. Seditious statements were prohibited, as was anyone preaching 'to the derogation of the
doctrine, discipline or government, of the established church'.[12]

Many at the time thought that Ashley had been the prime mover in
formation of the Declaration, that it had been 'shot' out of his 'quiver'.
The King and Clifford seem to have been the prime movers, but Ashley
certainly gave it his enthusiastic support. It was immensely unpopular, particularly in Parliament, but in November 1672 Ashley – by then earl of
Shaftesbury – became Lord Chancellor and defended it strenuously in
Parliament. In a speech in composition of which Locke may well have had
a hand, he argued that the King was a 'true defender of the Church of
England' but not convinced that 'violent ways are the interest of religion or
of the Church'. Faced by the claim that it gave to the King a prerogative
that was vested in Parliament, Shaftesbury defended the King's prerogative. He even went so far in one speech as to argue against the view that the
legislative power resided in the King and the two Houses of Parliament
co-ordinately, arguing that the 'sanction of laws' was in the King alone – as
he was 'commanded' to inform the House. In February 1673 the King
himself defended his Declaration stoutly in Parliament, and Shaftesbury
attacked both the doubts expressed by Parliament about the legality of the
measure and the allegation that the King's motivation was to secure toleration for Catholics rather than for dissenters. Parliament, however,
resolved once again that 'penal statutes, in matters ecclesiastical, cannot be
suspended but by Act of Parliament'.[13]

It was probably at least partly in response to this assertion by the
Commons that Shaftesbury had someone draft a manuscript which argued
that the King should stick by his Declaration, that Parliament should
accept it, and that the royal prerogative in ecclesiastical matters should be
tested in the House of Lords. This was surely also very importantly
intended as a response by Shaftesbury to Clifford and Lauderdale's advice
to the King to raise an army, dissolve Parliament and enforce his will.

12 PRO SP 104/177 fo. 11–12 entries March 5, 6 1672 (Minutes of the Committee for Trade
and Plantations); cf. L. F. Brown, *The First Earl of Shaftesbury*, New York (1933), 195;
PRO SP 104/177 fo. 14–17, 19–22; PRO 30/24/6B/427; PRO 30/24/6B/430; the text of the
Declaration is printed in F. Bate, *The Declaration of Indulgence 1672* (1908), 76–8.
13 PRO 30/24/6B/431; Bate, *Declaration*, 79–81; 106–27; Haley, *Shaftesbury*, 319–26; W. D.
Christie, *The First Earl of Shaftesbury*, 2 vols. (1871), I, 132–4.

Although a defender of the King's sole ecclesiastical supremacy, and willing to 'inform' the House that the King had sole 'sanction of laws', Shaftesbury never shared the monarchically absolutist proclivities of his Cabal colleagues. While exalting the King's ecclesiastical supremacy over the next few years in order to support religious toleration, Locke had also penned various declarations for Shaftesbury when he was Lord Chancellor, and as such the King's representative in Parliament, saying that the King intended only to secure the liberties and properties of his subjects, not to rule arbitrarily. Locke had celebrated the restoration of the ancient laws in 1660, and cited Magna Carta in the 'Essay' in 1667; in 1672, when he briefly visited France during Shaftesbury's tenure as Lord Chancellor, he recorded that he saw 'vast and magnificent buildings as big almost as others' dominions, preparing only for one man, and yet there be a great many other two legged creatures, but 'tis not the way of that country much to consider them'.[14]

Although only one of the manuscripts relating to the issuing of the Declaration appears to be connected directly to Locke, there can be no doubt that Locke was fully involved in Shaftesbury's affairs throughout this period and that he was therefore a committed supporter of the Declaration. Among the Shaftesbury papers are documents in Locke's hand relating to parliamentary business from the exact period in which the debates were raging in Parliament over the Declaration of Indulgence. Locke apparently wrote the Lord Chancellor's speech for 18 February 1673, four days after the Commons had petitioned against the Declaration. This declared the King unwilling to accept the reluctance to serve of the proposed Speaker (because of the Declaration) and declared that he [the King] 'not only hath, but ever shall inviolably maintain the Property, Rights, and Libertys of his people, and every individual person of them'. He would take 'every care' that justice was enforced and that the laws were put in force 'as far forth as consists with the good and safety of his people'. There can be no doubt that this last phrase, *restricting* the laws to be put in force to those consisting with the good and safety of the people, related at least in part in Locke's mind and in those of the hearers of the speech to the suspension of the penal laws against dissenters.[15]

II

In March 1673, short of money, Charles was forced by parliamentary Anglican opposition to withdraw his Declaration and 'surrender to his

---

[14] See the discussion of the *Letter From A Person of Quality* below; Haley, *Shaftesbury*, 276; 312; cf. PRO 30/24/47/30 fos. 32–5; *Correspondence*, I, 264.
[15] PRO 30/24/47/30 fo. 28; PRO 30/24/5/276–7; cf. PRO 30/24/6B/429; PRO30/24/47/30 fos. 32–5; Brown, *Shaftesbury*, 225–7; Haley, *Shaftesbury*, 368–70; PRO 30/24/6B/427

friends'. In November 1673 Shaftesbury was dismissed from the Lord Chancellorship, and Charles turned to the Earl of Danby to build parliamentary support for the monarchy from among the supporters of the narrow and persecuting church. By 1673 a number of members of the House of Commons had already become worried about popish and absolutist counsellors of the King, but there was not at this stage anything like a firm division into 'court' and 'country'. It was in many ways Danby's success at creating a firm body of support for the King over the next few years which led to the growth of a moderately consistent 'country' opposition in Lords and Commons in the mid-1670s. Although Shaftesbury had been the King's mouthpiece throughout 1673, and had thus been the supporter of alliance with Catholic France in war against Protestant Holland, he was already close to Charles' illegitimate Protestant son, the duke of Monmouth, had already suggested to Charles that he should 'own' the Duke instead of James, and had opposed James, duke of York over a number of other issues. James' Catholicism, effectively announced in 1672, rapidly became a focal theme of politics. By attacking 'Popery', and by pressing the need for a new Parliament, Shaftesbury became a central figure in opposition to the King's policies, especially to those fearful of the succession of James, and he was to remain one of the most important opponents in Parliament to Charles' policies over the next seven years. During these years, however, Shaftesbury's aim was to turn Charles away from absolutism and Catholicism, never to attempt to remove Charles.[16]

As Charles finally set himself against toleration, Shaftesbury began to build political opposition in Parliament and in the country in large part on the basis of support for a wide measure of religious toleration, attempting to unite moderate Anglican supporters of toleration and nonconformist supporters of toleration. It is possible that a manuscript entitled 'Excommunication' that Locke composed in 1674 reflects this new aim on Shaftesbury's part, or merely Locke's private sympathies soon after Shaftesbury's fall from ministerial position. It focused upon the need for toleration of different churches far more than any of Locke's earlier writings, declaring church membership 'perfectly voluntary', and recognising that in England the 'public established religion' was not received by all subjects since the 'religions' of presbyterians, Independents, anabaptists, Quakers and Jews were different from the 'governing' part of society. For Locke the civil magistrate could only punish someone for dif-

---

refers to the creation of a Vicar General, but I can find no reason to associate this with Locke.
[16] See Haley, *Shaftesbury*, 276; chs. 16–17.

ference in 'fide aut cultu' when 'fully persuaded that it will disturb the civil peace'.[17]

In 'Excommunication' Locke reasoned about the nature of the state in reasoning about the consensual basis of the church, but in order to indicate that the state was not similarly based upon consent and that authority of the state could not be challenged even if it had been originally consensual. In the state men were combined 'into civil societies in various forms, as force, chance, agreement, or other accidents have happened to constrain them'. Membership of the civil society was not perfectly voluntary with freedom for members to leave. The 'terms of communion' with, 'or being a part' of, the civil society were simply 'promise of obedience to the laws of it'. No limits to such obedience were described; the laws were supposed to be aimed at the civil happiness of the people, but punishments up to capital punishments for violation of the laws of the society were simply described as 'just' without any discussion of whether the actual laws had been made with the intention of fostering civil happiness. For Locke, since the breach of laws involved 'mostly the prejudice and diminution of another man's right, and always tending to the dissolution of the society, in the continuance whereof every man's particular right is comprehended' it was 'just' that 'he who has impaired another man's good, should suffer the diminution of his own'.[18]

Throughout 1675 the earl of Danby pressed forward with measures designed to link together through patronage as well as political commitment the supporters of the King and Church in Parliament, and Shaftesbury built his opposition on the basis of fear of absolutism and support of toleration. Opposition lines crystallised around Danby's proposal of an oath declaring the government of both church and state to be unalterable. The King was maintaining various regiments in time of peace that seemed to many to point towards a standing army, independent of Parliament, and to threaten that the King would rule by standing army and not Parliament – particularly to those such as Shaftesbury, who had heard just that policy recommended by Clifford. Danby's manoeuvres were opposed by a number of peers, prominently including Shaftesbury, in a way that linked the proposed oath to the use of patronage and the threat of a standing army as a combination tending towards absolutism.

Shaftesbury made many speeches against the oath which were then recapitulated in a full-scale assault upon Charles' absolutist tendencies in November 1675 in a 15,000 word pamphlet, the *Letter From A Person of Quality*. The *Letter* was anonymous, but there is very little doubt that it

---

[17] This manuscript is most readily available in King, *Locke*, II, 108–19; the opening quotation is from 108.
[18] *Ibid*., 108–16.

was issued from Shaftesbury's household, and for various reasons it is extremely likely that Shaftesbury had played a significant part in its composition and that Locke had helped him, although perhaps by little more than taking Shaftesbury's 'dictation'.[19] The focus of the *Letter*'s assault was 'An act to prevent the Dangers which may arise from Persons disaffected to the Government'. This 'state-masterpiece' was blamed on high Anglicans, being 'first hatched (as almost all the mischiefs of the world have hitherto been) amongst the great church-men'. There had been a plan to 'make a distinct party' of the 'high episcopal men and the old cavaliers' and for these to 'swallow . . . all the power and offices of the Kingdom'.

These high churchmen had designed to 'have the government of the church sworn to as unalterable; and so tacitly owned to be of divine right', an imitation of the 'prelate of Rome'. In 'requital' to the crown for their claim of a separate order of divine-right government they had declared 'the government absolute and arbitrary; and allow monarchy as well as episcopacy, to be *jure divino*, and not to be bounded or limited by any human laws'. In order that they 'might be owned by the prince to be *jure divino*' the bishops had 'trucked away the rights and liberties of the people'. The desired result was that 'priest and prince may, like Castor and Pollux, be worshipped together as divine, in the same temple, by us poor lay-subjects; and that sense and reason, law, properties, rights, and liberties, shall be understood, as the oracles of those deities shall interpret'.

According to the *Letter*, there were in fact only two types of Church which did not trespass upon civil jurisdiction and could properly recommend themselves to the civil government. These were the 'state' religion and the 'independent congregations' when the latter claimed no other jurisdiction than to expel unruly members of their own denomination 'and endeavour not to set up a Kingdom of Christ to their own use, in this world'. The ecclesiological attitudes that Locke had expressed in the 'Essay on Toleration' and 'Excommunication' could not have been more succinctly expressed.[20]

The *Letter* opposed Restoration Anglican persecution. Because many could not subscribe to the terms of the Act of Uniformity this had then created an Anglican clergy who were a 'sort of men . . . taught rather to obey than understand'. The ejection of ministers on St Bartholomew's Day 1662 was condemned as 'fatal to our church and religion', in throwing out

---

[19] The *Letter* is printed in *Works*, IX, 200–46. For the most convincing account in print of Locke's involvement in composition of the *Letter*, see Ashcraft, *Revolutionary Politics*, 120–2; on dictation see Wootton, *Locke: Political Writings*, 45 and more generally idem, 'John Locke and Richard Ashcraft's *Revolutionary Politics*', *Political Studies* 40: 1 (1992), 79–98.

[20] *Works*, IX, 200–1; 232; 246.

a very great number of worthy, learned, pious, and orthodox divines'. The *Letter* pointed out the danger of a 'rigid, blind, and undisputed' conformity in the Church of England making it susceptible to becoming Catholic if a popish Prince succeeded – an obvious reference to the likelihood of James' succession. The penal laws had made 'our church . . . triumphant', resulting in the persecution of dissenters but not of 'papists' since Catholics were thought by the bishops 'not dangerous . . . differing only in doctrine and fundamentals' but exalting church government to its highest.[21]

The *Letter* defended the Declaration of Indulgence, and the King's ecclesiastical jurisdiction that it had claimed. This was 'of another nature than that he had in civils', and had been possessed by Elizabeth, James I and Charles I. Although the evidence of the manuscript discussions before the Declaration and of Shaftesbury's support for the Declaration before its withdrawal both show that he viewed it as within the sole power of the King, in 1675 Shaftesbury wished to argue that he had only supported the Declaration as a measure permissible between Parliamentary sittings. According to the *Letter* toleration was also 'extremely' in the best interests of the Church of England. This was true because 'the narrow bottom they had placed themselves upon, and the measures they had proceeded by, so contrary to the properties and liberties of the nation' would have proven fatal to the Church 'in a short time'. Toleration would have led them instead to live peaceably with dissenting and differing Protestants and so to becoming by 'unavoidable consequences' the 'head of all Protestants, a place due to the Church of England'. Toleration did not require 'any diminution of the church; it not being intended that one living, dignity, or preferment, should be given to any but those that were strictly conformable'. It was held to be necessary to the preservation of liberty and property in 'this essentially trading nation' that articles of faith and matters of religion were not made necessary to civil rights. Indeed, Shaftesbury was declared to think toleration a duty from the care owed to 'those he was convinced were the people of God, and feared him; though of different persuasions'.[22]

In speeches in Parliament Shaftesbury protested strongly against the requirements to swear to government in the church as unalterable. He declared that this oath gave no 'regard to anything that rules of prudence in the government, or christian compassion to protestant dissenters' might require. Shaftesbury condemned the concentration of the oath upon defence of the discipline, pointed out the substantial differences that existed within the Church of England over issues such as predestination, declared that the catechism and homilies needed improvement, and sug-

[21] *Ibid.*, 202–4; 206; 208–11.   [22] *Ibid.*, 205–8.

gested amendment of the liturgy and abolition of the need for reordination. The liturgy was 'not so sacred' being 'made by men the other day'. It was suggested that it 'might' be the action of a 'very good protestant' to alter and restore the liturgy to its Elizabethan form. The *Letter* condemned the 'uncharitableness' of requiring reordination for Anglican ministry by those not episcopally ordained. In short, the *Letter* suggested the possible desirability of many of the exact changes in church discipline, liturgy and ordination that were required for comprehension as well as toleration.

In making his speeches and publishing the *Letter* Shaftesbury unquestionbly wished to gain the support of Protestant nonconformists, both inside and outside Parliament, but the support of many of these, and of many moderate lay Anglicans in Parliament, could be gained through support for comprehension within the church as well as for toleration outside of the church. A similar combination of moderate Anglican and nonconformist support was aimed at in the *Letter from a Parliament-Man to His Friend* in 1675, probably also issued from Shaftesbury's household. This assaulted the bishops as 'creatures' of the prerogative, attacked their 'harsh and irreconcilable spirit', and reminded Parliamentarians that they ought to represent dissenters as well as Anglicans in the straightforward statement that 'we were chosen by both, and with that intention we should oppress neither'. Shaftesbury was trying to build opposition to monarchical absolutism and high episcopalian persecution, and to mould a number of disparate groups together. Indeed, in the loose confederation of those opposed to the high Anglican collaboration of *jure divino* monarchy and *jure divino* episcopacy, Shaftesbury was even grateful for the support of Catholics such as Lord Bristol, and argued in the *Letter* that Catholics should be tolerated although deprived of any office.[23]

The *Letter* is most important as the political testament of country sentiment in 1675. It stoutly defended parliamentarily 'bounded monarchy', 'Magna Charta' and the 'liberties and properties of free Englishmen'. The *Letter* declared that the powers of the House of Lords had to be maintained because 'the power of a peerage, and a standing army are like two buckets, in the proportion that one goes down, the other exactly goes up'. The *Letter* condemned the engrossing of all places of 'profit, command and trust' being given to 'old Cavaliers', declaring straightforwardly that men could by office be made 'too much' for a king if that king was attempting to introduce 'absolute and arbitrary government' or to take any greater power than 'the law and constitution of the government had given'. The English government was said to be like all 'bounded monarchies, where the

---

[23] *Ibid.*, 215; 226–30; 207–8; *A Letter From A Parliament-Man to his Friend* (1675), 3–6; Lacey, *Dissent*, 80–1; Ashcraft, *Revolutionary Politics*, 117.

prince is not absolute'. These issues – and opposition to James' succession as a consequence – were to be the cynosures of the electoral platforms and parliamentary manoeuvres of the opposition to Charles II in 1675–79, and even in 1679–81, an opposition devoted to encouraging Charles to take a different course and with realistically high expectations that this would be achieved.[24]

The *Letter* asserted in opposing an oath declaring that it was unlawful upon any pretence to take up arms against the King that the fear of 'breaking the golden chain and contexture between' King and people was useful in making sure that the King maintained the interest that the people 'justly and rightly' claimed. It opposed declaration that arms could never be taken up against those commissioned by the King as legitimating 'arbitrary government' and a 'standing army' and an arbitrary 'law of property'. It did not declare, however, that the people could justly and rightly take up arms against the King himself (except when the King was captured). It opposed the actions of the Long Parliament in resisting the King – while making clear that the crown had wrongly perpetuated its sitting and thus altered the government – and argued that to take up arms against the King was treason. It contended, moreover, that any who invaded the King's person or right invaded 'his whole people' who derived from him all 'liberty, property, and safety'.

III

In late 1675 the *Letter* was ordered to be burned by the common hangman; shortly afterwards Locke left England for France, where he stayed for nearly three years. In exile Locke's tolerationism and hostility to absolutism received considerable further practical reinforcement as he saw Protestantism placed under increasing restriction, and observed very closely indeed the opulence of Louis XIV's government. Translating the Jansenist Pierre Nicole's *Essais* in 1676 with an initial intention of publishing them in England, Locke recorded Nicole's argument that men's faculties were especially inadequate when faced by the 'inexplicable mysteries' of religion; understanding most of the various points disputed and 'contested' among Christians was beyond the capacities of most men. For Nicole, the authors of the 'new heresies' of Protestantism had hubristically taught men to use their own wit to judge where the truth lay, instead of relying on the Catholic Church. Locke agreed that much in religion was above man's understandings and would never be fully resolved or understood, but

[24] *Letter*, 201–2; 212–17; 222; 234–8; 242–6. Cf. J. G. A. Pocock, *The Machiavellian Moment*, Princeton (1975), 406–16; Christie, *Shaftesbury*, II, xc–xcii; McNally, 'Levellers', 21; Haley, *Shaftesbury*, 382–4.

argued that men's business was to rectify mistakes upon the 'grounds of truth and evidence'. Locke attacked the 'monstrous presumption' of commanding interpretations of Scripture, claimed because the Church of Rome had found 'the sweet of dominion over men's consciences, and considered it as an advantage too great to be parted with', and defended the 'just right' of withdrawal from such 'slavery'.[25]

In France the issues of toleration did not centre upon comprehension or toleration among Protestants. Locke reiterated his support for toleration in a journal note on penal laws shortly after completing his translation of Nicole, and registered a more global focus in declaring the presumption of magisterial rectitude standing behind claims of enforcement damaging to true religion because magistrates in Europe varied so much in their religions. As in the 1667 'Essay on Toleration' and the 1675 *Letter From A Person of Quality*, this commitment to toleration did not indicate that Locke was no longer interested in English toleration through comprehension. In 1679 Locke discussed with Dr John Covel his bringing nonconformists 'back to conformity' at the church in Constantinople at which Covel had recently ministered by having allowed receipt of the sacrament kneeling or standing. Locke noted that he felt that this ought to 'be tried' elsewhere, clearly having England in mind.[26]

Although Locke was in France several years before the revocation of the Edict of Nantes in 1685 instituted the fiercest persecution of Protestants, he recorded carefully the corrosion of the toleration that the Edict officially provided. When he first arrived he noted that Protestants were 'only' deprived of office and still received 'common justice' – a distinction between toleration of worship and equality of civil rights on the one hand and qualification for office on the other that was reminiscent of Shaftesbury and Locke's 1673 support for both toleration and the Test Acts denying office to any who had not taken the sacraments in the Church of England. Over the next few years, however, Locke increasingly noted the closure of Protestant churches, the limitations upon the meeting of local Protestant estates and the exclusion of Protestants from offices and from sitting in the Estates. Just before leaving for England he noted that 'The Protestants within these twenty years have had above three hundred churches demolished, and within these two months fifteen more condemned.'

Locke asked French Protestants the question that one would expect from his earlier declarations of persecution's inefficacy, and obviously he

---

[25] *Discourses*, 2.41; 41n. in Hancock's edition cites Nicole's original argument as it was translated by the translator of the 1677 *Moral Essays*.

[26] *Essays*, 274–5; Lough, *Locke's Travels*, 252–3 (1 Jan 1679); MS Locke d1, 5; 9, 53; Locke's noted Covel's advice also in BM Add. MS 15642, 1.

received the answer that reinforced his views: 'Notwithstanding their discouragement, I doe not finde that many of them goe over'; 'they sometimes get and sometimes loose proselytes'. Another informant was convinced that 'the number of Protestants within these twenty or thirty last years are manifestly increased, and doe dayly, notwithstanding their losse every day of something'.[27]

An even more important political message was simultaneously being registered, increasing Locke's deep-seated fear of the Catholic doctrine that faith did not need to be kept with heretics: even when Catholic kings had officially provided for the toleration of Protestants, they persecuted their worship and limited their roles in office, in elected representation and even in trade. Catholic kings could not be trusted to keep their promises. One of the central issues in the fear of a Catholic king for most English Protestants, one of the central causes of his alleged inability to protect Protestant property rights, was the duty to restore the lands to the church that had been lost at the Reformation. This was a fear sufficient to force James, duke of York, to deny in a speech in 1679 that he would aim at their restitution when he succeeded. A Carthusian monk discussed with Locke in 1678 the future prospects for church lands in England 'when we came to be papists'; Locke said that they would be restored under a Catholic monarch since 'there could be noe reconciliation to their church without restitution'. The Carthusian declared him 'a good divine'.

In his time in Paris in 1678 and 1679 Locke repeatedly visited Versailles, drawn there partly by his intense disapproval of absolutist excess. Locke noted the emasculation of the provincial governors as Louis increasingly governed through the Intendants, and as the Estates ceased to have any real voice. As early as 1676 Locke noted that the Estates might have the 'solemnity and outward appearance of a Parliament' but that 'the difference' was that 'they never doe, and some say dare not, refuse whatever the King demands'. For Locke in the 1670s the increasing intolerance towards the Protestants of Louis XIV and his increasingly obvious absolutism gave flesh to the picture of the Catholic and absolutist King that was to be the central, fearful image of the politics of 1679–81, as attempts were made to exclude James, duke of York, from the succession on the ground that he was axiomatically untrustworthy and desirous of absolutism simply because he was a Catholic, but which was also increasingly feared of Charles himself as he resisted this Exclusion. When Locke apparently called the manuscript of the First Treatise or of the *Two Treatises* 'De Morbo Gallico', the French disease, it reflected his recent years in France.[28]

[27] Lough, *Travels*, 15; 22; 27; 41; 48; 89; 107; 113; 271.
[28] *Ibid.*, 30; 86; 97; 156; *Treatises*, 75–7. On the fear in England of Catholic lands being returned to the monasteries and abbeys under a Catholic King, and James' need to make a

On the only occasion on which Locke discussed the topic of obedience to government while in France, however, he repudiated armed resistance by subjects just as firmly as in his earlier manuscripts. In February 1676 he composed a lengthy note on virtues and vices. Some were described as antecedent to society, such as love of God and unnatural lusts; others, such as obedience to magistrates, were said to 'suppose society'. Human laws were purely penal, not obliging the conscience directly. Men were therefore not obliged directly by human laws 'but by that law of God which forbids disturbance or dissolution of governments'. The New Testament had only confirmed preceding civil relations, and when it said 'obey your superiors in all things' it had 'laid no new obligation' upon Christians. The end of civil society being civil peace 'the immediate obligation of every subject must be to preserve that society or government which was ordained to produce it'. He 'that obeys the magistrate to the degree, as not to endanger or disturb the government, under what form of government soever he live' obeyed to the utmost that conscience was obliged. The obligation on conscience was 'to preserve the government'. The magistrate could penalise men 'even to the loss of life' and the subject was 'in conscience obliged' to submit 'patiently to the penalty'.[29]

At first sight this seems to be unequivocal. Examined more closely, it might be thought significant that this note did not discuss the question of obligation in a situation where a 'government' was composed of more than one element, such as a monarchy and houses of parliament, which might clash among themselves. While the manuscript clearly enunciated the obligations to non-resistance of all subjects, it did not explicitly discuss the possibility of resistance by officers of the kingdom, an important distinction in sixteenth- and early seventeenth-century resistance theory that preserved significant room for resistance to monarchs while removing the rights of individuals to resist *qua* individuals. Nor did it explicitly discuss resistance to a government which changed its form from being limited to being absolute. It might therefore be thought that despite the clear thrust of its argument this note still implicitly left significant room for justifications of resistance. Yet we just saw that Locke's notes of this broad period in France recognised that the French monarchy had removed the powers of the Estates in effectively becoming absolute, and it seems very likely that

speech in 1679 to reassure Englishmen that that was not his intention see O. W. Furley, 'The Whig Exclusionists: Pamphlet Literature in the Exclusion Crisis', *The Cambridge Historical Journal* 1st series 13 (1957), 19–36 at 24.
[29] King, *Life*, II, 114–17; Dunn, *Locke*, 49. On the general contexts of Huguenot resistance theories of the sixteenth century see Q. Skinner, *The Foundations of Modern Political Thought*, Cambridge (1978), II; on Huguenot denial of these theories in the seventeenth century see G. H. Dodge, *The Political Theory of the Huguenots of the Dispersion*, Columbia (1947).

Locke was making nonresistance by all subjects required at a time when he recognised that the Estates were not in a position by force or by political means to oppose absolutism in France. Locke had surely thus very firmly rejected armed resistance by subjects in a situation where the clear and only alternative was absolutism. There was still a very considerable distance indeed, conceptually and psychologically, that had to be travelled before Shaftesbury and Locke would together attempt to prevent absolutism and Catholicism in England by plotting and defending armed resistance to the King by individual subjects.[30]

[30] Almost certainly before leaving England for France in 1675 and thus a few months earlier than this journal entry Locke composed a manuscript which he entitled 'Philanthropy or the Christian Philosophers'. In 'Philanthropy' Locke registered once again his belief that the high Anglican clergy were inclined both to re-institution of the Catholic religion in England because their own interest was exalted most highly therein, and to flattery of monarchical power. 'These thoughts' and a recognition that religion and virtue were promoted most by one's own immediate company and friends were then declared to have led an unspecified number described simply as 'us', but apparently a form of group of friends focused upon religion and not, say, a political organisation, to 'associate ourselves, with such as are lovers of truth and virtue that we may encourage, assist, and supporte each other in the ways of them'. This mutual assistance would be of help in 'preserving truth, Religion, and virtue amongst us; whatever deluge of misery and mischiefe may over run this parte of the world'. This unspecified group was declared not 'to intermeddle . . . with anything that concernes the Just and legall power of the Civill Magistrate; the government and laws of our Country cannot be injur'd by such as love truth, virtue and justice; we thinke ourselves obliged to lay downe our lives in the defence of it. Noe man can say he loves God, that loves not his neighbour; Noe man can love his neighbour that loves not his Country. 'Tis the greatest charity to preserve the Laws, and rights of the nation, whereof we are.'

The discussion here of the duty of charity to preserve the 'rights' and 'laws' of the 'nation' and the 'just and legall power' of the civil magistrate suggest the opposition to Charles' 'encroaching prerogative' that Shaftesbury and Locke had been engaged in promoting throughout 1675. They suggest moreover that the rights and laws are of the 'nation', political or legal rather than natural rights. These laws are the source of the power of the King. Nonetheless, this section of the manuscript does not specify any measures to be taken in the defence of these rights, and it could even be read as indicating that the group will not discuss the powers of the magistrate at all in not 'intermeddling' with them but instead concentrate upon mutual support of truth, religion and virtue. The comment about laying down one's life in defence of the government is not clear. It could be a rhetorical emphasis upon the extent of support for one's government when one would fight for it against foreign threats; a suggestion that one should lay down one's life if ordered to by a government that has become absolute as the 1676 journal entry describes; or, just possibly, a comment that one ought to fight to preserve the government against any threat from another part of the government. The last of these readings, reached by combining the middle and final sections of the quotation above, seems by far the least likely. This is particularly true in the light of the countenancing by Locke in 1667 and 1676 of men laying down their lives at the order of a government denying their rights, including the most crucial right of worship. It seems likely that this manuscript is one where Locke is arguing that it is desirable to preserve the laws and rights of England, woefully contemplating the imminent fate of Protestantism and liberty under a Catholic clergy and Catholic absolute monarchy, and supporting those who will oppose it by their mutual discussion of religion and virtue. The focus of the manuscript is upon the importance of a group of friends who will mutually assist one another in the pursuit of religious

IV

Between May 1679, when Locke returned to England, and early 1681 Shaftesbury campaigned energetically against absolutism and for the exclusion of James, duke of York from the succession in three heated national elections, helping to build a tolerationist coalition of nonconformists and moderate Anglicans against Charles' recent intolerance and Charles' moves towards absolutism as well as against James' succession. Shaftesbury's intention was to turn Charles towards compromise and exclusion and to resume his place as a royal minister, as he did briefly in 1679. In these years Locke once again recorded reading a large number of Anglican works supportive of toleration through comprehension as well as toleration outside of the church, and very few nonconformist works. Having once again stated his personal commitment to toleration in an entry in his *Lemmata Ethica* in 1679, Locke purchased several of the works of Archbishop Ussher, author of proposals for comprehension which had been used as the basis for Restoration plans, and the works of Chillingworth, which pleaded for a considerable degree of comprehension, although far more extensively in the arena of doctrine than ritual, and was cited repeatedly by the Latitudinarians for its eirenicism. Locke read and recommended to Shaftesbury the Anglican rector George Lawson's *Politica Sacra et Civilis*, half of which discussed the ecclesiastical constitution and advocated a form of comprehension, uniting government by bishops with a council of elders to satisfy presbyterians and with substantial autonomy for local congregations to attempt to satisfy Independents.[31]

truth and virtue under the 'deluge of misery and mischiefe' that will have overrun the country due to the clergy returning to Rome and flattering the monarch's power. Friendship was always extremely important to Locke; in 1675 he seems to have thought that it would have been even more important in a dismal future. See 'Philanthropy', MS Locke c27, fos. 30c–30c2; there is a more extended discussion of this manuscript in my 'John Locke in Context'. This manuscript is about to be most readily available in Wootton, *Locke: Political Writings*.

31 On toleration, MS Locke d1, 125–6; on Ussher, BM Add. MS 15642, 114; 117; 120; on Lawson, J. Franklin, *John Locke and the Theory of Sovereignty*, Cambridge (1978), 54; 58–9 and passim; C. Condren, 'Resistance and Sovereignty in Lawson's *Politica*: An Examination of a Part of Professor Franklin, His Chimera', *Historical Journal* 24: 3 (1981), 673–81. In 1680 Locke also bought Godolphin's *Epitome of Ecclesiastical Laws*, MS Locke f4, 192; Chillingworth's works, MS Locke f4, 95; and he was lending Boyle the *Journal des Scavans*, taking notes from Boyle on the Bible, and making comments upon a theological treatise by Boyle: BM Add. MS 15642, 113; 124; MS Locke c27, fo. 67. In December 1680 he bought *Liberty of Conscience in its order to Universal Peace*, (1681) a work pleading for comprehension and innatism; see *Liberty*, 10; 27–33; 46; 69; 115–42; MS Locke f4, 1 Dec 1680. In 1681 Locke read Stillingfleet's *Defence of the Discourse Concerning Idolatry* and Burnet's *Conference with the Jesuits*, continuing his long-standing interest in Latitudinarian arguments against Roman Catholicism. Locke's copy

Locke's journals suggest that he read few nonconformist works. In 1681 he did read the Independent Thomas Coleman's Civil-War sermon *Hopes Deferred and Dashed* and recorded the biblical texts for church government that Coleman had identified as insufficient to establish any form of *jure divino* church government, including independency. He then read the high-church Anglican William Cave's 1675 *Primitive Christianity*, a work which defended at length the primitive status of episcopacy, and the 1675 *Naked Truth* by Herbert Croft, ageing bishop of Hereford, which had sparked a major controversy between high-church and Latitudinarian Anglicans, both by proclaiming in direct contrast to Cave that church government was prudential and had originally been government by 'elders' not yet differentiated into 'bishops' and 'presbyters', and by arguing that a very wide comprehension on ceremonial issues was desirable. Of these three works, it was apparently Croft's work that seems to have made the most significant impression on Locke; it was one of only a few works that Locke was to cite in his works in the 1690s, declaring it then a work by an 'ornament of our church'.[32]

In 1680 Edward Stillingfleet had caused a major controversy by first preaching a sermon, the *Mischief of Separation*, and then writing a large book in its defence, the *Unreasonableness of Separation* attacking the dissenters for their 'unreasonable separation' from the Church of England. Owen and Richard Baxter were just two of a host of nonconformists who composed works in reply; almost every leading nonconformist controversialist of the Restoration published a defence of his own separation from the Church of England against the works of Stillingfleet as one of the Latitudinarian churchmen whom most had long viewed as among their most important Anglican sympathisers, both for his support of comprehension, and for his eirenic contention in his early *Irenicum* that episcopacy had not been the required primitive form of church government.[33]

In his two works Stillingfleet pressed the desirability of conformity to the

---

of Stillingfleet's *Defence of the Discourse* has a seven-page entry list inside the back cover on the subject of idolatry: Locke Room 8. 134 (*Library*, entry 2775); MS Locke f5, 23 on receipt of Stillingfleet's two works March 1681; MS Locke d10, 23, 149; 157 on reading in 1681. Locke bought a work by Falkland and Hales' *Tracts* at auction in December 1681, and read the latter in 1682: MS Locke b2, 31; 36; MS Locke f6, 84ff. In 1682 he bought Wilkins' *Natural Religion*: MS Locke b2, 40; on Locke and Hooker in this broad period see my 'Locke in Context', chapter five.

[32] T. Coleman, *Hopes Deferred and Dashed* (1645), passim and MS Locke f5, 49ff. from Coleman; [H. Croft], *The Naked Truth* n.p.p. (1675), passim and MS Locke f5, 52 for reading of Croft. MS Locke f5, 52 reading Cave; MS Locke f5, 53; 55–8 on Locke's reading of Ussher in May 1681; cf. MS Locke f5, 152 on Cosin.

[33] See my 'Ecclesiology' on this and the next paragraph. Stillingfleet, *Mischief*, passim; idem, *Unreasonableness*, passim.

Church of England by all Protestants, particularly the presbyterians, since the Church of England was the 'main bulwark against Popery'. Maintaining his support for comprehension, however, in the preface to the *Unreasonableness* he proposed either removing or leaving free those disputed ceremonial issues which most moderate nonconformists had long described as causing their separation from the Church of England, most notably kneeling at the Sacrament, the use of the sign of the cross in baptism, and the use of godparents. The *Unreasonableness of Separation* also countenanced the toleration of dissenters, but only with great reluctance. Stillingfleet pressed the obligation to conform on two grounds, the general duty of all Christians to seek the peace of the Church, and the specific biblical precept that all things were to be done decently and in order. Stillingfleet argued that if men were allowed to separate merely for an opinion that they would find better means of edification elsewhere, then the church would be torn apart. Noting the agreement of most Protestants on questions of doctrine, and emphasising the fortuitous coincidence of the established religion and the true religion, Stillingfleet stressed the role of the Church of England as the church established by law. This argument thus came perilously close to arguing that the obligation to conform lay in the legal establishment itself, and Stillingfleet was frequently accused of 'Hobbism' in a major series of nonconformist replies. In keeping with the elevated conception of episcopacy increasingly held by the Latitudinarians in the later years of the Restoration, much of Stillingfleet's argument also described episcopacy as the true primitive form of church government and condemned nonconformists for their lack of this primitive form.

It was almost certainly in early 1681, in the period between the dissolution of the first Parliament of 1681 and the meeting of the Oxford Parliament when Locke was ill at the Oakley house of his friend James Tyrrell, that he began a 167-page reply to Stillingfleet's work. This was the longest work of his life to date. It is very likely that he had completed at least the first hundred pages by February 1681, but he almost certainly continued to work on the manuscript in brief bursts until at least the middle of 1681, and thus was working on it in the period of his reading of the works of Cave, Croft and Coleman in May 1681. As he was working on it, then, he was taking notes from two works which illustrate the broad combination of the elements of his own preceding ecclesiological views, Coleman's Independent but rather erastian work and Croft's extremely Latitudinarian Anglican work – by comparison with the views of most Latitudinarians by 1681, far too Latitudinarian a work – as well as a high-church Anglican work by William Cave that both Croft's and Coleman's work opposed. Stillingfleet's work thus represented only one of the three versions of Anglicanism before Locke during the period when he was writing his attack on

Stillingfleet, a version that fell between the eirenicism of Croft and the hierocratic Cave.[34]

Locke's 'Critical Notes Upon Edward Stillingfleet's Mischief and Unreasonableness of Separation' was largely a page-by-page and often a point-by-point reply to Stillingfleet's two works; it is difficult therefore to assess which of its arguments were for Locke himself the most important. In an important development, in response to Stillingfleet's attack upon nonconformist separation simply for their view of edification, Locke came to describe edification as a duty that the individual owed to himself, and toleration thus became for Locke in part a right correlative of this duty. The 'Critical Notes' pointed out the incongruity of the use of force to institute ritual observance when Christianity was a religion of peace and immorality was not punished, but even though it had been hinted at as early as the end of the fourth draft on toleration and was present in some detail in the 'Critical Notes', Locke still did not mount a full argument that toleration was a duty of Christianity; that was not to come until the opening pages of the *Letter Concerning Toleration* in 1685.

---

[34] The 'Critical Notes' are MS Locke c34. 'Critical Notes' is a somewhat awkward title for a 167-page manuscript, but is used in the secondary literature and does convey its character of a point-by-point reply to Stillingfleet. The manuscript is largely in the hand of Locke's friend James Tyrrell and is generally identified as a joint composition by Locke and Tyrrell. There are, however, several reasons to suggest very strongly indeed that Locke was sole author and Tyrrell an amanuensis (like Sylvanus Brownover, Locke's amanuensis, in whose hand part of the manuscript is also written). In March 1685 Locke wrote to Edward Clarke about papers that he had left with Clarke, including a parcel 'whereof one part was of the Doctor's preparing . . . and the other of my own though for the most part marked by another's hand who was my operator when I kept my bed'. The last phrase was written over 'kept ill a bed'. The doctor referred to was almost certainly Stillingfleet, and the manuscript the 'Critical Notes'. Locke was ill at Tyrrell's house in January and early February 1681, recording that he had left Tyrrell's house 'after so long keeping my bed and being in almost constantly in a breathing sweat', and reflecting in June that he had been 'Constantly in bed for a fortnight'. Locke's sole responsibility for the manuscript is also suggested by Tyrrell himself, who wrote to Locke in 1686 in an attempt to persuade him to revise the work they had 'writ together': Tyrrell referred to it as 'your discourse' on toleration and not as 'our discourse'. It is further confirmed by many of the passages in Tyrrell's hand which are very close verbal parallels to passages in Locke's other writings on toleration. Passages in Tyrrell's hand also discuss details of French Protestantism that were known to Locke from his time there in the 1670s. The index to the manuscript was by Locke. Finally, it is suggestive that when Locke went abroad this manuscript went to Clarke and not to Tyrrell. Richard Ashcraft, who tentatively dated MS Locke c34 to May 1681, presumed in *Revolutionary Politics* that Locke's first journal reference to Stillingfleet's *Unreasonableness* denotes its arrival at Tyrrell's house. While Locke was ill, however, he made – uncharacteristically – almost no entries in his journal. It is therefore quite likely that Locke's first reference to the work in his journal reflects that he was still working on MS Locke c34 in May, but not that it had just arrived. References to various works in the later sections of the 'Critical Notes' and in Locke's journal also suggest that Locke worked on MS Locke c34 in May 1681. *Correspondence*, II, 615–18, 620, 815, 817, 820, 822–3; III, 889; Ashcraft, *Revolutionary Politics*, 491n.; MS Locke f5, 7–9, 39, 68. Ashcraft has now recognised that this manuscript is by Locke: Ashcraft, 'Latitudinarianism', n. 36.

The 'Critical Notes' unequivocally supported toleration of different religions, and particularly the toleration of Protestant worship outside of the national, established church. The 'Critical Notes' also indicate, however, that Locke's concern with 'latitudinism' in the 'Essay on Toleration' persisted into the early 1680s, with Locke strongly advocating comprehension. Locke explicitly identified himself at several points as a member of the Church of England who thought their sermons the best then in the world. Against Stillingfleet's elevation of episcopacy, Locke declared church government prudential, and argued that in the primitive era the church had been governed by a mixture of independency and presbyterianism in a consistorial form of government. Locke departed significantly from even the most eirenic of the Latitudinarians of the Church of England in this argument, and in the extent of his defence of toleration as well as comprehension. He was also, however, highly critical at several points of the views and behaviour of dissenters, and condemned unequivocally both their own pretensions to *jure divino* authority and their compulsion of other Christians and even of their own church members. Attacking both Anglican and dissenting clergy, the 'Critical Notes' raised the anticlericalism voiced in the *Letter From A Person of Quality* to a level unparalleled in its venom by any of Locke's other works. In short, Locke's continuing ecclesiological eclecticism, hostility to elements of nonconformity, apparent absence of reading of nonconformist works and lay anticlericalism in the 'Critical Notes' should prevent description of him as the ideologist of religious dissent in early 1681.

At two points early in the 'Critical Notes' Locke spoke of himself as 'I who am of the Church of England'. At many points throughout the 'Critical Notes' he spoke of nonconformists as dissenters from 'our' church. He declared that 'I can truly say that I think there have never been in proportion so many learned and devout bishops anywhere in the world as in the church of England'. He held that Stillingfleet had shown 'well enough against B[axter] that our church discipline is better than that of the Presbiterians', and argued that Stillingfleet had had 'so much the better' of John Owen about *jure divino* independency. He declared that there were 'many excellent preachers wee have in the Church of England whose lives as well as sermons I looke upon and verily believe, to be the most seriously Christian that are now in the world or have bin at any time in the Church'. Their preaching received 'a testimony even from the dissenters since many of them, who seem in earnest in Religion find it for their Edification to come and hear several of the Divines in our Church'. Locke was to remain an Anglican communicant until the end of his life, receiving the Sacrament at home in his last months. Given Locke's own stress upon the legitimacy – indeed, the duty – of searching out the church best for one's own edification in the 'Critical Notes' it is significant that he thus remained a member of the Church of England. Locke's opposition in the 'Critical Notes' was to a Church placing too much emphasis upon outward conformity and not enough upon morality; it was significantly to be the sermons on morality of several Restoration Anglicans that he singled out for particular praise in 1703 as the best he had ever read.[35]

Locke applauded Stillingfleet's proposals for the widening of Anglican communion by removing 'those bars' to communion that were easily removed, by discarding or leaving up to the individual communicant the performance of rituals such as kneeling at the Sacrament. He wrote that 'I readily agree with the Doctors modell of the Crosse, kneeling, and sponsors, and I doe it with great admiration of his ingenuity, temper, and Candour he being the first that I have ever met with of the side in power that would ever hearken to the least abatement of what they had once set up in departing from the precise rigour of their formes towardes an accommodation.' He lauded Stillingfleet's 'Christian largenesse of mind' over comprehension which meant, he noted, that on this he was arguing not against Stillingfleet but those 'who are of a contrary mind from his'.[36]

The desirability of moving towards an accommodation between the Church of England and dissenters was one of the major themes of the 'Critical Notes', voiced in a way that made clear that Locke thought that the dissenters as well as Anglican imposition had been responsible for the breaches between Protestants. Locke declared that he thought it 'the apprehension of many sober Protestants of the Church of England, that the setting up of all these outward formalityes . . . and narrowing the termes of Communion' at the 'King's happy restoration' had contributed more to Roman Catholic designs against Protestantism than 'the miscarriages of our dissenters, who I will not deny to have had their share in it'. Locke had 'often heard sober men, ev'n divines of the Church of England bemoane' its concentration upon ceremonial enforcement.[37]

It is probably accurate to identify the sober divines of the Church of England whom Locke identified as opponents of Anglican imposition as the Latitudinarians, but it should be stressed that if so Locke was here identifying himself with the most eirenic of the Latitudinarians such as Tillotson and Fowler – precisely the two Latitudinarians with whom his personal contact was most significant up to this date. Frustrated by what they perceived as nonconformist intransigence about matters that almost all agreed to be indifferent, increasingly believing that those who disagreed were unwilling to consider matters properly, finding episcopacy more

[35] MS Locke c34, 5, 8, 71, 96, 104, 147, 160; see my 'Locke and Latitudinarianism' on his recommendations of Latitudinarian sermons as the best works of morality.
[36] MS Locke c34, 31, 36.   [37] MS Locke c34, 8–9; 144–5.

defensible because of their own patristic research, and seeing increasing conservatism as the way to preferment, many of the other Latitudinarians were becoming increasingly unwilling by this point in the Restoration to expend energies demanding accommodation through genuine compromise.[38]

According to Locke, if the ceremonies confessed to be indifferent had 'bin lessened, and the borders of the Church enlarged, the Church of England must needs have had more Partisans and lesse contentions'. Severity had 'widened the breach; and kept it open' and the best way to bring them together was 'to enlarge its communion'. The way to union was not 'to require one side to submit to all: but to persuade both sides to remit something, and to meet in an amicable yielding to each other'. Probably having in mind his 1679 conversations with Covel about conformity in Constantinople, Locke queried why 'may not peace betwixt the kneelers and not kneelers at the sacrament be as well preserved were there no injunction about it as it is betwixt the bowers, and not bowers at the altar'. He argued that historically there had been no separation 'until after uniformity was presst with vigour', even though there had been many who 'all along . . . disliked many things in our church and wisht for a farther reformation'. He suggested that 'perhaps the wise and learned bishop Prideaux's rule had it bin observed had as perfectly cured the heats, and dissentions about these indifferent things in the church as well as it did in his parish about a Maypole' – a very important source of puritan disquiet in the early seventeenth century – 'viz those that would should, and those that would not should have none upon which . . . the controversy . . . fell of itself'. If uniformity could be preserved amongst several modes of worship it was 'to be wondered, why our church will not remit, or leave at liberty some not necessary modes of worship, when it would give admittance and quiet the minds, and certainly stop the mouths of so many dissenters'.[39]

Locke argued that at the beginning of the Reformation the people had been brought up in the superstitions of the Roman church 'and had bin taught to beleive them substantial, and necessary parts, nay almost the total of Religion'. Many ceremonies had therefore been kept at the Reformation in order 'to bring over as many converts as they could', to enlarge communion. Converts from Rome were now 'at a stand if not an ebbe'. There were many more shut out by retention of ceremonies. Thus, the problem over kneeling at the Sacrament was that many nonconformists thought it redolent of popish adoration. According to Locke, maintaining these ceremonies was directly counter to the intention of the reformers,

---

[38] See my 'Locke and Latitudinarianism'.   [39] MS Locke c34, 8–10; 37; 51; 60.

who had preserved ceremonies only in order to promote edification. In the time of Edward VI they had even reduced ceremonies on this ground. Since the only change since then had been in the opposite direction there was now reason for the 'Phanaticks' to think the church was 'under far different churchmen'. It was 'not onely prudent' but actually 'a duty incumbent on those whose businesse it is to have a Care of the salvation of men's souls' to remove ceremonies. Dissenters could be gained 'and the Church enlarged, by parting with a few things', purchasing union at 'so cheap a rate'.[40]

At times Locke's description of what he meant by the 'few' ceremonies that were to be removed was probably more capacious than that of even the most eirenic of the Latitudinarians like Tillotson and Fowler, although perhaps reminiscent of Croft. He declared it desirable to take away 'as many as is possible of our present ceremonies'. He presumably meant those that were contested, but he may have intended even more ceremonies should be removed than those currently contested because he restated a view that he had first voiced against Catholic worship in France, that ceremonies took up the minds of most men: 'I ask if this multiplicity of Ceremonyes be not apt in its owne nature soe to take up mens minds, as to make them rest satisfyed in these outward performances, and neglect the materiall, and necessary parts of religion.' This was because 'mens minds cannot be intent to a great diversity of things', as well as the influence of those who were guiding them and were 'so much concerned in a precise observance of them, more perhaps then of the great things of the gospel'.

Further underpinning Locke's hostility to ceremonial enforcements was Locke's view on man's susceptibility to superstition. In the 'Critical Notes' Locke wrote that superstition was 'thinking to please God with outward ceremonies, and bodily performances which he neither requires or expects'. The day that he left Tyrrell's house in May 1681, almost certainly at the end of one of his periods of working on the 'Critical Notes' during his six-day stay with Tyrrell, Locke wrote in his journal that mankind was governed by 'three great things . . . reason, passion and superstition'. Reason was said to only govern 'a few', but Locke did not identify passion as governing most of the remainder, as he had in the late 1650s. Instead, probably reflecting increased opposition to Anglican formalism and his years among French Catholics, it was superstition that he declared was 'especially powerful and produces the greatest mischiefs'. This argument was voiced in a work against Stillingfleet, and the number of ceremonies that he thought should be removed almost certainly exceeded the Latitudinarians' desire to reduce the current ceremonial emphasis of the Church of

[40] MS Locke c34, 142–57.

England, but fear that ceremonial emphasis left the substance of religion little regarded was frequently voiced not merely by nonconformists but also by Restoration Latitudinarians, including Tillotson, who argued that whenever 'the external part of religion is principally regarded, and men are more careful to worship God with outward pomp and ceremony than in 'spirit and in truth' . . . men embrace the shadow of religion and let go the substance'. John Smith, Cambridge Platonist and the mentor of many Latitudinarians, made a similar point in his analysis of superstition and when Locke read his *Select Discourses* in 1682 he was to declare one among the best treatises on superstition that he had ever read. Locke was thus still here expressing a theme that he was identifying primarily in the works of eirenic Anglicans who emphasised moral performance, even if with a more intense opposition than they expressed.[41]

For Locke, the ceremonies of the Church of England had wrongly been made the terms of communion 'whilst holynesse and sobriety of life is lesse regarded'. Locke questioned rhetorically whether Christ would approve of church discipline 'wherein a known drunken or debauched person, if he does not but bow at his name, and conforme zealously to other outward imposed ceremonyes shall be a good Member of the Church . . . when a sober, and devout Christian endeavouring with a sincere obedience to observe all the rules of the Gospel shall pass for a phanatick because he cannot bow at the name of Jesus or the like'. Locke would 'not say that the Laws of our church make such a distinction' but the 'Leading men of the church' gave the 'title of true sons of the church to those onely who are zealous for their instituted ceremonyes whatever their lives be'. The 'true conformity of the Gospel', in contrast, was of those who believed Christ's doctrine 'and by good lives conforme to his precepts'.[42]

Locke joined an unequivocal and a far more extensive defence of religious toleration to his advocacy of comprehension. Responding to Stillingfleet's stress upon the necessity of keeping the peace of the church, Locke declared that toleration would 'lesse cause endless contentions, then the imposeing uniformity' unless force was used to 'extirpate all dissenters', behaviour which was not 'agreeable to Christian religion'. Toleration was more likely than force to 'bring men into mutual forebearance, and charity, which is true unity'. Locke could 'not see why the Peace, and unity of the Christian church may not be as well preserved in distinct churches, as the peace of a parish in distinct families'. He thought that 'it suffices for the union of Protestants that they keep up a Friendship under different formes and modes of worship'.

Separation would remain while 'the different judgments of men, appear-

---

[41] MS Locke c34, 35, 51, 59–60; 142–3; MS Locke f5, 59.   [42] MS Locke c34, 142–5.

ances of things, and corruptions in all partyes remaine'. Locke here argued that the separation of different judgements was inevitable: it was no more 'to be hoped to have men all of the same mind in these things than to have them all of the same looks, or complexions'. The question 'what is the true religion' was likely 'to remain always the great debate of mankind'. He did nonetheless hold out hope that toleration might help to foster a conformity of practice and even to a large degree one of belief. Stillingfleet had cited the Brownists as examples of the inexorably fissiparous tendencies of the nonconformists. Maintaining the argument of peace through sectarianism first voiced in the 'Essay on Toleration' Locke argued that it was force that had joined them together. When they had got to Holland they had 'divided and subdivided'. They did not then threaten the government. But he also went on to suggest concerning the Brownists that 'the readyest way to bring men to their wits, and so back again to a reasonable conformity (next to kind usage) is to let them wander until they are weary for I think opposition and rigour works nothing upon them'. Separation was especially likely where persuasion was not used, presumably where the 'corruptions in all partyes remained'. According to Locke, even Stillingfleet did not think that force could persuade: 'I doubt whether the Doctor thought a cudgell ever convinced a man of any article of faith, or the lawfulnesse of any ceremony in worship.' Force might bring compliance, but not conviction. Force was not to be used because 'the proper instruments of the magistrate are altogether incapeable to convince men's minds'. Believing or not believing were 'the ungovernable actions of his owne mind, which he himself cannot command much lesse any other'. 'Therefore' the magistrate should not annex penalties to belief.[43]

For Locke, Stillingfleet had not chosen the path of persuasion. It was necessary for union that one seeking it 'though he betrays not the truth, yet takes care to say as little that offends, exasperates, or exposes as may be. He that would reconcile his friend or child to his duty, will scarce expose himself to publick shame, and he that meets not another in any difference, so as to perswade him he is his friend seldome prevailes upon him to be of his mind.' Locke had 'seldome observed any other effectual way of healing differences (especially in Religion) then by letting the controversy sleep and expressing kindness and good will to the persons, with charity and allowance to humane frailty which seldome failes in such controversyes to make mistakes or at least miscarriages on both sides'. Locke declared that there were few better than Stillingfleet 'in preaching or disputing' but thought that few were convinced by arguments 'though never so strong, and ration-

---

[43] MS Locke c34, 7, 56; 63–4; 15–25; 148; 41; 49; 78; 107; 119.

ally written', particularly where these were accompanied by 'any mixture of reproaches'.

Persuasion was the only effective means of conversion. It was also the only legitimate means. It had been Christ's method, whose ways were 'of meekenesse, and gentlenesse preaching of the gospel in simplicity, and exemplariness of life'. The union of Christians into one society 'by the common tyes of Charity, brotherly love and kindnesse I think is their duty and very much tends to the preserving and propagating of the Christian religion'. It was through persuasion and example that men were to be brought to religion, not by force. Even in attacking Stillingfleet's and the other Anglicans' use of persecution instead of persuasion, Locke did not, however, exonerate the nonconformists, declaring that 'I doe not overlook the carriage of . . . the other side, who I fear are much more to blame, and perhaps as the Doctor [Stillingfleet] alleges gave the first blow.' Stillingfleet's reproaches were inefficacious 'how justly so ever deserved, as those undeniable ones are which the Doctor proves out of their owne writeings'. The nonconformists' miscarriages were substantial, and Locke was highly critical of their behaviour, even when he recognised that they had greater cause to be recalcitrant as they were the ones being persecuted.[44]

Describing men's motivation to worship, Locke stressed God's power and particularly man's concern with his own happiness. According to Locke 'the light of nature' discovered 'to man that he is under the power and disposal of an invisible and supreme being'. It taught him also that he was concerned 'to behave himself as not to offend, or if he did, to find means to reconcile and recover again the favour of that being which over-rules all human affairs . . . dispenses good and evil in this world and on whom depends Eternal happiness' in another. This knowledge of a God and 'his absolute power over them puts all men everywhere upon thoughts of religion'. The 'great end of every man is happynesse which Religion is alwayes thought more directly to serve to'. Some of the actions that men had to perform were moral actions, but man also had to worship and to profess a faith. They had to 'honour and worship the God they served . . . by publick acts of devotion'. Men therefore had to join churches. Men had to perform worship that they judged acceptable. Nothing could be used in worship 'unless it be that which I in my conscience judge will be acceptable to' God. A man was to join whatever society he believed most conducive to his own salvation, and was free to leave it again 'if he thinks the order set up there not subservient to the ends for which he entered the society'.[45]

The 'great ends' of religion to be attained in such church societies were 'edification (which consists in informing the understanding and subduing

44 MS Locke c34, 8; 24–5; 108–10.   45 MS Locke c34, 22ff; 75ff.

of the will) . . . the public worship of God . . . the propagation of truth, and the continuation of the Gospel down to posterity. One of these containing my duty to God, the other to my neighbour, and the other to myself'. Stillingfleet had argued that separation upon pretence of purer worship or better means of edification was schismatic. In reply Locke stressed at many points that edification, the informing of the understanding and the subduing of the will, was vital and was a quite sufficient reason to depart from any church. For Locke, the Christian religion stressed that 'which other religions did not so manifestly concern themselves in . . . the particular edification of the members and the preservation and propagation of its truth'. That which had 'reasonably' to determine church communion was individual belief that a church had 'the truest worship . . . the greatest purity of truth and the best means of . . . edification'. The command of edification, was 'as great a command and of as strict obligation as let all things be done decently and in order'. Stillingfleet, like most Anglicans, placed much emphasis upon decency and order, but in his work of edification 'wee heare very little'. While peace was not to be neglected for edification, 'Edification is not to be neglected for peace and order when those are interpreted to consist in submission.' Edification was 'never mentioned by the zealous pleaders for Ecclesiastical impositions though it be oftener mentioned in the Scripture than Decency, and order perhaps because it was foreseen how apt it would be to be forgotten'. Locke did not mention that he had himself forgotten it until the 'Critical Notes'.[46]

While thus placing a heavy emphasis upon 'edification', upon this 'informing' of the understanding and 'subdueing' of the will, Locke did not expand upon this and describe his view of the status of the understanding or will, or the means of informing and subjecting them. Because of the unsystematic nature of Locke's manuscript it is not clear what Locke thought should be done to inform the understanding. While Locke did speak of choosing other churches for purer doctrine and preaching, and spoke at great length about the duties of persuasion through discourse and especially through example, the crucial element in informing the understanding appears to have been individuals' liberty. Christ had proclaimed the 'true liberty of the Gospel' which was 'to be tied up to the strictest rules of a good life but to be guided by his owne conscience in things of faith and worship'. Locke stressed once again that it was the duty of every individual to search out his own duties, and it appears to be enough room for the individual's search which is crucial for the understanding, as it had been since the early *Essays*.

In the case of the will, however, it was not liberty that Locke turned to,

[46] MS Locke c34, 22–3; 53; 59; 69; 77; 136.

but the power of custom and conversation disciplining man into living uprightly. Locke posed the purportedly hypothetical case of one who was of a church where the doctrines of faith and practice were all true and ceremonies indifferent but where those 'of most credit and reputation' were those 'most zealous and exact in the outward, and instituted Ceremonyes, whose lives otherwise savoured not much of true Christian piety, whilst at the same time others of exemplary good life, were neglected, yea and discountenanced too if they showed but the least doubt concerning any of those external rites'. The fellowship of this society was not 'so effectual to keep' a man 'up to the strictness of a good life . . . [who observed] . . . in himself irregular inclinations ready to lay hold on any pretence that might indulge them'. He should therefore quit this society where 'his owne natural corruption had too great subterfuges to be easily masterd' and go to a church where the common opinions and practice stressed a strict life. The way that human nature was wrought on, 'the great spring, and motive to good and bad, in man's actions is the credit they finde by it with their party and that that most governs the whole course of their lives is the reputation it gives them with the company they keep and the society they recommend themselves to'.[47]

It was at this point that Locke made explicit the identification of his hypothetical case with the Church of England. He declared that this was not meant to criticise the 'many excellent preachers . . . of the Church of England' whose sermons and lives were the best in the world and whose preaching was often attended by dissenters. He went on, however, that 'one maine reason' that even these divines 'must confesse with me' that their 'admirable and convinceing discourse' had left so many 'outside' Christians in their congregations was that many hearers contented themselves with the commendation that they found for outward conformity. A person was not to be blamed for adding 'the awe of his company or disciplin of his societie' to teachers' discourses in order to 'suppresse some vitious inclinations or habits'. In his journal in mid-1679 Locke had written that men were rarely prevailed upon by laws in reformation of manners, and that 'the chief thing' that was to be looked to was the power of custom.[48]

Locke once again also focused upon harmlessness as legitimating toleration. The name of religion was 'appropriated to those actions only which are referred . . . to pleasing . . . God without any concerning at all my neighbour, civil society, or my own preservation in this life. For my praying to God in this or that fashion or using any other ceremony in religion or speculative opinions concerning things of another life entrenches not at all upon the health or possession, Good name or any other right of my neigh-

[47] MS Locke c34, 43; 158ff.   [48] MS Locke c42, 66; MS Locke c34, 158–60.

bour'. Locke condemned the Church of England for appealing to the power of the civil magistrate. Those who persuaded the magistrate to 'stand at the door with whips and scourges to chastise' dissenters made their 'church power perfectly Erastian'. Locke's manuscript repeatedly questioned Stillingfleet's declaration of obligation to obey the Church of England as the church established by law. Legal establishment added no obligation to worship. Locke assaulted depictions of the role of the magistrate as 'nursing father' of religion; the christianisation of the Roman Empire had resulted in a confounding of civil and ecclesiastical jurisdictions and was 'one great occasion that the Christian religion is accused of so many disorders'. The true precedent was the first 300 years after Christ, where the Christian religion was often spread 'against all the opposition of the secular power'.[49]

Locke's criticism of the Church of England was not written as a defence of nonconformists' principles. Locke was as critical of the nonconformists' reliance upon the power of the civil magistrate as he was of the Church of England. When the Presbyterians had been 'in the saddle' and 'were like to have the quiet of their reigne disturbed by Liberty of Conscience' they 'were then of the mind that some Church men now are that Liberty of Conscience is worse than Popery'. They had wished to separate from the episcopal order of the Church of England, but not to allow men a right from separating from their own 'which it is pretty hard to find principles which will doe and I yet have not had the luck to light on any such'. There was little hope of peace and truth in the world, Locke declared 'untill this great and fundamentall popish doctrine of using force in matters of Religion be layd aside'. It necessarily followed from this doctrine that 'wee in England punish Phanaticks', that the Presbyterians had 'persecute[d] the Episcopat when they had power' and that 'the independent and Quaker clergy think' – and Locke's use of the present tense here should be particularly noted in the light of attempts to link Locke in this period to an ideology of dissent revolving around the Independents because of their supposed support for toleration – that 'they ought to use the magistrates power or have any temporal tyes to force men to keep them in their Churches'. Locke declared, indeed, that 'I know not whether they would be as dangerous reformers as Germany found the Anabaptists'.[50]

Against Stillingfleet's elevation of episcopacy, Locke argued that the first form of church government had involved congregations with a consistorial form of presbyterian authority based upon the consent of the members of the church in such a way that neither modern presbyterianism nor modern independency ran parallel. It was 'playne there were many Presbyters or

---

[49] MS Locke c34, 76–7; 14; 18; 101 and passim.   [50] MS Locke c34, 3–7; 103.

Bishops in one church and there was yet no subordination amongst them'. The names of presbyter and bishop were originally used 'promiscuously' for the same office, meaning merely 'elders'. In some cases the Apostles had appointed as preachers those 'most considerable for knowledge, prudence, or age'; in others 'History seems to justify by the practice of the primitive Church' the claim that the people had the right to elect their 'Bishops and pastors'. From this original mixture of independency and presbytery, episcopacy had gradually grown up, probably in part for 'dispatch', in part because of the veneration of new converts for their guides, and, of course, from clerical ambition. It was very likely that other churches would then imitate this for all 'churches held a correspondence one with another'. Those who claimed that church history demonstrated the Apostolic origin of separate offices for bishop and presbyter were relying on an untrustworthy source: church history had been written by bishops.[51]

The bedrock of Locke's argument against Stillingfleet's case for *jure divino* episcopacy from Scripture, however, ran along lines parallel to his assault in the First Treatise upon Filmer's case from Scripture for *jure divino* monarchy. He proffered his own interpretation of Scripture as not necessarily true, but declared that Stillingfleet's account could not explain the silence of Christ and the Apostles about such a supposedly necessary form of church government. It was simply incredible that 'our Saviour and his Apostles should omit to give plain directions' about something that was 'absolutely necessary to the Church'. Every church had the power to institute their own form of government as they desired since it was 'meerly prudential'. It was 'plain' to Locke that 'the forme of government of the church (whatever is said to the contrary) had bin managed, as a prudentiall thing, and not submitted to as a modell absolutely prescribed by God almighty'. For Locke this condemned not merely *jure divino* episcopacy but all claims to *jure divino* church government, including those claims long mounted by the presbyterians, and those mounted by many Independents in the Restoration as they sought to justify their nonconformity. Locke lauded Stillingfleet's demolition of Owen's arguments: 'I do not wonder that Dr S[tillingfleet] should have so much the better of Dr O[wen] . . . about the *jus divinum* of his congregational model . . . I fear 'tis a fate that attends all those who would persuade the world that any one form of church government is *jure divino* when the Scriptures say so little or nothing at all about it.'[52]

For Locke, all of these claims to *jure divino* authority were caused by clerical avarice. He suggested that were there 'no more power and interest

51 MS Locke c34, 39; 71–2, 88ff.
52 MS Locke c34, 3–4; 4, 71–2; 104; passim.

annexed to the being guides to the new Jerusalem, than there is to any other place they would as litle obtrude themselves with authority or require us to travel by their charts as other guides do'. Stillingfleet ought to look 'a little beyond the glittering scene of this world and the dazling splendour of Ecclesiastical Dominion, and great Church preferments, and consider what a tragical sight it will be to see men in Hell by takeing their pastors, and with them their Religion upon trust'. The image of shepherd and his flock was frequently evoked to show clerical domination. When Christians came 'under the notion of sheep' Locke declared with a strange image that 'it is no wonder they contend for the largeness of their flocks since they have the more to milk and shear and have often the selling of them'. One could not wonder 'that any pastor whose riches enlarge still with the increase of his flock should contend so mightly to have it believed that all sheep ought to be only in his fold'. Clerical power involved extending the metaphor of pastor and flock a little too far 'and treating men as if they were brutes in earnest'.[53]

Locke contended that there were 'very few' of 'all the instances' that Stillingfleet cited 'both ancient and modern of heats, animosities, breach of peace and charity amongst Christians' wherein 'the pastors were not on both sides the first movers and warm leaders in the quarrel'. The 'ambition of the clergy' was the 'cause of great schisms and divisions in the Church'. The example of New England where the government was 'in the hands of the clergy as it is in Rome' demonstrated that Protestant persecution 'for Religion' fell 'very little short' of Roman 'only Rome being the Elder – her nailes are grown a little longer and sharper'. 'Churchmen of all sorts with power', Locke concluded sweepingly, were 'very apt to persecute and misuse those that will not pen in their fold.' He thought that this might 'some time or other open the laity's eyes and make them consider that those men, who pretend a commission . . . to teach them the truths of God, have made little other use of that authority, but to make slaves of those that submitted to them, and miserable those that dissented'. Independent pastors were no exception. He found it very difficult to see how the leading Independent Vincent Alsop could argue as he had against Stillingfleet that men could not separate from those churches they had voluntarily joined. The bonds

given to their pastors in Independent churches shews how in this contest churches are made like bird cages with trapp doores which give free admittance to all birds whether they have always been the wild inhabitants of the Air, or are got loose from any other cages but when they are once in, they are to be kept there and are to have the liberty of getting out no more. And the reason is because if this be

[53] MS Locke c34, 5–6; 131; 148; 155.

permitted our votaryes will be spoild, but the happynesse of the birds is not the businese of these bird keepers.[54]

Locke's work was animated as much by disbelief that any clergy could be given power, Independent or Quaker as well as presbyterian, Anglican and Roman Catholic, as it was by support for toleration; support of a tolerant policy to be pursued towards dissent is not at all the same as expression of an ideology of dissent. Shaftesbury put the same central point to Charles in 1681 when accused of supporting presbyterian principles in his desire to exclude James: 'no Church nor clergy were but would impose upon the government' if given the opportunity. His biographer has justly remarked that this was Shaftesbury's 'constant attitude'. The same could be said of Locke.[55]

V

For Locke, Protestants needed to be united in early to mid-1681 because 'the Protestant religion required the united force of all sorts of Protestants to make good their ground against their common enemy'. This was a time when 'popery so threatens and so nearly surrounds us'. Locke noted that the Church of England might indeed be the main bulwark against Popery, but argued that it was very strange to fortify it by reviving disputes against those who wished to aid it against that common enemy. No general would reject the help of those 'that were hearty of his side . . . when the enemy was in sight . . . because they were perhaps so fantasticall, as not to be brought to wear red Coats with the rest of his Army'. According to Locke, 'every sober man would think it seasonable at this time that all dissenting Protestants should be brought to a good understanding and compliance one with another'. 'I think', declared Locke about the Catholics in one of the most striking statements of the 'Critical Notes', that 'all Protestants ought now by all ways to be stirred up against them as People that have declared themselves ready by blood, violence, and destruction to ruine our Religion and Government.' They could be looked upon 'as nothing but either Enemyes in our bowells or spies among us, whilst their General commanders whom they blindly obey declare warr, and an unalterable designe to destroy us'.[56]

This sentiment of the 'Critical Notes', a work composed almost immedi-

---

[54] MS Locke c34, 6; 44; 88; 148; 161.
[55] Haley, *Shaftesbury*, 634; cf. also 28–9; 66–7; 141; 734–46.
[56] MS Locke c34, 7–11. Locke did, however, also raise the possibility at one point of a 'regulated toleration' of Catholics while keeping out their priests: MS Locke c34, 26. He later made an attempt to find a way to tolerate English Catholics: MS Locke c27, 30a. I intend to write an article on this issue in the near future.

ately before the meeting of the Oxford Parliament in 1681 and continued later in the summer after its dissolution, indicates the very considerable force of Locke's anticatholicism in 1681. The Oxford Parliament was the third Parliament in as many years that was curtailed by Charles because of its demand to exclude James from the succession following the 1678 revelations of an alleged 'Popish Plot' to assassinate Charles and place James on the throne. Much of the politics of 1678 to 1681 had been focused on the dangers of the potentially imminent succession of James; much on the dangers of Charles' own moves towards absolutism, with his commitment to James itself being seen as a substantial sign of this tendency. In many passages of the 'Critical Notes' Locke explicitly declared Stillingfleet's erastian principles dangerous if a Catholic king should succeed and gain control of ecclesiastical appointments. One week before Locke had landed back in England in May 1679 Shaftesbury had declared in a speech in Parliament that 'Popery and Slavery, like two sisters, go hand-in-hand' and in 1679–81 he was a leading figure in a country and Exclusionist political grouping. James' Catholicism was cited repeatedly as sufficient proof of his absolutist and arbitrary designs, since Catholicism was held to make him bound to seek the destruction of Protestants' religion, estates and lives. As the anonymous 1680 *Letter From a Gentleman in the City to One in the Country* declared, it was 'an indispensable duty' of a Catholic Prince to destroy those subjects who disagreed with him 'in faith and worship'. For many, from 'Popery came the notion of a standing army and arbitrary power'.[57]

Here anticatholic argument firmly clasped hands with the antiabsolutist rhetoric of Locke and Shaftesbury's *Letter From A Person of Quality*, and extended the analysis of Marvell's 1677 *Account of the Growth of Popery and Arbitrary Government*. It is very likely that Locke helped Shaftesbury compose parts of his speeches declaring that Catholic monarchy was necessarily absolutist, and was fully committed to such a view. The third earl of Shaftesbury declared that the first earl had used Locke's 'assistant pen in matters that nearly concerned the State and were fit to be made public to raise that spirit in the nation which was necessary against the prevailing

---

[57] On erastianism, MS Locke c34, 7–11; Shaftesbury, House of Lords, 25 March 1679, cited in Ashcraft, *Revolutionary Politics*, 203; *Letter From a Gentleman in the City* (1680), 3 cited in Ashcraft, *ibid.*, 192; on monks and friars, and James' declarations of his intention to leave property unchallenged by monastic Catholic claims, *ibid.*, 202; Capel's famous comment is cited in J. Miller, *Popery and Politics in England 1660–89*, Cambridge (1973), 172. More broadly, see *ibid.*, passim; T. Harris, *London Crowds in the Reign of Charles II*, Cambridge (1987), passim; Ashcraft, *Revolutionary Politics*. J. Scott, *Algernon Sidney and the Restoration Crisis 1677–83*, Cambridge (1992), passim, seeks to broaden the understanding of the crisis of 1677–83 from one of the possible succession of a Catholic to the imminent dangers of Charles' absolutism, very largely persuasively.

Popish Party'; in its anticatholic arguments for toleration through comprehension and 'toleration' the 'Critical Notes', though probably initiated during illness at Tyrrell's house, was surely conceived by Locke as one such contribution to the campaign of Shaftesbury against the 'popery' of persecution common to almost all clerics and involved in too many of Stillingfleet's arguments as well as to the Catholicism of James.[58]

From the mid-1670s, and especially after 1679, high Anglican argument was increasingly, although not exclusively, absolutist. Absolutism was particularly supported by a number of high Anglican clerics who advanced claims to *jure divino* authority for episcopal church government and for *jure divino* monarchy in a *quid pro quo* that fulfilled precisely the fears of the 1675 *Letter*. For Peter Heylyn, whose writings were enormously influential around 1680, the King was the sole, omnicompetent and illimitable source of law. Parliament was subordinate, not co-ordinate, and its existence was by the King's gracious permission. Other high Anglican clerics, including George Hickes, John Nalson and Robert Falkner, agreed in works of the mid-to-late 1670s that the King had absolute and arbitrary power, that Parliament only advised and petitioned, and that English liberties were not rights but revocable privileges granted by the kings throughout history. To this was joined advocacy of *jure divino* church government. Falkner's *Christian Loyalty* of 1679 supported both monarchical absolutism and the exclusive powers of consecration, ordination and preaching that had flowed from Christ to the bishops, declaring that no earthly prince, however absolute, could alter the divinely appointed episcopal government of the church.[59]

The works of Robert Filmer, republished in 1679 and 1680 under the aegis of the Anglican hierarchy, carried support for monarchical absolu-

---

58 Amsterdam: Remonstrants MSS J. 20 cited in Cranston, *Locke*, 159; Scott, *Restoration Crisis*, passim; on popery, Goldie, 'Priestcraft and Politics', unpublished MS.

59 On this point, and the works discussed over the next paragraphs, see especially Goldie, 'Locke and Anglican Royalism', *Political Studies* 31 (1983), 105–19, passim, whose interpretations of the importance of Filmer and of Filmer as the most important representative of a more extensive clericalist royalism seem to me to be correct, and if anything to downplay the influence of Filmerian patriarchalism in 1681–3; also G. Schochet, *Patriarchalism in Political Thought*, Oxford (1975); Ashcraft, *Revolutionary Politics*, 186–7. Filmer's works were not merely cited by Locke as the most pervasive theme of royalist clerical preaching but also by other writers such as Tyrrell, for whom Filmer's *Patriarcha* and the theme of 'the divine and patriarchal right of absolute monarchy' had become the 'Diana' of modern 'churchmen': Tyrrell, *Patriarcha Non Monarcha*, preface; cf. also the arguments of 'Observator', the most important if crude voice of Tory thought, in Roger L'Estrange's serial publication *Observator*, on, for instance, 1 October 1683. For an account of the majority and particularly the mainstream of royalist thought as more moderate and constitutionalist than Filmer throughout the Restoration and even in 1679–83 see J. Daly, *Sir Robert Filmer and English Political Thought*, Toronto (1979), passim; cf. Dunn, *Political Thought*, 44 on moderate royalist views of Filmerian patriarchalism as 'a joke' and *ibid.*, ch. 6, on its efficacy.

tism to its zenith. *Patriarcha*, republished in 1680, was immediately useful in denial of parliamentary rights to alter the succession and more broadly and at greater length useful as Charles moved towards absolutism after 1681. It quickly became the 'palladium of the court' of Charles II. For Filmer, sovereignty was absolute and indivisible. Filmer's works tied this assertion to an account of the origins of monarchical authority that relied heavily upon biblical interpretation, especially of the Old Testament. The Bible was the central revelation of God's will containing all that it would ever be necessary to know about government and society.[60]

For Filmer, God had granted to Adam a 'natural and private dominion' which was the 'fountain of all government and propriety'. The first government was monarchical in Adam. Adam had 'dominion given him over all the creatures' and was thereby 'the monarch of the whole world'. Adam's posterity had a right to possess anything only 'by his grant and permission'. When Adam had died Adam's eldest son had inherited all his property as he inherited all his power to command. Having willed that human society began in this way, God had obviously meant to show that all other human beings were to be subordinated to Adam. Notions of consent or contract as the origin of political society were nonsense, and a state of nature absurd, because political society had originated with Adam's command and had never ceased. Adam's position as patriarch had been inherited by his eldest son and so by succeeding patriarchs down to Noah, who had divided the world up into separate states, each ruled absolutely by fathers. Although the authority to wield this power had been usurped in many cases since then, the nature of political power itself was still the same. Filmer attacked the view that Parliament had any legal right to meet or consent to legislation in England; they met and consented only by the King's grant. He derided the claim that men were originally free, which would give every man 'a liberty to choose himself to be his own King if he please; and he were a madman that being by nature free would choose any man but himself to be his own governor'. Filmer mocked explanation of private property that he alleged to have been constructed by Grotius, that while all property had originally been common it had become private property, possession exclusive of others, by a supposed general and unanimous consent of men; there had never been such a general consent. In one of his works Filmer summed up his views very briefly: there was 'no

---

[60] Dunn, *Political Thought*, ch. 6 is particularly effective in showing the providentialist nature of Filmer's arguments; cf. the argument of L'Estrange *Observator*, 1 October 1683, (issue 413): if government were the ordinance of man and not God then God's wisdom and providence would be defective. This is an impious suggestion. If men were originally equal they must stay equal; the first man of the World was therefore necessarily 'the First King . . . by divine commission'.

form of government, but monarchy only, no monarchy but paternal, no paternal monarchy but absolute or arbitrary, no such form of government as tyranny, and the people were not born free by nature'.[61]

Locke therefore had good reason to attack *Patriarcha* as the apotheosis of a form of argument for absolutism popular among the Anglican clergy, the view of 'a generation of men' who had 'sprung up among us' and flattered princes with 'an Opinion, that they have a Divine Right to absolute power'. Filmer's work alone, composed many years earlier, would not have been worthy of response but 'the Pulpit of late Years' had 'made it the Currant Divinity of the Times'. Filmer's work had become 'the perfect Standard of Politics' because the 'Drum Ecclesiastic' had beaten out the call of passive obedience, crying up their governors as 'Sacred and Divine'. It was necessary to show 'those Men, who taking on them to be Teachers, have so dangerously misled others' how little authority their 'blindly followed' author possessed. Very similar claims about the emerging dominance of monarchical theory by clerical support for absolutism and by Filmerian patriarchalism were voiced by both Tyrrell and Sidney in the early 1680s.[62]

For Locke, the clerical bases for absolute authority were deliberately obscure arguments 'Useful perhaps to such, whose Skill and Business it is to raise a Dust, and would blind the People, the better to mislead them'. His 'First Treatise' was a lengthy point-by-point refutation of Filmer's scriptural arguments, and it would apparently have been far longer if the greater part of Locke's pursuit of 'Sir Robert' through 'all the Windings and Obscurities' of his 'wonderful System' had not been lost (or destroyed) between composition and publication. It attempted to show that Filmer's works lacked 'what he so much boasts of, and pretends wholly to build on . . . Scripture-proofs'. According to Locke, matters of such consequence as government 'should be in plain words, as little liable as might be to Doubt or Equivocation'. 'It can never be understood, how a Divine Natural Right,

[61] Laslett, *Patriarcha and Other Political Works of Sir Robert Filmer*, Oxford (1949), passim.
[62] *Treatises*, preface; 1.1–5; 2.112; 224; 232–9; n. 59 above. Locke was also attempting to argue, of course, that it was only in 'This latter age' that the legitimacy of resistance had been completely denied and political authority had become *jure divino*. By using Richard Hooker, whose works supported *jure divino* episcopacy but only *jure humano* monarchy, and was thus a basis for 'their arguments' on church government, Locke was indicating that the elevation of monarchy as *jure divino* was particularly novel. Locke's citation of Bishops Bilson and Bancroft, who had attacked the Calvinist and Catholic doctrines of resistance to princes but had nonetheless founded political authority in the community, conveyed the same point. Sibthorp and Manwaring, Laud's devoted disciples, were indicted for their important role in formulating this doctrine in the early seventeenth century. This was all part of Locke's attempt to show that his defence of resistance was restorationist; on this, see chapter six below.

and that of such moment as is all Order and Peace in the World, should be convey'd down to Posterity, without any Plain Natural or Divine Rule Concerning it.' A 'clear positive Law' was necessary to establish subjection. The best understanding of Scripture was that 'which best agrees with the plain construction of the words, and arises from the obvious meaning of the place'. The 'Prejudices of our own ill grounded Opinions, however by us called probable, cannot Authorize us to understand Scripture contrary to the direct and plain meaning of the Words'. Where the meaning was unclear, according to Locke 'parallel places of Scripture are most probable to make us know, how they may be best understood'.[63]

Filmer had cited a number of biblical texts from Genesis in support of his argument. Locke indicated that they were at the least equivocal texts, insufficiently 'plain' to build government upon. On Genesis 1:28, God's grant of the things of the world, Locke urged that men 'consider the words' of the grant: 'all Positive grants convey no more than the express words they are made in will carry'. The words had nothing in them that could be 'wrested' to refer them to dominion over men. Cross-reference of Gen. 1:28 with Gen. 9:2 supported this interpretation. It was 'plain' that God's donation was not of man, and even if this was not accepted it was also 'evident' that the grant was to men in common because made in the plural. It was impossible for 'any sober reader' to find anything but that man as the image of God and 'chief inhabitant' of the earth was given dominion over the other creatures; this was 'So obvious in the plain words'.

For Locke, similar difficulties attended almost all of Filmer's interpretations, and in many different places Locke argued that 'It is too much to build a Doctrine of so mighty consequence upon so doubtful and obscure a place of Scripture, which may be well, nay better, understood in a quite different Sense', especially where 'nothing else in Scripture or Reason' could be found 'that favours or supports it'. Although Locke condemned Filmer for his 'doubtful expressions' and the 'intricacy of words' in his argument, his condemnations were directed against Filmer's deliberate obscurity rather than making an argument that the Scripture was not plain, or that its words were often necessarily obscure to modern readers. In many sections Locke argued that his own interpretations of Scripture were 'plain', 'evident' and 'obvious', appealing frequently to a 'sober' reader of Scripture. In other sections, however, the thrust of his argument was that it was to reason that men had to turn in default of biblical 'plain' directions, including those about a sole necessary form of government, and from reason that men if they had applied themselves properly could have derived

---

[63] On this and the next paragraphs see *Treatises*, passim; esp. preface; 1.25; 32–3; 36; 38; 46; 49; 108; 119; 121; 126; 1.21–9; 44–5; 1.11; 49; 60–1; 65; 112; 118; 145–7 (147 1st edn.); 2.4.

principles about God's wishes that God had later explicitly declared in Revelation. Locke's position appears to have altered slightly but significantly during the composition of these arguments, placing a greater stress upon the principles of reason and less upon interpretation of the biblical text, perhaps as a result of an increasing sense of the lack of perspicuity in the biblical text as he undertook an intensive investigation, or perhaps as the result of beginning to construct a more radical argument against Filmerian absolutism from the principles of reason, the argument of the Second Treatise.[64]

It is not certain when the First Treatise was written. Since *Patriarcha* was an extremely important text both during the campaign for Exclusion because it removed any possibility of parliamentary rights to alter the succession, and as a tract advocating absolutism from 1680 to 1683, Locke could have first decided to compose an attack on Filmer's arguments either to support Exclusion and to oppose advocacy of absolutism in 1679–81 or to oppose emergent absolutism in 1681, 1682, or even 1683. Locke's friend Tyrrell composed *Patriarcha Non Monarcha* to oppose absolutism among the clergy and to support parliamentary Exclusion of James in late 1680 and early 1681, and Locke knew of Tyrrell's work during its final stages of composition in early 1681 during their collaboration on the 'Critical Notes' at Tyrrell's house. Locke and Shaftesbury were discussing major texts of political theory in 1679–81, and these surely included *Patriarcha* and other crucial texts that Locke had bought in 1680 and read in 1680–1 and which he cited in the *Treatises*, such as Barclay's works. Locke may well have been commissioned by Shaftesbury or have commenced on his own initiative to compose the First Treatise against Filmer in order to support in a very general manner the principles on which Exclusion was to be based and to oppose the principles of absolutism and thus collaterally to oppose the persecution that in Locke's view helped to motivate high-church Anglicans to support absolutism.[65]

The 1675 *Letter* had decried clerical support for absolutism given in order to promote Anglican authority and thus their powers of persecution. In being thus direct and indirect attacks upon principles that would aid persecution, the 'Critical Notes' and First Treatise had in part a similar motivation. Nonetheless, the charges that Locke made against Stillingfleet of an erastianism that supported the 'popery' of persecution and of the danger when a popish king could make clerical appointments, his own celebration of Anglican preaching together with recognition that Stilling-

---

[64] *Treatises*, 1.4; 13; 32; the alterations are pointed out by Wootton, *Locke: Political Writings*, 64ff., esp. 76.

[65] On Locke and Tyrrell see below pp. 234ff.

fleet tried to work through persuasion and rational argument, and his desire for Stillingfleet's plans for comprehension to be followed, were very different responses than the attacks directed against clerics supportive of absolutism in the First Treatise. This suggests that Locke was clearly aware of the different strands in Anglicanism: on the one hand of the celebration of monarchy as *jure divino* and absolutist, backed by typological analyses of Scripture and obscure interpretations designed to blind the laity, and on the other hand of a Latitudinarian erastianism and support for passive obedience that was adopted in opposition to high-church sacramentarian clericalism and for pragmatic political reasons. Latitudinarian erastianism included the dangerous theoretical potential of indirect support for absolutism and Catholicism, but many Latitudinarians such as Tillotson, Fowler and Burnet supported the Parliamentary campaigns of the opposition to absolutism in 1679–81.

The differences in Locke's opposition to the two different types of Anglican argument might reflect an order of composition. When Stillingfleet wrote his work and when Locke composed the burden of the 'Critical Notes' the Oxford Parliament had yet to meet and comprehension seemed a significant possibility to many, including briefly even members of the Anglican hierarchy who thought that they would be forced to compromise and that toleration was about to be enacted by Parliament. After the dissolution of the Oxford Parliament it was the voice of high Anglican clerics advancing absolutist arguments about the twin sacred and divine regimes of government and supporting fierce persecution of nonconformity that became massively predominant, and it may well have been in these altered circumstances that Locke began to think it necessary to write the First Treatise against the high Anglicans' increasing monopoly on the current divinity of the pulpit. However, since both Anglican voices had been being expressed in the period before 1681, and since Tyrrell seems to have thought that his own attack on high Anglican absolutism in *Patriarcha non monarcha* and his help to Locke in transcribing the 'Critical Notes' were completely complementary exercises to be undertaken at the same moment in early 1681, simultaneous composition by Locke seems as likely on these grounds.

As David Wootton has emphasised, there are a number of reasons to think that Locke was at work on the First Treatise in or by 1681, and many reasons to be reasonably sure that the First Treatise significantly preceded the Second. The First Treatise includes no defence of resistance, contains relatively little on individual consent, and appears to accept in some sections both hereditary slavery and that men might consent to a complete subordination to their rulers, conceptions that were conventional among Locke's contemporaries in 1680–1, but which were crucially contradicted by the central arguments of the Second Treatise.[66] In this light, it seems likely that Locke had composed the vast majority of the First Treatise before desiring to advocate resistance and that this composition was undertaken to set out the broadly consensual basis of politics and the principles needed to combat *jure divino* absolutism in order to promote a policy of Exclusion and of Charles' return to a government of Shaftesbury's liking. It seems likely that the crucial alterations on the elements of his theory concerning subordination, resistance and slavery by the date of the Second Treatise were shaped by his having come after beginning or completing the First Treatise to have armed resistance as his primary purpose for composition of the Second Treatise. The reasons for this crucial transformation in Locke's thought and its dating will be examined in chapter six.

[66] See Wootton, *Locke: Political Writings*, 72–3.

4

The theology of a reasonable man
1667–83

I

Locke had read the broadly Arminian works of Hammond, Hales and Allestree around 1660. He was apparently interested in the case for a broadly Arminian view of the necessity of a working faith rather than Calvinist justification by faith alone by 1667. Among his manuscripts is an eight-page part of a draft for a sermon, most probably of January 1666/7. That this draft is among Locke's papers suggests that he had preserved it throughout his life and thus throughout the many moves of his papers. The manuscript of this draft is in a hand that is very similar in many respects to Locke's own hand, but a number of letters are formed in ways that Locke employed occasionally but not usually. It may just possibly be by Locke himself, although this seems unlikely. At the least, it suggests that Locke was aware by 1667 of arguments setting out a 'moral theology' similar to much Latitudinarian and Arminian thought; at the most it would indicate that these themes had already become important in Locke's own thought.

The text for the sermon was Gal. 5:6, on faith 'which worketh by love'. Against the Calvinist contention that Christ's righteousness was imputed to man (infused in man), having been apprehended by faith, this sermon declared that 'faith shall be imputed' (counted) to the individual 'for right-eousnesse'. The sermon stressed a working faith, and it seems to assert that this working faith was necessary for justification, rather than following justification, although the survival of only part three of the draft and its less-than-pellucid phraseology make the evidence for this too sketchy to be certain that this was its intended meaning. It was by faith, the sermon argued, that the individual would live, by this he shall be justified, by this he shall be saved . . . without the works of the law . . . but not without the works of the Gospell, not without the precepts of Christ, not without obedience and charity for tis faith workeing, workeing by love, and that alone, which thus avails'. Faith could not avail 'except it worke, nor if it worke, except it worke by love'. As we saw earlier, according to the sermon, man 'could not but follow happiness', and good was simply

119

'what' tended 'to the advancement of . . . happinesse'. Men loved God
because of his provision of 'rivers of pleasure' and from this love of God
came a desire to please him. It was this which created a love for one's
fellow man and thus resulted in all the good deeds that men did for each
other.[1]

[1] This draft is in MS Locke c27, 13–28; see esp. 19–22. I agree with Ashcraft (*Revolutionary
Politics*, 92–4) that this draft is of January 1667 rather than January 1666: Locke was
abroad in Cleves in January 1666. In January 1667 he seems to have been in London: MS
Film. 79. As the only scholar to have so far discussed this manuscript sermon, Ashcraft
describes it as 'notes' that Locke may have taken at a nonconformist sermon that he
attended (without any evidence that Locke *ever* attended a nonconformist sermon after the
1662 Re-establishment of the Church of England). Having read thousands of pages of
Locke's hand, he gives no indication that there is any doubt about whose hand the draft
was in: Locke's. It also seemed to me on first inspection of this draft that this was the case;
on re-examination, however, this seemed much less certain. Whoever was the author, in
terms of compositional flow it seems to me more accurate to call it a 'draft' rather than
'notes' on someone else's sermon, and the frequent alterations, marginal additions and
transfers of passages to rhetorically more effective locations strongly suggest authorship by
whoever physically wrote the draft itself. Even if the sermon was by Locke – and this is
doubtful – the tentative nature of the following comments on the draft needs to be noted.
Only a part of the draft (pt. 3) survives, and there is little indication of the contents of the
missing parts. Ashcraft describes the substance and language of the sermon as 'distinctly
sectarian and Non-conformist', citing Locke's usage of the terms brothers, sisters and
saints. I do not agree. I cannot locate anything in the sermon which could not have been
preached by Anglicans as well as nonconformists. Indeed, the arguments on faith being
counted for righteousness and the combination of James and Paul, without ascription of
James' statements to sanctification rather than justification, were far more characteristic of
Anglican than nonconformist preaching. The mere usage of 'brothers' and 'saints' at a
couple of points in the sermon is simply not exclusively nonconformist, as Ashcraft seems
to imply (and I cannot find any reference to sisters). 'Brethren' and 'Saints' is of course the
language of the Bible itself; the important point to define is the way in which they were
used, not to record the mere fact of their usage as though this was specific to nonconformity. Locke was to use both terms in the 1690s. The broad definition given to 'brothers' in
the sermon, where the brotherhood is explicitly defined as including all men and not
merely the regenerate, is more characteristic of Anglican than of nonconformist usage:
thus, 'this is evangelick charity which is not confined to those of our opinion, or party, or
brotherhood . . . makes every man a neighbour, and a neighbour a brother'. See D. D.
Wallace, *Puritans and Predestination*, Chapel Hill (1982) and J. Sears McGee, *The Godly
Man in Stuart England*, New Haven (1976), ch. 5 for discussion of the differences in tone
between Anglican and puritan attitudes. Locke's reading by the time the sermon was composed included a number of Anglican sources which defined the charity owed to the
brotherhood and to the household of faith in terms similar to the sermon, such as Hammond's *Pacifick Discourse* and Allestree's *Whole Duty of Man*. Although the sermon is a
commentary on Galatians 5:6, much of the commentary is explication of faith through
Matthew, particularly Matthew 12:33, 13:8, 13:23, 13:31, 13:33, 21:19, 22:37 and 23:8; also
Luke 13:18–21. It is possible that if the hand is Locke's, it represents Locke at least considering giving a sermon/lay lecture to 'try the pulpit', due to his recent consideration of
clerical offers. In January 1667 Locke had only very recently been excused from the
requirement of entering orders if he wished to remain at Christ Church, Oxford, had gone
to considerable trouble to avoid taking orders, and had showed considerable reluctance to
enter the clergy, but he had not yet decided to become Shaftesbury's personal adviser and
friend or gone to London to do so. The question of a clerical career was therefore not
necessarily completely closed, even if Locke's reluctance to enter such a career was already
palpable.

According to the sermon, this need for a working faith 'cut off' much of the faith 'abounding in the world'. 'Idle unactive faith' was rejected; faith was 'in its own nature . . . active and busy'. Condemned next was the faith which worked by pride, described in a way that made strict Calvinism a central target. The faith of pride was the faith of those 'who confineing the favour of God unto a very few, and supposeing him to reprobate, for his pleasure only, the greatest part of men, strongly conceit themselves . . . to be of the elected handfull'. A similar fate attended the faith which worked 'by hatred . . . by love to those who are of our way, our sect, our party, but by enmity to all dissenters'. This was identified as the faith of those who 'forget their fallible and imperfect nature' and proposed 'their own or others interpretations of Scripture and conjectures as necessary articles of belief'. Another passage in the sermon declared that 'evangelick charity' was 'not confined to those of our opinion, or party, or brotherhood, but is extended far and wide . . . makes every man a neighbour, a neighbour a brother and a brother neer as one's self'. Finally condemned at great length was the faith of those who 'joyfully listen to the mistaken explications of free grace, and are glad to hear it said that God justifies the ungodly, that we are sav'd freely by the alone faith in Christ without workes'. These antinomians believed that Christ 'died to save sinners . . . and apply his righteousnesse to their soules'. James had said that faith without works could never save, and Paul's statements on faith without works excluded 'only . . . works of the law of Moses' and not those of the Gospel.[2]

We noted in the previous chapter Locke's close friendship with Thomas Grigg. Locke's copy of this draft sermon was dated at 'St Andrews'; Grigg was rector of St Andrews Undershaft. It is at least possible either that Grigg was the author of the sermon, or, if it was given as a lay lecture by Locke, that it was at Grigg's parish that it was delivered. There is no clear endorsement of these views in any work of the period 1660–83 of which Locke was definitely the author, although the cumulative weight of his reading, friendships, already clear hostility to much of Calvinist thought, elevation of men's capacity to know natural law, and desire to restrain the anarchic implications of the necessity for the aid of the Holy Spirit, together suggest that these views were likely to have been appealing to him. We have already seen that in 1658 Locke declared that the way to make men follow truth was to make it their interest to follow their maker, but that this theme was considerably more muted in the *Essays*. If Locke was author of this draft sermon, he could hardly have carried out his earlier proposal more straightforwardly. If he was not its author but was interested in its argument, then the focus upon heavenly rewards that Locke had

---

[2] MS Locke c27, 22: 25–8; 17; 14–19.

met in reading Drexel's *Considerations Upon Eternitie* in the 1650s had apparently been supplemented by an even stronger argument that men were to act morally because of the pleasures provided by God. We will see later that much of Locke's later thought, including the *Reasonableness of Christianity*, *Paraphrase Upon the Epistles of St Paul*, and the *Essay Concerning Human Understanding*, articulated very similar stresses upon a working faith and upon rewards and punishments.

In its twin emphases upon a working faith and upon happiness the draft expressed very clearly much of the sentiments that were being supported by large numbers of the Latitudinarians in the Restoration, including those with whom Locke was friends and whose sermons Locke may already have been attending. Fowler's *Principles* noted that the Latitudinarians were frequently known as the 'Moral Preachers' precisely because they opposed the Calvinist doctrine that Christ's righteousness was imputed to the individual, having been apprehended by faith, and taught instead that the individual's faith was itself 'counted for' righteousness by God. Fowler declared, a little too synoptically, that the Latitudinarians were 'very careful so to handle the Doctrine of Justifying Faith, as not only to make obedience to follow it, but likewise to include a hearty willingness to submit to all Christ's precepts in the nature of it'. They held that justifying faith could not be divorced from works, assaulting 'idle, ineffectual faith' and extolling 'working faith'. On this issue they often cited Galatians 5:6, which spoke, Fowler declared, of justification by a 'faith that worketh by love; which takes in the whole of obedience'. Tillotson agreed, with Gal. 5:6 again prominent: the 'condition of our Justification' was 'a Faith which worketh by Love'.[3]

For many Latitudinarians revelation was largely the restatement of the precepts of natural law with the addition of strong incentives to obey. The precepts of natural law were held to be accessible by unaided reason, but they had been promulgated in revelation more clearly and backed by stronger incentives for obedience. As Fowler commented, the Gospel 'enforceth its precepts with infinitely stronger, and more persuasive Motives and Arguments, than were ever before made known'. Particularly heavy emphasis was placed upon God's rewards for the dutiful in the

[3] Fowler, *Principles*, 114, 117–30, 148–62, 188–9; idem, *The Design of Christianity* (1671), 213–22, 262; Tillotson, *Works* (1704), IV, 71, 142–5, 251–5; cf. Patrick, *Works*, Oxford (1858), V, 277; J. Glanvill, 'Antifanatical Religion and Free Philosophy' in *Essays on Several Important Subjects* (1676), VII, 22. For more cautious formulations closer to Calvinism see G. Burnet, *An Exposition of the 39 Articles of the Church of England* (1819), Articles 11 and 12; Stillingfleet's insistence that works were the fruit of justifying faith in Allison, *Moralism*, 147; on Barlow, *ibid.*, 141–4; on Barrow, *ibid.*, 148–50; on the developments in Restoration theology more generally, *ibid.*, chs. 5–9; Wallace, *Puritans and Predestination*, chs. 4–5.

works of Wilkins and Tillotson. Man was depicted as motivated by desire
for happiness, 'our chief end', and moral behaviour was commended as a
form of enlightened self-interest. According to Tillotson, 'Religion and
Happiness, our Duty and our Interest, are really but one and the same
thing considered under several notions'. Prudential appeals were seen as
'effective' or 'practical' preaching; one of Tillotson's most famous sermons
was entitled *The Wisdom of Being Religious.* In Wilkins' enormously
popular *Of the Principles and Duties of Natural Religion* the prudential
reasons for being religious included not merely heavenly rewards but also
terrestrial advantages. The work aimed to persuade men to be virtuous 'by
shewing how natural and direct an influence they [the virtues] have, not
only upon our future blessedness in another World, but even upon the
happiness and prosperity of this present life'. According to Wilkins, virtue
led to security, liberty and esteem, and to riches appropriate to the station
in which men were placed and sufficient to free them from want, although
his own account of the importance of the avoidance of a guilty conscience
and of the extent to which men would not receive physical riches commensurate with their virtue in this life undercut somewhat the sweeping
confidence of this declaration of the external terrestrial advantages of
virtue.[4]

According to Burnet it was largely from their allowance of 'great
freedom both in philosophy and in divinity' that the Latitudinarians
derived their name. Many Latitudinarians argued that man was fallible
and therefore ought not to seek to impose his own views on others. As
Whichcote put it in his *Moral and Religious Aphorisms*, 'our Fallibility
and the Shortness of our Knowledge should make us peaceable and gentle:
because I may be mistaken'. The Latitudinarians declared that the essential
doctrines of Scripture were few and plain and 'generally acknowledged
among Christians', but were 'not at all forward to give a Catalogue of
Fundamentals'. Depicting disagreement as inevitable because of the different constitutions of men's minds, tempers and educations, they generally
extolled a unity of spirit, not an uniformity of opinion, in Scriptural interpretation. For the most eirenic, heresy was an act of the will rather than a
failure of understanding, and sincerity in search for truth rather than
possession of objective truth was emphasised. They opposed the dogma-
tism of much religious sectarianism, indicting many of the Interregnum

[4] J. Tillotson, *Sermons* (1688), I, 217 cited in H. R. McAdoo, *The Spirit of Anglicanism*
(1965), 175; Birch, Tillotson, *Works*, cxix; Tillotson, *Works*, Edinburgh (1748), V, 253
cited in R. Sullivan, *John Toland and the Deist Controversy*, Harvard (1982), 65; Fowler,
Principles, 89; Tillotson, *Works* (1820), III, 68; Tillotson, *Sermons* (1688), I, 25 cited in
Cragg, *From Puritanism to . . . Reason*, 78n.; Tillotson, *Works* (1704), V, 424–5; Wilkins,
Of the Principles and Duties of Natural Religion (1674), preface, vii; 285–393 and passim.

sects for claiming infallibility and for desiring to impose their own doctrinal views on others. They depicted the Anglican Church as the most tolerant in practice, although as we have seen this tolerance was practically limited because it involved a distinction between liberty of judgement and worship.[5]

In their own Scriptural interpretation they emphasised literalism and a commonsense exegetical style which clearly displayed the train of reasoning behind the acceptance of beliefs, attacking 'mystical' or 'allegorical' interpretations. They made the search for religious truth directly analogous to the search for other kinds of truth, stressed that assent ought to be proportioned to the evidence, and expended much effort both on carefully reasoned analyses about the ontological bases of religious doctrines and on discussing the credibility of many testimonies in religion by careful study of patristic and biblical sources. These patristic researches and support for carefully reasoned expertise came, however, despite their recognition of their own fallibility and pleas for gentleness, to seem to some Latitudinarians to be reasons that others should accept their learned interpretations. They disapproved of appeals to faith against reason, and declared that beliefs could not be accepted that were contradictory to reason, but importantly maintained that many propositions in Christianity, such as the Trinity and Incarnation, were to be believed as 'above reason'.

Their accounts of credibility, reasoning, and assent proportionate to the evidence left very little room for the notion that the indwelling spirit of God brought with it a separate form and extent of conviction, and their descriptions of faith became inclined towards *fides*, the intellectual assent to theological propositions, rather than *fiducia*, the loving, trusting relationship with Christ that brought its own sense of conviction. In religious polemic they described many nonconformists as 'enthusiasts' who subjected reason to 'fancy', and associated this at times with a theology that stressed the personal union with Christ's spirit in regeneration bringing its own conviction of truths not revealed to others. Emphasising that men needed God's grace, they magnified the extent to which God graciously helped men through the natural processes of education, arguing

---

5 Burnet, *History*, 323–4; B. Whichcote, *Moral and Religious Aphorisms* (1753), aphorism 130. I owe this reference to Dr G. A. J. Rogers; cf. his article in Ashcraft et al. (eds.), *Philosophy*; Fowler, *Principles*, 307–9, 314–18; Tillotson, *Works* (1704), III, 60; XII, 267. On Latitudinarian epistemology see especially H. G. Van Leeuwen, *The Pursuit of Certainty in English Thought 1630–90*, The Hague (1963); R. Carroll, *The Commonsense Philosophy of Religion of Bishop Edward Stillingfleet*, The Hague (1975); R. Popkin, *The History of Scepticism From Erasmus to Spinoza*, Berkeley (1979). Cf. Glanvill, 'Antifanatical Religion', 11–12, 14, 25; Wilkins, *Principles and Duties*, bk. 1, ch. 1; B. Shapiro, *Probability and Certainty in Seventeenth Century England*, Princeton (1983), ch. 3; Keeble, *Literary Culture*, 177–86; Tillotson, *Works* (1704), III, 62–3; Sullivan, *Toland*, 54; Birch, Tillotson, *Works*, xxxvii.

that God could not have intended to overturn men's use of their faculties and so had not given them inspirations that would destroy their reason but had inspired them in the use of their reason.[6]

For Independents such as Owen throughout the Restoration, as in his many works throughout the Interregnum, God had eternally predestined men to savlation and to reprobation. His decrees were unconditional, made without respect to his foreknowledge of who would in fact act morally or his 'free grace' would have been compromised. The elect were justified by faith alone, and works were the result of such justifying faith. When the Apostle James had spoken of works he had been speaking of a false faith, or of men testifying before other men of the results of their previously justifying faith, and not of the faith which justified. As Owen's *Dissertation on Divine Justice* made very clear, only through payment to God's justice could God accept sinful men. The 'justice by which God punishes sin' was 'The very essential rectitude of the Deity itself'. Christ had paid this ransom for the sins of the elect and his righteousness was imputed to man, having been apprehended by faith.[7]

Placing a very heavy emphasis upon the effects of the Fall, Owen argued that men were extremely sinful and in need of God's grace. They could do nothing to gain his favour, but were purely passive recipients of the grace that made them believers. In his 1674 *Pneumatologia* and his 1679 *Christologia* Owen stressed the personal union of men with Christ, and the indwelling of his spirit, the Holy Ghost, in men. On the basis of these commitments Owen excoriated the Restoration Anglicans for moving away from even the moderate Calvinism of the Thirty-nine Articles, which clearly asserted predestination to election and the passivity of men in receipt of grace. Whereas for Restoration Anglicans the primary fear was of anti-

[6] See, for instance, Glanvill, 'Antifanatical Religion', 42–3; Fowler, *Principles*, 70, 96–7; Shapiro, *Probability*, ch. 3; McAdoo, *Anglicanism*, chs. 5–6; G. Reedy, *The Bible and Reason*, Pennsylvania (1985), passim; Burnet's description of the thought of the Latitudinarians commenced with the declaration that 'They declared against superstition on the one hand and enthusiasm on the other': Burnet, *History*, 323–4. On the polemics over enthusiasm and the theology of personal inspiration involved see S. Tucker, *Enthusiasm* (1972), passim; Keeble, *Literary Culture*, 177–86; J. Glanvill, *Philosophia Pia* (1671), 224; Parker, *Discourse*, 74–5; idem, *A Defence and Continuation of the Discourse of Ecclesiastical Polity* (1671), 665; W. Sherlock, *A Discourse Concerning the Knowledge of Jesus Christ and our Union and Communion with him* (1674), passim. Keeble, *Literary Culture*, ch. 8 argues convincingly that this debate and claims of both sides to a 'plain' interpretation of Scripture reflected important theological differences between the sides; cf. *Essay*, bk. 4 ch. 19; and Locke's early opposition to enthusiasm in the 'Essay on Infallibility' discussed above.

[7] J. Owen, *Vindiciae Evangelicae*, in *Works*, XII, passim; *A Dissertation on Divine Justice*, in *Works*, X, 498–506; *Truth and Innocency Vindicated* (1669) in *Works*, XIII, 416–26; *The Doctrine of Justification by Faith* (1677) in *Works*, V, passim; cf. the discussions of Owen's thought in Wallace, *Puritans*, 144–57 esp. 154–5; Allison, *Moralism*, 174–7; Toon, *God's Statesman*, passim.

nomianism and 'enthusiasm', for Owen the primary fear was of Socinian moralism and its denial of the atonement and regeneration by Christ. To Owen stress upon the exemplary role of Christ in bringing information about morality and offering rewards as incentives to its performance dangerously diminished Christ's satisfaction and the foundation of reconciliation of men to God through imputation of Christ's righteousness, and wrongly made men's self-interest instead of the indwelling of Christ's spirit central to motivation to obey God. His *Nature of Apostasy from the Profession of the Gospel* (1679) condemned the growth of Arminianism in the Church of England, assaulting the accounts of justification that made obedience necessary. For Owen by the late 1670s Independents should not join the current Church of England on doctrinal as well as disciplinary grounds since many of its ministers taught erroneous doctrine on fundamental points of theology.[8]

In the 1660s and 1670s Owen was joined in defence of strict Calvinist predestinarian thought, support for the personal union with Christ, and condemnation of Anglican accounts of justification, by his fellow Independent Ferguson. Ferguson's 1668 *Justification onely upon a Satisfaction* argued that justification involved a payment to his justice and not a 'forgiveness' of sin, that only Christ's righteousness imputed to man could make him just, and that justification followed sanctification. Ferguson defended these positions again in 1675 in *The Interest of Reason in Religion*, an important work bringing together support for Owen's view of the indwelling of Christ's spirit, defence of the use of reason in religion against the charges of enthusiasm and fancy, and the claim that it was the non-conformists who deployed 'plain' interpretations of the Bible while their Anglican opponents had degenerated into Socinian metaphor. Theologically, the *Interest* argued strongly that men were 'polluted, unholy, and incapable of doing anything' until the 'sanctifying spirit effectually, infallibly, and by an unresisted Operation' transformed men 'into the Divine Nature'. Christ's righteousness 'must be imputed to us for our Justification'.[9]

For Ferguson, reason was useful in proving that God existed, establishing to non-believers the divinity of Scripture, interpreting Scripture so that propositions contrary to reason were not accepted as faith, and gaining a sense of the words of Scripture themselves. He argued that it was

---

[8] Owen, *Pneumatologia or Discourse on the Holy Spirit* in *Works*, III, passim; Owen, *Works*, I, 41–4, 287, 302 cited in Wallace, *Puritans*, 155ff.; Owen's epitaph, cited in Toon, *God's Statesman*, 182–3; Owen, *On the Nature and Causes of Apostasy* (1679) in *Works*, VII, passim; cf. Keeble, *Literary Culture*, 256; Abrams, *Tracts*, 43.

[9] R. Ferguson, *Justification Onely Upon a Satisfaction* (1668), sig. a4r, 2–14; idem, *The Interest of Reason in Religion* (1675), 279, 391, 409–11, 427, 438–9 and passim.

in nonconformist accounts of justification, sanctification, predestination and the satisfaction that the 'plain' interpretation of Scripture was set out; the Anglicans were turning Christ's redemption and priesthood into 'metaphors' for his role in bringing the conditions of the Gospel to men and so supporting 'Socinianism'. Ferguson strongly upheld Owen's account of the personal union of believers with Christ. Ferguson expended enormous effort in attempting to make clear that this did not thereby deny the use of reason in the interpretation of Scripture, nor fall into the excesses of 'enthusiasm'. At several points he argued that the 'meer rational man' could gain exactly the same understanding of the 'literal' meaning of Scripture as the man regenerated by the indwelling spirit. His central argument, however, was that regeneration involved a renewal that made men 'feel' these truths, and that this made them 'saving' truths: 'The meer rational mind may discern the literal sense of Scripture propositions, but without a Supernatural Irradiation from the Spirit of life, there can be no saving knowledge of them. The spirit which breathed out the Scripture at first, is in this sense the only Interpreter of it.' Without 'auxiliary beams' the mind could never 'discern Spiritual things spiritually'. It worked to make men 'feel, rather than logically to discern the sense of such and such a place'. Much of this rhetoric was designed to point out the importance of *fiducia*, of a trusting, emotive relationship to God, against *fides* as the assent to the propositions contained in the Bible.[10]

Ferguson's distance from the description of assent as carefully proportioned to the establishment of proofs and reasoned connections between parts of Scripture that was increasingly advanced by many of the Latitudinarians was thus significant even when he argued that a new relationship to truth, but no new actual truth, was the result of the indwelling spirit. For Ferguson the mind in 'diviner things' was given illumination that was 'more Convincing than any demonstration'. At points Ferguson's argument also made it seem that new truths would indeed be discovered as a result of a heightened faculty of 'reason'. Men gained from the spirit a 'sagacity' of 'smelling out what is right and true and what is false and perverse' in their interpretations of Scripture by the spirit's purification of the heart in such a way that the Understanding was 'clarified' and 'elevated'. Even in a work constructed to show against Anglican accusations of enthusiasm and against Anglican associations of Independents and presbyterians with the 'enthusiastic' beliefs of such as the Quakers, that the nonconformists defended the use of reason just as much as Anglicans, and in a work in which the propositions to be understood were described as being capable of being understood in the same 'literal' sense by the regenerate

[10] *Ibid.*, 1–64, 129–42, 144–53, 161, 275–448.

and unregenerate, there was thus still support for what to many Restoration Anglicans was an 'enthusiasm' of assent and 'elevated' reason.[11]

II

In his 1671 *Drafts* Locke described faith in religious matters as a form of intellectual assent to propositions that could not be demonstrated with certainty. According to the *Drafts*, faith and opinion were distinct from knowledge. Whereas knowledge was 'immediate', faith was caused by something 'extraneous' to the thing that was believed. Treating faith simply as a form of intellectual assent, with no sense of faith as commitment to or trust in God, and with implicit opposition to the nonconformists' attribution to such *fides* of an illumination more convincing than any demonstration, Locke argued that faith was based on probabilty gained from the testimony of others, the agreeableness of the thing with either the experiences of the senses or the mind's reflection on itself, or a combination of these. All faith was ultimately grounded on experience. Belief in a written revelation was a particular kind of such faith. Revelation was handed down by men who vouched for its truth; the number, credit and condition of witnesses adduced in its support was important to its reception as probable.[12]

Locke's account here was similar both to that constructed by the Latitudinarians in the previous decade, and, probably more importantly in terms of influence upon Locke, similar to major texts which had inspired these accounts and which he had himself read either directly or in synopsis: Grotius' *De Veritate* and Chillingworth's *Religion of Protestants*. As with the Latitudinarians' works, and as with Locke's earlier 'Essay on Infallibility', there is here no direct denial of the need for grace to illuminate the meaning of Scripture in the *Drafts*, but there is present here a strong sense in which men are to accept Scripture by reasoned evaluation of its credibility and without conviction from God's grace. Locke's account stood apart from that of Independents such as Ferguson. Although Locke probably came to know Ferguson by the late 1670s, there is no evidence that Locke considered Ferguson a friend; indeed, we will see later that Ferguson recorded his opposition in these years to Locke's theology. In its limita-

---

[11] *Ibid.*, 59–60, 142–4, 152–3. Ashcraft cites the *Interest of Reason* as running parallel to Locke's thought in opposition to innatism, but this is highly questionable: Ferguson supported a form of dispositional innatism in arguing for a 'natural sagacity' that the idea of God 'was not otherwise inbred, than that the Soul is furnished with such a Natural Sagacity, that upon the exercise of her rational powers, she is infallibly led to the Acknowledgement of a Deity'. Men had a natural conscience and there was therefore an 'unalterable congruity betwixt some acts and our rational souls': *ibid.*, 22ff.

[12] *Draft*, passim esp. 56–67.

tions upon certainty in religion Locke's argument was farther from that of Ferguson than were the Latitudinarians. Locke did not follow the Latitudinarians in their development of a concept of 'moral certainty', a very high degree of probability, nor in the suggestion of some of them that the reasoned evaluation of Scripture and biblical and patristic studies by those with the time and learning to become experts ought to guide other men. For Locke in the *Drafts* faith and knowledge were radically discontinuous. Locke stressed in these *Drafts* the limitations of knowledge and the difficulties of interpreting Scripture, making it seem that for him it was very unlikely that men could give undoubting assent to many of the most important elements of religious truth. While he declared that man could be certain of God's existence and that he was a spirit, not merely was God's 'incomprehensible way of being' entirely beyond man's 'pigmy graspe' and understanding of the essence, nature and operations of God completely beyond man's natural capacities, but it was almost impossible for men since they needed leisure, books and languages to collect the testimonies necessary to make probable the propositions that they were 'most concerned to believe'. Locke did not make this comment specific, but he presumably meant here religious beliefs that men were 'most concerned to believe'. His distrust of the wrested interpretations of commentators in his early writings was becoming a far more extensively articulated doubt about the possibility of most men being able to make probable to themselves even central elements of religion.[13]

Locke's next significant extension of these arguments, in a series of journal notes in France in 1676, focused upon the difficulties in gaining reconciliation in religion without strict epistemological definition and the clear subjection of faith to the tests of reason. The limitations upon men's knowledge in matters of religion that he described were undoubtedly again intended to give further reasons for toleration of enquiry in religion, but they were also – and far more explicitly – aimed at securing *agreement* in matters of religion through a definition of the realms of faith and reason that effectively again denied the conviction of inspired faith central to the theology of Independents such as Ferguson. Locke was here working in two different directions; both supporting liberty of enquiry by recognising the near inevitability of disagreement about central religious issues, including definitions of faith, and simultaneously attempting to remove reasons for contention and disagreement by defining the relationships of faith and reason so as to reduce the claims to certainty of faith.

On 24 August 1676, the day after composing an entry on penal laws in

[13] *Draft*, passim; esp. 3–5; 7; 9–10; 20; 29–30; 48; 56–67; 72; generally, H. G. van Leeuwen, *The Problem of Certainty in English Thought 1630–90*, The Hague (1963), passim. esp. 21n.; Carroll, *Stillingfleet*, passim.

religion, he noted that it was desirable that 'in matters of religion' men would define how far they were to be guided by reason and how far by faith. 'The want of this' was said to be 'one of the causes that keep up in the world so many different opinions, for every sect, as far as reason will help them, makes use of it gladly, and where it fails them, they cry out that it is matter of faith and above reason'. The establishment of a 'strict boundary between faith and reason' Locke declared 'ought to be the first point established in all disputes of religion'. In propositions where men had clear and perfect ideas they did not need the assistance of faith; knowledge was the greatest assurance that men could have of anything. Faith could not convince men of anything that contradicted knowledge, because there could be no higher assurance than that which came from knowledge.

In support of this, Locke stated that it was impossible to conceive that God 'the bountiful Author of our being' would overturn 'all our principles and foundations of knowledge, render all our faculties useless, and wholly destroy the most excellent part of His workmanship, our understanding'. This would lower men below beasts. In matters above reason, but not in matters contrary to reason, revelation was to guide men: it was not to destroy 'the landmarks of knowledge'. According to Locke, if these distinct provinces were not set out then there could be no blame for 'those extravagant opinions and ceremonies that are to be found in the several religions of the world'. It was the 'crying up of faith in opposition to reason' that had led to many of 'those absurdities that fill almost all the religions which possess and divide mankind'. Men let loose their 'fancies and natural superstitions' to support 'extravagant practice' and opinions. These were 'so far from being acceptable to God' that they were even 'ridiculous and offensive to sober men'.[14]

One consequence of this distinction between faith and reason that Locke undoubtedly had very much in mind when making his comment in his journal, as in the *Drafts*, was that this denied the legitimacy of Roman Catholic insulation of their doctrines from critical examination. Transubstantiation was 'founded upon an interpretation of revealed truth'. Here, however, taking the words of Scripture in a literal sense – so often Locke's greatest desire – was 'inconsistent with all the principles of our knowledge'. The question was not a matter of faith 'but of philosophy'. It was impossible for a man to know bread to be flesh without destroying his ability to know anything. God always made use of the senses to convince men and never used miracles to destroy the senses.[15]

For Locke, men had very imperfect ideas, as of 'the first motions of our wills or minds, and much imperfecter yet of the operations of God'. Men

14 *Essays*, 275–7.   15 *Ibid.*, 277–8.

therefore ran into 'great difficulties about "free will", which reason cannot resolve'. Effectively prioritising what could be examined by reason over the testimony of faith about the relationship of faith to reason if that should set out a different picture, for Locke this was to give men the 'measure' of where to appeal to faith and quit reason, where 'for want of clear and perfect ideas, we find ourselves involved in inextricable difficulties and contradictions of our notions'. He continued that if men had 'such a clear and perfect idea of the operations of God as to know whether that power would make a "free agent", wherein, I think, lies the bottom of the question about predestination and free will, the dispute about it would quickly be determined by human reason, and faith would have little to do in the case'.[16] Locke gave no indication in this note of his own interpretation of Scripture on this point, his own belief about predestination and free will. His overt concern was epistemological. That he even posed the question in this way, however, suggests that he may have personally attempted to settle the question by reasoning about God and man. It seems likely that Locke had at this point, if not by the time of the *Drafts*, reached the position that he was to express in 1693 as his long-held resolution: that he was committed to men being free, and that he was equally sure that God was omnisciently omnipotent, but that he could not see how these were both possible, and had resolved to believe both without understanding how both could be true.[17]

Even without Locke's later comment to illuminate his position at this moment, his stress upon effortful intellectual enquiry and scattered comments upon the need for morality as the 'real' part of religion, comments in the *Drafts* on voluntary sins, his friendship with various Latitudinarians, his early reading of Allestree and Hammond and his possible authorship of the 1667 sermon combine to suggest that by 1677 his own interpretations of faith had yielded some form of broad support for man's free agency in a manner that looked towards Arminian (and Socinian) accounts that God possessed foreknowledge of who would freely obey him but had not predetermined that they would do so.

A similar picture of Locke's thought comes from his decision to translate three of Pierre Nicole's *Essais de Morale* in 1675–6 in order to publish them to serve 'truth and virtue'. Although a Jansenist, in various works Nicole was attempting to bridge the gap between Jansenism and Thomism. He raised many of the objections about Calvinist thought that were voiced by the Arminians and by most of the Latitudinarians, and supported views that were also broadly similar to their views in maintaining both a deep sense of men's loss in the Fall and a belief that men had free will and

[16] *Ibid.*, 276.   [17] *Correspondence*, IV, 1592.

needed to co-operate with a grace that worked largely through natural means. Nicole held that there was a grace 'sufficient' for salvation offered to all men, which men could refuse. Only by co-operating and undertaking moral endeavours could men gain the 'efficient' grace that saved. He strenuously opposed Calvinist theories, attacking especially their doctrines of assurance of salvation or reprobation as causing the immorality of presumption or of despair.[18]

The *essais* that Locke translated included the outlines of these emphases of Nicole although not the full details of his commitments that were set out in other works. Voicing a very common theme of the Jansenists, Nicole demonstrated man's weakness against the effects of pride in order to dispose men 'to seek that support and establishment – that strength and greatness, in God alone, which is not to be found in the narrow compass of his own being, nor in all those things that are tacked to him'. For Nicole, the mind was incapable of ever attaining much knowledge, and most men did not even extend themselves in thought beyond their bodily needs. The weakness of men's understanding was, however, nothing compared to the inability of the will. Reason was given to understand good and evil and govern desires and actions, but few used it. Nicole declared that instead of being guided by reason 'we float in the ocean of this world, under the conduct of our passions'. Men were led by reputation, beauty, honour and place.[19]

Nicole then gave this theme of men's weakness a stress that Locke had not registered at any point in his notebooks or works. In the clearest soteriological statement before the 1680s with which Locke associated himself – a statement far more forceful than any soteriological opinion that he expressed as his personal opinion – his translation of Nicole's argument at this point declared that the centre of 'corrupted nature' was

hell and fury. We struggle and bustle all we can, in this life, to keep out of it, but at last our strength fails, our weight prevails, death comes, and we tumble into this abyss of misery; if God, by his Almighty grace, hath not put into us another principle – another tendency, which raises us up towards heaven.

18 On Nicole's thought generally, see E. D. James, *Pierre Nicole, Jansenist and Humanist*, The Hague (1972); N. Keohane, *Philosophy and the State in France*, Princeton (1980), 293ff.; N. Abercrombie, *The Origins of Jansenism*, Oxford (1936). See the *Moral Essays* (1677), the second treatise passim on Nicole's deep sense of God's providential ordering of the world; on original sin, 77ff.; third treatise, passim on the need for God's enlivening grace. On resistance to grace and opposition to Calvinist assurance, the third treatise and Nicole, *Disquisitiones pauli Irenaei*, passim. Nicole was clear that man could resist grace ('potest dissentire si velit'). This means that divine grace does not necessitate men's actions, but allows men to perform morally if they cooperate with it.
19 *Discourses*, 2.1; 6–8; 10; 13–14; 2.42–5; 2.48–54.

Without God's assistance, what seemed great in men's will was 'nothing but weakness'. Men were 'full of sins, and transgressions; and corruption overspeads the whole man'. The result was that the 'good that is in us is very inconsiderable: And that little that is, self-love by too much reflecting on it, and overvaluing of it, makes a shift commonly to spoil'.[20]

Locke's translation of Nicole identified as a belief upon which men ought to establish their faith the deity of Christ – a belief that we will see in later chapters that Locke was later at least to doubt, and very probably to deny, but which he shows no clear sign of having doubted before 1683. His translation declared that those men ought to be strong who were filled with knowledge of 'the twofold end, the double eternity, of happiness, or misery, to which they are going' and the 'great and astonishing objects, of Hell, Heaven, Angels, Devils, and God himself dying for them'. But they were still weak, still concerned with the things of the world. They were still liable to a thousand passions, and biassed towards committing great crimes, with no strength of their own 'to hinder themselves from tumbling down that precipice, to which their natural inclination, if God should leave them to themselves, would certainly carry them'.[21]

While Nicole asserted the necessity of God's active grace in order for men fully to be able to act morally he described this grace as working largely by natural means and depicted men as needing to co-operate with grace and act morally in order to obtain their salvation. Nicole stressed that men's 'irregular motions' and their focus upon their own terrestrial pleasures and advantages rather than upon the needs of others were impossible to correct without God's help: 'Nothing but the grace of God can do this.' He importantly continued, however, that 'grace works upon us as men, and makes use of means'. Men could do much to aid themselves in overcoming their concentration upon the things of the world by learning to concentrate their energies upon God's rewards instead of terrestrial rewards, by learning to disengage themselves from the world firstly by the very process of recognising their own sinfulness and secondly by recognising 'the vanity of those beloved objects, we so much set our hearts upon'. He was clear, if somewhat terse, in arguing that such reformation of their behaviour by men's own actions was influential in determining their final fate. In this life men were 'marching forwards continually towards an eternity of happiness or misery', with 'each step, each particular word or action' potentially the occasion of turning towards one or the other. The 'chain of . . . election, or reprobation' could be fastened to a passage of life thought quite inconsequential. All men stood on the brink of a 'precipice, where the least jog is enough to tumble us in'. Complaining about the

[20] *Ibid.*, 2.54–5; 64; 3.2.13–14; 16–25; 29; 3.1.64.   [21] *Ibid.*, 2.64–7.

failures of other men to serve your own interests showed that you had not
expended the necessary effort in turning to God instead of the world, and
helped to make you one of the reprobate. Suppressing such complaints
about other men was the 'properest means to prevail with God to abate the
rigour of his justice; and, as the Scripture says, not to enter into judgment
with us'. Nicole queried how men could expect forgiveness from God for
their 'infinite debts' if they did not themselves forgive others – a notion
very different in emphasis from the Calvinist sense of men's relation to God
in salvation, in which there had to be a balance of the justice of God and
the satisfaction of Christ. Men's eternal happiness depended, Nicole was
clear, upon 'every good action'. The argument implicit throughout the
third discourse was thus that men's salvation depended in significant part
upon their own performance of morality, and not purely – as in Calvinism
– upon a predestined gracious transference to them of Christ's righteousness that they apprehended by their faith.[22]

In his journal on 15 August 1676 Locke wrote an introduction that he
obviously intended to be the preface to a published version of his translation of Nicole's essays. He recorded that

when we a little consider what our author says and experience vouches concerning
the shortness of our lives and the weakness of our understandings, what small
progress men of the quickest parts make in real knowledge, and how little of useful
truth we discover after a long search and infinite labour, we shall find there was
reason enough to desire all needless difficulties should be removed out of the way.

This note suggests that Locke agreed – as is unsurprising given his own
earlier writings – with much of Nicole's estimate of the degree of weakness
of men's understandings, and with Nicole's argument on this basis that
men ought to turn away from useless disputes in the physical sciences that
were often merely disputes about words, and instead use their reason to
generate the rules of good and evil and to direct their passions in order to
perform good actions.[23]

It is very likely that Locke also broadly agreed with Nicole's vision of
men's corrupted nature, the centrality of corrupt self-love among the
passions, and the essential role of God's grace in enlivening and saving
men even though at first sight Nicole's discourses present a picture of
man's weakness and need for grace not familiar to students of the *Two
Treatises* and the *Essay Concerning Human Understanding*. It is certainly
true that the picture of man in Locke's translation of Nicole is more pessimistic than that *explicitly* contained in many of Locke's later works and
that there is more stress on the need for God's grace than is explicit in
many of these later works. We will see later that Locke had moved deci-

<hr/>

[22] *Ibid.*, 3.2.1–10; 13–14; 16–25; 29; 3.1.64–7.   [23] *Essays*, 254–7.

sively away from orthodox accounts of men's inheritance of original sin from Adam by the time of the burden of composition of the *Essay* and publication of the *Treatises*, and to the broadly Socinian belief that men's sinfulness was developed from their own accretion of sins. This did not mean, however, that he then moved away from the picture of men as *in practice* extremely sinful. Socinians did not deny that almost all men were very sinful; they denied only that they had inherited this sinfulness from Adam. There was to be no point in Locke's life when he would declare or think that the vast majority of men were not extremely sinful. Nicole had nowhere here indicated that men cannot know the law of nature by reason, focusing very much on the extent to which their understanding is dark because their corrupt wills rule their understandings. He implicitly denied Calvinist assurance, and his comments on the need for continued grace even for those who had been given most grace suggested that grace was not irresistible, that it was something from which man could fall. There was much in the *Essais* that suggested that man needed to expend efforts to obtain and maintain the help of grace, and to reason about and perform their duties to other men.[24]

Intending to publish the *Essais* to serve truth and virtue, it is highly probable that in 1676 Locke held a number of views that he did not express at great length in any of his notebooks in these years: that men were in practice very corrupt and sinful, that man had suffered a very significant loss by original sin, but not as much loss as was believed by strict Calvinists, and that men had to co-operate with God's grace and act morally in order to attain salvation. Those authors that Locke read around 1660 and most Latitudinarians shared such a sense both of men's deprivation by the Fall and of men's need to co-operate with God's grace. Even Tillotson, the Latitudinarian who wrote the least about original sin, wrote repeatedly of mankind's 'degenerate and depraved condition' and argued that by Adam's transgression 'all Mankind suffers, and our Natures are extremely corrupted and depraved'.[25] Among Protestants it is difficult to find contemporaries of Locke outside of Socinians who did not have a deep sense of the seriousness of man's loss by the Fall, although there was significant variation amongst them in their shading of the picture of this inherited depravity. There is no evidence of Locke having read Socinian works before 1676, and even less to suggest that he agreed before 1679 at the earliest with their view of mankind's corruption as voluntary and habitual rather than inherited from Adam. There is very little evidence by this point in Locke's life of the kind of scrutiny of Scripture and theological works

[24] Nicole, *Moral Essays*, discourses 2 and 3; Nicole, *Disquisitiones*, passim.
[25] See my 'Locke and Latitudinarianism'.

that might have provided Locke with significant reasons to doubt these doctrines. Locke characteristically showed in France very little interest in or awareness of those Catholic sources – Jesuit and Thomist – which went beyond Nicole in elevating men's abilities to the point that they substantially diminished man's corruption from the Fall.[26]

That Locke probably maintained these broad beliefs, as on free will and omnipotence, but could not see how to prove them by reason, was probably not deeply troubling to him in the mid-1670s; it was enough for virtue that the Calvinist assurance and denial of free will that he associated with antinomianism was excluded, and he had seen major wars fought in part because of disputes on imposition of beliefs about these issues. Surely much more troubling to Locke was a personal recognition of difficulties attaching to proof by reason alone of the subject of the discourse which he chose to place first in his translation of Nicole's work signifying its importance to him on natural proofs of God's existence and the soul's immortality. Such natural proofs had, strangely, already been almost completely absent from the first two *Drafts* of the *Essay* in 1671. Nicole's discourse attacked the 'vicious and debauched part of men' who opposed Christianity by denying the 'two great points' of the 'being of a Deity, and the immortality of the soul'. The discourse acknowledged that some had defended these with 'refined reasons and the subtleties of metaphysics', probably a reference to Descartes' ontological proof of God's existence, and others by appealing to the testimony of prophecies and miracles, particularly influential in persuading the majority of people to believe. The subject of the discourse were arguments which lay 'nearer our senses, more comfortable to human reason'.[27]

According to Nicole, even atheists had been wholly unable to efface 'those characters that are stamped so clear, and are sunk so deep' of God's existence. These characters were 'naturally imprint[ed]' by 'the very view of the world'. Apprehension of a deity was at least a 'kind of intuition, not less forcible, not less convincing than all our reasonings together . . . we must do violence to ourselves, if we oppose it'. Nicole's original notion here seems to have been of a kind of 'sentiment', a kind of intuition, that was closer to contemporary notions of dispositional innatism than Locke rendered it in his translation, which described it as caused by the 'natural motion' of reason that led directly from 'the progress of nature, in an order never disturbed . . . the admirable connexion of all the parts . . . the variety

[26] J. Lough, *Locke's Travels in France 1675–9*, Cambridge (1953), 262.
[27] *Essays*, 254 (15 August 1676); *Discourses*, 1.1–1.4; the *Drafts* had included a little on proofs of the existence of God, but not much – see paragraphs 94 and 140 of *Draft B*, ed. B. Rand (1931); cf. bk. 4 ch. 10 of the *Essay*; *Discourses*, 1.1–4. See on the general topic, W. von Leyden, 'Locke and Nicole', *Sophia* 16: 1 (1971), 41–55.

[and] . . . the wonderful contrivance of the bodies of animals' to a creator of 'all things we see'. Paralleling Locke's declaration in the *Essays on the Law of Nature*, Nicole's discourse stated that it was 'impossible that reason, contemplating all these wonders, should not hear this secret voice, that all this is not the effect of chance; but the production of some cause, which possesses in itself all the perfections, which we observe in this most excellent piece of workmanship'. The original of matter and motion had to be 'an immaterial, intelligent Agent, who at first produced and continues to preserve both the one and the other'. The discourse declared it absolutely unequivocal that matter was insensible. Reason saw 'few things clearer, than it doth the impossibility that matter should think or reflect on it self'. The existence of thinking beings indicated that there had to be another, omnipotent spiritual being. In Locke's translation, Nicole concluded that matter, motion and spirit therefore all cried out 'with one very intelligible voice, That God is their Maker'. There was nothing in nature 'able to undertake such a piece of workmanship'.[28]

In an important note in his journal on 29 July 1676 Locke wrote, however, that while Nicole's arguments on the proof of God were 'very clear and cogent', they might be recognised as 'not yet perfect demonstrations' of the existence of a deity or the immortality of the soul. He continued not by indicating any way in which such arguments could be demonstrated, but by declaring that it was not 'reasonable' for anyone therefore to reject these beliefs. Anyone who rejected these without establishing some surer hypothesis had to be suspected of 'a secret and strong bias that inclined him the other way'. There were difficulties about matter and motion that were 'so great' that Locke thought men would 'never be able to resolve' them, but it was ludicrous for them to hold no views because they could not have certainty. Locke thought 'impossible' to think atheism more comfortable to reason and experience than belief in a God even if men were prevailed on 'by prejudice or corruption'; the understanding always followed the 'more probable side'. Even if men were motivated in consideration of an afterlife by prejudice and corruption the 'venture' ought to 'stick with a considerate man'. Everlasting happiness was 'the reward of the religious' if their belief were true and 'infinite misery' was the fate of the atheist. In contrast, annihilation or eternal insensibility was the best that could happen to an atheist if his beliefs were true, but it was the worst that could happen to a believer if there were no

---

[28] *Discourses*, 1.5–17; 21. The later point of the *Essay* was not that matter was not naturally insensible but that men could not know that God had not superadded to matter the power of thought. See M. Ayers, 'Mechanism, Superaddition and the Proof of God's Existence in Locke's Essay', *Philosophical Review*, 40: 2 (1981), 210–51.

God. According to Locke's argument, somewhat reminiscent of Pascal's famous 'wager', anyone who would 'pass for a rational creature' and who had the 'least care or kindness for himself' could not choose 'to venture the losse of infinite happynesse and put himself in danger of infinite eternal misery and that in exchange for and expectation of just noething'. Locke occasionally signed his own notes in his journals to indicate that something was his own opinion, rather than that of an author of a work that he was reading. This note bore the initials 'JL'.[29]

As a solution to the problem of demonstrating the bases for a secure morality, this contributed nothing; we will see that over the following years Locke was to find great difficulty in providing a better solution, and to rely increasingly upon this form of probabilistic argument. That he was utilising it at this point may only suggest that he thought it a useful collateral argument to the desired demonstration of the bases of morality, but probably also suggests that he already was thinking seriously about and could not at this point see how to construct such a demonstration.

III

During his time in France Locke began to show more interest in biblical interpretation, taking extensive notes from John Lightfoot's *Works* on biblical customs, discussing variations in translations of the Bible with Nicholas Thoynard and Henri Justel in Paris, and lauding Thoynard's privately circulated harmony of the Gospels which 'made evident' without 'explanations sought from elsewhere but simply by inspecting the Gospel narrative, its proper clarity, order, and meaning'. It is possible that a nascent critical sensibility provoked Locke to question the Trinity even before 1683. Locke recorded the absence of 1 John 5:7, a major trinitarian text, from the copies of a French Bible but without expressing anything like the view that Newton later propounded, that the text had been a fraudulent trinitarian addition to the text by Jerome. In January 1679 Locke read at least part of the Hungarian Socinian George Enyedi's *Explicationes Locorum Veteris et Novi Testamenti* – the first definite indication of Socinian reading in Locke's life – taking a note on Jesus' description of himself as the son of man and his use of this phrase to indicate that he was the Messiah, a neutral note in terms of the Trinity. Among the Shaftesbury papers are several pages of notes in Locke's hand summarising the arguments of Christopher Sand's 1669 *Nucleus Historiae Ecclesiasticae*, an Arian account of early Christianity. These are undated, and while they are

---

[29] *Draft*, 81ff. (29 July 1676); cf. chapters five; eight to ten below on the significance of this.

most probably from the period before 1682, when Shaftesbury died, there is no conclusive evidence to date them.[30]

In 1679 Locke did, however, take several notes suggesting that he was already broadly aware of Arian thought, recording that Ferrand's *Réflections sur la religion Chrétienne* said little for his position and 'much for the Arians'. He took one cryptic note on another French response to 'Socin a crellius'; another note suggests that he may have read a work on the lives of several of the Fathers, including Athanasius, the third-century credal formulator of trinitarianism. After his return to England Locke remained in frequent correspondence with Thoynard, and spent much time examining sections of the Bible closely in order to comment upon Thoynard's harmonies, which he claimed to have made him understand parts of the Bible 'much better'. He bought and started to read works of biblical criticism and patristic scholarship by Vossius, Cave, and several works by church fathers. He also probably started to read Richard Simon's *Histoire Critique du Vieux Testament*, an extremely important challenge to Protestant abilities to understand Scripture which will be discussed in chapter eight. His 1681 reading of Croft's *Naked Truth* not merely provided him with an extremely eirenic Latitudinarian account of the equality of bishop and presbyter in patristic times, but with a similarly extremely Latitudinarian view of the patristic requirements in terms of belief: Croft was a credal minimalist who asserted the necessity of belief by Christians only in the Apostles' Creed and thus, unlike many Latitudinarians, not in the trinitarian Athanasian creed. Locke probably registered this argument at his first reading in 1681 even though he did not then record it; he was to cite Croft precisely in defence of his own assertions of the necessity of only the Apostles' Creed in his works of the 1690s.[31]

It is possible that this reading was combined with further reading of unitarian works. In 1680 Locke made two notes in separate journals on a collection of unitarian works which may indicate that he had read these,

---

[30] MS Locke f14, 62–3; Locke's Bibles in the Bodleian Library, Oxford; Lough, *Travels*, introduction and 202; 252–5; BM Add. MSS 15642, 5; 12; 16; 27; 33–35; 63; 71; MS Locke c42, ii, 20, 26, 30; *Correspondence*, I, 428 and Locke's other letters to Thoynard (Toinard) and to Boyle about Thoynard; MS Locke f15, 129; 151; MS Locke c42, ii, 32–3 has notes from Toinard on the chronology of the Gospels which include the declaration that 'the word that was at the beginning with God is made flesh and dwelt among us', a note probably but not definitely of trinitarian intent; PRO 30/24/5pt. 3/278; PRO 30/24/47/30 fos. 17; 36–41; there are a number of manuscripts among the Shaftesbury papers in the PRO which date from after Shaftesbury's death, so there is no firm indication of the date of Locke's reading of Sand from the mere presence of his notes on Sand amongst these papers. On the extensiveness of Locke's reading of Lightfoot's works, see Locke's Bibles in the Bodleian. I am grateful to the anonymous referee of my article 'John Locke and Socinianism' for pointing out these notes on Sand's work.

[31] MS Locke c42, ii, 20; see chapter three above on Croft.

particularly given that he was reading the Socinian Enyedi's work in 1679, but which may merely indicate that he had purchased them, received a recommendation of them from a friend, or perhaps only procured them for that friend; the notes themselves merely list the titles of the works. In his 'Lemmata Ethica' there is a list bearing the initials 'D.T.' which describes as 'all contained in one volume' a number of unitarian works, from the *Racovian Catechism* itself, the quasi-official statement of Polish unitarianism, through to several works by John Biddle, the mid-century 'father of English Unitarianism'. Almost exactly the same list appears in Locke's journal for 1680. The initials 'D.T.' might indicate 'De Trinitate', but if so they would be the only such notation Locke made in referring to unitarian works, and there seems no reason for such a notation in his private notebook given that he was listing the books and could not therefore have been intending concealment of their topic. It is therefore surely more likely that they refer to David Thomas, Locke's Oxford friend for whom he frequently procured books while he was in London, and to whom he was sending pamphlets on the Exclusion Crisis and Popish Plot in 1681.[32]

If Locke did combine unitarian reading with his increasing awareness of issues of biblical interpretation, and with his patristic reading undertaken in order to oppose Stillingfleet's arguments about the early church in the 'Critical Notes', then it is possible that this combination fostered doubts about the doctrines that Socinians identified as being based upon the interpretations of various Fathers rather than Scripture itself, including the Trinity. Socinians held that the Trinity had become a doctrine of Christianity only in late patristic interpretations of Scripture, and that Scripture clearly indicated instead that God the Father was both superior and prior to Christ and the Holy Ghost. Locke's interest in the ecclesiastical history of the first centuries in order to reply to Stillingfleet, as well as his opposition to Stillingfleet's reliance upon patristic rather than Scriptural authority for the assertion of episcopacy, may well in itself have made this Socinian case more plausible to him. In Locke's assault upon *jure divino* episcopalianism he declared the Athanasian period not primitive; it is not a long step to thinking that the trinitarianism of this period was not 'primitive' enough to establish that the Apostles and their immediate followers were trinitarian.

It is thus possible that Locke became at least doubtful about the Trinity or even became committedly antitrinitarian in the years before 1683. A number of comments in the 'Critical Notes' very slightly suggest that he still believed in the Trinity, including repeated attacks on Stillingfleet's stress upon the established church by querying 'what would become of a

---

32 MS Locke f4, 10–12; MS Locke d10, 160.

poor Christian in such an age of the church, when . . . the whole world was become Arrian; must he either please [presumably God] for holding the Divinity of Christ by himself or be a Christian for denying it with them'. Since these passages were written in large part because Stillingfleet had argued that separation was not schism under idolatrous or Arian princes, and Locke wished to say that Stillingfleet's reliance on law as a basis for obligation would have legitimated antitrinitarianism, they are far from conclusive indications of trinitarianism. Holding that it was absurd to suppose that a magistrate of a true church should prescribe worship for a false church and yet more absurd that a magistrate of a false one should prescribe for a true, Locke said that it was unreasonable for a Christian magistrate to make laws concerning ceremonies to be used in a 'Mahometan mosque', or a 'Mahometan' for those in a Christian church. The same was true 'in a Socinian and Orthodox Magistrate and Church and soe in all lesser differences'. Continuing this passage with a reference that may have looked back to the divide between 'Mahometan' and Christian, but more probably referred to the Socinian and Orthodox division that he had just made, Locke declared that the absurdity was merely seen more easily 'because the difference between these two religious societies is soe wide and the opposition knowne and imprinted on every man's minde, but holdes as well and is as great, if you take Protestant and Papist'. The juxtaposition of Socinian and Orthodox, the apparent treatment of these as closer to the divide between Mahometan and Christian than to the divide between Protestant and Papist, and the suggestion that the division between Socinian and Orthodox was 'soe wide', combine with the repeated queries about enforced worship under Socinians or Arians to make it seem on balance improbable, but certainly very far from impossible, that Locke was himself antitrinitarian in 1681.[33]

A note in Locke's journal in 1680, however, suggests that Locke's view of men's sinfulness and original sin may well have moved very far in the direction of Socinianism by 1681, although there is no definite indication that this was a result of Socinian reading, and it is only by extension of Locke's argument beyond its explicit topic that it seems to support a more Socinian than Calvinist or Arminian view. On 1 August 1680 Locke composed a lengthy note in his journal, on the idea of God, characteristically proceeding not from an analysis of Scripture but from man's natural idea of God: 'Whatsoever carrys any excellency with it and includes not imperfection that must needs make a part of the idea we have of God.' Existence, 'all duration, power, wisedome and goodnesse' had to be 'ingredients of the

[33] MS Locke c34, 98; 160ff.; 45; 55; 75.113; 115; 130; cf. also 76 for apparent belief in eternal misery, frequently disbelieved by the Socinians and later by Locke.

perfect or superexcellent being which we call God and that in the utmost or an infinite degree'. Locke declared that unlimited power could not be 'an excellency without it be regulated by wisdom and goodnesse'. He continued with what he characterised as an explanation of this:

For since God is eternall and perfect in his own being, he can not make use of that power to change his owne being into better or an other state, and therefore all the exercise of that power must be in and upon his creatures, which cannot but be imploied for their good and benefit as much as the order and perfection of the whole can allow to each individual in its particular rank and station.

Locke's argument here appears to be that if God was not good to his creatures then he would have no one or thing to whom to be good, and therefore his power simply has to be defined by his goodness. Locke continued by asserting that looking on God 'as infinite in goodnesse as well as power we cannot imagin he hath made any thing with a designe that it should be miserable, but that he hath afforded it all that means of being happy that its nature and state is capable of'.[34]

There is nothing here that directly suggests that men should have immortality; the happiness in question is that of creatures' nature and state. Even if we presume that Locke thought that Adam was created naturally immortal, there is nothing in the passage just cited that precludes original sin; it is perfectly compatible with the notion that Adam's disobedience was freely committed and not caused by God. God had given to Adam the means to be happy, but he had chosen to sin. Locke continued, however, in a way that makes it very difficult to see how he could have made his note consistent with Calvinist or even Latitudinarian and Arminian accounts of the punishment for original sin, or of Christ's satisfaction. Justice was also a perfection

which we must necessarily ascribe to the supreme being, yet we cannot suppose the exercise of it should extend farther than his goodnesse has need of it for the preservation of his creatures in the order and beauty of that state that he has placed each of them in. For since our actions cannot reach unto him or bring him any profit or damage the punishments he inflicts on any of his creatures the misery or destruction he brings upon them can be nothing else but to preserve the greater or more considerable part and soe being only for preservation his justice is noe thing but a branch of his goodnesse which is faine by severity to restraine the irregular and destructive parts from doing harm.

To imagine God under any necessity of punishing for any other reason was 'to make his justice a great imperfection and to suppose a power over him that necessitates him to operate contrary to the rules of his wisdome and goodnesse'. God could not 'be supposed to make any thing so idely as that

---

[34] MS Locke f4, 145–9.

... it should be purposely destroid or be put in a worse state than destruction (misery being as much a worse state than annihilation as pain is than insensibility)'. The justice of God, then, could be supposed to extend it self 'noe farther than infinite goodnesse shall find it necessary for the preservation of his workes'.

The suggestion that none can be supposed to be made 'idely' to be purposely destroyed precludes at least strict, supralapsarian reprobation. Locke's comments can with very great difficulty be made compatible with a doctrine of original sin and punishment by arguing that when Locke speaks of us being unable to 'suppose' that justice should go beyond preservation he is not intending to preclude the information that we obtain from revelation that God justly punishes men for their sin. This interpretation of the note would argue that it merely suggests that by natural means we cannot come to this idea about God. It is, however, difficult to accommodate this kind of interpretation of this part of the note alongside the unequivocal statement that our actions simply cannot affect God. By far the more natural way to interpret the note leaves it difficult to see how either Adam or men since Adam can be punished for the offence of Adam except as this leads them actively to harm others now. Adam freely sinned and his children were sinful. This did not affect God because nothing that men did could affect God. God therefore punished them not because of their offence against his justice, but only because their offences were harmful to the preservation of his other creatures. Justice seems also to be limited to the harm of neighbours in this life: God's severity is to be used to restrain damage to the preservation of his creatures.[35]

This note, then, is hardly a well-thought-out or stable position on Locke's part, and it is quite possibly merely a momentary reflection upon the idea of God that Locke did not subscribe to in any meaningful sense in the longer term. This does not change the fact that the argument as it stands is a startling rejection of the view, common to Calvinists and Arminians, that men were punished for offending God by disobedience, and that Christ had had to die in order to satisfy for men's sins, to make a payment to God's justice equal to man's debt. It was this, indeed, that made Christ's deity essential: only as God could he make an infinite payment for sin. It is completely unclear what prompted Locke to compose this note, or whether he had thought out its implications for contemporary theology in this detailed way. Locke made no attempt to back his argument with any scriptural texts, and there is no indication that this note was prompted by reflection upon Scripture or by any reading of contemporary treatises, although texts such as Enyedi's *Explicationes* may well form part

---

[35] MS Locke f4, 145–9.

of the background. In the *Essay* and the *Third Letter Concerning Toleration* Locke was to assault any extrapolation from men's limited conceptions of God to the operations of God's grace; composition of this note therefore may well not have given rise to an extended consideration of its soteriological consequences. Yet at the very least it is difficult to believe that Locke could compose such a note without a sense that Scripture as usually interpreted by almost all of his contemporaries ran counter to this view of God's justice and without a consequent sense that Scripture needed to be examined in order to show how it could be compatible with this idea of God. It is possible that Locke had read those unitarian works indicated in his journal in 1680 in which original sin and the satisfaction were rejected before making this note as well as reading Enyedi's text. In a work explicitly published against Socinianism when Locke was a student at Christ Church in 1653, its then dean Owen had argued that God's justice meant that he 'necessarily punishes sin'; even if Locke had not read these unitarian works it is therefore very likely that he had at least a strong sense that the most natural extension of his argument, that God was not necessitated to punish men's original sin by his justice, was associated with Socinianism by Calvinists.[36]

In exile in Holland, as we will see later, Locke was to start collecting and almost certainly to start an extremely extensive reading of Socinian works. It would appear, however, that his own thought had started to point in the direction of 'Socinian' views of the satisfaction and original sin even before the extensive reading of Socinian theology that he was to undertake in Holland. This would suggest that Locke's theology in the mid-1680s and 1690s was partly motivated by his desire to find in Scripture confirmation of his 'natural idea' of God, and that it was this natural idea, as well as his extensive Socinian reading, that generated the firm commitment to unitarianism in the mid-1690s that will be suggested later. As important a point conveyed by this journal entry, however, is that for Locke preservation of God's creatures was the major concern of God himself. In the *Two Treatises* this was to be an overriding tenet. Behind the emphasis on this position in the *Two Treatises* it would appear that there was not merely Locke's sense that not preserving other men was failure to preserve God's property, but also that it was a thwarting of God's activities, God's goodness, in a way that would call forth God's justice.[37]

---

[36] Owen, *A Dissertation on Divine Justice* (1653) in idem, *Works*, X, passim, esp. 436, 496, 507, 550–72, 589–99.

[37] *Treatises*, passim.

IV

In the *Two Treatises* Locke declared at one point that men's natural community would have been sufficient were it not for the 'corruption, and viciousness of degenerate Men' and he spoke of men as 'very much, distant in condition' after the Fall from their condition before it. The *Two Treatises* say nothing that directly excludes the need to form a political society in order to remedy inherited sinful tendencies. However, Locke gave no indication that the changed 'condition' of man had anything to do with an infected nature, and did not interpret the texts frequently drawn to interpretation of original sin as implying original sin but rather the requirement of labour by Adam. His general picture of the state of nature, and his account of the stages of movement from the Golden Age to modern political society suggest a picture of sins as caused primarily by the accretion of voluntary and habitual sinfulness across time rather than due to the Fall.[38]

By the time of the *Treatises*' publication it is clear, as we will later see, that Locke opposed original sin in common with Socinians, and it is possible that this opposition had developed by the time that Locke first composed the *Treatises*, and helped to influence Locke's description of the state of nature as peaceable with initially little sin. It is also possible, however, that a brief recognition of inherited degeneracy at the time of composition had been excised by the time of publication, since Locke came clearly to oppose original sin in 1684; Locke's description of the development of political societies, men's corruption, and their covetousness, appears broadly in the works that other nonunitarian Whigs wrote against Filmer and absolute monarchy between 1680 and 1683, and Pufendorf's works, read by Locke in 1681, include a description of the state of nature and the

---

[38] *Treatises*, 2.128. Cf. *Treatises*, 1.16; 2.10–11; 16; 2.111; 1.58; 2.31; 36; 75; 107. Cf. Dunn, *Political Thought*; C. B. MacPherson, *The Political Theory of Possessive Individualism*, Oxford (1962), ch. 5. Although a strong argument from original sin was more easily associated with the need for rule by the will of a ruler given privileged coercive status by God, and perhaps also privileged epistemic status by God, than with Locke's description of the beastly rulers as not men, a resolution between a strong view of original sin and Locke's views in the *Treatises* could be constructed, for instance, in the following manner: All men are inherently sinful, and easily become degenerate, become then jurally 'beastly', but are still 'men' when they follow reason; therefore the law is established as an impartial artificial reason to correct this deficiency in all men. Two very minor further intimations that Locke's thought was not structured around a commitment to original sin were his limitation of the role of the father in the creation of his child to being the occasion of his being and particularly his argument that the children of those who have been the aggressors in a state of war bear no responsibility for it. [II, 82] In the second case, the 'brutishness of the father' is explicitly denied to affect the children, and thus no power over the children is said to accrue from unjust aggression by the father. Neither of these arguments is especially difficult to square with a strong view of original sin, but both tend away from a notion that children bear responsibility for their ultimate father's sin.

dangers of a state of war very similar to Locke's, that was explicitly but very briefly indeed tied by Pufendorf to men's inherited depravity. It would be unwise to attribute a Socinian impetus to composition of the *Treatises*.

If anything, it is more likely that composition of the *Treatises* furthered Locke's move towards Socinianism by first advancing his critical analysis of the Bible in order to attack Filmer's Old-Testament account of government, and secondly because as Locke came to assert strongly the necessity of individual consent and responsibility in the *Treatises* for political reasons that we will examine in chapter six, he encountered a significant problem with the doctrine of the Fall. In a work of November 1681 that Locke surely read, *Absalom and Achitophel*, Dryden drew a direct analogy between those who would wish to throw off divinely instituted government and supported the consent of all and the logic of objection to the orthodox accounts of the Fall:

> If those who gave the scepter could not tie
> By their own deed their own posterity
> How then could Adam bind his future race?
> How could his forfeit on mankind take place?
> Or how could heavenly justice damn us all
> Who ne'er consented to our father's fall?

It was a question that Locke may well have had in mind from the composition of the Second Treatise in about 1682, which he answered with a decisive rejection of original sin in his 1695 *Reasonableness of Christianity*, and which probably underpinned his clear rejection of original sin in the Netherlands by 1683–4, to be examined later.[39]

The deep sense of God's goodness to man communicated in Locke's journal note of 1680 was important on a more general level to Locke because it was crucial to his epistemology. Locke repeated in 1681 his arguments from the consequences of allowing faith to establish truths not called to the bar of reason; again a simple appeal to God's goodness provided the basis for men to be able to discriminate between truth and error by their reason alone. Locke declared in April 1681 that where reason was 'not judg' of the doctrines conveyed by inspiration immediately to an individual or by an inspired individual to others, then it would be 'impossible for a man himself to destinguish betwixt inspiration and phansy; truth, and error'. It was also 'impossible' to have 'such a notion of God' that one could believe that 'he should make a creature to whom the knowledge of himself was necessary and yet not to be discoverd by that way which discovers every thing els that concernes us'.

---

[39] Ashcraft, *Revolutionary Politics*, 214ff.; Dryden, *Absalom*, discussed in Wootton, *Locke: Political Writings*, introduction.

Reflecting not merely his epistemological stress upon the senses as the basis of all information, but also his acute sense of the range of absurd customary beliefs in the world, Locke declared that it could not be believed that truth was 'to come into the mindes of men only by such a way by which all manner of errors come in and is more likely to let in falsehoods than truths, since no body can doubt from the contradiction and strangeness of opinions concerning God and religion in the world that men are likely to have more phansys than inspirations'. Even miracles testifying to doctrine had to be judged by reason. It would always be a miracle for God to alter the 'course of naturall things' and overturn men's principles of knowledge, and so at most one miracle would challenge another when there was a contradiction between faith and reason. Furthermore, there were also many creatures above man which might be able to perform miracles against the true religion. Religion was the homage that men paid immediately to God. For Locke, this 'supposes that man is capeable of knowing that there is a god, and what is required by and will be acceptable to him thereby to avoid his anger and procure his favour'. That there was a God 'nothing can discover to us nor judg in us but natural reason'. Once again Locke simply does not countenance the possibility of God's goodness being manifested by regeneration of sinful and fallen men in a way that diminishes the role of their reason as that was infected and damaged by the Fall, and replaces it with a regenerate faith, or by a faculty of 'reason' that is heightened and altered by regeneration. Locke's argument runs again from the consequences of such a theology: reason alone is necessary for any discrimination of truth from error, therefore God must have provided that knowledge of himself and of men's duties comes to men, even after the Fall, through reason.[40]

In *Patriarcha* Filmer had described God as directly granting Adam sovereign authority, and he had described God as providentially ordering the events of the world to preserve this authority. In the *Treatises* Locke argued against the view 'that what happens in Providence to be preserved, God is careful to preserve as a thing to be esteemed by Men as necessary or useful'. Most of Locke's comments suggest that for him by the early 1680s providence was not equated with any direct active intervention in the world. Thus, the subjection of women to men that Filmer interpreted as supporting the sovereignty of fathers, Locke interpreted instead as foretelling what should be women's lot, 'how by his Providence he would order it so, that she should be subject to her husband, as we see that generally the Laws of Mankind and customs of Nations have ordered it so; and there is, I grant, a Foundation in Nature for it'. Providence for Locke

[40] *Essays*, 281.

seems to mean here 'laws of Mankind' and 'customs' which had a foundation 'in nature', a notion of God's creation of men and women as they were created, the natural foundation from which men's laws and customs would flow, rather than any active direction of events.[41]

Locke's political thought had long been moving to the creation of political society by men's consensual activity rather than the providential activity of God. His ethical thought had long stressed the perspicuous ordering of nature provided by God; the responsibility of each individual to search out his duties by arduous use of reason had been directed especially against the intervention of inspired grace, commencing with Locke's attempts to insulate religious inspiration from harmful 'enthusiasm'. It is likely that Locke's opposition to Filmer here brought to culmination a long erosion of his own view of 1660 of God's extensive active involvement in the world towards a view that God's providence operated almost exclusively by natural means.

We saw in the last chapter that in the 1681 'Critical Notes' edification was one of Locke's three main aims of church society, that it consisted of subduing the will as well as informing the understanding, and that it was not an extraordinary grace that Locke appealed to for the 'subdueing of the will', but the natural means of using the powers of credit and custom in a strict church society to correct man's 'natural corruption'. This is not, however, to say that Locke thought that these means were not part of God's providence as the result in some sense at least of God's ordering of the world. At another point in the 'Critical Notes', Locke declared that a man was not to accept any doctrine on the authority of others until 'god shall reveal it to him (whether by his reason better informed in a naturall way, or illuminated by revelation, I determine not)'. The important point to note here is that Locke conceived of men reaching an understanding of Scripture by 'reason better informed in a naturall way' as the result of an activity of God himself.[42]

Locke's meaning here is probably further revealed in his 1682 correspondence with Damaris Cudworth about the Cambridge Platonist John Smith's *Select Discourses*. Smith divided men ('brutish' Epicureans aside) into four 'ranks' to which corresponded 'a fourfold kinde of knowledge'. The fourth kind of knowledge was possessed by 'the True Metaphysical and Contemplative man . . . who running and shooting up above his own Logical or self-rational life, pierceth unto the Highest life'. For Cudworth, like Smith, there was 'something between' visions and reason, a 'Degree of Perfection to be attain'd to in this life to which the Powers of meere Unassisted Reason will never Conduct a Man'. She declared that men were not to lay reason aside, but she asked Locke in a letter whether by constantly employing reason men might not 'at length come to be acted by a Higher Principle', becoming the new creatures 'so often spoken of' by this higher principle and not by the application of reason 'alone'. This she thought to be both Smith's view and that of St Paul.[43]

It was probably the receipt of this question which prompted Locke to compose a lengthy note on enthusiasm. For Locke, enthusiasm involved any 'strong and firme perswasion' of any religious proposition which was received without sufficient proof from reason but rather as a truth 'wrought in the minde extraordinarily by God himself'. The consequences of such a view of faith, rather than any personal interpretation of Scripture or the faith itself, were once again the crucial shaping force of Locke's declaration that this could not be true faith: 'For . . . Christians, Mahumetans, and Bramins all pretend to it.' It was certain that no one 'of the true Religion could be assured of any thing by a way whereby those of a false religion may be and are equally confirmed in theirs'. He expanded upon this theme in his reply to the letter by describing a change in the end of men's actions but not a change in his faculties. Locke wrote that it was easily to be imagined that 'a love and practise of virtue may and naturally doth by imploying his thoughts more on heavenly objects give a man a greater Knowledge of God and his duty, and that reciprocally produce a greater love of them'. This was not another kind of knowledge 'or any knowledg at all above his reason'. Opinions or persuasions in the mind without foundation of reason were 'Enthusiasme which however you seeme to plead for and thinke St Paul to a degree allows yet I must still say is noe part of knowledge'. For Locke the 'new creature' did not consist 'soe much in notions nor indeed in any irrationall notions at all, but in a new principle of life and action, ie the love of God and a desire of being in holyness like unto him'. He continued that he could not 'determine what unassisted reason can or cannot do . . . since I thinke the faculty in itself in its severall degrees of perfection all the helps and improvements of it by education discourse contemplation or otherwise are all assistances from God and [are] to be acknowledg[ed] to the goodnesse of his providence'.[44]

Reason was like an eye which could grow very acute by 'constant imployment about any object', or see things better with the assistance of glasses, but still saw things with the natural faculty of seeing, however assisted. Whatever was known, 'however sublime or spirituall', was

[43] MS Locke f6, 18; *Correspondence*, II, 684; Smith, *Select Discourses* (1660); first discourse, passim.
[44] MS Locke f6, 20–5 printed in *Draft*, 119–21; cf. MS Locke f6, 33–8, printed in *Draft*, 123–5 and *Correspondence*, II, 687; MS Locke f6, 33–8 printed in *Draft*, 123–5.

known 'only by the naturall faculty of the understanding', reason. There was one significant difference between these cases, that one man 'perhaps has got an help to see and discerne heavenly objects which an other never soe much as lookd after'. Locke thought that men fell into three groups. There were those who acted as if they were only body and mind and never thought of the afterlife, those who thought as if they consisted only of a soul and not body and had visions, 'or more properly imaginations', and lastly those 'who considering themselves as made up of body and soule here and in a state of mediocrity make use of and follow their reason'. His preference for this last group was palpable.[45]

While thus opposing Smith's neoplatonic form of knowledge beyond reason, Locke declared that Smith's next discourse, on superstition, was 'one of the best I ever read', a declaration that his notebooks and his copy of the *Discourses* support. Smith declared that superstition developed from a false appraisal of God, fearing God as a 'dismal and sour' being. Locke copied out Smith's account of the cause of superstition and his definition of superstition as consisting in the belief flowing from this that by certain ritual observances it was possible to placate this fearsome being. We have seen that in the 'Critical Notes' Locke had himself defined superstition as an attempt to placate God by ritual observance; what Smith's discourse added was the tying of this explicitly to a dismal view of God. Against the background of Locke's belief that God was good, and his declaration in August 1680 that his goodness defined the parameters of his justice, Locke's approval of this account by Smith confirms the picture of Locke's thought as moving away from the essentially rigorous notion of God's justice and emphasis on fear of God's punishment that ran throughout Calvinist thought, and towards the softer views shared especially by Cambridge Platonists and Latitudinarians. The terminus of this path was Socinianism, and for strict Calvinists like Owen and Ferguson the Latitudinarians were in this sense already Socinian whether or not they believed in the Trinity. Smith was a trinitarian like his Latitudinarian followers. There is nothing in Locke's note which suggests that he pushed this thought any further than had Smith or the Latitudinarians, but also nothing to exclude such a possibility.[46]

In February 1682, while discussing Smith's *Select Discourses* with Damaris Cudworth, Locke also began to read Ralph Cudworth's *True Intellectual System of the Universe*, a monumental work which had finally

---

[45] *Draft*, 119–25.
[46] Smith, *Discourses*, second discourse, passim; *Draft*, 125; MS Locke d10, 161; MS Locke c33, 27rff.; Locke's copy of Smith's *Select Discourses* is one of those relatively few books in which he marked page references – noting the section on superstition: Locke Room shelved under 8.4.

appeared, unfinished at 800 pages, in 1678. Locke quickly became interested by Cudworth's proofs of the existence of a deity, noting the location of Cudworth's arguments against atheists' contentions, although without any comment on their efficacy. It was probably at about the same time that he was taking extensive notes in his journals from Smith's discourse on atheism. In both works proof of the immortality of the soul was discussed at length.

Either or both of these works may have provoked the note that Locke composed on 20 February on the immortality of the soul. As so often, his approach to the topic was through epistemology and not through the exegesis of any texts of Scripture or explication of any detailed theological position. According to Locke, the usual physical proof of the immortality of the soul was that 'Matter cannot think ergo the soul is immateriall; noe thing can naturally destroy an immateriall thing ergo the soule is naturally immortall.' This argument had been attacked by those who suggested that beasts felt and thought and so had to have immortal souls, and had led to their description of animals as machines in response. Locke felt that neither spoke 'to the point' and that both 'perfectly mistake immortality whereby is not meant a state of bare substantiall existence and duration but a state of sensibility'. The soul during sleep was 'certainly then in a man' but it did not have sense or perception, whereby it was evident that the soul could exist without sense or perception. An eternal duration of such a state was possible, and was inconsistent with 'such destinct states of heaven or hell as we suppose to belong to soules after this life, and for which only we are concernd for and inquisitive after its immortality'.[47]

Introducing Scripture into his discussion, but with the sense of an illustration of his argument rather than its foundation, Locke left it to those who have 'well considerd' the story of Lazarus to 'conjecture' whether death, which the Scripture called 'sleep', 'may not put the soules of some men at least into such a condition'. Both body and soul could lie dead and inactive to eternity 'which wholly depends upon the will and good pleasure of the first author'. The argument from the immateriality to the immortal sensibility of the soul was thus by men's 'experience dayly contradicted'.[48]

In composing the *Essays*, and in translating Nicole's *Essais*, Locke had recognised the importance of the immortality of the soul to persuading men to be virtuous, even though in translating the latter he registered his awareness that Nicole did not offer a perfect proof of this doctrine. Attack-

---

[47] MS Locke f6, 19–20 and 25–32 printed in *Draft*, 118–19 and 121–3; MS Locke d10, 3; Cudworth, *True Intellectual System* (1678), passim, esp. 745; Smith, *Discourses*, passim; cf. Ayers, 'Mechanism', 239.

[48] MS Locke f6, 25–32 printed in *Essays*, 266–70.

ing in this note the natural proof of such immortality, Locke recognised that this potentially created a problem of man's incentive to be virtuous. He declared, however, that the claim of a natural proof of immortality would not be effective to bring men to 'live comfortable to such a future state' who would not already do so 'out of the undoubted certainty tis that god [exists] . . . and the strong probability amounting allmost to certainty that he will put the soules of men into a state of life or perception after the dissolution of those bodys'.[49]

The approach of this note to religious doctrine and debate from a physical and epistemological angle rather than from an interpretation of Scripture is itself significant. Here Locke's account of the role of reason and of reason as preserved even where assisted by God is important in its legitimation of investigation by reason of even central religious doctrines from a naturalistic epistemological angle when they concerned elements of the natural and physical world. Even more important, however, is the approach of this note to the provision of a basis for morality. The immortality of the soul is a crucial doctrine because it is necessary to convince men to live 'comfortable to a future state'. For Locke, however, as in his comments after translating Nicole's *Essais* in 1676, in his private reflections of 1682–3 morality is apparently to be secured by focusing upon men's naturalistic, probabilistic expectation of sensibility of happiness or misery after this life, upon men's 'supposition' of states of heaven and hell and 'strong probability amounting allmost to certainty' that God would resurrect them. Locke was clearly not here arguing as though he thought that men could *know* that there was an afterlife with rewards and punishments; he was also not arguing as though they should receive the essential information from revelation.

If it was true, the natural proof of immortality from immateriality, which Locke had rejected, offered a secure basis for morality by maintaining an obvious continuity of physical being; if it was a different physical being that was resurrected, it was not clear why men should act morally. This, indeed, was to be the focus of Leibniz's opposition a decade later to Locke's attack in the *Essay* upon the natural proof of the sensible immortality of the soul from its certain immateriality; in the *Essay* Locke was later to argue that the soul was potentially material. For Leibniz this was one indication of Locke's Socinianism: Socinians disbelieved in the resurrection of the same bodies, giving no natural, physical security that one's own being would be resurrected and be that which was rewarded or punished. Locke's final answer to the problem, added to the *Essay* in 1694, was his philosophically famed account of personal identity through

---

[49] *Ibid.*, cf. *Essays*, 173

consciousness rather than physical identity. In his journal in 1683 he importantly presaged this argument in a note that suggested that he had recognised during, or at least very soon after, composition of his 1682 note on the proof of the soul's immortality that he had posed a problem for securing morality, a note which showed how he thought morality could be secured without such a natural proof of immortality. He wrote that 'Identity of persons lies not in having the same numerical body made up of the same particles, nor if the mind consists of incorporeal spirits in their being the same. But in the memory and knowledge of one's past self and actions continued on under the consciousness of being the same person, whereby every man own's himself.' To make a man concerned about his future state a continuity of any particles or spirits was not necessary; the continuity of consciousness was all that was needed. He was later to make clear that men could rely on God for resurrection of the appropriate individual consciousness.[50]

While this was apparently thought by Locke to be satisfactory as an answer to the problem of showing why men could be confident (but not know) that it was they who would be resurrected *if* there was a resurrection which did not involve physical identity, it did not advance any answer to the other problem raised by his previous note, of showing how men could *know* that there would be a resurrection or an afterlife at all. Here Locke's postponement in the *Draft* of consideration of proof of God's rewards and punishments was becoming very serious; the only answer that he had voiced up to this date, apart from the natural proof of immortality, which he had now undercut, was the probabilistic answer of the 'wager' upon morality from 1676. This argument was to be pursued further in the *Essay* and he did not therein show how men could *know* by reason alone that there was an afterlife and reward and punishment for virtue and vice. In the 'Critical Notes' Locke had noted in passing that one purpose of revelation was a 'plain discovery' of the afterlife. That theme was to be expanded in his later works, but at this point Locke was showing no inclination to rely upon it, and while that discovery could provide security for morality among Christians, it was the security of faith and not of knowledge. The problem of knowledge of reward and punishment and an afterlife was to remain a serious and, as we will see, an unanswered problem in Locke's account of morality.[51]

As with Locke's 1680 note on justice, these two notes give no sense of direct Socinian purpose in the construction of his arguments, and no indi-

---

[50] *Ibid.*
[51] MS Locke c34; D. Wootton, 'Locke', passim makes somewhat similar points to those made in this section of this chapter and later chapters, and I am indebted to his argument at significant points.

cation of Socinian reading having prompted his consideration of the topic.
To the extent that any reading seems to have prompted the notes, it was
not reading of *Sociniana*, but of the naturalistic accounts of the soul in the
works of the trinitarians Cudworth and Smith. In the background was
probably also Pufendorf's declaration that only from revelation could men
gain sure information of the immortality of the soul; Pufendorf attempted
to generate the principles of natural law from terrestrial advantages alone
as well as 'hopes' of an afterlife as a result. Locke was reading Pufendorf in
1681, and his conception of the state of nature probably owed much to
Pufendorf. It will be seen later that Locke did clearly express his disbelief in
the resurrection of the same bodies in the late 1690s, and that he did so at a
time when he had come to a broadly Socinian view of original sin and very
probably indeed also of the Trinity, but that up to the 1690s he had apparently still personally believed, unlike most Socinians, in the resurrection of
the same bodies. It will be suggested then that before this expression of
disbelief in the resurrection of the same bodies in the 1690s he was certainly
aware of similar Socinian arguments, but that, as these notes indicate, and
as he was then to claim, support for Socinianism was not then the reason
for his acceptance of these arguments. Together with Locke's note on
God's justice in 1680, these journal entries in 1682 and 1683 make it seem
likely that Locke was moving very significantly in the direction of major
elements of Socinian thought in the early 1680s, but also suggest, again like
the journal note of 1680, that the primary cause of his inclination to these
views was his own naturalistic epistemological investigations rather than
Socinian commitments or even significant Socinian reading. At the very
least, however, on a number of important issues the ground had been prepared so that when he began an extensive reading of Socinian thought in or
after 1683 he found in Socinian views a number of interpretations of Scripture to which he was already inclined by his own epistemological investigations.

Part II

RESISTANCE AND RESPONSIBILITY

5

Locke's moral and social thought 1660–81: the ethics of a gentleman

I

Locke's most important work from the perspective of political scientists and historians, the Second Treatise, was in significant part an exercise in moral philosophy. He wrote much on morality and the possibility of its proof and developed a theory of personal identity to anchor moral responsibility that is still influential today. It is extremely tempting therefore to attempt to associate Locke with a consistent extended and fully articulated moral vision. As we will see, however, Locke never wrote a treatise on anything like the full content of ethics despite the many requests of his friends and his own recognition of the importance of this task. His ethical views changed significantly during his life. His moral thought was often remarkably fragmentary and rudimentary. Several problems that he encountered in the way of establishing a demonstrable ethics were considerable, and he found no way of solving these problems. Locke's thought could perhaps be made more consistent by identification of elements of his works and jottings with the more extended thought about these issues of a number of authors whose work he recommended or translated, including especially Nicole, Cicero and Pufendorf, but he never adopted their thought wholesale, and his recommendations of each were always significantly limited. These and other authors, particularly the Latitudinarians, provided him with laudable accounts of significant elements of a broad morality of which he approved, but he held significant reservations about parts of their arguments and apparently did not see a way to improve as much as he desired upon these arguments. He ended his life by recommending the Bible above all of these works and by composing works of biblical exegesis.

For these many reasons it would be wrong to construct an account associating Locke with a consistent extended and articulated moral vision. The emphases of his thought and the attempts that he made to articulate the content of men's duties to other men are nonetheless central to an understanding of his social vision, and to an adequate understanding of his religious and intellectual identity, not least in showing the path that his thought travelled. They are essential to the explication of his social and moral purposes in composing the Second Treatise and many of his other works. This chapter and chapter seven will therefore survey these emphases and attitudes, describing and analysing both his very fragmentary and his more lengthy attempts to establish a morality, and examining his recommendations of various works by others. These chapters will also attempt to place Locke's ethics within an extended analysis of his social thought and identity.

Locke's moral thought focused especially upon the responsibilities of a gentleman such as himself. Analysis of this area of Locke's thought is therefore absolutely central to an understanding of his social commitments. It is true that Locke's arguments involved a substantial criticism of the current extent of practice by other gentlemen in his society of the duties that he specified, and an idealisation of his personal fulfilment of these responsibilities. Nonetheless, since Locke was himself educated as a gentleman and spent much of his life devoted to educating others to be gentlemen, and since much of his thought was based upon many relatively conventional assumptions about the behaviour of such gentlemen, his moral thought is best understood by commencing with analysis of the moral ethos of gentility in the education of gentlemen in his period.

II

A gentleman in seventeenth-century England was a political agent, a leader of his local community, and one of the ten to fifteen thousand substantial landowners who owned perhaps 65 per cent of the land yet were only about 2 per cent of the English population of approximately 5 million. Free of the need to labour for his own sustenance, he had a status that carried many social obligations and expectations. Service of the community at large was frequently declared to be a major part of gentility. William Harrison's famous description of the foundations of gentility in the late sixteenth century described a gentleman as one who 'studieth the laws of the realm . . . abideth in the university giving his mind to books, or professeth physic and the liberal sciences or [serves] in the room of captain in the wars, or [by] good counsell given at home, whereby his commonwealth is benefitted'. In addition to 'benefitting' the commonwealth directly by their offices, gentlemen were supposed to maintain the networks of beneficence and gratitude that dominated much of early modern English society and helped to hold it together. Among the upper ranks of the society kinship, marriage alliances, friendship, patronage and clientage were all frequently thought of as horizontal and vertical relationships of beneficence and gratitude. Much of gentry society, particularly in the south of England, lived lives dominated by these relationships. The importance of these relationships from the perspective of the upper ranks is indicated by the startling declaration of an early seventeenth-century lord lieutenant to the archbishop of Canterbury that a 'commonwealth' was 'nothing more than' a 'mutual exchange . . . of benefits'. It is revealing of the importance of this discourse that in seventeenth-century England a 'gentleman' was a 'generous' man, that 'ungrateful' was generally used to mean unpleasant, and that ingratitude was frequently viewed as the most degenerate vice; Locke was entered into the matriculation book at Christ Church as '*generosi filius*', the son of a gentleman, and frequently referred to things as ungrateful when he meant unpleasant.[1]

Beneficence and gratitude dominated much of the relationship of the gentry and nobility towards the lower orders in maintaining the traditional social bonds of paternalism, deference and loyalty through considerable patronage, through occasional but important hospitality and through fulfilment of charitable obligations to the 'deserving' poor. As Keith Wrightson has written, 'The paternalistic gentleman, the generous patron, legitimized and justified his position by his actions, in his own eyes, in those of the world and in those of God . . . Such beneficence cost little, and in return a price was tacitly demanded – in terms of deference, obedience and implicit recognition of the legitimacy of the prevailing social order.' In many cases, from the seventeenth century until well into the nineteenth century, such deference was forthcoming. England was very significantly a society of vertical identification and integration throughout this period. As many excellent social historians have indicated, however, expressions of deference from the lower orders towards their gentle patrons occurred perhaps most often in laments for a previous age when such idyllic relations were supposed to have been far more dominant than they now were. There were many moments of resistance and opposition from the lower orders towards the actions of gentlemen in early modern England, and many groups were relatively independent of these networks of co-

---

[1] J. Furnivall (ed.), *Harrison's Description of England* (1877), pt. 1 ch. 5; K. Wrightson, *English Society* (1982), chs. 1–2; idem, 'The Social Order of Early Modern England: Three Approaches' in L. Bonfield et al. (eds.), *The World We Have Gained*, Oxford (1986); P. Laslett, *The World We Have Lost*, Cambridge (1965), passim, esp. ch. 2; R. Kelso, *The Doctrine of the English Gentleman in the Sixteenth Century*, Urbana (1929); Chichester to the Archbishop of Canterbury, 23 October 1612 in 'Letter-Book of Sir Arthur Chichester 1612–1614', *Analecta Hibernica* 8, 5–155 at 56 cited in L. Levy-Peck, *Northampton: Patronage and Policy at the Court of James I* (1982), 90; Edmund Coles, *English Dictionary* (1676) 'Generosity'; Edmund Phillips, *New World of English Words* (1706), 'Generosity'; 'generous'; cf. *ibid.* (1671) and (1678) 'generosity'; [John Somers?], *A Discourse Concerning Generosity* (1693); also the many translations of Cicero's *De Officiis* on 'liberales' = gentlemen.

operation and subordination. Opposition to the massive inequalities that were in part protected by the system were voiced most strongly in the Civil War by a number of politically active groups, including some, but far from all, of the Levellers. The limited numbers of such radicals, the traditionalist and localist views and concerns of the majority of the English population, and the power of Cromwell, a gentleman committed to the social hierarchy, ensured that the social hierarchy was never turned upside down or levelled. To many gentlemen, however, these groups had provided a substantial challenge to the social order of hierarchy and deference, and the threat they had posed was the abiding nightmare of many Restoration gentlemen. The considerable celebration of beneficence and gratitude, and thus of the bonds of deference, in the wake of the Civil War was for many gentlemen consciously opposed to the social egalitarianism seem as being advanced by such groups in the Civil War and Interregnum.[2]

The importance of beneficence and gratitude in gentlemen's obligations and relationships was set out in many works on gentility; by many of the works that formed the standard education of gentlemen, including a host of classical works by authors such as Hesiod, Ovid, Martial, Sallust, Seneca and Cicero; by sixteenth- and seventeenth-century treatises still influential in the Restoration such as Guiccardini's *History of Italy* and *Ricordi*; by many of Shakespeare's plays, including *Coriolanus*, *Timon of Athens* and *King Lear*, each of which was revived in the Restoration with amendments that increased their already considerable stress upon beneficence; and by many contemporary works, especially the plays of John Dryden.[3]

[2] Wrightson, *English Society*, passim, quotation from 58; D. Underdown, *Revel, Riot and Rebellion*, Oxford (1985), chs. 2–3; E. P. Thompson, *Customs in Common* (1992), passim; cf. C. Hill, *The World Turned Upside Down* (1972), passim on some leveller and digger challenges to the social order and the threat and fear that they wanted to turn the world upside-down; and, as a starting-point on the celebration of beneficence after the civil wars, see the many works discussed in J. Wallace, 'John Dryden and the Conception of an Heroic Society' in P. Zagorin (ed.), *Culture and Society from Puritanism to the Enlightenment*, Berkeley (1980).

[3] Seneca, *De Beneficiis* (Loeb Classics, 1935), passim; T. Lodge (transl. and ed.), *The Works of Seneca* (1614), *On Benefits*, passim (significantly placed as the first treatise after the life of Seneca by Lipsius); 81st Epistle; Wallace, 'John Dryden'; Hesiod's *Works and Days*, Martial's *Epigrams*, Ovid's *Epistles*, Xenophon's *Cyropaedia*, and Sallust's *Bellum Jugurthinum*; on Guiccardini's influence in England see in addition to publication of his works themselves also, for instance, G. Fenton, *The History of Guiccardini* (1st edn. 1579), T. Purfoote, *A brief collection of all the notable and material things contained in the Historie of Guiccardini* (1591), R. Naninni, *Civil Considerations* (1601); R. Dallington, *Aphorismes Civil and Militarie* (1st edn. 1613); W. Shakespeare, *King Lear* (1606?), passim and its Restoration revision by Nahum Tate as *The History of King Lear* (1681); idem, *Coriolanus* (1608?) and its Restoration reissue by Nahum Tate as *The Ingratitude of a Commonwealth* (1682); *Timon of Athens* (1607?), passim.

At its height this discourse involved description of beneficence as quite literally the pulse of the society. This sentiment was voiced in one of the two most popular classical works on beneficence throughout the entire early modern period, Seneca's *De Beneficiis*. Between 1678 and 1700 a shortened version of *De Beneficiis*, edited under the title *Seneca's Morals By Way of Abstract* by Roger L'Estrange, went through ten editions. For Seneca, benefiting was a 'fellow like thing; it purchaseth favour'. The exchange of services bound men together into *concordia*. This was a low level of 'friendship', nurtured by the exchange of benefits, but it was absolutely vital because by creating mutual obligations of gratitude and fostering good will it preserved society. For Seneca, a failure of gratitude led to a collapse of society itself since gratitude was quite literally the social cement holding society together and the central form of social interaction. As L'Estrange declared, almost 'the whole business of mankind in society' was said to come 'under this head' of beneficence.[4]

De Beneficiis, written under an Emperor, made beneficence and gratitude the central social and political relationship and said nothing of justice as a virtue or as a political bond. In contrast, a second massively popular treatise discussing beneficence in early modern England, Cicero's *De Officiis*, was written by a republican and emphasised justice as the central political virtue and bond, making society thereby less fragile and making a rather more limited beneficence necessary than in Seneca's view. For Cicero beneficence was nonetheless extremely important and absolutely central to the behaviour of a gentleman (or '*liberales*') since it was 'close akin' to justice, a social virtue promoting the social solidarity of *concordia*, the most noble of actions, and required by men's 'natural fellowship'. For Cicero, beneficence had to be carefully proportioned to the degree of social relationship between individuals and the worthiness of the recipient. Men were said not to be born for themselves, but their country, family and friends all claimed a share. They did, however, have to maintain and develop their estate carefully in order to provide the means for liberality.

---

[4] Seneca, *De Beneficiis*, 19; R. L'Estrange, *Seneca's Morals by Way of Abstract* (1678), passim, esp. 2–3; cf. J. Dryden, *Absalom and Achitophel*, esp. the lines immediately preceding the description of Shaftesbury used as the opening of Haley's biography of Shaftesbury: 'Of these the false Achitophel was first / A name to all succeeding ages curst'; Sprat, *True Account*, passim. The importance of the *concordia* secured by exchange of benefits to the preservation of any form of 'res publica', perhaps given its most influential formulation in Sallust's *Bellum Jugurthinum*, but also noted in works such as Cicero's *De Finibus*, was reiterated time and time again in seventeenth-century tracts, and became proverbial. Cf. generally E. Catherine Dunn, *The Concept of Ingratitude in Renaissance English Moral Philosophy*, Washington (1946), which barely scrapes the surface of an enormous and relatively unexplored subject. I am very grateful to Dr F. Conrad for discussion of this theme.

Beneficence was thus a central use for justly acquired goods and it was a central purpose in their acquisition.[5]

De Officiis was the first classical text to be issued from the printing press, in 1456, and was published in fourteen English and many more Latin editions between 1534 and 1699. Written as a book of moral advice for Cicero's own young son, it was a basic text in the sixteenth and seventeenth centuries at schools such as Westminster and Eton, and at various Cambridge and Oxford colleges. According to Roger L'Estrange in 1681 it was 'one of the commonest School-Books that we have'. John Aubrey and John Toland similarly recognised the predominance of *De Officiis*, with 'the common fashion at schooles' being beginning the ethical education of 'young Gentlemen' with *De Officiis*.[6]

De Beneficiis and especially *De Officiis* were also extremely influential within late seventeenth-century moral philosophy because they were discussed at length in many of the important ethical treatises, including Pufendorf's *De Jure Naturae et Gentium* and Grotius' *De Jure Belli ac Pacis*; we will examine Locke's recommendation of Pufendorf's works later. The books that Robert Sanderson, whose early influence on Locke's thought was noted earlier, had studied most when laying the 'foundation of his great and clear learning' in moral philosophy included Cicero's works, but 'chiefly his *Offices*, which he had read over not less than twenty times, and could ... say ... without Book'. At the end of the century Thomas Cockham noted that 'some of the most eminent Writers in the World have ow'd [a] great part of their Credit to it ... the Sandersons, Grotiuses, Pufendorfs, &co are particularly oblig'd to it for their Skill in determining Moral Cases'. When Jean Barbeyrac, Locke's correspondent, came to write the history of morality in the early eighteenth century he both recommended Locke's works and lauded *De Officiis* as 'without

[5] Cicero, *De Officiis*, passim; cf. chapter seven below.
[6] MS Aubrey, 10 fo. 5ff. at 45r; R. L'Estrange, *Tully's Offices* (2nd edn. 1681), To the Reader, 5; Toland, *Cicero Illustratus* in Cicero, *Tusculan Disputations* (1715), xviii cited in J. Champion, *The Pillars of Priestcraft Shaken*, Cambridge (1992), 183; H. Bennett, *English Books and Readers 1603–40*, Cambridge (1970), 134; W. Costello, *The Scholastic Curriculum at Early Seventeenth Century Cambridge*, Cambridge, Mass. (1958), 42–3; 61; C. Wordsworth, *Scholae Academicae*, Cambridge (1877), 332, 340. For further intimations of the breadth of the importance of *De Officiis*, see the introduction to John Higginbotham's translation of *De Officiis* as *On Moral Obligation*, Berkeley (1967); A. Macintyre, *After Virtue* (1981), 214 on Hume to Hutcheson about *De Officiis*, 17 Sept 1739; G. Gawlick, 'Cicero and the Enlightenment', *Studies on Voltaire in the Eighteenth Century*, vol. 25 (1963), 657–82; N. Waszek, 'Two Concepts of Morality: A Distinction of Adam Smith's Ethics and its Stoic Origins', *Journal of the History of Ideas* 45: 4 (1984), 591–606; B. Willey, *The Eighteenth Century Background* (1967), 21.

Dispute, the best Treatise of Morality, that all Antiquity has produc'd . . . and what comes the nearest to a full and exact System'.[7]

III

John Locke was a gentleman. He published his works as 'John Locke, Gent.' For most of his life he was a landed proprietor in Somerset, inheriting his father's lands in 1661, and thus becoming the exacting absentee landlord of a large number of farmers and labourers; the majority of his correspondence with his relatives in Somerset concerned collection of rents. Declaring gentlemen the most significant members of the English community, he wrote a book on the education of sons of gentlemen that focused upon their moral education both in terms of preparing them for their responsibilities and in terms of advocating for their reading works which endorsed broadly neostoic views of beneficence. He composed and delivered lectures on morality for the sons of gentlemen at Oxford and set them other moral readings, and his two major works, the *Treatises* and *Essay*, were intended as partial contributions to the field of moral philosophy.[8]

Much of Locke's life was lived within the expectations and dependent upon the practical realities of the networks of beneficence and gratitude. He owed both his place at Westminster and his place at Oxford to his father's patron Alexander Popham. Locke described Popham in 1652 as to him 'my god' for his benefits, in a poem that is worth quoting in full:

> To gods proved kind do suppliants most repair
> They kiss the stones, redoubling prayer on prayer.
> Then, when they see their wishes prospering,
> New prayers, new incense are the thanks they bring.
> By these, too, gods are made; do thou condone
> My often asking; thus my god you're shown.

Throughout his life Locke was to argue that we could not know God's real characteristics and attributes, but had to ascribe to him in unlimited degree capacities or actions that were laudable in human life. It is therefore revealing of Locke's social attitudes that God was very frequently lauded as a

---

[7] I. Walton, *The Life of Dr Robert Sanderson* (1678), 179; T. Cockham's *Tully's Offices in Three Books* (1699), preface, vii; J. Barbeyrac, 'An Historical and Critical Account of . . . Morality' in S. Pufendorf, *The Law of Nature and Nations* (1729), esp. 59–71; the work itself, passim, esp. 'On the Common Duties of Humanity'; H. Grotius, *De Jure Belli ac Pacis* (1625), passim. Locke recorded a confused version of the report of Sanderson's debt to Cicero in *Correspondence*, V, 192.

[8] On the importance to Locke of gentility, see Cranston, *Locke*, passim and Laslett, *Treatises*, introduction.

benefactor in his works, a notion reflected rather than challenged by description of Popham as 'my god'. Locke was so deeply indebted to Popham, he declared in 1660, that he was 'a utensill in which' Popham was said to 'have a Propriety'. In other words, he was bound by the duty of gratitude to return services to Popham if he was able; he offered help to Popham's son.[9]

Among the many works saturated with the celebration of the exchange of favours that Locke himself had been made to read at Westminster, almost certainly for the purposes of imitation, were Seneca's *Epistulae Morales* and Cicero's *Epistles*. Locke almost certainly first read *De Officiis* among many of Cicero's works at Westminster, where *De Officiis* remained a part of the curriculum throughout the Civil War. Locke's reading of *De Officiis* would there have followed upon reading of Cicero's *Epistles*, and preceded reading of Cicero's *De Amicitia*. In a notebook that Locke kept on famous authors and works between 1658 and 1667, he noted recommendations of Cicero's *Epistles*, including Montaigne's suggestion that Cicero's *Epistles* were 'full of notable sayeings, and wise sentences by which a man doth not only become more eloquent but more wise, and that teach us not to say well but to doe well'. In order to express his awareness of the obligations of gratitude in his letters to Popham, Locke adapted passages directly from the epistles of Cicero. Locke was to continue to use Cicero's epistles to describe his personal friendships and exchanges of favours with other gentlemen throughout his life, and this was surely central to his later educational recommendations that Cicero's *Epistles* should be set as one of two models for all of the correspondence of gentlemen.[10]

[9] *Correspondence*, I, 6; 96. For a very different reading of the significance of these comments, informed less by the classical debates about beneficence within which Locke largely lived and thought than by the assaults upon dependence of later philosophers such as Adam Smith, see J. Dunn, 'Individuality, Clientage and the Formation of Locke's Social Identity' in idem, *Rethinking Modern Political Theory*, Cambridge (1985). Cf. Hobbes' analysis of the character of the right of God over man by creation that Locke supported: 'The right of nature, whereby God reigneth over men . . . is to be derived, not from his creating them, as if he required obedience as of gratitude for his benefits; but from his absolute power.' Hobbes, *Leviathan*, bk. 2, ch. 21.

[10] Cranston, *Locke*, 29; MS Locke e6, 7r; 11r; 13v; 18v; 19r; 20r; 20v; 21r; 21v; 22r; 39v; 47r; 50v; 52v; 53; 69r; 73r; 74r; 82r (all notes from Seneca's epistles); MS Locke c41 and b7 (the two vols. of Locke's herbarium), passim: I cannot agree with Axtell's declaration that Locke later condemned all of these exercises by his students as time-wasting (*Education*, 40); Locke continued to recommend for epistolary imitation the sources which he had already recommended to his students, including Cicero – on the importance of which, see chapter seven below. For notes by Locke on Seneca's moral teaching see MS Locke f14, 86 (from Balzac): 'All the wisdome of the pagans is containd in Seneca's Epistles'; and *ibid.*, 170 (from Boyle's *Usefulness*): 'Seneca . . . the severe teacher and perswasive recommender of the strictest virtue, whose eminent wisdome made him invited to governe him that was to governe the world, and who so excellently presses [us] to the husbanding [of]

Most of these classical texts, including those of Cicero and Seneca, distinguished between *honestum* and *utile*. If service was undertaken for gain, then it was a bargain and not a benefit, and deserved no gratitude in return. Only beneficence was laudable and only beneficence could unite society through gratitude. What was *honestum* was not what was *utile* in any purely self-interested calculations of the individual, but it was what was *utile* to the society. In the seventeenth century these classical texts emphasising the separation of *honestum* and *utile* in terms of individual motivation were, however, read alongside many Christian texts which suggested that it was legitimate to undertake service of other men for heavenly reward, or which attempted to show how men gained clear terrestrial reward for their virtue. A host of Restoration works by the Latitudinarians emphasised man's motivation to serve others through the enlightened self-interest of gaining heavenly pleasures and through the pleasures and plains delivered by the force of a conscience dependent upon innate ideas, while lauding the works of Cicero and Seneca as central ethical teachings and as better than most works of Christian ethics. The differences between these classical and Christian motivational accounts are extremely important, but here it is just as important to recognise that in their implications for social practice in seventeenth-century England both strongly emphasised the services that men owed to other men and stressed the virtues of beneficence and friendship.

In his first extended writings Locke was concerned with making men serve other men when it was not in their immediate terrestrial interest. In the late 1650s, and especially in the *Essays* in the early 1660s which were composed in Locke's role as censor of moral philosophy in Christ Church, of inculcating moral precepts into students destined as adults to set moral examples for their community as gentlemen or themselves to teach these principles as preachers, he argued for such service without focusing almost completely upon God's rewards. For the remainder of his life motivation through God's rewards was vastly predominant in his thought in providing most men with reasons to serve other men. In the 1659 draft letter to 'Tom', already briefly discussed in chapter one, Locke emphasised the extent to which men were self-interested – in most cases professing religious beliefs solely as a mask of this self-interest – and canvassed the idea that the way to motivate men to be virtuous was through imitation of the best men of the past as well as by making it clearly their interest to serve their fellow men by focus upon God's rewards.

In his letter to Tom, Locke did not give any indication of the extensive-

our time'; cf. also MS Film. 79, 36; Cranston, *Locke*, 20–1; BM Add. MS 28227, 126; MS Film. 77, passim, esp. 38.

ness or character of this duty to serve others, but at many points in the *Essays* Locke described all men as united in friendship and mentioned the duty of 'liberality'. The most extensive assertion of the importance of liberality and friendship came in the final essay, which opposed the notion that 'every man's own interest' was the basis of natural law. Locke argued against the view of Carneades, and of a 'number of people ever since', that all men were driven by their own interests and that it was 'folly' for them to be concerned for others and therefore to act justly against their own interests. The 'basis' of natural law had to be 'some sort of groundwork' from which other 'less evident precepts' could be derived. Pursuit of private advantage alone could not be such a basis.[11]

In an important formulation, Locke declared that a 'great number of virtues, and the best of them, consist only in this: that we do good to others at our own loss'. Almost certainly reflecting the classical works which Locke had been discussing with his pupils throughout his teaching, especially Cicero's *De Officiis*, and pursuing the imitative route to inculcation of virtue mentioned in his letter to Tom, he continued that 'By virtuous actions of this kind heroic men in former times were raised to the sky and placed among the number of gods, purchasing heaven not with a mass of riches brought together from all sides, but with toil, hazards, and liberality.' These men had not pursued their own advantage but the 'public interests' (*utilitati publicae*) and 'the good of all mankind'. None achieved greatness by being 'idle or covetous'. Locke's examples of men to be imitated were men such as Cicero himself, the 'father to his country' for preserving it from tyranny.[12]

According to Locke in these 1663–4 *Essays*, every man pursuing his own private advantage was an impossible basis for the other duties of natural law because all goods were static: 'The inheritance of the whole of mankind is always one and the same.' Goods had been provided for 'use and convenience' in a 'predetermined quantity' which did not expand as the population expanded. No one could become rich without others becoming poorer. In such a situation to make pursuit of private advantage the law would create only competition and fraud. Nothing could be the basis of natural law which would thus destroy 'all justice, friendship, and liberality' and make it impossible for any man to 'give anything to a friend, incur expenses on his behalf, or in any other manner do him a favour out of pure kindness'. This was absurd, 'contrary to reason, to human nature, and to an honourable conduct of life'.[13]

The central thrust of the final essay was thus to support service to friends

---

[11] *Correspondence*, I, 81; *Essays*, 162–3; 200–1; 205–15. Cf. chapter one above.
[12] *Ibid.*, 205–15.
[13] *Ibid.*, 205–15.

and to the public at individual terrestrial loss, describing these as the best of actions. Equally importantly, however, even in this final essay Locke did not deny that the *result* of such service to others, and of obedience to the law of nature when that was against one's immediate advantage, was a greater ultimate utility. He denied only that that ultimate utility was the basis of men's obligations to serve others. Obliquely discussing the role of punishment at the end of the essay, Locke introduced the possibility of such actions being undertaken because they were useful to the individuals undertaking them, recognising that they were useful because the law commanded them and that disobedience to the law would yield punishment. Avoidance of punishment was one of a list of advantages resulting from obedience to natural law, enumerated as 'peace, harmonious relations, friendship, freedom from punishment, security, possession of our property'. In sum, the result of combining service to others with pursuit of one's own advantage when that was legitimate was 'happiness'.

In addition to this clear statement of the resultant terrestrial as well as heavenly rewards for virtue, the essay also noted in passing that only through obedience to the law of nature and consequent security of possessions would men become able to pursue their own advantage. It was declared to be impossible without the law for a man to be 'master of his property and to pursue his own advantage'. Locke thus made pursuit of private advantage alone antagonistic to justice as well as to liberality and friendship. He was clear that theft was a sin against the law of nature, and his concern with property and theft was shown by repeated reiteration of the point. He argued that it was by the law of nature that men's rights to private property were protected, although he gave no indication how men came by such rights to property. 'Justice' was the 'chief law of nature' and the 'bond' of every society.[14]

Concentrating upon the denial that pursuit of private advantage to the exclusion of other concerns and service to others at one's own loss could be the fundamental law of nature, the final essay thus did not clearly delineate how men should strike the balance between service to others and legitimate pursuit of their own advantage within the bounds of the law of nature. It also did not discuss the possibility that pursuing one's own advantage within such legitimate bounds might give the means to be liberal in the first place. Since the *Essays* were also apparently composed to exclude the information of revelation from consideration, they did not thereby exclude the possibility that the addition of the information of revelation would make

---

[14] *Essays*, passim; esp. 140–1; 168–9; 170–1; 190–1; 194–5; 206–7.

clearer still the motivational importance to serving other men of avoiding God's punishment and gaining God's rewards.[15]

The virtue of liberality, or beneficence, was clearly also stressed in Locke's other teaching of his pupils during the early 1660s, as it had been central to his own moral education. The Latin exercises that Locke's students composed for him recognised these virtues and indicate that some of Locke's students were set works by authors for whom those duties were extremely important, such as Seneca. Liberality was also advocated by Locke in a 1666 letter to a former student at Christ Church, John Alford, which importantly made the pursuit of riches necessary to that virtue as well as to personal advantage. He advised Alford that 'though riches be not virtue, tis a great instrument of it, wherein lies a great part of the useful-nesse and comfort of life'. Men were mistaken in being 'too covetous, or too carelesse of it. If you throw it away idly, you loose your great support, and best freind. If you hugge it too closely, you loose it, and your self too.' It was good to be both 'prudent and liberall, provident and good natured'.[16]

This combination of riches as providing the means for the comfort of life of the gentleman to be prudently saved and the means for his liberality is a combination that was repeated throughout Locke's life, and there is nothing in the *Essays'* celebration of service to others at one's own loss that directly contradicts it. Striking another note that was to resound throughout his life, Locke declared that Alford's ancestors had left him 'a condition above the ordinary rank' but that he alone could 'advance your self to it: For tis not either the goeing upon two legs, or the liveing in a great house . . . that gives an advantage over beasts or other men: but the being wiser and better.' He was clear, with a degree of austerity which was also repeated throughout his life, that Alford could gain a 'title' to 'recreation' only through the need for rest from work, and not from idleness. Gentlemen were not to be idle simply because they did not need to undertake manual labour to support themselves, but rather to serve others.

Beyond the duties of friendship and liberality neither Locke's letter to Alford nor the *Essays* gave much indication of men's duties to other men. Included among the duties that were owed to other men were piety towards parents, and nourishment and care of children, both later to be important in the *Two Treatises*, a friendly disposition and speaking well of others in order to preserve their reputation, both later to be declared important in Locke's translation of Nicole's *Essais*, and finally nourishment and consolation in times of hunger and grief respectively. Such charity and con-

---

[15] On pursuing one's own interest in order to gain the means to serve others, see below; note the 'purchasing' of heaven by liberality, p. 166 above.
[16] See no. 10 above; *Correspondence*, I, 200.

solation were only duties when necessitated by circumstance; a love for one's neighbour Locke declared to be a disposition that men had to preserve at all moments. There was thus present in outline here – and perhaps in a deeper commitment that cannot be evidenced but which there is good reason to suspect from the outline alone – an important distinction limiting one's duties to other men and perhaps thereby allowing an arena for prudent concentration on one's own estate. Locke was to make such a distinction explicit fifteen years later, distinguishing duties of active service to other men, which were required only at certain moments, from duties required at all times, such as a disposition to help others whenever that was necessary.

For Locke, these were all duties which could be inferred from the two principles that he was later to claim could be made the foundations of a demonstrable ethics: God's possession of man as his property and the constitution of men's purposively created nature. Locke gave almost no indication in the *Essays*, however, of how these duties could be inferred from his faculties. Citing Aristotle in contending that all things had their own telos, and their own function appropriate to their nature, Locke argued that God had meant men 'to work'. Locke was clear that God had provided men with abilities to provide for themselves the means of existence, and that God had not intended men with 'agile' and able bodies to be 'idle and sluggish'. In this sense the clear implication of Locke's argument was the argument to be spelled out in his later works, that men were obliged to be industrious in their use of the world. Perhaps because his audience were the sons of gentlemen, in the *Essays* this theme did not receive much consideration in any emphasis other than upon man's epistemological duties. Unlike the beasts, men had reason to think and to contemplate upon the world and upon themselves. Sense-experience and reason impelled man to 'contemplate God's works and that wisdom and power of His which they display, and thereupon to assign and render praise, honour and glory most worthy of so great and beneficent a creator'. Man's 'pressing needs' and 'a certain propensity of nature' also inclined man to 'procure and preserve a life in society with other men'. Man was urged by 'an inward instinct' to 'preserve himself', and such self-preservation was an obligation. These three general themes were a completely conventional description of the content of natural law going back to Aquinas and in significant measure to Cicero; Aquinas had declared the three fundamental laws of nature to be the study of God, the preservation of oneself, and living in society. Locke declared that they 'embrace[d] all that men owe to God, their neighbour, and themselves'.[17]

---

[17] *Essays*, 110–13; 156–9; cf. Aquinas, *Summa Theologica*, Ia IIae q94 art. 2 cited in *Essays*, 159.

There is a strong sense in which the element of man's duty which Locke already felt most deeply in writing the *Essays* was the obligation which he was to expend most of his energies in encouraging for the rest of his life: the duty of investigation itself. According to Locke, 'Concealed in the bowels of the earth' were 'veins richly prepared with gold and silver', but not all were wealthy. It was only 'with great labour that those resources' could be brought to 'the light of day'. Men seldom delved 'into themselves' in order to search out 'from thence the condition, manner and purpose of their life'. Only a few made such a 'proper use' of 'the light of nature'.[18]

As Locke pursued many investigations of the capacities of the mind over the remainder of his life, he was, however, to see ever more difficulties in the creation of an ethics unenlightened by revelation than were signalled in the cursory *Essays*, and ever more ways in which a properly-directed mind could achieve greater conveniences of life. He was therefore to place greater emphasis upon this as legitimate because obviously intended by God. After the *Essays*, Locke never composed another work which placed as little emphasis upon the motivation to serve others from the pleasures attached to virtue. The importance of man's hedonic motivations may even have become central to Locke as early as the 1660s. Although the un-equivocal evidence for this being Locke's own view of man dates only from the mid-1670s, not merely did his 1659 letter recognise the importance of making virtue men's interest, but the 1667 'Essay on Toleration' probably involved at its conceptual centre a recognition that men inexorably fol-lowed their view of the path to happiness, and the draft sermon of 1667 focused upon man's hedonic motivations and made God's rewards and punishments central to men's service of other men. As we have seen, according to the sermon man 'could not but follow happiness'; good was simply 'what' tended 'to the advancement of . . . happinesse'; men loved God because of his provision of 'rivers of pleasure'; and from this love to God came a desire to please him which created a love for one's fellow man and resulted in all the good deeds that men did for each other. It is possible that this sermon was instrumental in making Locke emphasise more the pleasures provided by God in motivating men to serve others; it is as important that the overriding purpose of the sermon was to emphasise that men needed to serve other men to be saved and to utilise man's hedonic motivation for this purpose, not to justify solely self-interested behaviour.[19]

Locke thus entered Ashley's household not merely as a gentleman and landowner, but also as a moral theorist who had celebrated as a crucial part of his ethical views the necessity of considerable service to others and

---

[18] *Ibid.*, 134–5; cf. 112–5.   [19] MS Locke c27, 13–28; see chapters two and four above.

who thought of this service very largely in terms of the charity, liberality and friendship that described much of seventeenth-century gentlemens' understanding of their social relationships with each other and of their responsibilities towards the lower orders. He knew little about trade and economics, had apparently thought the amount of goods static when writing the *Essays*, and had then used that as a limitation upon the legitimate pursuit of private advantage. As we will see over the next pages, Locke did come in Ashley's service to recognise clearly that goods were not static, and it appears that as he did so his views of the extent to which men should pursue their private advantage increased, but it is important to emphasise before examining the development of Locke's social and economic views that Ashley's world was dominated by much of the devotion to social hierarchy, the role of the landowning elite, and services of liberality and friendship that already dominated Locke's thought. Ashley had been an opponent of the social levelling that was demanded in the Civil Wars and Interregnum and seen by many more as at least implied in the concentration by the Levellers upon equal natural rights and the proposal of a far more democratic franchise. As a moderate member of Cromwell's Council of State he had supported the imprisonment of the leveller John Lillburne. According to John Evelyn, Shaftesbury had declared to him that he would defend monarchy to his last breath, 'as having seen and felt the misery of being under a mechanic tyranny'. He was an extremely rich landowner who viewed such landowners as the foundation of English society and he supported an ideal of gentlemen who were benevolent, generous and hospitable. He attempted to live as such a gentleman, seeing no contradiction between these ideals and his energetic improvement of the land by new agricultural methods that were undertaken against his tenants' opposition and to their very probable short-term disadvantage. Rioters against Ashley's enclosures in the 1640s were whipped.[20]

Between 1667 and 1683 Locke lived in Ashley's homes in what could have been a subservient position in what was an extremely carefully ordered hierarchical environment; it may at some moments have felt to Locke to be uncomfortably subservient. Locke had to walk behind Shaftesbury's coach in ceremonial procession when Shaftesbury started his term as Lord Chancellor. He was designated as sitting at the steward's table and being

---

[20] Underdown, *Revel*, 22–3; 214. Cf. among many other accounts, Thompson, *Customs*, passim, esp. chs. 2–5. Ashcraft fails to indicate Ashley's early distance from the Levellers, and many other significant elements of Ashley's thought that point in the same direction throughout his life. For a valuable criticism of this failure which reiterates many of the elements of Haley's account of Ashley Cooper, see D. McNally, 'Locke, Levellers and Liberty: Property and Democracy in the Thought of the First Whigs', *History of Political Thought* 10: 1 (1989), 17–40; cf. also Wootton and Ashcraft's debate in *Political Studies* 40: 1 (1992), 79–115.

'allowed' wine during dinners in a household that often seated seventy or more for meals, in a carefully regulated order of service and seating at tables to respect social standing, with the scraps delivered to the poor at the door after the meal. In 1672 as Lord Chancellor Shaftesbury became an earl, and through him Locke came into social contact with many of the most powerful hereditary peers of England. Shaftesbury was extremely wealthy, with an annual income of approximately £30,000 to Locke's several hundred.[21]

Although there are moments when at first sight Locke does seem to have been treated as little more than a servant, as an impoverished gentleman serving a rich aristocrat, Locke had an independent income and status as a gentleman that allowed him to be a guest in Shaftesbury's household rather than a dependent servant. Crucially, their relationship seems generally to have been conceived as a relationship of mutual service, and not merely the service of beneficence and gratitude in the relationship of patron and client with Locke being grateful for far more favours received from Shaftesbury than done for him, but instead very significantly the service of friends sharing thoughts on a basis very close to equality. As we saw earlier, Locke had saved Shaftesbury's life through an operation and thus earned his undying gratitude. He was moreover consulted 'as a friend' on all the important business of a Minister of State, and wrote many of Shaftesbury's most important speeches. Shaftesbury may well have been largely responsible for prompting the crucial transition of Locke's thought from the *Two Tracts* to the 'Essay on Toleration', and he certainly possessed a remarkably forceful intelligence, but Locke was unquestionably aware that he performed services of great importance to Shaftesbury in advising him on many different subjects. The third earl of Shaftesbury, Shaftesbury's grandson and Locke's pupil, later remarked that Locke had frequently been in company with the great Lords at Shaftesbury's house, and had used them with 'a freedom' in discourse that could *only* have been used by a man of 'his genius'. It may have helped considerably in Shaftesbury's appreciation of Locke that while Shaftesbury was an earl he had risen to that title by his own talents from a status as a landed gentleman that was equivalent to that of Locke. It would be possible, indeed, to describe Shaftesbury's life as exemplifying a degree of social mobility within the ranks of gentility which was the reward for industry and ability within a generally stable overarching social hierarchy, and thus as exemplifying very much of what this book will suggest to have been Locke's ideal of gentility. Whether Locke thought this through consciously is debatable; what is important is that in Shaftesbury's household there is no sign that Locke found so uncomfort-

---

[21] Cranston's *Locke*, chs. 9–12; Haley, *Shaftesbury*, passim.

able a subservience that it led him to challenge the system of mutual services and deference in liberality and friendship, already celebrated in his correspondence with Popham, that helped to underpin the hierarchy.[22]

IV

In his first years in Ashley's household Locke's awareness of issues of trade, briefly expressed at the end of the 'Essay on Toleration', broadened substantially. In 1668 Locke wrote a manuscript for Ashley, then chancellor of the exchequer, on the charging of interest on borrowed money, his first, rather rudimentary work on economics. He added a further section to the manuscript in 1674, and he published an expanded and altered version nearly twenty years later in 1692 as the first of three works on economic policy, *Some Considerations of the Consequences of Lowering of Interest and Raising the Value of Money*.

The manuscript of 1668 displayed a new level of economic awareness and the implication of its central argument – that prosperity and land values depended in part upon the amount and velocity of money in circulation – was that Locke had clearly come to see the amount of goods as variable rather than static. Its general description of those who 'contribute at all to trade' as 'landholders, labourers, or brokers' was, however, based very firmly upon agricultural production, very small-scale artisanal production, and hostility to the commercialisation that expanded massively in England shortly after Locke's death, but which was already far more significant in England than in other contemporary societies. Locke opposed the 'multiplying of brokers' – shopkeepers and merchants – because they held too much of the money in their hands 'to the prejudice of trade', and consumed too 'great a share of the gains of trade'. Their behaviour was 'starving the labourer and impoverishing the landholder'. Locke declared straightforwardly that the landholder's interest 'is chiefly to be taken care of, it being a settled unmovable concernment in the common wealth'.[23]

[22] Cranston, *Locke*, 113–14. The balance of mutual service is difficult to capture synoptically. The extensiveness of Locke's service is indicated in the way in which Shaftesbury effectively ordered Locke out of sick-bed in early 1681 to arrange lodging for him in Oxford, and by the delicately ingratiating relationship indicated by the presentation copy of Nicole's *Essais de Morale* for the countess of Shaftesbury that is now housed in the Pierpoint Morgan Library. This has to be off-set considerably, however, by the combination of Locke's characteristics and position noted in the third earl's account of Locke's behaviour – that 'together with his serious, respectful and humble character he had a mixture of pleasantry and becoming boldness of speech. The liberty he could take with these great men was peculiar to such a genius as his.' Cf. Dunn, 'Individuality and Clientage'.

[23] The original 1668 manuscript version of and the 1674 additions to what later became *Some Considerations* are published by W. Letwin in *The Origins of Scientific Economics*

In order to prevent this starving of the labourer and impoverishing of the landholder, Locke proposed the hindering 'as much as is possible' of anyone from selling 'our native commodities but he that makes it'. Land was declared to produce 'naturally something new profitable and of value to mankind'; in contrast, money was naturally 'barren', transferring by compact 'that money that was the reward of one man's labour into another man's pocket'. Nonetheless, because money could 'drive a man's trade', it could be as valuable to production as was land, and loans were permissible if directed to increased production. Without any analysis of the origins of property-holdings, Locke was clear that great inequality of possessions was the foundation of the renting of both land and money. When one man had more land than he could 'manure', and another less, he gained a tenant; when one had more and another less money than was needed, the owner of the money similarly gained 'a tenant' for his money. Indeed, it was the usurer, not the landlord, who usually took less of another's labour: his 6 per cent was the fruit of another man's labour, 'yet he shares not near so much of the profit of another man's labour as he that lets land to a tenant'. There is no sign that Locke thought either situation to be unjust or avoidable.

Locke declared that the manufacture of 'artisans', 'labourers' and clothiers 'deserves to be encouraged'. His argument for this, however, was not that their standard of living needed to be or even could be raised, but that such encouragement was deserved because it was so low that in manufacture 'driven by labour and handicraftsmen' the amount of money that needed to be occupied in production was only one week's wages. This was precisely the proportion he described elsewhere in the manuscript as necessary for labourers who lived 'but from hand to mouth' and needed only to buy 'victuals', clothes and 'tools' purchased from 'other tradesmen as poor as themselves'. There was no sense that the encouragement of their manufacture was intended to reduce their poverty, nor that he thought their poverty capable of significant reduction.[24]

The emphasis upon the interest of the landowner in Locke's economic advice for Ashley was reflected again in the *Fundamental Constitutions*, which Locke helped to compose in 1668 and the one constitution during his life for which he claimed credit in designing. Carolina was to be divided

---

(1963), 273–300; the information in this note is from the 1668 text, 273–96. Letwin discusses the manuscript in *ibid.*, ch. 6. R. Ashcraft discusses the manuscript and debate in *Revolutionary Politics*, 101–4, but gives too much emphasis to the celebration of artisanal labour, does not note Locke's explicit recognition of the poverty of these labourers and downplays the wealth and influence Locke wishes to preserve for the large landowners. Cf. D. Wootton, 'John Locke and Richard Ashcraft's *Revolutionary Politics*', *Political Studies* 40: 1 (1992), 79–98.

24 Letwin, *Origins*, 274; 276; 278; 280; 282–3; 287–8.

into counties, one fifth of each then being divided amongst the eight Lords Proprietors, including Shaftesbury. A further fifth of each county was to be divided in equal amounts between a hereditary nobility composed of one 'Landgrave' and two 'Cassiques'. The Lords Proprietors were thus to own about 96,000 acres of each county between them; a Landgrave 48,000 acres of land in one county. The initial settlers of the colony, on the other hand, were offered up to 150 acres for each adult male, and lesser amounts for servants. In 1671 the Lords Proprietors granted Locke the title of 'Landgrave' in Carolina and the substantial lands that went with it.

The preamble explicitly declared that it was intended to avoid 'erecting a numerous democracy'. The legal and political provisions aimed at achieving a balance between the new aristocracy and the 'people', giving power to the Lords Proprietors and local nobility that was at least equal to the power of the entire rest of the 'people', with local court leets modelled on medieval English practices, and supreme courts with overall jurisdiction run by the Lords Proprietors or their representatives. A Parliament held every two years was to be comprised of the eight Lords Proprietors (or their deputies), each of the barons (three per county, or their representatives), and four elected freemen per county, each of whom had to possess at least 500 acres to qualify for election. Servants and anyone who owned less than fifty acres was denied even the vote. The colony fared badly, and by 1674 Locke was arguing on behalf of the Proprietors that colonists who were in debt should become hereditary serfs in a refounding of parts of the colony, and should be kept from gaining any political power for 'it was as bad as a state of war for men that are in want to have the making of laws over men that have estates'.[25]

It was a similar vision of a polity rightly dominated by great aristocratic landowners that Shaftesbury and Locke supported for England as well as the Carolinas in their arguments against absolutism composed in the mid-to-late 1670s, shortly after this colonial correspondence, as in the *Letter From A Person of Quality*'s declaration that the powers of the House of Lords must be maintained, because 'the power of a peerage' was necessary to forestall a standing army. In a case contemporary to the *Letter*, Shirley vs Fagg, Shaftesbury supported the role of the peerage as essential to 'the interest of the nation . . . for, let the House of Commons and gentry of England think what they please, there is no prince that ever governed without nobility or an army'. One or the other was necessary to prevent degeneration into 'a democratical republic'. Since the King was 'king by law, and by the same law that the poor man enjoys his cottage' it was the concern of 'every man in England', even one who had 'but his liberty', to

[25] *Works*, IX, 175–93; Haley, *Shaftesbury*, 243–4; 251–7; Cranston, *Locke*, 120.

defend both the King 'in all his rights and prerogatives' and the House of Lords as 'an essential part of the Government' established by the same law.[26]

In running the Carolinas via an extensive correspondence as Secretary to the Board Locke emphasised strongly the best utilisation of land by employing both the best agricultural techniques and the labour of the 'industrious people' whose voyages to Carolina were financed by the Lords Proprietors. The same attitudes prevailed towards Ashley's extensive lands at home. In the grounds of his country estate Ashley experimentally farmed fruit trees. When Locke accompanied Ashley into the country in 1674 they took with them a large number of books advocating and specifying the mechanisms for better exploitation of the land, including Gervase Markham's *English Countryman*, the same author's *Country Farmer* and William Blith's *English Improver, or a New Survey of Husbandry*. When Locke came back from a lengthy trip to France in 1679 he brought home for Shaftesbury a treatise on the cultivation of vines and olives. His journal for the three years that he spent in France was filled with entries on the differing crops and methods of farming in the different regions of France. Locke had thought the Somerset gentry ignorant and foolish on visits there from Oxford in the 1650s, and life with Ashley can only have intensified considerably that feeling; much later in life Locke was to compare the knowledge of the lazy and ignorant landowner in the country unfavourably with that of even the poor in major cities. He suggested that such landowners would justly lose their wealth and status and that others – though not the poor – would gain it through their industry.[27]

In the early 1660s, in collaboration with experimentally minded friends in Oxford such as Boyle and Sydenham, Locke had become acutely aware of the advances that could be made through experiment and through imitation of the best techniques and technologies used by other societies, particularly in medicine, but also more broadly in production of many items. Ashley aided Locke's experimental awareness by providing him with equipment and membership of the Royal Society. Locke's support for such methods in the *Essay Concerning Human Understanding* was to help to advance their usage in the eighteenth century and thus to aid in the formation of the wealth of some who were not gentlemen. Very many of those supporting trade and inventions in England in the eighteenth century, as in the seventeenth century, were themselves gentlemen, and most others

26 For a broader discussion of these themes, see McNally, 'Locke', passim; cf. Wootton, 'Locke', *Political Studies*, 79–98.
27 Haley, *Shaftesbury*, 218; 249–51; *Correspondence*, I, 197; Cranston, *Locke*, 108–9; Lough, *Locke's Travels*, passim; Wood, *John Locke and Agrarian Capitalism*, passim; Wootton, 'Locke', 79–98.

bought land as soon as they could and then gained both security and status and perpetuated rather than challenged the domination of English society by the landed gentry. As committed to experiment and trade as Locke and Ashley were in these years, and as important as Locke's investment in shares, bonds and private loans was to become, it is important to underline that their main income during their lives came from land and office, and that their favoured experimental methods were almost entirely based upon the harnessing of land to its best advantage – that is, to the best advantage of the landowner. Locke's central intended audience for the *Essay* were surely the many gentlemen who needed to be taught to reason correctly and to be industrious; having done so, they would have the means to perpetuate their dominance of the society.[28]

V

The development of Locke's awareness of the extent to which the sum of goods was variable, and of his beliefs that industrious labour on unused land and the use of the best techniques on ploughed land could raise production enormously, together made him emphasise the production of conveniences as a good use of man's purposively given faculties and thus helped to develop a very strong commitment to the view that the pursuit of terrestrial or civil 'happiness' from such conveniences was required by God. This belief may have been further underpinned by a more firmly articulated vision of men as hedonically motivated, although as we have seen Locke probably held such a view at least in outline and perhaps much more substantially as early as 1667. By the time of Locke's 1674 'Excommunication' happiness loomed very large indeed in his descriptions of the aims of both civil and religious societies. His analysis of church and state now started with the declaration that 'There is a twofold society, of which almost all men in the world are members, and that from the twofold concernment they have to attain a twofold happiness; viz that of this world and that of the other: and *hence* arises these two following societies, viz religious and civil.'[29]

The end of religious societies was 'the attaining of happiness after this life in another world'. Civil punishments were inappropriate because they were ineffectual: no temporal punishment could persuade a man to turn away from the way he thought led to 'everlasting happiness or misery'. They were also 'unjust' since in matters of 'faith and religious worship' no other man was hurt 'in any concernment of his'. Such 'civil happiness' was

[28] N. Wood, *The Politics of Locke's Philosophy*, Berkeley (1983), *passim*; Wootton, 'Locke', *Political Studies*, 79–98.
[29] *The Life and Letters of John Locke*, ed. P. King, II, 108–19.

to be secured by laws, but these could be passed only when the 'doing or omitting' of any moral or indifferent thing had a tendency 'to the end above mentioned'. 'The end of civil society' was only 'civil peace and pros- perity, or the preservation of the society and every member thereof in a free and peaceable enjoyment of all the good things of this life'. It is important that for Locke in this comment the preservation of the society remained as important as the peaceable enjoyment of the things of this life. We have by now seen at length that the duty of preserving peace and one's society was central to Locke's thought from his early life in the 'storms' of Civil-War and Interregnum England. It was central not merely to the politics of the *Two Tracts* in 1660–2 but also to the explicit denial in his tolerationist works of rights of resistance even when rights to liberty of worship were violated by the magistrate. Locke declared in passing, in an important note in his journal in 1677, that one very important use of man's knowledge was 'to live in peace with his fellow men and this . . . he is capeable of'.[30]

A very strong stress upon men's hedonic motivation, the duty and diffi- culty of preserving peace among men, and the need for hedonically moti- vated men to be persuaded to serve other men through liberality and civil- ity in order to keep the peace, were the linked themes of Locke's translation of the third of Nicole's *Essais* in 1676, by far the longest of the three that he translated. This *essai* identified many sources of disruption of the peace; all of these ultimately resolved into men's concentration upon their own pleasures and upon the world, motivated by self-love. Nicole has become famous among scholars searching for the origins of utilitarianism and a secular justification of a commercial society for having described society as joined together by men's wants and necessities, by their self-interest founded in their self-love. For Nicole, simply by being prudentially directed in an englightened calculation, men's self-love led to considerable co-ordination, building societies which provided many conveniences. Viewing men as being considerably corrupt, for Nicole such men created economically thriving but vicious societies. Even though the third *essai* that Locke translated recognised this possibility of basing society in calcula- tions of self-interest, however, it simultaneously and at greater length emphasised both the threats to peace that were based on self-love, and two forms of service of other men that were not founded on vicious calculations of terrestrial self-interest. It exhorted men to concentrate upon the service of God, and upon the service of other men as a way of serving God, both by giving them reasons for such an orientation in terms of heavenly reward, and by great stress upon the difficulties of gaining the kind of terrestrial rewards that self-love made men think their due. It also defined

---

[30] King, *Life and Letters*, ed. II, 108–19; *Draft*, 84–7.

the forms of virtuous behaviour that would secure the preservation of the peace in descriptions of the duties of considerable service to other men through gratitude, and especially through civility, a virtue which was given extensive discussion. These were duties that according to Nicole were required of Christians because of their obligation to 'goodness' rather than because of calculation of terrestrial benefit.

In 1704 Damaris Masham recorded that Locke had thought that 'civility' was a duty of far greater importance than was generally recognised, and had recommended Nicole's third discourse as one of the two best works on the subject. The other work that she then recorded that Locke had recommended was Whichcote's recently-published *Sermons*, which Locke had formerly 'heard', and her comment suggests that Locke had made the recommendation of both works in the recent past, almost thirty years after he had translated Nicole's *Essais*. It should not need emphasis after the previous chapters that up to this point in his life Locke saw contention over religious opinions and the attempt to force those religious opinions upon others as the central causes of the disruption of the peace. It was against religious contention and censure that Whichcote had developed his celebration of the virtue of civility. It was against many of the attitudes about one's opinions that led to such religious censure and contention that a significant portion of Nicole's argument for civility was directed. By 1676 Locke was committed both to the duties of bringing other men to salvation if at all possible and to the need for religious toleration. Men were not to command others to their own religion, but they still had a considerable duty of 'charity' to persuade them of its truth. We have seen that Locke advocated soft usage and courtesy in the 'Essay on Toleration' in 1667; we will see in chapter seven that Locke celebrated the duty of civility in various of his own manuscripts and works of the 1690s, not least in an extensive discussion in *Some Thoughts Concerning Education*, in a manner reminiscent of Nicole's *Essais*. In an undated note on morality which was probably composed between about 1676 and about 1680 Locke enumerated the major elements of morality apart from justice as liberality and civility, the topics of most of Nicole's third discourse.[31]

In now turning to give a fuller account of the description in the third discourse of the need to focus upon God, of the duties of liberality and civility, and of the ways in which being civil kept the peace, it appears very likely indeed from all of the varied intimations that have just been cited of Locke's agreement with Nicole's definition of the virtues, and particularly from his intention to publish his translation in service of the cause of 'truth

---

[31] On Nicole see N. Keohane, *Philosophy and the State in France*, Princeton (1980), 293ff.; Wootton, *Locke: Political Writings*, 107ff.; le Clerc, *Life of John Locke* (1706), 28; MS Locke c28, fos. 139–40.

and virtue' that Locke agreed with much in Nicole's arguments about the content of virtue; about its distinction from vice and its simultaneous recognition that vicious men predominated in the world; that vice contributed much in the way of conveniences to the society; and that if men were truly enlightened in their terrestrial calculations they would perform almost the same duties that Christians would perform, although not because of the Christian obligation and motivation to perform moral actions that Nicole's *essai* celebrated most: 'goodness' and celestial reward. It appears very likely that in delineating the arguments set out in Locke's translation of Nicole's third discourse one is specifying a very considerable part of Locke's ethics of service to others both in 1676, and for the rest of his life, especially but not merely in terms of civility.[32]

VI

Citing the biblical text that men were to seek the peace of the 'city whither I have made you to go', the third of Nicole's discourses that Locke translated suggested that all of the societies of which men made a part and which influenced the 'temper of our minds' were 'so many cities where we pass our pilgrimage'. On the most extended level this meant that the 'world is our city' because there was a chain tying 'the whole race of men together by their mutual wants'. Men were more particularly 'denisons' of the country in which they were born and lived. Men were also in 'some sense citizens of ourselves, and of our own hearts; where our divers passions, and multitude of thoughts, are the people with whom we are to converse'. For Nicole, the scriptural injunction to seek peace referred to all of these cities. Men were to seek 'the peace of the whole world, of our own country; of the place of our dwelling; of our society; and of ourselves'. Nicole held that there was little that individuals could do to help the world except pray. In contrast, there was much that could be done by men in order to preserve the peace of their particular society. Nicole argued that men were brought together into societies by the necessities of life. These needs plainly evinced that these societies were appointed by God's will, since it was God who had put them into men. His next step was to argue that 'Whatsoever then serves to the preservation of society, comes within that appointment.' The law of nature obliged each part 'to contribute to the preservation of the whole' and to this also 'every one ought to contribute his part, since every one derives from it great advantages'.[33]

For Nicole, love and respect were the bonds of society and necessary to its preservation. There were many things never bought and sold, the 'traffic

[32] *Essays*, 254 (15 August 1676).   [33] *Discourses*, 3.1.1.3.1.2; 3.1.90–1; 99.

of kindness', which love alone could 'purchase'. The law of 'charity' further required men 'to serve and oblige our neighbours'. The 'common obligation' of Christians was 'to do others all the good they can'. Scripture gave Christians 'charge of other men, to serve them all the ways we can'. Men owed to each other 'debts' of service, and owed gratitude when they had received services. Since gratitude, love and kindness were gained by serving other men and were the bonds of society, this serving of other men preserved the society as well as fulfilling one's duty to serve others. Love and respect were also gained and preserved by being civil to other men. At various points Nicole described civility as gaining love; at others, as merely avoiding hatred and thus preserving mutual kindness. In both senses, civility helped to preserve the peace.[34]

Civility was especially important because most quarrels between men came from 'our indiscreet stirring of other men's passions'. Men were not loved because they lacked 'the skill' to make themselves 'beloved'. The 'science' of avoiding giving offence was 'a thousand times more useful than all those which men bestow so much times and pains upon'. Men took pains to understand how to make the world and creatures useful to them, but little to understand how to make men useful. This study was for Nicole encouraged by reason as a rule of 'worldly wisdom', or terrestrial self-interest. It was also, however, required by faith and religion, Christ having bestowed two beatitudes on peace. St Paul had published a law expressly commanding peace with all men, and inculcated few precepts so often as those 'which concern the regulating ourselves in our conversation with others', encouraging a 'soft answer', being 'beloved by words' and – with phrases that were very reminiscent of Locke's conclusion to the 'Essay on Toleration' – 'soft words' and 'courtesy'. Emphasising the soteriological centrality of preserving peace through civility in conversation, for Nicole a 'peaceable tongue' was 'the tree of life', because it 'procures us quiet, both in this life and the other'.[35]

Civility was also vital because by preserving friendship it allowed the performance of other services. Although men did not have to serve each other at every moment, there was not a single moment when men were not obliged to do their part to remove the obstacles to serving each other: their duty to serve others extensively at certain moments made preserving friendship and peace with them necessary at all moments. Men's duty to serve others 'all the ways we can' obliged them to live peacefully with them since peace opened the door to the heart and aversion shut it. Even where an internal peace of unity of judgement and opinion among men was not

---

[34] *Ibid.*, passim, esp. 3.1.12; 48; 85; 90; 3.2.78.3.1.7–10; 3.2.1–10; 3.1.64–7.
[35] *Ibid.*, 3.1.7–10; 3.2.1–10; 3.1.64–7.

possible, men had to take care not to fail in the outward circumstances of civility. If men stood at a 'distance' from us because of incivility then they 'disrelish even truth, that comes from our mouths; and oppose right itself, when we appear for it'. It was impossible to serve others at all times with edifying discourses, but as long as one preserved the peace with them one could serve them by one's exemplary patience, modesty, and other virtues. Men were particularly to be blamed when their neglect of peaceable conversation disabled them from exercising the 'more spiritual part of charity' to another man 'in doing good to his soul'.[36]

Nicole was clear that only 'an overflowing charity' could fully and properly maintain one's peaceful, friendly relations with one's neighbours, which seemed for Nicole to mean a 'charity' so extensively concerned with the good of other men that it could result only from God's grace. Nonetheless there were many 'natural' means to help to maintain friendship with one's neighbours, among which was study of the ordinary causes of divisions in order to prevent them. One had to avoid giving offence, particularly by not 'contradicting their opinions, or crossing their passions' since men were 'naturally fond of their opinions'.[37]

Religious opinions were both the most difficult of all opinions to contradict, and those that men were most likely to attempt to force on others. Since men ought to have been humbled by religion it ought to have made them 'less conceited'. The true effect of prayer was 'to take us off from too great a reliance on our own judgements, and to dispose us the more willingly to be informed by others'. By prayer one could gain an inclination to learn the truth and the 'grace to make good use of it'. It often, however, did the contrary, as men who were diligent in prayer presumed that they understood more, and as they dressed up their 'false or ill-grounded opinions with reasons of conscience'.[38]

In face of all of these difficulties Nicole recommended that men should demean themselves 'with all the compliance that truth and charity can allow'. They certainly had to avoid the 'inbred ill-nature' which made them forward to contradict others, proceeded from a great 'corruption of nature', and tended to the disturbance of the society. Men should learn to bear with the errors of others without disturbance, 'To the end that we may never oppose them, but with a sincere desire, and when there is hope of doing good'. Christ himself, although aware of men's many errors, had only corrected those about God or their salvation – a point that Locke was later to emphasise in his *Reasonableness of Christianity*. There were only two ways of persuading, by reason or by one's authority, and since men adopted their opinions largely because of the belief in them of those that

---

[36] *Ibid.*, 3.1.13–16; 18–19.   [37] *Ibid.*, 3.1.20–3.   [38] *Ibid.*, 3.1.24–30; 34–41.

they were close to or those in authority, if one knew that one did not have the position significantly to influence others, then one could believe that God dispensed one from the duty of persuasion.[39]

This did not mean that dissent in judgement was never to be voiced. Men had to learn to discourse in a way 'so mild, so humble, so taking, that nobody may be able to take offence at them'. Men practised this art when they applied to great men for favours; it ought to be practised to all who were 'brethren', as though they were 'superiors, and grandees in the kingdom of Jesus Christ'. Men had to learn to contradict with submission and civility. Particularly to be avoided were dogmatic discourses delivered in a 'magisterial way'. Instead, men were to season their discussions with doubt, recognising that they could be wrong. This was because 'every one would have leave to be judge of his own opinions, and not have them forced upon him, without his own approbation. And the mind naturally swells against those, who would take from it the liberty of examining.' Men were to keep silent where no good could come of speaking, and to speak only with humility. There are many senses in which Locke's religious and epistemological works, designed to prevent the wars of religious opinion and the attempts to enforce these opinions on others, were to follow these instructions, couching their criticisms of current religious views in extremely humble terms in works like the *Essay*, and silent on disputed issues which seemed especially difficult to challenge, as in the silence on the Trinity of the *Reasonableness*; it is especially necessary to be alert to the depth of the changes that Locke was promoting in these works despite their proclaimed humility and their significant silences.[40]

To keep the peace it was not necessary to gain all other men's affection and love, but it was crucial to avoid their hatred. To do this, men had to be just and civil. This was difficult because men wished to be tyrants over their fellow men. If this was not always apparent it was only because they had been taught by self-love to veil their passions under the name of justice, pretending that they contended only for truth when what they really wished for was power. In addition to those things which were owed to men by the law of justice, properly called a law, others were owed by the 'law of decency', which was founded on the common consent of men who had agreed to condemn those who opposed its standard. Thus men had to pay certain civilities by the custom of a country which were not taken notice of by the laws of the country. Among these requirements by the duty of civility was the respect to be paid to the social status that individuals held within a society.[41]

---

[39] *Ibid.*, 3.1.27–30; 34–48.   [40] *Ibid.*, 3.1.38; 50–1; 54; 56; 63.
[41] *Ibid.*, 3.1.70–4; 83.

Nicole was clear that men's self-love made very difficult indeed the performance of the many extensive services of liberality, gratitude and
'charity' to others, and the civility that was necessary to gain love, maintain respect, and preserve the peace. Each man therefore had to attempt to
control his self-love in order to be able to perform these duties that kept
peace with other men. Internal peace came especially from 'governing well
our thoughts and passions', which also contributed to the peace of the
society 'there being little else, besides our passions, that disturbs us'.
Enmities and hatred grew from small beginnings and extinguished charity.
It was not enough in order to preserve the peace, internal and external, to
avoid giving offence to others by civility; it was also necessary not to take
offence when others failed to provide what you thought you deserved.[42]

While 'Nothing but the grace of God' could lessen men's concern with
their treatment by their fellow men, 'since grace works upon us as men,
and makes use of means' men were to 'furnish our minds with considerations, that may shew us the vanity of those beloved objects we so much set
our hearts upon'. Men were frequently concerned with gaining the good-
will of other men because of the influence that their affections had on their
temporal concerns, from hope, fear, or interest. According to Nicole, men
ought not to claim such love as a right, but rather to think that aversion
was their due, considering their faults. More importantly, they should
recognise that the love and esteem of others was never gained by compulsion. Men in general hated the covetous, selfish, proud and presumptuous.
For Nicole, men should do others all the service that they could, without
expectation of return, doing this only for God's sake. A man who thus
governed himself 'by that unerring and unchangeable rule the will of his
Maker, and the obedience he owes Him' would thereby avoid the hatred of
men, and in many instances he would also gain their love, without making
it his business.[43]

Such a man would also thereby gain his own internal peace when others
failed to love him or to return his services, as they were sure to do since
they were self-loving and corrupt men. Concern with gaining the love of
men was a force that 'captivate[d]' men, a snare that entangled them. Men
were bound to show gratitude towards each other, but this gratitude only
contributed to peace when it was founded in celebration of God's making
use of other men to convey his blessings to us, and not in an interested
desire to gain further services that would lead to antagonism as men's
self-love overvalued their services and gratitude to others and undervalued
the services and gratitude that they received in return. Any failure to return

---

[42] *Ibid.*, 3.1.4–6; 3.2.1–12; 3.1.64–7 and passim.
[43] *Ibid.*, 3.2.13–29; 3.2.36–47; 50; 57–9.

gratitude was described not as a cause for anger in the benefactor, but for rejoicing. When men received no return from men they were for Nicole even more certain to receive a return from God. 'Nothing' was said to show 'more the decay and utter extinction of faith in Christians' than their 'displeasure' with those who did not return services. Men's glory in services done for them was a robbery from God; the lack of return was a blessing since it stopped men from being concerned with men, and gave 'a title to an inestimable treasure'.[44]

Men were to serve other men in order to serve God, not to look for terrestrial recompense. Men should love nothing but the law of God. They were not to seek their 'satisfaction, content, and reputation, amongst the creatures'. Only by avoiding such immersion in the vanities of the world, while performing all their duties in the world, could they secure either terrestrial reward itself, or, far more significantly, the lasting and far greater heavenly rewards. This focus upon God was necessary because men were mainly corrupt and motivated by self-love; they would not return appropriate gratitude and services even when served with the intention of gaining these. The only 'way to a sure, unmoveable peace' in the mind was therefore 'wholly to possess it with the love of God: So that it may regard nothing but Him; desire to please Him alone; and place all its happiness only in obeying His will'.[45]

For Nicole, then, the only way to gain a secure reward, and to fulfil one's duties in the world, was to pray for grace to assist one's endeavours and to help oneself all that one could by focusing upon the service of God. This was very clearly for Nicole an extremely difficult task, but one could at least try to live life as a pilgrimage to a better place by understanding that only by doing this could one preserve the peace of one's society and even of one's self, and that if instead one focused upon the world both terrestrial unhappiness resulted and heavenly rewards were lost. He declared that 'if they [men] would but think a little on it, they would find, that faith and reason are agreed in the greatest part of the actions and duties of men'. The courses proposed by religion were as necessary to 'quiet in this world' as to 'felicity in the other'. Indeed, most of the things that religion proposed would lead to more temporal as well as ultimate happiness than the things that ambition and vanity made men pursue. The broad obligation to live at peace with other men was taught as 'an essential duty of Christian piety; and reason presses it, as most necessary to our particular interests'.[46] Here for Nicole terrestrial self-interest and morality have almost the same circumference even without requiring the argument that John Wilkins con-

[44] *Ibid.*, 3.1.81–9; 3.2.47–8; 50.   [45] *Ibid.*, 3.1.1–12; 3.2.47ff.; 78.
[46] *Ibid.*, 3.1.4–6.

structed in England to come to a very similar conclusion, that it was from adding in the costs of a guilty conscience that virtue became terrestrially rewarding. This is largely, however, because peace was elevated in Nicole's work over all other interests and because celestial rewards were never far from Nicole's mind, and not because of a focus upon or celebration of terrestrial advantages.[47]

It appears likely that Locke read various works by Gassendists, perhaps including works by Gassendi himself, and Pascal's *Pensées*, at about the time that he was translating Nicole's *Essais*. It is possible that their stress on men's motivation by the pleasures reinforced still further Locke's move towards a fully-articulated hedonic psychology. In mid-July 1676 Locke composed an important note in his journal declaring that almost all of the ideas produced by body and mind were themselves accompanied by two other ideas: pleasure and pain. Pleasure and pain were 'two roots out of which all passions spring and a centre on which they all turn'. If removed, the passions 'would cease'. Knowledge of the passions was therefore to be obtained through considering pleasure and pain and what produced these. Locke turned here not to an account of men as sinfully passionate because they were dominated by a corrupt self-love, but instead, as so often, to a naturalistic account of men based upon commitment to God's bounty. God had 'framed the constitutions of our minds and bodies' in such a way 'that several things are apt to produce in both of them pleasure and pain, delight and trouble, by ways that we know not, but for ends suitable to His good-ness and wisdom'. Thus most men were pleased by the smell of roses, by liberty, and by the acquisition of knowledge. Some things existed 'whose very being delights', such as one's children. Love was nothing but having in the mind the idea 'of some thing that is able ... to produce ... delight or pleasure in us'.[48]

Men were said to desire to preserve the things which produced pleas-ure, and in this sense they loved things such as fruit trees. Although the discussion of friendship in Locke's early *Essays* had not explicitly denied that there was a pleasure in service of others at one's own loss in money or expenditure of effort, it had contended that friendship was based upon service to others at one's own loss and honourable precisely as it involved an expenditure that was not balanced by any other gain, such as the pleas-

---

[47] Cf. J. Wilkins, *Of the Principles and Duties of Natural Religion* (4th edn. 1699), passim, esp. 312–13; 326–7; 330–40; 372–87 and the preface, iii–vii, by John Tillotson.

[48] See E. A. Driscoll, 'The Influence of Gassendi on Locke's Hedonism', *International Philo-sophical Quarterly* 12 (1972), 87–112; R. Kroll, 'The Question of Locke's Relation to Gassendi', *Journal of the History of Ideas* 45: 3 (1984), 339–61; J. Tully, 'Governing Conduct' in E. Leites (ed.), *Conscience and Casuistry in Early Modern Europe*, Cam-bridge (1988), 12–71 at 38–9; *Discourses*, 266–70.

ure of serving others, and certainly one that was not balanced by a calculation of pleasures that would be received by good offices done in return. In sharp contrast, in this note Locke argued that among the things which men were said to desire to preserve because of the pleasure that they gained were friends 'with whose good offices or conversation they are delighted, endeavouring and wishing their good, thereby to preserve to themselves those things that they have pleasure in'. Love of friends was mainly love of 'those good things' that they provided. This 'amor concupiscentiae' was 'only provident'.

Locke's exhortation to John Alford in 1666 to be provident *and* good-natured had apparently by this point undergone a transformation towards the notion that when most men were being good-natured, when they were giving to their friends, they were even then being 'only provident'. Locke did still importantly continue to divide this kind of 'providential' love or good nature from true love of others, however, writing that there were 'some wise minds . . . of a nobler constitution, having pleasure in the very being and the happiness of their friends, and some yet of a more excellent make delighted with the existence and happiness of all good men, some with that of all mankind in general, and this last may be said properly to love'. The clear implication was that these men, concerned with the happiness of men in general, were few in number, but that in their love of all men, it was they who were the more noble; Locke was obviously not generating an egoistic morality of purely strategic concern for others from the self-interested motivation of the majority of men, although he was recognising the prevalence of that morality and motivation in the lives of most men.[49]

Love could not be generated by reason, but only by 'the union of the mind with the idea of something that has a secret faculty to delight it'. Hatred was merely the opposite passion to love, except more virulent because 'the sense of evil or pain works more upon us than that of good or pleasure; we bear the absence of a great pleasure more easily than the presence of a little pain'. The extension of the ideas of pleasure and pain created the ideas of happiness and misery. That which produced pleasure was good, the *bonum jucundum*; that which procured us this was *utile* and *honestum* and good only because 'ordained by God to procure the *jucundum*'. Temperance was a good because it served to procure health and ease in this world and happiness in the other; gluttony an evil because it did the contrary. Repentance and sorrow were 'good' for some largely because they were 'a means and way to our happiness'.

The mind had ideas of pleasure that it could achieve by effort, and this

[49] *Ibid.*, 266–70 and 263 n. 7.

created an uneasiness in the mind, a 'desire' to obtain this pleasure. However, desire consisted largely of pain, of the impulse to remove some present evil. Men had no clear ideas of pleasures not felt by themselves. Men were 'immersed in the body and beset with material objects' and so had 'very little sense or perception of spiritual things'. This meant that men had only a 'very imperfect' idea of the happiness which the 'blessed enjoy and such as we are capable of'. Locke did not pass by the topic of eternal happiness, so central to the wagering on an afterlife that he had already suggested in his journal was a basis for all rational creatures to be moral, without noting that this lack of knowledge of spiritual pleasures did not stop it being the 'greatest folly' not to endeavour to obtain this happiness.[50]

It is important to note that when Locke became clearly committed to this account of men's motivation he did not describe it directly or indirectly as the consequence of the Fall and as axiomatically sinful; for Locke, God had 'framed the constitutions of our minds and bodies' in such a way that some things were 'apt to produce in both of them pleasure and pain, delight and trouble, by ways that we know not, but *for ends suitable to His goodness and wisdom*'. It was not being motivated by the passions that was wrong; indeed, that was unavoidable. As Locke was to make clear in his later writings, it was in being motivated to the wrong actions by the passions that man sinned, by not focusing upon God's rewards and instead pre-ferring terrestrial pleasures, allowing their reason to be led by the passions. Nicole's argument made men's general motivation by self-love far more explicitly sinful, and men's need for God's grace to be 'charitably' con-cerned with others far more clearly necessary.

After translation of Nicole's *Essais*, Locke was to focus increasingly upon men's God-given hedonic motivations, turning more and more to a naturalistic and Socinian religiosity. He increasingly made hedonic moti-vations legitimate bases from which to infer much of the content of man's obligations, and thus countenanced a greater legitimacy for men's pursuit of terrestrial happiness. Within a few years he was explicitly to view the capacity to protect a greater pursuit of happiness as a major advantage of English government over the French absolutism that Nicole supported, and to move further in the direction of an account of men's duties as strategic terrestrial self-interest.

Locke never, however, sought to construct an account of men's duties based upon their hedonic motivations alone, and while the reasons for this are unclear, it seems likely that it was in part because he never managed to separate himself from the intense sense in his translation of Nicole that the virtuous would not be properly rewarded in this life, except through the

---

[50] *Ibid.*, 266–70.

limited fact of peace. Such a conclusion was probably undergirded for Locke as for Nicole by the importance to them of the exchange of services, by belief that other self-interested men would not return appropriate gratitude or services, and by a consciousness of the limited happiness that could be attained by most men in this life.[51] Instead of seeing a way to advocate service to others as purely terrestrial self-interest because strategically self-regarding, once Locke had become clearly committed by the mid-1670s to a fully articulated strongly hedonic theory of motivation it seems to have been considerably more difficult for him to give adequate motivational reasons for the extensive service of others that he thought necessary than it had been when he wrote the *Essays* and could exhort the gentlemen and sons of gentlemen in his audience to serve others at their own loss because such behaviour was acting in keeping with the 'best' of human nature, because it fulfilled their role of being 'generous' men and thus being 'gentlemen', and because it imitated the 'bravest' or best men. Translation of Nicole's third *essai* was in a major sense the first work – or the second, if the 1667 sermon was by Locke – of a series that Locke would write to attempt in varying degrees to answer the problems of showing how men could be made to perform their duties of service to other men, given that they were obliged to serve other men extensively, that they were hedonically motivated, and that such services were not clearly individually terrestrially rewarding; heavenly rewards were to play a very large role in all such accounts.

On 1 September 1676, a few weeks after completing his preface for his translation of Nicole's *Essais*, Locke wrote in his journal that 'Men, by the common light of reason that is in them, know that God is the most excellent of all beings, and therefore deserves most to be honoured and beloved, because He is good to all his creatures and all the good we receive comes from Him.' This is not a statement that God wll be loved because he was good to men in the sense of provoking man's *amor concupiscentiae*, but a statement that God deserves to be loved for his free beneficence. Locke continued that 'By the same light of nature we know also that we ought to do good to other men, because it is good for ourselves so to do.' Again Locke made clear that the notion here was not the terrestrially instrumental one that could have been extrapolated from his journal note of mid-July diagnosing men's motivation by pleasures and pains, that men should serve those who bring them pleasure, but that this was good for men because 'Men are capable of it, it is the only tribute we can pay to God

---

[51] *Essays*, 266–70. *Discourses*, passim; cf. Dunn, *Political Thought*, chs. 15ff.; Wootton, *Locke: Political Writings*, 107ff.

for all the good we receive from Him, and it cannot but be acceptable to God, being done for his sake, and to men whom we cannot but know that He has the same kindness for as for us.'[52]

The focus here is slightly different from that of Nicole's *Essais*: Nicole had repeatedly argued that it was the law 'of charity' and of the obligations of Christians set out in Scripture that obliged men to serve each other as extensively as they could in order to serve God, and he did not attempt to provide a naturalistic basis for this obligation beyond recognising that self-interested, self-loving men needed society and owed service to the society because they derived great advantages from it and that God had placed these desires in men. Locke has combined the argument from a natural theological principle, that men should serve other men because God loves those other men equally to them, with Nicole's emphasis upon Christians serving God through serving men. Locke's note does not emphasise God's rewards for service, providing a clear basis for the obligation to such service, but not for the motivation to perform such service. It seems likely, however, that so soon after translating Nicole's *Essais* and composing his notes of July 1676 Locke thought that men should be motivated correctly to serve others by the rewards that God provided for such service, and that many others would be viciously motivated to such service by calculations of their terrestrial self-interest. There is again no sign that he thought an entirely terrestrially self-interested morality an acceptable way to define and defend men's duties.

Locke continued with a statement of confidence that he was to reiterate throughout the rest of his life, although he did not indicate whether God's grace was involved in gaining knowledge: 'They, then, that consider that they ought to love God and be charitable to men, and do to that purpose seek to know more of Him and His mysteries, that they may better perform their duty of love to Him and charity to their neighbours, shall no doubt find all that God requires of them to know, and shall run into no damnable errors.' Those who instead made themselves 'their own god and their own end', and who would not accept truths of natural and revealed religion until they had had all objections removed, sought truth unreasonably and would not find it. There is surely already here at least a tacit recognition of the problems that Locke was already recognising as plaguing his attempts to found a demonstrable morality given his removal of its basis in innate ideas and an immaterial immortal soul. Locke continued that God designed knowledge 'not as an improvement of our parts and speculations, but of our love of Him and charity to our neighbour, and that increase of our knowledge should make our lives better'.[53]

---

[52] *Essays*, 281.   [53] *Essays*, 281.

Again Locke ranged this declaration of men's ability to know their charitable duties of love towards others alongside stress upon their hedonic motivation and epistemological duty to pursue their own happiness. Early in 1677 he declared that 'Our minds' were 'not made as large as truth nor suited to the whole extent of things'. Recognition of this state of our minds was not to discourage endeavours but to redirect them. Men could attain knowledge by confining investigation 'within those purposes and direct-[ing] it to those ends which the constitution of our nature and the circumstances of our being point out to us'. Men were in an estate where they needed 'meat drinke cloathing and defence from the weather and very often physick'. Their 'conveniences' demanded 'a great deale more'. Labour 'art and thought' were needed to allow man anything above 'a poore and miserable life' Utilising the information gathered during his extensive correspondence with the West Indies in the early 1670s, Locke recorded that a 'sufficient instance' of the difference in provisions made by the application of inventions and discoveries was that 'large and firtill part of the world the west Indies' where the people lived 'a poore uncomforable laborious life with all their industry scarce able to subsist'.

Locke argued that there was a 'large field for knowledge proper for the use and advantage of men in this world viz to find out new inventions of dispatch to shorten or ease our labours'. The mind of man was well fitted for this although 'the essence of things their first originall, their secret way of workeing and the whole extent of corporall beings be as far beyond our capacity as it is besides our use'. Man's faculties were 'given him for . . . use' which must 'necessarily' be to 'procure him the happynesse which this world is capable of', nothing else but 'plenty of all sorts of those things which can with most ease pleasure and variety preserve him longest in it'. This could provide 'ease safety and delight' which were 'all the happynesse he is capeable of'. Men were concerned to have 'a plenty of the good things of this world and with life health and peace to enjoy them'. It is important to note here the ethical importance of the pursuit of peace with other men to the Locke whose thought was still shaped massively by the need to avoid further civil and religious war – that this was a concern as great as plenty – and yet to note simultaneously that the enjoyment of a plenty of the good things of life to the greatest extent that this can be achieved by the direction of men's intelligence had by this point become stressed as a central reason for such peace to matter.[54]

Locke then commenced his discussion of the knowledge necessary for happiness in *another* life with the declaration that 'it seems probable that there should be some better state' to which men could attain since a man that 'hath all that this world can afford . . he is still unsatisfied uneasy and

[54] *Draft*, 84–7.

far from happynesse'. Behind Locke's argument that there had to be another life because men were uneasy in this once again stands both a tacit reluctance to adopt a theory of solely terrestrial self-interest and a notion that God was bountiful, not making men to be unhappy. Gaining of this other life depended upon the 'ordering of ourselves in our actions in this time of our probationership here'. According to Locke, the acknowledgement of a God led directly to this view 'and he hath left soe many footsteps of himself, soe many proofs of his being in every creature as are sufficient to convince any who will but make use of their facultys that way'. Locke offered, however, no detailed account of these proofs, declaring instead that 'those only doubt of a supream ruler, and an universall law who would willingly be under noe law accountable to no judg, those only question another life hereafter who intend to lead such a one here as they feare to have examined and would be loath to answer for when it is over'. This was something that Locke suggested that he would always be convinced of 'until I see that those who would cast off all thoughts of god heaven and hell lead such lives as become rationall creatures or observe but that one unquestionable morall rule doe as you would be don to'. Locke unfortunately did not expand upon the meaning of this rule nor suggest a basis for it.

It was at least 'probable' that there was another life wherein men would have to account for their actions in this life, from which flowed the 'main concernment of mankinde and that is to know what those actions are that he is to doe what those are he is to avoid'. For Locke, men were furnished with faculties able to discover and 'his understanding seldom fails him in this part unlesse where his will would have it soe'. If men took a 'wrong course' it was 'most commonly because he willfully goes out of the way or at least chooses to be bewildered'. There were 'few if any that dreadfully mistake if willing to be in the right'. Locke thought it safe to say that 'where any one endeavoured to know his duty sincerely with a designe to do it scarce ever any one miscarried for want of knowledg'. It was necesary in order to be happy in this world and the next only to know 'the effects and operations of naturall bodies within our power, and of our dutys in the management of our owne actions as far as they depend on our wills ie as far also as they are in our power'. Men had light if they used it to distinguish good from bad actions. It was agreeable to God's goodness and our condition that we could obtain the conveniences of life and 'as proper to fill our hearts and mouths with praises of his bounty'. That his greatness exceeded men's capacity was 'the better to fill us with admiration of his power and wisdome'. Natural and moral knowledge could be obtained 'by moderate industry and improved to our infinite advantage'.[55]

[55] *Ibid.*, 87–90.

In an undated manuscript entitled 'Morality', probably composed between 1676 and 1680, Locke united the argument that there was a probability of an afterlife in this 1677 note in his journal with comments upon the content of ethics which are reminiscent of the third of Nicole's discourses that he had translated in 1676. According to 'Morality', morality was 'the rule of man's actions for the atteining happynesse'. The 'end and aime' of 'all men' was described as 'happynesse alone'; it was declared that therefore nothing could be a rule to them 'whose observation did not lead to happynesse and whose breach did not draw misery after it'. Good was what created or increased pleasure; or what took away or diminished pain. All men desired the enjoyment of happiness and the absence of misery, and men were said to act 'only . . . for what they desire'. Men were described as capable of 'some degrees of happynesse and great degrees of misery in this life'.

Locke argued that there was at least the possibility of life after death. He laid down two 'evident' truths: Man 'made not himself nor any other man', and 'man made not the world which he found made at his birth'. 'Therefor', Locke argued, 'noe man' had any more right to any thing in the world than any other. He made no reference at this point to the natural equality of men to be inferred from their faculties or characteristics, and gave no consideration to the possibility that God might have declared that there was some form of natural subjection among men. Locke argued that if all things were held in common, 'want rapin and force will unavoidably follow in which state as is evident happiness cannot be had which cannot consist without plenty and security'. For Locke in this manuscript, unlike the *Two Treatises*, to 'avoid this estate compact must determine people's rights'. If compacts were not kept, then 'want rapin and force' would result, unless one man were 'stronger and wiser then all the rest', which Locke implicitly denied. If compacts were kept, then 'Justice is established as a duty and will be the first and generall rule of our happiness.' Justice was the 'greatest and difficultest duty'. According to Locke, once established it would not be hard to establish other virtues 'which relate to society and so border on justice but yet are not comprised under direct articles of contract such as Civility, Charity Liberality'. Civility was the only one of these duties that Locke defined, and in a phrase reminiscent of the argument of Nicole's *Essais* it was declared to be 'noe thing but outward expressing of good will and esteem or at least of noe contempt or hatred'.[56]

---

[56] MS Locke c28, fos. 139–40 in 'Locke and Ethical Theory: two MS pieces' (ed.) T. Sargentlich (ed.), *Locke Newsletter*, v, (1974), 26–8; discussed among others by Tuck, *Natural Rights Theories*, 169; Colman, *Moral Philosophy*, 194–9; D. Wootton, 'John Locke: Socinian or

There is no sign that Locke pursued this method of establishing these
duties beyond this note, and he was to discuss a very different basis for the
duty of justice and men's equality in the *Two Treatises*, but there are
several very important features of this manuscript. Most obviously, it is
fragmentary and remarkably rudimentary, with Locke at least considering
a conceptual centre for ethics being provided by happiness. It is important
that the content of the ethics that he was intending to describe consisted of
justice, liberality, charity and civility – a list with significant echoes of his
earlier *Essays* and his translation of Nicole's *Essais*. It is equally important
that he was again attempting to accommodate the potentially extensive
duties of service to others of civility, charity and particularly liberality with
a strongly hedonic account of motivation in an account based around
consent and compact and the advantages of government in securing terrestrial happiness rather than in an account explicitly focusing on these as
required by God's will (although the manuscript is so fragmentary that
Locke may not have conceived of the full exercise of founding morality in
this manner). Perhaps most important of all in terms of Locke's view of the
content of ethics is that this account communicates a strong sense that his
commitment to the specific duties to be defended preceded rather than
followed from an articulated notion of how they were valuable due to their
importance in a terrestrial hedonism. The manuscript seems to suggest, in
other words, that Locke was attempting to think out how to base duties to
which he had long been committed in an overarching account of their role
in facilitating happiness, and not that he came to think that these were
duties as a consequence of an elaborated view that they facilitated terrestrial happiness and therefore were obligatory.

Most of the stresses by now apparent in Locke's ethical thought were
reiterated in several 1677–8 letters to and manuscripts for Dennis Grenville,
an anxious Anglican clergyman wandering around France (who may well
have been keeping track of Locke because of Locke's political affiliation
with Shaftesbury). Grenville's letters to Locke expressed a series of agonies
over not being able to fulfil his duties to God satisfactorily either in the
amount of time he spent in his devotions or in the ways in which he used
his leisure. Locke's replies consistently set out to reassure Grenville, and set
out again a strong view of God's goodness to man. In March 1677 Locke
wrote that God was merciful towards men, considering their 'ignorance
and . . . frail condition'. God 'delights not to have us miserable either in
this or the other world, but ha[s] given us all things richly and to enjoy'.
Man became tired from labour and his mind was 'naturally tender of its

Natural Law Theorist?' in J. Crimmins (ed.), *Religion, Secularization and Political
Thought: Thomas Hobbes to J. S. Mill* (1989), 39–67; P. Kelly, 'Locke and Filmer: Was
Laslett so Wrong After All?', *Locke Newsletter* 8 (1977), 77ff.

freedom' and sought variety. Repeating the austere argument that he had expressed to John Alford in 1666, Locke declared that men had a 'title' to recreation that they gained by wearying themselves in labour. Men were to secure their main duty 'which is in sincerity to doe our dutys in our calling as far as the frailty of our bodys or mindes will allow us'. This was all that God required of us, and we had a right to recreation, as long as this recreation was designed 'to put us in a condition to doe our dutys'. It is important to note at this point that even though some scholars have seen it as Calvinist, Locke's description here of men's 'calling' was not tied to any particular theology; later in life it was to be described in terms antithetical to Calvinist thought.[57]

Between March and May 1677 Grenville's enquiries prompted composition of a lengthy manuscript by Locke on 'Study'. This reiterated many of the views stated in Locke's earlier journal notes, stressing that men's existence was short and the subjects of knowledge vast; importantly it focused upon the need for study to be directed towards those areas which would yield service to others. Men were in a state 'of mediocrity'. A man therefore had much to do to clear the 'many doubts in religion', to establish to himself 'many rules' in morality, and to 'master his unruly desires and passions'. This should lead men to concentrate their studies on those things that were useful to them. The end of knowledge was 'practice or communication'. History was to be studied only for examples of living well and, once the rules of morality had been mastered, to show students that men 'really were' sinful.

Heaven was men's 'great business and interest'. The knowledge which would 'direct us thither is certainly so too, so this is without peradventure the study that ought to take the first and chiefest place in our thoughts'. Men's 'quiet prosperous passage' through this life, being happy in themselves and useful to others, made 'prudence' an important but clearly subsidiary object of study. The essences of 'substantiall beings' were in contrast 'beyond our ken'. Men were suited to 'the improvement of naturall experiments for the conveniences of this life, and the way of ordering' themselves 'so as to attain happiness in the other – ie moral philosophy, which, in my sense, comprehends religion too, or a man's whole duty'. Here the casual stress upon morality as the essence of religion, with no

---

[57] *Correspondence*, I, 326–9; 357; 366; 372; 374; 377; 411–12; 416; 421; 426; 447; 458. On Grenville keeping tabs on Locke see Ashcraft, *Revolutionary Politics*, 135–6. Dunn's *Political Thought* interprets Locke's views on the 'calling' as part of his Calvinist familial values. As Tarcoy has pointed out, however, his association of this view with Locke is very heavily dependent upon secondary sources rather than Locke's thought and is unpersuasive as an account of Locke's thought, which did not conflate occupation and vocation in a Calvinist providential manner: N. Tarcov, *Locke's Education for Liberty*, Chicago (1984), 127. Cf. *Third Letter*, in *Works*, VI, 342–3; *Paraphrase*, 1 Cor. 7:20.

mention of faith, is startling, but again the comment is insufficiently elaborated to gain any sense of the relationship between Locke's view of the
ability to perform moral actions and God's grace or faith. Study was also a
duty owed to God as the fountain and author of all truth 'and truth itself'.
Men were bound to search for truth with a 'mind covetous of truth'. The
intimation of employing the passions in searching for truth is significant;
Locke is apparently already attempting to indicate how men motivated by
pleasures and pains can be made to follow the path of duty by directly
harnessing their passions. The harnessing of the passions for the cause of
virtue was to become a central topic of his thought in the 1690s, as we will
see in chapter seven.

A year later Grenville was still pleading with Locke for reassurance.
Locke wrote that this continued anxiety was because Grenville wrongly
thought that men were 'obleiged strictly and precisely at all times to doe
that which is in it self is absolutely best'. God's infinite goodness, however,
took account of men's frailty. Love to God and charity to our neighbours
and ourselves was at all times 'indispensably necessary' but as long as men
kept these 'warme in our hearts, and sincerely practice what they upon
occasions suggest' they had a great latitude 'in the ordinary actions of our
lives'. Men found it difficult to know what was absolutely the best in their
'State of Mediocrity' and so God had 'compassion on our weakness and
knows how we are made'. He did not require us to consistently do what
was the best. Men were to avoid sinning, to do their duties to others at the
necessary times, and to furnish themselves always 'with habits and dispositions to those positive dutys in a readynesse against those occasions'.[58]

Still Grenville plagued Locke. Locke was by now becoming annoyed,
but his next reply set out in usefully summary fashion a number of important elements of his thought. He repeated his stress upon God's goodness
and compassion, and joined with these the arguments that he had set out in
his survey of the capacities and purposes of men's faculties in early 1677.
Men, he wrote, were not born in heaven but on earth where they· needed to
provide much for their preservation by 'care and labour'. God had put us
into a condition where we were 'obleiged to use all meanes to preserve
ourselves' by employing in search of the means of preservation 'the greatest
part of our time and care'. Locke then importantly declared that this was
especially true of the civilized world where men had to keep up their 'rank
and station' in order to be in a condition 'of doeing that good and performing those offices requird from one in that station'.

The duty of preserving one's ability to do good to others has been shown
to have been important in Nicole's *Essais*, where it was focused upon

[58] King, *Life*, I, 171–203; *Correspondence*, I, 374.

maintaining peace with and civility to others in order to be able to guide them to the paths of virtue and piety. Here Locke has connected this notion to that of keeping up one's position in society. The notion that one had to be industrious in order to maintain the ability to help others, so unfamiliar in descriptions of Locke's individualistic egoistic intentions on the basis of the *Two Treatises*, will be shown in later chapters to have been important to Locke on many occasions during his life, right up to his final work, the *Paraphrase upon the Epistles of St Paul*. Locke argued to Grenville that men also had to worship God with addresses to him of thanks prayer and resignation; and our concernments in an other world make it reason, wisdome, and duty so to doe'. Here the combination of interest and obligation suggests that at least at some moments for Locke 'reason' was little more than calculation of interest, although celestially-focused interest. For Locke, men were born 'with dispositions and desires of society, we are by nature fitted for it, and Religion increases the obligation'. Presumably the notion of obligation here is that men's dispositions were given to them by God and so following them was obligatory, as Nicole had argued in the *Essais*; it is exceedingly unlikely that Locke was trying to say that desires created obligations in themselves.

Presuming that Locke meant by commonwealths specifically political societies, the most usual contemporary meaning, Locke then took a line very different from that which he was to take in the *Two Treatises* just a few years later: Men were 'born members of commonwealths, beset with relations, and in need of friends, and under a necessity of acquaintance', requiring of men 'the mutuall offices of familiarity friendship and charity'. There is no necessary contradiction here between Locke's attempt in 'morality' to find a basis for society and justice in 'contract' among men born with no subjection; it was quite possible to argue that society originated in consent and contract, but that succeeding generations were born into political society, and that was the view held by almost all of Locke's contemporaries who argued that society had originated in consent. Unfortunately for the attempt to tease out of Locke's scattered comments upon morality a fully coherent account, Locke did not then expand upon the character or extent of the duties of familiarity, friendship and charity, but turned instead to one of the points on which Grenville had asked for advice, arguing that men could not spend all of their time in devotions to God. Recreation was necessary because men were like watches 'that have gon till their force is spent' and then 'move to little purpose, if not wound up again'. In a note in his journal in July 1678, 'Lex Na[tur]a', Locke was similarly reticent about the content of men's duties towards others in society, while being clear about their need for society and their duty to preserve the society itself. He declared that 'If he finds that God has made him and all other men in a state wherein they cannot subsist without society and has given them judgement to discern what is capeable of pre-serving that society, can he but conclude that he is obliged and that God requires him to follow those rules which conduce to the preserving of society.'[59]

In mid-July 1679 Locke developed these themes further. God had 'given man above other creatures . . . a knowledge of himself which the beasts have not'. This placed him 'under obligations that the beasts are not, for knowing God to be a wise agent he cannot but conclude that he has that knowledge . . . for some use and end'. Locke continued with a passage that extrapolated not merely the duties of worship and justice, but also appar-ently those of service to others, from the analogy between God and men and a father and his family:

> If therefore he comprehend the relation between father and son and find it reason-able that his son whom he hath begot (only in pursuance of his pleasure without thinking of his son) and nourished should obey love and reverence him and be grateful to him, he cannot but find it much more reasonable that he and every other man should obey and revere love and thank the author of their being to whom they owe all that they are. If he finds it reasonable to punish one of his children that injures another, he cannot but expect the same from God the father of all men when any one injures another, if he finds it reasonable that his children should assist and help one another and expects it from them as their duty will he not also by the same reason conclude that God expects the same of all men one to another

Locke again did not give any substantial indication of the content of men's duty to 'assist and help' one another, but it was here clearly distinguished from not injuring one another. This might merely indicate the duty to help by preventing others from injuring one's fellow men – a notion that we will later encounter in Cicero's thought and in Locke's annotations upon it – but such a notion is far more likely to have been expressed as 'protecting' one another than as assisting and helping one another, and so a more extensive form of service is very likely to have stood behind Locke's com-ments. It should be noted, for reasons that will become clear when discuss-ing the *Treatises* later, that Locke had here drawn a direct analogy between the duties of terrestrial families and the duties of all men as like a family under God.[60]

At some point in 1681 Locke made a further attempt to define virtue, once again using the notions of serving others and self. He wrote that 'Vertue as in its obligation it is the will of God, discovered by naturall reason, and thus has the force of a Law, so in the matter of it, it is nothing else, but doeing of good either to your self or others, and the contrary here unto vice is nothing else but doeing of harme'. He continued that 'thus the

[59] *Correspondence*, I, 426; MS Locke f3, 201–2.   [60] MS Locke f3, 201–2.

bounds of Temperance are prescribed by the health, states and the use of the time: Justice, truth and mercie by the good or Evil, they are like to produce, since every body allows one may with justice deny another the possession of his own sword, when there is reason to believe, he would make use of it to his own harme'. Men in society were in a 'farr different state' than 'when considered single and alone', and therefore the 'instances and measures of vertue and vice are very different'. If a man was a member of society, then temperance might 'according to the Station he has in it, receive measures from reputation and example'. The result was that 'that which was no vicious excess' in a 'retired obscurity' became one where people thought ill of it 'because by lessening his esteem amongst them it makes a man incapable of haveing that Authority and doeing that good, which otherwise he might'. Esteem and reputation were 'a kind of Moral Strength whereby a Man is enabled to do as it were by an augmented force, that which others of equall natural parts and natural power cannot doe without it'.

A man who lessened his reputation therefore did 'as much harme' as if he weakened his natural strength and this was 'equally vicious as doing harme to himself'. According to Locke, 'if well considered' this would give men 'better boundaryes of vertue and vice than curious questions stated with the nicest destinctions that being always the greatest vice whose consequences draw after it the greatest harme'. Locke continued that many things became vices in society which would not have been vices in a 'solitary condition', explicitly naming polygamy. In passages which are far more redolent of the thought of contemporary *libertins* than they are of contemporary Chrstian ethics, he declared that he could see nothing vicious in having children by several women 'separate from society since no body is harmed'. It became a vice of 'deep dye', however, 'in a socieitie wherein modestie the great Vertue of the weaker sex has often other rules and bounds set by custom and reputation than what it has by direct instances of the law of nature in a solitude or an estate seperate from the opinion of this or that societie'. If a woman brought a 'blemish' to her reputation she might lose the comforts of a conjugal settlement and 'therewith the chief end of her being, the propagation of mankinde'.

There is no indication of what prompted this remarkable reflection from Locke, which bore his initials to indicate that it was his considered opinion, and its dating to 1681 does not indicate a month. There is, however, at least a possibility that Locke was here pondering the arguments of Dryden in his late-November *Absalom and Achitophel*, because this poem began with a defence of ancient polygamy in order to defend Charles' notorious promiscuity, including his fathering of the illegitimate duke of Monmouth, by claiming that it reflected royal virility and had been legitimate behaviour in 'pious times, ere priestcraft did begin'. According to Dryden, the priests had imposed a later morality of monogamy because of their desires for power over society. If this was indeed what prompted Locke's response, his reflection on the changing standards of virtue propounded by priests managed both to endorse in effect Dryden's attack on 'priestcraft' and yet simultaneously to condemn Charles for a vice of 'deep dye' in blemishing the reputation of women in society. Locke was to be far happier with the morals of the court of William and Mary than with those of Charles, and we will see much later a shift in at least the rhetorical thrust of his tolerationism from arguing that morality should not be enforced by the magistrate to arguing that debaucheries and immorality should be discouraged by the magistrate's manners and prohibited by the magistrate's laws that may in part simply reflect this change of monarchs. Indeed, his personal moral austerity may well have been a major reason why Locke desired another monarch than Charles to rule in 1682–3, and a very minor reason indeed why he became willing to countenance armed resistance.

As importantly, as David Wootton has argued, Locke's specific argument here and the very nature of the reflection is markedly different than his argument in the Second Treatise about the need for a stable family life even in the state of nature. It will be suggested in the next chapter that the Second Treatise had not been significantly composed until early 1682 and perhaps even later; if Locke's note on virtue was in part a response to Dryden in late 1681 that would add a layer of support for such a dating of the Second Treatise, which will shortly be supported for entirely separate reasons. More generally, Locke's comments on morality even in this 1681 note seem far more the result of a series of broad commitments than of an articulated moral vision, more to be unfinished jottings and attempts to build small parts of such a coherent moral vision than elements of any secure, consistent position. They appear far more likely to have been musings preceding the Second Treatise than thoughts contemporaneous with or following that work. In 'Virtue' it is the morality of serving others in society that is Locke's primary concern, and its distance from the morality of a state when men were 'alone' – a state apparently far closer in conception to the solitary state that seemed to be countenanced as preceding political society in 'morality' than to the state of nature described in the Second Treatise and emphasised there to be similar to the political state of men.[61]

---

[61] MS Locke Film. 77, 10; see Wootton, *Locke: Political Writings*, 72–3 for an interpretation of Locke's view as the 'conventional view of the state of nature' expressed piquantly by Dryden but not composed by Locke in response to Dryden. Wootton argues that 'Virtus' precedes the support for a stable family life introduced in §86ff. of the First Treatise. He argues that this section (86–95) was added after Locke wrote the section 'Why heir?'. Even

In one note in mid-1681 Locke did construct a note far closer in tone at first sight to the form of argument of the Second Treatise, although not contradictory to the morality of 'Virtue' when examined closely, a note frequently cited by Locke scholars because it identifies politics as including a branch of moral philosophy. He declared in this 1681 journal note that he 'that has a true Idea of God of him self as his creature of the relation he stands in to god and his fellow creatures and of Justice goodness law happynesse &c is capeable of knowing moral things or having a demonstrative certainty in them'. In 'Some Thoughts Concerning Reading and Study For A Gentleman' in 1703, Locke similarly identified one part of politics as concerning the 'original of societies, and the rise and extent of political power' and recommended Hooker's *Laws of Ecclesiastical Polity*, Pufendorf's *De Jure Naturae et Gentium*, and the *Two Treatises*. In June 1681 Locke was reading both Pufendorf's *De Jure Naturae*, bought in France in the late 1670s, and Hooker's *Ecclesiastical Polity*. He was surely then reflecting upon the ways in which a political argument against Filmerian absolutism could be built as a part of moral philosophy with the demonstrability held to be possible in his epistemological drafts of the *Essay* (but not necessarily therefore composing this work).[62]

Pufendorf's works provided a further account of men's duties that allied justice and beneficence as the central requirements of 'sociality' or 'sociability', and Pufendorf explicitly and repeatedly cited both *De Beneficiis* and *De Officiis* in construction of these arguments. Asserting that these principles were law only as commanded by God, he discussed them centrally as precepts that could be derived from men's self-love, desire for self-preservation, and individual weakness, asserting their necessity for men's 'safety'. Pufendorf's discussion of men serving other men depicted this in significant part as strategically other-regarding activity – in serving others through beneficence one secured the assistance of these men in the pursuit of self-preservation and gained returned services. Although services to others and gratitude in return were vital to peace and central duties that

<hr/>

if this is accepted, it is equally possible that the argument from §86–95 is an addition that Locke composed later than 1681 as well as later than 'Virtus' and that 'Virtus' was thus a note of as late as late 1681. Cf. n. 39 chapter six below.
[62] MS Locke, f5 fos. 77–83, printed in *Draft*, 116–18. This passage has been the subject of much discussion; I agree with the interpretations offered most recently by Tully, *Discourse*, 29–30; R. Grant, *John Locke's Liberalism*, Chicago (1987), ch. 1; *Education*, 400 ('Some Thoughts Concerning Reading and Study'); *Correspondence*, I, 355 (Stringer promising to obtain books that Locke has asked for, including Pufendorf 'De Jure Naturae et Gentium* and *Officium hominis*'); Lough, *Travels*, 255 ('Pufendorf de Cive' in a list of 1678); MS Locke f5, 62, 67 on purchase of Pufendorf's *De Jure Naturae* in May 1681; cf. MS Locke d10, 26v; also the recommendations of Pufendorf by Locke, *Education*, 294; 400; MS Locke f5, fos. 77–83, printed in *Draft*, 116–18; *Treatises*, 1.10; cf. J. Yolton, *Locke and the Compass of the Understanding*, Cambridge (1970), ch. 8.

men owed to other men they were not enforceable by political authority. They were 'imperfect' duties. Political society was created by men because without it there was co-operation between men but not security from injury.

Pufendorf firmly distinguished his discussion of these principles as precepts of natural law from discussion of 'moral theology'. Natural law was based on reason alone; moral theology in contrast imposed its precepts of morality based upon revelation and backed them by rewards and punishments which depended upon a belief in the immortality of the soul, a belief that for Pufendorf could only be anchored by the information of revelation. Although Pufendorf argued that Christians would also perform the duties of sociability that he was advocating, like Nicole he firmly distinguished his establishment of terrestrially-focused, strategically other-regarding sociability from the requirements of 'goodness' and expectation of reward in the 'life to come' for which Christians would perform these duties. Locke's 1681 journal note, as we have just seen, declared that moral certainty depended centrally upon the ideas of God and of justice, *goodness*, law and happiness.[63]

Locke had purchased Pufendorf's works in France in the late 1670s, and may even have met Pufendorf in Paris. In *Some Thoughts* Locke recommended that the sons of gentlemen should read Pufendorf's *De Officiis Hominis et Civis* and in both *Some Thoughts* and 'Some Thoughts Concerning Reading and Study for a Gentleman' he further recommended Pufendorf's *De Jure Naturae et Gentium* as the best work for instruction 'In the natural rights of Men, and the Original and Foundations of Society, and the Duties resulting from thence'. It might be thought that Locke was thereby endorsing an account which made justice and beneficence as sociability required by natural law easier to combine with Locke's hedonic psychology than that of Cicero's separation of *honestum* and individual *utile*, and that this was therefore to Locke a preferable account. Continuing to look ahead for a moment, however, as we will see in chapter seven, it was Cicero and the Bible that Locke emphasised on teaching the precepts of morality, and Pufendorf only with careful restrictions. With the possible exception of *De Officiis Hominis et Civis*, for which the prose is rather unclear, in *Some Thoughts* Locke restricted his recommendation of Pufendorf to its teaching of the duties of 'civil law', a category of law that Pufendorf firmly separated from natural law since natural law depended upon reason alone and the civil law upon the legislation of political society. In 'Some Thoughts' Locke recommended Pufendorf's work for teaching the

---

63 Pufendorf '*De Jure Naturae et Gentium* (1672), passim; idem, *On the Duties of Man and Citizen*, ed. J. Tully, Cambridge (1991), passim, esp. introduction; 9–10; 33–6; 62–7; 115–19; 132–41.

duties flowing from the foundation of society in a paragraph explicitly on 'politics' – defined to include the moral bases of political society – rather than in a preceding paragraph explicitly on 'morality' more generally, where it was Cicero that was recommended. It thus seems likely that Locke was here recommending the reading of Pufendorf's work on the morality concerned with the establishment of political societies, not for its more general account of the precepts of natural law based in terrestrial self-interest.[64]

Locke's reading of Pufendorf in mid-1681 and 1682 very probably provided him with some significant elements of the form of his argument on the state of nature as co-operative, and of the reasons for establishing political society because that state was also insecure, that Locke used in the Second Treatise, and it may have provided him with some elements of his theory of property in ways that are too complex to trace here, although even in this area of his thought, as scholars such as Hont and Ignatieff have noted, there were significant divergences between the accounts of Locke and Pufendorf in such important dimensions of their accounts as the roles of consent and money in pre-political society. More importantly, for the purposes of this account of Locke's broader moral thought, Pufendorf's works do not seem to have provided him with an argument that he thought fully satsifactory about the wider content of natural law nor about its derivation from calculations of terrestrial self-interest and hopes of an afterlife alone, since for Pufendorf knowledge of the afterlife was impossible to obtain by reason alone. Like Nicole, Pufendorf placed very heavy emphasis upon peace and endorsed an absolutism that delivered peace. Locke increasingly opposed absolutism with demands for the concentration of political society not just on peace but also on the happiness of its subjects, and he defended mixed government. Although Locke himself relied in practice upon the hopes of an afterlife, he clung tenaciously to the potential demonstrability of an afterlife, he never seems to have felt that the virtuous were properly rewarded in any calculation that did not take celestial rewards as its conceptual starting point, and he never pursued an analysis of morality as constructed on the basis of terrestrial self-interest as distinct from 'goodness', although 'Morality' may have pointed in that direction. These were significant differences in emphasis and attitude between the thought about natural law of Locke and Pufendorf. While Locke probably agreed with elements of Pufendorf's accounts of the duties of beneficence and justice – particularly in terms of the identification of the external manifestations of these duties – reading Pufendorf's works may well have increased, not decreased, his sense of the difficulties of establishing these

---

[64] *Education*, 294; 400.

duties and men's motivations and intentions in the manner that he desired.[65]

[65] On the divergences of Locke and Pufendorf's accounts of pre-political society see I. Hont and M. Ignatieff, 'Needs and Justice in the Wealth of Nations: An Introductory Essay', in idem (eds.), *Wealth and Virtue*, Cambridge (1983), and the works that they cite and discuss; cf. Leibniz's criticisms of Pufendorf discussed in J. Moore and M. Silverthorne, 'Gershom Carmichael and the Natural Jurisprudence Tradition in Eighteenth-Century Scotland', in *ibid.*; Pufendorf, *Duties*, 7, 115ff. As Tully points out in his introduction, in '*De Jure Naturae* Pufendorf does at one point (vii.8.7) allow exceptional resistance, but in general that work supports absolutism, attacks mixed government and condemns resistance, while the *Duties* provides no defence of resistance and effectively equates citizenship and obedience.'

6

Resistance and the Second Treatise

I

Many reasons for Locke's opposition to Filmer's arguments are by now obvious.[1] Locke had no doubt that James would be an English Louis XIV when he succeeded to the throne, and had feared from the mid-1670s that Charles II was inclined towards absolutism. Filmer's works were among the most powerful which opposed historical Parliamentary rights to alter the course of the succession and the most powerful theoretical argument supported by clerics endorsing Charles' moves towards absolutism, especially in the years following the dissolution of the 1681 Oxford Parliament. As royalism came to be increasingly dependent upon clericalist and biblicist Filmerian patriarchalism instead of the more moderate and constitutionalist royalism of many Restoration legists, Locke would have had good reason to oppose Filmer's arguments even if his own thought had not developed at all from his commitments of the mid-1670s. He had long been opposed to any claim to *jure divino* absolute monarchy, and especially to those Anglican clerics who campaigned for *jure divino* monarchy in order to gain royal support for *jure divino* episcopacy.

It is possible to see Locke's arguments in the Second Treatise very largely as a series of natural responses, based upon Locke's preceding and developing commitments, to the precise problems posed by Filmer's arguments for patriarchalism, and particularly to the problems posed by Filmer's attacks on those previous commentators on natural law who had asserted that political society originated from consent. Locke's method of responding to opponents throughout his life – Bagshawe in the early 1660s, Stillingfleet in the early 1680s, Proast and Stillingfleet again in the 1690s – was through intricately detailed reply to each of their contentions. The impression given both by the surviving portion of the First Treatise, and by Locke's comment on its large missing section, is that he had undertaken

---

[1] This chapter replaces and corrects chapter eight of my Ph.D thesis, especially the characterisations of some of the arguments of R. Ashcraft therein.

exactly that extensive a form of response to Filmer. It is quite likely, given Locke's characteristically thorough approach to disputes, that he would have felt the need to reply to almost all of the issues that Filmer had raised, whether central to Filmer's case for absolutism or more peripheral assaults upon the consensually based arguments of other thinkers.[2]

The Second Treatise may thus have been generated simply as a piece of extremely intensive reflection upon the arguments of Filmer, as a purely conceptual, intellectual resolution of the problems set by Filmer, based upon Locke's preceding commitments and his desire when opposing Filmer to write at least a part of the kind of treatise of ethics that his epistemological writings were devoted to declaring possible. Much of the scaffolding on which Locke erected his arguments in the *Two Treatises* had clearly been established in his earlier thought: men as God's property by being his workmanship, the purposive nature of man's faculties, men's reason giving them superiority over all other terrestrial creatures, the plainness of the law of nature to 'rational studiers' of that law, an instrumental and secular conception of political society as established to achieve terrestrial public good and preservation, and especially the duty of preservation of the society and of other men – the centrality of securing preservation of God's property being elevated in a 1680 journal note into one of God's most important desires.[3]

That Locke's arguments in the *Two Treatises* were constructed as responses to Filmer's arguments is most obviously true of Locke's lengthy distinction between paternal and political power. He sought to show that while men were indeed born into families as dependent children, *pace* Filmer, this did not prevent them from becoming free and juristically equal as adults. Locke's thought on property in the manuscript 'Morality' composed shortly before he wrote the *Two Treatises* was rudimentary and he was attempting to base property upon compact rather than upon the theory of appropriation by mixing one's labour with the things of the world that is famously central to the account of initial appropriation in the *Two Treatises*. Locke's argument in the *Treatises* was a much more successful answer to Filmer's questioning of how it was possible for private property to have originated from God's grant of the world to men in common when appropriation through the simultaneous universal consent of all commoners was ludicrous, and when any men who had not individually consented to any lesser forms of agreement that established property could justly complain against such appropriation. Filmer's works highlighted a further series of problems about any consensual origin of

[2] *Treatises*, The Preface; cf. MS Locke c34; *Tracts*; *Second Letter Concerning Toleration*; *Third Letter Concerning Toleration*.
[3] See pp. 142–3 above.

government, all of which were resolved in the *Two Treatises*: how and why men came to be subject to government if men were indeed born free and equal, how a political society could hold itself together across generations if men were not subjected by their parents and all had to consent individually to join the society, and why a political society would not be dissolved even within any particular generation by the withdrawal of consent by those who had consented. Filmer attacked theorists of mixed monarchy such as Philip Hunton for their inability to provide an answer to the question posed particularly acutely by the Civil War: who would judge between the different elements of a mixed government where none was alone supreme or 'sovereign' and they clashed among themselves. For Filmer, any assertion that 'the people' were to judge – or, worse still, that individual citizens were to judge – would necessarily lead to anarchy. For Filmer, such an assertion (or even its implication) would – horrifyingly – align exponents with the anarchic arguments of the most radical of the sixteenth-century monarchomachs, such as George Buchanan.[4]

It is certainly *possible* to see each of Locke's arguments on consent and even those on resistance in the *Two Treatises* as a reply to this series of questions and arguments, and thus as a work that Locke could have composed when confronting Filmer in 1679–80. Men joined political society in order to avoid the disadvantages of the state of nature and the dangers of the state of war. Each individual adult had to consent to join the political society because they were born free as they were born to be rational, but there were substantial advantages to joining political society in terms of

---

[4] *Treatises*, 2, chs. 5 and 6. Put very simply and straightforwardly, in chapter 5, Locke's chapter specifically on property, paragraphs 25–39 are devoted to explaining how property in things can evolve from a grant of the world in common; 40–4 on the appropriateness of Locke's answer in paragraphs 25–39; 45–50 on the legitimate evolution of significantly differing amounts of property, and paragraph 51 is a recapitulation of the chapter. Cf. Filmer, *Patriarcha*, 273, cited in Dunn, *Political Thought*, 67n.; all of Filmer's works, but especially the following passages: Filmer, *Patriarcha*, 286 cited in Dunn, 41: '. . . the original freedom of man being supposed, every man is at liberty to be of what kingdom he please . . . and he were a madman that being by nature free, would choose any man but himself to be his own governor . . .'; Filmer, *Patriarcha*, 273, cited in Dunn, *Political Thought*, 67n.: 'If it were a thing so voluntary, and at the pleasure of men when they were free to put themselves under subjection, why may they not as voluntarily leave subjection when they please, and be free again?'; Filmer, *ibid*., 226, cited in Dunn, *ibid*., 69: theorists of consent need to 'resolve the conscience, touching the manner of the peoples passing their consent; and what is sufficient, and what not, to make, or derive, a right or title from the people' – a problem that Locke noted in his notebook MS Locke f38, perhaps in 1679; Filmer, *ibid*., 294–5 cited in Dunn 70n.: 'Now if you ask the author [Hunton] who shall be judge, whether the monarch transcend his bounds . . . his answer is ther is an impossibility of constituting a judge to determine this . . . controversy'; cf. Filmer, *Patriarcha*, 67 cited in Dunn, *ibid*., 70n.: '[Grotius'] mind may be that every private man may be judge of the danger, for other judge he appoints none.' On Locke's work as an answer to these and other elements of Filmer's thought see Dunn, *ibid*., ch. 6, 8–14.

protection and inheritance. Locke replied to Filmer that there was no possibility of dissolution of the political society within any particular generation by a simple withdrawal of consent because once a member had joined a political society he had to remain unalterably of that society as long as it subsisted. Government was not established as government by consent in such a way that the withdrawal of consent led to the dissolution of government, but instead as a trust, with the people free to resist and to reconstitute government only when it had violated this trust. In reply to the question of 'who shall be Judge' Locke argued that 'the people' – apparently as a collection of individuals rather than as a legal entity – were to judge when government had exceeded its bounds. It was denied that this would lead to anarchy because only when the 'mischiefs' of government were 'general' would individuals whose actions were usually based upon their customary behaviour be impelled to resist and be able to mount a significant resistance, and because such a right would prevent magistrates from invading their subjects' property arbitrarily. It is important to note here that Locke had not so much answered one of the questions most prominently asked by Filmer, of 'who would judge' in a situation of deadlock between coordinate elements of a mixed monarchy, as he had answered who would judge whether prince or legislative had exceeded their trust, and had provided reasons for believing that anarchy would not result from the answer that Filmer vilified, the power of 'the people' as individuals to judge.[5]

However, neither the fact that many of the concepts that Locke deployed and that much of the shape of the Second Treatise can be explained simply as the rehearsal of Locke's preceding views in response to Filmer and with a desire to write a treatise of ethics, nor the fact that Locke answered all of the questions set by Filmer, as his methodical approach to dispute would have dictated, mean that this was the only fashion in which Locke could have deployed these concepts and answered these questions. The structuring commitment of most of the political argument of the Second Treatise was the legitimacy of individual and collective armed resistance – of 'appeal to heaven' – against governments which had exceeded the trust that was placed in them. However many alterations there had been to the text of the Second Treatise before its publication in 1689 – and this will surely never be known, although there were probably very few indeed – it is difficult to believe that Locke could have composed any substantial initial version of the Second Treatise which did not contain a defence of armed resistance at its conceptual centre.[6]

[5] *Treatises*, 2.168; 176; 204; 224–30.
[6] The structural centrality of the right of resistance to the Second Treatise may be illustrated by attempting to subtract all passages bearing directly upon rights to resist unjust force by

It is easy to conceive of another work which attacked Filmer's works by arguing that government was initially based upon consent, that government was a trust, and that it was supposed to secure the liberties of subjects and their protection, but which did not justify individual resistance, nor articulate the need for continuing individual consent by all adult males in order for them to become part of the political society. Such a work would look very different indeed from the Second Treatise, and much more like Locke's own political thought from the late 1660s through to at least the mid-1670s, and apparently also up to the late 1670s when Locke still spoke of men being 'born into commonwealths' and of the unequivocal obligations of individual nonresistance – and the rationality of individual non-resistance – because such nonresistance was necessary in order to preserve political society. It would look similar to the arguments that were hinted at in the First Treatise. In order for Locke to answer Filmer's arguments, only the distinction between paternal and political power and the development of an argument to show how the grant of the world in common could legitimately lead to private property was needed to be added to such commitments. It is thus necessary to explain the generation in Locke's thought of the need for contemporary individual consent and particularly for individual resistance.

The commitment in the *Two Treatises* to individual consent can plausibly be explained as the result of the polemical force of Filmer's argument. The associated positions that were supported with minor variations by most of those of Locke's contemporaries who argued for government 'by' consent were that government was initially established by consent, that later generations were then subject to such government by birth, and that this nonetheless continued to be government by consent because all men had consented in their forefathers to an 'immortal corporation'. This was a form of argument that Locke can be shown to have read in 1681–2 because it was the argument of Hooker's *Ecclesiastical Polity*, upon which Locke took extensive notes, and which he cited in the Second Treatise as though Hooker had supported his own very different account of consent.[7]

As Locke needed to demonstrate the distinction between paternal and political power simply in order to answer Filmer's case for natural subjection by paternity, and chose to argue that men had equal rights and jural

---

force of arms and upon the current circumstances making resistance justified, and all passages whose formulation is necessary to such rights.
[7] Hooker, *Ecclesiastical Polity*, passim; Hooker was cited by Locke particularly on consent, jural equality and sociability as the sources of political society, but for Hooker current generations had consented in their forefathers ('we were then alive in our predecessors'), and only an unanimous consent could allow men to withdraw their consent to the established legislative. Hooker's state of men without political society was also that of a time of evil, with men 'in regard of his depraved mind, little more than a wild beast'.

freedom because of their (broadly) equal reason, it is quite likely that he would have come to think inadequate simply on polemical grounds this contemporary form of argument supporting government 'by' consent, since it came far closer to Filmer's position in its concession that individuals were subjected by their birth than would have seemed conceptually desirable. With the hindsight provided by the modern replacement of arguments from natural rights with arguments about civil rights, with the expansion of population over the face of the globe, and with the scorn that Hume directed against the Lockeian adult individuals who were supposed not to be members of a political society before they expressly consented to government, Locke's argument for individual consent by adults and a natural right of emigration may now appear to be slightly absurd, and Locke's own earlier comment that men were born into commonwealths by far the more sensible view. It is nonetheless possible to see why Locke could have come to think that the arguments for consensual government constructed by his contemporaries were an inadequate reply to Filmer on purely conceptual grounds, and why he could easily have felt the conceptual desirability of asserting the necessity of individual consent by all adults throughout time.[8]

Locke's theoretical generation of political authority by the argument that men had an individual power to execute the law of nature is also explicable as a natural conceptual resolution of the problem of generating political authority over life and death that had been posed acutely by Filmer and by a host of other seventeenth-century writers. Henry Hammond had focused upon precisely this question when assaulting the Independents and presbyterians in the Civil War, and had depicted this problem as showing the necessity of the immediate divine communication of power to rule. Most independents and presbyterians had not chosen in response to support an individual generation of this power, and had defended just as strongly as Hammond the divine communication of this power, although seeing it as communicated directly by God to the political society that was instituting government rather than as communicated directly to its rulers. Locke's long-standing tolerationist commitments and stress upon the secular and instrumental nature of political society would probably have made this option less attractive. Grotius, one of Filmer's most criticised authors, and before him Almain, had described an individual executive power that was transferred to the political society and thus to the government as the origin of governmental authority. Locke had read Grotius' works in the early 1660s, and *De Jure Belli* was cited with

---

[8] Cf. D. Hume, 'Of the Original Contract', in *Essays Moral, Political and Literary*, Indianapolis (1987).

approval in the *Letter From A Person of Quality*. Locke's adoption of this argument in response to Filmer is thus plausibly explained by his polemical needs, his instrumental and secular conception of political society, his awareness of Grotius' arguments, and perhaps by an awareness of debate over this question in mid-century England.[9]

Yet the shape of Locke's thought on the necessity of individual consent seems to be at the least the consequence of his construction of argument for individual resistance in the Second Treatise as it is an account against Filmer of the ramifications of consent for government, or as it is an account of how and why men came to be subject to government when originally free and equal. Locke's argument does not seem centrally directed to identify who is subject to government and a member of political society or why they are obliged to obey government – areas in which his account would be inadequate if he had been intending to compose a full conceptual resolution of these issues. Rather it seems intended centrally to indicate that men cannot give away a power that they do not possess since it is God's possession, the power to dispose of their own lives, and that they therefore may resist governments that unjustly claim that power.[10] Likewise, Locke's 'strange' doctrine of possession of the individual executive power of nature in the state of nature seems designed at least as much to show that individuals retain a power to resist unjust force once government has been established as it is to solve the conceptual issues of the initial generation of political power raised by Hammond and Grotius.

Moreover, at the very least Locke's support for the need for individual consent and the individual possession of the executive power of government does not explain the conceptual need for an individual right of resistance. The retention of an individual right 'to judge' is obviously not logically necessitated by its initial possession. One of the most constant elements of Locke's thought between 1660 and the late 1670s was the duty of individual non-resistance, however governmental authority had arisen. The *Two Tracts* had certainly spent the most space of all of Locke's works in delineating the centrality of obedience to politics and ethics, but we have seen that Locke had urged that men were to submit even to a magistrate who transgressed their rights in the 'Essay on Toleration'. Furthermore, in

---

[9] Cf. *Patriarcha*, 285, cited in Dunn, *ibid.*, 70n.: 'if no man can have power to take away his own life without the guilt of being a murderer of himself, how can any people confer such a power as they have not themselves upon any one man, without being accessories to their own deaths, and every particular man becoming guilty of being *felo de se*?'. Cf. p. 19 above.

[10] On consent see especially J. Dunn, 'Consent in the Political Theory of John Locke', *Historical Journal* (1967), 158–82; also I. Hampsher-Monk, 'Tacit Concept of Consent in Locke's Two Treatises of Government: A Note on Citizens, Travellers, and Patriarchalism', *Journal of the History of Ideas* (1979), 135–9; McPherson, *Possessive Individualism*; Wootton, *Locke*, introduction.

response to Parker in 1670 Locke had declared that the magistrate necessarily had an 'uncontrollable' power to ordain whatever he thought necessary – or declared that he thought necessary – for the public good and
peace. While the *Letter* had opposed emergent monarchical absolutism,
supported religious toleration, and flourished the possibility of resistance
when a magistrate denied to people their rights, like the 'Essay on Toleration' it had not suggested that there could ever be an individual right to
resist and kill a monarch. After the *Letter* was composed, in private in his
journal written in France in the late 1670s Locke had directly and forcefully
expressed the illegitimacy of any subject's resistance to any magistrate,
including an absolutist and Catholic King. Our familiarity with Locke's
defence of individual resistance in the Second Treatise should not blind us
to the dramatic transformation in Locke's thought on this issue. It is this
key transformation that still needs explanation.

   The best three scholarly accounts of the historical genesis of Locke's
political thought in the *Two Treatises* very usefully identify the elements of
Locke's thought and intentions that might have been involved in this
dramatic transformation of Locke's views on resistance. Since their discussions are useful in providing a framework for analysis of these elements
and for bringing out many of the most important features of Locke's arguments, as well as being the best available historiographical interpretations
of the development of Locke's political thought, they will be discussed at
some length in the course of this chapter. The contextual arguments of
Richard Ashcraft and David Wootton will be analysed later. In *The Political Thought of John Locke* (1969) it has been suggested by John Dunn
that Locke's intellectual confrontation with Filmer's case in the context of
the Exclusion Crisis, and his preceding religious individualism, together
('appear to') sufficiently explain the arguments concerning consent and
resistance in the *Two Treatises*. Dunn thus declares that

the key [to the individualist doctrines of consent and resistance in the *Two
Treatises*] appears to be the very intense confrontation with the positions of
Filmer. What appears to have gouged out of Locke his implicitly radical response
was . . . a horror at the idea that limitless royal power should be construed as a gift
of God . . . It was the confrontation of Locke's previously socially quietist religious
individualism . . . with the exorbitant claims of Filmerian absolutism which led
him to the assertion of a countervailing right in the conscience of every man to
judge the damage inflicted by the strong and wicked upon God's world.[11]

Dunn does not specify at this point in his argument what he means by
Locke's 'religious individualism'. There are two obvious possibilities. He
has earlier alleged that the 'Essay on Toleration' in 1667, while itself

[11] Dunn, *Political Thought*, 50–1.

opposing resistance, had 'defined the basis for a more subversive politics' by proclaiming the

necessary autonomy of individual religious judgement . . . The transposition of this theme from theology and epistemology to sociology and politics made each individual man the final judge of how far the society in which he lived had succeeded in avoiding force, the 'way of beasts', the avoidance of which was its sole end.[12]

It is not clear whether Dunn is here suggesting that Locke's conception of the necessity of individual religious judgement was causally involved in the development of his individualistic politics in the *Two Treatises*, or whether, despite his comment that this 'defined the basis' of a 'more subversive politics', the relationship he had posited is one of analogy, that in a way similar to his declaration in 1667 in one area (theology and epistemology) of the necessity of individual religious judgement, so he would later declare in another area (politics and sociology) the necessity of individual (still 'religious'?) judgement. The burden of Dunn's interpretation of Locke's political thought throughout his book suggests that he meant the latter, that it was men's enquiry into their duties in morality that was the causal determinant of his articulation of a right of resistance. Thus, Dunn argues at another point that the crucial element of the political division between Filmer and Locke – and the element that prompted Locke's assertion of individual equality and resistance – was Filmer's assertion of 'God's providential provision for human moral education in eternal structures of social authority'. It was in response to this, he argues, that Locke asserted God's imposition of individual 'religious' duties on all men by their intellectual capacity to know the relevant moral truths; they necessarily must have been empowered to decide when the political society that they had either instituted, or to which they had individually subjected themselves, had transgressed its legitimate boundaries.

The 'religious individualism' alleged by Dunn to be crucial to the development of Locke's political individualism might thus consist of his assertion of individual responsibility to search out the true religion (and consequently of the need for individual consent in the church) which was then transposed to politics, causing the alteration of Locke's political views. It is more likely to have consisted for Dunn of Locke's assertion of the individual's responsibility to search out and perform his moral duties. The next pages will scrutinise these two possibilities and will examine in broad outline the relationship between Locke's political individualism, religious individualism, and stress upon the duties of individual moral enquiry.

It can first be said that Locke's arguments for the necessity of individual

[12] *Ibid.*, 39, 50–1.

judgement in religion and his arguments for individual consent in the church did not create a need for individual consent in the state. Locke's tolerationist thought was structured around a forceful distinction between church and state. We have seen in earlier chapters that Locke's statement of the necessity of individual judgement in religion from the 'Essay on Toleration' onwards was based upon a series of positions, among them the limitations of men's understandings, their enormous fallibility in religious matters, the equal potential for fallibility of magistrates and subjects, and particularly the inefficacy of force upon the understanding (supplemented by an important hint of the necessity of authenticity in religious opinions in the sense of uncoerced generation of these opinions). Most importantly, religious opinions and actions Locke had described as intrinsically harmless; only a few opinions, falsely thought by others to be 'religious' opinions, were thought by Locke to threaten civil peace (although these were for Locke especially dangerous views).

To none of these arguments for the necessity of individual religious judgement was there a parallel case for freedom of moral opinions and actions. Morality could be known. Indeed, it was easily known in many of its parts and thus could easily be plain to magistates. Force could work on the will to gain obedience, although it could not work on the understanding to bring conviction. Most importantly, much of morality was necessarily enforced by any magistrate because it involved harm to others or was necessary to the preservation of the society and of the majority of its subjects. Locke's arguments for liberty in moral matters were always constructed with an acute awareness of the necessity of enforcement of significant parts of morality to provide any security and to prevent harm.

Locke was explicit: men could be represented in civil affairs but not in religious affairs because religious belief was not within their power to change and civil actions were within the power of their will. Men had to worship in the way that they believed best and they could not be prevented from doing so when they had overriding heavenly rewards in view. They could only become subject to church authority by consent, and they could leave a church at any time that they felt that it did not secure their best interests. Once men had given their express consent to become members of political society, in contrast, the *Two Treatises* themselves were clear that they no longer possessed the right to leave. They did not have the right to remodel their political society, except when government had dissolved. Men could not trust anyone in religion; political authority was centrally a trust.[13]

---

[13] *Ibid.*, 121; *Treatises*, 2.121, ch. xix; Dunn has written extremely perceptively on Locke and trust in *Rethinking Modern Political Theory*, Cambridge (1985), ch. 2.

In the *Two Treatises* government was limited by what men could not consent to when they joined the political society – most importantly in the sense that since they did not possess the right to alienate God's property, they could not consent to absolutism. There is no indication that for Locke it had to operate in any sense as government by consent because governmental commands had to follow individuals' beliefs. There is very little sense in Locke's text of a politics of actively political self-determination. It was important and necessary for Locke that men were not represented in religious enquiry and practice, but not important that this was the case in political affairs. Indeed, while Locke at one point in the Second Treatise described the possibility of a perfectly democratic political society, he described representation as crucial to the practice of civil affairs: 'every man [was] . . . under an Obligation . . . to submit to the determination of the majority . . .' because for practical reasons the 'consent of every individual . . . is next impossible ever to be had'. In many ways the crucial advantage of political society over the state of nature was precisely its substitution of the judgement of the community for that of its individual subjects. Locke was clear that a society is only a 'Political . . . Society, where every one of the Members hath quitted this natural Power [of judging breaches of the law of nature] resign'd it up into the hands of the Community . . . And thus all private judgment being excluded, the Community comes to be Umpire.' This is necessary because it is only the exclusion of miscitation and misapplication of the law of nature by replacing it with the judgements of the community that allows peace to be preserved and injury prevented. In such a situation, every subject has given a right to the Commonwealth to 'imploy his force, for the Execution of the Judgements of the Commonwealth, whenever he shall be called to it'. They are then 'his own judgments', but only as they were made 'by himself, or his Representative' through his consent to be subject to the legislature of the society.[14]

Locke's discussion of civil society in the 'Critical Notes' in early 1681 also made this clear, in statements that were paralleled in his other tolerationist works. He argued that no consent to authority was possible in the church further than the individual believed himself commanded by God to that consent, but that the consent of the majority in Parliament could oblige men in all civil matters. This was because 'what is done in Parliament . . . may be truely sayd to be the consent of the nation, because . . . done by their representatives who are impowered to that purpose'. Civil laws were made 'by common consent of the nation in Parliament'. Consent

---

[14] *Treatises*, 2.23; 87–8; 90–2; 96–8; 135–7; 149; 163–4; 168; 172; Dunn, 'Consent'; cf. *Treatises*, 2.87; 88; 96–8.

in the church had to be individual, and no one could make another his representative in religion; "'tis such a consent as cannot be disposed of by the Majority of a house of Commons'. Men might indeed 'chuse representatives to make civil laws for them, because they have power to submit all their civil rights to them and to dispose of their temporal concernments because they have a power to dispose of them themselves'. A representative was 'one that has a power to doe something in other men's names which by delegation he hath received from them'. It should be noted that in these passages in the 'Critical Notes' in 1681 Locke gave absolutely no indication of how members of Parliament had come to represent individuals, of how their authority was 'delegated', but simply presumed that this was the case. He gave no indication, in other words, of any tension between voting qualifications and Parliament's representing of *every* individual in the nation in civil affairs.[15]

In 1690 Locke was to write to Edward Clarke that the 'happyest' possible political situation was one in which representatives in Parliament took such 'care of affairs' that 'all others' acquiesced and thought it 'superfluous and impertinent to medle or beat their heads about them'. Politics in the *Two Treatises* was concerned with protection of property, including liberty from arbirary interference, and not with liberty by political participation. Liberty in political society in the *Two Treatises* involved simply not being subjected to a legislature that had not been established over you by your own express consent, not the necessity of being subjected to a legislature in which, or even in the election of the members of which, you have a necessary right of consent. Beyond the need for express consent to join the society, a singularly attenuated form of political activity, there was no need for political activity by the individual in the *Two Treatises* either through participation in the government itself or even by the exercise of the franchise.[16]

It was very clearly thought by Locke that it was an advantage of the English system that men could be said to have consented in the legislative actions of the political society by being represented in the franchise. This representation in Parliament, however, did not involve possession of the franchise by all individuals, but rather the representation of all adults by those who did possess the franchise. Even this limited representation in the legislature through representation by others in the franchise was not made necessary in the *Two Treatises* in order for men to be said to possess the liberty that made a political society legitimate.[17]

Not being intended to gain for men a form of society in which their own

[15] MS Locke c34, 113–14, 118.
[16] *Correspondence*, IV, 1326; *Treatises*, 2.132; Dunn, 'Consent'.
[17] *Treatises*, 2.21; 132; 138–40; Dunn, 'Consent' again points this out most clearly.

consent and beliefs were followed – indeed, intended in significant part precisely to avoid such a situation because of its potential for conflict – and not being based upon any of the epistemological arguments for the necessity in religious faith of individual belief, nor upon any arguments from the necessity to salvation of authentically individual beliefs in these areas, neither individual consent to the political society nor individual resistance against it were seen by Locke, even in response to Filmer, as being necessary on similar grounds to his religious 'individualism'.

It is, of course, true that the *Two Treatises* advocated liberty for all individuals by advocating the limitation of political authority. One of its central arguments was that men were supposed to be free because that was appropriate to their status as rational individuals. It is this combination of the assertion that individual men are responsible for their own actions and should be free because of their capacity to reason, with the limitation of political authority to the preservation of individuals' property, including their liberty, that gives rise to the classic view of Locke as a founder of liberalism. God was said to give to men their 'understanding' in order to direct their actions, and a 'freedom of Will and liberty of Acting as properly belonging thereunto'. The 'Freedom then of Man and Liberty of acting according to his own Will, is grounded on his having Reason, which is able to instruct him in that Law he is to govern himself by, and make him know how far he is left to the freedom of his own will'. It was the capacity to know the law which made men's freedom appropriate; it was the same capacity that made the exercise of their reason in search into their duties rational and a duty. By having reason, men were 'presumed' to know how far they were to be guided by law, how far they could use their freedom, and 'so' they came to have freedom to act for themselves and not to be guided in their actions by other men.[18]

The primary expression of this liberty in the *Two Treatises* was the type of liberty now classically known as negative, the freedom to follow the promptings of one's own will and not to be forced by other men to follow their will. It is certainly true that this was an enormously important part of Locke's reasons for limitations upon government intervention and coercion. The *Two Treatises* certainly justified resistance as the way to preserve such a limited government, arguing that when there is a recognised legitimacy of resistance to governments that transgress their legitimate bounds, governments will consequently generally stay within their legitimate bounds. In Locke's thought before the *Two Treatises*, however, obedience to the government (or at least nonresistance and passive disobedience) was among the most central duties of the law of nature. Locke's writings from

---

[18] *Treatises*, 2.56–63.

the *Essays* to the *Drafts* of the *Essay Concerning Human Understanding* had stressed moral enquiry and seen it as quite compatible with the un-equivocal rejection of individuals' active disobedience to government. Nonresistance was such a major element of the law of nature for Locke up to the late 1670s because without this obligation the preservation of society, men's lives and their estates could not be secured. Indeed, for Locke before the *Two Treatises*, without this duty of obedience (or at least nonresistance) such liberty as the government allowed could not be secured. Locke was clear that the liberty allowed by the government should be considerable – including in his tolerationist writings liberty of worship, liberty of indifferent civil actions, and liberty of non-harmful sinful actions. He was equally clear that when the liberty allowed by government was not considerable, even when government actively violated its subjects' rights in the worst possible way by persecuting peaceful religion, it should not be resisted by force of arms, because that would bring violence and anarchy and not peace and liberty.[19]

In terms of the content of Locke's thought on resistance before the *Two Treatises*, to say that Locke's strong advocacy of the need for liberty of enquiry and action free from coercion – that is, his individualism in moral enquiry and practice – generated the change in Locke's attitude towards the legitimacy or necessity of an individual right of resistance would be to elevate the liberty of acting without coercion over the practical conditions which he thought necessary for such liberty. Locke was very clear at all points in the *Two Treatises* that this liberty of acting in ways uncoerced by others was only a liberty of acting within the bounds of the law of nature. Men had a right to liberty of action but not to licence. Liberty of action was restricted by the second, 'positive' conception of liberty in the *Two Treatises*, of men being made 'free' in being directed to their true interests. Where they wished to transgress the law of nature they were made 'free' by being coerced to obey the law. Thus, being directed by the government to follow the law of nature was not a restriction of freedom, but its enhance-ment. It was appropriate for men to be free from others' command because they were capable of knowing the rules that they were to follow, but they did not have the right to be free from command when they did not follow these rules, and they were made free when they were made to follow these rules. Since obedience (or at least non-resistance) was a prime duty of the law of nature for Locke up to the late 1670s, to have defended individual resistance in order to establish the widest liberty of uncoerced action would

---

[19] *Treatises*, 2.226. The classic statement of negative and positive conceptions of liberty, since subject to substantial refinements by other scholars, is I. Berlin, 'Two Concepts of Liberty' in *Four Essays on Liberty* (Oxford, 1969).

have involved a reversal of the thrust of his argument for liberty in the *Two Treatises* itself.[20]

At this point it is convenient to return to Dunn's analysis of the causes of the individualist form of Locke's argument against Filmer, including the right of resistance, with which we started this section, because Dunn did there provide a possible intellectual reason for such a massive reorientation of the structural priorities of Locke's thought. Dunn suggests that the individualist shape of Locke's argument was 'gouged' out of Locke by his 'horror' at Filmer's argument that limitless royal power was construed as the gift of God.[21] Locke's assertion of an individual right of resistance as an individual moral right to judge the government's transgressions might thus be thought to have involved a conceptual revulsion from Filmer's argument so great that his thought recoiled to take up the individualist position that was its polar opposite. This is certainly conceptually possible, but it does not seem sufficiently plausible. This book has indicated that the duty of individual nonresistance was so embedded in Locke's thought and personal experience up to the late 1670s, seen as so necessary in practical terms to any *secure* liberty itself, that it is surely not biographically probable that 'horror' on an *intellectual* level alone about Filmer's argument, even during the intensive intellectual confrontation of Filmer's arguments that Locke had clearly undertaken, can sufficiently explain the defence of a right of resistance.

In describing the right to judge as an extension of Locke's preceding moral or religious individualism, Dunn has perhaps wrongly concentrated upon the form of Locke's argument for the right of resistance rather than the content of Locke's argument itself. It is certainly in some sense an individual moral right to judge the government that is defended by Locke. It is certainly seen as irrational for men to have entered into a society in which they gave the ruler absolute power, and this is presented as one argument – although far from the most important – that shows that absolutism is not a legitimate form of government. But the right to judge the government when it acts against its trust is not fundamentally presented as being necessary because men must possess this right in order to fulfil their individual intellectual responsibility to search out and thereby to perform their duties. It is presented overridingly as a direct derivative of the need for preservation – and while it is described as a right that is necessary to preserve rights to life, liberty and estate, these rights are presented as rights not because their control by the individual is of intrinsic intellectual or moral value separable from preservation, but because they serve to secure preservation of life. This is the theme to which Locke consistently connects

---

[20] *Treatises*, 2.56–63.   [21] Dunn, *ibid.*, 50–1.

the right to judge the government, and from which he overridingly derives the right to judge the government. When composing the Second Treatise he had only recently thought that it was rational for men to consent to government which was limited and thus not absolute, but which it was also perfectly rational that they could not resist because only through such a duty of individual nonresistance could their very preservation be secured.[22]

It was therefore surely not an intellectual kind of moral individualism that determined the individualism of Locke's argument for resistance. Rather, it was the change in his view of the conditions necessary to secure preservation and the protection of rights to life, liberty and estate that were almost always presented in the Second Treatise as a function of the duty of (and right to) preservation. The individualism of the argument for resistance in the *Two Treatises* is surely a symptom of Locke's belief that only through such a form of resistance could these other rights be secured, not a cause of the argument for resistance. To explain the transformation of Locke's thought it is then necessary to ask why, and when, his view of what was necessary to secure (or to maximise the chances of securing) preservation changed from commitment to nonresistance up to the late 1670s to individual resistance in rare circumstances in the *Two Treatises*.

There was surely no sufficiently plausible reason for Locke to have diametrically altered his views on individual armed resistance before he had good reason to think that Charles' and James' absolutist intent could not readily be stalled by legal means: therefore, not before Exclusion had failed to pass in 1681 with the dissolution of the Oxford Parliament, and arguably not before there was very little expectation of another Parliament being called in the foreseeable future, and thus later still in 1681 or even early 1682 since there was Whig canvassing in expectation of another Parliament in the summer and expectations of another Parliament into 1682.[23] Charles had been monarch for about twenty years and had, as Locke and Shaftesbury well knew, resisted earlier calls to dismiss Parliament and to

---

[22] *Treatises*, Second Treatise, passim. Dunn (*ibid.*, 92–3) presents a further suggestion for the intellectual switch to defending rights of resistance: that as Locke came to stand outside of power, and as Filmer came to redescribe the duties [of obedience] of the many as the rights [of command] of the few, so Filmer 'revealed' to Locke 'a possible practical bias' in his earlier thought. Locke had, however, no need for a revelation from Filmer that his thought had a practical bias such that the magistrate who had been established for the good of his subjects could rule for his own benefit alone. He had recognised this possibility explicitly in his tolerationist tracts since the early 'Essay on Toleration', and had answered bluntly that if a magistrate went beyond his own authority and commanded things which he should not have commanded, then men were to passively disobey, but to purchase heaven with their lives if necessary. It was surely not that Filmer's works revealed a possible practical bias to Locke's thought, but that Charles' behaviour made this long-acknowledged bias seem immediately and massively more threatening to Locke than defence of an highly circumscribed right of resistance.

[23] Haley, *Shaftesbury*, 666–8; 685–6.

establish absolutism when there were major incentives for him to do so, and many thought that he might be turned away from that course still, particularly since English kings had shown themselves unable to last too long without parliamentary supply because they could not fight major wars alone. There was no polemical reason for immediate individual armed resistance to Charles or James to have been justified as a legitimate act to prevent James' succession before these Parliaments had failed to secure Exclusion, and every reason, polemical and political, for such resistance not to have been justified. Many of the supporters of Exclusion in the Parliaments had every desire to avoid a repeat of the turmoil of the Civil War, and while a number of them threatened that if Exclusion was not passed then James would be resisted by force of arms *when he came to the throne*, it is very hard to find a single justification of armed resistance *to Charles* that was either published or composed before 1681, or evidence that any thought a pre-emptive strike against James by assault upon Charles justified or necessary. James could have solved the dilemma of his succession for everyone by dying before his brother. It is not conceivable as a practical action in Restoration England that Charles would have been attacked by force of arms solely in order to prevent James' succession. It is very hard to find any work which was clearly written and published during the years from 1679 to the dissolution of the Oxford Parliament in 1681 that either directly opposed Filmer and considered the topic of resistance to absolutism, or considered that topic without explicitly opposing Filmer, which supported an individual right of armed resistance to the monarch before James' succession. Works of this period threatened resistance to James at the moment of his succession if at all only because he could be said to have necessarily absolutist intentions as a Catholic. This is true even though there were many in the House of Commons in 1680–1 who came to think restrictions upon monarchical powers necessary, and many more in the city of London who supported these views and looked back fondly to the 'good old cause' of the mid-century Commonwealth.

In the years from 1679 to 1681 Shaftesbury was the leading supporter of the Exclusion of James, and gained much support in the City for this campaign through anti-popish demonstrations and propaganda, but he was not, as Ashcraft tends to depict him, as much the guiding figure of radical city politics as he was one of the leading opponents of radical city politics. He was the firmest opponent, other than the duke of York himself, against the proposals of Halifax and others to limit the powers of James when he succeeded, a campaign that drew more support among the radical London populace than did Shaftesbury's frustrated courtier support for Exclusion. Shaftesbury saw the campaign against absolutism being won through making Charles adopt other policies and excluding James; others saw more radical changes in the powers of the monarchy itself as necessary to limit James and perhaps Charles. Shaftesbury abhorred these principles as 'too like a republic' and far more 'prejudicial to the crown than the exclusion of one heir'. Shaftesbury was therefore increasingly isolated within and without Parliament as the period 1679–81 progressed. He pleaded with the city to elect only moderate men and not fanatics; he was rebuffed. His addresses before the Parliament focused on Exclusion; the addresses of others did not. His candidate for sheriff was defeated in favour of the republican sheriff Bethel, a far more important figure in city politics in these years than was Shaftesbury. Shaftesbury did gain enormous support in the city in late 1681, but this was created far more by the King's actions than his own, coming specifically from his imprisonment and trial, and only more broadly and far less substantially from his support for antipopery. Even then he showed himself willing to turn to support of the King if Charles would restore him to favour or allow his exile. It is not surprising that even in late 1681 he was willing to leave the city behind him if Charles would allow it; desirous of support for his campaign for Exclusion and for Charles' favour, his associations with the radical politicians in the city and in the lower house had formerly been fragile at best and in some cases so bad that the leaders of the Commons could not even bear to be in the same room as him.[24]

There is, in other words, no convincing political or polemical reason for Locke to have come to justify individual armed resistance to Charles II between 1679 and the dissolution of the Oxford Parliament in 1681 at the earliest, and many reasons in his own intellectual commitment to individual nonresistance and in the limited political aims with which he was associated by being the adviser to and client of Shaftesbury, for him not to have come to such a view. That the burden of composition of both *Treatises* had been undertaken by Locke in 1679–81 remains the view most notably of Peter Laslett, its first proponent.[25] It has, however, little to support it, and much against it.[26] (See page 224 for footnote text).

II

In *Revolutionary Politics and Locke's Two Treatises of Government* Richard Ashcraft has argued that the justification of resistance in the Second Treatise makes sense as a political position once Exclusion had

---

[24] These paragraphs are deeply indebted to Scott, *Crisis*. Cf. also Wootton, *Locke: Political Writings*, introduction.

[25] *Treatises*, Introduction, especially 46–66, also 123–6 in reply to Ashcraft in the 1987 edition, Cambridge University Press.

Laslett argues that Locke thought of both treatises as one discourse on government, not as two separate treatises at different dates. This is established externally on the basis of

Locke's description of them in the published preface as one work, and on Locke's apparent original intention in printing them to print them as one discourse, with the division into two treatises added during printing. He argues that they were both written against Filmer during the 'Filmer Controversy', which he dates to 1679–81, and argues that the parliamentary concerns of the Whigs during Exclusion were prominent in the *Treatises*. He argues that Locke's 'chief concern' in all but the last chapter of the Second Treatise was with the hindering of the legislature from being called or sitting once called. He valuably argues against composition of most of the work after 1683 by showing that the books that Locke referred to in the Second Treatise were in his possession in 1681–3 and probably not thereafter. He argues that between 1679 and 1682 Locke was reading voraciously on natural law. He indicates that Locke was reading Hooker's *Ecclesiastical Polity* in 1681 and that the quotations that he took in his journal alternated with his citations of Hooker in the Second Treatise, which he takes to be evidence that Locke was working on the Second Treatise in mid-1681, incorporating elements of Hooker's argument into the text.

Laslett gives several reasons for dating the Second Treatise before the First. There were cross-references from the First Treatise to the Second, but not *vice versa*: 'Every one of [Locke's] positions is assumed in his first Treatise', and 'Who would deliberately choose to begin the exposition of a complicated theme by the refutation of another man's premisses'. It seems to Laslett 'undeniable that the Second Treatise is logically prior to the First because its author never had occasion to cite the First in composing the Second'. Providing important collateral evidence for this date, Locke bought *Patriarcha* in 1680 with others of Filmer's works, and cited from that edition of Filmer on 200 separate occasions in the First Treatise, but cited from Filmer's *Observations on Aristotle* in their 1679 form in the *Freeholders Grand Inquest* on the one single occasion that he cited from Filmer's works in the Second Treatise. Given Locke's meticulousness, this is taken to mean that Locke had composed up to that point in his Second Treatise by the time that he made that citation, before he possessed the 1680 collection of Filmer's works. Laslett further observes that in a notebook Locke took a note from Filmer's *Observations on Aristotle* on a passage related to consent to government, a major subject of the Second Treatise. This note was recorded under the date 1679.

On these bases, Locke is argued to have reached paragraph 22, and perhaps even paragraph 232, by 1680, and to have written the First Treatise after the bulk of the Second, when *Patriarcha* appeared in 1680. Laslett accepts that the Second Treatise may have been rewritten after the 1681 dissolution of the Oxford Parliament, but sees this as only making 'modifications' and 'additions' to the bulk of the work already composed, not as the most significant part of the process of composition itself. Finally, Laslett notes with further circumstantial evidence that Locke had a work that he left with James Tyrrell in 1681, which by 1682 David Thomas thought to be Locke's own work, entitled 'De Morbo Gallico', the French disease. He recognises that this might have been a medical treatise and might have been referring to syphilis under its cant name, but he suggests that it was probably a treatise on absolutism, the French disease. Indicating that some text of that name was composed by mid-1681, and that Shaftesbury was interested in it, in July 1681 Shaftesbury's papers were searched and notes by Shaftesbury on a treatise 'Mor[bu?]s Gallicus' were seized.

That Locke read various works which he cited in the Second Treatise in 1681–3 gives reason to think that it was composed before 1689, but not before 1682–3. That Locke read Hooker in 1681 and cited Hooker in the Second Treatise does not suggest composition in 1679–80, nor even in 1681: Hooker's work was probably read in 1681 because of Locke's ecclesiological interests of early to mid-1681 (see chapter three above), and Locke read Hooker again in 1682, which Laslett does not note. That Locke intended publishing the *Two Treatises* as one discourse and then changed his mind does not mean that he conceived them and wrote them as one discourse at the same time, merely that they came to seem one text to him when writing them or after they were both written; Laslett's own argument suggests that the Second Treatise was written before the First, and there is no reason at all to think on the basis of Locke's conception of the text as one work in 1689 that it was all composed at once. The 'Filmer Controversy' did not only date from 1679 to 1681 as an Exclusion Controversy, as Laslett suggests, but continued in the early 1680s as Filmer's work became the ideology of Charles' Tory reaction after 1681. As Laslett himself notes, Sidney wrote against Filmer by 1683, but not necessarily by 1681, a point now reinforced by Scott's suggestion that Sidney's resistance arguments were probably added in 1682–3. As Ashcraft has pointed out against Laslett, the note from Filmer's work in his journal under 1679 was not the first note under that date on the page, and Locke's date may have referred only to the first note. Even if this note was taken in 1679, it does not show that Locke was composing the Second Treatise in 1679. It most probably does mean that Locke did not have his 1680 edition of Filmer by him when writing the passage in the Second Treatise, but that indicates at most (accepting that Locke's meticulousness makes clumsiness in referencing unlikely) only that the First and Second Treatises were not composed at the same time, not their order of composition.

That there were cross-references in the *published* text of the First Treatise to the Second does not mean that these were included in the first manuscript copy of the work; they may have been added with publication in mind, and Laslett does not give any reason for thinking that they were in the original. Even if they were in the original text, however, they could very easily suggest that Locke came to perceive in writing his demolition of Filmer's argument in the First Treatise that he had to answer certain questions. Locke could easily have included passages in his text of the First Treatise when it was composed first that referred to these as things to be done in another place – rather as Locke's 'Essay on Toleration' included at its conclusion a list of things to be done in the future, but which he never composed.

Laslett's recent response to Ashcraft has recognised that his citation of Locke's 1679 note from Filmer may not indicate the date on which the note was composed, but restates in reply the logical priority of the arguments of the Second Treatise to the First: who would choose to begin the exposition of a complicated theme by the refutation of another's premisses? This conclusion of Laslett's argument, however, is dependent on its own premiss. If Locke did not know that he was going to write a complicated exposition such as the Second Treatise when he commenced the First Treatise then he would not have been *choosing* to write a detailed prefatory refutation, but instead having the complicated theme grow in part out of the refutation itself. Indeed, Laslett's argument surely is more plausible when completely reversed: who would sit down to write a detailed refutation such as the First Treatise *after* composing the complicated exposition of general principles that was the Second? Most importantly of all, as Ashcraft's work has indicated, it is simply not the case that Locke's concerns were those of the Whigs during Exclusion. Their central concern was the Exclusion of James by Parliament because of his Catholicism; that theme was only mentioned by Locke in the Second Treatise as the failure to call Parliament when needed was an example of Charles' intentions to establish absolutism.

²⁶ M. Knights has shown that Locke was a signatory of the January 1680 petition calling for Parliament to sit. He further suggests that the Second Treatise was written in part in defence of the petitioning campaign and he interprets a number of its revolutionary statements as possible responses to Charles' 1679–80 denial of the right to petition and declaration that petitioning was seditious. He provides us with no reason to believe that Locke composed these passages in 1680 other than the possibility that Locke may have been made to consider rebellion the only option other than petitioning and that Charles was publicly denying the right to petition and the specific cause of petitioning, the requirement to call Parliament because of the plots against the monarchy. He recognises that there is no evidence that Locke came to write these passages in 1680, indicating that they may have been written 'later rather than contemporaneously'. None of the passages that he cites can be distinctively linked to the petitioning campaign, even as retrospective arguments about that campaign. He notes a reference to papers sent with Locke's treatise on vines; this is extremely conjectural and fanciful. His article thus offers no support for dating the Second Treatise earlier than 1682: M. Knights, 'Petitioning and the Political Theorists: John Locke, Algernon Sidney and London's "Monster" Petition of 1680', *Past and Present* 138 (1993), 94–111.

failed and once Shaftesbury and other 'Whig' leaders had decided to turn to armed resistance to the King. The first of his reasons – which has just been endorsed and suggested to be extremely important – is that Locke's justification of armed resistance while Exclusion through parliamentary legislation was the policy of Shaftesbury, would have been singularly inept. He further produces much contextual evidence concerning justification of and plans for resistance involving Shaftesbury and Locke which he dates to 1681–3. Some evidence comes from the trials of alleged conspirators who were accused of planning resistance to the King in 1682 and 1683, including the supposed plotters of the 'Rye House Conspiracy' when it was apparently planned to assassinate both Charles and James upon their return from Newmarket as they rode past the 'Rye House'. Further evidence of Shaftesbury's involvement (and therefore presumably of Locke's involvement) in planning resistance is culled from the confessions of other conspirators, confessions which were published as part of their exculpation. Ashcraft associates Locke and Shaftesbury with these plans through the explicit naming of Shaftesbury, although not of Locke, as one of the leaders of these plans and by showing that they both attended some meetings of the alleged conspirators at which plans were allegedly discussed. He associates Locke more directly with these plans by arguing that these conspirators called for justifications of their planned resistance, that the Second Treatise was such a justification, and that its arguments were paralleled by the arguments of other supporters of resistance.

Ashcraft connects Locke not merely to plans for resistance by assassination of the King – as at the 'Rye House' – but also to plans for a more widespread insurrection, which would have been supported by many in the lower orders in London, Taunton, Bristol and Scotland. Here it seems that for Ashcraft the different dimensions of Locke's thought all intersect. Support of the industrious involved significant support for the industrious artisans who were usually nonconformists. Support for nonconformity, with which Ashcraft associates Locke in a broad ideology of dissent, was in part support for political opposition to the *jure divino* absolutism that was promoted by the Anglican church, as well as support for the religious toleration that was opposed by the Anglican church. Assertion of individual rights or the rights of 'the people' was an assertion of the rationality of all men against the views of the people as a beastly multitude that was central to much Anglican and royalist argument, to Locke's own former absolutist argument, and to much 'conservative' Whig argument. Ashcraft suggests that as the radical Whig activity moved to armed resistance from support for Parliamentary Exclusion – which he describes as having been far more central to all Whigs in 1679–81 than is accurate because he does not recognise the importance to most Whigs but not to Shaftesbury of the alternative policy of limitation – the axis of their potential supporters shifted decisively down the social scale, to the artisans and tradesmen in areas such as Wapping in London. Although Ashcraft very importantly recognises that Locke's theory of property was not intended to promote social revolution, he implies that the Second Treatise and Locke's declaration of equal individual natural rights was composed in part in order to appeal to these lower social groups to gain their support for the armed resistance which Locke wished to promote. Having indicated that most gentlemen retreated into obedience after the 1681 dissolution of Parliament, and having suggested elsewhere that 'the gentry could hardly be expected to play a leading or active role' in the planned resistance, he speaks of Locke's text as written 'for a radical *minority* of individuals with whom he and Shaftesbury were associated'. He further suggests that Locke's revolutionary theory existed among the 'ranks of tradesmen, tinkers, or cobblers' and was intended to gain 'support among tinkers and cobblers' at the price of losing support among 'more conservative or aristocratic readers', by which he seems to mean almost all or all merchants and gentlemen as well as aristocrats. He declares that 'It makes no sense . . . in terms of the social meaning attached to the language employed in the *Two Treatises* by contemporaries in 1681–2, in terms of Shaftesbury's own political purposes and activities, or in terms of the social composition of the audience receptive to an argument for resistance to assume that Locke could only have imagined "members of the aristocracy" as the social actors implementing his theory of revolution.' Ashcraft describes the scholarly interpretations of Locke as a conservative revolutionary who envisaged resistance by a handful of aristocrats and did not support a 'real revolution' as '*the* single most unhistorical proposition in the secondary literature on Locke'.[27]

The next sections of this chapter will probe some of Ashcraft's associations of Locke with plans for and justifications of resistance, some of his comparisons of arguments of the *Two Treatises* and the published and unpublished arguments of others, and some of his suggestions about its intended audience. It will register a number of disagreements about some of these issues and will attempt to clarify, refine, or alter his arguments or emphases in a limited number of areas, most notably about its dating and primary intended audience; it is important to stress here both that much of Ashcraft's case will be endorsed, and that this author believes that Ashcraft has taken us far closer to the immediate contexts of composition of the *Treatises* than any previous scholar.

---

[27] The preceding and following paragraphs are a summary of the case that Richard Ashcraft presents about the *Two Treatises* and Locke's involvement in plans of resistance in *Revolutionary Politics and Locke's Two Treatises of Government*, esp. ch. 7, especially at

Ashcraft suggests that after the dissolution of the Oxford Parliament in 1681 Shaftesbury began to turn to plotting armed resistance. Ashcraft implies that Locke wrote at least a part of the arguments for resistance in the *Two Treatises* in 1681; that at least several other works published in 1681–2 show that radical Whigs had quickly turned to support resistance with a shared group of arguments; and that Locke's use of these arguments was therefore the use of a shared language of justifications of resistance. Crucial to these arguments, according to Ashcraft, was the complaint that Charles had failed to call another meeting of Parliament after his dissolution of the Oxford Parliament when it was manifest that another Parliament was needed in order to exclude James and thus to secure the common good.[28]

However, despite the parallels that Ashcraft draws between the arguments of other works and those of the *Two Treatises*, he gives no compelling reason for thinking that Locke wrote the arguments justifying resistance to support serious plans of resistance in early 1681. The works which he cites in *Revolutionary Politics* as paralleling Locke's arguments in 1681 did not defend rights of armed resistance by individuals to the government of Charles, and it is difficult to find evidence that the argument that government was dissolved and that the people had regained their rights of self-defence by force of arms was the 'viewpoint reflected in the Whigs' political literature' in early 1681. Ashcraft cites only two pieces of evidence for this suggesiton. One, by Robert Ferguson, was not published until 1688, and there is no evidence that it was written in 1681, nor before 1685, as it considered at length James' reign. The other is a petition from the Grand Jury of Middlesex, which did indeed argue that in the absence of a meeting of Parliament there would be a situation 'tending even to the dissolution of the constitution of the government'. The Grand Jury's argument was, however, simply a plea for the calling of another Parliament; it did not in any way suggest that there was a right of resistance if it was not called.[29]

304n.; 307n.; 309, 325–7; and in idem, 'The Two Treatises and the Exclusion Crisis', University of California, Los Angeles (1980), 80–1.

[28] Cf., for a different view, Laslett, *Treatises*, Cambridge (1987), 123–6, especially at 125: 'The rest of Ashcraft's submission turns on a point on which we agree, that Locke may well have written in some sense for Shaftesbury's purposes. For him, however, these purposes were exclusively political, apparently entirely propagandist. This is how he interprets Locke's function as Shaftesbury's "assistant pen". He cannot have written any justification of rebellion unless his master Shaftesbury had reached the point when rebellion was the proper next political expedient.'

[29] Ashcraft, *Revolutionary Politics*, 314–15, including description of the Grand Jury as holding the common Whig viewpoint which he had just before described as the view that a dissolution of obligations by a dissolution of government had made self-defensive resistance by arms legitimate; Robert Ferguson, *A Representation of the Threatening Dangers*

Ashcraft cites the *Just and Modest Vindication of the Two Last Parliaments*, (attributed, probably wrongly, to Ferguson), published late in 1681 and written in about April–June 1681, as supporting an appeal to 'the people' to 'judge' between the King and his Whig opponents. Advocacy of a 'right' of 'the people' to 'judge' between the King and the Whigs may seem to evoke the image of Locke's right of armed resistance that was, of course, described as a right of the people to judge when the government had violated its trust. The *Vindication*, however, did not support such a right. It did argue that if James succeeded – and not *until* James succeeded, *if* he succeeded – then the nation would be 'forced into a war in its own natural defence'. It did argue that the King was king by law, and that government ruled for the good of the people by whose consent it was elected. Its concluding argument of an appeal to the people to judge, was, however, an appeal to the people to judge between the arguments used in debate between it and those who published in defence of the King's speedy dissolution of the last two Parliaments. It argued that if the supporters of the King's dissolutions did not allow debate, but merely appealed to force, they would show that they did not use the arms of the rational – that is, argument. There was no implication in this plea to the people to judge that they could do so by taking up arms, which was of course the point of Locke's argument. The *Vindication* pleaded for the exclusion of James and for support of the Protestant religion. Beyond its significant threat about the result of self-defensive force of James succeeding, it said nothing about force being used against unjust force, and there is no indication that its comments about resistance to James were intended to be applicable to Charles; it looked forward to the meeting of the 'next Parliament'. It was written, it is being suggested, before the absolute need for immediate

(1688); *The Presentment and Humble Petition of the Grand Jury for the County of Middlesex, May 18, 1681.* I do not doubt that Whig language from 1681 spoke of the dissolution of government and that this language was continued into 1682–3 and was one very significant influence in the composition of the arguments of the Second Treatise, merely that it was connected to any serious plans for armed resistance in 1681 and that this connection was made in a 'Second Treatise' of early 1681. Ashcraft may base a date of as early as early 1681 for the Second Treatise also on interpreting the Protestant Association as intended to resist Charles by arms, on Locke supporting resistance in the 'Critical Notes' in early 1681, and on later comments by conspirators that Shaftesbury came to envisage or suggest resistance this early. However, the Protestant Association cannot be shown to have intended to take up arms against Charles but rather to have threatened to do so against James and was essentially a Parliamentary proposal. The 'Critical Notes' did not advocate resistance to absolutism, as the final section of this chapter indicates. This is surely a significant silence in a work that Locke wrote during early and mid-1681. The comments about Shaftesbury were made after his death when he was convenient to blame and when the government wished to find evidence that Shaftesbury had been a supporter of armed resistance as early as they accused him of this. They are contradicted by the account of Ferguson, the closest of all of the·conspirators to Shaftesbury who discussed this issue. See also notes 53 and 63 below.

armed resistance by Englishmen to Charles as well as later to James had fully crystallised in the minds of even the most radical of those who were to plan resistance in late 1682–3 since it was probably written, as Jonathan Scott has argued, primarily by an author far more inclined to commonwealth principles and far more predisposed to resistance than Locke; Algernon Sidney. That it was probably not written by Shaftesbury's client Ferguson further limits the association of its views and purposes with those of Shaftesbury and Locke at the date of its composition; Sidney and Shaftesbury apparently loathed each other, a loathing that had a lot to do with their markedly different political views.[30]

While Ferguson did later indicate that no conspiracy was 'set on foot' before the dissolution of the Oxford Parliament, as Ashcraft cites, he also suggested that no active planning of resistance was even begun until early 1682, after Charles II had initiated his *quo warranto* proceedings to alter by royal writ the charter of the corporation of London and gain control of their franchise and, more significantly, of the sheriffs who then had the power to appoint juries. A charge of treason against Shaftesbury had been quashed by a London jury appointed by Whig sheriffs in November 1681, and it was in direct response to this that Charles initiated his *quo warranto* proceedings in December; the Whigs who had most prominently supported Exclusion and opposed absolutism had very good reason indeed to fear for their lives and liberty because of the proceedings, particularly once Tory sheriffs were 'elected' in June 1682, and even more when they took office in September 1682. The Tory account of the plots of resistance that Thomas Sprat issued in 1685 was just as clear as the burden of Whig confessions in seeing the 'principal rise and occasion' of the Conspiracy as the royal attempts to 'rectifie the City juries and Elections', and declaring that once they had been 'driven from that Strength' they had resolved upon actual 'rebellion' instead of their 'lesser arts' of sedition and an association to protect the Protestant religion once James succeeded.[31]

As Ferguson declared in his *Impartial Enquiry*, published in Holland in 1684, it was as Charles' failure to call another Parliament was joined with

---

[30] Scott, *Crisis*, ch. 9; Ashcraft, *Revolutionary Politics*, 317–18 cites this argument in a section of quotations leading up to the declaration that 'Other examples could be cited to illustrate the prevalence of this viewpoint' [the right to use force to repel force]. This would be very useful. He cites the *Just and Modest Vindication* accurately as threatening resistance if James came to the throne, and accurately as pleading for the controversy over the succession to be settled by reason and the laws: *Just and Modest Vindication of the Two Last Parliaments* (1682), passim, esp. 1–2, 31, 47–8.

[31] T. Sprat, *A True Account of the Horrid Conspiracy to Assassinate the Late King Charles II at the Rye House* (1886 reprint), ed. E. Goldsmid, 1, 15–17. It may be worth noting that to Locke it was particularly important that he was a descendant of Sir William Locke: Locke had the latter's arms inscribed on his seal. Sir William had been sheriff of London in 1548. Cranston, *Locke*, 3.

his proceedings to alter the franchise and the juries providing justice that the Whigs came to have 'every reason to believe that the King as well as the Duke wanted to subvert the constitution'. Ferguson's later description of Shaftesbury's view that is cited by Ashcraft is that he came to believe that obligations to the King were 'dissolved' by Charles' failure to call Parliament after its dissolution at Oxford in March 1681, and that the people therefore regained a right to self-defence against the government. Even if the two points – dissolution and the right of self-defence by arms – are accepted as an accurate although later analysis of Shaftesbury's views, Ferguson's focus was not on the dissolution of the Oxford Parliament, but on the 'suborning of Witnesses' against Shaftesbury during the period leading up to and during his imprisonment and trial from mid-1681 to his release on 24 November 1681. The issue 'hereupon' which Ferguson said that it was thought by Shaftesbury that 'obligations' to the King 'had become dissolved' was the 'Courts suborning Witnesses to destroy those upon forged crimes whom they neither durst publicaly massacre, nor could means privately to assassinate . . . The bribing Witnesses to foreswear men out of their Lifes and Estates, was reconkn'd [sic] worse than the sending forth Bandits to murder them would have been; and therefore that whatsoever the Laws of Nature, Nations, or the Kingdom, made lawful in the latter case, was no less in the other.'

Ferguson continued his confession with a declaration that 'notwithstanding all that was discoursed to this purpose in confiding companies', and what was 'accounted to be allowable . . . yet so long as thro the enjoyment of honest juries they saw any likelihood of being acquitted . . . they resolved to submit to . . . false accusations, close imprisonments, and the being indicted'. There may have been 'a little lavish talk' in late 1681, as Ferguson noted would always be the case among 'indiscreet persons' – and here we probably hear the voice of Shaftesbury's client reflecting on the 'indiscreet' politics of the city rather than upon Shaftesbury or upon any indiscreet persons in his household (and few who knew him would describe Locke as anything but a very discreet individual). He was clear, however, that there were 'no endeavours used towards the disturbing the Government, till the Court fell upon plundring the City of their Charter, and the rendering themselves masters of returning what juries they pleased'.[32]

There are further reasons to believe Ferguson's declaration that serious plans for resistance were not begun until early 1682. Many Whigs were

[32] Robert Ferguson, *An Impartial Enquiry into the Administration of Affairs in England* (1684), cited in Ashcraft, *Revolutionary Politics*, 352; James Ferguson, *Robert Ferguson the Plotter*, Edinburgh (1887), 412–15 cited in part in Ashcraft, *Revolutionary Politics*, 314.

hopeful of another Parliament being called in 1681, even doing some expectant canvassing in the summer/autumn of 1681; such expectations persisted even into early 1682, and Halifax may have proposed an amnesty for Shaftesbury in early 1682. It would have been foolish of the Whigs to have plotted resistance after Shaftesbury had been arrested in July 1681 and while he was imprisoned and facing a trial from which he would almost certainly emerge victorious: this could have provided the prosecution with the evidence that they would have desired to convict him for treason. The main evidence against Shaftesbury at his trial were the proposals for a Protestant Association made in 1680 in Parliament itself – hardly a secret conspiracy – which had declared that James should be prevented from succeeding by parliamentary legislation or by force of arms if that was not possible while clearly hoping that parliamentary legislation would be successful, and having no implications of immediate resistance against Charles. During the period of Shaftesbury's imprisonment Whig efforts were focused on legal manoeuvrings and not revolution. Shaftesbury was, moreover, as quickly became widely known, offering his obedience to Charles and voluntary exile to the country or abroad in October 1681.[33]

It is worth noting that Shaftesbury's papers had been searched and seized by the government in July 1681, and that their case was based around the evidence from Shaftesbury's proposals in Parliament. In this search they found notes that were said to have been taken by Shaftesbury himself upon a manuscript called 'Mors Gallicus', quite possibly intending by that 'morbus Gallicus'. It is possible that 'De Morbo gallico' or 'morbus Gallicus' was how Locke described the manuscript of the *Two Treatises*. These notes from 'Mor[bu]s Gallicus' were part of Laslett's case for the composition of much of the Second Treatise in 1679–80, before the composition of the First Treatise. It needs now to be said that even if they suggest that some form of the *Two Treatises* was written by mid-1681 – and that is itself questionable – they then simultaneously suggest that notes from that form of the work were apparently not thought to be incriminating evidence against Shaftesbury in a trial for treason, which required as potential evidence only the countenancing of harm to the King. There are not many extensive sections of the Second Treatise on which notes could have been taken without them being just such evidence, although the First Treatise would not provide such evidence. Thus, to the extent that anything at all is suggested by this tangential evidence, it is the direct opposite of Laslett's conclusion: that the central commitment of the *Two Treatises*

[33] Ashcraft, *Revolutionary Politics*, 315, 327–9; Haley, *Shaftesbury*, 666–7. On 317–19 Ashcraft cites a number of other works which he sees as holding, apparently in 1681, that men had rights to resist with government having been dissolved; on these see below.

to armed resistance was at least not discussed in the notes that someone in
Shaftesbury's circle thought worth taking on what may as 'De Morbo
Gallico' in mid-1681 have been part of the *Treatises*, and that therefore if
any part of the *Treatises* was indeed the form of 'De Morbo Gallico' composed by 1681, that this was the First and not the Second or both Treatises.
Indeed, early to mid-1681 is perhaps a likely date for composition of the
First Treatise, in a period when arguments needed to be made against
absolutism through publications because Parliament was not sitting but in
expectation of it sitting again.[34]

Robert Ferguson's anonymous *No Protestant Plot* was issued as Shaftesbury awaited trial in 1681 in an attempt to show that there had been no
Protestant Plot against Charles, and that Shaftesbury could not have been
planning such resistance. Its central argument was that it would have been
ludicrous for any Protestant, Shaftesbury included, to have organised a plot
against Charles in order to prevent popish absolutism: such a plot would
have led to the succession of James. Placed alongside the later suggestion of
Ferguson, that it was in about early 1682 that Charles' absolutist intentions
came to be feared just as much as and separately from his brother, *No
Protestant Plot* perhaps adds to the suggestion of a state of consciousness
around the long-term courtier and advocate of mixed government Shaftesbury in which resistance to Charles did not yet have adequate – that is,
urgent and very considerable – reason to be actively planned in 1681 by
those few who were thus seriously to plan resistance in 1682-3.[35]

When Ashcraft declares that the forfeiture of the King's trust by his
failure to call a Parliament was 'the specific theoretical issue around which
any argument for resistance in 1681-2 was to be formulated', and does so
in the course of argument about defence of resistance in 1681 or early 1682,
it is unclear what he means by the phrase of 'any argument for resistance';
what can be said is that it is difficult to find any compelling evidence for
published or written but unpublished argument in 1681 for an individual
right of armed resistance to Charles based on this issue, and similarly difficult to find compelling evidence that there were active plans for resistance
to Charles in 1681. It was, it is being suggested, not merely Charles' failure
to call Parliament in 1681-2 that led to composition of arguments that men
could therefore resist him by arms in order to justify actively planned
resistance, but the combination of Charles' increasingly significant failure
to call Parliament with his suborning of witnesses in mid-1681, and his *quo
warranto* proceedings, initiated in December 1681, to alter the franchise

[34] PRO 30/24/VI A/349, paper 3 cited by Laslett in *Treatises*, 62-3.
[35] [Robert Ferguson], *No Protestant Plot* (1681), passim; cf. Ashcraft, *Revolutionary Politics*, 348-9.

and thus the juries that led to the beginning of such justifications and plans against Charles himself in early or mid-1682, plans that then focused not just on Charles' very significant failure to call Parliament but on his other legal manoeuvrings towards absolutism.[36]

To dismiss judges who did not support the monarch's absolutist vision of his authority, and to alter the franchise, and thus the appointment of juries, and to do this while Parliament was not sitting, and when the monarchy was seen as being increasingly dependent upon the Filmerian vision of property as belonging to the monarch, together formed a 'long train of actings' that seemed in December 1681 to pose a very obvious threat to the property of the subjects and to the lives of Whig leaders. It was in these circumstances that the failure to call Parliament became most immediately threatening and the increasing conviction about Charles' absolutist intentions became a certainty. Here many also surely recalled the forced loans and the 'arbitrary taxation' of Charles I in the 1630s; Locke's own sensitivity to the issue must have been considerable since his father had been a collector of Ship Money in Somerset as well as one of those who had briefly taken up arms for the Parliamentarians in the Civil War.[37] Charles II was not securing the common good by failing to call Parliament when it was needed to exclude James, but by 1682 in terms of precipitating significant planning of resistance that was probably not the most serious of his failures to secure the common good and to provide security of lives for his subjects. Resistance to James could have waited until he succeeded to the throne – when it did come in the form of the Monmouth rebellion of 1685. The apparently imminent threat of Charles' making himself absolute, however, when coupled with his clear intention to execute a number of Whig leaders and his already initiated organisation of execution of Whig propagandists such as Stephen College, made resistance to Charles in the short term seem as necessary to many radical Whigs, and most especially to those with good reason to think themselves threatened by imminent trial, as it was thought that it would be to resist James in the longer term if and when he succeeded.[38]

---

[36] Ashcraft, *Revolutionary Politics*, 322. Ashcraft's point is surely that of armed resistance; Whigs were of course defending resistance by legal and parliamentary challenges to absolutism in 1681.

[37] See on Parliament and ship money, inter alia, J. P. Kenyon, *The Stuart Constitution*, Cambridge (1966); C. Russell (ed.), *The Origins of the English Civil War* (1973) and idem, *The Crisis of Parliaments*, Oxford (1971).

[38] Ashcraft, *Revolutionary Politics*, 348–51 rightly stresses the importance of trial by jury to the Whigs, but does not depict this either as the last of a 'long train of actings' or the single most crucial in terms of precipitating serious plans for resistance.

III

Before turning to discussion of the active planning of resistance in 1682, it is necessary first to examine the significant possibility that Locke wrote the Second Treatise quickly in the middle of 1681 or in the 'second half' of 1681, the argument of David Wootton. By August 1681 Charles had not merely failed to call Parliament, but had tried and executed the Whig witness and agent provocateur Fitzharris and the Whig propagandist College, and by late 1681 he had attempted to try Shaftesbury, and had suborned witnesses against him. Charles' strides towards absolutism were already very considerable indeed. Locke had surely written part of the First Treatise at the very least by this date. He was reading Pufendorf and Hooker over the summer and thinking about the possibility of a demonstrable ethics utilising the basic conceptions central to his understanding of natural law. His journal indicates that by September 1681 he was thinking about issues of inheritance that were related to those that were to come up in the Treatises, if not in exactly the way that they were to be handled in the Second Treatise. There can be little doubt, then, that he was thinking very seriously about the juristic principles necessary to oppose Filmer's arguments.[39]

In June 1681 Locke purchased Tyrrell's newly published *Patriarcha Non Monarcha*, and he may have been reflecting on it. He may have been thinking about the advantages of a number of Tyrrell's arguments against Filmer over much previous argument, and yet about the inadequacy of Tyrrell's arguments against Filmer in the situation that opponents of absolutism now faced. For Tyrrell, as for Locke, men were not subjected by their parents' consent to political society, but could leave until they had

---

[39] Wootton, *Locke: Political Writings*, 49–88, esp. 53ff. and 73ff. For Wootton, the 'sensible conclusion' to be drawn from the failure of Locke to argue in the Second Treatise in the manner of a signed journal note of 18 September 1681 is that 'all or most'.of the Second Treatise was already written by September 1681. This journal note argued that 'in the inheritance of anything indivisible, the next of blood is the eldest son, for want of sons the eldest daughter, for want of issue the father, unless the inheritance came by the mother, and then she is next heir. This one rule (wherein is preferred the natural right of nearness of blood) being observed, there can be no dispute about the next heir.' I agree with Wootton that this note was probably written after composition of the chapter 'who heir?', the final surviving chapter of the First Treatise. It seems to me, however, to be more likely that Locke did not think that this kind of resolution of this issue was sufficient or valuable when he came to recognise the different kinds of claims that parents had to dispose of their own property and the different claims that children had upon it in writing the Second Treatise, and that he thought it sufficient in September 1681 precisely because he had not yet written that more complicated work and because he was still reflecting upon the central issues of the First and not the Second Treatise. He did not then add the argument to the Second Treatise because it was not valuable or because he no longer held to such a belief.

explicitly consented. For Tyrrell, as for Locke, men before the creation of political society had a right to punish that was then communicated to the political society. For Tyrrell, as for Locke, labour gave rights to property before political society (although Tyrrell also argued for rights through occupancy). For Tyrrell, as for Locke, tyrannical behaviour restored the natural equality of the state of nature. Yet for Tyrrell, there was only an inalienable right to life and not to property; men could alienate themselves to absolute authority to preserve their lives. Political society voided all preceding property rights, whether gained through labour or occupancy. Tyrrell refused to defend the tyrannicide Milton, for that was to defend 'Murder and Rebellion'.[40]

As Wootton further points out, in late November 1681 in his attack on Shaftesbury, *Absalom and Achitophel*, Dryden questioned if people could give away 'for themselves and sons, their native sway', leaving them 'defenceless to the sword'; and posed as the only alternative that the 'crowd' were 'judge of fit and just / And kings are only officers in trust / then this resuming covenant was declared / when kings were made, or is for ever barr'd'. That alternative for Dryden would make Kings slaves to the people, would have property 'mischievously seated in the crowd', and would have government itself 'fall / To nature's state, where all have right to all'. While Dryden did not publish this work until late November, in response to the failure of Shaftesbury's trial, he probably began its composition in about mid-1681, and for Wootton the currency of these ideas and need to find a response to them is thereby suggested. As we saw earlier, and as Wootton emphasises, the authors of the *Vindication* were proclaiming in late 1681 the need to justify their position against the dissolution of the parliaments by rational debate; again their work was written in roughly mid-1681. For Wootton, practical planning of revolution in 1681 did not call for defence of individual rights of resistance, but the combination of the political situation by mid-1681, and the intellectual situation in the wake of the 'remarkable intellectual event' of publication of Tyrrell's *Patriarcha Non Monarcha*, did call for such argument from Locke. The burden of Locke's Second Treatise was quickly written in summer or summer and autumn 1681 because Locke was writing 'to satisfy

---

[40] Tyrrell, *Patriarcha Non Monarcha* (1681), passim: Wootton, *Locke: Political Writings*, 49–88, esp. 57ff. sets out the parallels and differences between Locke and Tyrrell's arguments in an extremely valuable way and makes a case for Tyrrell's influence on Locke that is very largely persuasive. As such it stands as a further important reason for dating the Second Treatise after mid-1681. I suspect, however, that the influence of Tyrrell's work on Locke's work was more the result of a strong general sense of his arguments due to early 1681 discussions and reading or due to mid-1681 discussions than due to a detailed mid-1681 or 1682 reading. Locke bought *Patriarcha Non Monarcha* 'for' Tyrrell rather than for himself, and his journals do not indicate that he was reading Tyrrell in mid-1681.

his own curiosity ... driven onwards by the need to make intellectual coherence out of the arguments that had brought Fitzharris and College to the scaffold' and 'perhaps with some rash plan of resorting to clandestine publication'; he came to his argument because it was 'self-evidently right'.[41]

These arguments present a plausible description of Locke's intentions. The claim that Locke is responding to Tyrrell, taking over many of the arguments of Tyrrell, but revising them so that individual resistance to tyranny is justified, is surely largely correct. Further research may turn up evidence to vindicate this suggested dating and perhaps even an intention of clandestine publication. It is certainly very likely indeed that Locke was at least thinking very seriously about a large number of arguments that were to be developed in the Second Treatise by and during the summer and autumn of 1681 and that some of the journal entries from Hooker and on inheritance reflect at least this serious thought. There is a slight disjunction between Wootton's claim that Dryden's work reflects an intellectual situation to which Locke needed to respond at a time of alleged composition in 'summer and autumn' 1681 and the publication of Dryden's poem in late November 1681, but the problems that Dryden identified were obvious problems in political and ethical theory and Locke had read widely in resistance theories that included individual rights of resistance many years before, when he firmly opposed them, including George Buchanan's *De Jure Regni Apud Scotos*. The conceptual availability of the arguments that Locke combined in the Second Treatise has, moreover, been made readily apparent in Quentin Skinner's and Richard Tuck's magnificent exegeses of the background to Locke's thought, *The Foundations of Modern Political Thought* and *Natural Rights Theories*.[42]

The impetus that Wootton believes that Locke received from the 'remarkable intellectual event' of publication of Tyrrell's work is reduced in likelihood by Locke's very highly probable knowledge of Tyrrell's arguments in early 1681 since they very probably discussed them when composing the 'Critical Notes' – a page of Tyrrell's *Patriarcha Non Monarcha* ended up mispaginated into the 'Critical Notes', most probably because Tyrrell was composing his revisions to *Patriarcha* during the period of composing the 'Critical Notes' and was discussing them with Locke.[43]

---

[41] Wootton, *Locke: Political Writings*, 49–89, esp. 54–7 and ff. and 89.

[42] For a lengthy exploration of these themes see R. Tuck, *Natural Rights Theories*, passim; Q. Skinner, *The Foundations of Modern Political Thought*, Cambridge (1978), vol. II; also my 'John Locke in Context', ch. 7.

[43] MS Locke c34 between 5 and 6 – a page from the section of *Patriarcha* that Tyrrell added to the text in early 1681, and which has been mispaginated into the 'Critical Notes', which Locke composed with Tyrrell's help in early 1681. The most likely explanation of this is

Indeed, as various scholars have argued, Tyrrell may well have created his own last-minute addition of argument on property rights coming from labour in response to Locke's suggestion, although that does not mean that Locke had therefore yet composed anything like the articulated account of property that became chapter five of the Second Treatise.[44] Locke was apparently purchasing *Patriarcha Non Monarcha* in mid-1681 not for his own reading but on behalf of Tyrrell himself ('for' Tyrrell) since he was then near the bookseller and Tyrrell was not. While this reduces substantially the possibility that Locke gained impetus to composition by becoming first aware of Tyrrell's arguments in mid-1681, Locke may nonetheless have significantly refreshed his awareness of Tyrrell's case in mid-1681 or have now perceived the need to improve on a series of arguments that had initially seemed to him in early 1681 to be broadly adequate for the circumstances of Exclusion.[45]

Locke had, then, all the intellectual materials available to him by mid-1681 that he was to combine in the Second Treatise. He was an intellectual, and this dating offers the very seductive possibility of the philosopher Locke having composed the work because of intellectual curiosity and because it was 'self-evidently right'. Moreover, politically, there may have been enough reason for Locke to have come to think Charles' moves towards absolutism incapable of being successfully resisted without recourse to individual resistance by late 1681, and perhaps even enough for Locke to have thought this necesary given the potential danger to Shaftesbury. Ferguson described the discovery of the suborning of witnesses against Shaftesbury in mid-1681 as causing 'reasonings' and discourses in 'confiding companies' about the justness of resistance by whatever means the law of nature and nations allowed; Locke may very well have been one of those thus reasoning, whether aloud or on paper.[46]

There are reasons, nonetheless, that make anything before December 1681 – whether as early as June or as late as September to November 1681 – seem to this author a less likely date for composition of very much or all of the Second Treatise, especially of its interlocking arguments on resistance. Doubt about an earlier date is fostered by a combination of the testimony of such as Ferguson that active planning of resistance began seriously in 1682 with a more general sense of the degree of desperation that was required for active planning and written advocacy of immediate armed resistance by individual subjects to the King who by 1681 had ruled for

---

surely that Tyrrell was working on both jointly, and that Locke saw at least these additions to *Patriarcha* at that date.

[44] Tuck, *Natural Rights*, 169–70; Wootton, *Locke: Political Writings*, 57–89.

[45] Wootton, *Locke: Political Writings*, 57–89.

[46] James Ferguson, *Robert Ferguson the Plotter*, Edinburgh (1887), 412–15.

twenty-one years with frequent Parliaments, who might still be persuaded to turn back to them, and who had not yet won control of the London juries. It is furthered slightly by an impressionistic judgement about the depth of Locke's preceding commitment to individual nonresistance and to the axiomatic centrality of preservation. Plans for raising armed resistance by a collectivity of individuals required a considerable level of desperation for virtually anyone in Restoration England, but especially for individuals such as Locke whose vision of a desirable polity had long focused on a King with an extensive prerogative, and on opposition to the tumults of the mid-century commonwealth. Scholars familiarised before almost anything else with Locke's arguments for resistance when rights are denied in the Second Treatise have noted in survey of his earlier thought the tensions in his arguments between declarations of individuals' rights and denials of the right to resist those magistrates who were denying these rights. This should in fact testify not so much to Locke's conceptual incoherence, condemnation of which is the privilege of the armchair critic in a stable and liberal society, but rather to the depth of Locke's opposition to individual rights of resistance. It is difficult to imagine ourselves into Restoration England, into a culture dominated by its mid-century Revolution and by the religious and political butchery of sixteenth- and early seventeenth-century Europe. It is necessary, however, to do so in order to understand more than a small amount of early modern political and ethical thought, and particularly of late seventeenth-century thought in England. It is especially necessary to do this to understand the thoughts of Locke, who had grown up in the 'storms' of Civil War England and who had spent many years attempting to find a religion and politics and to define an ethics that would secure peace and preservation. There is a very major level on which Locke's arguments about resistance not causing turmoil or rebellion in the Second Treatise itself are arguments against his own formerly deeply felt positions on the axiomatic centrality of individual nonresistance in order to secure preservation.

It seems unlikely to this author that Locke came to the recognition of the absolute need for armed resistance by individuals *and* composed a work in justification of that action, endangering his life, until he felt absolutism so advanced and preservation itself threatened as decisively as we will shortly see that it was by early-to-mid-1682 *and* was simultaneously involved in actively planning to engage in armed resistance, rather than at the point before the King had attempted to have Shaftesbury tried or even when Shaftesbury still had the support of the city and its juries in late 1681. It is harder still to believe that while Shaftesbury was facing trial from 2 July – and he was not released by his sympathetic London jury until 24 November 1681 – that Locke would have thought composition sensible. Shaftesbury, in close contact with Locke, was still attempting to negotiate with the King about his release in October 1681, either after or during the period when Wootton suggests that Locke wrote the Second Treatise. It seems unpersuasive to this author to argue that the remarkably cautious and secretive Locke who had until this point in his life published only his poem on Cromwell's return as the bringer of peace, and who had refrained from publishing other works despite the wishes of his friends, would have seen good reason to compose a work advocating resistance by various individuals before serious plans of resistance had commenced, either because he thought that he could or should get it clandestinely published, or because he thought that he should write a text defending resistance because it was 'self-evidently right'.[47] By 1682 Locke was to have very good reason to be desperate; in mid-to-late 1681 neither he nor many even of those who were to plot resistance in 1682–3 seem to have yet reached the level of desperation that was then to fuel their overlapping planning to take up arms against the King. That the authors of the *Vindication* had Locke in mind when speaking of 'intellectuals' who would defend Whig principles in late 1681, which Wootton suggests as a possibility, is as unlikely as that their works would then have justified individual armed resistance to Charles rather than making the case against James, for annual parliaments, and for liberty. Their comments surely refer primarily to the work in progress of their probable primary author, Algernon Sidney – the *Discourses*, which included much on these themes but was in 1681 very probably still, as Jonathan Scott has argued, in a state which did not include defence of armed resistance. Other intellectuals thought to be composing similar cases are far more likely to have been Sidney's fellow authors than any in the separate circle around Shaftesbury.[48]

IV

Ferguson's *The Second Part of No Protestant Plot* of early 1682 suggests a very significant transition in Shaftesbury's immediate circle towards a con-

[47] Ashcraft, *Revolutionary Politics*, 315, 327–9; Wootton, *Locke: Political Writings*, 57–89.
[48] Scott, *Crisis*, chs. 10ff. There is a little difficulty specifying the exact period when Wootton thinks the Second Treatise was largely quickly written – he seems to suggest dates including June 1681; 'by September' 1681; 'summer and autumn', and the 'second half' of 1681. His suggested influences upon this writing include not merely purchase of Tyrrell's *Patriarcha Non Monarcha* (2 June) and purchase and reading of Hooker (13 June; 22 June) but the executions of Fitzharris and College (12 July and 31 August). In addition to the reasons given in the text for finding all of these datings of composition unpersuasive – while accepting that Locke was very probably reflecting in these months on a number of issues related to the arguments that were to be combined in the Second Treatise, and probably still working on the First Treatise – I can find nothing compelling in Locke having taken notes from Hooker in mid-1681 that are from passages close to but not the

siderably heightened fear of Charles' immediate intentions and of his
capacity to carry them out, although it still stopped short of defence of
armed resistance to Charles in treading a very fine line between threat of
such resistance and protestation of loyalty. Ferguson argued that when the
law ceased to provide security to men then men would be 'sorely tempted
to apprehend themselves cast into a state of war, and justified in having
recourse to the best means' to secure their shelter and defence. This
strongly implied threat, however, was unclear about the locus of such
rights of resistance when the law ceased to provide security. It was still
placed within a denunciation of the contemporary allegations of a Protestant Plot against the King, with Protestants declared to be loyal and
obedient subjects. It was said to be a 'blessing' of God that England was
not a nation where subjects' lives and liberties were subject to arbitrary
power, where judges were vassals of the King's will, and where juries were
not required for political convictions. There is only a short step to be taken
to turn this into the argument that England has become such a country,
and crucial to that step was the successful removal by Charles' *quo warranto* proceedings of the security of trial by Whig-appointed jury. When
Ferguson's work was published Charles had initiated but had not yet
carried through his actions; their success was debatable until mid-1682
itself. It was a work that was surely published to be intimidatory and to
persuade Charles not to pursue these steps and Shaftesbury's head; Charles
refused to be intimidated and instead intimidated Shaftesbury into very
actively planning to remove Charles' head.[49]

It is likely that in early 1682, after the *quo warranto* proceedings had
been started on 21 December 1681, but before the Tory sheriffs were
'elected' in June 1682 and took office in September 1682, that Shaftesbury
was discussing very seriously and planning armed resistance to Charles.
Although Halifax was suggesting a rapprochement between Shaftesbury
and the King in early 1682, Charles' intentions to find another way to

passages that he did use from Hooker early in the Second Treatise. Hooker and Locke's
arguments were different; when Locke did cite Hooker it was for cover for his position,
not because of significant influence; Locke read Hooker again in 1682; and Locke's short
citations in the Second Treatise could easily even have been added or first composed in
1682, 1683 or 1689.
49 [Robert Ferguson], *The Second Part of No Protestant Plot* (1682), passim, esp. 1–2; 19–20;
cf. Ashcraft, *Revolutionary Politics*, 322–3 where Ashcraft seems to be using Ferguson's
work to illustrate the arguments that defences of resistance did use in 1681–2, and thus as
a work defending current resistance, which it was not. It is possible that the arguments
about resistance not being justified because England still had trial by jury had been composed with awareness of Shaftesbury's discussions in early 1682 with Argyll about resistance, and that Ferguson would have been ready to turn his arguments about self-defence,
a state of war, and England not being a country under tyranny into service of resistance, if
that had materialised. The structure of the argument, however, remained – even if only
just – one of protestation of Protestant loyalty.

prosecute Shaftesbury rather than acceptance of such a compromise were made clear by his *quo warranto* proceedings and clearer still by the declaration in March 1682 of Dryden's court sponsored *Medal* that Shaftesbury's head would look best upon a 'Spike of the Tower'. The 'first Overture towards an Insurrection' of which Ferguson claimed to have knowledge he described as having been started in early 1682 'after the commencing a *Quo warranto* against the City of London'. This 'overture' was a discussion between Shaftesbury and the Earl of Argyll, a Scottish leader with support from Scots Covenanter opposition to Charles II. This overture apparently neither lasted very long nor got very far. This was not least because the two men did not get along well, but also very significantly because by this point no provisions at all had been made in England for 'recourse to arms'. Lord Grey, who was sick during the winter of 1681–2, later declared that he had not even heard of these discussions until the following summer. According to Ferguson, once the discussions between Argyll and Shaftesbury had stalled so did any and all designs for resistance 'that season'.[50]

There is certainly a very significant possibility that Locke came in late December 1681 to see the need for resistance to Charles, because of his own awareness, from his time in advising the King in the early 1670s, of advice from some counsellors to take absolute power, because of his sensitivity to the absolutism of Louis XIV from his time in France, and particularly because of his personal role as Shaftesbury's friend and adviser. Shaftesbury was acutely aware of the dependence upon the Whig-appointed juries of the main supporters of Exclusion and parliamentary rights who had thereby become 'obnoxious' to the King's 'wrath', and had particularly strong reasons to fear the results of the *quo warranto* proceedings as soon as they were instituted. Stephen College, whose initial indictment had been quashed by a London grand jury, had shown as early as August 1681 what could be expected of a jury successfully appointed and thus controlled by the King; he had been executed. The *Vindication* and, more significantly, Dryden's *Absalom and Achitophel* had been published in late 1681, putting their arguments more forcefully on the intellectual agenda at the very end of 1681 than they had been earlier in 1681. Locke's thinking about Filmerian issues in 1681 and his very highly probable composition of the First Treatise by or during 1681 had surely generated many of the arguments of the Second Treatise at least in Locke's head by the end of 1681. Locke may have begun to write the defence of resistance in the Second

---

[50] Ferguson, *Ferguson*, 414–16; Ford, Lord Grey, *The Secret History of the Rye House Plot* (2nd edn. 1754), 22–3.

Treatise in early 1682 as a piece of extended personal correspondence for Shaftesbury and for the purposes of justifying a resistance that his own patron was then discussing with Argyll with the intention that it could be published when such resistance was mounted – rather than as a work to be circulated to urge resistance as yet uncommenced, for reasons to be given in a moment.

All of the royal measures that formed the 'long train of actings', supposed in the Second Treatise to make clear to all that Charles was intent upon absolutism, were evident by early 1682 to Shaftesbury and to Locke, even if it was not until the mid-1682 replacement of Whig by Tory sheriffs that resistance came to seem an absolutely vital action to other Whig leaders. The threat of imminent execution does tend to concentrate the mind. Charles was hindering the legislature from meeting when it was needed, he was in the process of altering the means of election to Parliament, and – in a passage to which perhaps too little attention has been paid – it was put 'past doubt what he was doing' by his initiation of the *quo warranto* proceedings since these were surely what was meant by 'all the Arts of perverted Law made use of, to take off and destroy all that stand in the way of such a design, and will not comply and consent to betray the Liberties of their Country'. The removal of security of trial by jury, the removal of the security provided by the law, helps to explain both why Locke would have genuinely thought by early 1682 that preservation itself was immediately threatened, and even perhaps helps to explain why so much of the Second Treatise is constructed as a juxtaposition of the state of war, involving 'appeal to heaven', and the conditions where there is an 'appeal to law'. The rhetorical force of Locke's description of kings becoming lions and tigers preying on mankind in the Second Treatise, and of the epigraph that he later added to the Treatises describing tyrants as unwilling to be placated 'unless we yield to them our blood to drink and our entrails to tear out', is surely reflective of the extent to which Locke felt desperately threatened. Much of the Second Treatise has less the tone of the 'reasonable liberal' considering an appropriate form of government than the tone of a desperate man with his own head and especially that of his patron very near to the block. Locke had probably composed the First Treatise against Filmer to defend Exclusion by mid-or-late 1681, and his desire to oppose Filmer's arguments together with Shaftesbury's decision that there was a need for him seriously to plan for imminent armed resistance may have together provided sufficient impetus for Locke's composition of the Second Treatise for intellectual and political reasons in early 1682. He surely must at the very least have then been mapping out in his mind and perhaps on paper a number of the positions that he was to write in the Second Treatise, if not actually composing almost all of it then.

Early 1682 is a very likely date of composition of the burden of the Second Treatise.[51]

Shaftesbury's discussions about resistance with Argyll, however, seem to have been perfunctory and acrimonious and to have been held before there were any serious plans for resistance in England. At that moment Shaftesbury and Locke may not have thought resistance imminent, and it could be argued that it is still unlikely that Locke wrote very much of the Second Treatise without thinking of it as a work to be imminently published. Publication by printing in advance of resistance would have been very difficult due to seizure of books and the trial of printers and authors if they could be located. A plan for widespread unprinted circulation in advance of resistance when Shaftesbury and his friends were under close surveillance from various government agents is difficult to believe. It may thus seem more likely still that Locke began to write most of the defence of resistance in mid- or late 1682, a time when we will see in a moment that serious plans of imminent resistance had been started in England, when Shaftesbury was certainly desperate, when he was very prominently involved in these plans, and when plans for resistance were sufficiently advanced to make planning of works to be published when resistance had commenced or had been completed seem important. It also seems quite possible, then, in terms of a probable intention to publish, and in terms of the circumstantial evidence about his involvement in plans for resistance later in 1682 that will shortly be presented, that Locke did not start to write the Second Treatise until mid- or late 1682 after he had become involved in these plans.

According to Ferguson, after the failure of the negotiations between Argyll and Shaftesbury, the summer of 1682 had passed with various leading Whigs discussing their 'woful condition' but with 'nothing formally concerted about an Insurrection' until after North and Rich were declared Sheriffs in June. Lord Grey concurred, declaring that 'nothing worth mentioning came under our consideration that summer . . . till about the time of electing the sheriffs for London and Middlesex'. The vastly greater part of the evidence that Ashcraft produces from trials, from confessions, and from the interpretation of diary entries and correspondence, provides further evidence to support this suggestion that serious plans for armed resistance were laid in the middle of 1682, after the election of Tory sheriffs for London. The day after the Tory sheriffs were finally confirmed in November 1682, Shaftesbury very sensibly went into

---

[51] *Treatises*, preface; 2.222. Since Locke speaks of perverted forms of law rather than perverted witnesses or rewards for witnesses this seems far more likely to refer to the *quo warranto* proceedings rather than the allegations of suborned witnesses at Shaftesbury's trial.

hiding; although the Whigs had been able to fend off this final dénouement for months, and even though their candidates had registered more votes than the Tory candidates in the election only to have many discounted by highly questionable means, the possibility of imminent success by the Court in their campaign to strip Shaftesbury of his protection by a Whig jury had been clear for several months. The evidence of plotting resistance in this period is grouped by Ashcraft under the heading of the 'Rye House Conspiracy', and he suggests that this did not merely involve the plan to assassinate the King and his brother as they returned to London from New-market past a house at Rye that has long been familiar to historians if insufficiently associated with Locke until his work, but also serious plans for a far more widespread insurrection, involving uprisings in Taunton, Bristol, Scotland and London.[52]

It is not possible because of space to review here all of the evidence that Ashcraft presents for these conclusions. A healthy scepticism must be expressed concerning many of the trials and confessions from which he has largely gleaned such information. The possibility of at least the orchest-ration of the evidence of plans for resistance presented by the prosecution, the strong probability of concoction of some of the evidence by the govern-ment who had spies watching many of the alleged conspirators, and the records of trials which certainly did not adequately scrutinise the evidence, combine to make a significant portion of the evidence decidedly suspect. The possibility that the earl of Essex, another alleged conspirator, was murdered in the Tower of London by agents of the crown in order to avoid a trial for treason creates further doubt about the secure evidence of plots that the crown possessed.[53]

A portion of the evidence that Ashcraft cites to suggest that Locke's *Two Treatises* expressed a series of arguments for resistance that were shared both with other conspirators in the plans for resistance from early 1681 to 1683, and with a wider radical audience that was sympathetic to the plan-ning of resistance, is a little more limited than Ashcraft makes it appear to be, and it does not date from as early as 1681. It is worth reflecting on this layer of evidence very briefly here because it will help not merely to identify

---

[52] Ferguson, *Ferguson*, 414–16; Ford, Lord Grey, *The Secret History*, 22–3; Ashcraft, *Revo-lutionary Politics*, ch. 8.

[53] Ashcraft rightly recognises that this evidence is dubious in his introduction to chapter eight (*Revolutionary Politics*, 338–41); he is nonetheless still a little too trusting of the evidence that he gathers from the trials and confessions of various alleged conspirators. Cf. Ferguson, *Ferguson*, 413–14 on the printed Informations being 'extremely distant from truth' and the 'Tribe of Witnesses' who would have been 'ready enough to have expiated their crimes, and to have attoned for their lifes, not only in discovering all they had heard or known concerning that matter [plans for resistance] but in venturing to swear to all the lies that should have been suggested to them as the price of their pardons'.

the very significant similarities of some of their shared arguments and their limits, but also to throw into relief some features of Locke's argument and to emphasise that it is difficult to find any printed text in 1681–3 as radical as Locke's in its direct justification of individual armed resistance. Ashcraft suggests that the 'radical Whigs' came to base their right to resist with arms upon a natural law argument of private resistance and he cites Samuel Johnson's *Julian the Apostate*, William Denton's *Jus Regiminis*, and the anonymous *An Argument for Self-Defense*, as supporting the right of 'every man' to repel unjust force and defend rights against invasion. The first thing to note here is that Johnson's work was published in 1682, Denton's in 1689 although allegedly written several years before its date of publication, and the *Argument for Self-Defense*, most startlingly, was not published until 1710, although it was then published with the completely unsubstantiated declaration that it had been written before the Revolution of 1689, and with the argument even then that it had been written in about 1687. The *Argument For Self-Defense* will not be considered here because there is simply not a shred of evidence to connect it to the period 1681–3; the other works merit brief consideration.[54]

Samuel Johnson was the tempestuous chaplain to Lord Russell, who apparently persuaded Russell that he must not deny that resistance was theoretically legitimate in some circumstances when Russell faced execution in 1683 for his part in the Rye House Plot. Johnson certainly spoke in *Julian the Apostate* in 1682 of all men possessing 'both a Natural and Civil right and property in their Lives' till they had forfeited them by the laws of their country, and cited Bracton in support of the argument that illegal force could be repelled by force. His central theme, however, was the comparison of James, duke of York with Julian the Apostate, and thus of Catholicism with paganism, and his overriding purpose was to attest to the importance of the Protestant religion established by law being protected from a Catholic successor. His work was written, in other words, against the prospect of James' succession and not against Charles' form of rule. Johnson contended that if a religion was established by the Prince against the laws then resistance was possible, making the law in a general sense superior to the Prince's will, and making resistance possible to James if he attempted to establish a religion against that Anglican religion established by law, but also argued that if a religion was established by law then subjects were 'to lay down our lives for Christ's sake', as the first Christians had done. While arguing that inferior magistrates enforcing the illegitimate will of the King could be resisted, Johnson was also clear that the person of a Prince lawfully possessed of the crown was inviolable, and

54 Ashcraft, *Revolutionary Politics*, 318–19.

that if a man was reduced to losing his life or contracting guilt by directly attacking a Prince in order to keep it then 'he ought to die'. It should be noted that this was an extremely conventional attitude among many of those who had resisted the 'advisers' of Charles I during the Civil War, and who then did not believe it legitimate to execute Charles I at its conclusion; it did not prevent them from taking up arms against his government. It should also be noted that Locke himself argued in the Second Treatise that the inviolability of the person of the magistrate outside of a 'state of war' was a highly laudable position. In saying this, however, the Second Treatise was crucially unlike Johnson's work in then being clear that a state of war existed in England, that the King could be destroyed as a noxious beast, and that it was Charles who might now be resisted and not James who might be resisted if he sought to establish the Catholic religion in the future. The absence of arguments for resistance to preserve the Protestant religion in the *Two Treatises* will be discussed later; it is important to note here that the gulf between the arguments of Johnson and Locke was as significant as their shared argument, and that Johnson had not legitimated resistance to Charles or to the person of any King.[55]

William Denton's *Jus Regiminis*, not published until after the Revolution but allegedly written an uncertain number of years earlier, came closer still to Locke's arguments in defending the use of force to repel unjust force and by arguing that governors were trustees for the governed, that the power of government was originally in the people which delegated it to the governors only for their own benefit, and that it returned to the people if the trust was abused. Unlike Locke, however, Denton was very explicit that the chief care of government was to secure the glory of God. He did declare that where the King violated his covenant with the people and injured them the injured parties could seek redress and relief, and that it was necessarily legitimate to use force to repel unjust force. He also argued at one point, however, that it was good that the King had been exempted from being called to account and was viewed as being unable to do wrong; only his officers were to be required to give an account. Furthermore, he argued that the people had never had the power of life and death as individuals but only collectively, an argument that correlated with his denial of an individual right of resistance. Crucially, he was absolutely unequivocal that only the 'ordines regni' or inferior magistrates, and not private men, could resist. Arguing that 'all' of the people could resist, he asserted repeatedly that 'by people is not meant the many-headed Monster-

---

[55] Johnson, *Julian the Apostate* (1682), passim, esp. 71–7; 82–6; 92); Ashcraft, *Revolutionary Politics*, 318–19; *Treatises*, 2.203–7. Johnson's argument about the inviolability of the King himself might be related to Russell's apparent intention to have captured Charles II in order not to kill him but to turn him away from his present policies.

Multitude, but by the Universal People is to be understood those who have any share in the government, or any authority from the people conferred upon them by any laws made by public consent, as inferior magistrates'.[56]

Thomas Hunt's *Defence of the Charter . . . of London* of 1683, which Ashcraft cites immediately after discussion of Locke's individual right of resistance as a work 'also' defending the right of 'any single individual to prosecute those who violate the fundamental principles of the political community', defended no right of resistance at all. The passage referred to by Ashcraft was part of a discussion of a corporation within a body politic, and the allowance of an appeal to law was that of an individual who was unwilling that others should dissolve this corporation without his consent, 'prosecute' being apparently quite literally meant.[57]

Coming closer to defence of an individual right to resist Kings in the 1680s, and this time published in 1683, was the anonymous *The Complete Statesman*. This was an highly favourable biography of Shaftesbury. It argued unequivocally that 'every man' ought to destroy a ruler who had become a 'public enemy and destroyer' because he did not rule by consent, by pacts and agreements. It was declared against the 'law of nature' for any man to impose his will on others without agreement between them about the conditions of rule. This was probably intended as an indirect commentary upon the reign of Charles II, and as a defence of an individual right to resist even rulers themselves it was probably the most straightforward statement of that nature actually published in England in the 1680s, but it was presented as a description of Shaftesbury's attitude in 1656, when, as Anthony Ashley Cooper, he had opposed the usurpation of authority by Oliver Cromwell. Its argument was about the legitimacy of resistance to the taking of power without consent, not about the abuse of power legitimately possessed, and it did not discuss at all any limitations upon governmental authority arising from the need for consent. Its circumstances were therefore not directly applicable to defence of resistance to Charles in 1681–3.[58]

---

[56] Denton, *Jus Regiminis* (1689), passim, esp. 'to the Reader'; 1–2, 4; 16; 19; 22; 32–5; 37–40; 43–5; 48, 51–7; 59–60; 64; 68; 71; 74–5; 80; 86–7; 90; Ashcraft, *Revolutionary Politics*, 318–19.

[57] Ashcraft, *Revolutionary Politics*, 308; Hunt, *Charter*, 42. The Charter was directed to the citizens of London, denying the ability of some of them to exclude others (especially dissenters) from their rights.

[58] *The Complete Statesman* (1683), passim, esp. 16–20; cf. Ashcraft, *Revolutionary Politics*, 314. Despite its date of publication and its inappropriate argument *The Complete Statesman* is one of those works that Ashcraft seems to represent as indicating that Whigs had come to support individual defensive resistance against Charles in *1681* (314 and n. 112). It should perhaps be noted that there is no independent confirmation that the attitude identified in the work as that of Shaftesbury had been his attitude even after he had been forcibly excluded from sitting in Parliament in 1656, that Shaftesbury had sat in the

Ashcraft has further suggested that the arguments that the government was dissolved, that the people were returned to the state of nature, that all power devolved to individuals, and that the people had a right to reconstitute government, were identified 'with the views of the Rye House Conspirators', and that 'these doctrines' were attacked by writers who viewed them 'as the rationale for the Rye House Plot'. This may give an impression that there was a very widespread recognition that all of these positions were held by the conspirators and that there is significant evidence of contemporary arguments extensively similar to those of Locke. It is necessary to stress therefore that the work from which Ashcraft cites these four positions, Bartholomew Shower's *The Magistracy and Government of England Vindicated*, was published in 1689. The dissolution of government to which Shower referred was that of James' government in 1688, as was indicated by the commencement of the passage concerning dissolution with reference to the 'Vacancy' of the throne as well as the preceding text. These arguments were not explicitly identified as those of the Rye House Conspirators, but rather arguments that Shower mentioned in order to suggest that if they were accepted as the valid interpretation of the events of 1688–9 even they would not provide legitimation of punishment for 'acts done before the dissolution'. Shower was pleading for an indemnity for actions undertaken during Charles' and James' reigns.[59]

Ashcraft cites four other works as identifying these arguments as 'the rationale' for the Rye House Plot. John Dryden's 1683 *Vindication*, however, attacked only the doctrine that the 'People, or their representatives' were superior to the King with a 'power of Revocation' and the alleged consequence that 'when ever they please they may take up arms' against him. It said nothing of the dissolution of government, the state of nature, or individual powers in that state, and was unclear about what the people or the representatives could do once they had 'revoked' the magistrate's office. There is arguably a significant distance to be travelled between Locke's arguments and the argument that the people or their representatives may resist 'when ever they please' and between Locke's argu-

---

Barebones Parliament and in the Parliament and Council of state established by the Instrument of Government which made Cromwell Lord Protector, and that he had been one of the advocates in 1654 of making Cromwell King.

[59] B. Shower, *The Magistracy and Government of England Vindicated* (1689), passim, esp. 26/36; Ashcraft, *Revolutionary Politics*, 332–3. Shower's mention of these positions came only as part of a lengthy discussion of the need for indemnity for those who had been involved in supporting the legal actions of Charles and James, and was intended to show only that even if they were accepted in 1689 they did not give a right of revenge against actions committed before the dissolution of James' government. In his 1683 *Antidote against Poison* Shower had not mentioned these positions in attacking the views of Russell, but in defending Russell's execution he had associated Russell's views with those who thought that the people had a right of resistance based on self-preservation.

ment and the view that the people could 'revoke' government – a notion implying that government should be effectively dependent upon continuous consent by the people, and not upon Locke's notion of the maintenance of a trust, only the violation of which gave the right of resistance.[60] One of the two editions of Roger L'Estrange's *Observator* that Ashcraft cites makes no mention of any of the four arguments at all. The other attacked, in the voice of 'Observator', the view that the original power of the government was in the people and defended against this the view that government was 'ordained by God'. The voice of the 'Trimmer' who defended the people's agreement as the basis of government against 'Observator' did not, however, also defend the ridiculed view that the executive power of government was at any point possessed individually by the people, nor that government was dissolved, nor that the power to reconstitute government resided in the people.[61]

Even Elkanah Settle's 1683 attack on the one conspirator who had by then been publicly identified (at trial) as maintaining a significant number of these positions, Algernon Sidney, was restricted to declaring that if laws and oaths were not observed by the King then there was a danger of 'dissolving the whole Fabrick of government', and it was Settle himself who extrapolated from this (as did Sidney's prosecutors) that there was then a licence 'for the people to rebel, to cause this Dissolution in revenge of that Violation'. Settle's work argued against the right of the 'people' to take the King to court or take 'any shorter method', declaring instead that 'the Tribunal of God' was the 'only place' where the magistrate was called to answer for his behaviour. It will be indicated in a moment that Sidney did have some notion of individual rights of resistance and of a state of nature, but Settle did not mention these.[62]

It is thus clear that this layer of evidence does not fully substantiate a suggestion that these positions were the contemporaneously recognised views of the Rye House Conspirators, nor evidence extensively similar patterns of argument to those of Locke. Moreover, while the arguments of Denton, Johnson and the *Complete Statesman* did to a significant degree utilise arguments that were to be included in the Second Treatise, they did

---

[60] J. Dryden, *A Vindication: or the Parallel of the French Holy League and the English League and Covenant* (1683), 7–8; Ashcraft, *Revolutionary Politics*, 332–3.
[61] R. L'Estrange, *Observator*, 18 December 1682, 1 October 1683; Ashcraft, *Revolutionary Politics*, 332–3.
[62] E. Settle, *Remarks Upon Algernon Sidney's Paper, Delivered to the Sherriffs at his Execution* (1683); Ashcraft, *Revolutionary Politics*, 332–3. Ashcraft also cites a letter supposedly from one of the conspirators that was printed in the *Observator* in August 1684. Not merely is it dubious, as he correctly notes (333n.), but it says nothing about the positions that he is saying were identified as the rationale or arguments of the Rye House Conspirators. He also cites much more valuably from Robert Ferguson's *Impartial Enquiry* of 1684 (333–7); on that important text and its parallels with Locke, see his account and below.

not defend resistance to Charles II himself by private individuals, nor focus upon Charles as needing resistance, nor establish a pattern of argument for resistance significantly similar to the Second Treatise in arguing for individual rights of resistance, states of nature and war, consent, and preservation of God's property.

V

Ashcraft does, however, brilliantly provide a very considerable amount of other very suggestive evidence to indicate that between October 1682 and March 1683 there were plans both for insurrection to be raised in various turbulent and historically radical parts of England, such as Taunton and London, and for the assassination of the King and his brother, and that Locke was probably to some extent involved in both. It is true that much of this evidence comes either from later confessions of alleged participants, or from the arguments of the prosecutors of Sidney and Russell in 1683, and very considerable scepticism is needed in accepting the validity of any of this evidence. Indeed, even when any part of it is accepted as broadly valid, considerable caution is necessary in sifting through the material to interpret whether the charges and confessions involved attempts to place the blame on others for the confessors' own actions – most readily by placing the blame at the feet of the by then very conveniently deceased Shaftesbury.[63]

Correspondence, diaries, and the reports of various government spies do suggest that there were a series of meetings in late 1682 and early 1683 that included Shaftesbury and Ferguson until their joint flight to the continent, and Essex, Russell, Grey, Sidney, John Wildman, Nathaniel Wade, Robert West and John Locke. The later confessions of Grey and Ferguson contended that these meetings discussed various plans for resistance through insurrection or assassination, and give some indications of the content of these plans and of the form of the discussions that took place. Lending considerable credibility to the existence of these plans of resistance made at these meetings rather than to the fabrication of these plans by government spies, ministers, prosecutors and the monarch himself, are a number of suggestive circumstantial pieces of evidence, not least the commissioning of arms and disbursement of moneys by Shaftesbury and a number of his

---

[63] The evidence is mainly collected by Ashcraft in chapter 8 of *Revolutionary Politics*. The point about Shaftesbury's responsibility being increased in confession made after his death in 1683 has been made against Ashcraft by G. Schochet, 'Ashcraft on Locke', *Journal of the History of Ideas* 50: 3 (1989), 491–510; Schochet also shows that Ashcraft miscites some of the evidence in a way that makes the extent of Shaftesbury's participation in the plans greater than it might actually have been.

associates. While all innocent explanations for individual pieces of evidence should not be disregarded, a significant portion of the evidence Ashcraft has assembled does suggest that there were plans for resistance.[64]

Further credibility is lent by the alleged participation in these plans of a number of people who were to participate in actual resistance just over two years later in the Monmouth rebellion, although in saying this it should again be underlined that resistance to James was seen by many as a very different and more necessary action than resistance to Charles; very few had come with Ferguson and Locke to believe in 1682 that Charles had to be resisted as instituting absolutism. More importantly, the realisation of how dangerous a position the leaders of the opposition found themselves in once they had been stripped of the protection of juries packed in their favour, and faced the prospect of juries packed instead in the favour of the King, lends considerable further credibility to the suspect testimony of plans for armed resistance. Resistance by arms to Charles was a desperate measure, but many of these men can certainly be said to have had excellent reason to be desperate men by late 1682, and the further they went in discussing and planning resistance, the more desperate their plight became. As Grey noted, by December 1682 'we expected every day to be hanged'.[65]

Many of the later accounts of the conspiracy by those supposedly involved in it, including that of Grey, suggest that at least some of the arguments that were present in the *Two Treatises* were part of the extensive discussions of justifications of resistance in 1682–3. Russell was alleged by Grey to have asserted in one meeting in 1682 that 'The most necessary thing of all in our undertaking is a Declaration' that set out their aims and reasons for their resistance. Ferguson is alleged to have read out in another

---

[64] See especially Ford, Lord Grey, *The Secret History of the Rye House Plot* (2nd edn. 1754), passim; Ferguson, *Ferguson*, passim especially appendix (cf. the explanatory note on this confession in Ashcraft, *Revolutionary Politics*, 359 n. 89); and Ashcraft, *Revolutionary Politics*, chapter 8 on all of this evidence including the spies watching the various alleged conspirators. Various other participants in these meetings are suggested by Ashcraft; some are highly plausible and others quite possible, but those that I have named seem to have been the core of those meeting as conspirators, with the significant addition of the Duke of Monmouth, the extent of whose participation and commitment is singularly difficult to specify. Three examples of Ashcraft disregarding innocent alternative explanations of the circumstantial evidence of resistance that he produces will have to suffice here. He argues that Shaftesbury borrowed much money in order to finance resistance; he could have been gathering it with the intention of fleeing from England. He argues that as a plantation owner Robert West could gather arms under pretence that these were to be shipped abroad; West's collection of arms could just as easily have been munitions for the colonies. He makes much of Locke's correspondence once he had gone into exile that is said to be in a 'canting' language of planning walks and planting seeds and importing sheep that was a code for raising the resistance that culminated in the Monmouth rebellion. See on this last especially Goldie, 'John Locke's Circle and James II', *Historical Journal* 35: 3 (1992), 557–86; Wootton, *Locke*, introduction.

[65] *Secret History*, 49 cited in Ashcraft, *Revolutionary Politics*, 363.

meeting a 'pretty large paper', perhaps of 'eight sheets', including a discussion of the ends of government. Sidney is alleged to have produced another long 'discourse' on the necessity and legitimacy of taking up arms, although it seems that this occurred after Shaftesbury's flight. Nathaniel Wade and Robert West are supposed to have drawn up further declarations, and John Wildman is supposed to have been commissioned to write a declaration of 'fundamentals'. According to Grey, discussions centred upon showing the dissolution of the government and that the people therefore had the freedom to settle another government. Ferguson was said to have declared that the people were free to settle another government because the King had violated the terms of his contract.[66] While there is little or no direct evidence of the detailed form of these arguments, it does seem extremely likely from the prominence of these concerns in the other published Whig argument which did not justify armed resistance that such legitimation of resistance would have focused upon indictments of Charles's failures in not calling Parliament when this was needed by the nation, and in altering the franchise and juries in order to secure absolute power.[67]

These arguments were all, as Ashcraft rightly emphasises, very similar to very major parts of Locke's case against Charles in the Second Treatise, but there is insufficient evidence from the confessions of various conspirators to go very far beyond these broad surmises about the broad patterns of argument employed in the discussions in 1682–3. It is probable that much of the detailed indictment of Charles' actions in the Second Treatise was paralleled very closely by the arguments of others in this group, and it is just possible that the stresses of earlier Whig Exclusion argument on the values of industry, commerce, and money alongside a view of political society as centred on the protection of property was also voiced, but there is so little surviving evidence of these discussions that there is not a substantial clear indication of this. There are two surviving lengthy works other than the *Treatises* which may have been works composed at least partly as a result of the discussions in these meetings: Sidney's *Discourses*, probably largely written between late 1681 and 1683, with their final sections probably written after mid-1682, and Ferguson's *Impartial Enquiry*,

---

[66] Grey, *Secret History*, 30, 47–8, 59, 63, 67; Add. MS 38847, fos. 91, 96, 102, 112; Ferguson, *Ferguson*, 132; T. Sprat, *A True Account and Declaration of the Horrid Conspiracy against the Late King* (1685), appendix, 50; all cited in Ashcraft, *Revolutionary Politics*, 390–3.

[67] It is not intended to challenge Ashcraft's argument that many of Locke's indictments of Charles were suggested to him by these arguments in Whig works and in discussions with other conspirators; indeed, dating the Second Treatise to late 1682 or 1683 instead of 1681 would make this influence upon Locke likely to have been even greater than Ashcraft depicts it as being.

published in Holland in 1684 after its author had fled there in 1682, and *perhaps* largely composed in 1683; it will be worth examining them very briefly to indicate both their significant parallels to and divergences from Locke's arguments.[68]

Sidney's *Discourses Upon Government*, like the *Two Treatises*, was written primarily against Filmer's *Patriarcha*. Again like Locke, Sidney attacked Filmer as one representative of the absolutist tradition of 'Laud, Manwaring, Sibthorp, Hobbs, Filmer and Heylin'. He assaulted the 'followers of Filmer and Heylin'. Much of Sidney's attack on Filmer's absolutism was also similar to Locke's, from analysis of the differences between paternal and political authority through to argument that even if Adam was sovereign, his heirs were impossible to identify. For Sidney, as for Locke, men were naturally free and equal, all being born to the 'same condition'. They had a natural right to 'liberty' as freedom from the dominion of another's will and natural equality was planted 'in the hearts of men'. Sidney stressed the necessity of government because of the lack of security and of conveniences when 'every man has equal right to everything'. In this state the liberty of one thwarted the liberty of another, and so men consented to set up government. Legitimate government was based upon consent, and governed for the benefit of the governed; 'salus populi' was the supreme law. Government was established to do justice and to secure the welfare of the people. Since the Fall men's nature was only 'fruitful in vice and wickedness'. God had, however, declared in Scripture and written in the 'heart of every man' that it was better to prefer the benefits of society to solitude, and therefore to establish laws necessary to the preservation of society. Men had been given reason to establish government and could raise themselves up towards God by use of that reason.[69]

Although Sidney spoke of every one having a right 'to everything' as a cause of government, and focused upon liberty as self-determination, he also argued that the law of nature preceded government and that there was a power to punish transgressions of the law of nature in a pre-political state. Sidney was not very explicit about who possessed this power, but Cain had been subject to punishment for murder before any civil law, and men had to conclude that there was 'some way' appointed by God 'for its execution, tho unknown to us'. This involved at least an individual right to self-defence, and perhaps also an individual right to punish transgressions of the law of nature which caused injury. Men had a 'natural right of defending themselves' of which they could not be deprived and which they could not alienate. Since 'every man has a right of resisting some way or

[68] The analysis of these arguments of Ferguson and Sidney cannot, of course, disprove a more extensive sharing of theoretical positions with Locke by other conspirators.
[69] Sidney, *Discourses*, passim; Scott, *Crisis*, ch. 10ff.

other that which ought not to be done to him', a man was justified who killed another who offered violence to him. This right extended to defence against 'injustice' when 'the ways prescribed by public Authority cannot be taken'.

Sidney argued that God had commissioned servants to resist and destroy kings who were tyrants. Saul had been chosen by the people but then became a tyrant, slaying priests and oppressing people, and 'so overthrew his own right'. God had declared the Kingdom abrogated, giving a right not only 'to the whole People of opposing him, but to every particular man' and thus to David. This apparently did not involve a special commission, however: war was made by David upon Saul 'upon the common natural right of defending himself against the violence and fury of a wicked man'.

Sidney did not set out any lengthy account of the content of the law of nature. He did nonetheless argue that government was bound by the law of nature to 'preserve the Lives, Lands, Liberties and Goods of every one of their subjects'. Men had by the law of nature a 'right' to 'liberties, lands, goods and co' as necessary for preservation. According to Sidney, kings had all their authority by contract. If they acted against the terms of this contract, then they lost authority. The 'people' retained the right of judging if their contract was violated and of 'abrogating', 'deposing', 'restraining' or 'chastising' the King if their trust was betrayed. Magistrates were subject to the judgement of 'all or choicest men of them'. Governors who could not provide justice and protection 'give the People a right of taking such ways as best please themselves in order to their own safety'.[70]

In declaration of an individual right of resistance to injustice, and in statement of men's rights to secure their own preservation, Sidney came close to the central themes of the *Two Treatises*. Nonetheless, even in the groundwork for these positions, Sidney had spoken of a right to all before government, had provided no account of the transfer of powers to government, and had only very cursorily discussed a state of nature. He had instead provided a much more extensive account than Locke of the need for liberty as an expression of God's reason and as something with which men could make themselves approach closer to God in creating ever better societies to frame their moral natures. More importantly, Sidney's central concern was with the shaping and development of political man by governments which ought to be the best possible. For Sidney, people could correct, reform or abolish a government in favour of one they 'found more convenient to them'. Most strikingly, sedition, tumult and war were declared good if they led to a better society. For Sidney, the government of

---

[70] Sidney, *Discourses*, passim; Scott, *Crisis*, ch. 10ff.

the English Commonwealth from 1648 was good firstly because it attempted to build a good society and secondly because it was militarily powerful and governments were largely to be judged by their military effectiveness. It was also a government of parliamentary sovereignty, for which Sidney made a strong case. Sidney was concerned not so much to vindicate the right of the people to remodel government, nor with a specific answer to the general question 'whether people, senate, or any magistracy made by and for the people can have such a right' as that of resistance, as he was concerned with the consequences of this right for government. For Sidney, Parliament was called into existence not by the king's prerogative alone but by some individuals in 'the poeple' who saw the need for this, and then was able to remodel society and to make and unmake kings. Parliament had legislative sovereignty, and 'popular government' was explicitly declared to be better than that of 'princes'.[71]

It was not until after Ferguson had fled to Holland that he published a work which paralleled a significant amount of Locke's argument, his *Impartial Enquiry into the Administration of Affairs in England*, published anonymously in 1684. Even then, Ferguson's arguments were wedded to a religious account of the origins and purpose of government. Ferguson assaulted a court conspiracy against the 'religion, liberties and laws'. Government was declared to be appointed by God with all 'ruling authority derived from God'. When a Prince withdrew a people's fealty from God he 'ipso facto' deposed himself. Ferguson did also argue in the *Impartial Enquiry*, however, that God gave political authority to reign only in order to secure the common good and that whenever a ruler departed from this standard, and ceased to protect his subjects, then he 'deposed himself'. Men had a right to their own safety from God, and could not 'grant them [rulers] a right to Rule over them as they please'. God prevented alienation of their rights; rulers could only rule for the common good. Acquiescence in tyranny gave no right to rule, and men always retained the right to vindicate themselves from tyranny. Men had a duty to preserve themselves. For Ferguson, echoing the exceptions to absolutism propounded by Bracton, subjects had a right to resist and defend themselves against a ruler who sought the ruin of a vast number of innocent people. He made, however, no more substantial or detailed argument that resistance was justified by the threat to individuals of subversion of the safety provided by the law.[72]

---

[71] Sidney, *Discourses*, passim; Scott, *Crisis*, ch. 10ff.

[72] Ferguson, *Impartial Enquiry*, passim, esp. 3, 13–14, 26–7. These themes were expanded in Ferguson's works of the late 1680s. *A Brief Justification of the Prince of Orange* (1689) continued to argue that government was the 'ordination and institution from God', with rulers under 'pact and Confinement' to exert their power for the service and Honour of

The arguments of Sidney's *Discourses* and Ferguson's *Impartial Enquiry* did thus replicate a significant number of the central themes of the *Two Treatises*, and importantly defended the arguments that individuals could resist a tyrant, that governments were established by consent, and that governments had to seek the common good and 'salus populi'. Apart from the right of resistance, however, these parallel elements should not be over-emphasised: views such as the necessity of rule for the common good and government from consent were singularly conventional views among the Whigs in broad outline, and on their detailed exegesis Sidney and Ferguson diverged somewhat from Locke. As striking as the shared form of the defence of the right of resistance by Ferguson, Sidney and Locke were the elements where the three works were discontinuous each from the others. Divergent from Locke's arguments were Ferguson's emphasis upon preservation of religion and the ordination and empowerment of government by God, and especially Sidney's emphases upon the building of a good society that looked back with longing to the austerity of the English common-wealth, militarism, and explicit support for popular government. Both Sidney and Ferguson lacked any extended conception of Locke's state of war, of an individual executive power of the law of nature continuous between pre-political society and political society, and the other linked themes central to resistance in Locke's *Treatises*: workmanship, the duty of preservation of others, and the inability to give away the property possessed by God.

The lack of detailed description of the positions taken by the various conspirators who produced papers declaring the purpose and legitimacy of resistance in the later confessions of Grey and Ferguson may well reveal that it was little more than hostility to absolutism and willingness to resist that was shared by the conspirators. Thomas Sprat's extremely hostile 1685 *True Account of the Rye House Plot* argued that while the conspirators' declarations of their aims agreed in opposition to tyranny and taxes and support of trade and toleration 'touching the new Form of Government to be set up' the conspirators were 'not altogether so unanimous', noting

---

God, and for the safety, welfare and prosperity of the people. Men could not consent to a power greater than the boundaries God had put in the 'Charters of Nature and Revelation'. The people could set the boundaries of government at the institution of government, and could 'abdicate' the ruler from his trust. Ferguson's *A Representation of the Threatening Dangers* (1689) again implied that men simply could not legitimately consent to the exercise of absolute power, declaring that this dissolved government 'and brings us all into a state of nature', by discharging men from the ties they were under from stipulations and laws. James II had done this by claiming all legislative power and by annulling by royal will and pleasure alone the Test Acts and the oaths of supremacy and obedience.

sourly that this was usual in conspiracies which sometimes agreed 'in what they would ruine' but never long 'in what they shall settle'.[73]

While there were some significant parallels to Locke's arguments in arguments for resistance by Sidney and Ferguson, there is no clear evidence that their thought was significantly influential on the detailed shape of Locke's arguments, whose premises seem instead to be owed to his own preceding commitments, his response to Filmer, and to the situation in which he found himself defending resistance. Nor is there any convincing evidence that Locke's thought was significantly influential upon the arguments of the other conspirators. The other conspirators do not seem to have thought that Locke had produced a work that expressed their views in such a way that they would not then need to write their own declarations and justifications of resistance. Indeed, there is no sign that they were even aware that he had produced such a work at all. There is certainly not enough similarity in the arguments of other authors nor enough detail in the confessions to infer that any parts of Locke's text were circulated in order to provide other conspirators with arguments or to influence them to the support of resistance, and the failure to identify Locke in the confessions as involved in composition of a justification of resistance makes it seem unlikely that Locke's text was circulated or discussed even in part by these conspirators. If Locke largely wrote the work in early 1682 then Locke was apparently attending some meetings and observing the formulation of justifications of resistance somewhat similar to his own work, but without these influencing that earlier work. The earlier dating, with composition largely for Shaftesbury in the hopes that he would manage to raise resistance, would certainly help considerably to explain why Locke was, strikingly, not named among the many authors of declarations or more extended works who were mentioned by the conspirators who dominated the later meetings.

Locke's Second Treatise may, then, have been written with an awareness from meetings with other conspirators in late 1682 of the different agendas of the various co-conspirators, as a text constructed with deliberate reticence or ambiguity about the form of government to be re-established in a conscious effort to encompass their various stated desires and principles. In this situation, Locke's text could be said to stand broadly as a statement of those points about which the conspirators seemed to Locke to be agreed, and as an expression of their desire to gain the most widespread support for their planned insurrection. Even then, it would be important to stress that the minimal changes to government after resistance allowed by Locke's arguments and the rarity of resistance emphasised by Locke –

---

[73] Sprat, *True Account*, II, 9.

features of Locke's text which will be analysed at greater length in a few moments – would have given to any readers of Locke's text a rather different picture of the kinds of resistance justified and the kind of government desired by its author than the image which would have been gained by those reading Sidney's more extended conception of the requirements for a desirable government. The Second Treatise may, alternatively, have been written earlier in 1682 as a statement of Locke's view of the arguments necessary for a justification of resistance before he became involved in the planning for resistance of Sidney and others and thus extensively aware of their views. It would then have been written as a text prioritising the need for resistance and reticent about the government to be re-established while carefully allowing the possibility of changing no more than the personnel who were currently attempting to establish absolutism. In both situations, as Ashcraft emphasises, Locke's text would be an 'outgrowth' of the need that was identified in the groups planning resistance to provide a justification for that resistance.

VI

There seem to be several different reasons for composition of the Second Treatise as an entire text to be published by printing or widespread circulation (leaving aside the possibilities that it was a piece of personal correspondence with Shaftesbury, an extended personal reflection which Locke had never shown and never intended to show to anyone in late 1681 or early 1682, or a text composed to advance a series of positions that were primarily intended to be circulated only in part and verbally in order to provide arguments for the other conspirators). It may have been intended to urge others to resist in advance of resistance – to support resistance that was planned but had not yet occurred, to indicate that people could resist and re-establish government, and, to a much lesser degree, to indicate what kind of government they should then re-establish. It may instead have been intended to justify a resistance that had occurred, to show the legitimacy of this resistance, to appeal for others not to oppose the consequences of this, and to show how government could then be satisfactorily re-established. This would be an explanation of the Second Treatise as composed primarily with an assassination in mind, or with an exorbitantly confident assumption that a wider insurrection would face little opposition. Or it may have been composed as something in between these two possibilities – as a manifesto of resistance to be published when such resistance had already commenced but before this resistance had succeeded in removing Charles from the throne and from his life, and to indicate that government could be easily and securely re-established. This would most naturally be the case of resistance by an insurrection led by London, Taunton, Bristol and Scotland in which the King was being fought but had not yet been killed; it could also describe a situation perhaps envisaged by Locke in early 1682, of resistance from Scotland and from unspecified numbers of people in England if Locke thought that the resistance that was allegedly then discussed between Shaftesbury and Argyll had any likelihood of occurrence.

It seems very unlikely that Locke intended the first of these three possibilities, that Locke composed the Second Treatise in order to circulate the work to urge others to resist in advance of resistance. We have seen that it is very difficult to find any works justifying individual resistance to Charles printed in England before 1683, although Ferguson's *Second Part of No Protestant Plot* of early 1682 came close to that extreme step in its threat of resistance. In that age of largely effective control over the press and of sedition trials this should not be surprising: printed works justifying immediate resistance would have been eagerly sought out by Charles II's agents and burned, and their printers and authors executed if found. Publication does not necessarily involve printing, and so it might be suggested that the *Two Treatises* was intended to circulate widely in manuscript to those whose support for resistance was desired. This, however, seems only slightly more plausible than the notion that they would be printed and then ordered through booksellers or distributed free of charge. It is very difficult to believe that the innately cautious Locke, who knew that he and the other plotters were being watched carefully, and whose papers and letters were subject to seizure and search, would have been distributing the work widely.[74]

What the conspirators seem to have intended to circulate just before or at the immediate point of raising resistance was a short 'declaration' of the aims of resistance – not a lengthy and bulky treatise such as the Second Treatise. It is conceivable that composition of such a 'declaration' of the aims and legitimacy of resistance in order to urge people to resist was Locke's primary intention only if we believe that he was the kind of intellectual who, when he sat down to turn out a short declaration, could not stop himself from generating a large and complicated text. That is simply

---

[74] Ashcraft stresses the extent to which all correspondence of the conspirators was subject to search and that their canting language was a necessary expedient. Composition of the Second Treatise with plans for it to circulate widely in advance of resistance are in these circumstances highly doubtful. Sidney's *Discourses* would have been slightly more capable of circulation than the *Two Treatises* because their discussion of resistance to particular Kings in history was less 'bare-fac'd' as an argument for resistance than Locke's argument, and at least allowed Sidney to try, unsuccessfully, to argue that his historical examples of the removal of Kings were not intended to refer to Charles. Even with that work, however, circulation in advance of resistance seems beyond belief.

not the kind of intellectual that Locke was, having advised a leading minister for many years.

Explanation of an intention to circulate in advance of resistance also fails to explain why not one reference to the *Two Treatises*, or to 'De Morbo Gallico', or to any other work by Locke that could have been a version of the *Two Treatises* survives in the various confessions of the planning of resistance. That there is no surviving reference does not necessarily mean that the work was completely unconnnected to the plans for resistance because written much earlier, as Laslett argues in his recent response to Ashcraft's claims, although it may well indicate that Locke's work was written very much for Shaftesbury when he was planning resistance, and that it was never part of the discussions that were undertaken in late 1682 and early 1683 after Shaftesbury had fled into exile. It does strongly suggest that the secretive and cautious Locke had shown the manuscript of the Second Treatise to very few people (at most), and certainly not circulated it widely even amongst the various conspirators, let alone amongst those outside of the small inner circle of conspirators.

It is very much more likely that the *Two Treatises* were intended to be published at the moment that resistance commenced in order to gain support for and prevent opposition to that resistance if such resistance took the form of a general insurrection, or that they were intended to be published to defend resistance already completed, to show that the people had the power to take the next step of re-establishing government, and to hint at the desirable form of that government, if assassination were the form of resistance that had been successfully undertaken.

Lending some credibility to this view, Shaftesbury seems to have had ready, and possibly even at the printers, a pamphlet with similar purpose in late 1682. Some of the conspirators claimed that various dissenting ministers sympathetic to resistance had prepared sermons showing the legitimacy of resistance that were to be preached when resistance was undertaken. It is likely that Ferguson's *Impartial Enquiry*, if it .had been composed by then, and Locke's *Two Treatises* were intended by their authors to be issued once resistance had been undertaken; Sidney's *Discourses* may have had such an intention but seems to have had little or nothing to do with Shaftesbury's plans. The extended assault upon Filmerian views in both Locke's and Sidney's works would have been very useful in such circumstances – and far more useful than in circulating to convince the lower orders to resist in advance of resistance.

Obviously, if an assassination of the King and his brother could have been planned which was not thought to have needed support from a widespread insurrection, then there would have been no need for Locke to have urged others to resist even in works published at the date of resistance, but merely to point out the legitimacy of resistance, and the way forward: the power of the people to re-establish the government and the desirable broad balance of executive, legislative and federative powers that ought to be re-established. So much of the genesis of the *Two Treatises* is shrouded in obscurity, and so little about the consciousness of the plotters of resistance at the crucial moments can be ascertained, that this highly circumscribed intention cannot be ruled out as a plausible possibility. It is possible that the conspirators around Shaftesbury could have thought that if Charles and James had been killed then their resistance would face little opposition. It is likely that this method of resistance was thought preferable by a significant number of the conspirators for that reason, among others. Ferguson himself noted that assassination was thought the preferable form of resistance by Shaftesbury because it was cheaper, safer, and more 'compendious' in achieving their ends. It is obvious why it would be cheaper and safer – far fewer people would have had to know about it than about an insurrection, and far fewer weapons and other supplies would have had to have been provided. Its 'compendiousness' may also have been an estimate of its likelihood of success – far fewer people were likely to have opposed by arms the perpetrators of resistance with Charles and James dead than with them living and fighting against a widespread insurrection that prompted memories of the social turmoil of the Civil War. This may also have seemed true because the most probable candidate for monarch in a revived ancient constitution, the duke of Monmouth, had seemed extremely popular on his 'progresses' around various areas of the country in 1681–2.

It is likely that assassination was also thought by Shaftesbury to be more compendious because it stood a much better chance of being controlled and directed to re-establishment of the mixed monarchy which he had long supported, probably with hopes that Monmouth would be elected monarch, instead of to the potentially more radical commonwealth principles that might have been supported by republicans such as Sidney in a widespread insurrection. Monmouth was to frustrate these hopes when Shaftesbury sought his support, apparently desiring the incredulous Shaftesbury to capture the King but not harm a hair on his head in order to pursue only Exclusion, thus allowing his succession instead of James and yet allowing him to remain 'a son' to Charles. Shaftesbury knew that the animus of Charles against him would leave no security for him in such a situation.

It is thus possible that Locke had in mind *only* an assassination without a widespread insurrection when writing the Second Treatise. It seems unlikely for several reasons, however, that this was the case. It seems intrinsically less likely that plotters of assassination would have thought that they would face no resistance in the deeply legitimist culture of post-Civil-War England than that they would have thought that some form of significant armed force would have had to be raised after assassination to support the re-establishment of government with a Whig candidate. The fragmentary evidence that we do possess from the later confessions of conspirators suggest that plans for assassination overlapped with plans for insurrection in late 1682 in Shaftesbury's circle and in early 1683 after his flight into exile. It seems very likely, given the limited range of his choices and the exigencies of his situation, that Locke would have supported resistance through insurrection as well as assassination, although no account of the meetings registers Locke's attitudes. The Second Treatise said nothing that would clearly exclude either form of resistance, but its rhetoric seems marginally more calculated as an appeal for support of an ongoing insurrection than of an already completed assassination. If Locke did compose the work in early 1682, insurrection seems to have been the only form of resistance then being proposed; later in the year assassination probably became the first preference of Shaftesbury but insurrection was still apparently seen as potentially necessary.[75]

Writing with a just anxiety to show that Locke intended to advocate a form of resistance in which many of its supporters would probably have been artisans and tradesmen, Ashcraft gives the impression that the Second Treatise therefore included an appeal directed at these men by utilising the language of equal natural rights. Ashcraft further emphasises the closeness of Locke's arguments to those of the mid-century Levellers, whose social base during the English revolution had been drawn from similar groups and which was animated in part by socio-economic grievances. That the Second Treatise included appeal significantly directed at such groups and groups lower still in the social scale seems also implied by Ashcraft's suggestions about the socio-economic core of revolutionary radicalism, by assertion that Locke's revolutionary theory existed among 'tinkers and cobblers', and by suggestion that the gentry could not have been expected to play a leading or active role in supporting revolution.

Ashcraft seems further to think that Shaftesbury and Locke were to a degree predisposed to make an appeal to artisans and tradesmen, tinkers and cobblers by their preceding association with an ideology of dissent, and commitments to trade, and to the politics of Exclusion. We have seen in earlier chapters, however, that Shaftesbury and Locke's support for toleration was that of lay anticlerical rationalist Anglicans, perhaps even of already unitarian Anglicans, and that their advocacy of trade was com-

---

[75] On the overlapping nature of the plans for insurrection and assassination see Ashcraft, *Revolutionary Politics*, ch. 8; on Monmouth, Scott, *Restoration Crisis*, 274.

bined with support for the role and riches of the industrious landowner and rather unblinking recognition of the poverty of the artisan, let alone the tinker. We have seen that while Shaftesbury's role in campaigning for Exclusion had made him an important figure in city politics, the city had been inclined to commonwealth principles in 1679–81 as well as to anti-popery and exclusion and that Shaftesbury had opposed the first set of principles even though supporting the latter. Shaftesbury's enormous support in the city in late 1681 came from his imprisonment and trial, and from his support for anti-popery, and even then he showed himself willing to turn to support of the King if he would restore him to favour or allow his exile. Shaftesbury and Locke's preceding identification with dissenting artisans and craftsmen, tinkers and cobblers, was rather more limited than Ashcraft tends to suggest.[76]

Shaftesbury did nonetheless apparently move significantly towards expectation of and desire for support of resistance from among artisans and craftsmen in London in 1682, as the King pursued preparations for his retrial and execution, and he hid in the city in late 1682. If the Second Treatise was not intended to have circulated widely before resistance commenced, however, there was no need for it to have contained an appeal to those that Ashcraft suggests that Shaftesbury was relying upon to support the first moments of resistance, including the 'ten thousand brisk boys' from Wapping in London; that they were apparently simply relied upon rather than being seen as needing to be convinced about the justness of resistance should itself give pause to any attempt to associate the Second Treatise with particular appeal to them.

That resistance – even through assassination – would probably have needed widespread support once it had been initiated, and that the Second Treatise was probably intended to be published to help to gain wider support once resistance had commenced, may nonetheless suggest that artisans and tradesmen, tinkers and cobblers may have been significant among its intended audience. Even if this were to be accepted, however, that the text would have been intended or thought by readers to contain such appeal because it contained an egalitarian language of natural rights of resistance is not clear. Locke was extensively aware of ethical treatises, including those of Grotius and Pufendorf; he desired to write a treatise of ethics when he wrote the *Two Treatises*, and the language of natural rights was appropriate because of that intention. Locke's arguments for individual natural rights of resistance had been foreshadowed in the previous century by writers whom Locke had read, such as Buchanan. Locke argued

---

[76] Scott, *Crisis*, ch. 8; Haley, *Shaftesbury*, 666–7; Ashcraft, *Revolutionary Politics*, 304n., 307n., 309, 325–7; idem, 'The Two Treatises and the Exclusion Crisis', University of California, Los Angeles (1980), 80–1.

for a natural jural equality in order to demolish Filmer's case for divine subjection and to defend resistance by private individuals rather than by political personalities. He argued for this as possessed equally by all private individuals in order to defend this right in polemically the strongest fashion and ethically in the fashion most satisfying to one who had long argued for individual non-resistance because of its necessity for preservation. A clear restriction of rights of resistance to only the materially propertied would have made difficult an avoidance of the possibilty raised in Tyrrell's account, of the alienation of property in order to preserve life; Locke's account made defence of material property by the propertied necessary to preservation itself. Resistance was made just as it was necessary to the preservation of life; it would have been difficult to exclude those with life but without material property from equal rights of resistance. Since he needed to make use of that egalitarian language for these purposes, no further commitment can be inferred from his adoption of the language; it needs to be shown convincingly that the way in which Locke used that language supported particular positions on issues that would have been intended to be significantly appealing to artisans and tradesmen, and perhaps especially to 'tinkers'. Furthermore, Locke's text made no declaration of rights of political agency within political society. To the limited extent that a case was directly made in a text of this period for 'popular government' in 1683, it was made by the man who had been associated with popular government and republican city politics in 1679–82, Sidney. It was not made by Locke, servant of a former leading opponent of radical city politics, whose case was instead for a popular revolutionary sovereignty which could very easily give way in practice to a mixed monarchy without any resulting political participation by the people at large.

It is far from clear not merely that a bulky and complicated book such as the *Two Treatises* would have been an effective type of appeal in convincing the lower social orders to support resistance, but also that they are the group whom it would have been most necessary for even such conspirators as the republican Sidney, let alone Locke, to convince to support an insurrection or assassination. The most obvious groups whose support would have been desired, and certainly those who would have been needed to be convinced by such a text in the wake of the Civil Wars and Interregnum, are the members of the gentry and yeomanry who had been Whiggish in 1679–81 and who were possessors of most arms and power in the country at large, together with the merchants of London and other cities who had the money to finance a fight against the crown, the historic experience of fighting against the crown in mid-century, and leading roles in defence of Shaftesbury, the city charter, and juries in 1681. While their situation had made Whigs such as Locke and Shaftesbury desperate men by

1682–3, they would surely have known that the fate of any widespread armed resistance would be very likely to be crucially dependent upon the attitudes and participation of the gentry, yeomen, and merchants. If all opposed it, then such an insurrection would be very likely to fail. It is the gentry, yeomanry, and to a lesser extent leading merchants, more than artisans or tradesmen, and especially more than 'tinkers', who the next section of this chapter will suggest would have been hoped to have had most reason to find attractive the combination of arguments in the Second Treatise on resistance, property and government, and for the calming of whose fears about resistance it will now be suggested that the rhetoric of the Second Treatise seems significantly designed. While Ashcraft's apparent implication of primary intended appeal to artisans and tradesmen will be suggested to be not particularly persuasive, especially as it extends down the social scale from master craftsmen to 'tinkers', his recognition earlier in *Revolutionary Politics* of Locke's intention to appeal to industrious gentlemen in the chapter on property is far more convincing, and will largely be endorsed and refined in what follows. The account of the purposes and implications and of the primary intended audience of the Second Treatise that follows in the next section remains largely unchanged whether a date of composition of 1681, early 1682, or late 1682–early 1683 is preferred.

VII

Locke's account of property in the Second Treatise has been the subject of more study since the *Two Treatises* were published than any other part of the *Two Treatises*, and much of that study has provoked diametrically opposed views of what Locke intended to support, or what could be supported by his arguments, his intentions having been simply ignored. Obviously, it is impossible here to provide any lengthy account of the divergent views of scholars about Locke's theory of property. Equally obviously, a few words about Locke's discussion of property are required in order to identify what this account suggests to have been Locke's central purposes in composition of this account, its relationship to Locke's earlier thought, and particularly its relationship to the political and social purposes of composition of the Second Treatise.[77]

---

[77] It is impossible to list more than a few of the more important books on Locke's thought on property here; in addition to Ashcraft's *Revolutionary Politics* and Dunn's *Political Thought*, see especially MacPherson, *Possessive Individualism*, ch. 5; Tuck, *Natural Rights Theories*; J. Tully, *A Discourse on Property*, Cambridge (1980); N. Wood, *John Locke and Agrarian Capitalism*, Berkeley (1984); J. Waldron, *The Right to Private Property*, Oxford (1988). The account of property that follows is overly schematic and these

A number of broad purposes of composition of the account of property are relatively uncontroversial. Locke needed to reply to Filmer, particularly to two contentions of Filmer; that Adam and later fathers had had a right to all property as well as the right to rule, and that it was not possible for a consensually based politics legitimately to generate individual rights in property from God's alleged grant of the world in common. Locke also intended in replying to Filmer to compose his answer as an ethical treatise along the lines set out in the *Essay*. His ethical commitments before the *Two Treatises* were therefore likely to be important in the shaping of the argument that he chose in order to reply to Filmer. It is possible that Locke had composed his own account of property in the Second Treatise against Filmer and as an ethical treatise before the arguments for resistance outlined in this chapter, and thus with only these two motivations in mind. We are inhibited by the lack of manuscripts of the *Two Treatises* from showing that this was not the case, but there is no significant evidence that Locke composed the chapter on property before arguing for resistance, and the chapter as we have it appears to be an intrinsic part of the general defence of resistance in the Second Treatise and constructed to calm fears about property raised by defence of a right of resistance as well as to answer Filmer's argument that private property could not legitimately be generated from God's grant of the world in common.[78] This chapter has suggested already that almost all of Locke's Second Treatise was probably

accounts should be read for more substantial analyses. The last two named seem to this author to be especially persuasive accounts.
[78] Locke's chapter on property appears to have been composed as an intrinsic part of the defence of resistance for several interlinked reasons. The generation of the right to appropriate property and the definition of its limitations are part of the argument from preservation that is the basis of argument for resistance in the Second Treatise. The argument sets out to show that men come by rights to property from labour and natural rights separate from the compact establishing society and this argument involved a dramatic change from the view of Locke's manuscript 'Morality', that the same compact established both property and government. This change in Locke's view would have been necessary for obvious reasons if support for resistance is seen as his primary purpose since such a separation was necessary in order to allow resistance to government which did not allow assault upon property. Locke thereby also constructed an argument that could defend substantial inequality in property from the results of a challenge to government. These arguments do not mean that Locke could not have constructed his argument on property as a response to Filmer before he wished to defend resistance and then integrated it with this defence, but the form of this argument and the changes in his views that were involved are both more readily explicable following a desire to defend resistance than if they are seen as caused purely by desire to formulate an answer to Filmer. The point about the usefulness of Locke's form of argument in the Second Treatise and its alteration from 'Morality' *because* he wished to defend resistance to government but not any enforced alteration of or challenge by resistance to the property then held in Stuart England was made by Patrick Kelly, although in defence of a different dating of the Second Treatise than is proposed here, in 'Locke and Filmer: Was Laslett so Wrong after all?', *Locke Newsletter* 8.

written as one connected work in 1682–3, although Locke may have been musing on property and labour earlier and making suggestions to Tyrrell in early 1681. It will be suggested in what follows that this makes excellent sense as an explanation of the chapter on property as we now have it and thus that Locke's third intention in composing his account of property was to defend individual natural rights of resistance to government. Locke clearly intended to construct an argument that would appeal to his desired audience for the *Two Treatises* in 1682–3; the suggestion already made is that this was primarily the gentry, yeomanry and perhaps leading merchants.[79]

It is not necessary to rehearse at length here Locke's ethical and economic views before the *Two Treatises*, set out in previous chapters. Locke had long based his ethics upon a view of man as God's purposively created property, his workmanship; this was central in the Second Treatise. He had long argued that men needed to utilise the world by employing their God-given talents upon it, had particularly focused in his epistemological writings upon the application of inventions and discoveries to nature in order to increase the yield of necessities and conveniences, and had particularly emphasised the associated duties of industriousness in his series of ethical, economic and epistemological writings. His own friendship with Shaftesbury had involved his advocacy of the application of various methods to increase the yield of the land. He had long recognised the massive differentials in wealth in his society without showing the slightest sign before the *Two Treatises* of thinking about any legitimate challenge to the political system that was protecting these property holdings, or of redistribution of this wealth through measures such as Harringtonian land laws, enhancing the common law rights of commons, or legislation to control imprisonment for debt – nor, anachronistically, through redistributive taxation. Instead, in his service of Shaftesbury he had been associated with argument that the equality of the law was as useful to the poor cottager as to the rich because it protected his limited property too, he had been partly responsible for the constitution of the Carolinas setting up enormous differentials in landholdings and defending these against the possibility of Harringtonian redistribution, and he had accepted the gift from the proprietors of a noble title and landholding there. He had thus helped to create a constitution which would provide extra representation of the richest so that the poorer groups with property would not form a majority, and described the danger of rule of the numerically preponderant poor over those with extensive property since it would cause a 'state of

---

[79] On Ashcraft's analysis of Locke's intended audience, see in addition to his works cited above *Political Studies* 11 (1992), 99–115.

war'. He had never shown any significant sign of thinking that a more equitable distribution of property would increase the overall amount of production in society. He seems to have thought the poverty of many simply ineradicable by any action whatsoever, an unsurprising conclusion given the view that greater political power for the poor would cause a state of war.[80]

Although Locke's analysis of the origin of property rights in the initial stages of appropriation altered from the compact described in 'Morality' to the famous labour theory of appropriation, that men gained property in goods from the common by mixing their labour with them, the thrust of the arguments in the *Two Treatises* continued and extended this series of preceding attitudes or commitments. The Second Treatise argued, in direct reply to Filmer's ridicule of the allegedly Grotian account of private property as derived from consent and occupation, that property in things was legitimately gained from a grant of all things in common by the mixing of labour with the goods of the world. Locke was particularly clear in showing how significantly different levels of property ownership could thereby be gained in the things of the world: due to different levels of industry men quite legitimately accumulated different levels of possessions in the state of nature, limited only by the obligations not to destroy unnecessarily God's property and to leave enough and as good – but not enough and as much – to others. The invention of money, accepted by consent, then made these differences in ownership substantial but still legitimate. The transmission through time of enormously unequal amounts of material property by inheritance was then legitimate. The central thrust of this argument showed that enormously different levels of property were legitimately now held in society despite property having begun through appropriation of the world given by God in common. Locke was clearly ethically perturbed by the covetousness that was increasingly brought about by money, but he was also clear – perhaps echoing the Nicolean insight into the contribution of vicious self-interest to provision of the conveniences of the world – that the increased production that money had

---

[80] See above, chapters three and four; Wootton, *Locke: Political Writings*, 42; *Treatises*, 2.42: 'that Prince who shall be so wise and godlike as by established laws of liberty to secure protection and incouragement to the honest industry of Mankind against the oppression of power and narrownesse of Party will quickly be too hard for his neighbours'; cf. Dunn, *Political Thought*, and Wood, *Agrarian Capitalism*. It should be noted that in his economic writings of the 1690s Locke was concerned that speculators were not allowed to profit from the misery of the poor by governmental policies on recoinage, that his manuscript 'Labor' (discussed below) did apparently countenance governmental regulations to reduce the working day of the industrious poor and to extend that of idle gentlemen, and that he may have supported taking land away from proprietors in Virginia who did not farm it at least once every three years: R. Ashcraft, 'Political Theory and Political Reform: John Locke's Essay on Virginia', *The Western Political Quarterly* 22: 4 (1969), 742–58.

facilitated had helped to make an economy like England's perhaps a hundred times more productive than that of America, with the desirable result that the day labourer in England was better off than the king in America.[81]

Labour was what had originally appropriated the goods of the world, and it was for Locke still what increasd the value of the products of labour – certainly far more than any other factor. Locke was clear, however, that men's labour could be sold, and that day labourers were doing just that in contemporary English society, with the product of their labour going to those who hired them; they received in return wages that were considerably less than the value that they had added to the products of nature. Locke certainly held that the world was given to the 'industrious and rational', and not to the 'covetous' and 'quarrelsome'. This condemned covetousness was not acquisitiveness, however, but desire for what another's 'honest industry' had given to that person. Although there are passages where Locke approached a theory of desert that would have been appropriate to an ethical belief that the industrious would be rewarded in this life, Locke did not create a theory of labour entitlement to property through desert. Locke made no suggestion that after the initial stages of appropriation rewards commensurate to individual industry were necessary, and his suggestion of natural rights of inheritance precluded an important part of the construction of such an argument. Among the industrious uses of the world, Locke was very forceful in argument that the landlord who improved and enclosed his land acted legitimately and desirably, benefiting himself and the community by such actions.

Men had set up political society in order to protect their property (their lives, liberty and estate). Political society regulated such property, but property was not surrendered to it and then partly returned. For Locke, government was instituted precisely to protect property in markedly different levels of possessions, as well as property in life and liberty. Through inheritance these different levels would be transmitted down to following generations, and often increased. Although Locke did not accept that the practice of primogeniture was divinely necessary, *pace* Filmer, he also did not argue that unequal inheritance was an illegitimate practice as long as children gained the necessities of life and perhaps conveniences too, a requirement that could be fulfilled without much property being removed from the inheritance of the eldest son.[82]

[81] *Treatises*, ch. 5; cf. n. 5 to this chapter above; Wood, *Agrarian Capitalism*, passim; Parry, *Locke*, 43–55; J. Waldron, *The Right to Private Property*, Oxford (1988), ch. 6.
[82] *Treatises*, ch. 5; Parry, *Locke*, 53–5; Wood, *Capitalism*, ch. 4; on wage labour see esp. *Treatises*, 2, para 28; Tully, *Discourse*, 104–18, 135–45; and Wood, *Agrarian Capitalism*, 88–92; *Treatises*, 37, 87–98, 111–12, 119. For Tully (*Discourse*, 169, and cf. also 134, 143,

Although for Locke government was instituted for the welfare of the people, the government could not legitimately be dissolved by the people at large for a majority conception that the betterment of their economic condition required the alteration of the pattern of holdings of private property. The government was dissolved in the *Two Treatises* not through 'revocation' when the people at large decided another government could best serve their interests but only when it dissolved itself by acting beyond its trust or unjustly – that is, by arbitrarily taking property, or by removing or corrupting the legal processes by which such arbitrary action could be prevented and thus directly threatening the people.[83]

Men did not have the right to resist whenever they felt like it, nor the right to revoke a contract (compact) and depose the government, the kind of political theory suggested in the hostile account of consensually based politics in Dryden's *Vindication* in 1683. Locke thus attempted to stand apart from the implications which could perhaps be drawn from the thought of the major mid-century theorists of tyrannicide, such as John Milton and the Leveller Richard Overton, of an expansively revocable consent based on equal natural rights. He stood apart from Sidney's vision of establishing the best possible society to make men as good as they could be moulded to be. This point needs emphasis: for Locke, men had the right to resist when the trust had been violated by the government and it had dissolved, centrally by attacking property or altering the legislature and laws protecting that property. Political society was not set up to be a revocable consent in the name of greater social justice, or of other conceptions of a better (more virtuous) society, nor did political society establish government by contract. Rather, it was set up with a much more minimal conception of government as a trust to establish security and protect property, whereby only the violation of that trust would dissolve government and allow the people to then re-establish the government. It would be remarkable to construct a theory in which government dissolved centrally because

146), 'His undermining of primogeniture clearly would have the effect of redistributing landed property into much smaller estates.' For Ashcraft (*Revolutionary Politics*, 283n.), Locke made a 'direct and sustained attack' upon primogeniture by arguing that all children have the same title to property because of their right to nourishment, and since it was a right not merely to bare subsistence but to 'the conveniencies and comforts of life' it was a rights claim to '*all* the property owned by the father' (his italics). With a large estate to be inherited, however, the conveniencies of life could be secured for all by a still markedly unequal distribution of property. The more accurate analysis is that of Wood, *Agrarian Capitalism*, 79–80.

[83] The government could also dissolve under foreign invasion: *Treatises*, 2.211. Ashcraft (*Revolutionary Politics*, 394–6) makes much of the rhetoric of invasion in Locke's thought having been paralleled as part of a language of conspiracy by radical Whigs planning insurrection. It was also, however, present in Locke's thought in the *Letter From A Person of Quality*, as Schochet has pointed out in 'Ashcraft on Locke'.

it violated or threatened the security of property and then declare that property became subject to the will of the people with all having a right to all when government dissolved, and Locke did not do this. Locke's purpose here was surely the exact opposite, to show against the accusation by such as Dryden's *Absalom and Achitophel* that natural rights involved such potential and in reply to the questioning on this issue that had proved so difficult for Leveller leaders and their military associates to answer at the Putney debates, that men had a natural right to their property equal to that in their lives and liberty which was not voided by establishing government or by government's dissolution. Protection of the subjects' material goods by government (and their lives and liberties) was vital, and a government that would protect these goods was to be re-established when the first government had violated its trust by taking or threatening this property by acting arbitrarily.[84]

Locke combined this series of arguments on property with a series of very broad and rather vague positions on the form of government and political society that could be established, in which the primary emphasis was unquestionably on the legitimacy and need for resistance and the right to re-establish government rather than on the form of government to be re-established. This reticence may have been intended to join together disparate elements of the opposition to Charles with their own agendas for government, but it is important to note that even if this was the case the form of Locke's arguments managed to make legitimate no change other than that of personnel within a mixed monarchy and to place considerable emphasis on the extent to which the current executive within that mixed monarchy was forcing his subjects to resistance by not restricting himself to proper use of his justly considerable powers.

Moreover, Locke's silences were as crucial as his explicit arguments. While Locke defended the need to consent to political society he did not argue from this juristic necessity for the need to consent to, or in, government through participation in the legislature, nor even in the vote for representatives. This silence is extremely significant: there was no theory of the need for participation as self-expression of every individual's property and personality, as had been implied in the Leveller Overton's writings in mid-century, or of the need for democracy for which other Levellers had at certain moments argued more explicitly. We saw at some length earlier in this chapter that in other writings Locke explicitly denied the need for consent of all in the state, in direct contrast to the church. His recommendations on the franchise in the Second Treatise called for a 'fair and equal'

---

[84] *Treatises*, 2, passim; cf. the Putney debates in Wootton, *Divine Right and Democracy* (1986), 285–317 and the reading recommended on 334–5.

representation to be established, but that fairness was explicitly depicted as involving representation proportionate to both numbers and wealth, as wealth was a contribution to the public good, and not as being democratic.

Locke's argument was supportive of a monarch with a substantial prerogative remodelling a franchise that Locke simply seemed to take for granted as the recent franchise, and which he saw as needing amelioration because of occasional rotten boroughs, and not as needing to be defended in its significant restriction to the propertied possessors of freeholds. In one passage, probably designed to assure the gentry of the conservatism rather than anarchism of the people, Locke intimated the desirability of a hereditary House of Lords, and a House of Commons, and a Monarchy in England, the kind of government that his account 'supposed' in considering resistance. He held that this was the only lasting constitution to which 'the people' had returned after each revolution in government in the past. Recognising the possibility of settling a new form of government, he simultaneously recognised the possibility of changing only its personnel. While Locke expressed the desirability of frequent parliaments and of parliaments being able to sit when they were needed for the 'exigencies' of the nation, he did not clearly support the call for annual parliaments that was central to the views of many of the radical Whigs who became known in 1689 as the 'true Whigs'.[85]

Locke indicted Charles for not calling Parliament when it was needed by the nation (to exclude James), and he indicted him for altering the franchise in order to support his authority. Yet he did not argue that the executive should not in future maintain the power to call and dissolve Parliament and to remodel the franchise to make it more numerically proportionate when areas had suffered population loss or had grown enormously. His argument was perfectly compatible with a renewed mixed monarchy in which the monarch still had the power to call and dissolve Parliament as a trust in his prudence. Locke may here have been hinting at his view of the desirable balance of government to be re-established as well as condemning Charles, supporting the form of government that had long been established in England according to the ancient constitutionalist views of the vast majority of 'Whigs', as well as fashioning an important element in a very substantial general depiction in the Second Treatise of Charles as the true rebel for his failure to call Parliament when needed. Shaftesbury had been an important supporter of the King's prerogative in speeches in Parliament probably written by Locke, describing the preroga-

---

[85] *Treatises*, 2, passim, 143–6; 149, 151, 157–9; 212–3; 220; 222; 225; 230; for a somewhat similar argument cf. D. McNally, 'Locke'. Cf. Wootton, 'Leveller Democracy', passim.

tive as intricately interwoven with the English system of government. Locke and Shaftesbury had been avid supporters of the King's prerogative to secure toleration when Parliament had been against this policy. Locke had good reason to oppose unrestrained parliamentary sovereignty, even without being aware of Sidney's arguments by the time of composition, and more reason still if he had become aware of these.[86]

Having attempted to protect unequal property from equal natural rights, and having 'suppose[d]' the English constitution as it had been functioning until the aberrations of Charles II, the Second Treatise expended significant effort in showing that justifying resistance by individuals would not legitimate anarchy or frequent resistance. Some scholars have treated these sections as Locke's additions to the text in 1689. However, they make excellent sense as a very major part of the process of composition, especially when they are contrasted to the arguments of Sidney for 'rebellion' being very frequently justified by the consequent establishment of better governments. We have seen that for Locke the re-establishment of government was allowed to the people only when government had dissolved. Once consent had been given, men could not leave an established political society, and they had only the choice of emigration or of joining an established political society with an established legislature in all generations succeeding the establishment of government (except when it had dissolved). These were major limitations upon the change of government, but far from the only limitations that Locke trumpeted. Locke wished to make it clear both that resistance would be rarely mounted and that it had now become unavoidable. According to Locke, the people were generally very apathetic, dominated by custom, and would not revolt whenever government was tolerably concerned with the common good. As long as government governed reasonably well it would secure affection. Even though by this theory any single individual could resist attack on their property, they ought to calculate the cost to society and not resist if this was greater than the benefit. Any revolt of an anarchic few would be easily and 'justly' crushed. It was only when mischiefs had become general or when the attack on particular individuals by the government was so threatening to all that resistance would be raised. When a 'long train of actings' had convinced men that absolutism was being advanced and was now almost established in a society used to liberty it was, however, impossible, according to Locke to expect obedience. Surely thinking of the very probable reactions to Shaftesbury's role in resistance, Locke argued that while some might blame ambition for any resulting commotions, it was the

---

[86] *Treatises*, 2.157–68; Ashcraft, *Revolutionary Politics*, 239; see above, pp. 86–7.

monarch who was forcing resistance, and as such the true rebel deserving condemnation for the most heinous of crimes.[87]

These arguments, occupying significant paragraphs of the Second Treatise, were very probably part of Locke's initial text. They are surely natural reflections of Locke's deep ethical, political and psychological concern with the preservation of the society and the peace and of his own social attitudes surveyed over previous chapters. These commitments, indeed, would make this part of the argument as vital to the Locke described so far in this book as was the defence of resistance itself. Moreover, and surely most crucially of all, there was pressing need for such an argument for a gentry worried about reviving 1649–53, and about creating the potential for frequent resistance. Rhetoric on the quiescence and conservatism of the people in almost all circumstances other than those which were now described as forcing resistance is surely an indication of an aim to persuade the formerly Whiggishly inclined gentry and yeomen to support or at least not oppose this resistance, rather than the rhetoric of a text aimed significantly at the body of 'the people' themselves. A desire to calm the fears of many such gentlemen was likely even if Locke did not know that Sidney had composed a defence of 'rebellions' that were not merely resistance in order to restore a disturbed balance in government, and if Locke composed the Second Treatise with awareness of Sidney's work, then there was even more acute need for such arguments in an initial text of the Second Treatise because just such a revival of the commonwealth and broad justification for rebellion was being set out by one of his co-conspirators.[88]

Reassuring as all of Locke's many efforts to limit the consequences of arguing for resistance was surely designed to be to the Whiggishly inclined gentry, Locke did, however, support in the Second Treatise the right of 'the people' to re-establish and therefore potentially to remodel significantly the government. This potentially undermined the argument that it was possible to resist and then to re-establish the same form of government with different personnel without thereby legitimating either social reform or any but the rarest, while now necessary, political resistance. It potentially undermined his considerable efforts to protect property by making it a natural right and legitimately used for the maintenance of the government, let alone redistributable, only with the consent of 'the people' through their representatives.

---

[87] *Treatises*, 2.160–8; 176; 203; 205; 207–10; 223–7; 230; Dunn, *Political Thought*, 178–9. See Laslett, *Treatises*, Introduction on the dating of publication and the fate of the manuscript of the *Treatises* between 1683 and 1689.

[88] It is not hereby intended to suggest that the majority of the gentry would in fact have been persuaded by Locke's arguments had they been published in 1682–3, merely that they were directed in significant part at the Whiggishly inclined gentry.

These arguments could have proven insufficient as principles to prevent a levelling desire by 'the people' at large setting up an egalitarian franchise and thus a much more egalitarian society.

To look ahead for a moment, that Locke accepted that the Convention of 1689 was 'the people' suggests the flaccidity in his thought about the need for the consent of the people at large to the re-establishment of the government after the dissolution of government. He was apparently happy that the 'consent' of 'the people' was involved when only those currently represented by their possession of freehold property had elected the Convention. Charles Leslie was to point out the disjunction in Locke's thought between an individual consent and rights to participate even by voting shortly before Locke's death, querying astutely in *The new Association of those called moderate Church-Men, with the modern Whigs and Fanaticks* 'when did all the people of England (for example) choose the free-holders to be worth so much per annum? If they did not, then not only every individual had no vote, but much the major part of them had none. And they all had lives and liberties to dispose of, as well as the rest.'[89]

It has been suggested by Wootton, partly on the basis of Locke's 1689 willingness to accept the Convention as 'the people', that he may have meant the Second Treatise to be read as supporting only this limited a 'people' in first writing of 'the people' in 1681. In *Politica Sacra*, which Locke read in 1681, Lawson seems to have thought that power would revert to the people as a collective legal entity, and thus only to the propertied individuals represented in the English franchise, and not to all men in the society, when government dissolved. Locke may have had in mind just such a legal entity in writing of 'the people', and he may have been relying in part upon the extent to which most of the elite in the seventeenth century considered the poor as non-persons and simply excluded them from consideration when speaking of 'the people'. Under English law only freeholders had the right to sit on juries, and in former times they had been the only ones allowed to take oaths of allegiance, acts of explicit rather than tacit consent that may have been part of the background to Locke's arguments on this issue (even if the immediate source of this distinction seems more likely to have been the work of Tyrrell).[90]

Locke did not, however, make clear such a circumscription of the people in the Second Treatise. He was surely conscious that his own argument that people had property in lives and liberties as well as their property and

---

[89] *Treatises*, 2.88–90, 93, 95–122; 132; 140; [C. Leslie], *The new Association of those called moderate Church-Men, with the modern Whigs and Fanaticks, to undermine and Blow up the Present Church and Government* (1703), pt. II, 5 cited in Parry, *Locke*, 127.
[90] Wootton, 'John Locke and Richard Ashcraft's *Revolutionary Politics*', *Political Studies* 11 (1992), 179–98.

needed to consent individually and expressly to join political society fully deserved the kind of riposte that was later to come from Leslie. That consciousness should not, however, be taken to show that Locke therefore was articulating a commitment in 1682–3 to the consent of 'the people' in a sense that was grounded on any new and significant commitment to adult male democracy. We saw at length at the beginning of this chapter the significant limitations on the role of consent and on the necessity of consent in politics that Locke saw as desirable as well as legitimate both before and in the Second Treatise. It appears far less likely that Locke had come to favour a significantly more egalitarian or democratic set of principles even under the pressure of requiring support for resistance than that he saw no satisfactory way of resolving the problem of establishing a more restrictive right to resist and to re-establish government than that of 'the people' at large while articulating in its most forceful and ethically justified form the extensive natural right that was essential to his argument because it was necessary to show that because of the requirements of preservation of life itself individuals could resist the King as individuals rather than as officers of the kingdom. It is likely that he was relying in practice on the nebulousness of his argument about the agency of re-establishment involved in declaration of that right and the likelihood of that agency being assumed primarily by the significantly materially propertied. He was pleased to find that a restrictive body 'representing' the people could meet as 'the people' in 1689, and would have desired broadly such a group to meet in 1682–3 if resistance took a course that made that possible. He was writing at a moment when he could not know who would form a representative body of 'the people' able to restore government once resistance had been undertaken and did not wish to make the agency of this re-establishment clearer, but this absence of specification also allowed him to avoid endorsement of a parliamentary sovereignty that would have removed the precarious balance of mixed monarchy that he probably wished to see revived.[91]

It is being suggested, in other words, that Locke's juristic egalitarianism was constructed primarily for the strongest defence of resistance by a collectivity of individuals, in the situation facing him when composing the Second Treatise of the immediate priority to oppose emergent absolutism by force of arms even over his long-standing desires and commitments

---

[91] For views stressing Locke's commitment to an extended notion of the people see Ashcraft, *Revolutionary Politics*, 181–337; P. Rahe, 'John Locke's Philosophical Partisanship', *The Political Science Reviewer* (1991), 1–43 at 13–16. For views which suggest the limitations of Locke's notion of consent see Dunn, 'Consent in the Political Theory of John Locke', *Historical Journal* (1967), 158–82; I. Hampsher-Monk, 'Tacit Concept of Consent in Locke's Two Treatises of Government: A Note on Citizens, Travellers, and Patriarchalism', *Journal of the History of Ideas* (1979), 135–9; Wootton, *Locke*, introduction.

about the precise form of government to be set up thereafter. Locke could not then close off the possibility that the people at large would have re-established a government without adhering to his own desires and expectations, that they would have established a democracy or a near-democracy in the franchise and parliamentary sovereignty, and that they then would have redistributed property by the consent of the representatives of all in more socially egalitarian fashion (perhaps even a communistic fashion). This would have been a situation that Locke's juristic principles did not render illegitimate. However, this was not a form of government that Locke recommended in the Second Treatise. It was a form of government which he thought that the people who would actually support resistance would very probably themselves have rejected in favour of the English ancient constitution and distribution of property. It surely would not have been a form of government that he would have himself supported if it had occurred, and it is very likely that it would have been a form of government that he would have thought doomed to extremely rapid failure as it evoked precisely the situation where the poor ruled the rich which he had declared in his correspondence of the mid-1670s would create a 'state of war'.[92]

The failure of Locke to discuss explicitly in the *Two Treatises* the arguments about the historic ancient constitution of English government, the primary way of thinking about the desirable form of political government for Whigs throughout the Restoration, has troubled commentators ever since it was identified many years ago by J. G. A. Pocock. This absence has been explained in various eminently sensible ways, particularly by Locke's desire to write a treatise of ethics and his consequent concentration upon assertions of men's natural rather than historical rights. This explanation can now, however, be put more forcefully: while the ancient constitution did provide a way for Exclusion to be supported, for deposition or alteration of the succession, that was not Locke's primary purpose by the time that he came to write the Second Treatise. Ancient constitutionalism did not provide for individual rights of armed resistance to the monarchy. Historical ancient constitutionalism was simply not the appropriate form of argument for Locke to have employed in defending resistance.[93]

As has just been indicated about Locke's views on prerogative and mixed government, however, this absence of argument from the ancient constitution does not in any way show that Locke did not himself support a Whig vision (or conscious mythology) of English constitutional history

---

[92] As Hume pointed out, Lockeian principles were much more subversive everywhere outside of 'this single kingdom' of England (except, perhaps, in the Netherlands): Hume: 'Of the Original Contract'. Cf. M. Thompson, 'Hume's Critique of Locke and the Original Contract', *Il Pensiero Politico* 10 (1977), 189–201.

[93] J. G. A. Pocock, *Ancient Constitution*, passim.

and the desirable and historically evolved balance of monarchy and Parliament that most moderate 'Whigs' described as the 'ancient constitution'. Even during the period of the *Two Tracts* when Locke did not believe that there were any rights possessed by subjects against the combined legislative body of King and Parliament, he seems to have viewed this combined legislature as the ancient form of English government, and his later manuscripts and the *Letter* were more clearly supportive of this view. Locke was to recommend James Tyrrell's *General History of England* (1697–1700) and William Petyt's *The Ancient Right of the Commons of England Asserted* (1680) as essential reading for English gentlemen; more significantly, he recommended especially the relatively obscure John Sadler's *Rights of the Kingdom* (1649) on the 'ancient constitution'. As Wootton has emphasised, this expressed a type of 'ancient constitutionalism' that was rare before the 1680s, describing monarchy as initially based on a contract and elective.[94]

The ancient constitutionalism derived from a compound of Tyrrell, Petyt and Sadler may be said to have been radical in depicting monarchy as elective, but it was simultaneously opposed to parliamentary sovereignty and to annual parliaments, the causes of the 'true Whigs' of 1689. Locke's recommendations of these authors were not made until after the publication of the Second Treatise, but it is quite likely that Locke would have supported an elective monarchy in 1683, as again in 1689, within the type of mixed monarchy with a hereditary monarch that he 'supposed' for his discussions of resistance and which he had clearly supported before 1681 and was to support equally clearly after 1688. Such a monarch could then pass his crown on to his children and they to theirs and so on as long as they governed within the bounds of their trust; the people in all years after the election would be bound to obey this government as long as they did not choose to emigrate because this would be the only government to which they had the choice of consenting when they became adults.[95]

This analysis of Locke's intentions in writing the *Two Treatises* explains why he thought that they could be published almost completely unchanged in order to support his political and social aims *in 1689*. The *Two Treatises* were published by Locke in 1689 to legitimate and interpret the 'Glorious Revolution'. The central political message of the *Two Treatises* as published was that there should be a constitutional assembly to reconstitute government because of the right of the people to re-establish government since that had dissolved. There is no sign in the *Two Treatises*, however, that Locke wished to see the constitution itself remodelled. His

---

[94] Wootton, 'Locke', *Political Studies*, 179–98; 'Some Thoughts Concerning Reading and Study For a Gentleman', in *Education*, 397ff.

[95] See chapters two to five above; 'Some Thoughts Concerning Reading and Study For a Gentleman', in *Education*, 397ff.

expressed wish was to make the title of William clear.[96] The 'ancient government', he declared in 1690, had been 'the best possibly that ever was', and it was that constitution which should be revived: 'the settlement of the nation upon the sure grounds of peace and security' could be done 'noe way soe well . . . as by restoreing our ancient government' and thus providing a constitution 'that may be lasting for the security of civill rights and the liberty and property of all the subjects of the nation'. He was to serve in the 1690s in several advisory and administrative positions for a number of leading Whig ministers and Members of Parliament, and he shows every sign of approving the form of government that had been changed in very little but the different rulers, after James had 'abdicated' by fleeing.[97]

Locke did not approve of the failure of the Convention to declare that the government had been dissolved because that made into rebellion and sin the resistance that Locke knew very well had been attempted in 1682–3, 1685 and 1688, in which he had participated or for which he had helped to gain finance, but which the Convention sought to ignore. The prevailing interpretation of 1688–9 was of an abdication within the bounds of the constitution, and Locke's published argument was therefore treated as irrelevant or as politically too radical. Its radicalism, however, lay in its criticism of the political route that had been taken to arrive at a very highly desirable destination, and its declaration of an individual right of resistance, and not in criticism of the destination itself. Locke surely implicitly recognised this by deliberate omission of these arguments in a paper supporting William's then precariously established rule in 1690. In 1689 he wrote to Edward Clarke that if the ancient constitution had 'not been invaded' then Englishmen had done 'very ill' in 'complaining', and in his manuscript in support of William he argued that if there had been no miscarriages by the government, then 'Our complaints were mutiny and our redemption rebellion.' This was the central source of Locke's complaint about the different route taken to the desirable destination. By putting together with this comment the psychological importance to Locke of his ethics of individual non-resistance and preservation up to (about) 1681, and with the psychological and ethical importance to him of the form

[96] *Treatises*, The Preface.
[97] Locke, *Correspondence*, III, 1102; MS Locke e18 cited in J. Farr and C. Roberts 'John Locke on the Glorious Revolution: A Rediscovered Document', *Historical Journal* 28: 2 (1985), 385–98. One of the unfortunate consequences of the redating of the *Treatises* to 1679–81 by Laslett and to 1680–3 by Ashcraft is that the 1690s has become too little studied a period of Locke's life; it was during that period that Locke revised and republished them. Cf. Cranston, *Locke*, chs. 24–5; P. Laslett, 'John Locke, the Great Recoinage and the Board of Trade 1695–8' in J. Yolton, *Problems and Perspectives*; Dunn, *Political Thought*, pts. IV and V.

of the argument in the *Two Treatises* about how rarely resistance was justified, it may be seen that Locke had reason not merely to think that the *Two Treatises* could be published in 1689, but also to think that they ought to be published. It was only through acceptance of their form of argument that his own behaviour would be recognised publicly as legitimate resistance and not sinful rebellion. It was that view of his own actions that the Whigs and Tories in the Convention combined to deny; it was to that view of his actions that he was to be deeply commited until the end of his life, albeit anonymously.[98]

VIII

The overall pattern of arguments on property, government and resistance in the Second Treatise can now be seen to clearly reflect the series of commitments that it would have been natural for Locke to have expressed in the Second Treatise on the basis of his social, economic, political and ethical attitudes in the late 1670s, and based upon the need to oppose Filmer in such a way as to justify a resistance that required defence of 'the people' as individuals but which would simultaneously come as close as possible to delegitimating any social upheaval, and suggest the unlikelihood of 'the people' desiring a change in the form of government and being anarchic. Locke had managed to combine in the *Two Treatises* arguments from individual consent and natural rights that were necessary to resistance to government with arguments showing both how a government established through individual consent was obligated to protect widely differing levels of property-holding (unless the representative body of the propertied in that society could be thought to be one that would consent to redistributive taxation), and that it could not be resisted or have its authority revoked in order to overthrow the property-holdings in that society. Filmer had argued against the views of such as Pufendorf that the compact setting up property was also the compact setting up the political society; we saw earlier that something like this had apparently been Locke's own view in the brief manuscript 'Morality', probably in the late 1670s. The need to abandon this form of argument is at this point fully explained. Needing to justify resistance to government, Locke also needed to show against Filmer that men did not lose their rights in their property by resisting government.[99]

Ashcraft implies that Locke's discussion of the productive significance of labour in his discussion of the value added to goods in his account of

---

[98] Locke, *Correspondence*, III, 1102; Farr and Roberts, 'Rediscovered Document'.
[99] Cf. McNally, 'Locke', passim.

property in the *Two Treatises* was intended as an appeal to those artisans and tradesmen whose support for Exclusion and then for resistance was necessary in 1680–3, while his general stress on industriousness and use was intended to appeal to the industrious gentry and aristocrats who used their land for productive purposes, and to condemn courtiers and wasteful landowners, particularly aristocrats.[100] There is much that is surely accurate in this account of Locke's ethical intentions in constructing his account of property. Because of Locke's deep ethical commitment to industriousness, Locke surely did wish to urge industriousness and to condemn those who were not industrious and whose lands were allowed to go to 'waste'. As Ashcraft recognises, Locke denied that there was any right of alteration of the property established by law, including that of inheritance, except through representative consent, and broadly justified the enormous differentials in property holdings in English society. Locke did clearly condemn in many other writings any landowners who were wasteful and he did think that the wastefulness of such landowners in England would lead to a decline in their property-holdings as the industriousness of others would lead to an increase in their property-holdings, but as a natural process of wastefulness leading to diminished income, and not a political process that involved the legal removal of the land of those who used it wastefully on the basis of that wasteful usage. Only for one colony in America, which was dependent upon the regulations of the English government, did Locke suggest a redistribution of property without the consent of the owners if they allowed it to go to waste and the purpose then was to ensure the viability of the colony and not to facilitate a more egalitarian society.[101]

An exhortation to the duties of industriousness which concentrates massively on defence of the extensive exploitation and enclosure of the land, and which also clearly denies that labourers should be rewarded commensurate with their labour and by extension denies that this is true of

[100] Ashcraft, *Revolutionary Politics*, ch. 6, esp. 264, 281. Ashcraft's comments upon members of the aristocracy as wasteful seem to be based largely upon an identification of the aristocracy with the Court and, perhaps, a presumption that since they had more land to waste, they would be more wasteful. However, it could as easily be argued that association with the Court in the Restoration gave you greater information about how to use your land, that greater money from office gave you greater ability to use the land than was possessed by rural landowners who did not hold office, and that greater landholdings gave more chance for the kind of economic experimentation in application of the different soils and methods that Locke and Shaftesbury were together engaged in promoting and utilising. The general attempt to construct a social ideology out of Locke's condemnation of waste that discriminates more than very broadly a wasteful aristocracy from an industrious gentry is questionable. Locke wished neither aristocrats nor gentlemen to be idle; he wished both to be generous; and he thought that industriousness on each of their parts would give them the means to be generous.

[101] See the Ashcraft–Wootton debate in *Political Studies* 40: 1, 79–115; Ashcraft, 'Exclusion', 80–1.

all who labour, is not an argument that seems primarily calculated to appeal to many urban artisans and tradesmen, although the self-identification of some of these men, particularly master craftsmen, as materially propertied individuals against the materially unpropertied should not be denied because many of them also expressed hostility to the rich.[102] On a general level, and as a subsidiary argument, Locke surely intended to support the industriousness of artisans and tradesmen; his general ethical celebration of industriousness would have made this a natural part of his ethical intentions. In socio-economic terms, however, the only direct appeal that the Second Treatise made to such a group was through an argument that they could only secure their property against arbitrary taxation by means of resistance to Charles II.

At this point the suggested intention to appeal significantly to the concerns of the gentry, yeomanry and merchants in Locke's construction of his entire set of arguments is hopefully more persuasive than the suggestion that artisans and tradesmen were the central elements of his intended audience; among artisans and tradesmen master craftsmen also seem a more likely audience than 'tinkers'. The Whiggish gentry were the most obviously desirable audience for arguments that were constructed to be issued at the moment of resistance in 1682 or 1683 in terms of the aid that they could give to further and support any resistance already commenced, in terms of the opposition to resistance that they could raise, and in terms of the probable desire on Locke's part to re-establish government along the lines of the 'ancient constitution'. They were also the desirable audience in terms of the social values of almost all of the conspirators, and in terms of Locke's own social commitments. Locke had tried to show that the extensive property held by the gentry would not become subject to alteration by the lower social orders if they supported the form of resistance being advocated, he had legitimated the acquisitive agrarian capitalism of many yeomen who were frequently thereby becoming gentlemen in seventeenth-century England, and he had argued that their property would become subject to the arbitrary taxation feared from many of the Stuart monarchs throughout the seventeenth century if they did not support resistance to Charles.

We saw earlier that for Ashcraft the scholarly description of Locke as a conservative revolutionary, reluctant to advocate resistance, and consider-

---

102 McNally, 'Locke' perhaps overstates the socio-economic grievances of the Levellers, while Ashcraft tends to overstate the extent to which the Levellers were agreed in support of a clearly restricted propertarian franchise and to understate the extent to which some Levellers were animated by socio-economic grievances.

ing resistance only by a few aristocrats, was the 'single most unhistorical' scholarly view of Locke. For Ashcraft, Locke meant to support a 'real revolution'. It is time now to reformulate very considerably the scholarly view that has been condemned by Ashcraft. Locke intended to support armed resistance to Charles II, and he almost certainly intended to support a form of resistance that would have extended far beyond a few aristocrats and gentlemen, but he probably would have preferred resistance by assassination that did not involve a substantial insurrection, and surely hoped for and had every reason to expect leadership and direction of insurrection by aristocrats and gentlemen – including Shaftesbury, Essex, Russell and Monmouth. His case for resistance suggested certain minimal while significant conditions that had to be met for a government to be legitimate, and advocated resistance when these were not met, rather than advocating the desirability of a virtuous or militaristic republic à la Sidney, or of a democratic government. Although he defended the legitimacy of a change of the form of government if that was thought to be necessary by 'the people', various hints in the text suggested the desirable potential for a restoration of a mixed monarchy, attacked by the true rebel, Charles, and that he thought – or at least hoped – that 'the people' who would support resistance would prefer such a government. He may have wished to declare monarchy elective in these very limited and very rare circumstances. If that is what is meant by a 'real revolution' – and it is a very considerable amount indeed – then Locke was a supporter of a real revolution. It needs equal emphasis, however, that he did not clearly intend to support a 'real revolution' in the sense of one that would definitely change the form of government that was to be established because of a radical vision of what government should achieve as a regime of virtue, nor one that would achieve a democratic society of the people enfranchised because resistance by the people was justified, nor the political remodelling of the enormously inegalitarian property-holdings of the society. Locke himself tried to establish a distinction between legitimate resistance occurring in limited and rare circumstances and rebellion in the Second Treatise; the distinction is perhaps very slightly blurred by Ashcraft's description of Locke's 'revolutionary politics' and by the degree of his emphasis on Locke's 'radicalism'. In the *Two Treatises*, while being very far indeed from the supporter of only an aristocratic *coup d'état*, Locke was in some ways close to being as conservative a revolutionary as a revolutionary could be: he was a theorist of resistance who had been pushed into a defence of resistance by Charles' actions, and who probably wished to see no more change to English political life than the restoration of a trustworthy mixed monarchy with a still restricted franchise and religious toleration, even though he composed a work whose principles could have led to still greater change.[103]

IX

The Anglican hierarchy was uniformly hostile to Exclusion of James and very few clerics of the Church of England were openly supportive of Exclusion. Almost all clerics of the Church of England were hostile to any form of armed resistance. All of Locke's friends and acquaintances among the Latitudinarians completely rejected resistance. Indeed, it was Tillotson who wrote the important 1683 condemnation of Lord Russell's unwillingness to denounce resistance in all circumstances before Russell's execution for alleged involvement in the Rye House Conspiracy. According to Tillotson, 'The Christian Religion doth plainly forbid the resistance of Authority.' The law of England establishing the Protestant Religion had added to this general condemnation of resistance its own explicit condemnation of taking up arms 'on any pretence whatsoever' and these particular civil laws would have been enough to tie the conscience to nonresistance, even if natural law had left men at liberty to resist. Tillotson was unequivocal that natural law did not in fact leave men at liberty to resist 'Because the Government and Peace of Human Society could not well subsist upon these Terms'. In moving to justifying resistance in 1681–3, Locke thus moved decisively away from his clerical Latitudinarian friends, reinforcing the hostility to their erastianism voiced in his 'Critical Notes' and his already substantial distance from even the most eirenic of the Anglican clerics.[104]

Much of the support for Exclusion in the Parliaments from 1679 to 1681 was drawn from nonconformists. Locke was a signatory of the 1680 petition for the calling of Parliament. Many of these petitioners were dissenters and seven of those signing the sheet that Locke himself signed were dissenters. Locke was clearly thus associated with a significant number of dissenters in

---

103 Cf. the Wootton–Ashcraft debate in *Political Studies* 40: 1, 79–115. D. Underdown presents in *Revel, Riot and Rebellion*, Oxford (1980), passim a superb analysis of the multitude of factors determining allegiance in Civil-War Somerset. It is perhaps worth noting that Locke's own personal experience of the determinants of allegiance in Somerset was significantly shaped by deference to Alexander Popham, by his gentleman father's commitment to Parliament as well as to his patron Popham, and by the parliamentarianism and puritanism of yeomen in the region. On yeomen becoming gentlemen see Wrightson, *English Society*, passim. The plans to raise a force in Somerset, particularly around Taunton, were said to have included the raising of several hundred horse, a proposal that is likely to have involved mainly yeomen and gentlemen. Dunn, *Political Thought*, brilliantly presents the extent to which Locke was concerned with establishing certain minimal juristic conditions for government.
104 J. Tillotson, *A Letter Written to My Lord Russell in Newgate, 20 July 1683* (1683), passim.

this campaign. Equally, however, many of those that signed the petition and supported Exclusion were Anglicans and Locke was here – as since the 1675 *Letter* – once again associated with a lay Anglican and dissenting alliance in support of parliamentary measures to exclude James and to prevent absolutism. Locke certainly became closer to a number of non-conformists as Shaftesbury attempted to build this alliance, but in the 'Critical Notes', written in early-to-mid-1681, he was critical of clerical nonconformists as well as Anglicans. Many – though not necessarily most – of those who were alleged to have supported resistance were non-conformists. Most nonconformists, however, did not move on to support of resistance to the King when Exclusion failed. Many had spent the entire Restoration denying that their nonconformity made them any the worse subjects, and in the early 1680s many of them suffered the most vicious persecution of the entire Restoration without legitimating resistance. Richard Baxter was (for once) representative of the vast majority of non-conformists in his 1683 declaration that 'private men may not defend their lives or other rights by any act injurious to the honour or power of the King, much less by a war against him'.[105]

While many supporters of resistance were nonconformists several of those whom we have identified as supporting resistance were Anglicans or free-thinkers far closer to Anglicanism than to nonconformity. If Russell was indeed a conspirator who defended resistance – and that is likely despite his protestations of innocence at his trial – he had been educated by presbyterians, but he went to his execution protesting that he was a member of the Church of England and pleading for comprehension. This was a plea that his chaplain Samuel Johnson was to repeat in 1687. Among the other plotters John Wildman had Deist leanings, and his close friend John Hampden had not merely been a presbyterian but in the early 1680s was a free-thinker who questioned the entire authority of Scripture.[106]

The closest ecclesiological affinities of several of the significant support-ers of resistance in 1681–3 appear to have been with Independency. It was alleged that John Owen was himself a supporter of plans for resistance, and that a few Independent preachers, including Owen, had prepared sermons to be preached should the resistance to Charles II planned in 1682–3 have been raised. In that age of dissemination of most information and propaganda from the pulpit, it is likely that such sermons were soli-

---

[105] M. Knights, 'Petitioning'; Baxter MS IV, fos. 61–2, Dr Williams Library, London, cited in Ashcraft, *Revolutionary Politics*, 295.

[106] *The Last Speech and Behaviour of William late Lord Russell* (1683), 2 on his having lived and died 'in the communion of the Church of England, though I could never yet comply with, or rise up to all the heights of some people', wishing that 'the Churchmen would be less severe, and the Dissenters less scrupulous'. On Wildman and Hampden, see Lacey, *Dissent and Parliamentary Politics*, 400–1; Goldie, 'Anglican Royalism'.

cited by some of the conspirators with the design of gaining support for a widespread insurrection if that was needed. Nonconformist clerics had far more reason to be willing to abandon their Restoration protestations of nonresistance and suffering than did any Anglican preachers, and would have surely formed the majority of any such preachers. John Owen had been the chosen preacher before Parliament in 1649 on the day after the execution of Charles I, and there is some indication that his brother Henry Owen was on the periphery of those involved in planning to support resistance. Nonconformist congregations would doubtless also form the majority of those who could have been expected to take up arms as a result of preaching – but that is not the same as saying that they were necessarily therefore the majority of those who it was hoped would take up arms to support resistance if an insurrection were needed, nor that they would guide resistance.[107]

The ecclesiological attitudes of two of the most prominent supporters of resistance in 1681–3, Algernon Sidney and Robert Ferguson, were closest to Independency. Gilbert Burnet summed up Sidney's religion in characteristically hostile fashion:

he was a christian . . . but he hated all sorts of church-men, and so he never joyn'd himself to any, but to ye Independents; he kept up very little of an outward profession of Religion . . . he thought devotions . . . were but slight things, and that good Morality was all that was necessary.

Sidney was committed throughout his life to the cause of religious toleration, but this commitment centred upon belief in a neo-Platonic personal inspiration that Locke would have labelled enthusiasm, concerned with the freedom for worship dictated by the Holy Spirit which 'discovers truth unto us by the wings of love and faith'.[108] Ferguson was an Independent and close to John Owen but, in stark contrast to Sidney, he was a fierce Calvinist and had won Owen's favour by a swingeing attack on reducing religion to moralism. Ferguson was many years later to accuse Locke of corrupting Shaftesbury, just before the latter died, with his Socinianism and thus, presumably, his moralism. This judgement was not passed until after Locke had been accused, with good reason, of Socinianism in the 1690s. The basis on which Locke converted Shaftesbury to Arianism and Socinianism in Ferguson's account was his chapter in the *Essay* on God, which said nothing that supported Socinianism (or trinitarianism), and Ferguson's story thus seems false, but the attack suggests tension over theo-

---

[107] Ashcraft, *Revolutionary Politics*, 374–5 points out the connections between Owen and Ferguson and the possible peripheral involvement of Henry Owen in plans for resistance.

[108] Burnet Add. MS 63057, pp. 137–8 cited in J. Scott, *Algernon Sidney and the English Republic 1623–1677*, Cambridge (1988), 27 and passim.

logical issues among the fellow plotters of resistance, and particularly between the stridently Calvinist Ferguson and Locke. Employed by Shaftesbury as a chaplain throughout the Exclusion crisis and the plans for resistance, Robert Ferguson must have known Locke well, but there is no indication of any friendship between them. Although they had a number of mutual acquaintances, such as John Mapletoft and Benjamin Furly, there is similarly no direct evidence that Locke met Algernon Sidney outside of the meetings of the conspirators and nothing to suggest friendship. Shaftesbury and Sidney, moreover, disliked each other intensely.[109]

A broad sympathy with Independency among the plotters of resistance whose arguments turned to natural rights would not be surprising. Although throughout the century many of the Independents had stressed very strongly the need for government from men's sinfulness, they had historically also been the most willing to employ discussions of natural rights of all of those religious groups which during the Restoration became nonconformists. In order to defeat the parliamentary presbyterian attempts to impose a national ecclesiastical discipline that made 'new Presbyter but old Priest writ large' Independents had had to seek a source of political authority outside of Parliament itself, and they were the most willing to argue that political society was constructed for men's temporal benefit alone because the exclusivity of their predestinarianism made them acutely aware that political society would necessarily be composed of many who were unregenerate.[110]

It might be alleged that in turning to arguments from natural rights against absolutism Locke was consciously utilising an ecclesiologically specific language in terms of those identified with natural rights arguments in the Civil War, and in terms of those willing to use them in 1682–3. In Locke's support for toleration from 1667, and especially in 1681, a number of significant affinities with Independency have been noted. There is no reason to think, however, that this is why Locke utilised these arguments. Locke needed to use them to answer Filmer, to defend resistance, and to write a treatise of ethics. He was aware of much of their ethical usage by authors of other religious denominations in other countries. It would not be logical to suggest that Locke's arguments were adopted because of any ecclesiological sympathies, even if he had had such ecclesiological sympathies in a more systematic sense than previous chapters have shown to be

---

[109] Bodl. MSS Smith 141 fo. 65; Rawlinson D 824 fo. 64; T. Cherry to T. Hearne, 25 July 1706; *Letters Addressed to Thomas Hearne*, ed. F. Ouvry, (1874), 9 cited in Haley, *Shaftesbury*, 732. Haley notes that the identification of the source of Shaftesbury's Arianism or Socinianism in Locke's *Essay* was a later description by Ferguson; he does not pronounce upon its validity. On the mutual dislike of Shaftesbury and Sidney, Haley, *Shaftesbury*, 718; Ashcraft, *Revolutionary Politics*, 178ff.
[110] M. Sommerville, 'Independent Thought', chs. 6–7.

the case, and even if the Independents had been the only people to have
used these arguments historically; the wide variation between the nature of
the sympathy with Independency of Locke, Sidney and Ferguson makes
any significant ecclesiological agreement among them seem very doubtful
at best, and Locke's criticisms of Independency in the 'Critical Notes'
reduces its plausibility still further.

There is no question that the years from 1679 to 1683 saw Locke moving
in circles made up of dissenters to a greater degree than earlier in his life,
and that his life in exile in Holland continued his association with a
number of English nonconformists. His own enforced exile for political
dissent and these associations must have made more personal to him the
suffering of those who were persecuted for religion in the 1680s in England,
and the *Third Letter on Toleration* in 1692 included a deeply felt account
of the viciousness of persecution in England. Such sympathy with those
who were persecuted and the possibility that most of those who were
willing to employ natural rights arguments were ecclesiologically Independent are, however, not enough to suggest that Locke was an ideologist of
dissent in the 1680s because of his support for toleration and resistance
without obscuring as much as is revealed about his thought and about the
widely varied religious views of his co-conspirators.

One further element of the *Two Treatises* which has long puzzled scholars can now be addressed: the complete absence of arguments for religious
toleration. Some have even suggested that the 'Critical Notes' were themselves the papers that would have 'filled up the middle' of the *Two
Treatises*. In general terms, this view owes much to the anxiety of commentators about the absence of arguments for toleration in the *Two Treatises*
when the Treatises were a work of political philosophy, when toleration
was such a deep commitment of Locke's and he must have been opposed to
the fierce persecution of Protestant nonconformity that Charles supported
in 1681–5, and when the *jure divino* teachings of the Anglican church were
such an important element of what Locke explicitly set out to oppose in the
Two Treatises.[111]

There are probably several layers to Locke's failure to argue for religious
toleration in the *Two Treatises*. Given that the *Two Treatises* were
intended to be published in order to gain support for resistance in 1682–3,
and given that the gentry have now been suggested to have been among the
most significant targets of this appeal, on a practical basis there was considerable reason for Locke not to lose the support for resistance of any who

[111] See, for instance, J. Waldron, 'Locke, Toleration', 73: 'Religious toleration was one of
Locke's abiding preoccupations and one of the most contested political issues of the age.
It is odd that he should make no reference to it in a treatise concerned with the functions
and limits of government'; Pocock, *Ancient Constitution*, 347.

would have opposed or questioned the grounds of his arguments for full-scale religious toleration. The institution of that policy could wait for the Parliaments and monarchs to be elected after resistance and the re-establishment of political authority. As Aschraft indicates, the majority of those who supported both resistance and toleration thought it advisable to wait for such a body to promulgate toleration rather than including it explicitly in their demands. As importantly, the form of Locke's own support for toleration, if it had come complete with anything like the assaults upon nonconformist clerics and suspicion of their arguments for 'liberty of conscience' expressed in the 'Critical Notes', would have been very likely to have alienated many nonconformists. By explicitly tying to toleration the defence of resistance of the *Two Treatises*, support for toleration both when he composed this defence, and especially in 1689, might very well have declined. He probably published the Second Treatise very quickly in 1689, without time to integrate argument for toleration within it.

Locke's tolerationism, ecclesiological eclecticism, and fear of persecution by nonconformists, were, however, probably important in determining the secular shape of Locke's argument for resistance. We have seen that unlike Ferguson, Denton and others, there were no significant arguments in the *Two Treatises* that men had to defend and establish their religion as well as defend their liberties, lives and properties.[112] There are two reasons which very probably help to explain why Locke did not advocate resistance to Charles on religious grounds, even though Charles was persecuting Protestant nonconformists and therefore acting against one of Locke's deepest political commitments: because he had spent his entire intellectual life trying to find ways to avoid warfare over religion, and because he did not believe that many of those nonconformists who would resist Charles on such grounds would then institute any adequate form of religious toleration, not least because as an eclectic tolerationist Anglican already close to Socinianism he accurately thought that that church at least allowed broader doctrinal disagreements than most nonconformist congregations would allow.

There is only one point at which the 'Critical Notes' considered resistance in order to alter the religion established by the monarch. Locke spoke of men who 'in defence of their natural and evangelical right, of takeing care of their owne salvation, and not oweing the beliefe of what they did, or could not believe, often resisted that force, which would unreasonably, and contrary to the Methods of the Gospell, compell them to a profession

---

[112] *Treatises*, II, 209 presents a practical argument that it will be difficult to hinder men from resisting when they think that their lives, liberties and estates and 'perhaps their Religion' too is threatened but it does not justify resistance on the ground of religion.

of that Religion or those doctrines, which they did not believe or could not assent to'. He went on to argue that if Christianity were left to 'the real convictions of men's minds and their free submission to the doctrine, and discipline that they judgd right', then 'there would not be roome for those dangerous questions about reformation which have so shaken the Governments of civill states'. When it was 'askt whether the people may reforme if the Magistrate does not' he argued that 'it in bottom meanes this: whether the People may use force against the Magistrate to alter either the doctrine, or discipline of the Church which he by force has established or maintained'.[113]

For Ashcraft, although this question was not answered, the implications of this are 'rather clear': Locke has raised the question of whether 'the people may use force against the magistrate' and has presented the 'general and the specific grounds for a theory of armed resistance, as developed in the *Two Treatises*'. It is true that Locke has not here repeated the clear denial of rights of resistance of his 'Essay on Toleration', nor repeated its argument that the dangerous view that the people might reform religion if the magistrate does not should be suppressed. Nonetheless, nothing Locke says clearly suggests a right of resistance, nor that Locke had gone beyond his earlier opinions that there was a right to toleration, that if this was denied men would in practice resist, that such resistance was illegitimate, and that the view that the people could forcibly reform religion was wrong and to be avoided. He spoke of 'bloud', 'confusion' and 'popular commotions' as the result of men using force to defend their right to take care of their own salvation in introducing that right, and went on, as we will see in the next paragraph, to reject the behaviour of those who would use force because they would use it in order to impose their own forms of religion. He declared that the only true reformation was that of the individual by 'peace' and 'quiet'. He spoke of men 'often' rather than 'justly' resisting. The subject of the entire section was not the existence or non-existence of a right to resist, but the calamitious consequences of non-toleration, due to the iniquities of magistrates and dissenters alike, committed to the 'popeish doctrine, of using force in matters of Religion'. The 'Critical Notes', discussing resistance only as something to be avoided, were, moreover, concerned exclusively with resistance for religion. They set out no arguments for resistance to absolutism, let alone the specific grounds for the argument in the *Treatises* in terms of property, consent and a private law theory of resistance for preservation. It is only by discussing the passage in unduly abstract terms and making it have a clear positive implication that it becomes analogous to the *Treatises*. Instead of setting out the grounds of

---

[113] MS Locke c34, 102; cf. Ashcraft, *Revolutionary Politics*, 490ff. esp 497–8.

resistance of the *Treatises*, the 'Critical Notes' underscore the necessity for Locke, when he was at last driven to formulate a right of resistance, of framing that right in political and not religious terms.

Locke continued in the 'Critical Notes' by arguing that reformation did not 'much mend the matter whilst the Reformers commonly proceeding upon the same ground desire only to have the secular Arme' and use 'the same force to compel others'. Locke's indictments of the intent of all groups to establish their own brand of religion, including the Independents, were cited at length in chapter three. The *Letter Concerning Toleration*, as we will see later, continued the assault upon those who argued for toleration only until they had received power and then sought to establish their own religion: there is absolutely no reason to think that Locke had changed his mind on the consequences of justifying resistance to Charles by nonconformists on religious grounds between the 'Critical Notes' and *Two Treatises*. Locke did not defend resistance in order to secure toleration in the *Two Treatises* because it would have lost him support for both resistance and toleration, and because he did not believe that those who would resist in order to secure 'toleration' desired or would establish genuine toleration. Instead, they would return England to the regimes of the Civil War, its commotions and confusions. Locke could never forget the 'storms' in which his childhood had been spent, and how the greatest pleaders for liberty had been its 'greatest engrossers' too. In its silence on toleration, and almost complete silence on resistance for religion, the *Two Treatises* were indirectly another work produced by Locke's anxious eclectic combination of elements of extremely Latitudinarian Anglicanism (now very close to Socinianism) and of Independent thought.[114]

---

[114] MS Locke c34, 102–3. Ashcraft, *Revolutionary Politics*, 490–8.

7

Locke's moral and social thought 1681–1704

I

Locke's *Essay Concerning Human Understanding*, largely composed in exile in the mid-1680s and published in 1689, declared in expanding upon his 1676 journal account that 'Nature' had put into men 'a desire of Happiness, and an aversion to Misery'. These were innate 'practical principles' which influenced 'all our Actions, without ceasing'. According to the *Essay* 'That we call good' was what was 'apt to cause or increase pleasure, or diminish Pain in us; or else to procure, or preserve us the possession of any other Good, or absence of any Evil'. Men were obliged, physiologically and morally, to pursue their own happiness.[1]

The *Essay* simultaneously assaulted innate ideas. For almost all of Locke's English contemporaries, Anglicans or dissenters, such innate ideas informed men that they had to serve others and provided an influence of conscience to help to bring them to practise that duty. While accepting significant elements of Locke's empiricism, many eighteenth-century philosophers, including Locke's own pupil, the third earl of Shaftesbury, were to develop an account of men's minds that described a natural 'sympathy' or 'benevolence' towards other men. Locke's analysis of the mind left no room for such an account and was criticised by these philosophers because they thought that it was difficult on Locke's premises to provide a basis for an ethic of mutual service, or even for the lesser mutual concern necessary to establish justice.[2]

In the *Two Treatises* Locke argued that the purpose of political society was the preservation of individual rights, even if these individual rights

---

[1] *Essay*, I, iii.3; II, xx.2, xxi.29 (1st edn.), xxi.39.

[2] On innatism see Yolton, *Way of Ideas*, passim; see particularly the works of the third earl of Shaftesbury, Francis Hutcheson and David Hume on benevolence and sympathy. Spellman, *Locke and Depravity*, valuably indicates that Locke's view of the actual character of men in the world was more pessimistic than that of most eighteenth-century philosophers and lacking the 'benevolence' and 'sympathy' thought essential by many of these later philosophers.

were depicted as duties to God and derived far more explicitly and significantly from the duties of preservation in order to preserve God's property than from any argument about the maximisation of those individuals'
pleasure or interest. This description of the basis of political society presented an obvious problem for the generation of political duties to serve
other men. Although the *Treatises* argued that political society was to
secure the common good, they did not extend this conception to the good
of the community beyond the prevention of injury or injustice and the
preservation of the society. Locke tended to identify the public good of the
community with the aggregate goods of individuals, arguing for instance
that laws were made for the 'public good, ie the good of every particular
member of that society'.[3]

It is therefore unsurprising that there are descriptions of Locke's thought
in the *Two Treatises* and the *Essay* as expounding 'possessive individual-
sim', as concerned above all with the protection of individuals' rights and
interests, or their material possessions. Locke's concern with the development, responsibility and reward of the individual was unquestionably
extremely important. His religious and epistemological thought stressed
the responsibility of the individual to study and practise the religion that he
thought best and not to accept opinions from custom, education and party.
His epistemological and ethical thought placed much emphasis upon personal responsibility, stressing the duty of every individual to labour, to
study, and to reason. His ethical and social thought was manifestly concerned with the provision of reward for individuals who had thus fulfilled
their duties in labouring industriously, although his recognition of the
limited rewards that would in this life go to the virtuously industrious,
given the arguments on property of the Second Treatise, is likely to have
sharpened his already pronounced sense of the need for celestial virtue to
compensate the industrious adequately.[4]

It is not the intention of this chapter, which concentrates on analysis of
Locke's ethical and social thought in the period of composition, publication and republication of the *Treatises* and *Essay*, to de-emphasise these
features of Locke's thought, nor to suggest that there is very much sense in
which for Locke men were *politically* obligated, or ought to be politically
directed, to service of the common good and of other men beyond those
measures necessary to secure justice, the preservation of life, and the preservation of society. In the *Treatises*, the laws were to provide an umpire

[3] J. Gunn, *Politics and the Public Interest in the Seventeenth Century* (1969), 292–4.
[4] C. B. MacPherson, *The Political Theory of Possessive Individualism*, Oxford (1962). For
many important correctives to MacPherson's account, see Dunn, *Political Thought*, passim.
Parry, *Locke*, is the best straightforward account of these aspects of Locke's thought.

between men's rights, not to civilise men into a more extensive service of others.[5]

It will, however, be indicated that none of these commitments of the *Treatises* and *Essay* led Locke to deny that men were obligated to serve the common good and their fellow men in ways beyond what he himself declared in his political thought to be the 'narrow measures' of 'mere' justice. More broadly, it will be underlined that Locke's political and religious individualism was not based on social or ethical egoism. We have seen that up to 1681 Locke thought that service was owed by those with means to an extent that he thought to be considerable (which is not to say that such service will appear to modern eyes to have been considerable).[6] While the *Two Treatises* was composed to set out a part of ethics, and to be consistent with the principles established in the *Essay*, it was intended by Locke to set out very little of the content of such ethics. Locke explicitly said in the Second Treatise that he was not going to discuss the content of natural law in any detail.[7] The *Essay* may originally have been conceived by Locke as including a section on the content of morality; as published it included little more than mention of the foundational principles on which a morality could allegedly be based. Locke's friends who had good reason to think that Locke had written the *Treatises* as well as the *Essay* did not think that by writing either Locke had constructed his projected account of the duties that men owed to each other; instead, they plagued him throughout the 1690s to compose just such a book of offices.[8]

Although the *Essay* declared men's duty to pursue pleasures since God had purposively placed these in them, even in the first edition of the *Essay* Locke did not argue that men ought to follow their terrestrial pleasures in an unrestrained and undirected manner, and he opposed ethical egoists and 'Hobbists' as not recognising very many plain duties of morality. He contended instead that God had blended pleasure and pain together in

---

[5] The point is made in order to contrast Locke with those theorists of a pre-political state of nature as solitary and wandering, with laws or the persuasion of an orator to make men civilised and sociable, including Cicero in *De Oratore*; it is not intended to deny that since Locke thought that habits were extremely important in making men virtuous or sinful the framing of men's habits so that they were just would probably lead to them being more beneficent.

[6] Locke genuinely thought that men should serve their country as much as they were able, or they did not deserve to eat, and he emphasised the duties of family and friendship and service of the community by gentlemen. In a society that was built, especially among the gentry, upon the networks of kinship and friendship, and upon the elitist assumption that society should be governed by those very few 'able' to govern it, such services could indeed be seen as considerable. Yet such services, as chapter five emphasised, helped to preserve the hierarchy and to legitimate a level of self-congratulation for very minor services indeed when contrasted with means.

[7] *Treatises*, 2.12.

[8] The most important of these were Tyrrell and Molyneux; see below pp. 386ff.

order for men to find dissatisfaction and want of complete happiness and thereby be led to 'seek it in the enjoyment of him, with whom there is fullness of joy, and at whose right hand are pleasures for evermore'. Men were said to be determined by the 'greatest good'; they therefore ought to be led to service of God and thus to service of other men since God offered them true happiness.

In 1694 Locke amended his earlier view that the 'greater good' in view determined the will by focusing upon men's uneasiness, and recognised the extent to which men would not fulfil their duties of service to others even if they recognised the possibility of heavenly reward. If men had been moved by the greater good then they would have been unable to 'get loose' from the infinite eternal joys of heaven once proposed, even if these were only considered as possible, since terrestrial pleasures were infinitely outweighed by heavenly pleasures even if the attainment of terrestrial pleasures was considered more probable. According to Locke, in practice the attainment and continuation of the 'pittance' of present goods of honour, riches and pleasure was less likely than the possibility of eternal durable joys. Men, however, little considered 'absent goods' such as heaven. The ordinary necessities of life filled their lives with uneasiness. Very little time was left for thought about absent goods because to these natural necessities was added 'fantastical' uneasiness for riches, honour, power and a thousand other desires derived from fashion, example and education and settled by habit. These 'irregular desires' were made 'natural' by custom.[9]

While Locke now asserted that in most cases the greatest uneasiness and not the greatest good determined the will, and thus increased rather than decreased his problems in motivating men to perform duties to God and fellow men, he crucially now declared that the mind could suspend the pressures of desires and could consider and weigh various objects. Such 'liberty' allowed the understanding to direct men to the true good, identifying their 'true' and 'real' happiness. Men had to forbear 'too hasty' a 'compliance' with their desires, and to moderate their passions so that they could examine freely. Indeed, men were to 'employ our chief care and endeavours' in disposing themselves to this activity, creating a 'hunger' for righteousness that would overcome their uneasy concentration on their own terrestrial pleasures. It was plain that men could give a relish to actions that had none before through due consideration, 'practice, application, and custom'. Fashion and common opinion settled wrong notions and education and custom bad habits. Men were therefore to settle 'contrary habits', including the love of virtue. If they then made the wrong decisions men were answerable for vitiating their 'own palate'.[10]

[9] *Essay*, II.xxi, esp. 31, 37–8, 44–5.   [10] *Essay*, II.xxi, esp. 35, 47–53, 69.

While the *Essay* never came close to indicating extensively how duties of
service to others could be combined with its hedonic psychology or how
they could even be recognised given its assault upon innatism, these arguments were designed by Locke to make men able to serve others and *thus*
their true happiness. Many of Locke's other writings in these years, as we
will see in the rest of this chapter, were devoted to providing further parts
of the answer to the problems of recognition of and motivation to performance of these duties, although none were fully to answer many of the
serious problems that Locke undoubtedly recognised in making these
attempts.

While for Locke politics was not concerned with civilising men into
service to others, his political works themselves recognised the importance
of such service. In the *Letter Concerning Toleration*, composed in 1685 and
published in 1689, Locke declared that men were not to stop at the 'narrow
Measures' of 'bare' justice, but to add 'Charity, Bounty, and Liberality',
(the first being apparently the general Christian concern for others rather
than the specific gift of surplus goods to prevent starvation of the
Treatises). Locke declared that this extended service of others 'the Gospel
enjoyns, this Reason directs, and this that natural Fellowship we are born
into requires of us'. It is particularly frustrating that Locke did not give any
extended account of how men's natural fellowship or reason required such
service, but it is important to recognise that he wished to make certain that
his readers did not think that by concentrating upon justice and the limited
nature of political society he was intending to deny these forms of service,
and to restrict morality to the 'narrow Measures' of justice. According to
the *Letter*, not merely were such duties required by natural fellowship but
any man 'if he be destitute of Charity, Meekness, and Good-will in general
towards all Mankind, even to those that are not Christians, he is certainly
yet short of being a true Christian'. Christians had 'Duties of Peace, and
Good-Will towards all men; no man could be a Christian 'without Charity,
and without that Faith which works, not by force, but by Love'.[11]

There was important endorsement of a communitarian ethos based
upon the exchange of services and gratitude even in the *Two Treatises*
themselves. Locke's analysis in the *Two Treatises* of men as social before
they were political, and of the state of nature as a state that was social
rather than solitary, facilitated an extended conception of duties to others
which were social or natural rather than political. The *Two Treatises*
themselves made explicit at a few points the extensiveness of duties that
they did not describe at length. The most substantial duties to other men
discussed in the *Two Treatises* were, of course, those of the family.

---

[11] *Letter*, passim, esp. 31; cf. also MS Locke c34, passim.

Filmer's argument that men were born into political society as they were born into the family made Locke construct this extended account; but there is also no question that Locke thought that in his contemporary society the family was the basic social, ethical and economic unit, the major locus of mutual services and support.

The various elements of men's familial duties are too obvious in the text itself to need much discussion here. Children were initially unable to preserve themselves. They had a right to their preservation as God's property, and so their parents were obliged to preserve them. This duty was essentially a sub-set of the general duty of charity as the duty to secure preservation that Locke derived directly from God's ownership of men, with parents having special responsibility for their children because of their role in their procreation and because of their 'naturally tender love of their offspring'. This general duty of charity extended only to preservation, but Locke also importantly spoke of children having a right to the conveniences of life if their parents had the ability to provide this.[12]

Parents were further obliged to educate their children so that they became rational and therefore responsible adults who were free to make their own choices. This duty was depicted as stemming from God's purposive creation of man with understanding. Until children had reached the stage of rational responsibility, parents were to think for them and to govern their actions. According to Locke, to give to children the liberty to follow their uneducated wills was to thrust them amongst 'brutes'. To follow an unreasoning will was to be enslaved in the understanding, which ought to be the freest part of men. In the comment which did not receive any extended explanation, but which the passages cited above are already enough to indicate might very well have been intended to hint at many social duties, Locke made it a duty of parents to educate children not merely so that they might be 'most useful to themselves' but also so that they might be 'most useful . . . to others'. We will see in a few moments how Locke thought in the 1680s such educational formation might be achieved for the children of gentlemen, those from whom most service outside of the family was in practice to be expected.[13]

---

[12] *Treatises*, 2, chs. 5 and 6; Dunn, *Political Thought*, 113ff. See Cranston, *Locke*, passim and the *Correspondence*, passim for indications of Locke's own view of his own responsibilities in his extended family and the extent to which his own social world was shaped by this family. Laslett's declaration in his introduction to the *Treatises* (44) that 'Locke the individualist was an individual . . . The remarkable thing about him was his freedom from engagement: family, church, community, locality' obscures as much as it reveals about Locke's social identity, shaped throughout his life by a defined social status and consequent responsibilities and relationships, and lived within an extended family, and within a series of crucial friendships.

[13] *Treatises*, 2, ch. 6, esp. 64.

In response to this parental care, children were declared to be under 'a perpetual obligation of honouring their parents'. By inward esteem, reverence and outward expressions, children were to foster the happiness of their parents. This engaged them in 'all actions of defence, relief, assistance and comfort'. They owed 'honour, respect, gratitude and assistance', and 'respect, reverence, support and compliance'. It is this step in making filial relationships not those of obedience and command but those of exchange of care – of intended service by the parent, and of the return of gratitude and service by the children – that is very important as a hint of the kind of social ethics that Locke thought should obtain not merely in the family but also in the society at large. The comparison that Locke made with the filial duty of 'assistance' of their parents, and of return to 'gratitude' for the intentional service of 'care' from their parents was that of a man who might owe 'honour and respect to an ancient or wise Man, defence to his Child or Friend, relief and support to the Distressed' and 'gratitude to a Benefactor to such a degree, that all he has, all he can do, cannot sufficiently pay it'. The obligation of children was thus for Locke one form of a general duty of gratitude for benefits received – was, indeed, a duty of 'Gratitude . . . for the highest Benefits he is naturally capable of' – and could also be one form of charitable service of the distressed.[14]

In an extremely important but shamefully neglected paragraph of the Second Treatise, Locke wrote that

Though I have said above . . . that all men by nature are equal, I cannot be supposed to understand all sorts of Equality: Age or Virtue may give men a just Precedency; Excellency of Parts and Merit may place others above the Common Level; Birth may subject some, and Alliance or Benefits others, to pay an Observance to those to whom Nature, Gratitude or other Respects may have made it due; and yet all this consists with the Equality which all men are in, in respect of Jurisdiction or Dominion one over another, which was the Equality I there spoke of, as proper to the Business in hand, being that equal Right every man hath, to his Natural Freedom, without being subjected to the Will or Authority of any other Man.[15]

In speaking of a natural but not political subjection by birth, Locke may have been thinking merely of the subjection of children to parents. It is also quite possible, however, that he was thinking of social stratification. We saw in chapter five that in the late 1670s Locke described society as divided into 'particular callings' with differing responsibilities; Locke articulated at

---

14 *Treatises*, 2, ch. 6, esp. 65–74.
15 *Treatises*, 2.54. Dunn, *Political Thought*, 121, is one of the few to give the existence of this passage the stress that it deserves, but he does not explore its content or its relationship to the forms of social interaction in seventeenth-century England. Cf., however, for an exploration of some of these themes which is different than that here, idem, 'Individuality, Clientage and the Formation of Locke's Social Identity' in idem, *Rethinking Modern Political Theory*, Cambridge (1985).

length the duties of a 'gentleman's calling' in letters in the 1680s and in the 1690s in *Some Thoughts Concerning Education*. Major degrees of social inequality and their transmission through time were recognised as legitimate in the *Two Treatises*, not merely as the result of individual labour, which the text emphasised, but also through inheritance, which gained less explicit consideration but which was of course by far the most significant source of social inequality in Locke's time, and which depended upon birth. While one could certainly become a gentleman and advance to aristocratic status in England far more readily than in other European societies, the vast majority of gentlemen were, like Locke, the sons of gentlemen, and Locke supported the social superiority of gentlemen throughout his life, even when he advocated that some industrious individuals would advance by their industry to that status. Locke wrote to the countess of Peterborough in 1697 that her son's birth 'without any more adoe tels every one what he is to be in the world and directs us to consider what may conduce to make him an accomplished and great man in his country'.[16]

In paragraph 54 of the Second Treatise Locke further recognised that his defence of juristic equality in no way denied subordination through 'Alliance or Benefits . . . and Gratitude'. We have just seen that the family involved exchange of many benefits and gratitude, and that Locke explicitly compared such beneficence and gratitude to wider social relations, including that of friendship. We have seen in chapter five the importance of these relationships both in Locke's thought and in seventeenth-century English society, particularly as seen from its upper ranks. It is important here simply to underline that in explicitly recognising the legitimacy of subjection by 'Alliance or Benefits' in paragraph 54 of the Second Treatise, and in there denying that his support for men's juristic equality in any way affected such forms of dutiful subjection, Locke was supporting one of the central elements of social co-operation through giving favours and subjection through gratitude in late seventeenth-century England, and that this would have been so clear to his contemporary audience that it simply did not need to be expressed at any length in the *Treatises*.[17]

II

We saw earlier that Locke had first read *De Officiis* at Westminster, had modelled his letters to friends and patrons upon Cicero's *Epistles*, and had almost certainly used *De Officiis* and Cicero's *Epistles* in his moral teaching at Oxford. There is no clear evidence that Locke re-read *De Officiis*

---

[16] *Correspondence*, VI, 2320; IV, 1693.   [17] See chapter five above.

again until 1677, when he took a note from book II of *De Officiis* which declared that it was 'a duty to make money, but only by honourable means, and a duty to save and increase it by care and thrift'. It is difficult to believe that Locke did not broadly endorse this view as well as think it significant enough to record. It is likely that Locke was then once again using *De Officiis* in his moral teaching of a son of a gentleman whom he was in charge of educating as they travelled around France together. Further discussions of Cicero's moral thought may have taken place in Thoynard's Paris circle, which numbered the moral philosopher Pufendorf among its members, and Thoynard recommended editions of Cicero's *Epistles* to Locke in 1679. Between 1679 and 1681 Locke purchased an edition of Cicero's works in which *De Officiis* formed volume 9. By the time that he made up his catalogue of his books in Oxford in 1681 they also included *De Officiis* in two single editions, and separate volumes of Cicero's *Epistles*, *Epistulae ad Familiares* and *Academicae Quaestiones*.[18]

Exile in Holland in 1683–9 saw Locke living in an environment where Cicero's thought was as clearly at the centre of moral discussion and of the conceptualisation of social relationships of friendship as it was in England. In the 1680s Locke's correspondence with the man who became his closest friend in the Netherlands, Philipp van Limborch, was conducted in direct imitations of Ciceronian language and conceptualisations of their relationship as one of *amicitia*. Locke became friends with van Limborch's friend Graevius, then undertaking a massive critical edition of Cicero's works which Locke purchased as the volumes appeared. Locke moved into the European 'Republic of Letters' by moving to Holland in 1683, becoming a contributor to the Continent's learned journals in which Graevius' edition was much discussed. It was probably with Graevius' edition of Cicero in mind that Locke composed his attack on the Stationers' Company monopoly in 1694 because it kept out of England good Dutch editions of Cicero's works. Locke also discussed Cicero with Jean le Clerc, and may have discussed Cicero with Benjamin Furly; Furly's library included many works by Cicero and several editions of *De Officiis*.[19]

Locke very carefully re-read *De Officiis* in 1684, taking detailed notes; he had been carefully reading through all of Cicero's works since 1681. In the

---

18 See chapter five above; MS Locke f2, 361–2; MS Locke f3, 94; MS Locke f28, 27; MS Locke f15, 32; 77; MS Locke b2, 20r; MS Locke f28, 20; 22; 31; 121; 123; 143; 161; MS Locke f8, 44, 68–9; MS Locke b2, 36, 40, 50; MS Locke f15, 82.

19 MS Locke b2, 43r; 44r; 50; 70v–72v; 77v; 86v; 89r; MS Locke f9, 331; MS Locke f10; 53; MS Locke f29, 90; King, *Life*, I, 377–80; Jean le Clerc, *Bibliothèque Universelle*, XX, Amsterdam (1691), 79; *Ars Critica*, Amsterdam (1697), II, 328; 368 see the copy in the Locke Room under 7.361a–b for Locke's listing of le Clerc's comments upon Cicero; *Bibliothèque Furliana*, Rotterdam (1714), 297, 299, 300, 306; *Correspondence*, IV, 1541; 1586; 1641; 1657; V, 1809; 1831.

1680s Locke added a passage to the drafts of the *Essay* on the demonstrability of morality declaring that 'the Truth and Certainty of moral Discourses abstracts from the Lives of Men, and the Existence of those Vertues in the World, whereof they treat: Nor are Tully's *Offices* less true, because there is no Body in the World that exactly practices his Rules, and lives up to that pattern of a vertuous Man, which he has given us, and which existed no where, when he writ, but in Idea.' In 1693 Locke published *Some Thoughts Concerning Education*, a treatise on the education of sons of gentlemen that was based upon a series of letters that Locke wrote to his friend Edward Clarke from the Netherlands in the mid-1680s, the period of detailed reading of *De Officiis*. He declared in *Some Thoughts* that a boy should only read the Bible and no other discourses of morality 'till he can ready Tully's Offices . . as one that would be informed in the Principles and Precepts of Vertue, for the Conduct of his life'. In a letter to his close friend Lady Peterborough in 1697 Locke recommended that her son read history and 'With the reading of History I thinke the study of Morality should be joynd, I mean not the Ethicks of the Schools fitted to dispute, but such as Tully in his Offices'. In 1703, in 'Some Thoughts Concerning Reading and Study For A Gentleman' Locke declared that 'the Morality of the Gospel' exceeded all, but that if a gentleman 'hath a mind to see how far the heathen world carried that science, and whereupon they bottomed their ethics, he will be delightfully and profitably entertained in Tully's treatises "De Officiis"'. In both of these education recommendations, the Bible was the only other work that he suggested for the teaching of morality.[20]

By the time of Locke's death Cicero had become the author of whose works Locke possessed most copies after Boyle and himself, including at least seven different editions of *De Officiis*. The quotation on the title page of the *Essay* was from Cicero's *De Natura Deorum*. Perhaps most remarkable of all indications of the importance of Cicero to Locke in the last twenty years of his life, however, is the existence among Locke's manuscripts on Cicero of several pages in which he worked out an exact chronology of Cicero's life and major works. This is one of ony two such chronologies that Locke composed. The other was of Jesus Christ.[21]

Locke's general recommendations of *De Officiis* suggest that he found the content of Cicero's ethics highly attractive, but they also frequently registered disagreement with the motivational and obligatory analyses of Cicero. For Cicero, moral actions were to be undertaken because they were

---

[20] MS Locke f5, 92–7; 151; MS Locke f6, 97; MS Locke c42, ii, 120, 128, 142, 204; MS Locke f7, 16–18; 22–3; 35; 36; 90; *Essay*, title page; *Education*, para 185; *Reasonableness*, in *Works*, VII, 141; *Correspondence*, VI, 2320; *Works* (1801), X, 306; *Library*, 711ff.

[21] MS Locke c31, 140–6.

honourable and appropriate to man's dignity as a rational creature. For Cicero, choice of immoral actions on the grounds of expedience was foolish because no pleasure was worth the dishonour of such activity. In the *Essay* Locke famously described the difference between the basis of obligation for Christians – the will of God –, for Hobbists – the will of the Leviathan –, and for 'Heathen' philosophers – the dignity of moral rectitude. It is extremely likely that Locke had Cicero's argument in his mind when composing this passage in the *Essay*. In 'Of Ethicks in General', a manuscript of the 1680s which was apparently initially intended to be a chapter of the *Essay*, Locke echoed the description of the insufficiency of heathen philosophers who had often discussed morality but had seldom derived duties 'up to their original'; instead of invoking the will of God their utmost enforcements were 'reputation and disgrace'. Locke made clear that it was only through the pleasure and pain that were annexed to laws that actions were made morally good or evil. Thus, as drinking to excess caused sickness it was a natural evil, and as it brought punishment for transgression of a law it was a moral evil. Philosophers who discourse 'ever so acutely of temperance or justice, but show no law of a superior that prescribes temperance, to the observation or breach of which law there are rewards and punishments annexed' lost 'the force of morality'. He stressed that 'properly and truly the rules of good and evil' were the declared will of God, 'sufficiently promulgated and known to all mankind', although he did not continue and show what this will contained or how it had been promulgated.[22]

In the *Reasonableness of Christianity* in 1695 Locke argued that various heathen philosophers had articulated significant portions of ethics, particularly because of the 'evident beauty' of morality. He argued, however, that they had not been able to produce sufficient reasons for men to obey their precepts in terms either of obligation or of motivation. Cicero was listed among these philosophers, and Locke described this failure as crucial. To make known the obligation of a law, it was necessary to make known a lawmaker with power to reward and punish. The same reservations about Cicero's work – that it showed the height of heathen ethics without the obligation to God and the motivation of heavenly rewards and punishments – were implicit in *Some Thoughts Concerning Education* and in 'Some Thoughts Concerning Reading and Study for a Gentleman'. Yet Locke recommended Cicero on teaching the principles of ethics in advance of and more broadly than those texts that attempted a generation of ethics in part on the basis of terrestrial self-interest, such as Pufendorf's works,

---

[22] *Essay*, I.iii.5; *The Life and Letters of John Locke*, ed. P. King (1884), 308–13.

and particularly instead of the works of 'Hobbists', since they did not recognise 'many' duties of morality in service of others.

By an exegesis of Cicero's ethics we can thus see what Locke recommended as the primary text including the principles and precepts of virtue which was to be set for the education of the son of a gentleman, Locke's own status and the status that he thought by far the most crucial to morality and to society. Such analysis will clearly need to recognise, however, those areas of disagreement between Locke's and Cicero's ethics which follow from their differing accounts of the bases of morality. In order to present as full a picture of the content of Locke's ethics from the mid-1680s to his death as is possible, in the next pages Cicero's thought will therefore be examined in detail to indicate what Locke wanted gentlemen to read on the principles and precepts of virtue, if not its sources or motivational underpinning, and this presentation will occur in tandem with extensive analysis of Locke's own arguments in *Some Thoughts*.[23]

In *De Officiis* Cicero argued that there were four elements of moral rectitude. The first part of such *Honestum* involved the search for and 'full perception of' the truth, or wisdom and prudence. *Honestum* included the 'greatness and strength of a noble and invincible spirit', or fortitude, and 'orderliness and moderation' in action and speech, variously described as involving 'decorum', 'temperance' and 'self-control'. Most importantly, there was the element concerning the 'conservation of organized society', or justice, which itself involved both rendering to every man his due and faithfully discharging obligations assumed. These were interwoven duties, since the search for truth, for instance, often involved the search for the ways to maintain relations between men, and decorum was required in the performance of all other duties.[24]

Man's search for truth called forth little discussion from Cicero in *De Officiis*. Only men among the creatures possessed reason in addition to the instincts of self-preservation. The search for truth was therefore peculiar to man, and men alone were able to appreciate the harmony and order of the universe. Cicero strongly stated that in searching for truth men had to avoid two errors: accepting too readily the unknown as known, and expending too much effort on matters that were both obscure and useless. Locke was very familiar with these themes, and the citation of Cicero's *De Natura Deorum* on the title page of the *Essay* was emblematic of his deep

---

[23] *Reasonableness*, in *Works*, VII, 140ff.; *Education*, paras 54, 185 and pp. 319–21.

[24] *De Officiis*, I.v.15–17. I have taken the four elements in different order than Cicero in this exegesis for convenience. Translations follow the Loeb Classics unless their translation seemed inadequate.

agreement with Cicero. In the mitigated scepticism of both, men could make few advances in natural philosophy and should redirect their attention from metaphysics and logic to ethics and practical wisdom. Importantly underpinning condemnation of the study of useless knowledge in *De Officiis* lay a strong emphasis on moral activity as the primary end of knowledge. Men were to be careful to devote themselves to study of moral rectitude, things which conduced to a good and happy life, and the pursuits of learning and science which could help men secure their preservation and conveniences.

For Locke in *Some Thoughts* curiosity, man's natural 'appetite after knowledge', was to be encouraged as much as possible. It was to be kept 'active and vigorous' by giving intelligible answers to enquiries. The end sought was the adult who could reason for himself, who could take responsibility for his own actions, and Locke urged that as children grew older they were to be treated more as friends to be reasoned with and less as children who simply ought to obey. A temper in a child 'curious resolute and good natur'd' if thus 'set right' would be able to 'produce anything'. While he stressed in the first edition of *Some Thoughts* in 1693, and even more in later editions in 1695 and 1699, that it was very difficult to construct the chain of demonstration needed to establish morality, Locke was adamant that children were to have duties proposed to them in 'few and plain' words, and to discuss particular moral cases. Locke's ideal result of such an education was the virtuous practice of duties inferred from the light of nature. In his 1684 notes Locke recorded Cicero's definition of 'sapientia', which declared that 'the more clearly' anyone observed the most essential truth in any given case, and the more accurately and quickly he could give reasons for this, 'the more prudent and wise he was esteemed'. Locke commented that this was 'a very loose definition of wisedome which takes in the speculative sciences where in a man may be very knowing without being wise wisdom referring as I thinke to the conduct of a man's actions in reference to his owne happynesse or his great concernments as prudence does to those of lesse moment'.

Locke thereby stressed even more than Cicero the superiority of practical to speculative wisdom and massively extended the focus of knowledge on men's concern with happiness. For Locke, 'The true Principle of . . . virtue' was 'the Knowledge of a Man's Duty and the Satisfaction it is to obey his Maker in following the Dictates of that Light God has given him, with the Hopes of Acceptation and Reward'. While Locke was thus clear that the dignity of moral rectitude was not the basis of virtue, *pace* Cicero, he may well have heard an echo of Cicero when penning the declaration that children should gain a 'temper' such 'that on all occasions it may be disposed to consent to nothing, but what may be suitable to the Dignity and Excellency of a rational Creature'.[25]

The next part of *honestum* for Cicero was decorum, in which there was considerateness for others and temperance, subjection of the passions, and moderation. Decorum was 'that which harmonized with man's superiority of nature to other creatures'. It manifestly embraced 'temperance' and self-control, and in Locke's notation of these arguments it very importantly described the kinds of behaviour which became a 'gentleman'. According to Cicero, 'Nature' had made men such that men ought to be steadfast, temperate, self-controlled and considerate of others. If men possessed decorum this would shine forth in their conduct and meet with the approval of other men. Decorum varied depending upon one's age and circumstances; it was proper, for instance, for gentlemen to jest only in an appropriately witty and refined manner. In conversing they were to avoid giving offence, and to be courteous and considerate. Gentlemen were to avoid trades unbecoming to their status, such as tax-gathering, trade on a small scale, or menial labour. They were instead to engage in study, the professions, trade on a large scale, or, best of all, agriculture. It was the function of justice not to do wrong to other men, but of considerateness not to wound their feelings. In such considerateness 'the essence of propriety' was 'best' seen.[26]

Locke's 1684 notes recorded this definition of considerateness, the declaration of its importance, and many of the rules for appropriate behaviour. Much of *Some Thoughts* could be considered an extended dissertation on how to teach the forms of decorum in the behaviour of a gentleman of late seventeenth-century England, particularly its account, reminiscent of Locke's translation of Nicole, of civility. In *Some Thoughts* civility was described as necessary to a gentleman specifically as a social grace or 'good breeding' and more broadly in order to prevent social discord, to facilitate persuasion and the doing of good to others, and to bring others to your own service.

Employing only the negative part of civility expressed in his earlier manuscript fragment 'Morality', Locke defined civility as in expression 'nothing but a care not to show any slighting, or contempt, of any one in Conversation'. It was from a disposition of mind 'not to offend' that men were called civil. Inward civility, from which the expressions of civility flowed, was, however, based in an apparently more extensive 'general Good will and Regard for all People'. Civility had to be based in the

---

25 *Ibid.*, I.v.16; I.vi.18–19; *Correspondence*, II, 822; 829; 844; III; 906; 929; 1098; MS Locke f8, p. 8; *Education*, paras 80–2; 98, 118–21; 159, 185ff.
26 *De Officiis*, I.xxvii.93–I.xlii.150; I.xxvii.96–9; I.xxxv.126–8; I.xxix.104; I.xl.142.

natural temper of the child, in 'a sweetness of mind, and a well turn'd disposition' with 'Respect and good will to all People', or it became artificial and displeasing. Education was therefore not to aim at rules of manners, but at cultivating this inward respect. This would establish an 'habitual and becoming easiness'.

Such civility or 'good breeding' was necessary to set a gloss on all other qualities. According to Locke it was only possession of civility that rendered other qualities useful in procuring 'the Esteem and Good will of all that he comes near'. Without it 'Courage' would appear 'brutality', learning pedantry, and 'Good nature Fawning'. Like diamonds, men had to be polished to gain a good reception, and it was therefore a principal care of educating a child to settle 'an habitual Gracefulness, and Politeness in all his Carriage'. Men could not 'but be pleased with an Humane, Friendly civil Temper, wherever we meet with it'. Civility was the 'most taking of all the Social Virtues'. A man who aimed to help others, but made them uneasy in doing so, 'recommends himself ill to another as aiming at his Happiness'. His advice or help was therefore likely to be disregarded, and any potential to do good was thereby lost.

Children's governors therefore had to be well bred and to understand the 'Measures of Civility' in the variety of places and among the variety of persons that the child would meet. Although based in a general respect of all mankind, Locke was clear that expressions of civility should keep the respect and distance due to Rank and Quality. Men were to express civility according to the 'Fashion' of the 'country', showing respect and value to people 'according to their Rank and Condition'. Locke identified a number of causes of incivility, including contempt, censoriousness and natural roughness – a brutality of temper which was not softened to 'compliance and accomodation'. In a manner reminiscent of Nicole's strictures on pride and self-love, however, he condemned particularly 'pride and ill-nature'. For Locke, natural pride turned to contempt caused 'Oppression and Cruelty'. Men were not to think meanly of others or of themselves, nor to stand upon a view of their own importance. They were to maintain civility in their 'Language and Deportment' towards 'their Inferiors and the meaner sort of people, particularly servants'. This made it even more necessary that they developed a 'gentle, courteous, affable Carriage towards the lower Ranks of Men' and did not lose 'the Consideration of Humane Nature, in the Shufflings of outward Conditions'. Here the consideration of service was given as one reason for such courtesy since servants would more willingly serve a civil master. That Locke personally had a reputation for courtesy or complaisance to all ranks of men and was genuinely concerned with the consideration of human nature does not mean that he ever lost sight of others' 'Inferiority', or of the gains of his civility in preservation of deferential service.[27]

Locke emphasised the importance in *Some Thoughts* not merely of the considerateness and propriety that Cicero made central to decorum, but also of temperance and modesty, and their link to preserving the reputation of a good man in order to do good to others. Locke argued in *Some Thoughts* that the child's needs were to be provided for, but that wants of 'phansy, and affectation' were never to be complied with. The more that the children themselves 'practised modesty, and temperance in this', the more they were to be rewarded with appropriate things, but as a natural consequence of general good behaviour, and not as a bargain. An early habit of silencing desires would settle in them behaviour which would in the long run make greater liberty permissible: they would become more 'moderate' in the extent of their desires, and particularly in their ability to restrain their desires, and then could be allowed to direct themselves. Thus, by providing them with a 'sober, plain' diet, they were not educated into placing their pleasures in 'epicurism', in drunkenness and gluttony. The temperance necessary to health, and the 'modesty' of desires necessary to virtue, could thereby both be secured. Locke recognised that in recommending this he was going against the prevailing fashion for the gentry, which placed much of a man's happiness in eating and drinking. It was also for Locke to go against the dispositions of the 'meaner sort', whose temperance was guaranteed only by their scanty fortunes.[28]

For Locke such temperance 'moderating' men's desires was not enough. Locke had a much stronger sense than Cicero of the physiological imperatives of the pursuit of immediate pleasure. He argued in *Some Thoughts* that 'Good and Evil, Reward and Punishment' were 'the only Motives to a rational Creature: these are the Spur and Reins, whereby all Mankind are set on work'.[29] It was therefore necessary to Locke not just to legitimate much of men's pursuit of happiness, but to find other ways than temperance to control men's desires since a man who did not know how to 'resist the Importunity of present Pleasure, or Pain, for the sake of what Reason tells him is fit to be done' lacked the true principle of virtue. The 'great Principle and Foundation of all Vertue and Worth' was 'placed in this, That a Man is able to deny himself his own Desires, cross his own Inclinations, and purely follow what reason directs as best'. Men's 'Natural Propensity' was to 'indulge Corporal and present Pleasure', the 'root from whence spring all Vitious Actions'. It was vital therefore that

---

[27] MS Locke f8, 30–3; *Education*, passim, esp. paras 67; 93; 109; 117; 143–5.
[28] *Correspondence*, II, 829; III, 929; *Education*, paras 103–8.
[29] *Education*, para 54.

'This temper' of denial of desires, 'so contrary to unguided nature', was planted early in men 'as the true Foundation of future Ability and Hapiness'. In order to 'make a good, a wise, and a vertuous Man' Locke declared that 'he should learn to cross his Appetite, and deny his Inclination to riches, finery, or pleasing his Palate, &c when ever his Reason advises the contrary, and his Duty requires it'.[30]

This task was enormously difficult, but it was possible since the mind at birth was a *tabula rasa* and since they were extremely concerned – as Nicole had pointed out so forcefully – with how others viewed them. The primary danger in educating children to form desires for the morally good and to control their appetite for evil but pleasurable things was that parents and tutors would try to teach such mastery by exactly the wrong methods, methods which would increase the concentration on present pleasures and pains or break children's natural curiosity and 'spirit'. Use of either the rod or rewards directly connected to specific actions would only reinforce children's motivation by the most pressing of pleasures and pains. This was 'to cherish that principle in him, which it is our business to root out and destroy'.[31]

Parents were therefore to employ the child's natural love of praise and commendation and to foster this love. Parents were to use 'all the arts imaginable' to make their child's 'minde as sensible of credit and shame as may be'. Good actions were then to be met with esteem from those whom the child respected until children grew to be able to judge for themselves and to make use of their reason. Although reputation and shame were not the true principles of vertue – 'for that is the knowledge of a man's duty, and the satisfaction it is to obey his maker in following the dictates of that light he has given him, with the hopes of acceptation and reward' – yet they came 'nearest to it'. The 'testimony and applause that other people's reason give to virtuous and right actions' was the proper guide until children attained the use of their own reason and took satisfaction in obeying God. Children were not capable of 'reasonings from remote principles' and 'long deductions', so motivation was to be provided by making it a 'discredit and disgrace to them'.[32]

Children were therefore to be taught by 'sober' and 'good natured' tutors, and to be kept away from the bad influence of servants. With an argument that was stated hyperbolically, but which revealed clearly his own attitudes towards most servants, Locke declared to his friend Clarke, a rich gentleman with many servants, that the flattery and insinuations of servants were so corrupting that it was to them that the depth 'to which mankind is degenerated' was 'more than to any one thing owing'. It was by

---

[30] *Education*, passim, esp. paras 33, 45–8, 115, 200.
[31] *Correspondence*, III, 929; *Education*, paras 48ff.
[32] *Correspondence*, II, 844; III, 929; *Education*, paras 56ff., 200.

example and not by precept that virtue was most easily taught, so the 'most efficacious' way to teach virtue was to 'set before their Eyes the examples of those things you would have them doe or avoid'. Servants provided too many examples of viciousness.[33]

For Cicero, the third of the four main elements of virtue, fortitude, was that part of 'virtue which champions the cause of right'. Just as knowledge which was divorced from justice deserved the name of cunning rather than wisdom, courage which was not inspired by a public spirit, but instead by selfish interests, was to be called 'audacity' rather than 'fortitude'. In sections from which Locke took extensive notes in 1684, Cicero defined a truly courageous soul as being indifferent to outward circumstances, as convinced that only moral rectitude deserved to be striven for, and as performing great and particularly useful deeds which required great labour and substantial danger. For Cicero magnanimity existed only when accompanied by justice. Without justice, such courage was likely to fuel ambition for power in ways dangerous to the '*res publica*'. Men were particularly to strive to avoid the allurements of pleasure and ambition for wealth. There was nothing so characteristic of 'narrowness of soul' as 'love of riches', and nothing was more honourable than indifference to money if it was not possessed, and the devotion of money to beneficence if it was possessed.[34]

While for Locke men were to cross, to control and to direct rather than, *pace* Cicero, to extinguish desire, Locke was clearly in agreement with Cicero in thinking that motivation by fear had to be extinguished in almost all cases. Defending 'True Fortitude' at length Locke defined it as 'the quiet Possession of a Man's self, and an undisturb'd doing his Duty, whatever Evil besets, or Danger lies in his way'. 'Fortitude' was 'the Guard and Support of the other Virtues; and without Courage a Man will scarce keep steady to his Duty, and fill up the Character of a truly worthy Man'. According to Locke, the English 'Nation' was 'so naturally brave' that it had become considerable in the world, and such valour was 'not the least part' of fortitude. Honours were 'justly due to the Valour of those who venture their Lives for their Country'. Nevertheless, true fortitude required more than 'Courage in the Field, and a Contempt of Life in the Face of an Enemy'. Men were also attacked by 'pain, Disgrace and Poverty'. 'True Fortitude' was 'prepar'd for Dangers of all kinds'.[35]

---

[33] *Correspondence*, II, 844; III, 906; 929; 1098; *Education*, passim.

[34] *De Officiis*, I, xix, 62–3; xx, 66; xx, 68; xxiii, 80; xxxvi, 90; MS Locke f8, 25–7. The first of Locke's three notes simply recorded Cicero's definition of 'Libertas' as 'properly to live as one pleases'. The second noted Cicero's declaration that it took a 'truly brave and resolute spirit not to be perturbed in difficult times', to keep presence of mind and keep to 'the path of reason'. The final note recorded that it involved as much weakness to give way to feelings in times of success as in times of difficulty.

[35] *Education*, para 115.

For Cicero, men were naturally social and sociable, associated with other men through reason and speech, prompted by a natural social instinct to join together with other men in companies and to form public assemblies. The duties of maintaining such society centred upon justice, the 'crowning glory' of the virtues, on the basis of which men were called 'good men'. For Cicero, the primary office of justice was preventing one man from harming another, unless provoked by injury, but justice also involved men using common possessions for the common good and private property for their own. Injustice included not merely the infliction of wrong, but also the failure to protect those who were being injured by another when this lay within your power. For Cicero, avarice, revenge and ambition motivated men to be actively unjust by harming others. The causes of failure to protect others from injury by others were more varied, but included indifference, indolence, incompetence, self-interest and unwillingness to incur expense to help others. Cicero was clear that even if men were just in all of their own actions, controlling completely their own avarice, revenge and ambition, they would nonetheless be 'traitors to the social life' if they did not prevent injuries by others to others when they were able. They were to expend the efforts and money involved in preventing injury.

Justice was, however, not the only duty that men owed to other men and which was necessary in order to maintain society. 'Close akin to justice', and recognised alongside it in Cicero's initial definition of justice, was 'beneficence', which was also called 'kindness or generosity'. Cicero cited Plato in declaring that 'we are not born for ourselves alone, but our country claims a share of our being, and our friends a share'. Since, 'as the Stoics hold', everything that the earth produces was created for men's sake so that they could mutually help each other, men ought to 'follow Nature' and contribute to the general good 'by an interchange of acts of kindness, by giving and receiving'. In an indication that social *concordia* would follow from such behaviour Cicero argued that the result of this use of 'men's skill, and industry' would be 'cement[ing] human society closely together'. Cicero provided a lengthy discussion of kindness and generosity, arguing in a manner of which Locke's eighth essay on the law of nature of 1663–4 had been highly reminiscent, that 'Nothing' appealed more to the 'best in human nature' than beneficence. Gratitude was an imperative duty, and men were to 'Imitate the fruitful fields, which return more than they receive'. Failure to requite a benefit was 'not allowable to a good man', unless such requital would violate others' rights.[36]

Cicero condemned those who looked to reward for benefits, putting

---

[36] *De Officiis*, I.vii.20–3; I.viii.28; I.ix.29.

themselves at the service of those from whom they expected the greatest favours. He recommended instead that assistance was given in proportion to need. Services were to be given not to those who were more wealthy, as by most men, but to the deserving poor who would be grateful as recipients, and even if not recipients would esteem those who were benefactors of the poor. For Cicero, this would promote social peace in a country of massive differentials in wealth and status. Cicero simultaneously argued, however, that the needs of society were best served when beneficence was shown in proportion to the closeness of the relationship between benefactor and recipient, and he concentrated his discussion (as the entire text) on the elite who participated in public life. Men were related to all other men as members of the same species, more closely to their own people, and more closely still to their fellow citizens. They were very closely related to kin, the first bond of human society being that between man and wife, then that of parents and children, and then of households. Of all the bonds of fellowship, Cicero described the intimate friendship of good men of similar character as the finest and strongest. This was *amicitia*. A lesser but strong bond of fellowship was itself created by the mutual interchange of services. This was *concordia*. Finally, for Cicero there was no bond more close than that linking each man with his country (or political community).

Men were to serve their country with their life if necessary. Service to country and parents came before any other duty, since their previously rendered services had created the greatest obligations. Service to children and family followed, and then to kinsmen. Friendship did not have a call of gratitude for services rendered similar to that of country or parents, but intimacy, 'counsel, conversation, encouragement, comfort', and 'even reproof' where necessary, flourished best in *amicitia*, a vision of friendship similar to many celebrations of the support of sincere and sober friends in enquiry, especially religious enquiry, that Locke composed over the final twenty years of his life. Cicero was equally clear, however, that men had to make sure that no injury was performed on account of beneficence, and that beneficence was proportioned to the means of the benefactor. Liberality was only to be employed if it did not hurt anyone by encouraging theft. Men who gave more than they could afford robbed their own kin of the services that were due to them, often induced or were involved in actual robbery of others' goods in order to pay for their beneficence, and were commonly motivated by desire for ostentation rather than by kindness.[37]

Cicero recognised very clearly that men would devote much of their time and effort to securing their own goods. An entire book of *De Officiis*,

---

[37] *Ibid.*, I.vii.20–3; I.viii.25; I.xi.34–5; I.xii.37; I.xiii.41; I.xiv.42–xv.48. Cf. MS Locke f8, 11.

focused on *utile*, or expedience, and described those kinds of duties relating to men's conveniences, the acquiring of things which made life enjoyable, influence and wealth. Cicero clearly thought that this could be pursued when its attainment did not lead to moral transgressions, failures of service, or an increase in one's motivation by sensual passions or uncontrolled appetite. In a passage that we have already seen that Locke cited in 1677, Cicero declared it legitimate to make money, but only by honest means, and to conserve and increase it by thrift and care. It was also a duty to study your own constitution and to preserve your own health. The vast majority of the book was concerned, however, with arguing that honourable behaviour was necessary to gain desired goods, and that there was no doctrine more pernicious than that things could be expedient which were not morally correct or 'honourable'.

According to Cicero, the vast majority of goods used by men, particularly those on a large scale such as canals or harbours, were only created through co-operative labour. It was through association of men that cities had developed, and from the laws and customs that then evolved that men developed consideration for others, with the result that greater wants were met through giving and receiving, and through monetary as well as benficent exchange of commodities. Cicero then proceeded to identify the means to gain the co-operation of other men as precisely the development of those virtues discussed in book I: wisdom, temperance, justice and beneficence. It was the 'peculiar function of virtue' to win others' hearts and 'attach them to one's own service'. While men aided each other from fear, hope for favour, or promise of payment, good will, esteem and confidence were both better and more secure.

Men had been impelled by nature to associate, but according to Cicero they had established a republic primarily to secure individual property rights. It was in the 'hope of safeguarding their possessions' that they had estabished the 'protection of cities'. The administration of public affairs was like the office of a trustee, for the benefit of those entrusted to one's care and not of those to whom it was entrusted. Those administering public affairs were to ensure the fair administration of courts of law in order to secure protection of property, to protect not merely the poor from oppression but also the rich from alteration of their property. Philippus deserved 'Unqualified condemnation' for proposing the equal distribution of property, as did agrarian laws which had destroyed the concord necessary to maintain society because they had involved the transfer of property without the owner's consent.[38]

According to Cicero, the chief end of men ought to be making the inter-

---

[38] *De Officiis*, II, passim, esp. iii.11–17; vi.21–2; xxi.73–4.

est of the community the interest of each individual. If expedience in the sense of personal advantage was preferred to morality, then kindness, generosity and justice would perish. The more a man preferred a life of service to others before a life of pleasure, the better he was. It is important at this point to capture the balance of Cicero's argument. Cicero's argument that the interests of the individual were to be made the interests of the community had much to do with defining justice, as protection of individual rights, as the queen of the virtues and the central interest of the community. Cicero made clear that every man could consider and pursue his own interests, but he was equally insistent that apparent advantages such as political power, riches and sensual pleasures, should never be preferred to the obligations of friendship. He argued that service of one's country was to be preferred to all sensual pleasures, although there were things that a just man would never do even to save his country. Cicero cited Hecaton of Rhodes, a Stoic pupil of Panaetius, who combined declaration that it was a wise man's duty to take care of his private interests, while doing nothing contrary to the civil laws, with argument that men's purpose in seeking prosperity was not to be rich for themselves 'alone, but for our children, relations, friends, and, above all, for our country'. Moreover, Cicero argued in discussing Hecaton's view that a man deserved little praise who sought only his own profit and refrained only from what was expressly forbidden by law. He noted, however, that if a good man was defined such that a good man was one 'who helped all he could and harms noone', without using any deception or even concealment, it would be difficult to locate a good man.[39]

While Cicero distinguished *honestum* and *utile*, he may be said to have provided several answers to the question of why men should thus be beneficent, only one of which – if the most important – was that it was praiseworthy. He also argued that such beneficence was owed because of the natural fellowship between men. His analysis of *utile* made very clear that by services men gained each other's help in creating and coming to possess the goods necessary to a comfortable life: expedience was the recognised result of service of others that was undertaken because it was *honestum*. Cicero's thought was thus unquestionably distant from Locke's view of men as motivated by pleasures and pains, but Locke could have come to perceive the gap as significantly narrowed by emphasis upon elements of Cicero's arguments – his account of the duties of natural fellowship, his opposition to the pursuit of dishonourable individual terrestrial expedience, and his contention that general terrestrial expedience was the result of service to others. These arguments could be aligned with his own

[39] *Ibid.*, III.v.24; vi.26–8; x.42–xi.46; xv.63–4; xxxiii.119.

emphasis upon men serving God, and his stress adopted at the latest in and after his translation of Nicole that by serving God men thereby also gained the love and services of others. The apparent distance between their accounts could be further narrowed by recognition of Cicero's very heavy emphasis upon the careful restrictions of beneficence by means, worthiness and social ties. The gap was narrowed further still by Cicero's emphasis upon the acquisition of goods for oneself that would be gained through industry and commercial exchange and not through beneficence; that justice was given such importance by Cicero made clear how extensive could be such commercial forms of exchange legitimately existing alongside beneficence.

In 1684 Locke noted Cicero's tripartite definition of justice as not causing harm to another; as leading men to use common possessions for the common good and private possessions for their own interest; and as not preventing a man from harming another when you had the means to do so. He recorded Cicero's argument that it was from justice that men were called 'good men'. Cicero had, as we saw, importantly described beneficence as linked to and 'close akin' to justice. Recognising the importance of this, Locke remarked shortly that 'I suppose benignitas must be taken in too which he makes alyde to justice.' Locke further noted in a book of memoranda Cicero's definition of a good man in his discussion of Hecaton of Rhodes as one 'who helped all he could and harmed none'. Locke did not then record in his memoranda Cicero's declaration that few such men could be found, but, as we saw earlier, when he added a passage in the manuscript of the *Essay* in the 1680s about the truth of Tully's definition of a good man, he referred to this definition as being 'true' even if such a man may never have existed in real life but only in 'idea'. It is likely that he was aware that he was here echoing Cicero's own declaration that few such men could be found.[40]

---

[40] *Ibid.*, II.iii.11–17; II.vi.21–2; II.vi.25; II.ix.34; II.xii.43; III.xiv.60; III.xv.63–4; III.xvii.68; III.xvii.71. For Cicero, in pursuing such prosperity, it was vital that nothing was done with misrepresentation, deception or unfairness. Even if civil law permitted such practices, and contemporary opinion found nothing wrong in them, they were against the 'universal law'. Cicero defined the function of wisdom as discrimination of good from evil; it was cunning, not wisdom, that preferred evil to good. Locke took down this definition of wisdom and cunning in his memoranda: MS Locke c33, 17–18. For Hont and Ignatieff, Locke's 1695 manuscript 'Venditio' was in part a paraphrase of the classical parable of the Alexandrian merchant who sailed to rich but famine-ridden Rhodes and, according to Cicero in *De Officiis*, ought to inform the Rhodians that other ships were currently sailing towards Rhodes rather than extract the highest possible price by dissembling. Locke's 'Venditio', concerned to establish a consistent concept of the 'just' price, defined this essentially as the consistent price in a particular market. It defended as 'just' the sale of corn in one market suffering famine at a much higher price than corn was currently being sold elsewhere. 'Venditio' did not, however, address the issues of dissembling that were central to Cicero's account (and also to Pufendorf's dis-

In the light of his disagreements with Cicero over issues such as the divine basis of morality and the reasons that motivated men to its practice, that Locke strongly recommended Cicero's ethics surely suggests at least a general approval for its arguments about the contents of beneficence as well as justice. It suggests that Locke may have thought valuable not merely Cicero's account of the advantages to *concordia* that beneficence brought – with beneficence thus necessary to Locke's conception of duties that were advantageous to the preservation of society – but also Cicero's careful account of the relationship and balance between justice and beneficence and his cautious series of restrictions upon beneficence, with beneficence having to be carefully proportioned to the benefactor's wealth, to the worthiness of the recipient, and to the gratitude that it returned, and with men having to gain the means of beneficence justly in order for it to be legitimate. The limitations of such service in Locke's own recommendations owed a considerable amount not merely to the personality that Locke famously revealed in keeping exhaustingly detailed accounts of the minutest expenditure throughout his life in his scores of notebooks, but also owed much to his zealous concern with the maintenance of estates by gentlemen throughout his life – from his advice to John Alford in the 1660s to republications of *Some Thoughts* shortly before his death – as a concern that gentlemen had to maintain the ability to serve others in the ways that appeared to him to be significant. In Cicero's careful exegesis of the boundaries of beneficence as much as in his exaltation of such services Locke surely found a form of argument replicating many of his own obsessive concerns with balancing service of oneself and others and the responsibilities of a gentleman.

In *Some Thoughts* Locke attempted to find ways to plant liberality and justice while recognising men's hedonic psychology in a way that Cicero had not. According to Locke, children loved liberty and dominion. Love of dominion was 'the first originall of most vitious habits that are ordinary and natural'. This love of 'power, and dominion' showed itself very early. Children had two 'humours', which for Locke by the time of this correspondence seem to have been natural humours which were not sinful in themselves, but which led to the majority of sinful actions if they grew into vicious 'natural habits'. Children wished to have their desires submitted to

cussion of it). 'Venditio''s argument was marked by a significant concern not to exploit the needs of individuals, and it identified strongly a duty of charity more extensive than that of 'strict justice'. Hont and Ignatieff's separation of Cicero from Locke is a little overstated. See I. Hont and M. Ignatieff, 'Needs and Justice in the Wealth of Nations: An Introductory Essay' in idem (eds.), *Wealth and Virtue*, Cambridge (1983), 38; J. Dunn, 'Justice and the Interpretation of Locke's Political Ideas', *Political Studies* 16 (1968), 68–87; Pufendorf, *Nature and Nations*, 5.3.4.

by others, and became peevish if they were not, and they claimed 'pro-priety, and possession; pleasing themselves with the power that seemes to give, and the right they thereby have, to dispose of them, as they please'. These were the 'two roots' of almost all injustice in the world. They had to be replaced both by desires that were intrinsically more restrained, and particularly by the ability to restrain the remaining desires, with 'contrary habits' introduced. Men were 'all from our cradles vain, and proud creatures' but by 'weeding out' the love of dominion tutors could provide the basis of a 'good and worthy man'.[41]

Children were to be taught to avoid cruelty to animals. The custom of treating animals badly would 'by degrees harden their minds even towards men, and they who accustom themselves to delight in the suffering and destruction of inferior creatures' would not be 'very compassionate or benign to those of their own kind'. In an argument that implicitly stressed the same duties of justice and charity of the *Treatises*, Locke declared that children were particularly to be taught not to destroy any living creature 'unless it be for the preservation and advantage of some other that is nobler'. Indeed, Locke remarked that if the preservation of all were the persuasion of all 'as it is the true principle of religion, politics and moral-ity' the world would be 'much quieter and better natured than it is'. By teaching care of animals children could be taught 'diligence and good nature'. For Locke children ought to be 'accustomed from their cradles to be tender to all sensible creatures, and to spoil or waste nothing at all'.[42]

Children were also to be taught to 'part with what they have easily, and freely to their friends'. By experience they were to find that 'the most liberall has always most plenty, with esteem and commendation to boot'. They would quickly learn to 'practise it'. Such liberality was important to develop kindness for others. It was also crucial for Locke in *Some Thoughts* because it would combine with civility and temperance to secure justice by reducing the covetousness that undermined it. When children contested to have their wills, then whoever began this should 'be crossed in it'. Children's crying was often 'Contention for mastery'. They were to be taught instead to 'have all the deference, Complaisance, and civility one for another imaginable'. This was to be done by approval for civility, for def-erence to others' desires, and for liberality. When children saw that this made them grow in 'love and esteem' they would take pleasure in it, and see that they lost no 'superiority' by it. They would then become just and liberal.[43]

Locke's vision of his own service to the public in various official posts

---

[41] *Education*, paras 103–5; *Correspondence*, II, 829.   [42] *Education*, para 116.
[43] *Education*, paras 109–10.

and through composition of his works when his health did not allow him to serve in such a manner was that this was both required and considerable. In *Some Thoughts* he argued that 'I think it every man's indispensable Duty, to do all the Service he can to his Country: And I see not what Difference he puts between himself and his Cattel, who lives without that Thought.' Locke's commitment to service to the community was given broadest expression, however, in a declaration to the Dublin philosopher William Molyneux in 1694 that 'I think every one, according to what way providence has placed him in, is bound to labour for the publick good, as far as he is able, or else he has no right to eat.' Exemplifying his own view that by publishing his works he was himself serving his country the first passage followed after the declaration that *Some Thoughts* was published because he had been pressed to publish to serve the public which 'had touch'd upon what will always be very prevalent with me'.

Locke advocated service by gentlemen energetically in the 1690s. *Some Thoughts* was published specifically for similar children to those of his prosperous friend Clarke, and thus to describe the education necessary for 'our English Gentry'. Locke declared that 'The well Educating of their Children is so much the Duty and Concern of Parents, and the Welfare and Prosperity of the Nation so much depends on it' that every one should promote it 'with regard to their several Conditions, which is the easiest, shortest, and likeliest to produce vertuous, useful, and able men in their distinct Callings'. He continued that that 'most to be taken Care of, is the Gentleman's Calling. For if those of that Rank are by their Education once set right, they will quickly bring all the rest into Order.'[44]

Locke did not explain the nature of 'Order' that he thought would be obtained by properly educated gentlemen, but he probably had in mind moral as well as social and political order. Locke also did not spell out in *Some Thoughts* how gentlemen were supposed to bring 'all the rest into Order', but behind this statement three separate notions were very probably combined: the power of the example of the gentry in setting manners, the moral investigations and propagation of morality by writing as well as by example, and finally the ruling of society in terms of making and interpreting laws. For Locke 'a Gentleman's Calling' involved having 'the Knowledge of a Man of Business, a Carriage suitable to his Rank, and to be Eminent and Useful in his Country according to his station'. It was clear that much of this usefulness came in making and interpreting law. According to Locke, an English gentleman had to be learned in the law of his own country: 'This, whatever station he is in, is so requisite, that from a Justice of the Peace, to a Minister of State, I know no Place he can well fill without

---

[44] *Education*, 'To Edward Clarke'; *Correspondence*, IV, 1693.

it.' To this he was to add history, the 'great Mistress of Prudence and Civil Knowledge' and, perhaps most importantly in terms of a gentleman, being 'serviceable to his Country', he was to read of 'our Law' and of 'our English Constitution and Government, in the ancient books of the Common Law; and some more Modern Writers, who out of them have given an account of this Government'. This theme was to be reiterated in Locke's suggestions for the reading of a gentleman in 1703, when Locke named Tyrrell, Petyt, Atwood and Sadler among the authors to be read. As was noted earlier, the absence of argument on the basis of the ancient constitution in the *Treatises* did not signify in any way a denial of the ideals of government and the largely mythic account of English history of which the ancient constitutionalism of Tyrrell, Petyt, Atwood and Sadler consisted.[45]

In his accounts of the liberty of contemplation, of harnessing the powers of education, custom and esteem in the *Essay* and *Some Thoughts* by the mid-1690s Locke had articulated a number of techniques to combine his hedonic psychology with his view of men's duties to other men. In the early 1690s several notes in his commonplace books suggest that he was trying to find further ways to accommodate an extended social ethic with his hedonic theory of motivation. In 1692 he composed perhaps the most hopeful of these writings in a note entitled 'Ethica'. This recognised that men were motivated by pursuit of happiness and argued that this could be a basis for loving one's neighbour as oneself because from doing good turns to one's neighbour men received enlarged and secure pleasures and an 'undecaying and uninterrupted pleasure'. Thus, the memory of a good turn lasted, while the memory of an eaten meal decayed quickly. Going without a meal in order to aid a friend therefore gave more pleasure than its consumption. Briefly stating the insight which was shortly to become central to his thought in the *Reasonableness*, however, Locke recognised that some men would not take pleasure from acts 'of love and charity' and would only be motivated to help their neighbour by God's reward in another life 'wherein God may put a distinction between those that did good and suffered and those who did evil and enjoyd by their different treatment there'. He recognised that for all to 'love all the world as you doe your child or self and make this universal' required a level of virtue that was unrealistic in this life: 'how much short will it make the earth of heaven'.[46]

Another manuscript note of 1693, again entitled 'Ethica', developed a slightly different approach, declaring that there were 'two parts of Ethicks'.

[45] *Education*, paras 94, 182–7; p. 295n.; pp. 397ff.   [46] MS Locke c42, ii, 224.

The first was 'the rule which men are generally in the right in though perhaps they have not deduced them as they should from their true principles'. This suggestion received no expanded analysis, but it probably referred to no more than the notion stated in the *Essay*, that in the standards of morality held by most societies most of genuine morality was accepted. The second part of ethics was 'the true motives to practise' virtues and 'the ways to bring men to observe them'. In contrast with the generally accepted virtues, these motives and means were 'generally either not well known or not rightly applyd'. Without these motives 'moral discourses' were heard 'with pleasure ... The minde being generally delighted with truth espetially if handsomely expressed', but did not result in 'practise, which will never be till men are made alive to virtue and can tast it'. Locke argued that 'To doe this one must consider what is each man's particular disease, what is the pleasure that possesses him.' 'General discourses' were ineffective here, but 'by all the prevalencys of friendship all the arts of perswasion' a man could be brought 'to trie the contrary course ... and soe by habits establish a contrary pleasure'. When 'conscience reason and pleasure' could be made to 'goe together' then virtuous behaviour was 'sure to prevaile'. The 'waye to doe this in particular cases' was 'easier for a prudent man to find when the case offers then for any to foresee and determine before the case happens and the person be known'.[47]

We will see in the next chapters that there were many reasons for Locke's 1695 composition of the *Reasonableness of Christianity* and 1700–4 composition of the *Paraphrase on the Epistles of St Paul* that related particularly to Locke's burgeoning theological interests and to his failure to find a way to prove the immortality of the soul, the existence of an afterlife and the rewards and punishments that God offered for virtue. It is important to note here that concern with motivating men to be virtuous was prominent among his reasons to compose these works, and that the virtues that Locke specified reiterated his long-standing commitment to the duties of liberality, charity, civility, temperance and fortitude as well as justice.

It is not necessary to quote from either of these sources in full; Locke's discussions included many of the emphases that have been established so far. In the *Paraphrase* Locke described the requirements of Christianity as those of 'temperance' and a 'sober and prudent Demeanour'. More generally, in the *Reasonableness* he argued that all 'worldly cares' which displaced concentration on the afterlife were sinful and that Christ had commanded 'self-denial'. 'Pride' and 'covetousness' were forbidden, but covetousness was described by Locke as usually the name given to the

---

[47] MS Locke c28, 113r.

desire for another's property which led to theft, and very importantly thereby implicitly distinguished from the legitimate behaviour of acquisitiveness. Indicating parts of the content of Locke's sin of 'incivility' in *Some Thoughts*, 'Morality' and his translation of Nicole's *Essais*, Christ was said in the *Reasonableness* to have condemned 'words of contempt . . . swearing in conversation, as well as forswearing in judgment [and] censoriousness'. Christ had commanded men instead to be 'reconciled and kind towards their adversaries', 'loving our enemies, doing good to those that hate us, blessing those that curse us, praying for those that despitefully use us'. Men were to have 'patience and meekness under injuries' together with 'forgiveness, liberality, [and] compassion'.[48]

Both the *Reasonableness* and the *Paraphrase* stressed serving God and not man, and in so doing made men's terrestrial advantages not merely less important as an aim of service to others but even less important as a result of service. In the *Reasonableness*, Locke argued that when a dinner was made, friends were not to be invited 'lest . . . recompense be made'. Men would instead 'be blessed' for giving to the 'poor and maimed'. In the *Paraphrase* Locke argued that charity was to be not 'at all self interested', and that Christians had to help others 'in want according to their necessities'. Locke paraphrased Rom. 12:8, 'he that giveth let him do it with simplicity' as 'he that giveth let him do it liberally, and without the mixture of any self interest'.

Locke was, however, equally clear in the *Reasonableness* about God's rewards to men, which made virtue 'visibly' the 'best bargain', and argued in the *Paraphrase* both that God made charitable gifts 'redound to your advantage', and that the 'true and sure way' for a man 'to get an excellency . . . above others' was 'the enlargeing himself in Charity'. Locke recorded that 'he that lays out the stock of good things he has, onely for the satisfaction of his own bodily necessitys, conveniencys or pleasures, shall at the harvest find the fruit and product of such husbandry to be corruption and perishing. But he that lays out his worldly substance according to the rules dictated by the spirit of God shall of the spirit reap life everlasting.'[49]

The *Reasonableness* and *Paraphrase* once again carefully balanced service to others and to oneself, both circumscribing such service and arguing that industriousness was in part a duty as it was necessary to provide the means to serve others. The command to one man to 'sell all thou hast and give it to poor' was described by Locke in the *Reasonableness* as 'not being a standing law of his kingdom; but a probationary

---

48 MS Locke c27, 121vff.; *Reasonableness*, 115–20; *Paraphrase*, preface; Eph. 4:25–5:2; 5:18–19 and n. cf. Tarcov, *Locke's Education*, 143.

49 *Reasonableness*, 118–20; *Paraphrase*, contents, 1 Cor. 12:1–14:40; 1 Cor. 13:6; Rom. 12:8; Rom. 12:13; Gal. 6:8; Eph. 4:19; see Tarcov, *Locke's Education For Liberty*, 142–3.

command to this young man; to try whether he truly believed him to be the Messiah'. On 1 Cor. 10:24, 'let no man seek his own but every man anothers wealth', Locke's *Paraphrase* inserted the legitimacy of seeking of one's own wealth alongside serving others without denying the need to serve others: 'Noe man must seek barely his owne private particular interest alone but let every one seek the good of others also.' Inserting into the *Paraphrase* the need to labour in 'some honest calling', Locke indicated that such labour was necessary partly in order to be able to relieve others. Describing Ephesians 4:25–5:2 as pressing 'several Particulars of those great Social Virtues, Justice and charity', Locke recorded that instead of stealing men should 'labour in some honest Calling, that he may have even wherewithal to relieve others that need it'.[50]

More generally, Locke recorded that John 13:34 included the 'new commandment', 'That ye love one another: as I have loved you, that ye also love one another.' All of the duties were summed up in two general declarations. The first of these was the golden rule, Matt. 7:12 'All things whatsoever ye would that men should do to you, do you even so to them.' The second was Luke 10:25: 'Thou shalt love the Lord thy God with all thy heart, and with all thy soul, and with all thy strength, and with all thy mind; and thy neighbour as thyself.' In the *Paraphrase* Locke exhorted mutual charity, 'good will', a 'kind and tender heart', and particularly 'liberality' and 'general beneficence' at many points. As men had 'oportunityes let us doe good unto all men, espetially to those who profess faith in Jesus Christ'. On Cor. 8:3, 'But if any man love God, the same is known of him', Locke inserted the love of one's neighbour: 'But if any one love god and consequently his neighbour for gods sake such an one is made to know or has got true knowledg from god himself.' Locke recorded the general exhortation to love 'which is in effect the fulfiling of the whole law'. His paraphrase of Romans 13:8 expanded: 'Owe nothing to anybody but affection and good will mutually to one another, for he that loves others sincerely as he does himself has fulfilled the law.' Men's 'Social dutys' were comprehended 'in this Thou shalt love thy neighbour as thyself'. Such love did not allow men to do 'harm to our neighbour, and therefore is the fulfilling of the whole law of the second table'.

The apotheosis of this theme of service to others was reached in Locke's discussion of Gal. 5:13–14, a text which exhorted men not to fulfil the 'lusts of the flesh' but to 'serve one another in Love'. Locke's paraphrase indicated that 'the whole law concerning our duty to others is fulfilled in observing this one precept "Thou shalt love thy neighbour as thyself"'. His note to this passage perhaps expresses better than any of the other

---

[50] *Paraphrase*, Eph. 4:25–5:2, contents; Eph. 4:28; 1 Cor. 10:24.

passages focused upon throughout this book the error involved in describing Locke as an egoistic 'possessive individualist'. Locke pointed out that the notion of serving others had 'a greater force in the Greek than . . . English' because it signified 'the opposite to freedom'. This meant that Paul was 'elegantly' informing the Galatians that 'though by the gospel they are called to a state of liberty from the law yet they were still as much bound and subjected to their brethren in all the offices and dutys of love and good will as if in that respect they were their vassals and bondmen'.[51]

In a manuscript of the late 1690s entitled 'Of the Conduct of the Understanding' Locke argued that there were 'fundamental truths that lie at the bottom' of morality, 'the basis upon which a great many others rest, and in which they have their consistency'. These were 'teeming truths, rich in store, with which they furnish the mind, and, like the lights of heaven, are not only beautiful and entertaining in themselves, but give light and evidence to other things, that without them could not be seen or known'. Locke argued that one such 'bottoming' principle in morality was 'Our Saviour's great rule, that "we should love our neighbour as ourselves"'. This was 'such a fundamental truth for the regulating human society, that, I think, by that alone, one might without difficulty determine all the cases and doubts in social morality'. He said nothing about the practical demonstration from reason of this bottoming principle, however, appealing to it as a precept of revelation. In contrast, he suggested a naturalistic basis for another bottoming principle as the appropriate response to the question of whether 'the grand seignour', the archetypal absolute monarch, could 'lawfully take what he will from any of his people'. This question could not be resolved, Locke argued, 'without coming to a certainty, whether all men are naturally equal; for upon that it turns, and that truth well settled in the understanding, and carried in the mind through the various debates concerning the rights of men in society, will go a great way to putting an end to them, and showing on which side truth is'. Once again, it was the limited principle of justice that Locke thought easy to ground naturalistically, the more extensive principle of love that seemed to require appeal to revelation.[52]

In 1693 Locke composed a strange note entitled 'Labor' in one of his commonplace books. Not published by him, and probably never shown to anyone else, its composition was probably prompted primarily by Locke's attitude towards his own ill health in 1693 and by desire to extrapolate on the basis of this sickness and his central commitment to man's purposive

[51] *Holy Bible*, 16.25, p. 750; *Paraphrase*, John 13:34; *Reasonableness*, 121; *Paraphrase*, 1 Cor. 8:3; 1 Cor. 12:31; 2 Cor. 8:3–12; 2 Cor. 9:7; Gal. 5:13–14; 6:6–10, contents; 2 Cor. 9:10; Rom. 13:8–14.
[52] Locke, *Of the Conduct of the Understanding*, passim.

nature an appropriate balance between types of activity that men ought to undertake in their industrious service of God. 'Labor' began with the declaration that

We ought to look upon it as a marke of goodness in god that he has put us in this life under a necessity of labour not only to keep mankinde from the mischiefe that ill men at leisure are apt to doe: But it is a benefit even to the good and the vertuous which are thereby preserved from the ills of idleness or the diseases that attend constant study in a sedentary life.[53]

By not labouring in physical occupations, the studious were deprived of the natural preservative against diseases and the virtuously 'busily studious' – such as Locke himself, of course – suffered from gout and spleen as much as did the 'lazily voluptuous'. A scholar such as Locke became thereby a 'useless member of the commonwealth in that mature age which should make him most serviceable', whereas a 'sober and working artisan and the frugal laborious countryman', performed 'his part well and cheerfully' and went on 'in his business to a vigerous old age'.[54]

Locke recommended that every man in the society should therefore spend 'six hours of labour' every day 'in some honest calling'. If all men were thus to spend 'Half the day imploid in usefull labour' this would 'supply the inhabitants of the earth with the necessarys and conveniences of life in a full plenty'. Instead, the 'Luxury of courts and by their example inferiour grandees' had 'found out Idle and useless imploymts for themselves and others subservient to their pride and vanity, and soe brought honest labour in usefull and mechanicall arts wholy into disgrace'. He continued, however, that

if this distinction of the twelve hours seem not fair nor sufficiently to keep up the distinction that *ought* to be in the ranks of men let us change it a little. Let the gent and scholer imploy nine of the twelve on his minde and the other three in some honest labour. And the man of manual labour nine in work and three in knowledg.

This would deliver many poor men 'from that horid ignorance and brutality to which the bulk of them is now everywhere given up'.[55]

Locke concluded that if his proposals were not put into force that was 'owing to the carelessnesse and negligence of the Governments of the world' which were 'wholly intent upon the care of aggrandizing themselves' and neglected 'the happynesse of the people' and with it 'their owne peace and security'. These governments should 'suppresse the arts and instruments of Luxury and Vanity and bring those of honest and usefull industry into fashen'. This would prevent 'temptation to Ambition where

[53] MS Film. 77, 310–11; cf. Dunn, *Political Thought*, 235–6.
[54] MS Film. 77, 310–11; cf. Dunn, *Political Thought*, 235–6.
[55] MS Film. 77, 310–11 (my emphasis); cf. Dunn, *Political Thought*, 235–6.

the possession of power could not display itself in the destinctions of useless pride and vanity'. It would thereby also prevent the ignorant poor from being turbulent since 'the well instructed minds of the people' would not 'suffer them to be the instruments of Aspireing and turbulent men'. Locke concluded that 'this is certain that if the labour of the world were rightly diverted and distributed there would be more knowledge peace health and plenty in it than now there is. And mankinde would be much more happy than now it is.' The note was signed 'JL'.[56]

This was one of two manuscripts in the 1690s in which Locke argued for governmental action to direct labour and make many men more industrious. Locke's recommendations to the Board of Trade in 1697 notoriously argued that the idle but able-bodied unemployed were to be forced into service at sea and that orphaned children were to be placed in workhouses and forced to labour from the ages of three for boys and five for girls. These children were to receive in return for twelve or fourteen hours of labour a day a 'watery gruel'.[57] This singularly distasteful proposal has correctly been identified by many scholars as revealing Locke's exceedingly limited notions of justice and of the charity in dire need that had been supported in the *Two Treatises*. In a manuscript 'Venditio' in 1695 Locke condemned those merchants who would only sell their foods in times of scarcity at inflated prices which were beyond the means of the poor as just but nonetheless guilty of 'murder'. As in the *Treatises*, justice was to be bounded by charity, but, as in the *Treatises*, there was no suggestion that the right of charity to take others' surplus goods extended one iota beyond those surplus goods physiologically necessary to preserve life itself. In these proposals Locke identified the problem of the idle poor as the result of the 'relaxation of manners'. For Locke, the idle and able-bodied poor were both depriving the community of their own labour and also were not leading industriously sober lives. It is important to underline that Locke's educational programme in *Some Thoughts* and the *Essay* was intended to create gentlemen who led 'sober' and 'Honest' as well as 'industrious' lives and who would thus fulfil the duties of their calling in a similar way to others fulfilling the duties of their less exalted callings. When Locke wrote to Molyneux in 1694 that he thought that those men who did not serve the public good according to the station in which providence had placed them did not have a right to eat, his argument could not merely be used to condemn those gentlemen who wasted their estates and ignored their duty to 'do something' but equally to condemn those poor people who failed in their 'main' duty in life, which was to labour industriously in their par-

---

[56] MS Film. 77, 310–11; cf. Dunn, *Political Thought*, 235–6.
[57] Cranston, *Locke*, 424ff.; MS Film. 77, 268–9.

ticular calling to secure their own means of subsistence and to support their family.[58]

Locke's proposals of governmental coercion of the poor into industriousness apparently did not for him breach his injunction to 'love thy neighbour as thyself'. They suggest that since for Locke the proper realisation of one's love for oneself was to set oneself upon a strictly sober and industrious life there was no reason for others in the society to be helped in any way that would allow them to avoid setting themselves upon such an industrious life, however poor they might be. In important contrast to the able-bodied but idle poor, for Locke the old and ill who could no longer work deserved not merely sustenance but also 'the conveniences' of life. While living at Oates, Locke frequently visited the poor who were sick, disbursing charity. His will provided for a plain burial for himself with the money saved as well as some of his clothes going to various 'deserving' poor of his parish.[59]

In the light of these proposals and all that has been said about Locke's (and Cicero's) conception of the limits of service to others because of means, social status, degrees of social ties, the worthiness of recipients, and benefits formerly received, there can be no doubt that being obliged to be others' 'vassals and bondmen' in the *Paraphrase* was an expression considerably more imperative in feeling than it was extensive in its requirements for practice. The service that Locke himself celebrated was a very limited sharing of resources by those who possessed the vast majority in a society of massive inequality, and it served to perpetuate that broad distribution of resources. Locke's recognition of the responsibilities of utilising property that the gentleman owned for service conceptualised these as 'imperfect' duties, with the recipients' 'rights' to what was due to them from that property being unenforceable; it was not recognition of the common rights that the people defended as customary in an increasingly unsuccesssful series of legal battles with their rich landlords over the seventeenth and eighteenth centuries. Locke's vision of liberality, civility, charity and justice may strike a modern reader as the morality of a gentleman appallingly self-congratulatory about his actually extremely limited concern for others. It does not do much to soften that judgement to recognise that this morality had been in large part designed to stop the widespread butchering of others for religion, that it was intended at least to preserve lives when securing sustenance was still precarious and others in Locke's society, such as Baxter, were opposing even that limited a charity, and that it was designed to oppose ethical egoism as the way in which

---

[58] 'Venditio' is cited and discussed by Dunn, 'Justice'.
[59] This is briefly discussed in Cranston, *Locke*, 480ff.; cf. le Clerc, *Life*, passim; MS Locke b5, 14.

gentlemen would best be encouraged to serve the community and in which the society could best be directed to the preservation of a peace, stability and continued employment for the poor with less onerous burdens upon most of them than had followed (if not necessarily followed from) attempts at a more substantial reformation in mid-century. It nonetheless remains vital to an understanding of Locke's ethics and social identity to recognise that that imperative feeling of duties of service and the attempt to establish them firmly in the minds of other gentlemen in England was extremely important to the way that he lived his entire life.[60]

[60] On the battles by the lower classes to obtain the means of preservation see especially E. P. Thompson, *Customs in Common*, passim.

Part III

HERESY, PRIESTCRAFT, AND TOLERATION: JOHN LOCKE AGAINST THE 'EMPIRE OF DARKNESS'

Theology, epistemology and toleration: against the 'Empire of Darkness'

I

Before his exile in the Netherlands in 1683 Locke had shown some first glimmerings of interest in doctrinal theology in the mid-1670s, and these glimmerings had then probably been very significantly developed by several influences between 1679 and 1683 – the reading of unitarian works in 1679 and perhaps in 1680, Locke's own increasingly biblically and patristically astute criticisms of Stillingfleet and Filmer and the reading that composition of these necessitated in 1681–3, and his discussions with Thoynard and Damaris Cudworth in the early 1680s. In exile in the Netherlands this burgeoning interest turned very rapidly into very deep interest indeed. Locke's correspondence, notebooks, journals, and book purchases in his first years in the Netherlands are filled with theology. Cudworth declared shortly after Locke's arrival that his time in the Netherlands had already 'Certainly been Advantageous to you, since I cannot but Fancie . . . that you have learnt more Scripture there than ever you Knew in your whole life before'.[1]

There are many reasons for this transformation. Theology was central to Damaris Cudworth, with whom Locke had just fallen in love. While it is likely that Locke supported the attempt at revolution in England in 1685 by helping to finance the ill-fated Monmouth rebellion, he very probably thought that he was destined to remain in exile for the rest of his life. More importantly, freed from the political duties of Shaftesbury's campaigns and intrigues, Locke's restless intelligence found a substantial new area of interest in the extensive theological debates of the Netherlands, where the questioning of central theological doctrines both reflected and furthered Locke's own long-standing anticlerical suspicions of clerical 'orthodoxy' and his support for toleration. Enquiry into the nature of the patristic church had become for Locke with the 'Critical Notes' a major necessity in order to challenge the powers claimed by priests; opposition to priestly

---

[1] *Correspondence*, III, 787.

traditions manipulable in whatever direction interest led the priests had led Locke in 1682 in the midst of a series of epistemological notes on reason to attack clerical 'tradition' and to suggest that pursuit of the content of divine law needed to be undertaken by men's 'natural light' (not, it should be noted, supernatural light). The initial attempt of the First Treatise to find 'plain' messages in Scripture had increasingly turned even within that treatise towards an attempt to determine the precepts of natural reason before revelation, and Locke had followed the latter tack almost exclusively in the Second Treatise. In theological debate in the Netherlands Locke found learned allegations of far more widespread abuses of the powers of what was already coming to be called 'priestcraft' in theological works that opposed the Trinity and satisfaction and thus the status of the 'priests' of Protestantism as well as Catholicism as mediators of Christ's sacrifice. These works indicted the self-interested motivations of various Fathers in adopting trinitarianism, and challenged claims to authority of biblical interpretation that derived from command of languages and of patristic sources.

Locke quickly became an avid reader and contributor to various of the Continent's journals reviewing recent publications on theology throughout Europe and discussing central issues of theology, toleration and epistemology. The most important of these journals was the *Bibliothèque Universelle et Historique*, founded in these years by an impetuous Calvinist and Huguenot refugee turned Arminian, Jean le Clerc. The *Bibliothèque* frequently discussed issues of theological orthodoxy and reviewed the best new critical scholarship on the patristic period. Le Clerc indicated something of the impact of these journals in his smugly self-satisfied 1700 declaration that the 'republic of letters is at last become a country of reason and light, and not of authority and implicit faith as it has been too long'. It was to the *Bibliothèque* that Locke contributed his first significant publications – an article on his method of taking adversaria and an extract of the *Essay Concerning Human Understanding*; he may also have contributed a number of book reviews on theological works, including Bayle's *Commentaire Philosophique*. In the 1690s Locke himself tried to extend critical theological debate in the *Bibliothèque* by supplying for review the new English unitarian challenges to orthodoxy.[2]

Locke was placed into the vortex of theological debate because he spent

[2] BM Add MS 15642, 124 for an example of Locke's interest in learned journals before 1683; Le Clerc in Colie, 'John Locke', 111–29; van Limborch's letter of introduction of Locke to Joannes Graevius, *Correspondence*, II, 793; J. le Clerc (ed.), *Bibliothèque Universelle et Historique de l'année 1686–93*; cf. the marks and notes and page lists by Locke in his own copies of the *Bibliothèque*.

his early years in Holland hiding from arrest under assumed names in the houses of various leading members of the Arminian community, and his later years in the household and in the library of the theologically learned and free-thinking Quaker Benjamin Furly, whose hatred for the priestly 'druids' outdid even Locke's own detestation and who found even Quakerism too restrictive and too priestly a religion. Furly's house was at the epicentre of the early Enlightenment.

Locke struck up a particularly close friendship with Philipp van Limborch, Remonstrant Professor of Divinity and their leading theologian. Within a few months of their first meeting in 1684 Locke was reading van Limborch's works before publication and making suggestions for improvements, and the rapid pace of growth in Locke's interest in theology is suggested in van Limborch's letters of introduction to Locke to his friends as having few equals in knowledge of theology. Within a few years Locke was lauding van Limborch as the 'best of friends' and 'the best of men', and recognising his importance as a friend who supported and advised him. In a 1677 manuscript 'Study' Locke had stressed that friends were crucial to discuss and re-examine received ideas, and in the *Essay* Locke described 'rational discussion' with a close friend as an example of a simple idea of pleasure; van Limborch quickly became exactly the kind of friend that Locke had lauded.[3]

When twenty years later Damaris Cudworth noted that Locke had studied 'when Calvinism was the fashion in England' and had described the opinions that as Ralph's daughter she had grown up with and 'always' found prevalent in the University 'and among the clergy' as being new to him, she continued – with a comment that suggests that for her Locke had wrongly been hostile to all clergy before going to the Netherlands because he associated them all with the Calvinism of his youth – that he had had 'only very little contact with clergymen' before going to Holland, and 'imagined' that he had found the opinions of the Remonstrants particularly pleasing, being unaccustomed to hear 'theologians speak in such a reasonable manner'. That Locke found elements of Arminian thought attractive immediately after his arrival in the Netherlands is also suggested by a comment of van Limborch that when Locke first arrived in Holland he had been 'surprised' to find how much he agreed with in Arminian thought,

---

[3] Klibansky and Gough, *Letter*, introduction; Ashcraft, *Revolutionary Politics*, chs. 9 and 10; *Correspondence*, II, pp. 648–51 on the Remonstrants and van Limborch; *Correspondence*, III, p. 39 on Furly and his many letters to Locke in the 1690s in vols. IV and V for Furly's anticlericalism, theology and Quaker unorthodoxy. *Correspondence*, II, 793; 831; 833; 834; III; 865; 868; 877.

having long attributed to them views 'very different' than they actually held.[4]

It is possible that Locke's rapid support for Arminianism was prompted by their advocacy of religious toleration and their practice of this toleration through doctrinal comprehension: giving practical effect to van Limborch's views on the limited requirements of Christianity, the Arminians admitted to communion with them as fellow Chrsitians a number of Socinians who had fled from Polish persecution and were allowed to settle in the Netherlands but were not permitted their own churches for public worship. On 30 July 1684, Locke went to an 'Armenian' service and recorded that 'They admit to their communion all Christians, and hold it our duty to join in love and charity with those who differ from them in opinion.' While some English Arminians were supporters of toleration, very many English Arminians were high-church Anglicans and strong supporters of religious persecution. It still seems unlikely, however, that van Limborch's comment about views that Locke found surprising but congenial referred to toleration: as a contributor to English tolerationist debates which clearly enunciated the comparative tolerationism of the Dutch, it is not easy to believe that Locke would have been surprised by Dutch Arminian support for toleration.[5]

By as early as April 1684 Locke had purchased and begun to read a large number of Arminian works, including works by the leading Arminian of the previous generation, Episcopius, and had purchased several works explicitly debating predestination and grace such as Velthusius' *Doctrina de Gratia et Praedestinatione Tradita Novo Methodo*. Locke may have been surprised to find that the Arminians were trinitarians who defended the satisfaction and original sin as well as man's free will and reason since in England the Arminians were often accused of elevating men's free will and ability to act morally too greatly, an accusation that was voiced, for instance, in Hammond's *Pacifick Decrees*, which Locke read in the early 1660s, and in Fowler's *Principles and Practices*, which Locke probably read in 1674–5. The logic of Locke's August 1680 journal comment on God's goodness and Damaris Cudworth's comment opposing Arminianism to Calvinism, however, make support for Arminian trinitarianism and belief in Christ's satisfaction and original sin seem very unlikely to have been what Locke found appealing.[6]

---

[4] Amsterdam: Remonstrant MSS J57A, cited and very variously translated in many works, including Klibansky and Gough, *Letter*, xv–xvi; Fox, Bourne, *Life*, II, 6; le Clerc, *Life*, passim.

[5] MS Locke f8, pp. 100–1, 30 July 1684.

[6] MS Locke f8, 36–9; 41–2; 49; 52; 57; 75; 78–9; 203; 210; 268–9; 287–93; 305–9; MS Locke f9, 1–9; 18–19; 82, 93; 117; 124; MS Locke c33, 27v; MS Locke b2.43–4; 50–; 81r; 84–6; MS Locke f29, 18; 90–1; cf. MS Locke f17, 1–5v; 45vff.

If it was Arminians' detailed theology that was found attractive, then this attractiveness very probably came from their emphasis on reconciliation of grace and freedom, firstly through elevation relative to most English theologians of men's capacity to reason, and secondly through emphasis upon co-operation with grace in the moral activity of a working faith. Locke read carefully and commented upon during composition in 1685 van Limborch's *Theologia Christiana*, a systematic exposition of Arminian theology which argued that Christ's death was of universal intent, that it was necessary to co-operate with God's grace, and that it was possible to resist this grace. It declared that justification was a merciful act of God whereby he absolved men of sin on account of their faith in Jesus. God remitted sins, graciously counting faith as righteousness.[7]

Although he read Arminian theology in 1684–5 and commented prepublication on *De Veritate*, however, Locke was apparently ignorant of the five points of Remonstrants' disagreement with Calvinists, the essence of Arminian theology, when he was working on the *Paraphrase Upon the Epistles of St Paul* in the late 1690s. Although Locke turned his epistemological drafts into the published version of the *Essay* in the mid-1680s during his reading of Arminian theology, his work included no detailed discussion of soteriology and only came close to discussing soteriological issues directly in condemnation of those who presumed to define whom God would save. Discussing 'changelings', creatures who were part man and part beast, Locke declared that there were zealous men who would seek to define the potential of these beings for salvation. They should avoid being 'peremptory' in defining others' fate since the 'Faithful Creator and bountiful Father' did not dispose of his creatures according to men's 'narrow thoughts or Opinions'. Locke similarly argued against those who supported innatism by contending on the basis of God's goodness that he had provided men with innate ideas. Men were instead to argue that things were good because God had done them, and not to identify what they thought to be best and then assert that that had to be how God had made the world.[8]

While the form of attack upon peremptoriness in defining who was saved was unquestionably closest to that adopted by the Arminians and some Latitudinarians when they assaulted Calvinists who presumed to define God's soteriological activities, and while Locke complimented van Limborch for his harsh attacks on Calvinism in the *Theologia*, and suggested that this could have gone farther in declaring that 'even German

---

[7] P. van Limborch, *Theologia Christiana*, Amsterdam (1686), passim and idem, *De Veritate religionis Christianae amica collatio cum eruditio Judaeo*; cf. Spellman, *Locke and Depravity*, 131ff.; *Correspondence*, III, 905 and De Beer's notes to that letter.
[8] *Essay*, IV.iv.15; I.iv.11–17; I.iv.21.

theology' did not look 'utterly unlovely' in his work, Locke did not extend his arguments into a positive account of how God did operate on the basis of scriptural analysis and interpretation, and therefore provided nothing remotely resembling the more general account of God's relationship to man in the process of salvation that these divines did at times attempt to articulate. Discussing men's inability to gain clear ideas in many areas, Locke repeated his earlier declaration that men had only 'imperfect ideas' of the operations of their own minds and more imperfect still of God's operations. Men therefore 'ran into great difficulties' about free created agents which reason could not 'well extricate itself from'.[9]

This left room for resolution in Revelation. However, two sets of commitments that Locke expressed in the *Essay* were surely in these years making any personal definition of the manner of men's salvation even through interpretation of revelation as well as reason extremely difficult for him. Locke clearly felt that neither God's omnipotence nor omniscience could deny men's freedom. In his model to illustrate the correct connection of ideas in a demonstration in the *Essay*, Locke set out an argument from punishment to man's freedom that seems to leave no room for strict Calvinist predestination to reprobation, although Locke did not explicitly point this out. The connected ideas for Locke ran as follows: 'Men shall be punished – God the punisher – just punishment – the Punished guilty – could have done otherwise – Freedom – self-determination.' The first edition of the *Essay* was thus clearly committed to man's freedom in terms of being able 'to do otherwise'. In analysing this freedom and its relationship to men's motivation, however, the first edition of the *Essay* created a significant problem for its own declaration of such freedom and for a broader soteriology which it did not resolve. For Locke, men's freedom was a freedom of the agent and not of the will. The longest chapter of the *Essay* in all editions, and the chapter that Locke was to change most in the second edition of the *Essay* in 1694, was Book II, chapter 21, 'Of Power'. In all editions of the *Essay* the will and understanding were defined as powers of the mind, and Locke condemned those who identified them as real and separate agents within the soul. Men found in themselves the power to begin, continue or stop some of their actions. The power of the mind to prefer an action to its forbearance, or *vice versa*, was the Will. Men were free agents as they had the power to think or not, to move or not; liberty was the power to do or forbear actions according to a thought of the mind. For Locke this rendered the question of whether the will was free 'unintelligible'. Liberty and will were both powers belonging to an agent; the proper question was whether the man was free, and Locke declared that he was.[10]

---

[9] *Correspondence*, III, 905.   [10] *Essay*, IV.xvii.4; II.xx; xxi, esp. 5.

As we saw in the last chapter, however, Locke also declared that 'Nature' had put into men 'a desire of Happinesse, and an aversion to Misery', innate 'practical principles' which 'constantly' operated and influenced 'all our Actions without ceasing'. In the first edition of the *Essay* this hedonic motivation was depicted in very strong terms. Willing was defined as preferring to do one thing or another; preferring was 'nothing but being more pleased with the one, than the other'. The first edition declared that it was not in men's choice which things pleased them more. It was therefore easy to know what determined the will: 'happiness'. Adopting what he described in the second edition as the 'general maxim', Locke declared that the will was determined by 'the greater good'. He held that this determination was not an abridgement of freedom, but the perfection of it. The end of liberty was to secure happiness; the more certain the determination of the will by happiness, the greater the perfection of the will.[11]

God having omnisciently annexed pleasures and pains to the things in the world, and having made men in a way that made their will follow their perception of their greatest pleasure in a strikingly mechanistic manner, it was not easy to see how God had left their salvation or damnation within the realms of their free agency. It is true that men were free when they followed happiness because the following of their happiness was defined as free activity, but if they could not choose but to follow this happiness, and if, as Locke argued, the degrees of happiness attached to the things around them had been provided by the omniscient omnipotent God who knew all past, present and future events, even though Locke had declared that the understanding could choose to act or not to act, it became difficult to see how he had left men free to choose their salvation or damnation, and free to do otherwise than they did actually choose to do.[12]

Locke was unable to resolve this problem to his own satisfaction in the first edition of the *Essay*; he later resolved the problem by asserting that men could suspend their will in order to consider actions. That Locke had a problem which he could not resolve was clearly by 1693 to make him unhappy with his own account, but at this point we have also here reached a reason central to Locke's psychological account of men for his own personal worries in the 1680s about the conventional reconciliations of men's freedom and God's omniscient omnipotence in Latitudinarian and Arminian accounts of salvation; they explained this element of the combination of freedom and omnipotence insufficiently, if at all, to resolve the problems posed by the analysis of men's motivations that Locke set out in the *Essay*. It seems once again to be the extent of Locke's personally reasoned separa-

---

[11] *Essay*, I.iii.3; II.xx; II.vii.3–6; II.x.3; II.xx; II.xxi; Epistle to the Reader; II.xxi.28 (1st edn.); II.xxi.49.

[12] Cf. *Correspondence*, IV, 1544, 1579, 1592, 1643, 1655.

tion from even those contemporary accounts to which he was closest that is most noteworthy here.

It seems most likely, therefore, that Locke was surprised by Arminian views but found them congenial not because of their specific resolutions to the problems of free will and salvation but because of their reticence in defining these matters and their even greater reticence in enforcing their views on others – that he had formerly thought that they professed a rigorously defined soteriology and now found that they held broad commitments to man's freedom and the necessity of God's grace but encouraged an extremely wide range of more detailed theological opinions within these very broad commitments. It was the Arminians' doctrinal freedom and support for toleration that was to be by far the most important topic of Locke's letters to van Limborch after Locke's 1689 return to England, and it seems to have been the central message that he took from Arminian works when first reading them. Locke announced to van Limborch in 1685 that he was 'everywhere in search of the truth alone' and that 'to the best of my understanding' he embraced it 'with equal readiness whether I find it among the orthodox or the heterodox', an important and explicit statement of theological eclecticism that he was thereafter to repeat on many occasions. In other letters Locke lauded van Limborch as one who embraced 'truth from whatever source it comes', and as one who used reasoned arguments and could be convinced of views different from his own by reasoned arguments, being free from 'Party spirit'.[13]

It may well have been van Limborch's personal support for a credal minimalism far beyond that of most Latitudinarians and his willingness to accommodate antitrinitarianism that Locke found surprising and congenial, or which, if Locke had not yet become very doubtful about the Trinity, helped considerably to lead Locke towards antitrinitarianism. In the *Theologia Christiana* van Limborch declared that the only absolutely necessary belief of Christianity was that Jesus was the Christ. Van Limborch went further still in the same year in composing *De Veritate Religionis Christianae Amica Collatio cum Eruditio Judaeo*, a work against a Jewish controversialist, Orobio, which attempted to show that Christ's coming was prophesied in the Old Testament. In the course of this argument van Limborch was willing to say that Christ's divinity was not explicitly advanced in Scripture and that belief in it was not necessary to salvation. Van Limborch's two 1685 compositions could thus be read as indicating in tandem that the sole necessary belief of Christianity, that Jesus was the Christ, did not explicitly indicate that Christ was God. Locke

---

[13] *Correspondence*, II, 834; *Five Letters Concerning the Inspiration of the Holy Scriptures* (1690), 105; *Correspondence*, II, 834; III, 868.

may well have met the identification of Jesus as the Christ as the 'Unum necessarium' first in Hobbes' *Leviathan*, as his opponents were to claim in the 1690s, and he may well have been registering the non-trinitarianism of the minimal belief that Jesus was the Messiah in taking his one note from Enyedi in 1679, and also aware of argument for such a minimal creed in reading Croft's *Naked Truth* in mid-1681. In reading Limborch's *Theologia Christiana* and *De Veritate* he surely became even more conscious of, and probably firmly committed to, the argument for a credal minimalism focused on belief that Jesus was the Messiah that was to be central to his own *Reasonableness of Christianity* a decade later. The message was further reinforced and presented in combination with another major feature of Locke's thought in the *Reasonableness* in William Popple's *Rational Catechism*, which Locke read in 1687. This emphasised that the only belief necessary to salvation was that Jesus was the Messiah, the son of God raised from the dead, and it argued that the reinforcement of morality by Christ was necessary since the duties of natural religion required 'deep meditation'. They were therefore both beyond the 'vulgar' and, in their 'fine-spun' consequences, beyond even those who could reason well. Popple was to become a very close friend indeed of Locke immediately upon his return to England and was the translator of Locke's *Epistola de Tolerantia*.[14]

II

The latitude that the Remonstrants promoted in theological enquiry and belief helped to provide an atmosphere of free intellectual enquiry in which Locke undertook his studies of theology in the Netherlands. The critical ferment in the Netherlands in these years, however, owed rather more to debates provoked by several French and English works than to Arminianism itself. A series of critical debates followed publication of Richard Simon's *Histoire Critique*, focused on but not restricted to Jean le Clerc's response *Sentimens des quelques theologiens*, Simon's defence of the *Histoire Critique*, the *Response aux sentimens*, and le Clerc's *Défens des sentimens*.

A notebook on the Old Testament which Locke very probably began in the early 1680s, and possibly began in 1680–1 even before coming to the Netherlands – which would date it at about the time that he was composing his attacks on Filmer's treatment of the Old Testament – starts with twenty-two pages of notes on Richard Simon's *Histoire Critique*. These

---

[14] MS Locke c33, 19; Klibansky and Gough, *Letter*, introduction, xxii; Spellman, *Locke and Depravity*, 135.

summarise Simon's argument that several books of the Old Testament were collections of other more ancient writings recorded by public scribes from Moses' time, and that while these writings were divinely inspired, over time many careless errors and alterations had been made. Simon's overall point was that Protestants who argued that 'the Scripture is plain of itself' were ignorant or prejudiced. The textual problems of Scripture, and particularly the errors that had been made in its transmission, necessitated for Simon an extrascriptural tradition and thus Catholicism. Showing great interest in examining these claims for himself, in his years in the Netherlands Locke took extensive notes from several works of sophisticated interpretation of the customs of the biblical period, such as Stephanus le Moyne's *Varia Sacra*, Sir John Marsham's *Chronicus Canon Aegypticus, Ebraicus, Graecus, et Disquisitiones*, and, most importantly, John Spencer's 'very learned and . . . very dangerous' *De Legibus Hebraeorum*, which indicted Mosaic practices that had then been continued in Christianity and were major elements of priestly authority, including even tithes, priestly vestments and sacrifices, as priestly 'accomodations' to 'superstitious' gentile practices. Instead of being divinely required, for Spencer in these practices God had allowed Moses to comply with pagan folly. Spencer had, just possibly with some foresight of these attitudes, been one of those clerics that Locke had preferred in the Church of England in his time as Secretary to the Clergy in the early 1670s.[15]

Simon's work was written to defend Catholicism; its critical corrosion of Protestant clerics' hermeneutic authority and its emphasis upon the difficulties of interpreting the Bible were substantial. Reading it was to propel John Hampden into free thought around 1680, and Locke may well have been reading it and moved further towards criticism of clerics' arguments about orthodoxy as a result in 1680–2. The works of Spencer and Simon focused on the Old Testament. Le Clerc's *Sentimens* in response to Simon was a far more direct explosive attack on theological orthodoxy. While le Clerc attacked Simon's dependence upon the church as an interpretative authority, he extended Simon's argument that not all of Scripture was divinely inspired very forcefully from the Old Testament to the New Testament. The eleventh and twelfth letters in le Clerc's *Sentimens* argued that in prophecies, in recording history, and even when discussing doctrine itself, the Apostles had often not been inspired by a particular revelation from God. The scriptural identification of the Apostles speaking 'with the Holy Spirit' had often meant no more than their being influenced by a

---

[15] MS Locke f30, passim; MS Locke f32, passim, esp. 25; 30v; 43r; 54v; 61r; 64r; 82v; 106r; 137v; 146r; 160r; MS Locke f8, 305ff.; MS Locke f9, 4ff.; cf. Reedy, *Bible and Reason*, 105–6; MS Locke c27, 238–9. I concur with M. S. Johnson, *Locke on Freedom*, Texas (1978), 160 n.7, on the dating of most of these entries and interest in these issues.

general spirit of piety. The Apostles were not 'secretaries of the Spirit' taking down the Spirit's dictation. Contradictions between the Gospels showed that not everything they said was inspired; the Apostles had dissembled, and had made mistakes in recording their Gospels. Le Clerc declared that this account of variation and mistake in the New Testament was supported by St Jerome, and by the critical scholarship of Erasmus, Grotius and Episcopius. According to le Clerc, to ignore these points was to lay religion open to attack from libertines who could point out the contradictions between the Gospels and therefore refuse to accept anything in the Gospels. Recognition of these problems did not necessitate an oral tradition, as Simon claimed. Rather, the important elements of Scripture had been recorded plainly, were agreed upon by all of the Evangelists, and could be seen clearly in all of their Gospels; *contra* Simon, they were even plain in all translations.

Among the major consequences of le Clerc's argument was a diminution of the importance of the Apostles' epistles. By both locating the important truths as contained in the Gospels, and declaring that in writing the epistles the Apostles had not been divinely inspired, but instead had largely followed their own opinions, le Clerc substantially lessened the role of the epistles as sources of doctrine. Le Clerc simultaneously criticised the neglect of the substance of the Gospel, the observation of 'gospel morals', for the 'outside' of 'opinion'. The passion for orthodoxy of opinion was a human cloak for inability to behave morally, while the 'severe' morality required by the Gospel was little suited to men's 'way of living'. A refugee from Genevan orthodoxy who had been converted to Arminianism by reading the work of Stephen Courcelles, le Clerc showed how far he had travelled by arguing that men 'should apply our selves wholly to the obeying Christ's precepts, which is the only thing God indispensably requires from us'.[16]

Locke read le Clerc's *Sentiments* in 1685 with feelings apparently mixing considerable anticlerical hostility to those who he had no doubt would attack it immediately with reservations about the incaution of le Clerc's expression of the arguments – an attitude that may well reflect far more Locke's commitment to Nicole's strictures on challenging religious opinions with careful humility than opposition to the arguments themselves. He wrote to van Limborch that upon reading the eleventh letter he had heard cries of protest 'as if it meant the end of all religion'. The ways of critics Locke proclaimed all too well known to van Limborch: the less they are able to refute some heterodox opinion, the more they are roused, in their

---

[16] J. le Clerc, *Sentimens des quelqes theologiens*; quotations from translation of the eleventh and twelfth letters in *Five Letters*, passim, esp. 13–27; 35; 42; 44; 60; 77–85; 93; 108–17.

anxiety not to appear idle in God's cause, to outcries, accusations, and calumnies'. Locke recognised that urging that Scripture was entirely of divine authority was to leave all of religion open to the assault of the philosophers. Although not spelled out by Locke, his notion here may have included the view that much belief about natural philosophy in the Bible is erroneous, but was uncorrected by Christ in accommodating himself to gentile and Jewish views in order to concentrate on fundamental points, a notion mentioned in le Clerc's work, and later to be central to Locke's *Reasonableness of Christianity*. If every word of Scripture had to be treated as of divine authority in order to allow any to be of divine authority, then all would fall together. Locke recognised, however, that accepting that all was not of divine authority raised the question of the criterion to distinguish that which was from that which was not. This was a question 'in the utmost degree fundamental', and for Locke it was therefore proper 'to proceed with the greatest caution, prudence, and moderation', which le Clerc had signally failed to do.[17]

Locke wrote to van Limborch that he found some of le Clerc's detailed arguments unconvincing, but that he recognised that there were a number of passages which cast doubt on the general infallibility of Scripture to which he could not find an answer, and about which he asked van Limborch for his opinion. Locke's doubts and questioning were surely furthered when he discussed theology with le Clerc and Furly after 1685; by the later 1680s, Locke was corresponding with le Clerc directly on various points of biblical interpretation, and his later correspondence with Furly suggests that their intellectual discussions in the late 1680s revolved around the need to interpret Scripture with humility and careful scholarshp, swingeing criticism of almost all clerics for following neither course, and emphasis upon morality almost to the complete exclusion of doctrine. By 1688 Locke was recommending le Clerc's *Defens des sentimens* to Benjamin Furly as demonstrating that there had been many alterations in the Gospels themselves.[18]

The clear implication of Locke's correspondence with van Limborch, le Clerc and Furly is that Locke had become very interested by his reading of le Clerc's work in developing a way of discriminating between passages of the Scripture of divine authority and those which were not, the question to 'the utmost degree fundamental'. Ten years later, in the *Reasonableness of Christianity* he was to proffer an interpretation of Scripture which argued

---

[17] *Correspondence*, II, 834.
[18] Le Clerc (ed.), *Bibliothèque*, passim; MS Locke f30, passim; MS Locke f32, passim; MS Locke c33, passim; MS Locke f9, passim; MS Locke f10, passim; *An Account of the Life and Writings of Jean Le Clerc* (1712), 16; S. A. Golden, *Jean Le Clerc*, New York (1972), 63.

that Christ had deliberately neither confuted errors of natural philosophy nor announced his own role in order to be able to deliver his message of eternal life achieved through faith and moral behaviour. He was to argue that this general theme was identified clearly in the Gospels themselves, and that the epistles were relatively unimportant in delivering the main points of Christianity. He was to argue that the only essential belief of Christianity was that Jesus was the Christ. There is an important sense in which this interpretation was an amalgam of van Limborch's credal minimalism with an answer that largely followed le Clerc's own arguments to a problem that le Clerc's work had posed in a particularly acute form for Locke in 1685.[19]

The *Sentimens* had argued that the Apostles had had the assistance of the Holy Spirit at certain moments only, and had itemised its means of inspiration, such as visions and voices. Christ alone was identified as receiving the Spirit without measure, as having the Godhead dwelling bodily in him. In Locke's notebook on the New Testament, which was very probably indeed used by Locke during the 1680s, there is a note which discusses at length the means of communication that God employed, which discusses passages to which le Clerc had been referring in his discussion, and which was therefore probably created in this period; the note bears the initials J.L., indicating that it is Locke's own interpretation. Interestingly, its comments upon Colossians 2:9, a passage often interpreted as support for the Trinity, interpreted that passage in a way that did not ascribe to Jesus a divine nature. Only Jesus of all of the prophets had been given the highest degree of revelation 'expressed here by the Spirit given not by measure'. There was no period when Christ did not have the assistance of the Spirit 'whereby every thing he said was of divine authority every thing he did was according to the will of God. And by this I think we may understand that expression of St Paul Col II.9 for in him dwelleth all the fullness of the Godhead bodily viz that the Spirit of God without stint or measure was as certainly and constantly in him to be the source of all his words and actions, as our souls are annexed to our bodys as the principle of action in us.'[20]

In not identifying the passage as testifying to the deity of Christ, this interpretation comes close to that favoured by most unitarians, rather than that of most trinitarians. If this note was made in the mid-1680s, it is possible that Locke was simply unaware of the more usual trinitarian explication of the passage. It is also possible, however, that it was constructed with both a desire to distinguish fundamental truths of Scripture and with detailed unitarian arguments that the Trinity was not among these at the

[19] See chapter ten below.   [20] MS Locke f30, 42r.

front of Locke's mind. In the Netherlands Locke's general awakening of substantial interest in theological issues and his particular interest in the debates over the arguments of Simon and le Clerc helped to reinforce his pre-existing interest in Socinian works. By as early as April 1684 Locke had purchased the leading Socinian Johann Crell's *Ethics* and *De Spiritu Sancto* and his pseudonymous *De Trinitate*, although there is no indication that he read these then. In 1685, however, he bought Johann Volkel's *De Vera Religione*, a synopsis of Socinus' thought by his amanuensis, and Johann Crell's *De Uno Deo Patre*, and there are several indications that he probably began to read each of these in 1685 and 1686. In a short manuscript entitled 'Volkelii Hypothesis De Vera religione', Locke started a synopsis of Volkel's work which was primarily concerned with the debate following Simon's analysis of the Old Testament.[21]

A lot of the notes in two notebooks on the Old and New Testament come from these two Socinian works, bound together, that Locke had purchased in 1685, as do many of the notes in a number of bibles that Locke was probably composing at this time. The vast majority of the notes in these notebooks and bibles concerned biblical customs and chronology. A Greek New Testament, probably the one that Locke purchased in 1685, also includes, however, many lengthy notes from Crell's *De Uno Deo Patre* and from Volkel's *De Vera Religione*. Many of these were complementary to Locke's many other notes from Arminian works in emphasising morality and working faith as necessary to justification, but many others diverged from them significantly in setting out lengthy Socinian analyses of the passages of Scripture that were the basis of dispute between trinitarians and unitarians. Most crucially, Locke copied out Volkel's interpretation of the beginning of St John's Gospel, the central text in the entire trinitarian arsenal: 'In the beginning was the word, and the word was with God, and the word was God.' In classic Socinian fashion, Volkel's interpretation referred 'In the beginning was the word' to the beginning of the Gospel, not to eternity. The presence of the word with God was taken to indicate that God had not yet explained his Gospel to man. That the word was God was taken to mean that the Gospel was God's wisdom, a divine virtue, but not a person of the Godhead. Locke was thus recording Socinian arguments on the Trinity at the same time as reading critical debates about

---

[21] MS Locke f8, 36–9; 41–2; 49; 52; 57; 75; 78–9; 203; 210; 268–9; 287–93; 305–9; MS Locke f9, 1–9; 18–19; 82, 93; 117; 124; MS Locke c33, 27v; MS Locke b2, 43–4; 50–; 81r; 84–6; MS Locke f29, 18; 90–1; cf. MS Locke f17, 1–5v; 45vff.; MS Locke c27, 238–9; MS Locke f30, passim; MS Locke f32, passim, esp. 25; 30v; 43r; 54v; 61r; 64r; 82v; 106r; 137v; 146r; 160r; Johnson, *Locke on Freedom*, 160n.7.

patristic theology in the learned journals and having his critical views of the Gospel refined and reinforced by Simon and le Clerc.[22]

Locke's *Methodus Adversariorum*, published in the July 1686 edition of the *Bibliothèque*, illustrated Locke's methods of taking notes with several sections from works that explicitly discussed the Trinity. It is unclear whether Locke himself provided the illustrative texts, or someone connected with the journal, such as le Clerc himself. At the least, they show Locke's familiarisation in the mid-1680s with patristic debates over the Trinity, and they suggest that Locke probably thought that the Trinity was a particularly appropriate subject on which to compile adversaria. Among Locke's notes in this period from the *Bibliothèque* and from the Leipzig journal, the *Acta Eruditorum*, are further notes on Arianism and on the variation between 'six separate creeds' all described as Athanasian. In December 1686 James Tyrrell wrote to Locke about Aubert de Verse's *Protestant Pacifique*, responding to the work as by 'your' author. The implication is that Locke had at least suggested that Tyrrell should read this eirenic work, and perhaps that he approved of its arguments. This is interesting not so much because of the indication of Locke's continued but completely unsurprising interest in works advocating toleration, which was one theme of the *Protestant Pacifique*, as because among Locke's notes there is an undated note from Verse's work which identifies Jonas Schlichting's *Confessio* and his work *Contra Meisneorum* as containing 'the sum of Socinianism'. Locke appears to have purchased Schlichting's *Confessio Fidei* in 1686. There is no direct evidence that Locke read Schlichting's work, even in later years, but the interest in Socinianism once again suggested by this note and book purchase suggest very strongly indeed that Locke's undated reading of Crell and Volkel took place in the 1680s rather than the 1690s. Locke's intellectual curiosity and the admittance of many Socinians to the worship of the Arminians who were sheltering Locke would make examination of Socinian thought likely even without there being any clear indications in Locke's journals that he had undertaken reading of their works in these years; the evidence of interest in Socinian works and thought in his journals and the extent of his purchases of Socinian works made it exceedingly difficult to believe that Locke was not reading at least some of these works in these years.[23]

As early as 1684, in a letter to his English friend Edward Clarke, Locke had clearly and explicitly adopted the position towards which his 1680 note on God's goodness had already pointed, recording an argument that is exceedingly difficult to reconcile with any Calvinist or Arminian account

[22] MS Locke f8, 67; MS Locke f17, 2v; *Testamentum Graecorum*, shelved under 9.40 in the Locke Room (Library, 2862); 74v and passim.
[23] MS Locke b2, 81r; 86r; MS Locke f9, 82; MS Locke c33, 27v; *Correspondence*, III, 889.

of original sin but perfectly compatible with Socinian denial of original sin. He identified the virtuousness or viciousness of almost all men as almost entirely dependent upon their good or bad education. He argued that 'of all the men we meet with, nine parts of ten, or perhaps ninety-nine of one hundred, are what they are, good or evil, useful or not, by their education. 'Tis that which makes the great difference in mankind.' Children's minds were 'easily turned', like the fountains of rivers, where 'a gentle application of the hand turns the flexible waters into channels that make them take quite contrary courses'. Little impressions early in life had 'very important and lasting influences', and because of these impressions men arrived 'at places quite different and opposite'.[24]

We have seen that in 1682 Locke declared that all improvements of men's minds were to be ascribed to God's providence, listing education among the means of improvement. To argue as Locke was doing that almost all men became what they were, good or evil, by their education was therefore not in itself to deny outright that God's grace defined whether men became good or evil, nor to deny that men had been corrupted by original sin in such a manner that they needed God's grace, provided through education to become good. Crucially, however, the few men that Locke explicitly recognised whose virtue or vice did not depend on their education were the naturally virtuous. According to Locke, some men's bodies and minds – one in ten, or perhaps one in a hundred, were so well framed 'by nature' that their strength of 'natural genius' carried them towards 'what is excellent'. This is exceedingly difficult to accommodate with any notion of original sin corrupting Adam's posterity; even the most attenuated version of original sin amongst the Arminians in Holland declared that all men had a backwardness to good and were naturally prone after Adam to do evil.[25]

Even allowing that for Locke education was a form of God's providence, an expression of his grace, it is clear that in his argument a regenerative faith in Christ whereby the Holy Spirit inspires and dwells in men to renew them from the corruption of Adam's sin had been removed from its central location in most Protestant thought: from the date of this letter at the latest Locke's thought was very clearly focused not upon man's only possible hope of acting morally through regeneration by faith in Christ and the immediate operations of the Holy Spirit, but upon the natural means, par-

[24] *Correspondence*, II, 782.
[25] *Correspondence*, II, 782; cf. chapter one above. Spellman's *Locke and Depravity* notes correctly that many Latitudinarians saw education as crucial in determining men's goodness or badness, and wishes to assimilate Locke's comment here to their view of original sin; however, his argument fails to take account of Locke's comment on the one in one hundred naturally carried towards the excellent.

ticularly education, by which men could develop control of their desires by reason, and by which the development of the love of virtue would itself allow them to act morally.

Locke's argument had thus clearly moved away from Calvinist and Arminian accounts of original sin and towards the effective denial of original sin, a denial whose explicit statement was particularly associated with Socinianism. There is no direct sign that this argument was the result of detailed scriptural analysis or theological reading. In the light of Damaris Cudworth's comment in early 1684 that Locke had come to know more of Scripture than he had ever known before, however, it is very likely that he had been examining parts of the teaching of Scripture before contending for his view of the role of education. It is also quite likely that reading of some theological works was influential upon his views, both directly in making him question the doctrine of original sin, and indirectly in increasing his awareness of issues of biblical scholarship that made much of the Bible seem more difficult to understand, and which made many of the patristic and contemporary interpretations of the Bible that set out orthodox views of original sin seem to be suspect. Amongst the works which may have directly influenced Locke's view of men's nature were Socinian works which denied original sin. However, the most suggestive evidence of substantial Socinian reading by Locke seems to date – and no more decisive characterisation is possible – more from 1685–6 than from 1684, after the purchase of Crell and Volkel's works.

It therefore seems likely that Locke had moved by 1684 in the direction of Socinian views in his implicit denial of original sin in his letter to Clarke after some reading of Socinian works, such as his 1679 reading of Enyedi's *Explicationes*, but before the extensive reading of *Sociniana* which he was to undertake from 1685–6, rather as his thought of 1680–3 had pointed in the direction of Socinian views on the satisfaction after some Socinian reading but before extensive reading of Socinian works. In the 1690s Locke was to respond to accusations of Socinianism by arguing that he sought truth in an unbiassed manner from Scripture itself and that he did not follow any system. While this was a debating tactic as well as a description of method of enquiry used by many unitarians in the 1690s, it would appear not merely that Locke's commitment to theological eclecticism was extremely pronounced during his extensive Socinian reading in the 1680s – and surely long preceded it in his hostility to priestly power, in his reading and approval of authors like Hales and Chillingworth, in his assaults upon party and custom in various ecclesiological and epistemological writings, and in his very early opposition to the supine acceptance of wrested interpretations of commentators – but also that his own 'Socinian' views on man's sinfulness were developed in tandem with, and perhaps just before, detailed and extensive theological reading which then massively reinforced them.[26]

III

The *Essay*, turned from drafts into its published version during the mid-1680s and revised substantially during the period of Locke's letter to Clarke and of his Socinian reading, set out an account of men's capacity to know the duties of morality and of the reasons that men did not in practice come to such knowledge which was based upon opposition to Calvinist and Arminian accounts of original sin, and compatible with, and probably influenced by, Socinian views. The *Essay* never commented on the understanding having been clouded by men's Fall in Adam or being unable to function because of a significant inherited disposition towards sin; Locke's account of the understanding as a *tabula rasa* at birth and of the will as a power left it unclear how either could have been in any sense damaged by inherited sinful dispositions. Locke gave many reasons in the *Essay* for men's failure to establish in practice a certain and accurate morality upon a certain foundation, but gave most extensive consideration to most men referring their actions to the standards of their society and not to God's will, and to the many failures to construct the chain of reasoning required for establishment of a known morality. Locke did declare that men did not contemplate morality because 'vices, Passions, and domineering Interest' opposed contemplation. In comparison with the stress laid upon referring morality to the wrong standard, and to not examining ideas because of accepting the words of one's society, only a very minor role was given in the *Essay* to this opposition to morality of vice and passion. There was no suggestion that these intemperate passions needed supernatural cure.

In these emphases upon the potential eradicability of sinfulness through proper education and enquiry Locke's *Essay* thus helped to foster the optimism about creating virtuous individuals (at least individuals among the elite) which was to spread massively in England in the early eighteenth century. It is important therefore to note again here that unlike the philosophers and poets of the eighteenth century the *Essay* did not proclaim men's 'good nature' or natural benevolence, recognised that most men would fail even to come to knowledge of morality, and said nothing about the extent to which men would act morally even once they had come to knowledge of morality. There was nothing in Socinianism which denied men's sinfulness; Socinians saw that sinfulness as caused by men's individual actions but not original sin. There was nothing in the *Essay* even when Locke had

---

[26] *Correspondence*, II, 834; III, 868.

clearly come to be broadly Socinian in his views in the mid-1690s that indicated that most men were not in fact severely deficient both in their knowledge of the content of morality and in the extent of their practice of morality; the *Essay* was therefore to be compatible both with the argument of Locke's later *Reasonableness of Christianity* that no men had ever come to knowledge of the full content of morality by unassisted reason alone, and with a deep pessimism about men's actual behaviour that he expressed in his later *Third Letter on Toleration* and *Paraphrase*.[27]

In the 1690s Bishop Edward Stillingfleet attacked the *Essay* for supporting Socinianism. His attacks focused not upon its ready compatibility with Socinian denial of original sin, but upon the discussion of the concept of substance. For Locke, men's ideas came only from sensation and reflection and they could not gain knowledge of the real essences of things in the external world, being limited to denominating them from the information about their properties conveyed by the senses. Men could therefore only know of substance that it was something we 'know not what' which supported those qualities which produced simple ideas. Stillingfleet's attacks did not accuse Locke of taking a position directly antithetical to the Trinity in emphasising the obscurity of men's idea of substance, but rather of favouring Socinianism by compromising trinitarians' ability to construct extended explanations of the Trinity. Despite Locke's reading of Socinian works in the Netherlands, Locke's stress upon the limits of the idea of substance in the *Essay* was almost certainly neither Socinian in intent nor directly Socinian in effect. Locke was generally hostile to discussion of the nature of God, and expressed that hostility on many occasions throughout his life as well as in muted form in the *Essay*. This hostility was not, however, necessarily antitrinitarian. On the one occasion when Locke explicitly recorded his belief in the Trinity, in the 'Essay on Infallibility' in 1661–2, he stated that he believed in the Trinity although he did not understand how it was true, and attacked those who tried to comprehend the nature of God. The way that the Trinity was true could 'not be expressed in discourse nor grasped by the mind' in words 'other than those in which God has revealed it'. Even if Locke had read Sand, Enyedi and perhaps some of Biddle's works before composing these revised drafts of the *Essay*, and also read Crell and Volkel at about the time of finishing these drafts, there is no evidence of any reading by Locke of Socinian works before composition of the 1671 drafts of the *Essay*. These stressed the limits of the idea of substance in a manner that directly foreshadowed the *Essay*.[28]

---

[27] *Essay*, passim; cf. Spellman, *Locke and Depravity*, passim.
[28] *Essay*, II.xiii.15–19; II.xxiii.2; E. Stillingfleet, *A Discourse in Vindication of the Trinity* (1696), ch. 10; idem, *The Bishop of Worcester's Answer to Mr Locke's Letter* (1697); idem, *The Bishop of Worcester's Answer to Mr Locke's Second Letter* (1698). On Locke

The essential element of the argument concerning substance was, then, surely composed long before Locke had any Socinian motivation for composition. The *Essay* itself was probably largely composed before Locke had extensively read Socinian works, and it may well have been published before Locke came to the Socinian view of Christ which he very probably held by 1695–7. Even when Locke probably did come to argue for a Socinian view of Christ, in a 1695–7 manuscript entitled 'Some General Reflections Upon the Beginning of St John's Gospel', his antitrinitarian argument was – appropriately for an agnostic about substance – entirely historical and hermeneutic. Among Locke's many notes from unitarian works in the early 1690s and in the 'General Reflections' there is almost no comment upon the nature of God. There is no sign that Locke ever felt able to assert that there could not be three infinite persons of the Godhead in only one infinite space, as other unitarians were to assert in the 1690s. Locke did assert that there could only be one body in any particular space in the *Essay*, but there is no indication that he felt able to assert the same about spirits. Indeed, as Locke noted in reply to Stillingfleet, accepting the obscurity of the idea of substance limited unitarians' argument that the Trinity could be said to be impossible simply because they understood the nature of God, as much as it restricted trinitarians' explanations of the Trinity. The *Essay*'s comments upon the idea of substance were, then, surely animated by Locke's assessment of the limits of men's understandings, as any straightforward reading of the *Essay* would suggest, but not invested with Socinian purpose.

Stillingfleet's charge of Socinianism for its comments on substance was only one of two major accusations of Socinianism that were levelled at the *Essay* in the 1690s. As was noted in chapter four, the philosopher Leibniz joined Stillingfleet in attacking the *Essay* as Socinian because of Locke's recognition of the possible materiality of thinking substance and therefore of the soul. For critics like Leibniz it was the soul's certain immateriality which proved its immortality; Locke's recognition of the possibility of materiality was, for Leibniz, presumably intended to favour mortalism, a doctrine held by many Socinians. Again, Locke was apparently to become at least doubtful about the soul's natural immortality in the 1690s. Again, however, Locke's argument concerning the possible materiality of the soul did not have any direct Socinian purpose.[29] Locke's comments on the pos-

and substance see especially Ayers, 'Power and Substance'; M. Tindall, *Letter to the Reverend Clergy* (1694), 22; Locke, *A Letter to the Reverend Edward Lord Bishop of Worcester* in *Works* (1801), IV, passim, esp. 67–9; idem, *Mr Locke's Reply to the Bishop of Worcester's Answer to his Letter*, in *Works*, IV, passim, esp. 147; cf. W. Sherlock, *A Vindication of the Doctrine of the Holy and Ever Blessed Trinity* (1690); Yolton, *Way of Ideas*.

[29] N. Jolley, *Leibniz and Locke*, Oxford (1984), esp. ch. 2.

sible materiality of the soul were misrepresented by critics like Leibniz, who described these as though Locke had identified the soul as material, and by more cautious critics like Stillingfleet, who argued that Locke had canvassed the *ontological* rather than merely the *epistemological* possibility of a material soul. Locke's actual argument was carefully agnostic: men could not know whether the soul was material or not because their ideas were insufficient. Men had the ideas of matter and thinking, but might never be able to know whether any material being thought, or not. It was not possible to discover without revelation whether God had given to some systems of matter 'fitly disposed, a power to perceive', or joined to matter 'a thinking immaterial Substance'. Men were 'very far' from knowing what their soul was, it seeming to Locke 'put out of the reach of our Knowledge'. It was impossible to examine the 'dark and intricate part of each hypothesis' and to determine fixedly for or against the soul's immateriality. In the *Essay* Locke held that as far as men could tell God could 'superadd' thought to matter as well as to finite immaterial beings. Locke's point was not that the soul was definitely material, nor even that it was clearly *ontologically* possible that the soul was material. It was merely that men could not know from their ideas that it was definitely immaterial: it was epistemologically possible that thinking substance – and therefore the soul – was material. Locke's attitude here has been accurately characterised by Michael Ayers as the view that things which were not observed to happen, but which could not be known to be actually impossible because of what we did know, were to be regarded as within God's power. In the 1690s Locke was to challenge Stillingfleet to show that there was a 'manifest repugnancy' in material things thinking, or to recognise that it was he (Stillingfleet), and not Locke, who was actually restricting God's omnipotency to the limits of man's ideas.[30]

In his comments in the *Essay* Locke declared that he did not canvass the possibility of material things thinking in order to 'lessen belief of the Soul's Immateriality: I am not here speaking of Probability, But Knowledge.' The *Essay* itself inclined towards the view that it was probable that men's souls were immaterial. In replying to Stillingfleet in the later 1690s Locke was still willing to declare it to the 'highest degree probable' that the thinking substances in men were indeed immaterial. Even if Locke had not believed in the immateriality of the soul, as it appears that he did, Leibniz's assault is also surely mistaken in seeing this assertion of the possibility of the materiality of the soul as intended by Locke to support mortalism. Locke had from 1682 thought that the soul's immateriality was not capable of

---

[30] Jolley, *Leibniz*, passim; *Essay*, IV.iii.6ff.; Locke, *Second Reply*, in *Works*, IV, 462ff.; brilliantly, Ayers, 'Mechanism, Superaddition', passim, esp. 217ff., and 224ff. to which I am indebted.

proving it to be immortally sensible (such sensibility being the only significant thing about immortality). Put simply, if he did not believe that the soul's immateriality proved its immortality in 1682, there was no reason for him to have had to remove the grounds for belief in its immateriality in order to support the mortality of the soul in 1685 or 1690. In fact, it seems likely from the *Epistola de Tolerantia*, which declared without any qualifiaction or apparent shadow of doubt that the soul was immortal, that Locke did believe that men had a naturally immortal soul both in 1685 when composing *Epistola*, and in 1689 when it was translated into English with Locke's knowledge even if without his active assistance. Although Locke probably did not continue to believe in a naturally immortal soul in the late 1690s, and although he probably did not see how it could be *proven* from his epistemological principles as early as the early 1680s, there is no evidence that he did not believe in it when composing the *Essay*.[31]

IV

Although Locke thus apparently did not intend to provide direct support for Socinian beliefs of mortalism or antitrinitarianism in composing the *Essay*, and depicted his positions as preventing only claims to knowledge about these principles and not belief in them, the *Essay* was written during years when he was made extremely aware of the massive disagreements in belief about the meaning of central theological passages of Scripture and when he had personal sympathy for Socinian positions on toleration, on a working faith and on original sin. These personal sympathies may well have extended to denying the Trinity; at the least he was very acutely aware of Socinian opposition to the Trinity. Locke clearly composed much of the *Essay* in order to remove false pretensions to theological knowledge and to promote toleration in theological enquiry, and he probably had all claims on ontological 'proofs' of trinitarianism – very importantly together with attempts at ontological 'proofs' of unitarianism, and of many other theological doctrines – among his conscious targets as early as composition of the *Essay* during the mid-1680s.

It is also very likely indeed, given his apparently contemporaneous Socinian reading and composition of the *Essay*, that Locke had the Trinity in his mind in composing in the *Essay* a series of linked arguments about the difficulties of assenting to a true faith. The *Essay* opposed many bases for certainty asserted by theologians and its analysis of men's epistemological limitations meant that (with the exception of God's existence) in areas

---

[31] *Letter to . . . Worcester, Works*, IV, 33; 37; *Essay*, IV.x.10; IV.x.16; Jolley, *Leibniz*, ch. 2; *Letter*, 47; Ayers, 'Mechanism', 246ff.

about which theological doctrine pronounced men could not achieve a reasoned certainty. Locke further described substantial difficulties in regulating assent correctly in those many subjects in which only probability was possible, from the interest of witnesses and 'strict gards' to the need of most men for leisure to study sufficiently. Particularly emphasised as susceptible to legitimate and very probably irreconcilable disagreements were the manifold difficulties of interpretation of words, including religious words. Recognising the possibility of claims to authority of expertise, he argued that acceptance of and obedience to an external authority if that authority used force rather than using persuasion based upon goodwill was not 'reasonably' to be expected. Very few theological doctrines were specified by Locke in the course of these arguments, but the cumulative effect of these arguments – especially when read in the context of the theological debates which dominated both the years of their composition and of their publication and republication – was to suggest that no theological doctrines beyond the existence of God were beyond legitimate debate and widely differing interpretations and assents. It was in this important sense that Stillingfleet had good cause to think that the *Essay* 'favoured' Socinianism in England in the 1690s. It was surely in part for this cumulative effect of the *Essay* that Molyneux celebrated Locke in the 1690s for abridging the priestly 'empire of darkness, wherein ... the subjects wander deplorably yet the rulers have their profit and advantage'. It was for his 'Rules of Criticism' in studying 'ancient authors' that le Clerc cited the *Essay* in his programme of rationalist interpretation of Scripture.[32]

According to the *Essay*, in most of the affairs of life men could operate only upon probability, or 'likeliness to be true', and not upon knowledge, a term that Locke applied only to that which was understood with certainty. For Locke, there were many problems in regulating assent properly because when men could not establish (or follow) the connection of ideas that constituted knowledge they were limited to examining the conformity of any thing with their knowledge, observation and experience, and to the credibility of others' testimony which depended not merely upon the number of such witnesses but also upon whether the witnesses had any possible interest in the acceptance of what they testified. Most theological doctrines were extremely difficult to assess by these standards. In many matters men could not be sure that they had 'all the Particulars before us, that any way concern the Question'. Men lacked the 'leisure, patience and means' to collect all the proofs relevant to an issue, but had to make decisions about them in order to conduct their lives. It was therefore unavoidable that men would have 'several Opinions'. For the tolerationist Locke

---

[32] *Essay*, passim. *Correspondence*, vi, 2221.

this ought to lead all men 'to maintain Peace, and the common Offices of Humanity, and Friendship, in the diversity of Opinions'.[33]

Locke did accept that the highest degree of assent was required by 'bare Testimony' without any support from observation or witnesses when the Testimony was 'of God himself'. This revelation, and man's assent by faith 'as absolutely determines our Minds, and as perfectly excludes all wavering as our Knowledge it self; and we may as well doubt of our own Being, as we can, whether any Revelation from GOD be true'. For Locke, however, men had to be sure that such a revelation came from God, and in order to exclude the 'Extravagancy of Enthusiasm', men's assent to revelation could come no higher than the evidence that it was a revelation, and their assent to any proposition contained in revelation could be no higher than the evidence that the meaning of it was correctly understood. Locke thereby ignored but implicitly denied the view that men were inspired by the Holy Spirit to believe the Scripture to be the word of God or to believe the terms of the Scripture with an inspiration that provided greater certainty than came by knowledge or reasoning about the evidence of the truth of propositions. Faith was not knowledge, and involved probability and not the certainty of knowledge. Furthermore, while God could imprint new ideas in the mind of a person by immediate revelation, these could not then be communicated to any other men because they had only the simple ideas of sensation and reflection as sources for their ideas: they had no way of understanding what was not based upon ideas derived from their senses. After being 'rapp'd up into the third Heaven', St Paul had therefore been able only to say to other men that he had seen things 'as Eye hath not seen', and heard things that 'ear had not heard'. It was illegitimate for men to receive for true anything that directly contradicted their knowledge. For instance, men clearly 'knew' that one body occupied one space. If revelation seemed to argue for one body in two places at once then it could not be accepted: it was not revelation, or its meaning was misunderstood. Locke argued that without this scrutiny of revelation by reason there would be no grounds on which to discriminate the true from the false. Faith could therefore never convince men of what contradicted their knowledge. It could not be as certainly known, and it could not be conceived to come from that 'bountiful author' who had given men their faculties, since it would 'destroy' these faculties.[34]

There were many things of which men had at best very imperfect notions, and many matters of fact which would not be known in any other way than by revelation. Reasoning from analogy was not a powerful aid in these matters. These things, which were above but not contrary to reason,

---

[33] *Essay*, IV.xv, xvi.   [34] *Essay*, IV.xvi.14; IV.xviii.3–5.

were the proper matter of faith. Such were the fall of the angels, and the resurrection of the dead. What was thus revealed carried assent even against probable reasoning, but the revelation itself was judged to be revelation by probable reason. Without even discussing the possibility that once men had come to accept that a particular revelation was the word of God they were then aided by the Holy Spirit in interpretation of that word, Locke declared that 'reason' was also judge of the signification of words wherein it was revealed. Whatever God had revealed was certain; no doubt was possible. But 'whether it be a divine revelation, or no, Reason must judge'.

Locke was explicit in the *Essay* in describing as the result of this distinction what his earlier journal notes have already clearly revealed to be largely the motivation for this distinction: setting the proper boundaries between faith and reason would eliminate the cause of 'great Disputes' in religion. It would prevent every sect from using reason as far as it supported their principles and then crying out that things were matters of faith above reason. The understanding of these boundaries between faith and reason would leave no room for 'those extravagant Opinions and Ceremonies, that are to be found in the several Religions of the World', the absurdities which filled almost all 'the Religions which possess and divide Mankind'. The principle that men did not have to consult reason had let loose man's fancies and natural superstition and led them to very strange opinions which were offensive to God and even to 'a sober, good Man'.[35]

The *Essay* made such reasoned interpretation of Scripture an extremely difficult task likely to lead to a wide diversity of opinions because of the problems associated with the use of words. In most usages in 'civil' conversation that were fitted to the 'conveniences' of life words were used in a very loose and obscure manner that was adequate for communication but not for precise knowledge. Men therefore generally had only a confused and obscure understanding of the signification of words. Even those who studied and gained more precise notions very often had different notions than those of other equally intelligent and studious men. Since the signification of words in all languages at any time depended 'very much on the Thoughts, Notions, and Ideas of him that uses them' these were 'unavoidably of great uncertainty, to Men of the same Language and Country'. This was magnified in 'different Countries and remote Ages, wherein the Speakers and Writers had very different Notions, Tempers, Customs, Ornaments, and Figures of Speech'. Making explicit the bearing of this argument for religion, Locke declared that many men, 'well satisfied of the

[35] *Essay*, IV.xviii.1–11.

meaning of a text of Scripture' had 'By consulting Commentators, quite lost the sense of it' and 'drawn obscurity upon the place'.[36]

This natural obscurity was then magnified by several 'wilful faults and neglects'. Many words were used which did not stand for any clear ideas even in their original usage, a fault of many words introduced by 'The several sects of Philosophy and Religion'. The 'authors or Promoters' of these words had coined 'insignificant' words in order to affect 'something singular, and out of the way of common apprehensions', to support 'strange Opinions', or to cover 'weakness' in their hypotheses. These words then became the distinguishing characters of churches or schools because men did not examine the precise ideas that they stood for and find them absurd or meaningless. The schoolmen and metaphysicians were particularly prone to this kind of 'insignificant' speech. According to the *Essay*, the 'mischief' of perplexed meanings had infected not merely remote 'speculations' but had even 'obscured and perplexed the material Truths of Law and Divinity', which Locke unfortunately left undefined. This might not have destroyed the 'two great Rules, Religion and Justice', but it had 'in great measure' rendered them useless. These problems were even further exacerbated by the desire of some to keep others in ignorance in order to foster their own power. There were many 'strict guards' upon knowledge who did not wish others to enquire 'lest, knowing more, they should believe the less in them'.[37]

For Locke, coming to understand these imperfections of language, to which an entire book of the *Essay* was devoted, ought itself to lead to the cessation of 'a great many Controversies' and open the way to greater Knowledge 'and, perhaps, Peace too'. Instead of turning to the inspiration of the Holy Spirit as providing elected hearers or readers of the Word with a correct understanding of Scripture, or even to claiming with le Clerc's *Sentimens* and most Latitudinarians that, whatever the obscurity of some parts of Scripture, the kernel of essential doctrine remained clear through time and translation, Locke turned to natural religion and lauded tolerance among fallible interpretations of Scripture. Scripture was infallible, but men could not 'but be very fallible in the understanding of it'. It would 'become us to be charitable one to another in our Interpretation or Misunderstandings of those ancient Writings' which were liable to great doubt and uncertainty. In discourses of 'Religion, Law and Morality, as they are matters of the highest concernment, so there will be the greatest difficulty'. The 'Volumes of Interpreters, and Commentators on the Old and New Testament' were 'but too manifest proof of this'. Men should instead 'magnify' God's 'Goodness, that he hath spread before all the World, such

---

[36] *Essay*, III, passim, esp. chs. ix, x.   [37] *Essay*, III.x, esp. 1–12.

legible characters of his Works and Providence, and given mankind so sufficient a light of Reason, that they to whom this written word never came could not (when-ever they set themselves to search) either doubt of the Being of a God, or of the Obedience due to Him'. The 'precepts of Natural Religion' were plain and 'very intelligible to all Mankind', unlike the truths revealed in 'Books and Languages' and so liable 'to the common and natural obscurities and difficulties incident to Words'. For Locke, it 'would become us to be more careful and diligent in observing the former, and less magisterial, positive, and imperious, in imposing our own sense and interpretations of the latter'.[38]

Locke was clear that men were obliged to think for themselves. The *Essay* argued that this search was a vital duty to God and would be recompensed. In doing so he voiced an attitude that was to be developed further in his religious works and manuscripts in the 1690s, where the sincerity of the search was clearly depicted as far outweighing the objective truth sought, but which had already been set out in outline in his journal in the 1670s. Locke declared in the *Essay* that a man who sincerely and effortfully searched for truth but did not find it would certainly 'not miss the Reward', while one who did not search but by luck held the correct opinion might well miss such reward. In addition to the motivation of enquiry by such reward for search, Locke provided a further glimmer of hope for the undertaking of the search rather than the acceptance of ideas from custom and party in describing the search for truth as naturally pleasurable. Mentioning simple ideas of pleasures and pains that he could have discussed at greater length, Locke gave as examples the pain of captious wrangling, the pleasure in rational conversation with a friend, and the pleasure of the discovering 'of a speculative truth upon study'. In later editions the search itself, as well as any resultant discovery, was described as pleasurable. Later editions of the *Essay* were also to recommend the expenditure of much effort in developing love of truth.[39]

Locke recognised, however, that men most commonly adopted views from 'the opinion of others'. Although 'there cannot be a more dangerous thing to rely on, nor more likely to mislead one; since there is much more Falsehood and Errour amongst Men, than Truth and Knowledge', men frequently judged opinions by the credit of their proposer with their party or in their society, or from an opinion that the person was in some manner inspired by God. He combined his acute sense of the sociological formation and acceptance of belief that he had expressed over many years with his tolerationism by arguing that it could not 'reasonably' be expected that men should renounce their own opinions, *even if* these were adopted

---

[38] *Essay*, III, passim, esp. chs. ix, x.   [39] *Essay*, epistle to the reader; IV.xvii.24; IV.xx.4.

on the false bases of party and custom, in order to submit to an authority that they did not recognise. According to Locke, it was unreasonable to expect even those many men who had not regulated their assent correctly to accept the authority of others if they suspected that those who wished them to renounce their opinions were motivated by 'Interest, or Design', a suspicion which Locke then asserted there 'never fail[ed] to be, where Men find themselves ill-treated'. Men would 'do well to commiserate our mutual ignorance, and endeavour to remove it in all the gentle and fair ways of Information; and not instantly treat others ill, as obstinate and perverse' because they would not accept our own opinions'. The necessity of believing in this 'fleeting state of Action and Blindness' ought to make men 'more busy and careful to inform ourselves, than constrain others'.

Arguing implicitly against the contention that the cumulative wisdom of men over time and the wisdom of experts who had correctly analysed matters should be put into the balance against the interpretation of fallible individuals, and on at least some and perhaps very many occasions should be preferred to those individuals' interpretations – a contention that was effectively voiced in varying form and degree despite their stress upon fallibility by a number of the Latitudinarians and other Anglicans in the Restoration – Locke first asserted that those who had not 'thoroughly examined to the bottom all their own Tenets, must confess' themselves to be 'unfit to prescribe to others'. He then asserted that these were in fact 'so few in number' – which is unsurprising since he had set the standard without discussion for its necessity at the ridiculously high level of examining to the bottom 'all' views – that almost no one had any legitimate pretence to prescribe to others. He further added that those few who had examined their views thoroughly found so 'little reason to be magisterial in their opinions' that 'nothing insolent and imperious is to be expected from them'. Behind this last contention was presumably the notion that the examination of issues by these men revealed their own ignorance and the extreme difficulty of deciding matters with full awareness of all the relevant particulars and thus made them avoid any imposition of belief upon others.

Locke did declare towards the end of this lengthy series of arguments that these very few men who had thus examined would have had a 'juster pretence' than others to require others to follow them. The inexactness of his language here was probably deliberate; the strong impression of the form of his argument, as it proceeded from the unreasonableness of any being expected to accept the authority of others to command to discussion of the few who had thoroughly examined, is firstly that because of Locke's tolerationism this thorough examination would still not have constituted for him a 'just' claim, merely one that was a more just ('juster') 'pretence' than that of men who had not examined, and secondly that he wished to make it seem by this lengthy argument alone that there were absolutely no conditions in which men could reasonably be expected to submit to others, but that it was difficult to see how to preclude in principle the claim to authority of experts from the premises of argument about men's largely reducible ignorance. Without the strong *implication*, conveyed more by the form of his argument than by its detailed content, that the acceptance of expert authority was itself unreasonable even when the imposers had thoroughly examined all issues and others had not, Locke's case on probability could in principle still have been used to support intolerance through the claims of expertise, even if its very clear and vastly predominant practical orientation was to support toleration.[40]

v

Locke had been concerned about increasing restrictions upon French Protestants during his years in France. In England in the early 1680s he followed their worsening position. In 1685 Louis XIV finally revoked the Edict of Nantes, which had officially provided toleration for Protestants for the past century, and instituted a vicious persecution in the name of true religion. Refugees flooded into England and the Netherlands. Before the Revocation, Protestantism had already lost substantial territory and force to Catholicism throughout Europe during the seventeenth century. Locke had long feared an absolutist and Catholic monarchy in England under Charles or under James. The cause of European Protestantism, whose dependence upon the English King as the strongest Protestant King had been noted in Locke and Shaftesbury's *Letter From A Person of Quality*, seemed doomed if England as well as France became committed to Catholicism. Looking at France and England in 1685, the year of Louis' revocation and James' succession, surrounded by Protestant refugees from France and living under an assumed name to avoid extradition for treason by an English monarch that he was convinced was to be a Catholic absolutist, Locke had good reason to fear that Catholicism was about to reconquer Europe.[41]

It was in this atmosphere in the winter of 1685 that Locke composed a Latin argument for toleration, probably as a piece of private correspon-

---

[40] *Essay*, IV.xv.6; IV.xx; IV.xvi.4.

[41] MS Locke f5, 54 on Locke lending to James Tyrrell in May 1681 a work on the policy of the clergy of France 'to destroy the Protestants'; *Letter*, in *Works*, X, 206–7 and 229 on the place of the King and Church of England as Head of all Protestants being 'due' to them as the church in favour and of 'nearest approach to the most powerful prince of that religion' and as giving the greatest protection that that party could receive throughout Christendom; Scott, *Restoration Crisis*, passim.

dence for van Limborch, whose *Theologia Christiana* of 1685 described toleration as a duty of Christianity but did not proclaim it as a right or describe its principles at length. Locke's *Epistola de Tolerantia* was not published until 1689, when it appeared anonymously in several languages as the first major publication of his life. Written and published in Latin, written in the winter of 1685, and composed for van Limborch, the *Epistola* was undoubtedly written with the European fate of Protestantism and the universal principle of toleration, not just English events and the forms of toleration most suited to England, at the forefront of Locke's mind.

The case that the *Epistola* mounted in defence of religious toleration was largely a reiteration, in considerably fewer pages, of many of the arguments that Locke had used against Stillingfleet in the 'Critical Notes'. It was altered significantly, however, by the additions of a strong assertion of the Christian duty of toleration, and a very cautious implicit argument for resistance to Catholic monarchs in countries where they established a 'strange' religion. It was further altered by the diminution, almost to complete absence, of arguments for comprehension.[42]

The *Epistola* defined the commonwealth as 'a Society of Men constituted only' for 'procuring, preserving, and advancing of their own Civil Interests', which were 'Life, Liberty, Health, and Indolency of Body' together with possession of 'outward things'. The magistrate's 'Duty' was to secure the just possession of the things 'belonging to this Life' by the 'impartial Execution' of equal laws. We have seen that Locke had declared this assertion of the secular ends of civil society 'foundational' to toleration in the 'Essay on Toleration' in 1667. The *Epistola* argued that the specification of the different ends of civil and religious society was 'above all things necessary', but it did not explicitly argue that it was itself 'foundational'. Locke argued in the *Epistola* 'that the whole Jurisdiction of the Magistrate reaches only to these Civil Concernments' and that it 'neither

---

42 Klibansky and Gough, *Letter*, introduction on the composition of the *Letter* for van Limborch and the European focus of its concerns; Ashcraft, *Revolutionary Politics*, 475ff., for a largely unconvincing attempt to read it as a comment on English politics which 'necessarily assigned to the *Letter* a particular location along a spectrum of political perspectives that emerged' in England during the period 1686–9. The *Letter* was written in Latin by Locke for van Limborch and as a reflection upon European issues; there is no sign of Locke having intended it to be circulated in England or to be a direct commentary upon English political discourse. Ashcraft wishes to depict Locke as necessarily a political radical in these years for his opposition to toleration through royal prerogative. Locke was certainly a political radical in these years, but his fear of James' true intentions was surely far more important to him than was worry about the route taken to toleration. While Ashcraft points out that Locke's argument was opposed to Anglican views, and the considerable extent to which Locke's argument was continuous with his argument against Stillingfleet, he fails to point out that it was perceived by Locke as also discontinuous with the views of almost all current supporters of toleration, whether these were opponents of prerogative toleration or not. Cf. Goldie, 'John Locke's Circle'.

can nor ought' to be extended to the Salvation of Souls' was 'abundantly . . . demonstrate[d]' by three 'Considerations'.[43]

It is not entirely clear from this phraseology whether Locke had by this point in his life come to think that these considerations were themselves the necessary premises of the conclusion that political society had purely secular ends or were merely sufficient 'demonstrations' as 'illustrations' or as collateral evidence that would be sufficient evidence if that were necessary that the political society, which could be shown on other grounds to be established solely for such civil ends, neither could nor should interfere in religious worship. The declaration that these considerations were enough 'abundantly to demonstrate' the limited ends of political society suggests more than a sufficiency of demonstration but it does not clearly suggest a necssity of demonstration in order for the conclusion to be true. Later in the *Epistola*, Locke spoke of the considerations as 'sufficient to conclude' that the limits of civil society were as described, and later still he spoke of having already 'proven' in the *Epistola* that the civil society had purely secular ends. It seems clear from these comments that he did think that these considerations were sufficient by themselves to prove the limited ends of civil society, but again they do not definitely indicate that the considerations were necessary to that conclusion or the only way in which this could have been shown, and he explicitly argued that there were 'many other' considerations that he could have 'urged to the same purpose'.

Other arguments in the *Epistola* suggest that for Locke the intrinsic harmlessness of religion properly defined and the desirability of a liberty of 'conscience' compatible with peace and justice remained conceptually and motivationally foundational to Locke's case. The *Epistola* repeated in outline the analysis of the *Two Treatises* that civil society had been set up to resist foreign invasion, to prevent injury, and to protect property, and that its means were limited to securing these ends. Men had temporal lives which needed outward pains and industry to support. The 'pravity of Mankind', which made men prey upon others' goods rather than labour themselves, created the need for government to preserve men 'in the Possession of what honest industry has already acquired, and also of preserving their Liberty and strength, whereby they may acquire what they further want'. This was the 'original' and set the 'bounds' of the legislative power. As civil penalties were legitimate only against illegitimately harmful actions, and as religious worship and belief could not harm a neighbour, so civil penalties were not appropriate in religion. Speculative opinions were free because they did not affect civil rights. Even if false and absurd, as belief in transubstantiation, or doubting the New Testament to be the

---

[43] *Letter*, 26–9; 34–6.

Word of God, these opinions did not affect the 'security of the Commonwealth, and of every particular man's Goods and Person'. The overall
impression, then, is that for Locke his three 'considerations' were peculiar-
ly powerful arguments showing that the magistrate should not interfere in
worship, but that they were not absolutely essential arguments.[44]

According to the first of these considerations, there was no indication
that God had given any one authority to compel others in matters of faith.
At this point in the argument Locke simply ignored the responsibility and
authority claimed upon the basis of Scripture to interpret that Scripture
and at the very least to prevent heresy and idolatry, including both the
Roman church's claim from Matthew 16:18 and the duty of regenerate
Christians to establish the true religion central to much Civil-War puritan
thought. He simply asserted that 'it appears not that God has ever given
any such authority to one Man over another, as to compel any one to his
Religion'. The alternative source for the interpretative authority of a
magistrate that Locke then described, the consent of its members, was then
denied to be able to create an interpretative authority because men could
not conform their faith to the dictates of others. In worship men had to be
fully satisfied in their own mind that their form of worship was true. It was
not possible for men to consent to the authority of another by 'blindly'
leaving it to him to prescribe their faith and worship.

Locke's reasoning here was that 'no man can, if he would, conform his
Faith to the Dictates of another', and that no man could abandon 'care of
eternal salvation' to another to embrace under compulsion the worship or
faith that they prescribed. The point here seems, unsurprisingly, in significant part to be that of the 'Essay on Toleration' and also of the first
edition of the *Essay*, that men physiologically determined by their perception of the greater good simply cannot choose to follow any other religion than one they perceive, rightly or wrongly, to lead to eternal happiness.
Their perception may be changed, but they cannot guarantee that it will
change in line with a magistrate's dictates.[45]

For Locke, the use of force in religion was improper because it was
axiomatically inefficacious: 'such is the nature of the understanding, that it
cannot be compell'd to the belief of any thing by outward force'. Laws
were of no force without penalties and penalties were 'absolutely im-

---

[44] *Ibid.*, 26–8; 34–9; 47; compare the argument of J. Waldron, 'Locke: Toleration and the
Rationality of Persecution' in S. Mendus (ed.), *Justifying Toleration*, Cambridge (1988),
61–86, on Locke's three considerations. Although I disagree with Waldron in thinking
that Locke still wished to utilise his functional definition of political society as well as and
separate to arguing that his three considerations proved or demonstrated ('demonstrare';
'probavimus') that political society had limited ends, the rest of Waldron's argument has
very significantly influenced the discussion which follows.
[45] *Letter*, 26.

pertinent; because they are not proper to convince the mind'. Force was applied to the will; belief was not within the influence of the will. In the *Epistola* this case was not clearly presented as an account of the type of actions that could influence the will and thus the understanding, but apparently as part of an argument that the will could not influence the understanding. According to Locke, 'to believe this or that to be true, does not depend upon our Will'. Only the 'light of evidence' was held to be able to change men's opinions, which light 'can in no manner proceed from corporal sufferings, or any other outward Penalties'. Locke also declared in the *Epistola*, however, that truth had 'no such way of prevailing, as when strong Arguments and good Reason, are joined with the softness of Civility and good Usage'. By recognising that civility and good usage prepared men for considering arguments Locke was tacitly admitting that what affected the will could at least indirectly influence what was believed. It would seem that it was not that for Locke the will could not influence the understanding, but rather still that only certain influences – those that were positive – could prove effective in making men consider the arguments offered.

Locke's point may well have been that only a positive influence upon the will allowed it to consider the arguments proposed, because as he separately believed men were naturally averse to those that harmed them, but the effective admission that the will had a role in promoting consideration and thus belief made the argument that 'only' light and evidence could alter belief without further argument about positive and negative influences upon the will a weak link in the chain of Locke's argument for toleration. This weakness is revealed clearly when the *Essay*'s parallel assertion that belief was not within the power of the will is examined. The *Essay* declared that the mind could see only what was presented to its senses when it considered the world, and that much of belief was therefore not voluntary, but it explicitly recognised that the choice of what was considered was within the power of men's will and was therefore to some extent voluntary.

In the *Epistola* Locke's long-standing assertion, going back to the *Two Tracts*, that the understanding cannot be influenced by the will is thus in tension with his equally long-standing and acute perception of the influence of external forces upon the formation and acceptance of beliefs. Part of the background to the argument of the *Epistola* was doubtless Locke's lengthy documentation of evidence that men had not in practice been convinced by the use of force, his frequent recognition of the power of custom and party influencing men far more than any external penalties, and particularly a psychological sense, very probably heavily influenced by Nicole, that persuasion was the only effective means of convincing people because of their love of their own opinions, liberty in adopting these, and hatred of contradiction. Men were only willing to accept or consider the arguments of those that they trusted. The *Essay*, as we have just seen, argued that it was unreasonable to expect men to accept the authority of others if they used force, and attempted to suggest that this was true even when those others had examined an issue correctly. Locke's argument is not so much that the will cannot influence the understanding as the weaker but still not negligible assertion that only those who treat men well can persuade them to consider their arguments. It seems far more likely that this case would be able to amount at most to the argument that in practice most people would not reconsider their views under coercion in such a manner that they would genuinely change their minds, than that it could be shown *in principle* that none would do so, and a pessimist would suggest that many people probably could be made to change their views under duress if only by an enforced extension of the realm of issues considered. Unsurprisingly, Locke's opponents in the 1690s, such as Jonas Proast, were to exploit this unmercifully by arguing that force as well as good usage could be used to make men consider what they were otherwise unwilling to think about, and so could indirectly influence men's minds. On the simplest level, force could be used to make men read works that they otherwise would not read, and thus come to views to which they would not otherwise have come.

Locke's third argument, again presaged in the 'Critical Notes', pre-emptively answered this assault by indicating that 'even if' force could be used to convince, such use of force would result in damage to the cause of truth: 'though the rigour of Laws . . . were capable to convince and change Men's minds, yet that would not help at all to the Salvation of their Souls'. There was but 'one way to Heaven'. If religion was instituted by the magistrate, then true religion would suffer in the world, because magistrates varied in their religious beliefs – and entire religions – from country to country, had no special knowledge of the way to heaven, and were in practice very susceptible to secular interests and to promoting religions which advanced these secular interests.[46]

For Locke in such a situation 'most men' could not have 'hopes' to reach heaven; therefore, such magisterial authority could not be granted. This was not an arugment that most men would need to be saved for any form of religion to be true, and if it was a lesser argument based on quantity that the most men possible would be saved without magisterial imposition it was not supported by anything more than the (for Locke) obvious probabilistic declaration of the likelihood of magisterial corruption and variation. The central point for Locke, although not fully articulated, may

[46] *Ibid.*, 27–8; 33; 37; 46; *Essay*, IV.xiii; Waldron, *Locke*, 79ff.; J. Proast, *The Argument of the Letter Concerning Toleration Briefly Considered and Answered*, Oxford (1690).

have been that since most men could not 'hope' to gain reward by this distribution of authority and since religious commitment was significantly based upon individuals' calculating the rationality of being religious, magisterial authority (derived from any source other than every individual's revocable consent) could not be legitimate.

To this Locke then added what appear to have been the beginnings of an argument about the necessity of reward for exertion, arguing that the 'absurdity' of magisterial claims to religious authority was 'heighten[ed]' by men owing their eternal happiness in such a situation to the accident of their birth. For Locke, voicing an objection that was central to his way of thinking about God and his designed rewards for men in all of his ethical, epistemological and most of his most recent political and religious writings, and thus surely crucial on a motivational level to his objections to this argument, salvation because of accident of birth and not desert 'ill suits the notion of a Deity'.[47]

For his opponents, however, this entire argument about the likelihood of magisterial error and corruption opened the possibility of replying that Locke's global perspective was irrelevant when the issue was the use of force in a country where 'true' religion was evidently established; this had been the argument of Stillingfleet's *Unreasonableness*, and it was to be the argument of Proast's replies to Locke. That magistrates of a false religion did not have the right to enforce their religion on all subjects was generally agreed (although the erastianism of the Latitudinarians had led several of them, including Stillingfleet when he had been young, into incautious arguments that the magistrate's duty to promote and establish religion gave him the duty of establishing the religion that he *believed* to be true). That magistrates of the true religion *in principle* could not establish religion because magistrates of the false religion could not legitimately establish religion needed for these authors a further argument than Locke provided by simply pointing out that there were many magistrates of false religions and that magistrates were susceptible to secular interests in order to respond adequately to the Anglican clerics' focus upon a country with 'evidently' true religion. In the *Epistola*, however, Locke went a considerable way towards such a further argument by contending that the ascription of power to the orthodox church over the erroneous or heretical was 'in great and specious Words, to say just nothing at all. For every church is Orthodox to itself; to others, Erroneous or Heretical'. Each church believed its religion true and the claim to orthodoxy of either of any two such churches in dispute was 'on both sides equal'.[48]

In order to meet the obvious response to this, that all claims to ortho-

---

[47] *Letter*, 27–8. Cf. Wootton, *Locke*; introduction.   [48] *Ibid.*, 32; cf. Rogers, 'Locke'.

doxy were not equally valid since some magistrates, men, or churches, had examined religion more extensively or more accurately than others because of their greater abilities, efforts, or assistance from God, it would have been valuable to show at least one, and preferably more than one, of several things: that even if men (magistrates) did indeed believe the objectively true religion it was impossible for them to know that they had indeed examined properly or accurately; that it was impossible because of the nature of religion for there to be an 'evidently' true religion and for any man to know as well as to believe that he believed the true religion; or that it was impossible if any man did have such knowledge or merely far greater expertise to show to others that this was the case in a way that ought to persuade them of that fact and make them legitimately consent to his interpretative authority. In this sense, Locke's argument for the equality of claims to orthodoxy against knowledge, expertise or illumination, would have been buttressed by a convincing analysis of men's irreducible fallibility in religion, of men's limitation to faith and not knowledge in religious affairs in such a way that it could never be evident that any one held to the true religion, or of their inability to show to others the truth of their religious views if they could certainly know the truth (as did those who were immediately inspired by God). We have seen that when Locke wrote the *Epistola* he was separately and contemporaneously committed to the necessary fallibility of almost all men in many religious issues; to their epistemological limitation in intepreting revealed religious doctrine to faith and not knowledge; to their inability if immediately inspired by God with religious knowledge to communicate this to others; and to the unreasonableness of the claim of almost all men to enforce religion because they had not thoroughly examined their views, which he set out in such a way that he attempted to make it appear that even the very few experts also could not reasonably make such a claim to command others. Locke was to expand upon some of these arguments in the *Third Letter on Toleration* in 1692 in response to the repeated assertion by Proast of the evident truth of Anglicanism. The *Epistola*, however, did not expand in these directions upon his assertion that a claim of orthodoxy was specious, concentrating instead upon declaration of equality of claim to orthodoxy and to the assertion of the different religions of magistrates, the fallibility of all magistates, and the susceptibility of magistrates and their advisers to secular interests.[49]

As in the 'Critical Notes', churches were described in the *Epistola* as voluntary societies with the power to institute order and appoint officials. Since men entered churches voluntarily, they could leave whenever they

---

[49] *Third Letter on Toleration* in *Works*, VI, passim, esp. 143ff.; Waldron, 'Locke', 72.

chose. Locke argued that there was no 'express and positive Edict' setting up any church order as necessary *jure divino*. Men could join societies where they believed that the order set up was *jure divino*, but this was by their own choice and they had no power to compel others to join such societies. A church could give power to make laws to the civil magistrate, but this gave no power to the magistrate over other churches. Magistrates could impose indifferent things if they were for the public good, but nothing in worship was indifferent unless believed to be so by each individual. Church power was limited to exhortation and advice, and, if these failed, to expulsion of recalcitrant members. They had no right to 'prejudice another Person in his Civil Enjoyments' because he was of another church. Clerics were bound not merely not to persecute others but also 'to admonish . . . Hearers of the Duties of Peace, and Good-will towards all men; as well towards the Erroneous as the Orthodox'. Far more restrained in its comments about the clergy than the 'Critical Notes' had been, the *Epistola* nevertheless condemned clerical zeal or 'Craft' and argued that those clerics who claimed the power to use force betrayed ambition and showed that what they really desired was 'temporal Dominion'.[50]

Locke declared that he intended to prevent the claim of liberty of conscience legitimating licentiousness, and he continued to argue that much of morality had come under the magistrate's inspection because it was necessary to the peace and preservation of men and society, but he also suggested that there was much of morality that the magistrate would not enforce. It did not belong to the magistrate to 'make use of his Sword in punishing every thing, indifferently, that he takes to be a sin against God. Covetousness, Uncharitableness, Idleness, and many other things are sins, by the consent of all men, which yet no man ever said were to be punished by the Magistrate. The reason is, because they are not prejudical to other mens rights, nor do they break the publick Peace of Societies.' The magistrate did not, however, have to tolerate any opinions contrary to the peace and preservation of the society on the grounds of religious conscience. He did not have to tolerate churches which claimed religious powers which undermined the preservation of peace, as the Roman Catholic claims that the Pope could dispense with oaths, and depose rulers, and that faith was not to be kept with heretics. Atheists were not to be tolerated because they could not be bound by promises. Promises were the oaths which bound society, and had no hold upon an atheist. 'The taking away of God, tho but even in thought, dissolves all.' Atheists also had no claim of religious right to toleration.[51]

Locke then posed a problem that he had not pursued in the 'Critical

---

[50] *Works*, VI, 28–34.   [51] *Ibid.*, 26–8; 34–5; 39–40; 44–51.

Notes', or even in the *Two Treatises*, and which he had answered in a different way in his earliest writings on toleration. If the magistrate attempted to enforce matters not for political ends of the public good but for religious ends – if, for instance, the magistrate attempted to enforce a 'strange Religion' which all subjects had to 'join in the Worship and Cere- monies of' – or if he altered property solely on account of religion, then he exceeded his authority. God would judge between the supreme magistrate and the people, and was the only judge between them where the bounds of rightful legislation had been left behind, but until they reached this divine tribunal men were to take care firstly of their own soul, and then – only then – of the public peace. Apparently reluctant explicitly to pursue this argument to its fullest extent by declaring in simple words that these people had a right to resist such a magistrate, this was the implication of taking care of one's soul first, and Locke did explicitly recognise that contests by force always began where the law could not settle a dispute. When Locke wrote the *Epistola* James had come to the throne in England and Louis had recently revoked the toleration formerly provided by the Edict of Nantes. The *Epistola* was written against Catholic kings forcing their subjects to the worship of Catholicism and taking their property because of religion.[52]

It is important to note that it remains as difficult to speak of this argu- ment as evolving out of an ideological commitment to the principles of religious dissenters in England as it was to speak thus of the *Two Treatises*. Nor is it possible to speak of a unified theory of religious toleration in the Netherlands. Many dissenters in England and many of Locke's friends opposed resistance and supported James' toleration of both Protestants and Catholics in 1685–7, including in Pierre Bayle the other major theoreti- cian of toleration in the Netherlands. Equally, in speaking of resistance to the imposition of a 'strange' religion by force on a nation Locke did not voice the arguments then being proffered by many recent Calvinist refugees in the Netherlands, such as Jurieu and Abbadie, as by over a century of Calvinist theoreticians, that there was a religious duty incumbent on those of the *true* religion to oppose the imposition of a false religion, and that the agents of such resistance were the inferior magistrates. Locke's arguments generally cleaved instead most closely to those of the Arminians and Soci- nians, and they were unhesitantly attributed to the Arminian Jacques Bernard when published in 1689, but the arguments of those authors tended to postulate an untyrannical magistrate and not to countenance resistance by subjects in even as muted tones as had Locke.[53]

[52] *Ibid.*, 48–9.
[53] Klibansky, introduction; R. Colie, 'John Locke in the Republic of Letters' in J. Bromley and E. Kossman (eds.), *Britain and the Netherlands* (1960), 111–29; Wootton, *Locke: Political Writings*, 94ff.

VI

The major argument that Locke used in the *Epistola* that had not been used at length in the 'Critical Notes' was the unequivocal statement that it was a duty of Christianity to tolerate others. While the 'Critical Notes' had recognised the importance of edification as a duty owed to oneself, and persuasion and propagation of the truth of the Gospel as a Christian duty owed to others, it had not strongly asserted that toleration was a duty owed to others; Locke's earlier tolerationist writings had not even included the duties of edification and propagation of the truth, let alone the Christian duty of toleration. There is a sense in which an unequivocal interpretation of the requirements of Christianity as tolerationist had finally become an important component of Locke's commitment to toleration; as such, it was to remain extremely significant for the rest of his life. In the Netherlands Locke was for the first time an intimate of many Protestants for whom toleration and moral behaviour were the two central duties of Christianity and who cited several texts of Scripture repeatedly to convey this message, Locke was not merely friends with van Limborch, but he seems to have participated in yet another of his many intellectual circles of friends in the late 1680s with Benjamin Furly and others who emphasised the Christian duty of toleration; Locke drew up rules for this group of 'Pacifick Christians' which included citation of many of these texts in justification of toleration.[54]

According to the *Epistola*, any man 'if he be destitute of Charity, Meekness, and Good-will in general towards all Mankind, even to those that are not Christians, he is certainly yet short of being a true Christian'. Christians had 'Duties of Peace, and Good-Will towards all men; as well towards the Erroneous as the Orthodox; towards those that differ from them in Faith and Worship, as well as towards those that agree with them therein'. Christianity required a faith which worked by 'love'. Here Locke put into a published work for the first time, in a passage on the very first page of the *Epistola*, a citation of Gal. 5:6, the passage interpreted by the draft sermon of 1667 and cited frequently by all of those who stressed a working faith, including notably many Latitudinarians, Arminians and Socinians. Locke was to return to the passage many times in the course of his own works of religious intepretation in the mid-1690s, the *Reasonableness* and its *Vindications*.[55]

Much of the account of the duty of toleration was embedded in the argument sharpened against Stillingfleet but now stated without specific

[54] Tully (ed.), *Letter*, 23–5; 34; MS Locke c27, fo. 80a–b. Cf. MS Locke c33, 24v, on which Locke compiled a list of scriptural texts supporting toleration in 1688.
[55] *Ibid.*, 23–5; 34.

target: it was incongruous to prosecute those who were moral but could not conform to the entirety of worship, but to leave alone those who were immoral and conformist. This theme made very clear that morality and toleration were the centre of Christianity. The opening pages of the *Epistola* resounded with the declaration that 'I esteem . . . Toleration [among Christians] to be the chief Characteristical Mark of the True Church'. In an attack whose terms applied to Catholics, and to most Anglicans and most dissenters in England, esteem not merely of antiquity of places and pomp of outward worship but also of reformation of discipline and the 'Orthodoxy of their Faith' were declared 'Marks of Men striving for Power and Empire over one another'. The business of true religion was 'the regulating Men's Lives according to the Rules of Vertue and Piety'. It was vital 'above all things' for men to make war upon 'lusts and Vices'. Much of religion consisted of 'a Good life'. Immorality was 'more contrary to the Glory of God . . . and to the salvation of souls, than any conscientious Dissent from Ecclesiastical Decisions'.[56]

The *Epistola de Tolerantia* also saw a major development from the 'Critical Notes' in being a straightforward advocacy of toleration with almost no argument for comprehension. This was no doubt partly because it was stated on a far more general level than the 'Critical Notes', concerned with European events and not focused on the politics of toleration in England. Locke's extensive awareness of the theological debates of the Netherlands, the degree of theological disagreements countenanced in the *Essay*, his close contact with more radical separatists than in England, such as Furly, and probably the consciousness of the distance that his own theological views had already travelled from those of his contemporaries and of his youth, had surely helped to generate in Locke a markedly pessimistic estimate of men's prospects for ever reaching agreement in religion. At one point in the *Epistola* Locke did still pose 'by the way' the question of whether it 'were more agreeable to the Church of Christ' to make the 'Conditions of her Communion consist in such things, and such things only, as the Holy Spirit has in the Holy Scripture declared, in express Words, to be necessary to Salvation' than it was to impose 'their own Inventions and Interpretations upon others, as if they were of Divine Authority, and to establish by Ecclesiastical Laws, as absolutely necessary to the Profession of Christianity, such things as the Holy Scriptures do either not mention, or at least not expressly command'. Locke's own implied preference was thus still that there should be one church with very wide terms of communion, similar to the ideal that he had first canvassed in 1667. Even this was only a very minor argument in the course of the *Epistola*, however, and when in 1689 van Limborch arranged for publication of the *Epistola* at

---

[56] *Ibid.*, 23–4; 46–7.

Gouda in a joint edition with Strimesius' *De Pace Ecclesiastica*, he was quite correct in depicting Locke's work as a plea for toleration outside of the established church, and Strimesius' work as a plea for comprehension, although also thereby seeing them as complementary rather than opposed visions of the desirable state of the church.[57]

When the leading unitarian merchant and friend of Furly, William Popple, translated Locke's *Epistola de Tolerantia* into English in 1689 as the *Letter Concerning Toleration*, very probably with Locke's knowledge but without his active assistance, he prefaced the *Letter* with a page of his own composition addressing its relationship to English thought and events. He declared that England had seen much written on the subject of toleration but still needed works like the *Letter* because of the failure of most nonconformists to argue for such toleration to be extended impartially. Not only had the government been partial in religion, but even those who had suffered under that partiality and had therefore vindicated their own 'Rights and Liberties' had 'for the most part done it upon narrow Principles, suited only to the Interests of their own Sects'. It was 'Equal and Impartial Liberty' that England needed, but which had not been practised either by the government to the people in general 'or by any Dissenting Parties of the People towards one another'. Popple condemned the 'narrowness of Spirit on all sides' as the principal cause of England's miseries. He declared that the Declarations of Indulgence and Acts of Comprehension 'practised or projected' in England were insufficient, indicting comprehension in a forceful declaration as likely to 'encrease our Evil'.[58]

In condemning the lack of consistent support for the principle of toleration amongst dissenters as well as Anglicans, Popple was echoing another of Locke's arguments in the *Epistola* itself. Again the passage was stated in very general terms, but it was unmistakably the universalisation of Locke's condemnation in the 'Critical Notes' of the dissenters' use of force whenever they gained power. It was 'worthy to be observed, and lamented' he wrote 'that the most violent . . . Defenders of the Truth, the Opposers of Errors, the Exclaimers against Schism, do hardly ever let loose . . . their zeal for God . . . unless where they have the Civil Magistrate on their side'. As 'soon as ever Court-favour has given them the better end of the Staff . . . Peace and Charity are to be laid aside; Otherwise, they are religiously to be observed.' It was only 'Where they have not the Power to carry on persecution, and to become Masters' that these churches 'desire to live upon fair Terms, and Preach up Toleration'.[59]

The Toleration Act of 1689 (I Wm and M. c.18), which passed into law

[57] *Ibid.*, 29; *Correspondence*, III, 1131.
[58] Tully, *Letter*, 21; MS Locke c33, 19; Klibansky and Gough, *Letter*, introduction, xxii; Spellman, *Locke and Depravity*, 135.
[59] *Ibid.*, 32–3; cf. pp. 107ff. above.

on 24 May, granted toleration of worship to Protestant trinitarians. It excluded unitarians, Roman Catholics and atheists, and it legalised toleration in the form of a revocable exemption from the penal laws against dissent. There was no recognition, in other words, that the community did not have the right to abridge peaceful forms of worship. Proposals for comprehension to be joined with this toleration failed to become law. Locke's correspondence with van Limborch in 1689 shows that he both felt that the toleration act as passed was too limited, and that he had increasingly limited hopes for comprehension as anything but a long-term aim. On 6 June 1689 he declared that toleration was now established by law although it was 'Not perhaps so wide in scope as might be wished for by you and those like you who are true Christians and free from ambition or envy'. He hoped that 'with these beginnings the foundations have been laid of that liberty and peace in which the church of Christ is one day to be established'. Three months later he declared that the settlement of a 'certain measure of indulgence' had not yet resulted in a 'complete settlement of the differences between minds and parties', but that the granting of liberty led to those who differed 'conducting themselves much more peaceably and moderately than I had expected'. Discussing comprehension, however, which van Limborch was still energetically supporting in his letters to Locke, he wrote that he could not 'feel any hopes that ecclesiastical peace will be established in that way. Men will always differ on religious questions and rival parties will continue to quarrel and wage war on each other unless the establishment of equal liberty for all provides a bond of mutual charity by which all may be brought together into one body.' Here toleration creating a bond of mutual charity is seen as necessary before comprehension can work at all.[60]

VII

Jonas Proast was a high-church former chaplain of All Souls, Oxford; close both to the high churchmen Henry Dowdwell, George Hickes and Thomas Hearne, and to Locke's later fierce opponent Jonathan Edwards; and a formidable opponent of the Latitudinarians, including Tillotson, who were then actively keeping him out of his position at All Souls. In 1690 and 1691 he composed two works that voiced the high-church Anglican case against religious toleration, the first of which assaulted Locke's *Letter Concerning Toleration*. In these Proast argued that while force could not directly work on the understanding, it was not completely inefficacious: it could be used to make men 'consider' their religion. Proast argued that men's nature was

[60] *Correspondence*, III, 1147; 1182.

'depraved' and 'corrupt' and that if left to a free choice of their religion they would choose a religion which legitimated their 'lusts'. He argued that the magistrate was empowered by the law of nature to do all possible good for his subjects, and that this included the spiritual good of enforcing their consideration of the 'true religion'. He added that by the duty of charity under the New Testament the civil sovereign was obliged to use such force. By applying 'moderate' penalties the advantage that false religion derived from its legitimation of men's lusts would be removed, and then the light of the Gospel would be able to prevail.[61]

Locke's *Second Letter on Toleration* (1690) was a reply to Proast's criticisms of the *Letter*; his *Third Letter on Toleration* (1692) was a response to Proast's reply to the *Second Letter*. While the *Second Letter* was even shorter than the first *Letter*, the *Third Letter* swelled to over 400 repetitive pages, and is consequently both almost entirely unreadable and very rarely read. As controversial works, the *Letters* concentrated upon pointing out the deficiencies of Proast's arguments far more than on setting out a clear version of Locke's own arguments and add very little to the case for religious toleration. Disdaining the possibility of suffering bringing religious conversion, Locke argued that where all magistrates used force true religion would obviously be more damaged by force than helped. Locke devoted considerable space to continuing to allege the absence of a commission for the magistrate in religion, and pointed out the difficulty of limiting the force used against dissenters to the 'moderate' penalties that Proast proposed. He argued that since Proast explicitly based the need for force in its counterbalancing of those lusts of men which had led them to choose a false religion, penal laws in religion were ineffective. They promoted only conformity, and conformists would simply be able to preserve their lusts within the bounds of the church instead of outside. It was inequitable to punish moral and considering dissenters for their alleged failures to consider religion properly, and not to punish unconsidering and immoral conformists, and these laws were therefore illegitimate.[62]

The *Second* and *Third Letters* were, however, concerned with English ecclesiastical politics as well as universal principles of toleration, and indicated that Locke continued his personal confessional allegiance in the early 1690s, twice identifying their author as a member of the Church of England. In the *Second Letter* he declared to Proast that 'I confess of myself' membership of the Church of England. In the *Third Letter* he noted Proast's argument: 'You tell me "If I own with our author, that there is but one true religion, and I owning myself to be of the church of England, you

---

[61] *Works*, VI, 142; 150; 152; 170; 262ff.; 351; 374.
[62] *Ibid.*, passim, esp. 134–5; 142ff.; 374.

cannot see how I can avoid supposing, that the national religion now in England, backed by the public authority of the law, is the only true religion.'" Locke argued that 'If I own, as I do, all that you here expect from me' this would not lead to Proast's conclusion, because while he was of the Church of England and held that the true religion was taught in the Church of England, it was not the only true religion since it made things necessary to communion which were not made necessary in the Bible. In the later 1690s Locke attempted to gain a clerical position in the Church for le Clerc. He lived for most of the 1690s and early 1700s in the house at Oates of Damaris Masham, the Anglican daughter of an Anglican cleric, and his correspondence during these years shows that he attended the local parish church and encouraged visits by friends by asking them to the sermons and services at the parish church there. When he became too sick to attend at the very end of his life, he received the sacrament at home, as was then the custom in the church.[63]

With phraseology that was strongly reminiscent of the 'Critical Notes' Locke declared against Proast that 'the present Church of England [has] a greater number in proportion than possibly any other age of the church ever had, of those who by their pious lives and labours of their ministry adorn their profession'. This was not merely applause that was intended to soften his own criticisms of other Anglican preachers for their intolerance or failure to preach effectively, but also a reflection of his own continued personal attraction to the views of many Latitudinarian Anglican churchmen, and of Chillingworth and Hales, their intellectual forefathers. In part this was approval merely for the Latitudinarian willingness to preach and teach in a plain style and in the words of Scripture, and thus for their attempts to avoid placing men's restrictive definitions upon the concepts conveyed in Scripture. This was reflected in his approval in *Some Thoughts* of the style of Tillotson and Chillingworth, and in his recommendation of the Cambridge Platonist and Latitudinarian John Worthington's *Catechism* as having 'all its answers in the precise Words of Scripture, a thing of good example, and such a sound form of words, as no Christian can except against, as not fit for his child to learn'. In part it was approval for Chillingworth's eirenicism, support of intellectual enquiry, and firm distinction of faith and knowledge; Locke read Chillingworth's *Religion of Protestants* again in Holland, and re-read it several more times in the 1690s.

His approval also extended, however, to much more significant elements of Latitudinarian thought: their descriptions of morality, their encouragements of moral behaviour through prudential arguments that recognised men's motivation by desire for happiness, and, as we will see in a few

[63] *Ibid.*, 100; 320; *Correspondence*, VI, 2202; McLachlan, *Religious Opinions*, 80.

moments, their animus against 'debaucheries'. In 1703 Locke was to recommend to his relative Peter King the sermons of Tillotson, Barrow and Whichcote for their 'view of the parts of morality' which he thought nowhere else 'so well and distinctly explained, and so strongly enforced'. He declared them to be 'masterpieces in this kind'. Locke's memoranda of books in Holland suggest that he was reading Barrow's sermons there in the late 1680s, and his annotated bibles include a number of notes drawn from these sermons. He had possessed an early volume of Tillotson's sermons before his exile to Holland, and his bibles show that in the 1690s he read several of the further collections of these sermons that were published when Tillotson became archbishop. A few years before his death he read a volume of Whichcote's sermons, which he then recommended on the role of civility. In one of his bibles he recorded from Whichcote the simple but important summary of their view of faith: 'the reforming our lives is the way to believe the Gospel'.[64]

As importantly, Locke maintained his friendship with the Latitudinarian clerics to whom he had been close before his exile, a friendship that was still far closer than that with any other English clerics. When he was very ill in 1703 Locke was visited at Oates by Fowler, and before Tillotson's death in 1694 Locke visited him several times. In 1694 Locke recorded his approbation of Tillotson as a 'candid friend' whom he had consulted on all 'doubtful points of divinity'. Some of the volumes of Tillotson's sermons that Locke received were personal gifts from the author, and he sent copies of some of his own works to Tillotson and Fowler. He personally brought van Limborch's works to Tillotson, securing Tillotson's patronage for their publication. Tillotson and Fowler were among the Anglicans most readily attracted to the post-Revolution settlement because of their erastianism and eirenicism, but probably also by some degree of Whig commitment, although not a commitment that had sanctioned armed

[64] *Works*, VI, 172; *Education*, 262; 296; 377; 399; *Works* (1801), X, 306; *Correspondence*, IV, 1398; 1429; V, 1507; 1509; 1518; 1572; 1601; 1826; 2011; 2012; 2029; 2031; 2023; 2939; 3332; le Clerc, *Life*, 44; MS Locke c25, 50; 51; 53r; 53v; 54r; 54v; MS Locke c33, 20, 27–9; cf. MS Locke f30, 1, 7–9; 43; 47–50; 83; 90; 93; 110; 118; MS Locke f32, 15; 66; 119; 130; 157; Sir Thomas Pope Blount, *Censura Celebriorum Authorum* (1690), shelved under 15.38, 15; 19; 22–3; 40; 43; 54; 72; 100; 119; 125; 132; 138; 160; 200; 219; 221; 252; 370; 500–1; 532; 570; 628; 636–7; 644–5; 652; 676; 684; 695; 701; 725; 745; *Le Nouveau Testament*, Mons (1673), shelved under 9.103–7; IV, 4–5; 58; 82; 99; 102; *Holy Bible* (1648), shelved under 16.25, 28; 82; 88; 96; 102–3; 167; 183; 192; 219; 449; 455; 465; 496; 513; 529; 562; 667; 682; 689–90; 711; 729; 731; 733; 750; 754; 773; 787; 789; 791–6; 807; 813; 819; 824; 828; 830–1; 837–8; 841–2; 844; 847–50; 852; 854; *Holy Bible* (1654), shelved under 10.59–60, 3; 76; 88; 99; 151; 189; 245; 253; 329; 450; II, 536; 573. *Library*, under the names Barrow, Boyle, Burnet, Cudworth, Fowler, Lloyd, Patrick, Stillingfleet, Tenison, Tillotson, Whichcote, Worthington, Chillingworth, Hales and Smith; *The Trinitarian Scheme* (1692), 28; [R. Howard], *A Twofold Vindication* (1696), 47–8, cited in Firpo, 'John Locke', 115.

resistance. As we saw earlier, Fowler had been a frequent guest at Shaftesbury's house in the later 1670s and was tried in an ecclesiastical court in 1684 for his association with Whiggism, and Tillotson was still in contact with Locke in 1681. Locke remained close to the eirenic lay Anglicans, Edward Clarke and James Tyrrell. Locke's friendship with a number of unitarians, including Isaac Newton, Peter King and William Popple, will be shown in the next chapter to have been very significant to him during the 1690s. It is worth noting at this point therefore that while these men were all theologically unorthodox, all remained members of the Church of England, as, indeed, did almost all contemporary unitarians, a fact they repeatedly trumpeted.[65]

Locke assaulted the punishments whose removal by the Toleration Act of 1689 Proast regretted as ruining many 'in their fortunes'; causing others to lose 'their liberties, and some their lives in prisons'. He anatomised at length the growth of penal laws under Queen Elizabeth which had eventually 'reached men's estates, liberties and lives'. Unlike Proast, however, the Latitudinarians had supported the (limited trinitarian) toleration established by William, and had accepted preferment by William to the top ranks of the church hierarchy. They attempted to secure comprehension in 1689 but failed because of the strength of high-church opposition among the lower clergy. For the Latitudinarians the post-Revolution Church of England was consequently still too insistent upon ceremonial. It was therefore in common with Latitudinarian desires that at many points in the *Second* and *Third Letters* Locke condemned the use of the cross in baptism and the requirement of kneeling at the Sacrament, both of which he recognised as still 'matter of great scruple'. Locke strongly praised those Anglican clerics who had not persecuted dissenters, although noting the 'possible' failings of most Anglicans: 'I have heard of those, and possibly there are instances of it now wanting, who by their pious lives, peaceable and friendly carriage, and diligent application to the several conditions and capacities of their parishioners, and screening them as much as they could from the penalties of the law, have in a short time scarce left a dissenter in a parish, where, notwithstanding the force had been before used, they scarce found any other.'[66]

Partly because they were faced by inability to force men to church and thus to instruction, and feared – in common with many dissenting ministers – that the Toleration Act had made it easy to attend no church at all, and partly because of their long-standing commitments, the Latitudinarian clergy attempted to extend the proselytising instruction that had been prac-

[65] On Fowler and Whiggism see p. 80 above; on Tillotson and Locke in October 1681 see, amusingly, Dewhurst, *Locke*, 206; Cranston, *Locke*, 134.
[66] *Works*, VI, 261; 328–330; 422ff.; 154–6; 388; 289ff., 322; 463; 286–8.

tised and advocated in the Restoration by Firmin and various of the Latitudinarians. Burnet's *Pastoral Care* (1692) encouraged the local parish clergy to be energetic in proselytising. In the *Third Letter* Locke noted that he had heard 'very sober people even of the church of England' say that current Anglican instruction was insufficient to teach the Christian religion, that Anglican ministers complained of the ignorance of the laity in religion more than of anything else, and made repeated use of the *Pastoral Care* in order to indict the failures of Anglican preaching and thus, like the Latitudinarian hierarchy, to encourage a proselytizing ministry. Locke cited approvingly Burnet's declaration that preachers should visit parishioners at home and his encouragement of 'the discoursing with men seriously and friendly about matters in religion, by those whose profession is the care of souls; examining what they do understand and where, either through laziness, prejudice or difficulty, they do stick'.[67]

Locke's citation of Burnet's work was in part the adoption of a screen to protect himself from the charge of 'ill-will' to the clergy with which Proast assaulted him. In most of his comments Locke avoided the strident anticlericalism of the 'Critical Notes', and he was careful not directly to insult preachers. His anticlericalism still surfaced at a number of significant moments, but it was directed especially against those of the high-church party rather than the proselytizing Anglicans. Proclaiming the need of all individuals to consider, search and examine the Scripture, Locke noted both that Proast was 'backward in putting men upon examination of the Scripture' and that it was 'convenient' for ministers that men should 'receive no instruction but from the ministry ... examine no arguments, hear nothing of the gospel, receive no other sense of the scripture than what that ministry proposes'. Locke broadened the attack at a few points in the manner of the *Letter From A Person of Quality* and *Two Treatises*, attacking 'our churches' for altering their preaching, sometimes venting antimonarchical principles and sometimes preaching up nothing but absolute monarchy and passive obedience; again high-church Anglicans are the primary target as preachers of *jure divino* monarchy. Accusing Proast of writing for 'party' and for 'preferment', Locke argued that the only party that he wrote for were those who 'in every nation fear God, work righteousness, and are accepted with him; and not those who in every nation are zealous for human constitutions'.[68]

Locke further argued that those were most 'authors and promoters of sects and divisions, who impose creeds, and ceremonies and articles of men's making ... who narrow christianity within bounds of their own

[67] *Ibid.*, 330; 302–3; 201–2; 391; 173; 527; 433; 524–5; 462.
[68] *Ibid.*, 356–7; 473ff.; 542ff.

making, which the gospel knows nothing of'. He contended that the 'bond of unity might be preserved, in the different persuasions of men concerning things not necessary to salvation, if they were not made necessary to church communion'. Pointing out the doctrinal latitude of the church, he queried 'What two thinking men of the Church of England are there, who differ not from the other in several material points of religion, who nevertheless are members of the same church, and in unity with one another'. He continued by noting that if one of those points were made necessary to communion then division resulted and by arguing that in such circumstances the sects were created by the imposers. He declared pointedly that many imposers had 'established sects' under 'specious names of national churches', and queried of the division between presbyterianism and episcopalianism what a 'sober sensible heathen' would think of finding an island 'where christianity seems to be in its greatest purity' but where the south and north parts established churches upon the differences of 'only whether fewer or more, thus and thus chosen, should govern' and each then denied the other to be a true church of Christ. The criticism here extended beyond its most obvious target, Anglican imposition, to dissenters' unwillingness to compromise, and Locke condemned the 'sects which so mangle Christianity'.[69]

While these passages suggest that a very broad comprehension remained a desire for Locke, this theme was generally muted within the text. These few very general passages aside, there was no appeal for comprehension in the *Second* and *Third Letters*. Instead, Locke stressed at the majority of points that each man had to follow his conscience in doctrine and ceremonial, and repeated the pessimism about ever achieving intellectual argreement between men that he had voiced to van Limborch in 1689. The ideal that he held to be practicable in the *Third Letter* was that of 'An agreement in truths necessary to salvation, and the maintaining of charity and brotherly kindness with the diversity of opinions in other things'. This was 'that which will very well consist with christian unity, and is all possibly to be had in this world, in such an incurable weakness and difference of men's understandings'.

VIII

We have seen in earlier chapters that from 1667 in his writings on toleration Locke restricted the morality to be enforced by the magistrate. In his 'Essay on Toleration' in 1667 he argued that the magistrate was not to enforce morality except as this was necessary to secure the public good, the

[69] *Ibid.*, 239–40.

preservation of the society and of the individuals in society. Any such injunction would be 'injustice'. Locke took it as evident that men ought not to be forced to be healthy or wealthy; indeed, the rhetorical force of his argument against religious enforcement owed much to querying why, since this was so evident, men should think that they ought to force others to take care of their supernatural welfare. While these private civil concernments probably included merely indifferent matters, they also clearly included significant parts of Locke's morality; industrious labour, whatever one's calling, was for Locke a prime duty of morality, and preservation of health and wealth in order to secure the means of subsistence and to do good to others were also very significant duties. The *Letter Concerning Toleration* similarly argued that the magistrate was not to enforce morality unless necessary to prevent injury, preserve society, and secure the common good. Locke argued that 'Covetousness' and 'Idleness' were recognised to be sins 'by the consent of all men, which yet no man ever said were to be punished by the magistrate. The reason is, because they were not prejudical to other men's rights, nor do they break the publick peace of Societies'. 'Nobody', Locke intoned 'corrects a spendthrift for consuming his substance in taverns.'[70]

Both the *Second* and the *Third Letter on Toleration* continued the central arguments of these earlier tolerationist works in defending the argument of the *Letter* that civil society was established only for civil interests against Proast's claim that it was empowered to secure any good, including spiritual good. In both the *Second* and *Third Letter* the burden of Locke's argument also continued to be that the magistrate had no commission to enforce religion and that almost all of morality remained beyond the bounds of magisterial authority. Against Proast's argument that the magistrate was to establish true religion because false religion was an offence to God, Locke queried why, if all offences had to be punished, the magistrate was not to punish 'envy, hatred, and malice, and all uncharitableness'. It was clearly not judicial proof that was the issue, for 'why does the magistrate never punish lying?' He declared that it was not the 'sense of mankind' that the magistrate had a duty to punish all offences against God. Using the same form of reply to the same form of argument by Proast, later in the *Third Letter* he queried how Proast would 'prove that God has given the magistrates of the earth a power to punish all faults against himself? Covetousness or not loving our neighbour as ourselves, are faults or sins against God. Ought the magistrate to punish these?'[71]

Other passages of the *Second* and *Third Letter* were far less clear on the

---

[70] *Letter*, passim; *Treatises*, passim. Tully (ed.), *Letter*, esp. 34 and 44.
[71] *Works*, VI, 295; 535.

question of the enforcement of morality by the magistrate, however, and some even seem to imply that the magistrate had a duty to use force to promote morality *in order to* promote religion. The first of these passages came in the *Second Letter*. Proast had quoted various passages of the Bible to argue that the magistrate should enforce religion, among them John 7:17, 'if any man will do his will, he shall know of the doctrine', a passage that Locke had himself quoted in emphasising moral behaviour as the way to gain knowledge of Scripture in his 1688 'Pacifick Christians'. In the *Second Letter* Locke suggested that this text proved that 'a good life is the only way to seek as we ought; and that therefore the magistrates, if they would put men upon seeking the way of salvation as they ought, should, by their laws and penalties, force them to a good life; a good conversation being the readiest and surest way to a right understanding'. Thus far, Locke's comment could be seen as merely an extension of his argument that penal laws in religion made men conform but did not prevent them from continuing in their 'lusts'; Locke is not necessarily agreeing with Proast that there is a magisterial duty of *forcing* men to seek *salvation* in pointing out that Proast's method is not suited to Proast's own ends, and it is not entirely clear whether the 'ought' in his statement refers to a magisterial duty of putting men upon the seeking of salvation or to the way that those men ought to seek salvation. Locke concluded this passage, however, by declaring that 'Punishments and severities thus applied . . . are both practicable, just and useful.' The most natural way to read this comment is that the justness, practicableness and usefulness of penalties comes from their effectiveness in securing the subjects' effective seeking of salvation, which would imply a religious reason for the magistrate to have promoted morality. The entire passage is, however, phrased with sufficient lack of precision that Locke may have meant by it that these penalties were 'just' as they separately procured other, purely civil interests that were connected with a good life. It could also be argued that Locke's approval of force to ensure a 'good life' and 'good conversation' referred only to a good life as it involved the prevention of injustice and securing of preservation.[72]

In the *Third Letter* the picture becomes more obscure. Although he specifically did not defend the magistrate imposing morality when it extended beyond justice to issues such as envy, uncharitableness, lying or covetousness, other passages suggest either that Locke was arguing for a magisterial duty to enforce morality when it was not clear that this was injurious to others or seditious, or, more probably, that the morality that he thought was to be enforced as necessary to justice and preservation was being very significantly expanded in a way that was in tension with his

[72] *Ibid.*, 66; cf. chapter six.

earlier statements on not forcing men to be healthy or wealthy and not preventing them from being 'idle'.

Proast had condemned Locke's support for toleration as leading to 'epicurism' as well as to atheism. Locke responded that the toleration of 'corrupt manners' and of 'the debaucheries of life' was not pleaded for in the *Letters*: it was 'properly the magistrate's business by punishments to restrain and suppress' these. Making an effective point, he declared that it was 'in the magistrate's power to restrain and suppress them by more effectual laws than those for church conformity'. Locke reiterated his argument from the *Second Letter* in citing John 7:17, noting that he had 'argued already' that the way to seek salvation was a 'good life'. He concluded that the severity of the magistrate against vice should 'promote a good life' and that this was 'another means besides imposing of creeds and ceremonies, to promote the true religion'. Proast argued that religious 'seducers' would be 'hearkened to' because they taught 'opinions favourable to men's lusts'. Locke's reply was, 'Let the magistrate, as is his duty, hinder the practices which their lusts would carry them to, and the advantage will be still on the side of truth.' He gave no indication of the source of this magisterial duty, but his comment that the magistrate was to hinder 'the practices' caused by lusts clearly suggests that he did not have in mind sinful lusts in and of themselves but only their external results. That punishment was thus to be directed as sinful action and not at sin itself suggests that he *may* have had in mind the prevention of sinful practice only as this was also injurious, and that the duty to punish may therefore still have been that of the protection of property and peace stated elsewhere in the *Third Letter*.[73]

Proast argued that men's lusts would prevent them from accepting the true religion without being forced to 'consider' by the magistrate. In a manner similar to that of the *Second Letter*, Locke argued in the *Third Letter* that the way in which force 'can and ought to be serviceable' to religion was 'in subduing of lusts; and its being directed against pride, injustice, rapine, luxury and debauchery, and those other immoralities which come properly under his cognizance, and may be corrected by punishments'. This was the magistrate's 'duty, in reference to religion'. It is again possible to read the passage as arguing that these were only punishable in those instances where they came 'properly under the magistrate's cognizance' by causing injury and injustice, although by far the more natural way of reading the passage is that *in addition to injustice*, pride, luxury and debauchery were 'properly' punishable by the magistrate, as were other 'immoralities'; the question in such a reading then becomes

[73] *Ibid.*, 416; 485–6; 373.

whether they were directly threatening to the civil peace or thought by Locke to lead inevitably to injustice or sedition.[74]

Proast argued that the prejudice of corruption against the true religion, which required mortification of lusts, had to be counterbalanced. According to Locke this meant that a 'drunkard must part with his cups and companions; and the voluptuous man with his pleasures. The proud and vain must lay by all excess in apparel, furniture, and attendance; and money (the support of all these) must be got only by ways of justice, honesty and fair industry: and every one must live peaceably, uprightly and friendly with his neighbour.' It was 'here' that Locke argued that the magistrates 'may and ought' to 'interpose their power, and by severities against drunkenness, lasciviousness and all sorts of debauchery; by a steady and unrelaxed punishment of all the ways of fraud and injustice; and by their administration, countenance, and example, reduce the irregularities of men's manners into order, and bring sobriety, peaceableness, industry, and honesty into fashion'. According to Locke, 'This is their proper business everywhere and for this they have a commission from God, both by the light of nature and revelation.' 'If men were *forced* by the magistrate to live sober, honest and strict lives, whatever their religion', then the advantage would be on the side of truth since the gratifying of lusts was not gained by forsaking her.[75]

Much of what the magistrate was to secure, according to this lengthy passage, was unquestionably merely justice, and much of his way to secure honest, sober and upright lives was clearly through the influence of the magistrate's own example and encouragement. Locke was also, however, projecting laws and punishment – indeed, 'severities' – against 'drunkenness' and 'debauchery'. The substantial possibility is raised that when Locke argued that the magistrate should enforce a good life in the passage of the *Second Letter*, and that he should prevent 'corrupt manners' in the passage in the *Third Letter*, that were both cited earlier, he was in fact thinking there of force being used to make men lead 'honest' and 'sober' lives.

It might seem possible that as Locke came to believe that men's sinfulness was the result of custom, habit and the power of the flesh, rather than a necessity of sinning inherited from Adam, and as he came to accept fully

---

[74] *Ibid.*, 468.
[75] *Ibid.*, 468–70 (my emphasis); on fashion and custom being more effective than laws see 'Atlantis' in MS Locke c42, 36ff.; cf. also *Correspondence*, IV, 1336, Benjamin Furly to Locke: 'We laugh at your politicks; if your Parliaments would never trouble their heads about 2 things, thats Religion and Trade, we should grow both Religious and Rich. Provided the Laws might be rigorously executed against immorality and debauchery which I plead not for.'

the scriptural teaching that the way to know more of the will of God was to act morally, he also came to believe that the magistrate should enforce more of morality than he had formerly thought as a way to promote his subjects' religious understanding. His arguments in the *Treatises* that individuals and thus the magistrate possessed the executive power of the law of nature, and that all men had the capacity to gain certainty in morality, although initially designed to support an individual right of resistance and liberty, could have come to seem to him to show that there was a way in which religion could legitimately be promoted by the magistrate without the magistrate attempting to force belief or worship, with all the dangers and reasons that he was still completely convinced made any such enforcement of belief and worship illegitimate. However, Locke had long believed that obedience to God's law was the way to a better understanding of that law; he continued to argue at a number of points in the text that the magistrate had no commission to seek the spiritual good of his subjects; he articulated so little of an opposing argument directly that it seems very unlikely that he had come to believe in it; and if he had come to such a view, it becomes difficult to see why he would then still have thought that no attempts should be made to punish other parts of immorality.

It seems more likely that several factors stood behind this set of arguments. First, in order to rebut Proast's charge of 'epicurism' on a controversial level, Locke blurred over the distinctions between a magisterial duty to promote religion by force and a duty to institute the parts of morality necessary to secure justice and to preserve the society which would *incidentally* help to promote religion. The magistrate would be doing his duty of helping others seek salvation, a duty that he possessed along with every other man in the world, but his use of force would actually be legitimate *only* on separate civil grounds. Second, Locke had come to think that governmental regulation to force people to an honest and sober life was itself necessary to justice and/or to the preservation of the society. In works such as *Some Thoughts* and his translation of Nicole's *Essais* Locke argued that pride would lead to injustice and oppression. As we saw in the last chapter, he argued in 1697 for forcing the able-bodied poor to labour in the navy or workhouses. In his notebook entry 'Labour' in 1693 he suggested that governments ought to 'suppresse the arts and instruments of Luxury and Vanity And bring those of honest and usefull industry into fashen', arguing both that aristocratic competition should be prevented and that the government should 'divert' men into honest labour. This would prevent 'temptation to Ambition where the possession of power could not display itself in the destinctions of useless pride and vanity' and would encourage 'honest labour'. He asserted that if governments neglected to do this they neglected 'the happynesse of the people' and with it 'their owne peace and security'.[76]

Placed alongside the passages of the *Second* and *Third Letter*, these two recommendations of enforcing honest and sober lives and reasons for preventing luxury and pride and 'debauchery' make it seem likely that in the 1690s Locke had come to think that luxury, debauchery, vanity, drunkenness and lasciviousness ought to be prevented by the force of the magistrate because if these things were not prevented they would lead not merely to attack upon honest labour but also to injustice and to the undermining of the peace. Administration of the poor law throughout the seventeenth century was explicitly concerned with maintaining the public peace; these were Locke's first years of such administration. As the 1690s progressed Locke became increasingly convinced of the difficulties of making men understand morality and practise it, including gentlemen, and declared that most men had to believe and not to know. Locke's efforts to show how men could govern their own conduct in liberty were increasingly focused on the need for outside agencies to govern them: tutors, parents and preachers.

In these senses, a more acute awareness of the extent of morality needing to be enforced by the magistrate seems the culmination of a number of factors within Locke's own thought. The argument was also very probably the result of his identification with the Latitudinarian programme of moral reform promoted by Tillotson, Burnet, Fowler and others, who had long complained of the viciousness allowed under Charles II and James II; Locke's own probable criticisms of Charles in 1681 were discussed in chapter five. Many in 1689 celebrated the coming of William and Mary as bringing a new moral order to England. Mary, very close to many Latitudinarian churchmen, issued proclamations with their support against 'vicious, debauched and profane persons' in 1692, and the Latitudinarian churchmen then set about defining these over the next decades as necessary to the preservation of the peace and therefore enforceable by the magistrate rather than as necessary to spiritual redemption. Locke's complaint in *Some Thoughts* that his society had been becoming increasingly 'vicious' was a common complaint of the period; he was identified with many of the Latitudinarians who also believed this and were involved in the founding of 'societies for the reformation of manners', and he was visiting Tillotson frequently during approximately the period that he composed the *Third Letter.*[77]

It thus seems most likely that Locke had not contradicted the central

---

[76] 'Labour', MS Locke Film. 77, 311; cf. Dunn, *Political Thought*, 235ff.
[77] Goldie, 'Proast'; S. Burtt, *Virtue Transformed*, Cambridge (1992).

argument of his writings since 1667 that the magistrate was limited to enforcing only those measures necessary to the public good, preservation and justice, but that he had come to expand the content of those necessary measures of moral reformation in such a way that he had contradicted the thrust of his argument in 1667 that it was evident that noone ought to be forced in their 'civil concernments' to be healthy or wealthy and in the *Letter* in 1689 that the 'idle' and the spendthrift in the taverns were committing sins whose punishment lay beyond the magistrate's penal authority. A massively coercive regime of industriousness and sobriety was quite legitimate and, indeed, required in this new vision.

The contexts of The Reasonableness of Christianity

I

Many of Locke's contemporaries had argued that it was necessary to morality to show that the soul was immortal: only by evidence of their own continuity into the afterlife could men be given adequate reason for behaving morally. In 1682 Locke had, however, denied the 'usual' proof of immortality from immateriality because it was not mere existence but the preservation of a state of sensibility that was important. The *Essay* was agnostic on the immateriality of the soul and argued that it did not matter if men could attain certainty about the soul's immateriality because 'All the great ends of Morality and Religion, are well enough secured, without philosophical Proofs of the Soul's Immateriality.' He continued that this was because 'it is evident, that he who made us at first begin to subsist here, sensible intelligent Beings . . . can and will restore us to the like state of Sensibility in another world, and make us capable there to receive the Retribution he has designed to Men, according to their doings in this Life'.[1]

Apart from this declaration of men's 'evident' restoration to sensibility in another world by God, however, the *Essay* crucially gave no indication of how men could gain certainty of the existence of an afterlife, of their own resurrection, or of God's punishments for sin. Locke's personal commitments were probably such that a very simple belief stood behind the 'evident' nature of this restoration to life, a view that was highly conventional in arguments proving punishments for natural law: God had created men with a purpose and he was just; it was therefore 'highly rational' to think that as men used their talents they would be rewarded. Some men were vicious but relatively successful in this life and others virtuous but relatively unsuccessful: an afterlife was necessary to rectify the accounts. However, since that view was dependent upon a knowledge of God as just, since Locke had nowhere shown in the *Essay* how men could know that God was just, and since he additionally argued that men should not define

---

[1] *Essay*, IV.iii.6; King, *Life* (1884), 308ff., cf *Essays*, 173

how God would dispose of men by their own narrow views and thus made it difficult to see how he could have constructed any extended argument on the basis of men's knowledge of God's justice *even if* that justice could indeed be demonstrated, there was a very serious problem in demonstrating punishment for sin and an afterlife at this point of Locke's account.[2]

Two arguments of the *Essay* may have been in significant part a result of Locke's worry as early as the 1680s about his failure to anchor a demonstrable morality. Locke reiterated much of his 1676 'wager' argument and extended the suggestion of the 'supposition' of states of heaven and hell in his journal notes of the early 1680s. When the eternal state was considered 'but in its bare possibility, which no body can deny', then, according to Locke, the pleasures and punishments *possibly* offered by God ought to be sufficient to determine men to act in expectation of an afterlife. Locke argued that a virtuous life was clearly preferable to a vicious one, even on simple hedonic principles, because the best to which the vicious could attain with their principles was the worst that could attend the virtuous if they were wrong: annihilation. For Locke, this was true even if a virtuous life here brought only pain, and he contended that in fact the vicious here had 'not much the odds to brag of'. The 'sober' man would venture nothing against the possibility of infinite happiness. Very lamely, Locke declared at the end of this argument that he had 'foreborn to mention' anything about the 'certainty or probability of a future life' since his concern was simply to show that even on their own principles the vicious judged wrongly by preferring the 'short pleasures of a vicious Life . . . whilst he knows, and cannot but be certain, that a future Life is at least possible'.[3]

The second argument whose formulation may have owed something to Locke's failure to see how to demonstrate the afterlife and reward and punishment by reason alone was part of the argument about the standards by which men measured morality. Moral good or evil was 'the Conformity or Disagreement of our voluntary Actions to some Law, whereby Good or Evil is drawn on us, from the Will and Power of the Law-Maker'. This good or evil was 'Reward and Punishment'. Locke declared that men generally created their ideas of morality by comparing actions with three such 'laws': 'divine law', 'civil law', and a law that was described as 'philosophical law' in the first edition, and as the 'law of Opinion or Reputation' in subsequent editions. The civil law was the rule set by commonwealths, which used rewards and punishments to 'protect the Lives, Liberties and

---

[2] *Essay*, IV.iii.6; King, *Life* (1884), 308ff. On this topic in the next paragraphs see especially Wootton, 'Locke: Socinian', passim; *Essay*, IV.xiv.
[3] *Essay*, II.xxi.70.

Possessions, of those who live according to its Laws'. The 'philosophical law' involved denominating actions as good or evil which were not taken notice of by the civil law but rather 'by approving or disapproving' of them. Broadening this analysis in subsequent editions of the *Essay*, Locke declared that the law of opinion was the attribution of the names virtue and vice to actions in each country and society which were there 'in reputation or discredit'. While what was in esteem varied between societies and over time, this public esteem generally approved that which was advantageous to the public, and 'in a great measure everywhere' corresponded to 'the Unchangeble Rule of Right and Wrong, which the Law of God hath established'. Even in the 'corruption of Manners' the 'True Boundaries of the Law of Nature' were 'pretty well preserved'. Elsewhere in the *Essay* Locke argued that men were motivated to recognise and observe much of natural law even when they did not recognise the authority of the lawgiver, God, because God had 'by an inseparable connexion, joined Virtue and publick Happiness together; and made the Practice thereof, necessary to the preservation of Society, and visibly beneficial to all, with whom the Virtuous Man has to do'.[4]

Two very serious problems for morality in these arguments of the *Essay* were raised by Tyrrell's report to Locke of the beliefs of various friends that by speaking only of the 'divine law' in the first edition he had left no room for natural law, and that since any natural morality appeared to be based instead either in the 'civil law' or 'philosophical law', men's duties other than those that were necessary to the peace of society might not be established as duties. In the light of Locke's stated but unfulfilled intent to show what God's will required of men in a manuscript 'Of Ethick(s) in General' that was projected initially as a chapter of the *Essay*; of Locke's fragmentary manuscript notes in the early 1690s on ethics surveyed in chapter seven; and of Locke having had his amanuensis copy out his early *Essays* which Tyrrell suggested could be the basis for a book of offices, it is likely that Locke was attempting to find a way to establish men's duties to other men beyond those of justice and preservation in the early 1690s, and attempting to accommodate them with his hedonic psychology. We saw in the last chapter, however, that Locke's comments on morality are, to put it kindly, fragmentary and very unfinished attempts at such a reconciliation.[5]

The second problem that Tyrrell had identified in Locke's account was equally acute: Locke's inability to demonstrate men's immortality and knowledge of rewards and punishments in the afterlife and thus to found a 'natural law' that was separate from revelation. Locke replied rather irri-

---

[4] *Essay*, II.xxviii.5–10; *Essay*, II.xxviii.9–12 (2nd edn.); I.iii.6.
[5] *Essay*, II.xxviii.5–10; *Correspondence*, IV, 1301; 1307; 1309; MS Locke f30.

tably that he had intended to describe in the *Essay* only the way that men came by their moral ideas, 'whether true or false', and not to establish the true morality. He argued that his discussion of divine law had not been meant to exclude natural law from the *Essay* but had been constructed to refer to all standards of 'divine law' to which men referred their moral ideas – and thus, for instance, to the Koran as well as to the Bible. He revised the *Essay* so that it declared in subsequent editions that he meant by the divine law 'That Law which God has set to the actions of Men, whether promulgated to them by the light of Nature, or the voice of Revelation'. The 'rule prescribed by God' was 'the true . . . measure of Vertue' and 'the true touchstone of moral rectitude'. Locke wrote to Tyrrell to question whether nothing would then 'passe with you in Religion and Morality but what you can demonstrate?' He declared that he thought that demonstration in those matters 'may be carried a great deale farther then it is' but then continued with the declaration that there were millions of propositions in mathematics which he could not demonstrate and which were nonetheless demonstrable. He then added that 'the probability of rewards and punishments in another life I should thinke might serve for an inforcement of the Divine law if that were the business in hand'.[6]

Showing a similar fear that he would not be able to demonstrate morality, but not a belief that it was undemonstrable, Locke wrote to Molyneux as early as September 1692 that 'Though by the view I had of moral ideas, whilst I was considering that subject, I thought I saw that morality might be demonstratively made out, yet whether I am able soe to make it out is another question. Every one could not have demonstrated what Mr Newton's book hath shewn to be demonstrable.' He had then promised to use 'the first leisure I can get to employ some thoughts that way', unless the *Essay* 'stir'd up some abler to prevent me, and effectually do that service to the world'. In early 1694 he repeated that 'the first leisure I get to myself, I shall apply my thoughts to it', but added also that 'I know not whether the attempt will exceed my strength.' Since between September 1692 and January 1694 Locke had been occupied by publishing *Some Thoughts*, and revising and publishing the second edition of the *Essay*, this delay in occupying his 'first leisure' should not necessarily be taken to indicate that Locke had no intention of composing such a work. Nonetheless, Locke did not develop an argument from God's justice or a proof of the soul's immortality in his revisions to the *Essay* in order to show that men could know that there was an afterlife in which they would be rewarded and punished. It remains likely that he still believed in the possibility of

[6] *Correspondence*, IV, 1309; King, *Life* (1884), 308ff.

demonstration of God's justice and therefore of an afterlife in which men would be rewarded and punished, but that he still could not see how that could be demonstrated any more successfully than men's immortality, once his own epistemological principles had been accepted.[7]

In 1695, then, Locke was acutely aware of severe epistemological problems attached to the demonstration of morality. To this awareness was added an equally acute perception of the practical problems attached to obtaining assent to proofs and consequent practice of morality even if it were demonstrable. When published in 1693 and revised in 1695 *Some Thoughts* had provided a technology for making gentlemen who were properly educated able to serve virtue, both in terms of reasoning to the content of virtue and in terms of controlling and directing their passions, but it had simultaneously emphasised how difficult this was, and recognised how few had been thus educated even among the tiny part of society that were gentlemen, let alone among the rest of society. As a member of the Board of Trade, Locke was at this time very much concerned with the problem of making the poor recognise their duties of industrious labour and dependence. The *Essay* had argued that men could come to knowledge of their duties by reason alone, but it had not suggested that men had in fact done so, let alone that they possessed the ability to perform these duties, and in Locke's debates over toleration with Proast in the early 1690s he had argued very forcefully indeed that most men were in practice extremely sinful. Locke's denials of original sin, like those of the Socinians, had never been designed to remove recognition of men's sinfulness, merely to advance different reasons for its occurrence than Adam's initial act of sin.

There were thus many practical reasons for Locke to find attractive in 1695 a picture of Christianity which provided arguments for the existence of an afterlife, heavy emphasis upon the rewards and punishments for virtue, and plain testimony about the content of virtue, even while not wanting to declare that this revelation was the only route to such knowledge. As we will see in the next chapter, these claims were to be a very major element of Locke's works of biblical interpretation from his 1695 *Reasonableness of Christianity* to the *Paraphrase Upon the Epistles of St Paul*, and were surely among his most pressing reasons for composition of the *Reasonableness* in 1695. Locke also wrote these works at the end of many years of deep theological interest, however, and before examining these works it will be valuable to delineate these interests and discuss the other dimensions of Locke's theology in these years.

---

[7] *Correspondence*, IV, 1538; 1693.

II

Between 1687 and approximately 1700 there was a major debate over the Trinity in England which became known as the 'Unitarian Controversy'. This controversy began when the unitarians took advantage of the relaxation of the press under James II to disseminate their views and it burned particularly fiercely in the early 1690s when many Anglicans, including leading Latitudinarian Anglicans such as Tillotson, Fowler, Burnet and Stillingfleet, wrote lengthy accounts defending the Athanasian Trinity and in turn provoked further unitarian works. The Unitarian Controversy was sparked by publication of Stephen Nye's (anonymous) *Brief History of the Unitarians*, which first gave the term 'unitarian' prominence in England to indicate all those who accented the superiority of God the Father to Jesus Christ and the Holy Ghost, and thus joined the Arians who believed after Arius in a pre-existent but not eternal Christ with the Socinians who followed Socinus in believing that Christ was neither pre-existent nor eternal.[8]

It appears very likely indeed that Locke followed the Unitarian Controversy from his return to England in 1689 at the latest. Locke's interest was undoubtedly partly animated by Jean le Clerc's request that Locke send him any important new works published in England for review in the *Bibliothèque Universelle*. In 1689 Locke sent Nye's *Brief History* to le Clerc. Over the next few years other works in the controversy followed, such as Arthur Bury's *Naked Gospel*. The *Naked Gospel* voiced a very common unitarian theme in showing 'how the primitive chastity of the gospel was defil'd with the . . . vain philosophy of the pagans; how Platonic enthusiasm was imposed upon the world for faith', and indicting this accretion of trinitarian doctrine for slowing the spread of the Gospel. Publication of the *Naked Gospel* caused a major part of the Unitarian Controversy. It cost Bury his rectorship and was officially condemned by Convocation.

Locke apparently discussed Bury's work with James Tyrrell, and he sent a copy to le Clerc, which then received a favourable review in the *Bibliothèque Universelle*. Locke's frequent and lengthy correspondence with le Clerc itself often touched upon the Trinity. Le Clerc was personally trinitarian, but was highly critical of some of the texts used to support trinitarianism, discussing these with great historical and interpretative sophistication in his correspondence with Locke, in his *Bibliothèque Universelle*, many volumes of which Locke owned, and in a commentary upon the beginning of John's Gospel that Locke also possessed. From 1690

---

[8] See my 'Locke and Socinianism'.

Locke similarly obtained copies of unitarian works for Benjamin Furly, and Furly's letters to Locke often discussed the arguments of various works issued during the Unitarian Controversy. Furly was a trinitarian, but he thought that he would never see the Trinity 'demonstrated to be of the number of those things that are necessary to be believed in order to salvation'.[9]

Locke quickly struck up a friendship with Isaac Newton shortly after his return from Holland in 1689. Newton was a frequent visitor to Locke at Oates in the early 1690s, and Locke's interleaved bibles and correspondence show substantial collaboration in biblical interpretation. Newton was one of those to whom Locke turned in 1692 when seeking information on the role of miracles in the early church. Newton was an Arian. As early as 1690, soon after they first met, he sent Locke two lengthy manuscript criticisms of texts frequently deployed in support of the Trinity as fraudulent insertions into the Bible. Locke copied these criticisms into his own hand and forwarded them to Jean le Clerc with a view to publication in his *Bibliothèque Universelle*, but Newton decided against publication. Although these manuscript criticisms are the only direct evidence of discussion of the Trinity by Locke and Newton, it is extremely hard to believe that they were their only discussion. Locke's cousin Peter King, author of the Arian *Enquiry into the Constitution of the Primitive Church* of 1691, was probably a significant recipient of Locke's praise of Newton as 'a very valuable man . . . in divinity . . . and his great Knowledg in the Scriptures, where in I know few his equals'.[10]

In 1690 Locke's notes show that he either discussed three unitarian works with Newton or procured them for him. It is quite possible that Newton's willingness to send Locke his manuscript criticisms of trinitarian texts as early as 1690 indicates that Locke had revealed to Newton that he was antitrinitarian by that date. It is also possible, however, that Locke had merely shown a receptivity to sophisticated historical investigations of the Bible, including trinitarian texts. Le Clerc was trinitarian, but would have been interested in publishing Newton's manuscripts on just such a basis. Locke's closeness to Peter King was itself to be important by the time of his death, and it is possible that Locke and King themselves discussed the Trinity and the history of trinitarianism in the primitive church as early

---

[9] [A. Bury], *The Naked Gospel* (1690), preface; *Correspondence*, III, 889; 1090; 1120; IV, 1248; 1256; 1325; 1329; 1344; 1684; V, 1702; 1832; 1855; 1880; 1933; 1961; 1999; VI, 2459; Sullivan, *Toland*, 721–3; MS Locke f29, 124; *Library*, 768.
[10] R. Westfall, *Never at Rest*, Cambridge (1980), 310–19; *Correspondence*, IV, 1338; 1357; VII; 3275; MS Locke f29, 126; *Holy Bible* (1648), 629; 744; 859; 861–2; McLachlan, *Religious Opinions*, 131–4; *Correspondence*, IV, 1405; 1457; 1465; 1499.

as the early 1690s, when King published his Arian *Enquiry*. At his death Locke left King all of his theological manuscripts.[11]

Locke had known the unitarian merchant Thomas Firmin since 1671 at the latest, and was probably a member of the circle of intellectuals that Firmin hosted in the 1670s and 1680s. In the late 1680s and early 1690s Firmin was the 'great promoter of Socinianism' who commissioned Stephen Nye's *Brief History of the Unitarians* and many of his other works, financed several collections of unitarian tracts, and almost certainly financed their free distribution as well. No direct evidence of Locke and Firmin discussing the Trinity survives, but Firmin sent Locke unitarian works such as Matthew Tindall's *Reflections* in the late 1690s. He also sent Locke a request for information upon the conversion to Judaism by a Dutch woman because of her disbelief in the Trinity, and her reconversion to Christianity by van Limborch in 1695 when he did not require her to believe in the Trinity. It seems likely that Locke and Firmin discussed the Trinity, and Firmin was among Locke's nominees to receive copies of his books from his publiser, including his replies to Stillingfleet's accusations of Socinianism. A more significant friend still was another unitarian merchant, William Popple, the English translator of Locke's *Letter on Toleration*. In the early 1690s Locke founded with Popple yet another of his societies for intellectual discussion, the 'dry club'. When ill health forced Locke to miss their meetings Popple sent him accounts of their discussions, and was one of Locke's visitors at Oates. Popple also served with Locke on the Board of Trade and may well have owed his position as Secretary to the Board to Locke's influence. When Locke's amanuensis Sylvanus Brownover married in 1696 Popple took him on as clerk. There is again no direct evidence of Popple and Locke discussing the Trinity, but it seems very likely.[12]

It is impossible to be certain exactly when Locke came to possess many of the works issued during the Unitarian Controversy. It is clear that by his death Locke owned many of the works published during the Controversy, and it appears highly likely that many of them were purchased shortly after their respective publications. By 1700 Locke possessed eight works by Stephen Nye, including the *Brief History of the Unitarians*. He owned a shoal of slim anonymous tracts like the 1690 *Brief Notes Upon the Creed of St Athanasius*, and its redaction *The Acts of Great Athanasius*, which

---

[11] *Correspondence*, IV, 1405; 1457; 1465; 1499.
[12] *Library*, introduction; *Correspondence*, V, 1955; MS Locke c25, 50; 53r; 53v; 55r; H. Stephenson, 'Thomas Firmin', Oxford DPhil. thesis (1949), *passim* and p. 509 for the description of Firmin as the 'great promoter' by Narcissus Luttrell. *Letter*, (Klibansky and Gough), 43–51; *Correspondence*, V, 1906; McLachlan, *Religious Opinions*, 102–3; MS Locke c25; 56.

assaulted Athanasius, the fourth-century credal formulator of co-equal, co-eternal and consubstantial persons in the Godhead. More significantly, Locke owned five works by Arthur Bury, including the *Naked Gospel*. In the 1690s Locke owned John Biddle's *The Apostolical and True Opinion Concerning the Trinity*, perhaps most famous for its assault upon trinitarians' delusions of 'personalities, moods, subsistencies, and such-like brain-sick notions' hatched by Platonists to pervert the worship of God. Locke unsurprisingly owned and praised enthusiastically his cousin and heir Peter King's Arian 1691 *Enquiry*. Completing his extensive holdings of unitarian works published before 1695, Locke possessed each of the three collections of unitarian tracts that were issued in the early 1690s. The first and most significant of these, *The Faith of One God* (1691), brought together in one volume several of John Biddle's works which had originally been published in the Interregnum.[13]

It is possible that Locke owned many works by the major Socinian authors by 1695. Certainly by the time of his death in 1704 Locke had amassed a large collection of works by all of the most important Socinian authors, several of which he had definitely purchased during the 1680s in Holland, and several more of which may have been purchased during the late 1680s or early 1690s. Locke's possessions included eight titles by Faustus Socinus himself, nine works by John Crell, Socinus' most important follower, six by Jonas Schlichting, publisher of the Polish church's confession of faith, five by Valentine Smaltz, joint editor of the *Racovian Catechism*, the closest that the Socinians came to an official statement of doctrine, and two books by Socinus' amanuensis John Volkel, including the 716-page compendium of Socinus' thought, *De Vera Religione*. His collection was rounded out by the ecclesiastical histories of Christopher Sand, various works by John von Wolzogen, George Enyedi, Martin Ruar and Andreas Wissowatus junior, and in the late 1690s by the *Bibliotheca Fratrum Polonorum*, a nine-volume collection of the major writings of Socinus, Crell, Schlichting and von Wolzogen.[14]

Locke also purchased or was given several of the Anglican defences of the Trinity published in the early 1690s. He received as a personal gift Tillotson's very restrained *Sermons of the Divinity and Incarnation of our Saviour*, owned the non-juror Charles Leslie's assault upon this restraint, *The Charge of Socinianism against Dr Tillotson*, and possessed the *Vindi-*

13 *Library*, entries 142–142a; 2069; 543–4; 785; 2988–92; 3017–20; 3022; 2702; 336; 2107–9; 3021; 3008; 3013; 3019; 3010; 3012; 1636; 3022a; 3010; 3007; J. Biddle, *The Apostolical and True Opinion Concerning the Holy Trinity* (1653), fA48; J. Force, *William Whiston, Honest Newtonian*, Cambridge (1985), 99.
14 *Library*, entries 2704–12; 876–83a; 2574–7; 1062; 3009; 2693–7; 3103–4; 2549–51; 3174; 2508–9; 1052; 3170; 331; 723.

cation of Tillotson from Leslie's attack by John Williams, future bishop of Chichester. Tillotson was the most moderate amongst the Latitudinarians in his reticence about proofs of the Trinity but like all of the Latitudinarians who had become the hierarchy of the church after 1689, from the placatory bishop Fowler to the less temperate bishops Burnet and Stillingfleet, he defended the Anglican orthodoxy of Trinity and satisfaction. Locke also purchased Fowler's *Certain Propositions in Defence of the Trinity*, and Stillingfleet's much more robust defences of the Trinity and satisfaction. He possessed three of the attempts by William Sherlock, Dean of St Paul's, to explain the Trinity in terms of three distinct intelligent persons with a mutual consciousness which drew upon Sherlock the charge of tritheism, the creation of three separate Gods, from his fellow Anglican Robert South, much to the joyful scorn of the unitarians and the derision of Furly.[15]

It is very likely that Locke was reading these unitarian and trinitarian works in the early 1690s as they appeared, although there are no notes from unitarian works in Locke's notebooks, manuscripts and interleaved bibles that were definitely taken between 1690 and 1693. In 1694–5, in contrast, there is clear evidence that Locke was taking notes from a number of unitarian works because in 1694 he started a large manuscript book which he entitled 'Adversaria Theologica' in which he recorded many notes from unitarian works. Dividing his pages into two, he listed arguments for and against the Trinity, and for and against the propositions that Christ was the most high God, that Christ was only a good man, that the Holy Spirit was God, and that Christ had satisfied for man. Each of these discussions was composed from the arguments of unitarian works, and the burden of each was unsurprisingly antitrinitarian. Locke was a meticulous and assiduous commonplacer, who filled volume after volume with arguments on matters from cannibalism to skin disorders, from schooling to stooling, and contributed an article on his method of commonplacing to Jean le Clerc's *Bibliothèque Universelle*. It would be wrong to suppose that Locke subscribed to even many of the opinions in these books, and this is as true of his 1694–5 entries upon the Trinity. The 'Adversaria Theologica' and Locke's other manuscripts and his interleaved bibles do suggest, however, that at the very least many of Locke's unitarian holdings were read carefully in the mid-1690s, and provided him both with arguments against the Trinity that he wished to consider more deeply and with information about sources in which to pursue his investigation.[16]

---

[15] *Library*, entries 2569–60; 2657; 1165–6; 2787–90; 1526; 76; 299; 475; 1214; 2912; 2905; 3163; 2722.
[16] MS Locke c43, 1ff.; it was indicated earlier – when considering MS Locke f14 – that Locke's dates of notebooks are not always reliable, and it is possible that he started this

Under the heading 'Trinitas' Locke marshalled two textual arguments. These were answered, and eleven further arguments were recorded, under the opposing heading 'Non Trinitas'. A similar imbalance in favour of antitrinitarianism marked the other entries on the propositions 'Christus Deus Supremus', 'Christus merus homo' and 'Spiritus Sanctus Deus'. Almost all of the arguments that Locke deployed under these headings came from two works by John Biddle, the *Confession of Faith touching the Holy Trinity according to the Scripture* and *Twelve Arguments Drawn Out of the Scripture wherein the Commonly received opinion touching the Deity of the Holy Spirit is clearly and fully refuted*, which together made up Biddle's *Apostolical and True Opinion Concerning the Trinity*, but were also available to Locke in *The Faith of One God*. Although culled from Biddle's tracts, Locke's list of arguments were paraphrases rather than extracts, and were gathered together from different parts of Biddle's texts, suggesting at the least that Locke had read Biddle's works very carefully.[17]

Under the heading 'Satisfactio Christi Aff[irmatur]' later in the 'Adversaria Theologica' Locke recorded no arguments at all. This blank side of the page faced a lengthy argument that Christ did not satisfy for man's sins in the sense of a 'true and adequate payment to the justice of God' but rather was 'a voluntary expiatory sacrifice' only as an 'oblation or application to the mercy of God . . . And for this reason tis said all along in the Holy Scripture that God forgives to us our sins and not that he received a satisfaction or an equivalent for them.' As well as suffering as an application to God's mercy, rather than a payment for sin, Christ had suffered in order to 'recommend mankind to the mercy' of God on 'the condition of faith and newness of life on our parts'. He had also suffered in order to obtain his own glorious reward. Once again Locke's source was a unitarian work, this time the anonymous 1694 assault upon Stillingfleet, Tillotson, Fowler and Burnet, *Considerations on the Explication of the doctrine of the Trinity*, probably by Stephen Nye.[18]

A few pages later in the 'Adversaria' Locke recorded a note entitled 'Redemptio and Ransom', a note that he neither signed as his own opinion nor recorded a source for, but which once again set out the Socinian understanding of the satisfaction. This argued that

---

book earlier. Perhaps the strongest evidence that Locke did not commence this 'Adversaria Theologica' before 1694 is that his 1692 and 1693 notes on man and the Fall and on the imputation of Adam's sin were recorded in his 1661 commonplace book – which would have been highly unusual for the exceedingly methodical Locke if he had already started the 'Adversaria Theologica'. The notes include notes from works published in 1694 itself, or which Locke can be shown to have purchased in 1694–5. Finally, they also appear to have been written as Locke was engaged in the studies which led to the *Reasonableness*.

[17] MS Locke c43, 1–7; 12–13; 26–31.   [18] MS Locke c43, 42–3.

Christ by his death redeems us from sin in that his death is a demonstration of the truth of his doctrine and the great argument to bring them into an obedience to the Gospel whereby they leave sin and soe scape punishmt. To restore the law of nature or natural religion almost blotted out by corruption god yields his son to death which is therefore called a ransome . . . The first and principal end of Christ's death is by being a proof of the gospel to be a motive to holynesse, and for all such as it thus works on God accepts it as a Sacrifice and forgives their sins . . . Tis Gods acceptance not its merit makes it expiatory.[19]

Locke also took a number of notes in several manuscripts and books from other unitarian works, including *Dr Wallis's Letter touching the doctrine of the Blessed Trinity answerd by his friend, Observations on the Four Letters of Dr Wallis Concerning the Trinity, and the Creed of Athanasius,* once again available to Locke in *The Faith of One God,* and the *Letter of Resolution concerning the Doctrine of the Trinity and Incarnation; giving the general Reasons of the Unitarians against those Doctrines,* the first tract in *The Second Collection of unitarian tracts.* These notes frequently focused on the association of Platonism and trinitarianism. Under 'Patres', an entry that Locke created on the interleaved pages of his copy of Sir Thomas Pope Blount's 1690 *Censura Celebriorum Authorum,* and again although in abbreviated form in his 'Lemmata Ethica', Locke noted the association of Plato and the Fathers' views from Nye's declaration in the *Defence of the Brief History of the Unitarians* that 'Anyone that is never soe little acquainted with the writeings of the fathers of the three first Centuries, cannot deny, if he be but sincere; that those fathers follow the ideas of Plato concerning the three principles, and therefore speak rather like Arians than Orthodox . . .' The source of this entry on 'Patres' was Stephen Nye's *Defence of the Brief History of the Unitarians,* a work once again republished in *The Faith of One God.* Locke also recorded this entry in rather more succinct form in 1695 under the heading 'Unitarian' in his 'Lemmata Ethica'. Other notes directed readers to Ralph Cudworth's *True Intellectual System* for insight into 'the Original of the Trinitarian doctrines, from whom they are derived [or] . . . by whom they were invented'. In the *True Intellectual System,* a massively erudite work from which Locke took copious notes in his manuscripts and bibles, the Cambridge Platonist had given a 'parallelism betwixt the Ancient or Genuine Platonick, and the Christian Trinity' in the hope that doubters would be convinced of the Trinity by finding that 'the best philosophers' amongst the pagans were 'fond' of the Trinity. The unitarians could not have wished for better ammunition for their association of the Trinity and Platonic corruption of Christianity, and they made much of Cudworth's claim.[20]

[19] MS Locke c43, 46.
[20] MS Locke d10, 167–8; 177; *Library,* entry 902; McLachlan, *Religious Opinions,* 105–6. Locke's citations of Cudworth were legion throughout *Le Nouveau Testament,* Locke Room (9.103–9); *Holy Bible* (16.25); *Holy Bible* (10.59–60).

The testimony of Locke's private biblical interpretation confirms the impression given by his theological manuscripts and notes of significant reading of unitarian works. All of Locke's notes in his Bibles are undated, and it is possible that they date from as late as the period of composition of the *Paraphrase*, but it seems likely that Locke recorded these notes when also taking notes from some of the same works in the mid-1690s. Among the many works cited by Locke in these Bibles were Biddle's *Confession of Faith*, and the *Considerations on the Explication of the Trinity*. Perhaps the most significant of these were recorded in his 1673 *New Testament* in French, Greek and Latin, consisting of general statements about the genesis of John's Gospel that suggest that Locke was giving serious personal consideration to this central text of trinitarianism, notes that supplemented Volkel's Socinian analysis of the text that we saw earlier that Locke had probably copied into his bible in the mid-1680s.[21]

From the *Considerations on the Explication of the Trinity* Locke noted that 'very many of the ancients who lived nearest to the Apostles times, and some of them in those times believed that Cerinthus', a first-century Gnostic heretic against whose denial of the deity of Christ the trinitarians argued that John had written his Gospel, was in fact 'the true author of the Gospel imputed to St John'. Several notes on contradictions between John's Gospel and the other three gospels followed from the *Considerations*. An entry from Eusebius' *Ecclesiastical History* completed the notes in this bible, and show that Locke was interested in a simpler account of the purpose of John's Gospel than the need to expound the Trinity: 'The other Evangelists haveing committed to writeing only' Christ's actions 'dureing one years space: therefor the Apostle John . . . declared in a Gospel according to him the time that was passed over by the other Evangelists, and what was done by our Saviour therein.' It should be noted at this point that many of the unitarian works discussed the role of Cerinthus in the genesis of John's Gospel, as did Locke's correspondence from Jean le Clerc in the early 1690s.[22]

Further suggestion of private considerations of the Trinity by Locke in early 1695 comes from a letter of 24 March from Alexander Beresford, who had previously visited Locke at Oates. Beresford sent Locke John Williams' *Vindication* of Tillotson, remarking that he had intended to send it sooner but had delayed with 'an expectation of having Eusebius and Epiphanius to peruse . . . being . . . desirous to report' to Locke whether they were 'as

[21] Blount, *Censura*, 1, 613, 620–1, 687, 340; cf. also 663; 19; MS Locke d10, 177.

[22] *Testamentum Graecorum*, 5, 10–12; 17; 54; 74ff.; 76; 78; 85; 124; 126; 128–9; 132; 135; 142–3; 146–7; 156–7; 161–2; 168–9; 174; 176; 178; 180–1; 190; 196–7; *Nouveau Testament*, 31; 344; *Holy Bible* (1648), 416; 441; 477; *Holy Bible* (1654), I, 18; *Correspondence*, V, 1832, 1855, 1880.

much misrepresented as Irenaeus', whose writings were actually 'more against than for' trinitarianism. He hoped Locke would produce 'more than a private Consideration' of the issue, sending Locke his 'own thoughts of the Trinity-texts of Scripture' and asking him for the opportunity to visit again 'to know your farther thoughts of the great Point'. No record of this proposed meeting and no correspondence from Locke to Beresford survives, but Beresford remained a visitor to and correspondent of Locke and Locke recommended him to others.[23]

In his commonplace book in 1693 Locke composed a lengthy journal entry, 'Homo Ante et Post Lapsum', bearing his initials. This argued clearly that Adam's posterity received mortality but not inherent sinfulness from his original sin. According to this manuscript,

man was made mortal put into a possession of the whole world. where in the full use of the creatures there was scarce room for any irregular desires but instinct and reason carried him the same way and being neither capable of covitousnesse or ambition when he had already the free use of all things he could scarce sin.[24]

God had given man 'a probationary law whereby he was restrained from one only fruit'; the punishment 'annexed to this law was a natural death'. Although Adam had been made mortal, yet the tree of life 'should after haveing observed this probationery law to a sufficient testimony of his obedience have clothed him upon with immortality without dieing'. Adam had sinned, and was sentenced to death by being 'excluded from that which could cure any distemper . . . and renew his age'. The result was that 'he and in him all his posterity were under a necessity of dyeing and thus sin entred into the world and death by sin'. God had then instituted 'a new

---

[23] *Correspondence*, V, 1865, 2195; VI, 2216; 2225.
[24] MS Locke c28, 113. Cf. Locke's *Third Letter*, (*Works*, VI, 409–12) where Locke argued in 1692 that a man of the Church of England could 'raise to himself such difficulties, concerning the doctrine of original sin, as may puzzle him though he be a man of study; and whether he may not push his studies so far, as to be staggered in his opinion?' He might 'question "whether it may be truly said that God imputes the first sin of Adam to his posterity?"' It is likely that this was a personal description of Locke's own thought, as was its immediately preceding comments that there were difficulties in interpreting the Athanasian Creed and that he could not pronounce any damned on the basis of not understanding it (*Ibid.*, 261, 409–12). It is perhaps the central failing of Spellman's *Locke and Depravity* that he argues that Locke was not Socinian/Pelagian because of his view of man's extensive sinfulness, and that he attempts to align Locke's mature thought with the Latitudinarians in still seeing men as very sinful from some unorthodox version of original sin; Socinians and Pelagians did not deny that men were extremely sinful in practice; they disagreed about its genesis and whether it was essential to men. Cf. H. Chadwick, *Augustine*, Oxford (1986), 108–9, on Pelagius and Augustine: 'The two men were agreed on far more than that on which they disagreed. Both saw humanity as locked into a corporately sinful social tradition. Pelagius insisted that sin is not physically hereditary, and therefore by free choice one can escape . . . The grace of God would give illumination to know what was right, and extra assistance, short of doing absolutely everything.'

covenant of grace' which offered man 'eternal life but not without dyeing'. Locke argued that 'for men to be born mortal after that was no punishment'. By their 'sin Adam and Eve came to know good and evil ie the difference between good and evil for without sin man should not have known evil'. Locke then concluded with an analysis which emphasised the widespread nature of sin as a result of men's voluntary acts, built up into the power of 'fashion and example', but not from an inherited necessity of sinning:

> upon their offence they were afraid of God. this gave them frightfull Ideas and apprehensions and soe infected their children, and when private possessions and labour which now the curse on the earth had made necessary, by degrees made a destinction of conditions it gave roome for covitousnesse pride and ambition, which by fashen and example spread the corruption which has soe prevailed over man kind.[25]

From 1693 at the latest this view of man, effectively denying original sin, stood behind Locke's account of the need for government, and was voiced explicitly in that fashion in Locke's *Third Letter on Toleration*.

III

It was very probably therefore in an atmosphere of readings questioning the Trinity, and associatedly questioning doctrines such as the immortality of the soul, and after continuing his 1680s rejection of original sin, that Locke revised the *Essay* in 1693 and published its third edition in 1694. He added an entirely new discussion of personal identity, locating this not in any necessary physical continuity of substance, whether material or immaterial, but in consciousness. Consciousness always accompanied thought 'and 'tis that, that makes every one to be, what he calls self; and thereby distinguishes himself from all other thinking things, in this alone consists personal identity, ie the sameness of a rational Being'. Locke recognised that the 'more probable Opinion' was that consciousness was annexed to and the affection of 'one individual immaterial Substance'. He argued that it did not matter, however, whether it was the same identical substance that always thought or a succession of several substances, or whether that substance (or substances) was (or were) material or immaterial. Consciousness alone was significant; it was necessary to the provision of a basis for morality only that there was something in all intelligent beings which was sensible of happiness and misery, and which each individual was 'concerned for, and would have happy'.[26]

It was consciousness alone that led to identification of the 'self', provid-

[25] MS Locke c28, 113.   [26] *Essay*, II.xxvii.1–25.

ing concern for happiness or misery and a locus of responsibility for actions in ways that would draw happiness or misery as reward or punishment. The sentences of the 'Day of Judgement' would be justified by the consciousness of the 'persons' resurrected that they were the same 'persons' who had committed the actions that deserved the judgements, whether or not their bodies or spirits exhibited any physical continuity. There was no need to know of the existence of, or even to believe in, either the resurrection of an identical body or a soul that was immortal because immaterial, the views of Locke's theologically orthodox Protestant contemporaries whether Calvinist, Arminian, or Latitudinarian. On the basis of Locke's account of consciousness, it could be conceived that the same 'Person' was resurrected 'though in a body not exactly in make or parts the same which he had here'.[27]

This account of personal identity was therefore compatible with disbelief in the resurrection of the same bodies, a disbelief that was associated with the views of Socinian authors, although not a disbelief that was shared by all Socinians. It was compatible also with disbelief in a naturally immortal soul, as long as the same consciousness was resurrected in some substance – which Locke was willing to call men's 'Soul'. Again, many Socinians spoke of man having a soul or spirit, but disbelieved that this was naturally immortal, holding that between the end of earthly life and the resurrection men were dead; this belief was known as mortalism. As we have seen earlier, for Leibniz, by rejecting the necessity of the resurrection of the same body and by rejecting the proof of the natural immortality of the soul in favour of his account of personal identity in consciousness, Locke had left morality insufficiently supported. Men could have no certainty of their own existence in an afterlife without a proven physical continuity. At points Leibniz described Locke's motivation in construction of this argument as an inclination towards Socinianism.[28]

By the late 1690s and early 1700s Locke was willing to say explicitly in print in the *Paraphrase* – although even then anonymously, and, as it turned out, posthumously – that the same bodies were not resurrected. His paraphrase of 1 Cor. 15:50, the central text for those who supported the resurrection of the same body, described Paul as declaring 'that we shall not at the resurrection have such bodies as we have now. For flesh and blood cannot enter into the kingdom which the saints shall inherit in heaven: Nor are such fleeting corruptible things as our present bodies fitted to that state of immutable incorruptibility.' In the fourth edition of

---

[27] *Essay*, II.xxvii, passim, esp. 15–17, 26.
[28] *Essay*, II.xxvii.15; Jolley, *Leibniz*, passim, esp. chs. 2 and 5.

the *Essay* in 1700 Locke spoke only of the 'Resurrection of the Dead' and not of the resurrection of their bodies.[29]

Locke had almost certainly come to disbelieve that the same bodies were resurrected by the time that he wrote the *Reasonableness of Christianity* in the winter of 1694–5, when he wrote that men's 'frail mortal bodies' were changed into 'spiritual immortal bodies' at the Resurrection. The combination of personal belief and personal doubt which very probably lay behind this statement in the *Reasonableness* in 1695 was recorded privately by Locke in two signed notes in his 'Adversaria Theologica', probably composed in 1694–5, on the possibility of the materiality or immateriality of the 'spirit'. Locke's second of his two signed arguments in favour of the immateriality of the spirit clearly expressed his own belief that the same bodies were not resurrected. He noted that spirit in Scripture often referred only to 'animal life and thought' and not to any 'material or immaterial' being in whom that life and thought resided. He then contrasted men before and after the resurrection as discussed in 1 Cor. 15, declaring that before the resurrection man seemed to be a 'body animal corruptible mortal', whereas after the resurrection he seemed to be a 'body spiritual incorruptible and immortal'. Locke was clear that the Apostle had not spoken, as most contemporary theologians apart from the Socinians argued, of an immortal soul and a mortal body but 'of the whole man dyeing and the whole man as raised'. This meant that 'immortality is not at all oweing nor built on immateriality as in its own nature incorruptible'. The Apostle had not known 'that argument which is so much insisted on [nowadays] but quite the contrary'. Showing an interpretation of Scripture as central, the note declared this 'plain' in Scripture. Locke's note indicated that 2 Cor. 5:1–4 could not support an 'immaterial immutable substance' in man distinct from the body because by analogy he would then have to interpret a 'grain of wheat' as possessing an 'immaterial substance'. At this point Locke noted that it was 'further remarkable that in the whole new Testament there is noe such thing as any mention of the resurrection of the body how ever it crept into the creed but every where the resurrection is spoke as of the whole man'. Although this was listed under the heading of argument for the immateriality of the spirit of man, it had ended without supporting immateriality, and, apparently recognising this, on the opposite page of arguments supporting materiality Locke noted that he should see 'the other page'.[30]

By 1694–5 Locke thus had apparently reinforced his epistemological doubts about men's ability to know the nature of thinking substance, come

---

[29] *Paraphrase*, 1 Cor. 15:50; *Essay*, IV.xvii.23; IV.iii.29; IV.xviii.7.
[30] *Reasonableness*, 107; MS Locke c43, 32–3; *Paraphrase*, I, 468.

to disbelieve the resurrection of the same body, and continued to oppose proof from immateriality alone of the natural immortality of the soul. This might be thought to provide evidence for Leibniz's suggestion that Locke was motivated by direct support for the mortalism associated with Socinianism in composition of his account of personal identity. There is evidence, however, that Locke's account of personal identity in the *Essay* was not forged in order to support a belief that resurrection involved only consciousness and not a continuity of identical substance (whether body or immaterial soul) because Locke personally believed when composing his account of personal identity with the Socinians in mortalism, nor because he personally thought that the soul was material, nor even because he thought in 1693 that the same bodies were not resurrected. In all editions of the *Essay* Locke continued to declare that the 'most probable opinion' was that men's consciousness resided in an 'immaterial' substance. Furthermore, at the time that the account of personal identity in the third edition of the *Essay* went to press, including its account of personal identity, Locke apparently still thought that the same body was resurrected. The first three editions of the *Essay* all spoke at various points of the resurrection of 'the bodies' of men; it was only in the fourth edition of 1700 that these references were changed to the 'resurrection of the dead'. The third edition of the *Essay* went to press in late 1693 and was published in 1694. It therefore went to press before Locke's note in his 'Adversaria Theologica' and his statement in the *Reasonableness* were composed, and long before composition of the *Paraphrase*.[31]

The immediate impetus for composition of the account of personal identity seems to have lain with requests from the Dublin philosopher William Molyneux, who had gained Locke's friendship by lauding Locke's reasoning as 'somewhat angelic'. In 1692 Molyneux's suggestions for improvements to the *Essay* had included the desirability of a discussion of 'Principium Individuationis'. In 1693 Locke wrote to Molyneux noting that his new chapter on identity was composed solely to comply with that request. Locke's long-standing belief in the inadequacy of proof of the immortality of the soul from its immateriality was surely a major factor that made him desire to develop an account of personal identity that showed that it did not necessarily reside in, and certainly did not consist of, continuity of an identical immaterial substance; the argument had been constructed in outline in his journal note as early as 1683. The result was an argument about personal identity that was compatible with mortalism, but which did not logically entail that belief. Even the *Paraphrase* was to leave unclear whether Locke supported the mortalist view that men would

---

[31] *Essay*, IV.xvii.23; IV.iii.29; IV.xviii.7; MS Locke c43, 32–3; *Paraphrase*, II, 675ff.

be dead between the end of their earthly life and the resurrection, or merely thought that to be a strong possibility, although the former view seems the more likely.

Locke may have wished in constructing his account of personal identity to make his argument compatible with mortalism because of a general sympathy for Socinian argument and awareness that many Socinians were mortalist, but his account of personal identity was the logical extension of his own account of men's very limited knowledge of substance and of a desire to provide reasons to be moral which did not depend upon proof of immortality from immateriality, a proof that Locke had opposed before any direct sign either of any Socinian belief or of any degree of disbelief in the immortality of the soul. In the light of his apparent belief in the resurrection of the same body in composing the account of personal identity in 1693 and his rejection of that belief by the time that he composed the *Reasonableness* and his adversarial note, the fourth edition of the *Essay*, and the *Paraphrase*, it seems likely that instead of sympathy for Socinian belief directly motivating his account of personal identity, Locke's epistemological investigations in 1693 were themselves part of what prompted his consideration of the exact doctrine about the resurrection delivered in Scripture. It seems likely, in other words, that Locke's personal construction for primarily philosophical reasons of an epistemological argument about personal identity, which he began to build in the 1680s, and expanded rather than altered in 1693, was influential in his coming to rejection of a significant element of contemporary theological orthodoxy in rejecting with the Socinians the resurrection of the *same* body, and that it may also have helped him towards a belief in mortalism that was also associated with Socinianism, if he came to such a belief, which seems probable.[32]

Locke made two other alterations significant to his theological views in preparing the third edition of the *Essay*. Again, Locke's primary motivation seems to have come from correspondence with Molyneux. Molyneux depicted Locke's discussion of the will as motivated by the greatest (hedonic) good in the first edition of the *Essay* as too 'fine spun', making 'the Great Question of Liberty and Necessity' seem 'to Vanish'. The problem for Molyneux was that Locke seemed to 'make all Sins to proceed from our Understandings, or to be against Conscience; and not at all from the Depravity of our Wills'. It seemed harsh to Molyneux to argue that 'a Man shall be Damn'd, because he understands no better than he does'. Molyneux's point was apparently that if the will was a power that was determined by the greater good, and it was the understanding that

---

[32] *Correspondence*, IV, 1609; 1620; 1655; 1661; 1685; V, 1712.

identified that greater good, then a simple failure to identify this correctly would lead to sin and thus to damnation. Molyneux also forwarded to Locke some comments upon the *Essay* by William King, Bishop of Derry, raising a similar problem from a different direction: since in Locke's empiricism ideas were created by circumstances ordered by God, this included all ideas of good, leaving no room for liberty.[33]

In January 1693 Locke initially responded to Molyneux's criticism with a declaration that 'if you will argue for or against liberty, from consequences' he would not answer:

For I own freely to you the weakness of my understanding, that though it be unquestionable that there is omnipotence and omniscience in God our maker, and I cannot have a clearer perception of any thing than that I am free, yet I cannot make freedom in man consistent with omnipotence and omniscience in God, though I am as fully perswaded of both as of any truths I most firmly assent to. And therfore I have long since given off the consideration of that question, resolving all into this short conclusion, that if it be possible for God to make a free agent, then man is free, though I see not the way of it.[34]

In revising the *Essay* for its second edition later that year, however, Locke gained 'a new view'. He shifted from determination by the greater good – which he declared the common opinion – to uneasiness as the motivation for action. Unless men were uneasy, either through the presence of evil, or the absence of a desired good, they would not act. Whatever good was proposed whose absence did not carry pain did not evoke desire, and therefore did not evoke vigorous use of the means to attain it, but instead only some 'faint wishes'. However much a man was convinced of the advantages of action, until he desired something he would not act to obtain it. This helped to explain why men had the 'unspeakable joys' of heaven set before them and acknowledged them as probable, but focused on their terrestrial happiness. While in practice the attainment and continuation of the 'pittance' of present goods of honour, riches and pleasure was declared by Locke to be less likely than the possibility of eternal durable joys, men little considered 'absent goods' such as heaven. The ordinary necessities of life filled their lives with uneasiness. Very little time was left for thought about absent goods because to these natural necessities was added 'fantastical' uneasiness for riches, honour, power, and a thousand other desires derived from fashion, example and education and settled by habit. These 'irregular desires' were made 'natural' by custom.[35]

The second major change made in the second edition of the *Essay*, and the change necessary to satisfy Molyneux's queries, was Locke's assertion that while in most cases the greatest uneasiness determined the will, the

[33] *Correspondence*, IV, 1579; 1544.   [34] *Correspondence*, IV, 1592; 1643.
[35] *Essay*, II.xxi.31ff.; 34ff.; *Essay*, II.xx.6.

mind could suspend the pressures of desires and examine its choice of actions. Indeed, while Locke continued to maintain that being determined by the greatest good was no abridgement of freedom, he asserted in the second and later editions of the *Essay* that it was precisely in man's power of suspending desires that his liberty lay. This power was the 'source', the 'hinge', the 'inlet' of all liberty, giving men the ability to identify their 'true' and 'real' happiness. It was from not using this liberty correctly, but not from simple failures of understanding, that 'all' faults stemmed. Men frequently engaged their wills before examination of possible actions.[36]

Although Locke had presumably been made broadly aware of the attempts at reconciliation of grace and liberty in his reading of the works of various Latitudinarians and especially in his Arminian reading in the Netherlands in the 1680s, his correspondence with Molyneux and the form of his own argument in the *Essay* both suggest that Locke thought that in his amendments to the *Essay* he had solved much of the major problem of liberty and necessity, of men's free will and God's omniscient omnipotence, while having found no satisfactory answer in his reading of theology. Once again, Locke's epistemological investigations seem to have spurred his further examination of theological discussions of the issues, rather than the other way around. Locke corresponded about the relation between his account of liberty and theology with le Clerc in 1694 and in his 'Adversaria Theologica' in 1694 Locke took several notes from Episcopius' *Opera Theologica*, including a note supporting the freedom of fallen man: 'Homo Lapsus liber'. Significantly, however, Locke ended his note on this freedom with his own argument: men's freedom came from his power ('potentia') to act or not to act, to suspend or to cease actions. The facing page, 'Homo lapsus non liber', was blank.[37]

Locke's further reading on theologians' arguments about freedom underlined the extent to which, Episcopius included, they interpreted Scripture in the light of philosophy. In his 'Lemmata Ethica' Locke took a lengthy note, dated 1695, from the unitarian Stephen Nye's *Discourse Concerning Natural and Revealed Religion*, which was a compound of several sections of Nye's published text, and probably also from several sections of Nye's manuscript, which Locke read before its publication. Nye was a strong advocate of man's freedom who commenced by noting that the question of 'Liberty and Necessity' had divided philosophers and theologians. He then listed all of the ancient philosophers who had discussed the subject and the location of their discussions; Locke copied this list into his 'Lemmata'. He contended that all Christian writers before St Augustine had defended man's free will but that most since had either directly or

[36] *Essay*, II.xxi.47ff.	[37] MS Locke c43, 36–7.

implicitly denied free will. Again, Locke recorded his argument. Nye next surveyed various opinions about man's freedom, including the view of Simplicius, who had argued particularly against those philosophers who supposed that men were physically necessitated to perform actions by their circumstances. Simplicius had argued that external objects, the temptations of the body, and custom were the 'occasions' of many actions but were never 'fatal causes'. They inclined men to actions but men's reason governed when men wanted it to; they had the power of deliberation. Locke recorded Simplicius' argument, an argument that was significantly similar to Locke's form of response to King's criticisms of the first edition of the *Essay*. Finally, Nye surveyed opinions concerning the reconciliation of God's foreknowledge and men's freedom. Ammonius of Hermas, in exposition of Aristotle's thought, had argued that God foresaw certainly in what manner every free agent would dispose itself, but did not make these actions necessary by such foresight. Nye described this as also his own opinion. The Remonstrants and Socinians, however, Nye described as rather following Maximus of Tyre in interpreting Scripture as saying that God foresaw all possible actions of free agents, but did not foresee certainly exactly which of these actions they would freely choose. Again, Locke noted this discussion. Although much of Nye's discussion set out the views of various necessitarians, Locke in contrast did not take down any notes of these discussions.[38]

Locke's new account of liberty had thus apparently sent him to condemnations by theologians of other theologians' philosophic prejudices, an attack on theologians very similar to the claims of many unitarians that the doctrine of the Trinity was based on the philosophic prejudices, usually Platonic, of patristic theologians. More broadly, these arguments were part of an increasing identification by a number of laymen that much of theology had been generated by self-interested clerics concerned far more with building up their authority than with the disinterested truth of religion. As Justin Champion, Peter Harrison and especially Mark Goldie have recently emphasised, by the mid-1690s this case was being repeatedly stated in a series of works anatomising the growth of 'priestcraft', such as Robert Howard's *Natural History of Religion*, which discussed 'how religion has been corrupted, almost from the beginning, by priestcraft' and argued that 'priestcraft had contrived notions and opinions, to engage people to submit implicitly to their directions'. Howard further described priestcraft as centring on persecution by powers of creed-making, excommunication, and attack on heresy. Similar claims about the description of powers of creed-making as central to persecution and as symptoms of priestcraft were

[38] MS Locke d10, 93–5; [S. Nye], *Discourse Concerning Natural and Revealed Religion* (1697), 64–76.

central to many other accounts issued between 1657 and 1694, and 'priest-craft' was anatomised in Dryden's *Absalom and Achitophel*, and Charles Blount's *Great is the Diana of the Ephesians*, among other works.[39]

By the time that Locke was undertaking his theological investigations the accusation had reached the point where Burnet described 'priestcraft' as a 'common word in fashion'. Locke had probably encountered the term in Dryden's attack on Shaftesbury, which placed in the voice of a sceptic a description of 'pious times, ere priestcraft did begin', and it was almost certainly part of the background to his attack in the *Essay* on priestly auth-ority. Furly assured Locke in 1694 that the *Essay* would help 'priestcraft . . . fall' since it could not 'stand long against the light, that has so far opened men's eyes to see through' their authority. The *Letters'* attack on creed-making and denunciation of 'heresy' were motivated by recognition that these were central to the powers of clerical persecution.[40]

Locke's reading of Scripture and composition of the *Reasonableness* in 1695 was thus undertaken with many attacks on priestcraft focused on creed-making and the addition of extraneous philosophy to original beliefs in his mind to add to the long-standing suspicion of many theologians' creed-making which had underpinned his already deep-seated toleration-ism. In the process of defending toleration against Proast Locke had faced an argument that the church now needed to use force to replace the mir-acles that God had originally provided to spread Christianity. In order to diminish the need for replacement of miracles by force, a significant portion of the *Third Letter* was devoted to a diminution of the role of miracles in the early church by arguing that very few early Christians were 'wrought on' by miracles because most had been converted to Christianity by preaching and the report of miracles. Locke therefore constructed an argument in 1693 that the Gospel had prevailed then and prevailed still 'by its own beauty, force [of argument], and reasonableness'.[41]

The *Epistola* had been constructed around the premiss that there was one true religion, one 'way' to salvation. Locke did, however, note in the *Epistola* that there would be less or no legitimacy to persecution if there were more than one way to heaven. This is not a particularly satisfactory argument for toleration on the most general theoretical level: even if a variety of ways to heaven can be specified, that still leaves the question of those who do not follow any of those routes. It did, however, have very considerable practical potential indeed, which was important to Locke in

[39] J. A. I. Champion, *The Pillars of Priestcraft Shaken*, Cambridge (1991); P. Harrison, '*Religion*' *and the Religions in the English Enlightenment*, Cambridge (1990), passim, esp. 77–85; M. A. Goldie, 'Priestcraft and Politics', unpublished typescript.
[40] Goldie, 'Priestcraft'; Dryden, *Absalom*, lines 1–2; Locke, *Letters*, passim.
[41] *Works*, VI, 442–53; *Correspondence*, IV, 1465; 1499; 1473; 1485.

the 1690s when Proast was pressing the case of enforcing the recognised 'true religion'. If a core of beliefs, or a core belief, can be specified, with other beliefs identified as all being possible ways to heaven, then the practical question of who is to be tolerated even on the grounds of those who claim the right to enforce the 'true' religion simply has considerably less purchase. Here it is important to distil Christianity into its most refined essence in order to remove many arguments for persecution. There is even the second possibility that objectively false belief may be held without this preventing salvation, perhaps but not necessarily as long as some core belief(s) are also held; this would involve the maintenance of only one 'true' religion, but the possibility of several ways to heaven. Whereas the first form of argument leads to specifying a minimal creed, the second thus leads to elevating sincerity in the search for truth over the attainment of truth, perhaps but not necessarily in tandem with support of a minimal creed. Locke canvassed the latter form of argument both in the *Essay* and in a 1698 manuscript entitled 'Error'. The specification of a minimal creed surely recalled for Locke the works of Croft, Popple, van Limborch and le Clerc which had interested him in the 1680s, among other reasons, precisely for their desire to differentiate fundamental truths of Scripture from other propositions, by concentration on the gospels and Christ's own preaching rather than the apostolic epistles, and by specification of the only essential belief of Christianity being that Jesus was the Christ, a text that van Limborch interpreted as not requiring belief that Jesus was God.

By 1695 this minimal belief was, however, being defended by unitarians in England not merely from many trinitarians desirous of imposing a more extensive meaning of that article and often also a more extensive creed, but also from a growing number of deists who depicted Christ's mission solely in terms of republishing natural law and not as preaching a minimal creed. While many limited their attacks on priestcraft to heathen practices and beliefs (including some adopted by the Christians), some attacks involved a full-scale assertion of deism, treating 'all mysteries in religion as the contrivances of priests', as Burnet sorrowfully noted.

The first half of Nye's *Discourse* was devoted to setting out the content of natural religion known by reason against atheism and scepticism, but the second half was equally significantly devoted to showing the advantages of revealed religion specifically against the deists. Nye argued with the deists that all men could attain to knowledge of all duties of morality by natural reason. Christianity was an added light offered to some men, particularly useful at the moment that it was offered because of the degenerate state of mankind before Christ. For Nye, however, the faith required by Christianity was faith in God the Creator and in the Lord Christ 'as the Messias; which is to say, the anointed and the Sent of God'.

He argued that various testimonies showed that Christ was divinely sent, particularly the miracles that he had done and which the Apostles after him had been enabled to do by the Holy Ghost, but also the fulfilment of scriptural prophecies, the 'Sincerity' evident in Holy Scripture, and the fact that the most probable explanation of the world was that given by Scripture.[42]

There is a letter of friendly criticism on the *Discourse* by William Popple, written to an unnamed correspondent, most probably Locke since it came to lodge among his correspondence and was endorsed by Locke 'Mr Popples Observations'. Its date was 22 May 1695. Exhibiting no more sense than had Nye that Christ had come to teach any articles of faith, or to provide a satisfactory redemption, Popple declared that 'the end of Jesus Christ's Coming into the world, was . . . only to revive, explain and enforce those general Laws of Nature, which God had laid upon all men from the beginning. And from thence I conclude, that no Commandment of his can properly be called new.' The ground of such obligations was in 'the nature of things, and in the relation in which we stand towards God and towards one another'. Nye had urged that miracles testified to the divine mission of Christ. Popple declared that by showing his promotion of the law of nature men 'therein infallibly demonstrate[d]' the divine authority of Christ. For Popple, it was simply not necessary to establish this divine authority separately. The test of all new precepts was simple: whether they promoted 'a greater reverence to God, and greater Good-will to our Neighbours? Those I think are the only foundations of Piety and Virtue. And Piety and Virtue, I am sure, are the only foundations of our true happiness.'[43]

Among Locke's manuscripts are three pages of undated friendly suggestions for alterations to the *Discourse* for its publication. In describing the advantage from preaching to moral behaviour in the world – emphasising that morality was often ignored in the corruption of men before Christ – Nye had declared that without preaching 'the Christian religion had come to nothing before now'. Locke's note described this as 'A dangerous saying and well to be considered unlesse the Author will by this one sentence make all that he hath said insignificant to the Deists'. Arguing against the Deists was Nye's stated intention throughout the second half of the *Discourse*, and even on the title-page of the work itself; Locke's comment indicates that he (Locke) was thinking about ways of arguing against the Deists, and that he was probably thinking about this issue in early to mid-1695.

Locke had long been familiar with the deistic arguments of Herbert of Cherbury, citing them in the *Essay* itself, and he was very probably familiar

---

[42] Burnett, *History*, II, 649 cited in Goldie 'Priestcraft'. Nye, *Discourse*, passim. Cf. Waldron, 'Locke', 69–70.
[43] *Correspondence*, IV, 1906.

with the arguments of Charles Blount, Herbert's most important deistic follower in England before John Toland. Blount's thought became particularly influential in the year of his death, 1693, with publication of his *Oracles of Reason*, and several of his books were republished in 1695 together with a collected *Miscellaneous Works*. Locke possessed several of Blount's books, including the *Works*, by the time of his death, and possibly several years earlier. He certainly knew (and became friendly with) a number of Deists during the later 1690s, including Matthew Tindall and Anthony Collins. At some point in 1695 Locke noted that Acosta was the 'father of the deists'; he possessed Acosta's argument that there had been 'no need of revelation at all', because it was printed – with a refutation – in van Limborch's *De Veritate*, which Locke had commented upon during composition.[44]

Locke had met John Toland, who had come recommended to Locke by le Clerc and van Limborch, and whom Locke initially thought 'ingenious'. In 1696 Toland published *Christianity not Mysterious*, which combined Locke's epistemology with Deism by arguing that men should not accept anything which could not be confirmed by one's 'clear Perceptions' and thus should not receive as revelation any proposition above reason; his arguments could be read as challenging the acceptance of the Scriptures as revelation. Locke's epistemology came under fierce attack from Stillingfleet for this association, forcing him to distance his own arguments from those of Toland. It is quite likely that Toland had expressed deistic notions to Locke when they met, and that Locke was in part intending to reply to Toland in the *Reasonableness*. Although Locke's own manuscript notes from *Christianity Not Mysterious* were dated 1696, Locke seems to have been sent 'papers' or a 'Tract' by Toland in March 1695.[45]

Locke was to argue in both of his *Vindications* of the *Reasonableness of Christianity* that the *Reasonableness* had been 'chiefly' written for the conversion to Christianity of the Deists, a group whose name was heard in 'the pulpit and the press . . . so often'. This is extremely likely. Locke's reading of Nye's arguments against the Deists, which limited Christ's role to that of the reviver, with divine authority, of natural religion, and to the reform of ritual, and which did not mention the satisfaction or the Trinity, does suggest that Locke may have had an example of silence on the Trinity and satisfaction being a good way to answer Deists when composing the *Reasonableness*, which was itself silent on these issues. It is very difficult indeed to believe, however, that Locke did not also know that the author

---

[44] MS Locke c27, 92–3; 107r; 213; *Library*, 353–7; *Correspondence*, IV, 1657; V, 2173; VII, 3278; *Essay*, I.iii.15ff.

[45] J. Toland, *Christianity not Mysterious* (1696), passim; J. Biddle, 'Locke's Critique of Innate Principles and Toland's Deism', *Journal of the History of Ideas* 37 (1976), 410–22.

of the *Discourse*, like his correspondent Popple, was an unitarian and that
therefore one major motivation for Nye's failure to describe the Trinity
and satisfaction in the *Discourse* was disbelief in those doctrines. The same
was probably, but not definitely, true of Locke's *Reasonableness*.

IV

Locke argued in his *Vindications* that another major contemporary religious debate also influenced his composition of the *Reasonableness*. A
major nonconformist debate over justification had been started by the
republication in 1690 of the Civil-War antinomian Tobias Crisp's *Christ
Alone Exalted*. Daniel Williams, close to Richard Baxter in ecclesiological
and theological sympathies, attacked Crisp's antinomianism in *Gospel
Truth* and set out an account of justification as including repentance and
the promise of a new life, an account that was therefore markedly similar
to the accounts of justification which many of the Latitudinarians had been
advancing for many years. He was supported in print by two other old
presbyterians, John Howe and William Bates. Samuel Crisp, Tobias' son,
was joined by Isaac Chauncey, Richard Davis and Stephen Lobb in supporting Crisp's book and accusing their opponents of Arminianism. They
argued that works at most followed justification, that men were freely
justified by imputation of Christ's righteousness, and that men apprehended this righteousness by faith alone. In late 1694 and early 1695 this
debate over justification came to a head with a spate of pamphlets and the
withdrawal of the presbyterians from the Pinner's Hall lectureship that
they had formerly shared with their Independent colleagues.[46]

Confined with nonconformist ranks, this debate caused fewer waves that
the Unitarian Controversy, and it was apparently not a debate that Locke
felt to be important enough to inform le Clerc about it, in sharp contrast to
the Unitarian Controversy. Indeed, in September 1693 it was le Clerc that
wrote to Locke discussing Daniel Williams' *Gospel Truth*, which had been
sent to him by John Toland and which he had reviewed in the *Bibliothèque
Universelle* in December 1692. It is unclear when Locke became aware of
this debate, although it may even have been through le Clerc's correspondence or the *Bibliothèque*, and it is unclear which of the many works
published in this controversy Locke read – if, indeed, any. In the Preface to
the *Second Vindication of the Reasonableness of Christianity*, however,
Locke wrote of the genesis of the *Reasonableness* that 'the controversy that
made so much noise and heat amongst some of the dissenters, coming one
day accidentally into my mind, drew me, by degrees, into a stricter and

---

[46] *Works*, VII, 187–7; 158; see on this especially Wallace, 'Socinianism'.

more thorough inquiry into the question about justification'. Near to the end of the *Reasonableness* itself Locke noted that 'justification' was the 'subject of this present treatise'.[47]

In May 1695, however, approximately five months before the *Reasonableness* was published, Locke wrote to van Limborch with a long description of the *Reasonableness* that deserves to be quoted in full:

> this winter, considering diligently wherein the Christian faith consists, I thought that it ought to be drawn from the very fountains of Holy Writ, the opinions and orthodoxies of sects and systems, whatever they may be, being set aside. From an intent and careful reading of the New Testament the conditions of the New Covenant and the teaching of the Gospel became clearer to me, as it seemed to me, than the noontide light, and I am fully convinced that a sincere reader of the Gospel cannot be in doubt as to what the Christian faith is. I therefore set down my thoughts on paper, thereby the better to survey, tranquilly and at leisure, the agreement of the parts with one another, their harmony, and the foundations on which they rested.[48]

It is important to underline several points here. Locke was reiterating the claim he had made to van Limborch in the late 1680s, that he read the New Testament setting aside the opinions and orthodoxies of systems and sects. Locke has further argued that 'a sincere reader' of the gospel could not be in doubt as to the content of Christian faith. This is important because there is no suggestion that the help of the Holy Spirit was necessary to appreciate this sense of Scripture and because it contrasts to Locke's recognition in his *Third Letter On Toleration* that most people could not understand long or difficult arguments concerning Scripture. He thinks that any sincere reader could not be in doubt as to the content of 'the Christian faith'. We will see in a moment that Locke in fact based his interpretation of Scripture in the *Reasonableness* in part on the illiteracy of the Apostles and in part upon the ignorance of the bulk of mankind. Finally, and most importantly, Locke has also indicated to van Limborch, in a letter before publication of the *Reasonableness*, and thus when there was no reason for him to have misrepresented the case, that he had been composing a work which he thought set out the content of the Christian faith. Locke's descriptions in his *Second Vindication* of the *Reasonableness* as a work intended to discuss justification, like his description of it as intended to reply to Deism, was intended to deflect criticism that he had left the Trinity out of the *Reasonableness*. The implication of Locke's letter to van Limborch is that he had composed an interpretation of the content of 'the Christian faith', and not one that simply discussed justification and replied to Deism.

Locke continued his letter to van Limborch by declaring that:

[47] *Correspondence*, V, 1901.   [48] *Correspondence*, V, 1901.

when everything in this creed of mine seemed everywhere sound and conformable to the word of God I thought that the theologians . . . ought to be consulted, so that I might see what they thought about the faith. I went to Calvin, Turrettini, and others, who, I am compelled to admit, have treated that subject in such a way that I can by no means grasp what they say or what they mean; so discordant does everything in them seem to me with the sense and simplicity of the Gospel that I am unable to understand their writings, much less to reconcile them with Holy Writ.

Under the title 'Electio' in his 'Adversaria Theologica' in 1695 Locke composed a signed note which declared that 'I cannot see of what use the Doctrine of Election and Perseverance is unlesse it be to lead men into presumption and a neglect of their dutys being once perswaded that they are in a state of grace, which is a state they are told they cannot fall from.' He continued with an analysis that suggests that this note at least was composed after his reading of Calvin's *Institutes*:

For since noe body can know that he is Elected but by haveing true faith and noe body can know whan he has such a faith that he can not fall from Common and Saveing faith . . . being soe a like that he that has faith cannot distinguish whether it be such as he can fall from or noe. Vid Calv Inst 13c2 para12 Who is elected or had faith from which he cannot fall can only be know [sic] by the event at the last day and therefor is in vain talked of now till the marks of such a faith be certainly given JL.[49]

With 'better hopes' Locke declared that he had then turned to van Limborch's *Theologia Christiana* and read 'not without very great joy book V, chapter VIII, from which I perceived that one theologian was to be found for whom I am not a heretic'. The chapter of van Limborch's book was 'De Fide in Jesum Christum; ac primo de actu eius antecendente, Scientia', whose arguments were briefly discussed earlier when it was also noted that Locke had been consulted by van Limborch during the composition of the *Theologia Christiana* in 1685, that he had then made suggestions for improvements, and that he had probably at least absorbed its general lines of argument even if he had not become completely familiar with its detailed soteriological picture.

Since van Limborch was a more moderate critic of theologians than other friends of Locke like le Clerc and Furly it is possible that in his private correspondence Locke was not telling van Limborch the truth about the order of his investigation, that he had only studied the name 'theologians' after studying the Scripture. In the Preface to the *Reasonableness* itself the order was reversed: 'the little satisfaction and consistency that is to be found, in most of the systems of divinity I have met with, made me betake myself to the sole reading of the Scriptures . . . for the understanding the Christian Religion'. In his private correspondence, then,

---

[49] *Correspondence*, V, 1901; MS Locke c43, 44.

Locke gives the impression of checking in works by specific theologians, including Calvin, the interpretation to which he had already come, and even of being somewhat surprised with the distance between his interpretation and that of Calvin and Turretini; the preface to the *Reasonableness* makes it seem rather that Locke was unhappy with the interpretations that he had found in the works of various unnamed theologians and had turned to Scripture as a result.

It is not possible to arbitrate between these accounts. Whichever order of reading Locke had undertaken – of the Scripture and then of various theologians or vice versa – it appears extremely likely that Locke's notes in his 'Adversaria Theologica' reflect a process of general interpretation of the Christian faith, as Locke had described to van Limborch, which may have become focused in Locke's mind upon questions of justification and arguments to oppose Deism, but which was started with a much broader remit. It also appears very likely indeed that Locke's many notes from the unitarian works discussed earlier in this chapter were taken during this process of investigation and provided a very significant part of his reading in this period. The 'Adversaria' commenced with a broad list of theological topics, suggesting that Locke had intended a wide survey of Scripture, but its notes rapidly became heavily concentrated on consideration of the Trinity and satisfaction, and far more extensively concentrated on that issue than they were on justification, although there was at least one note directly on justification recorded on one of the later pages of the 'Adversaria'.[50] Despite Locke's later reasons for the absence of the Trinity from the *Reasonableness*, it is highly probable that that silence was the result of lengthy and detailed consideration of the Trinity, and that in issuing the *Reasonableness* Locke was consciously willing to give succour to the unitarian side in the Unitarian Controversy, albeit anonymously.

[50] *Reasonableness*, 3; MS Locke c43, 1–46; these notes on Rom. 3:27, entitled 'Lex Operum/ Lex Fidei', were placed immediately before his notes from the *Considerations* assaulting the doctrine of the satisfaction.

From the Reasonableness to the Paraphrase: an unitarian heretic

I

The opening pages of the *Reasonableness* straightforwardly opposed original sin. Locke declared it 'obvious to any one, who reads the New Testament, that the doctrine of redemption . . . is founded upon the supposition of Adam's fall'. It was therefore necessary to consider what was lost by Adam in order to discover what Christ had restored to men. Locke declared that identifying Adam's loss required a 'diligent and unbiassed search' of Scripture because the 'two extremes, that men run into on this point, either on the one hand shook the foundations of all religion, or, on the other, made christianity almost nothing'. Some 'would have all Adam's posterity doomed to eternal infinite punishment, for the transgression of Adam, whom millions had never heard of, and no one had authorised to transact for him, or be his representative'. Others – surely Deists such as Acosta – had found this inconsistent with 'the justice or goodness of the great and infinite God' and so had 'thought that there was no redemption necessary', making Jesus Christ 'nothing but the restorer and preacher of pure natural religion'. Locke condemned these last interpreters of doing 'violence to the whole tenour of the New Testament'.

For Locke, it was 'visible' to the 'unbiassed' that what Adam had lost was 'bliss and immortality'. The declaration of 1 Cor. 15:22 that 'in Adam all die' was interpreted by some as 'a state of guilt, wherein not only he, but all his posterity was so involved, that every one descended of him deserved endless torment, in hell fire'. This was for Locke a 'strange way of understanding a law which requires the plainest and directest words, that by death is meant eternal life in misery'. These words were also said to describe Adam's posterity as in a state 'of necessary sinning', which for Locke was 'a yet harder sense of the word death than the other'. It would have been 'strange' if death had been put to mean the 'corruption of human nature in his posterity'. Locke declared simply that 'Every one's sin is charged upon himself only.' Opposing not merely the view that Adam's fall resulted in the necessity of all men afterwards sinning, but also the

414

belief that the wicked suffered eternal punishment, Locke wrote that 'I must confess, by death here, I can understand nothing but a ceasing to be.' The wicked suffered an exquisite torment before death as punishment for their sins, and they suffered this in an eternal fire, as one of Locke's theological manuscripts made clear, but after that they ceased to be; the fire was eternal, but not their torment.[1]

Loss of bliss and natural immortality was not an injury to men who came after Adam because they had had no right to anything or to eternal life; they received the world and dominion over the creatures as gifts of God and therefore had no right to complain about the requirement of labour. He then joined to this analysis of the results of Adam's fall an argument that was in a sense an extension of his 1680 argument in his journal note on God's goodness and justice, agreeing with the deist and unitarian opponents of Calvinism that a necessity of sinning and thus of eternal misery was not an acceptable interpretation of Scripture *because* it would have involved an injury which Adam's successors had not deserved, and was not consistent with the notions of God's goodness and justice that men were said to derive from revelation or from reason. Opposing equally the Deists, however, Locke declared that it was by belief in an article of faith that had been revealed by Christ, that Jesus was the Christ, that men could attain eternal life without perfect obedience to natural law, and so Jesus was not merely the reviver or 'preacher of natural religion'.[2]

Locke had thus opposed original sin and the eternity of punishment of the wicked in the *Reasonableness* in a way directly parallel to major arguments of the Socinians, and opposed not merely to Calvinists and Deists but also to Arminians and Latitudinarians. These arguments were to help to provoke many charges of 'Socinianism' over the next few years. The accusations that Locke was 'all over Socinianiz'd', particularly in the three works of the extreme Calvinist John Edwards, *Some Thoughts Concerning the Several Causes of Atheism* (1695), *Socinianism Unmask'd* (1696) and *The Socinian Creed* (1697), however, focused even more upon his omission of the satisfaction and the Trinity from the *Reasonableness*. Enumerating the advantages brought to men by Christ, Locke did not include Christ's satisfaction for sin. He declared that he did 'not remember' that Christ ever assumed the name of priest 'or mentions anything relating to his priesthood'. Even van Limborch criticised the *Reasonableness* for its failure to include Christ's priesthood and thus any notion of Christ's satisfaction for men's sin. Edwards declared that Locke 'gave proof of his being Socinianiz'd by his utter silence about Christ's satisfying for us, and purchasing salvation by virtue of his death'. Even more serious for Locke's accusers

---

[1] *Reasonableness*, 4–7; *Paraphrase*, II, 679ff.   [2] *Reasonableness*, 7ff.

was the possibility that behind this silence on the satisfaction lay a disbelief in the Trinity. They feared that for Locke Christ had not come to satisfy for man because he was not a person of the co-equal, co-eternal and consubstantial Godhead, but instead only a divinely inspired prophet who had come to teach morality and to offer incentives for its practice.[3]

Throughout the *Reasonableness*, Locke was silent about the Trinity in the midst of the 'Unitarian Controversy'. He supported Socinian explications of the Bible more overtly in explaining the purpose of John's Gospel as showing that Jesus was the Messiah, ignoring its supposedly central purpose of proclaiming the Trinity, and not even mentioning John 1:1 – as Edwards forcefully pointed out. Every text that trinitarians usually interpreted as supporting the Trinity that Locke mentioned in the *Reasonableness* was not interpreted in a way that included any support for the Trinity. The phrase 'Son of God' was explained as indicating 'the Messiah' but not as signifying that Christ was God. The union of Jesus Christ and God was described as 'such an union that God operates in him and by him'. Like the Socinians, Locke declared that Jesus 'being conceived in the womb of a virgin (that had not known man) by the immediate power of God, was properly the Son of God'. This paralleled the sonship of Christ with that of Adam in an interpretation that located the cause of Christ's sonship in his birth rather than in his eternal generation.[4]

Locke's awareness of the 'Unitarian Controversy' in his correspondence, reading and note-taking shows that Locke was aware of the importance of these silences and assertions. In the light of these silences, his manner of interpretation of texts used to support the Trinity, his extensive unitarian reading and his friendships with various unitarians, it is very likely that Locke held some form of unitarian belief about Christ when writing the *Reasonableness*, as well as broadly Socinian understandings of original sin, the satisfaction, and the eternity of punishments not being the eternity of any individual's punishment.[5]

Locke's two *Vindications* of the *Reasonableness* in 1695 and 1697 against the accusations of Socinianism added very little in direct argument about the Trinity, satisfaction or original sin. Locke refused to proffer any trinitarian sentiments in either *Vindication* of the *Reasonableness*, describing these as doctrines which Edwards had 'collect[ed] out of' the beginning of John's Gospel. He argued that his description of Son of God to mean

---

[3] See my 'Locke and Socinianism'.

[4] J. Edwards, *Some Thoughts Concerning the Several Causes of Atheism* (1695), 113 and passim; idem, *Socinianism Unmask'd* (1696), 24, 28, 100, 108 and passim; idem, *The Socinian Creed* (1697), postscript; *Correspondence*, VI, 2222; *Reasonableness*, 113; 101–7; and passim.

[5] See above pp. 389ff.

only Messiah and not that Christ was God was supported by the Bible, and cited Simon Patrick's *Jesus and the Resurrection* (by its subtitle, the 'witnesses to Christianity'), and a sermon by the 'never sufficiently admired and valued' 'ornament of our church and every way eminent prelate' Archbishop Tillotson, as also interpreting the phrase Son of God in that way. In the process, however, he excised or ignored the support that Patrick and Tillotson both gave to the Trinity. He pointed out that the Apostles' Creed omitted all declarations of the Trinity and noted that the Church of England baptised on the basis of belief in the Apostles' Creed alone.[6]

Locke argued that his description of the restoration to life by Christ in the *Reasonableness* 'sounded somewhat like' or was usually 'taken to imply' satisfaction for sin, equivocations that John Milner scorned as Socinian in *An Account of Mr Lock's Religion* in 1700. At one point Locke declared that there was 'not any such word in any one of the epistles, or other books of the New Testament, in my bible, as satisfying, or satisfaction made by our Saviour' and that he could not therefore have put it into his book on 'Christianity as delivered in the Scripture'. Describing the attributes of God seen in the redemption, he included 'wisdom, goodness, mercy and love' but did not mention justice. Christ's motivation for enduring the cross was described as 'plain from Scripture . . . for the joy set before him' – that is, the joy of gaining a kingdom, not of paying for sin. Locke asserted in the two *Vindications* that the *Reasonableness* had not included 'one word of Socinianism', conveniently ignoring the fact that he had been charged with Socinianism for a series of significant omissions. He simultaneously attacked the Socinians for approaching Scripture with their own doctrinal prejudices and for zeal for their own 'orthodoxy', although he did not specify any points at all where he thought that their scriptural analysis was erroneous. The focus of Locke's reply to the accusation of Socinianism was that he had derived his thought from Scripture alone and not from any systems of theology.[7]

In the light of the reading of unitarian works evidenced in his manuscripts and bibles and very highly probably undertaken before and during composition of the *Reasonableness*, this argument was somewhat disingenuous, nowhere more so than when Locke declared that he had not 'read a page' of the works of Socinus or Crell. The mental reservation in the case of Socinus was presumably that he had read the summary of Socinus' thought by his amanuensis, Volkel, and in the case of Crell that he had read much more than a page.[8] During the time that Locke wrote the *Reasonableness* he had probably approached Scripture with Socinian

---

[6] *Vindication* and *Second Vindication* in *Works* (1801), VI, passim, esp. 166–72; 362, 365–74; 416–17; 270–8; 281; 179ff.
[7] *Ibid.*, 267, 374–5; 417–18; 228; 235; 166 and passim.   [8] *Ibid.*, passim, esp. 290ff.; 359.

works, or at least English unitarian tracts, in hand as well as in mind. We have seen that Locke's thought had, however, been pointing in the direction of Socinian views about several issues before any evidence of his having any Socinian beliefs, and on others his thought was misinterpreted when it was accused of being Socinian. Locke's repeated and significant assaults upon the credulous acceptance of scriptural interpretations from commentators and his support for seeking the 'plain' meanings of Scripture both went back many years.

Locke was a surprisingly flexible interpreter of Scripture when he did examine it in detail in the decade after 1695, even altering his views on a number of biblical texts that were significant to some of the main arguments of the *Reasonableness* of 1695 and its two *Vindications* of 1695 and 1697, when he wrote the *Paraphrase* in the late 1690s and early 1700s. On one important interpretation, on the mortality of men after Adam, Locke's view apparently changed even during composition of the *Reasonableness* itself. In the mid-and-late 1690s, then, Locke was very probably 'Socinian' in terms of the complexion of his actual beliefs on original sin, the satisfaction, and very probably the Trinity, and in terms of significant influences of reading and friends upon his coming to these beliefs. He was also, however, not a Socinian by any simple derivation of thought or crude typology, and had reason both from his own opposition to systematic theology and from his genuine desire and attempts in practice to identify the teaching of the Scripture itself to think that he was not thus 'Socinian'.[9]

II

Although the 'Unitarian Controversy' died down a little in the later 1690s, particularly after the new archbishop of Canterbury, Thomas Tenison, discouraged debate in 1695, it was still the subject of a very large number of works published between 1695 and 1704. Locke continued to follow both sides of the controversy, coming to possess among other works the future Deist Matthew Tindall's *Reflections upon Edward Fowler's Certain Propositions in Defence of the Trinity* and Tindall's *Letter to the Reverend Clergy concerning the Trinity*, Gilbert Clerke and Samuel Crell's *Tractatus Tres*, Thomas Smalbroke's *Judgement of the Fathers Concerning . . . the Trinity*, John Smith's *Designed End to the Socinian Controversy* and Thomas Emlyn's *Humble Inquiry into the Scripture Account of Jesus Christ*, the last of which saw the development of unitarianism among the presbyterians. In addition to the vindications of the Trinity in the assaults

[9] See the preface, 'An essay for understanding St Paul's epistles by consulting St Paul himself', to the *Paraphrase* in *ibid.*, I, 103ff.; and cf. II, 665–6.

upon his *Reasonableness* by John Edwards and John Milner, Locke also obtained the rather more restrained defences of the Trinity by John Howe, Pierre Allix, Thomas Beverly, Francis Gastrell and Joseph Boyse.[10] Locke's correspondence and notes show that he read a significant number of these works. He continued to be visited by and correspond with a number of unitarians, including not merely Popple, Firmin, Beresford and Newton but also Samuel Crell, grandson of John Crell, who stayed with Locke at Oates longer than originally intended because Locke found him so congenial.[11]

It was in these years that the charge of Socinianism was increasingly directed against Locke's own works. In addition to the assaults of Edwards already mentioned, Jean Gailheard and the Grand Jury of Middlesex also attacked the *Reasonableness* as favouring Socinianism in 1697 and Stillingfleet lent his episcopal weight to the accusation that Locke's works favoured Socinianism, while Stillingfleet's works unsurprisingly turned increasingly towards questioning whether Locke believed in the Trinity. In his replies Locke was unwilling simply to state that he believed in the Trinity, only denying that he had ever *publicly* denied the Trinity. Locke's unwillingness to defuse what was becoming a very serious accusation of Socinianism, an accusation directed not merely at the anonymous *Reasonableness* but also at the *Essay*, by a simple declaration of belief in the Trinity in either of the two *Vindications* of the *Reasonableness* or in his three *Letters* and *Replies* to Stillingfleet, led many of his contemporaries to conclude that Locke at the least had unitarian sympathies. Modern scholars have endorsed that judgement. Locke's public silence over the Trinity has, however, generally prohibited them from ascribing a definite anti-trinitarian complexion to Locke's theology.[12]

---

[10] Locke, *Library*, entries 2659–60; 2657; 1165–6; 2787–90; 1526; 76; 299; 475; 1214; 2912; 2905; 3163; 2722; 142–142a; 2069; 543–4; 785; 2988–92; 3017–20; 3022; 2702.

[11] *Correspondence*, V, 1865; 2195; VI, 2216; 2225; VII, 2775; MS Locke c27, 107r.

[12] Locke, *A Letter to the Reverend Edward Lord Bishop of Worcester* in *Works* (1801), IV, 67–9; 147ff. For the unitarians' claims about the Trinity being palpable nonsense, see Tindall, *Letter to the Reverend Clergy* (1694), 22. M. Montouri, *John Locke on Toleration and the Unity of God*, Amsterdam (1983), 175–219, argues that Locke's comments to van Limborch on the unity of God (*Correspondence*, VI, appendix II) clearly commit him to an unitarian position. This seems very doubtful since trinitarians accept the unity and omnipresence of God in much the same way as Locke does in these letters, arguing that there was no division of place between Christ and God the Father but a difference between begetter and begotten. His difficulties in seeing how there could be two 'beings' with a unity of will and understanding and action and place may, however, point in a unitarian direction. See also E. Stillingfleet, *The Bishop of Worcester's Answer to Mr Locke's Second Letter* (1698), 4–5; *Correspondence*, VI, 2518; John Milner, *An Account of Mr Lock's Religion* (1700), 34ff.; Yolton, *Way of Ideas*, 10; Reedy, *Bible*, 138; M. Firpo, 'John Locke e il Socinianismo', *Rivista Storica Italiana* 92 (1980), 35–124; McLachlan, *Religious Opinions*, 69–114. As a general point about much Christian theology, patristic, early modern unitarian and modern unitarian disbelief in the satisfaction very often

Locke never committed himself in print to an unequivocal antitrinitarian position before or during composition of the *Reasonableness* or its *Vindications*. There is, however, an entry in one of Locke's manuscript books which sets out a Socinian view of Christ as a divinely inspired prophet who had come to teach morality, but not as God. This is entitled 'Some General Reflections on the Beginning of St. John's Gospel'. Of the two scholars who have so far very briefly discussed this manuscript, M. S. Johnson apparently simply presumes that it was by Locke, and Arthur Wainwright declares that 'it is unclear to what extent Locke was responsible for [its] contents' and then restricts his analysis to one line.[13]

These 'General Reflections' are written almost entirely in the hand of Sylvanus Brownover, Locke's amanuensis, but have emendations, Greek words and one marginal addition (among many marginal additions by Brownover) in a hand that resembles Locke's own hand. In this combination they are similar to many manuscripts of Locke's composition that Brownover copied for him in the 1680s and 1690s, including the 1685 'draft C' of the *Essay* itself, the final draft of his 1692 *Some Considerations*, part of the 1695 draft of *Further Considerations*, 'Of Ethick in General', and a copy of the *Essays on the Law of Nature*. There are a significant number of arguments in the 'General Reflections' which parallel the arguments of the *Reasonableness*, and one that parallels a major theme of Locke's ecclesiological writings. Some of the sources cited in this manuscript – such as Patrick's *Jesus and the Resurrection* – are cited in the *Vindications*; others are of works that Locke can clearly be shown to have read. The 'General Reflections' discussed at length the context of composition of John's Gospel, very frequently indeed the subject of Locke's many entries in his bibles and notebooks from Socinian and unitarian works, and from patristic studies. The role of Cerinthus was a central topic of debate in the 'Unitarian Controversy' since for many trinitiarians John's Gospel had been written to confute Cerinthus' heresy. Beresford's and le Clerc's correspondence with Locke discussed Cerinthus. Beresford had hoped in early 1695 that Locke would produce 'more than a private Consideration' of the issue, seemingly knowing that Locke had produced a private consideration. This also seems very likely due to the specific accusations of Edwards about Locke's failure to allege in the *Reasonableness* that the central purpose of John's Gospel was revelation of the Trinity on the basis of John 1:1.[14]

proceeded from prior disbelief in the Trinity; this is thus likely in Locke's case, but it cannot be proven.

[13] MS Locke e17, 175–223; Johnson, *Locke*, 150–1; *Paraphrase*, I, 39n.1.
[14] MA 998 Pierpoint Morgan Library, New York, 7, 14.16, 21, 24, 36–7, 45, 48, 65, 67, etc.; MS Locke d2; MS Locke b3, 39–46, 62ff.; MS Locke f30, 122ff.; MS Locke d3; MS Locke

For these reasons – that the 'General Reflections' were definitely in Brownover's handwriting and appear to have some words and one emendation by Locke; that that was a characteristic form of manuscript for Locke's own writings; the location of the text in Locke's manuscript book; the citation of books possessed and read by Locke; the substantial and significant reiteration in the manuscript of a number of arguments used by Locke in the *Reasonableness* and its *Vindications*; and his interest in the subject, both generally and specifically – it appears probable that Locke was the author of 'Some General Reflections'. As such, it would be the only surviving occasion on which Locke committed distinctively Socinian views of the Trinity to paper.

That the 'General Reflections' were by Locke cannot be shown conclusively. It is possible that they were copied by Brownover from another author, even though it is unlike almost all of the very few occasions when he copied others' works for Locke's perusal in not containing an indication that this was being done; even though there was no indication of such a manuscript being sent to Locke or discussed by Locke; and even though a substantial reading of the arguments of Locke's unitarian friends and of contemporary unitarian tracts has not turned up any closely similar text and has found occasions on which Locke's unitarian friends composed arguments that were discordant with or directly antithetical to the argument of the 'General Reflections'. More generally, Locke usually refrained from discussing commentators upon the Bible in favour of interpretation of the Bible itself, and in his replies to Stillingfleet Locke declared that he was insufficiently learned in patristics to debate the Trinity. That reply to Stillingfleet, however, was a natural polemical argument to make in an attempt to deflect Stillingfleet's persistent questioning of Locke's beliefs. The 'General Reflections' are an account of trinitarianism perverting the interpretation of John 1:1, they necessarily therefore focus on the writings of the Fathers as well as John's own intentions. Locke's notes indicate that he had undertaken a significant reading of the Fathers themselves, and Locke was willing to discuss their views extensively where this was necessary, doing so in his reply to Proast on miracles. On one point at least his *Paraphrase* has recently been claimed by its editor, Arthur Wainwright, to differ from

c28, 52–60, 119–21; 146–21; MS Locke c34, 35, 51, 142–3; *Vindication* in *Works*, VII, 179–80. The confluences of Locke's arguments in the manuscript and other works, in addition to that of extensive argument from the phraseology Son of God and Messiah in both the *Reasonableness* and his manuscript, and citation of Patrick and Tillotson on both in both, include the argument in 'Some General Reflections' that ceremonies that had been kept prudently at the Reformation to bring over converts should now be removed prudently to bring over converts to the Church of England, a parallel to the 'Critical Notes'. The works cited in the manuscript, by such as Tertullian, Grotius and Vorstius, were largely of works that Locke can be shown to have read.

the 'General Reflections' in expressing a belief about Christ that stands between Arianism and Socinianism rather than being Socinian. This point will be discussed in the next section of this chapter, when it will be suggested that it is not entirely clear that there is such a contradiction between the 'General Reflections' and the *Paraphrase*, and that even if it is accepted that such a contradiction existed there is reason to believe that Locke had come to the view stated in the *Paraphrase* only during composition of that work. While it cannot be shown beyond a significant possibility of doubt that the 'General Reflections' was indeed composed by Locke, these objections do not seem to this author to be substantial enough to counter the reasons given above for thinking that it was probably composed by Locke.[15]

'The beginning of St. John's Gospel being the sheild of the Trinitarians', the first sentence of this manuscript declared, 'I design to clear it by some general reflections.' The manuscript attacked the accounts of John's trinitarian intent given by several of the Fathers who recorded 'wonderful deeds' to make people think that John had been divinely inspired to write 'concerning the Eternal Divinity of Christ against Cerinthus'. There was, however, no need 'of so much . . . labour to bring to light a Mystery which Plato himself tho a Heathen, had easily and very clearly explained'; Christ's divinity was unknown to all of the Evangelists; and 'Cerinthus's Heresy . . . did not consist, as it is now a days believed in the denyal of the Eternal Divinity of Christ . . . Cerinthus maintained that eternal Divinity.' According to the 'General Reflections', Cerinthus had believed that Jesus was 'the Son of Joseph and Mary as other men are only that he was more Excellent than they in holyness and wisdom' and that 'after his Baptisme Christ came down from heaven into him'. Cerinthus was thus 'the first Author of all their new doctrine concerning the Divinity and pre-existence of Christ'. The only difference between them was that Cerinthus maintained that 'heavenly person came down to Jesus only at his baptism' while trinitarians assigned 'that miraculous Incarnation to the very moment of his conception'. If John was writing against Cerinthus, he therefore intended to show 'that God, and the word which made the world are one and the same thing . . . that when God was about to create the world, he made use of his word or Command . . . but . . . that word was internal and essential to him, being his power, one of his chiefe attributes . . . not a person distinguished from God as Cerinthus and the whole school of Plato pretend'. God had sent a 'bringer of the promise of life', Christ, who was

---

[15] Cf. MS Locke d10, 177–8; Locke, *Vindication* in *Works* (1801), VII, 179–80. Although Brownover left Locke's service in 1696 he continued to visit Locke after that date.

'with respect to his office, the true word of life . . . in the world as God's interpreter and the teacher of men'.[16]

John was writing to show that 'Jesus the Son of Mary was already the Christ the word and the light before John had baptized him'. Interpreting 'apud deum' in a manner similar to several English unitarians, including Biddle's notes recorded in Locke's 'Adversaria Theologica', and to Socinus and Schlichting, the manuscript argued that Christ had been taken up into heaven in a pre-Ascension ascension. In order to oppose Cerinthus' views John had only needed to assign 'the beginning of Christ's Installation in the Office of Messiah to that time wherein he was taken up into heaven'. The 'antients' suggested a simpler motivation than the need to expound the Trinity against Cerinthus. Eusebius, in an account that we have already seen that Locke partially copied into one of his bibles, was 'Expresse' about the need for John to relate 'what our Saviour had done in the beginning of his preaching'.[17]

John did not say that he was writing to prove the Trinity. Rather, 'These things says he are written, that ye may believe that Jesus is the Christ the Son of God.' 'If therefor', the manuscript continued in a passage redolent of the *Reasonableness of Christianity*, 'St John designed to prove that Jesus is the Christ the Son of God as it appears by the end of his Gospel, 'tis manifest he had no other scope in the beginning of the same Gospel and consequently the word is the same with the Christ the Son of God; the Messiah; the King of Israel.' The manuscript cited in support, as Locke had in the *Vindications*, Simon Patrick's *Jesus and the Resurrection Justified by Witnesses in Heaven and Earth* (1677), conveniently – as Locke in the *Vindications* – excising support for the Trinity in part of the passage he was citing from: ' "The Son of God" says he, is a name in the holy Stile not so much expressing his nature as his authority and Soveraigne power.' Once it was granted that Christ and Son of God were 'termes of the same signification' it was, according to the manuscript, 'evident' that St John had

not writ his Gospel to make us believe that Jesus is the Supreme God, or an eternal Spirit of the same nature with his Father but to instruct us in that essential truth that Jesus is the Messiah or if you will the Son of God in a sense of office and commission.[18]

---

[16] MS Locke e17, 175–86. Johnson argues (*Locke*, 150–1) that the manuscript was not Socinian because it suggested that he had a pre-existent divine mission, although not pre-existent as a person. Whatever many modern unitarians believe, this was a view accepted by many seventeenth-century Socinians.

[17] MS Locke e17, 187–92; cf. G. Williams 'The Confessio Fidei of *Jonas Schlicting*' in L. Szczucki (ed.), *Socinianism*, Warsaw, 1983, 108–9.

[18] MS Locke e17, 192–4; S. Patrick, *Jesus and the Resurrection* (1677), 8–9.

It was 'not without reason that St John says that the word was in the beginning'. Had he intended to teach an eternal Divinity 'he would have said in the time past that the word was God. He would undoubtedly have exprest himself more emphatically, thus from all Eternity the word is God, from all eternity it was with God.'[19]

III

Between 1699 and 1704 Locke composed a series of paraphrases on the epistles of St Paul which were gathered together and published post-humously and anonymously as *A Paraphrase Upon the Epistles of St Paul to the Romans, Galatians, Ephesians and Colossians* in 1707.[20] Representatively, the biblical text of Romans 1:3–4 spoke of 'his Son Jesus Christ our Lord, which was made of the seed of David according to the flesh / And declared to be the Son of God with power, according to the Spirit of holiness, by the resurrection from the dead'. Many commentators interpreted this contrast of the flesh and the spirit of holiness as referring to the 'union of the two natures' in Christ, to use Luther's phrase, and as indicating the necessity of both of these natures to salvation, Christ's divinity possessing the righteousness which was conveyed to men by his humanity, as Calvin emphasised in his commentary. Locke paraphrased the text without avowing a divine nature in Christ:

concerning his Son Jesus Christ our Lord, who according to the flesh, ie as to the body which he took in the womb of the blessed virgin his mother, was of the posterity and linage of David, according to the spirit of holyness ie as to that more pure and spiritual part, which in him over-ruled all, and kept even his frail flesh holy and Spotless from the least taint of sin and was of an other extraction with most mighty power declared to be the son of god by his resurrection.

---

[19] MS Locke e17, 197–8.
[20] References in this chapter are to the excellent edition of the *Paraphrase* by A. Wainwright, including all references to the explanatory notes, but they are given by biblical text so that other editions of the *Paraphrase* can be consulted. Cf. Rom. 3:24; Rom. 5:12 and its explanatory note for contrast with Calvin and others; contents 5:12–19 and explanatory note. Locke also paraphrased Rom. 3:25 as speaking of Jesus as the 'propitiatory seat', the way in which God had spoken of redemption, and not as a 'propitiation', which would imply payment, and of God 'passing over' sins, not as receiving payment for them. His paraphrases of and notes upon 1 Cor. 15:35–50 declared that men *could* be raised in bodies 'of very different constitutions and qualityes than they had before' culminating in his paraphrase of 1 Cor. 15:50, which reiterated the theme of his 'Adversaria' note, describing Paul as declaring that they would not be raised in identical bodies, saying in answer to his 'Brethren to satisfie those that aske with what bodys the dead shall come, that we shall not at the resurrection have such bodys as we have now. For flesh and blood cannot enter into the kingdom which the saints shall inherit in heaven: Nor are such fleeting corruptible things as our present bodies fitted to that state of immutable incorruptibility.' See 1 Cor. 15:35–50, especially 1 Cor. 15:35, 38–39, 42, 50, and explanatory notes by Wainwright.

One of Locke's notes expanded that the spirit of holiness meant 'that more spiritual part he was in him, which by divine extraction he had immediately from God'.[21]

At no point in the *Paraphrase* did Locke give any support for the Trinity. In one extended footnote in the *Paraphrase*, however, Locke interpreted two texts that were the subject of debate between Socinians, Arians and trinitarians in a way that seems to imply that Christ was pre-existent as a person to Jesus. These texts were discussed in a note to the interpretation of Eph. 1:10 'That in the dispensation of the fulness of times he might gather together in one all things in Christ, both which are in heaven, and which are on earth, even in him'. Locke noted that the Greek for this passage meant to 'recollect or reduce' all heads of a discourse under 'one Head'. Developing from this philological point, he identified this head as Christ, and that it was 'plain in Sacred Scripture, that Christ at first had the Rule and Supremacy over all, and was Head over all. See Col.i.15–17 and Heb.i.8.' Locke located this headship before the Fall of Satan, which clearly predated the birth of Jesus. Locke declared that Christ was 're-instated' in this headship after his victory over Satan at his resurrection.[22]

This discussion is important both for the interpretation of Locke's final views on Christ, and because if it indicates that Christ was a pre-existent person to Jesus then it would contradict the Socinianism of the 'General Reflections'. It will therefore be necessary to examine it very closely. In an excellent recent edition of the *Paraphrase*, Arthur Wainwright declares this note to be an 'unequivocal declaration of Christ's pre-existence' as a 'distinct person'. It is quite possible that, as Wainwright argues, Locke came at the end of his life to believe that Christ was a pre-existent person to Jesus.

---

[21] *Paraphrase*, Rom. 1:3–4. M. Luther, *Lectures on Romans*, Library of Christian Classics, XV, ed. W. Pauck (1961), 12–13; J. Calvin, *Commentaries on the Epistles of St Paul to the Romans*, transl. J. Owen, Edinburgh (1849), 43. Wainwright correctly notes that Locke's interpretation of this text was different from that of Biddle recorded in his Bible, which referred to Christ's holy spiritual body after the Resurrection, and argues that Locke's interpretation was like that of Hammond, who interpreted the spiritual part as opposed to flesh. However, Hammond – as Wainwright quotes – talked of the spiritual part 'in respect of that other nature in him called his eternal spirit'. Locke's comment did not refer to an eternal nature. Wainwright correctly notes that Locke's usage of 'declared' is neutral on the question of when Christ was appointed Son of God, being consistent with the belief that Jesus is the Son of God before the resurrection; if Locke had used 'appointed' by the resurrection this would have implied that he was not the 'Son of God' until the resurrection. This does not mean, however, that Locke was not Socinian – Locke clearly believed that Christ's sonship was from his extraordinary birth by the Spirit of God, but that was not necessarily a trinitarian view; *Paraphrase*, Rom. 9:5; 1 Cor. 1:2; 1 Cor. 7:6; 2 Cor. 5:19; Eph. 3:9 and Eph. 4:9–10; Luther, *Romans*, 260; Calvin, *Romans*, 342; cf. *The Racovian Catechism*, ed. T. Rees (1818); see Wainwright's explanatory and manuscript notes. As Wainwright notes, Biddle's interpretation of the text of Romans was recorded in MS Locke c43, indicating that 'god over all' did not signify his supreme deity.

[22] *Paraphrase*, Eph. 1:10 and notes.

This would have been a non-Socinian position. It is important to stress at this point that it is not necessarily therefore a trinitarian position, because it does not indicate that Christ was pre-existent to the world, let alone eternally God. Indeed, in Wainwright's interpretation, Christ's appointment to this headship came after the existence of men, since Locke went on to argue that Satan's fall 'perhaps' occurred at Christ's exaltation, and spoke elsewhere of men as having been initially in the Kingdom of God but then rebelling to the Kingdom that Satan set up. Such an interpretation of the passage would make Locke's belief about Christ non-Socinian, but not fully Arian, and certainly not trinitarian. It would be a view of Christ somewhere between Socinianism and Arianism. Here, then, is evidence that Locke was antitrinitarian at the end of his life, whether or not the 'Reflections' are attributed to Locke. The theological journey that Locke had begun in Calvinist trinitarianism had ended at the least in anti-Calvinist antitrinitarianism, even if not definitely in Socinianism.[23]

If Locke did thus believe Christ pre-existent as a person to Jesus, and thus did not believe in a Socinian antitrinitarianism, it is quite possible that this was a very recent interpretation. The entire theme of Satan's role had been very little discussed in any of Locke's previous writings or reflections, and it was not rendered particularly clear in the *Paraphrase* itself, perhaps because Locke died before its completion. The footnote itself has the appearance of such a recent interpretation by Locke, starting the interpretation of Christ's 'reinstated' headship on the basis of a translation of a passage that it is likely that Locke had only made when he was intending to paraphrase the passage. The note was also explicitly declared to include material that Locke had 'in my small reading' found nowhere 'sufficiently taken notice of'. In the *Reasonableness* Locke had interpreted Col. 1:15, of Christ as 'First-born of all Creatures', part of one of the texts that he declared in the *Paraphrase* 'plain' in showing that Christ at first had rule and supremacy, as referring to him being 'first born from the dead'. The text was thus interpreted in the *Reasonableness* as post-resurrectional, as it was interpreted by most Socinians.

It is quite possible that Locke had only come to believe Christ a pre-existent person to Jesus between 1695 and 1704 – and between the 'Reflections' and 1704 – and that this involved reinterpretation of texts that he had earlier thought post-resurrectional to refer to a headship possessed 'at first'. There is evidence that Locke changed his mind in writing the *Paraphrase* about the interpretation of other texts that were central to his view of Christianity in the *Reasonableness*. Such an amendment of Locke's views would certainly confirm Locke's professed independence of Socinian

[23] Wainwright, *Paraphrase*, Introduction, 37–9; Eph. 1:10 and notes; *Reasonableness*, 106–7.

systems of theology, not merely in approach to Scripture, but also in the substance of its most central belief, and such a change might even have been promoted in part by these accusations. It would suggest that if the 'Reflections' were indeed by Locke they marked a view of Christ that he held for only a few years.[24]

Locke's reference to Col. 1:15 in the *Reasonableness* to the resurrection from the dead, however, raises the possibility that Locke was interpreting the text in the note in the *Paraphrase* in his earlier manner, and that the declaration of Christ's headship possessed 'at first' referred to his headship as 'foreseen' and 'appointed' by God. When Locke argued in the note itself that Satan 'perhaps . . . fell at' Christ's exaltation, he cited as evidence for this exaltation of Christ that Satan had 'perhaps' fallen at a text that the note itself had only just referred to Christ's post-resurrectional headship. This suggests the possibility that Locke thought Christ's initial supremacy to be his later supremacy as foreseen, and that he would have continued to possess this supremacy as foreseen without diminution if it had not been challenged by the fall of Satan. It was not impossible, although it was unusual, for Socinians to speak of Christ eternally possessing the 'glory with which he was glorified' at his resurrection as this was foreseen by God, as Schlichting had declared in his *Confessio Fidei* (a work which Locke had noted in 1687 as containing the 'sum of Socinianisme' and had then purchased). The 'Reflections' themselves had spoken of Christ as allegorically pre-existent, being in God eternally as his word. Such an interpretation of Locke's note would leave it possible that Christ did not preexist as a 'distinct person', and thus that Locke was broadly Socinian in his view of Christ as well as his views of the satisfaction and original sin in writing the *Paraphrase*. The evidence seems insufficient to this author to be certain with what kind of antitrinitarian view Locke ended his life; it is most important to emphasise with Wainwright that it was unequivocally an antitrinitarian view.[25]

IV

Locke's anti-Calvinist interpretation of justification and his credal minimalism in the *Reasonableness* and the *Paraphrase* also provoked broader charges of Socinianism. Declaring that it was plain in Scripture that men were justified for faith, Locke devoted the majority of the first one hundred pages of the *Reasonableness of Christianity* to the contention that it was 'plainly set down in the Gospel' that there had been only one article of

[24] Wainwright, *Paraphrase*, Introduction, 37-9; Eph. 1:10 and notes; *Reasonableness*, 106–7.
[25] *Paraphrase*, Eph. 1:10; *Reasonableness*, 106–7; Williams, 'Schlichting'; MS Locke b2, 81r (Locke's note on the *Confessio*).

faith declared to be necessary to salvation by Jesus and by the Apostles. This article was that Jesus was the Messiah, or the Christ, which Locke explained as indicating that Christ was the 'King' of all those who would gain eternal life. Locke surveyed the gospels and Acts, indicating that this was the 'one proposition' that was 'to be believed for justification', the fundamental doctrine taught in all of the preaching of the Apostles. It was 'the sole doctrine pressed and required to be believed in the whole tenour of our Saviour's and his Apostles' preaching'. Locke had certainly found in this interpretation of Scripture an argument that was extremely useful to the cause of religious toleration: if that single article was all the belief that Christ had made necessary to salvation, then that was all the belief that any Christian church should require of communicants.[26]

Locke combined with this argument the contention, set out at great length, that although belief in the Messiah was taught by Christ as necessary to salvation, Christ had not declared himself to be that Messiah in plain words until shortly before his crucifixion. The Jews had expected a temporal Messiah and if Christ had taught plainly that he was the Messiah they would have raised tumults, subjecting Christ to punishment for sedition. He had therefore not taught that he was the Messiah in direct and plain words in order that he could fulfil the Old Testament prophecies of his reign. The Apostles had been chosen precisely because they were ignorant and illiterate and would not therefore reveal that Christ was the Messiah before the appointed time. Indeed, many of the Apostles had not known that Christ was indeed the Messiah for much of his life, and some only became certain of this after his death and resurrection. People were taught to believe Christ's doctrine by the miracles that were done in its confirmation, by his fulfilment of the prophecies of the Messiah in the Old Testament, and by the divine wisdom and blameless life that Christ displayed. It was the lengthy theme of the constraints upon Jesus' preaching, occupying approximately half of the entire *Reasonableness*, which Locke himself described in the *Vindication* as one of two themes in the *Reasonableness* that he had found insufficiently discussed in books of divinity. Van Limborch went further and declared it to be 'peculiar' to Locke. At least in this major element of his interpretation, Locke would thus seem to have indeed been interpreting Scripture with the opinions of sects and systems set aside.[27]

That the only fundamental article of faith preached in the Gospel as necessary for salvation was that Jesus was the Christ or Messiah was one of two central arguments of the *Reasonableness*, a credal minimalism that

[26] *Reasonableness*, 16–100; especially 19; 28–30, 51, 98–102; 84–6; 40.
[27] *Ibid.*, passim, esp. 35, 42–5, 82, 93; 32–5, 40–2, 82; *Correspondence*, VI, 2222.

rendered the 'priest's' authority that of preacher of one simple article and that led his defenders to celebrate Locke as setting out a 'true and free reasonable religion' which rescued it from the 'great trade of priestcraft'. A wide doctrinal toleration was thereby, if largely implicitly, promoted by Locke. The second major theme of the *Reasonableness* was that this faith had to be combined with obedience to the commandments pressed in the Gospel, an account that made a 'working faith' necessary to justification. Locke made clear that obedience to the law of the Gospel was necessary to salvation, indicating for instance that Christ's preaching had shown the way of admittance into the kingdom of God: 'Viz repentance and baptism; and teaches the law of it, viz good life, according to the strictest rules of virtue and morality'. Belief in Jesus as the Christ alone could not save: repentance was 'as absolute a condition of the covenant of grace as faith' and consisted in attempting 'a sincere obedience to the law of Christ, the remainder of our lives'.[28]

Locke was in part considering the nonconformist arguments for justification by faith without works, and its culmination in the antinomianism of Tobias Crisp, when he wrote the *Reasonableness*; his 1695 letter to van Limborch suggests that he also had opposition to Calvin in mind. He made clear that God could never justify those who 'had no regard to justice at all, whatever they believed'. It was important that men did not 'mistake' the doctrine of faith, 'grace, free-grace, and the pardon and forgiveness of sins, and salvation' by Christ: what men did was as vital as what they believed, and in every place in the Gospel where the day of judgement was spoken of, it was men's obedience and not their belief that was discussed. St Paul's doctrine, the locus of salvation by 'faith alone', did not contravert this, since simetimes faith could be put for both faith and works: 'St Paul often, in his epistles, puts faith for the whole duty of a christian. But yet the tenour of the gospel is . . . "Unless ye repent ye shall all likewise perish".' When asked about faith Paul had therefore reasoned of 'temperance and justice'. Although Paul had not pressed the 'duties of the moral law' everywhere, it had to be remembered that most of his sermons had been preached to Jews, 'who acknowledged . . . the law . . . what they needed was faith'.[29]

Locke was here paralleling many contemporary accounts of the need for a working faith, including those of the Latitudinarians, Arminians, Socinians, and some of the moderate presbyterians, against strict Calvinist accounts like those of Owen. He cited in support of this position the favoured texts of many of these theologians, Gal. 5:6, Titus 2:14 and the Epistle of James: 'And that faith without works, ie the works of sincere

---

[28] *Ibid.*, passim, esp. 42; 48–50; 101–5; 124. Correspondence, VII, 2775.
[29] *Ibid.*, 127; 101–5; 124–5.

obedience to the law and will of Christ, is not sufficient for our justification, St James shows at large, chap ii.' The *Vindications* and the *Paraphrase* reiterated each of these positions and very many of the biblical texts
on which they were based. The *Paraphrase* amended the account significantly only in strengthening considerably the assertion that faith was
trust in God, described only in very muted form in the *Reasonableness*.[30]

V

At no time before the mid-1690s does Locke seem to have given Paul's
thought on predestination and God's foreknowledge the very close attention that was absolutely central for so many Protestants. Damaris Cudworth had declared her surprise in 1684 that Locke had written a letter to
her which could not be understood without turning to Paul's epistles; she
had thought before then that Locke's opposition to 'enthusiasm' had been
opposed not merely to her own neoplatonic religiosity but also to Pauline
views of men's sinfulness and need for inspiration by the Holy Ghost;
Locke's reference to Paul's thought in his letter of 1683 need not have
shown any significantly detailed confrontation with Paul's thought in that
context to have provoked Damaris' reply. Locke probably read many
Arminian and some Socinian arguments on the subject in the 1680s, and
was interested in 1695 in the passages of Nye's *Discourse* which discussed
the views of Arminians and Socinians on predestination. We have seen that
Locke was, however, still willing in 1693 to admit that he could not reconcile men's freedom and God's omnipotence but was committed to both,
and even his 1695 attempts to reconcile these seem to have been primarily
naturalistic rather than scriptural. The *Reasonableness* concentrated upon
the Gospels and Acts, to the diminution of the epistles, including Romans,
and included almost nothing on predestination. Strikingly, in a letter that
Locke wrote in 1701 to van Limborch when composing the *Paraphrase* he
asked van Limborch to inform him of the content of the five points on
which Remonstrants and strict Calvinists disagreed about men's freedom
and man's predestination. Van Limborch wrote back in astonishment –
and with seemingly not a little irritation – that Locke did not know these
points of disagreement, providing references to discussion of these central
points in Arminian works.[31]

---

[30] *Ibid.*, 110–12; 235; 283–8; Wainwright, introduction.
[31] *Correspondence*, VII, 2935, 2953 (Locke to van Limborch, 1 June 1701: 'There is one
thing that I feel the want of in your book, namely those five articles of the Remonstrants
of which there is such frequent mention. I confess that I do not know them . . . Please,
therefore, be so good as to inform me where I can read them . . .'; van Limborch to Locke
8 July 1701: 'I believed that our five articles . . . were known to everybody . . .').

It is thus likely that the *Paraphrase* itself represented Locke's first attempt to interpret Paul's thought in intricate detail, motivated in significant part by desire to reply to those of his critics who attacked the *Reasonableness* for its failure to examine the epistles. In the preface to the *Paraphrase* Locke explicitly declared that he had been unable to understand Paul's epistles until he had evolved the new method which prompted composition of the *Paraphrase* of reading and re-reading each epistle in order to establish Paul's 'drift and design'.

The result of this reflection between 1699 and 1704, undertaken alongside reading of a host of unitarian, Arminian and Latitudinarian works by authors such as van Limborch, Hammond, Allix, Whitby, Whichcote and Tillotson, which all concurred in opposing Calvinism, was an analysis of Romans which was unsurprisingly unequivocally opposed to Calvinist notions of absolute predestination to salvation and reprobation. Locke interpreted God's election spoken of by Paul as that of nations and not of individuals. God's foreknowledge and predestination was that he would offer salvation to the gentiles through Christ, and that those who accepted the offer and obeyed with a sincere endeavour to keep his law would be conformed to the image of Christ by becoming immortal. Even in the *Paraphrase*, having closely examined Arminian thought, Locke still did not set out clearly whether God actually knew which individuals would be saved, and had therefore, as most Arminians argued, predestined those particular individuals that he foresaw would accept his offer of grace, or whether his predestination was limited to providing eternal life for all those particular individuals who then happened to accept the Gospel; it is possible that Locke had still not settled on either of these beliefs.[32]

For Locke, Christ had thus brought redemption to men, the ability to gain eternal life through belief of a faith which would gain forgiveness for failures of obedience as long as obedience was sincerely attempted. In the *Reasonableness* and *Paraphrases* Locke declared that he had also brought the offer of the assistance of the Holy Spirit, but did not make clear the extent of the operations of the Holy Spirit. He was clear, however, that men could resist and fall from grace. Locke argued in interpreting Rom. 6:8

---

[32] On the *Paraphrase* as a natural response to the criticism of diminution of the epistles directed at the *Reasonableness* see Wainwright, *Paraphrase*, introduction, 1–3; on reading Paul see the preface, 'An essay for understanding St Paul's epistles by consulting St Paul himself', in *ibid*., I, 103–16; II, 665ff.; I, 24ff.; 108; Introduction, passim, esp. 12 and 12n.2, 14 and 14n.3 and the notes cited in the explanatory notes to both volumes of Wainwright's edition; *ibid*., Rom. 8:29–30; cf. also Romans 6 + 7; note f to Eph. 1:4; Rom. 9:1–10:21 'contents'; Rom. 9:21–2; Rom. 12 'contents'; and the explanatory notes on all of these texts. Calvin and Beza provide the sharp contrast, identifying foreknowledge as referring to the election of particular individuals; everyone thus foreknown was saved. Whitby gives the classically Arminian position, that God had foreordained and called to salvation those who he knew would truly love him.

that Paul's business in the chapter was 'not to tell them what they certainly and unchangeably are, but to exhort them to be what they ought . . . to be by becomeing Christians. viz that they ought to emancipate themselves from the vassalage of sin not that they were so emancipated without any danger of returne'. Locke also made absolutely clear that the most significant operation of the Holy Spirit was the communication to the Apostles of the Gospel that they taught. Men were then to interpret the Gospel using their reason. In keeping with his assault upon enthusiasm in the *Essay*, published while he was working on the *Paraphrase*, Locke limited the aid offered by the Holy Spirit in exegesis of the Scripture, describing Paul as arguing that men were not to think or claim that they interpreted Scripture by the immediate gifts of the Holy Spirit.[33]

Although Locke denied that men had inherited any propensity to sin from Adam, he declared in all of these works that they had all sinned. He gave no explicit account of the origin of such sin, but was especially clear in the *Paraphrase* that men's 'carnal appetites' were particularly important causes. The 'frailty of their flesh', which meant 'all those vitious, and irregular appetites, inclinations, and habitudes whereby a man is turnd from his obedience to that eternall law of right', had caused men to sin. The 'bodily state' was 'the sourse from which all our deviations from the strait rule of rectitude doe for the most part take their rise, or else doe ultimately terminate'. In discussing the gentiles' turning away from God Locke made much of the influence of customs and habits in promoting these carnal appetites. He argued that it was by 'custome and contrary habits' that the principle of the 'spirit', here equivalent to the direction of reason, was 'very much weakened' among the gentiles. They were therefore exhorted by St Paul to put off the old man 'ie Fleshly corrupt habits' and to put on the new man by renewing their minds, by understanding the Gospel.[34]

On Rom. 7:14 Locke even went so far as to declare that men were 'enslaved' to sin by their 'carnal appetites', paraphrasing Paul as declaring – of himself, and through his description of himself, of all other men – that 'I am so carnal, as to be enslaved to them, and forced against my will to doe the drudgery of sin as if I were a slave that had been sold into the hands of that my domineering enemy. For what I doe is not of my own con-

[33] *Ibid.*, Rom. 6:8n; Rom. 12:6. Recognising that Paul had received his revelation immediately from God, Locke argued, as he had in the *Essay*, that Paul could only communicate this revelation to others by words and according to their ideas. Interpreting 2 Cor. 12:4, which other commentators saw as declaring that it was not lawful for Paul to inform others of his full revelation, Locke argued that Paul could not utter what he saw when in the third heaven. Cf. also Gal. 3:1–5, 'contents'.
[34] *Ibid.*, Rom. 8:9 and n.; 1 Cor. 12.3; cf. 2 Cor. 4:12; Gal. 4:6; Rom. 8:2; Rom. 8.3n.; Rom. 9:1; Rom. 7:22–5; Rom. 7:14–24; Gal. 5:16–17n.

trivance. For that which I have a mind to, I doe not; and what I have an aversion to, that I doe.' Since his understanding recognised the law, but he did not perform its requirements, 'it is not I a willing agent of my free purpose, that doe what is contrary to the law; but as a poor slave in captivitie not able to follow my own understanding and choise forced by the prevalency of my own sinfull affections, and Sin that remains still in me notwithstanding the law'.

At this point of the *Paraphrase* a greater explicit stress had been laid upon the power of men's sinfulness than at any other point during Locke's thought, with the possible exception of his translation of Pierre Nicole's *Essais de Morale* in the late 1670s. There seems little doubt that in his study of Paul's thought Locke did come to place a heavier stress upon man's sinfulness, a stress that his substantial reading of Paul's thought helped to create, as it had helped to create that of Luther, Calvin and Nicole. Locke had here set out an account of men whose 'natural inclination' led to the 'satisfaction of . . . irregular desires' even when these were not approved by the judgement of their understandings. Man was said to be forced 'against my will' to 'doe the drudgery of Sin' in such a way that the understanding was itself coerced by carnal affections.[35]

It is very difficult indeed to reconcile this with the *Essay*, whose fifth edition was published in 1700 when Locke was working on the *Paraphrase*. In the *Essay* men were still said to do what they 'willed' unless prevented by physical handicap. The *Essay* allowed that men could be taken over by some 'passionate uneasiness' in such a way that they did not have the power to reflect, but described this as a temporary phenomenon. There is unquestionably a terminological contradiction between the *Essay* and *Paraphrase* in the latter's assertion that men did what they did not will. It is possible that Locke was coming to have great difficulty at the end of his life in reconciling the *Essay*'s almost entirely natural theology, to which his concentration upon epistemological issues, rejection of the religion and politics of much of Calvinism, and significant avoidance of interpreting Scripture in his middle years, had jointly carried him, with his newly detailed concentration upon Pauline thought.

It is important to emphasise here, however, that the point of the *Essay* was not that men could not or did not 'enslave' themselves to sin by not conquering or at least properly channelling their affections, but only that their minds were capable of knowledge of those things necessary to their 'pilgrimage' on earth, and that men were responsible for not 'vitiating' their palates by settling desires for vices. The point of *Some Thoughts*, which went into its fifth edition in 1700, was similarly that men did in fact

---

[35] *Ibid.*, Rom. 7:22–5; Rom. 7:14–24; Gal. 5:16–17n; I, introduction.

voluntarily give themselves up to many vicious habits, and thus to sin, but that they should attempt to settle virtuous habits and create 'regular desires' through education. His proposals were made with the recognition that few had settled such habits and that most men, particularly in the lower orders of society, had 'given themselves up' to their carnal appetites. In writing the *Paraphrase* Locke clearly expected all men to sin, even when helped by the inward regeneration of the Holy Spirit, and located the cause of such sin in their carnal affections or the desires of the 'flesh'. Much of his argument, however, still stressed that men could conquer at least the 'prevalency' of their carnal appetites and their 'irregular' desires. On Rom. 6:6 Locke declared that the 'prevalency of their carnal sinful propensitys which are from our bodys' should be destroyed, and that many phrases of St Paul referred to 'the giveing our selves up to the conduct of our sinful carnal appetites'. He spoke of sin not having control over men 'unless by your own free choice you inthralle yourselves to it and by a voluntary obedience give it the command over you'.[36]

VI

Although Locke was clear in the *Reasonableness* that God accepted faith in place of a full obedience, he was equally clear that God did so only when men sincerely attempted to obey his law: 'a complete obedience and freedom from sin, are still sincerely to be endeavoured after'. Locke was adamant that 'no part of the eternal law of right' could be 'abrogated . . . whilst God is . . . just . . . and man a rational creature. The duties of that law, arising from the constitution of his very nature, are of eternal obligation.' They could not be changed without 'changing the nature of things' and throwing all into 'confusion'. Men had failed to keep all of God's commands, so God had instituted by grace offers of salvation in Mosaic law and then in Christianity, but the moral requirements of each dispensation did not abrogate the law of nature. The law of works under Moses was conformable to the 'eternal law of right' and was therefore 'of eternal obligation'. Christ had reinforced but not altered the content of the moral law. He had confirmed 'and at once re-enforce[d] all the moral Precepts in the Old Testament'.[37]

Locke extended this line of argument in the *Reasonableness* to the thorny problem of those who had never heard of Jesus, pronounced to be damned by Lutherans and Calvinists on the basis of Acts 4:12 ('Neither is there salvation in any other name'), but frequently described by most

[36] *Ibid.*, I, Introduction, 57; note on Rom. 7:14, 17; Rom. 6:6; 6, 12–14&n. *Essay*, II, xxi.71.
[37] *Reasonableness*, 111–15; 122–3; 132–3.

Latitudinarians, Arminians and unitarians as left to the 'mercy' of God. Locke interpreted the text as indicating that God had sent no other mediator. For Locke it was so 'obvious and natural' that men could only be expected to believe what was proposed to them, that he could not see how any 'reasonable man' could raise a question about the fate of those before Christ. Before Christ, those who had heard that he would come would be justified for their belief that he would come, and for their acknowledgement of God's 'peculiar providence and benignity' to men.[38]

At that point Locke noted that God's works of nature alone showed his 'wisdom and power' (the attributes of God that he had focused upon in the *Essay*) but that his promises 'most eminently' showed his goodness. Philosophers studying Locke's thought have questioned how Locke thought many of God's attributes, particularly his goodness, could be derived from the works of nature. Locke gave no satisfactory answer to this question, but he would probably have given an answer of the form common among his contemporaries; man's exalted status on the earth as rational and therefore possessing dominion showed God's mercy and goodness. Considering those who had never heard of God's particular promises of a Messiah, Locke held straightforwardly in the *Reasonableness* that 'god had, by the light of reason, revealed to all mankind, who would make use of that light, that he was good and merciful'. God's 'goodness and mercy' was 'over all his works'. The 'same spark of the divine nature and knowledge in man, which making him a man, showed him the law he was under, as a man, showed him also the way of atoning the merciful, kind, compassionate Author and Father of him and his being, when he had transgressed that law'.

Any men who had made use of the 'candle of the Lord' therefore could not have missed the way to reconciliation with God for their sins. Even those who had not heard that Christ would come could thus have learned how they could be saved. The law of nature was the 'eternal, immutable standard of right'. Without showing how it could be derived from reason, Locke declared that part of that law was that a man should forgive his enemies upon repentance and asking for pardon. Men therefore could not doubt that the author of this law, God, who was 'rich in mercy' would fail 'his frail offspring'. The 'light of nature revealed this'.[39]

Having argued that the only faith required as necessary in the preaching of the Gospel was that Jesus was the Christ, and having held that the morality of the Gospel was a reinforcement of the morality of the Mosaic law and the law of nature, Locke then faced the problem of answering what need there had been of Christ's coming. He declared it was 'enough'

[38] *Reasonableness*, 128–33.   [39] *Reasonableness*, 128–33.

simply to say that it was a requirement of the divine wisdom, but went on to enumerate five 'great . . . advantages' to man in Christ's coming. It was the omission of the satisfaction from this list which caused many of the accusations of Socinianism against the *Reasonableness*. For Locke, Christ had brought the promise of assistance of the Holy Spirit, the reform of Mosaic worship, and the refutation of pagan polytheism. Christ had also brought information about the content of men's duties and the nature of their obligation, and he had brought an encouragement to be virtuous by bringing information about rewards and punishments and testimony of the existence of an afterlife. It is the description of these last two advantages conferred on man by Christ that has led to Locke being depicted by various scholars as turning to fideism instead of to natural law accessible by the light of reason in 1694–5.[40]

According to Locke, before Christ a 'clear knowledge' of their duties was 'wanting to mankind'. Locke gave a number of reasons for the 'little footing' that morality had 'among the people', emphasising the historical failure of men to demonstrate morality. This failure was largely the result of the division of religion and philosophy. Before Christ, 'priests made it not their business to teach . . . virtue' and very few men 'went to the schools of the philosophers to learn virtue' since 'lustrations' were far easier than a 'clean conscience', and 'an expiatory sacrifice that atoned for the want of it, was much more convenient than a strict and holy life'. Religion had been 'every where distinguished from, and preferred to virtue'. 'Natural religion, in its full extent, was no where, that I know, taken care of, by the force of natural reason'. Some morality was taught by the civil laws of commonwealths, but this was only 'So much virtue as was necessary to hold societies together, and to contribute to the quiet of governments'.[41]

Morality had also not been demonstrated before Christ because the philosophers themselves had not managed – or even attempted, Locke suggested at one point – to establish a full body of morality. The 'attempts of philosophers . . . before our Saviour's time' had very visibly come short of the 'perfection of a true and complete morality'. The law of nature was the 'law of convenience too' and so some men 'of parts, and studious of virtue' had 'by meditation' settled 'on the right even from the observable convenience and beauty of it', but even then they had failed to make out 'its obligation from the true principles of the law of nature, and foundations of morality'. 'Human reason unassisted' had 'failed men in its great and proper business of morality. It never from unquestionable principles, by clear deductions, made out an entire body of the law of nature.' A full

---

[40] *Ibid.*, 134–5; 138ff.; 147ff.   [41] *Ibid.*, 138ff.

'body of ethics, proved to be the law of nature, from principles of reason, and teaching all the duties of life' Locke thought 'nobody' would 'say the world had before our Saviour's time'. No philosopher had managed to demonstrate all of morality, and even the collected moral principles of all of the philosophers came 'short of the morality delivered by our Saviour'. Sending men for their morality to the philosophers before Christ was to send them to a 'wild wood of uncertainty'.[42]

Locke underlined particularly heavily the difficulty for these philosophers in providing 'a complete morality, that may be to mankind the unquestionable rule of life and manners' because they had had no authority. Men were under no obligation to accept their views. According to Locke, morality could only be 'settled' either by 'showing' that it was built 'upon principles of reason self-evident in themselves' and that 'all the parts of it' were deduced 'from thence, by clear and evident demonstration', or by the commission from heaven that could be shown by revelation. Jesus Christ had given man an 'unquestionable' rule of morality, a 'full and sufficient rule for our direction, and conformable to that of reason'. The 'truth and obligation' of his precepts was 'put past doubt' by the 'evidence of his mission' from miracles and his resurrection.[43]

Locke allowed that 'some' men would say in response to this argument that 'men were negligent' and therefore had not made out the full morality. His answer was to reiterate the *historical* necessity of Christ's mission. Natural reason had 'then' not been likely to cure the 'corruption of manners'. Locke's argument was up to this point clearly that of men's historical failure to generate moral knowledge, and not the theoretical impossibility of such knowledge. It was the *historical* need for Christ's mission that he was to declare in the *Vindications* to be one of two central elements of the *Reasonableness*.[44]

He also argued, however, that 'It should seem, by the little that has hitherto been done in it, that it is too hard a task for unassisted reason to establish morality in all its parts, upon its true foundation, with a clear and convincing light.' This is clearly a stronger statement about the difficulty of gaining moral knowledge on a theoretical rather than purely an historical level, but it is immediately apparent that Locke had spoken of the difficulty of *unassisted* reason establishing *all* of the parts of morality by reason, and of establishing them not merely with a clear light, but also with one that was *convincing*. Locke made a distinction in his letters to Molyneux in 1692–4 between the demonstration of morality to oneself and the ability to demonstrate this to others which is also very significant here, for Locke continued his comment in the *Reasonableness* by declaring that 'it is at

[42] *Ibid.*, 139ff.   [43] *Ibid.*, 138–46.   [44] *Ibid.*, 138–46; 187.

least a surer and shorter way, to the apprehensions of the vulgar, and mass of mankind, that one manifestly sent from God, and coming with visible authority from him, should, as a king and lawmaker, tell them their duties; and require their obedience; than leave it to the long and sometimes intricate deductions of reason, to be made out to them' – not, it should be noted, made out 'by them'. Such trains of reasoning Locke declared that 'the greatest part of mankind have neither leisure to weigh; nor, for want of education and use, skill to judge of'.[45]

Locke declared that even if reason had gone on to give men an ethics

in a science like mathematics, in every part demonstrable; this yet would not have been so effectual to man in this imperfect state, nor proper for the cure. The greatest part of mankind want leisure or capacity for demonstration; nor can carry a train of proofs, which in that way they must always depend upon for conviction, and cannot be required to assent to, until they see the demonstration . . . you may as soon hope to have all the day-labourers and tradesmen, the spinsters and dairymaids, perfect mathematicians, as to have them perfect in ethics this way. Hearing plain commands, is the sure and only course to bring them to obedience and practice.'[46]

Locke argued that 'were all the duties of human life clearly demonstrated, yet I conclude, when well considered, that method of teaching men their duties would be thought proper only for a few, who had much leisure, improved understandings, and were used to abstract reasonings. But the instruction of the people were best still to be left to the precepts and principles of the gospel.' The ordinary apprehension could conceive miracles done by divine power better than it could even follow let alone create a chain of proofs. The 'surest, the safest, and most effectual way of teaching' was therefore by revelation. Locke declared that 'the greatest part cannot know, and therefore they must believe'.[47]

According to Locke, 'the christian philosophers' had 'much out-done' heathen philosophers 'yet we may observe that the first knowledge of the truths they have added, is owing to revelation: though as soon [as] they are heard and considered, they are found to be agreeable to reason; and such as can by no means be contradicted'. Every man had to recognise that a great many truths had been received at first from others which were hard 'and perhaps beyond his strength, to have discovered himself'. Truth seemed easy to men when it was delivered 'dug and fashioned' but it was difficult to 'mine'. Nothing seemed hard to the understanding once it was known, and the notions which had grown familiar to us 'and, as it were, natural to us, under the gospel . . . we take for unquestionable obvious truths, and easily demonstrable; without considering how long we might have been in doubt or ignorance of them, had revelation been silent'. Some

[45] *Ibid.*, 138–46.   [46] *Ibid.*, 138–46.   [47] *Ibid.*, 138–46.

parts of truth lay too deep 'for our natural powers easily to reach, and make plain and visible to mankind; without some light from above to direct them'. It was 'no diminishing to revelation, that reason gives its suffrage too, to the truths revelation has discovered. But it is our mistake to think, that because reason confirms them to us, we had the first certain knowledge of them from thence; and in that clear evidence we now possess them.'[48]

Locke had thus argued in the *Reasonableness* that men had lacked a certain knowledge of all of the principles of morality before Christ, but he had not depicted men as unable in theory to gain such knowledge. He had described Christ as providing an 'unquestionable' morality, one 'put past doubt' not by the certainty of men's knowledge of the precepts of morality as a result of a demonstration of these precepts by Christ but by the evidence of Christ's mission, evidence primarily provided by miracles. More generally, he had argued that men were started by the prompting of revelation on the examination of many principles, and set on the study of the correct nature of obligation to the law of nature as an obligation to obey God, but that once these principles were examined (by 'assisted' reason) men had then come to 'certainly know' these principles. Locke spoke of men 'knowing' principles in the sense of being 'informed of' them at various points in the *Reasonableness*, but also spoke of 'certain knowledge' in distinction to such 'knowledge' and thus preserved the notion of 'knowledge' by demonstration of the *Essay*. Locke's comment that most men could not 'know' but had to 'believe' becomes inexplicable without recognising that this distinction was being made. Locke's argument was thus that Christ had provided those men who were capable of abstract reasonings with the topics on which to reflect in order to build a demonstrable morality, and had provided for most men an 'unquestionable' morality that was known in the sense that they were informed of it, but which was not a morality 'known' in the sense of the *Essay* until it had been examined by those individuals with the necessary leisure and mental ability.[49]

Locke was a fideist in the *Reasonableness* in the sense that he thought that men would be saved only by their faith being accepted in place of their failures to live righteously (excepting those who had not heard of Christ but had lived as righteously as they could and repented for their failures). He was also a fideist in the very important practical sense that he thought that most men would have to accept their morality from the Gospel. He was fideistic to a considerable further degree in arguing that without Christ's revelation in the Gospel even the intelligent, educated and leisured

[48] *Ibid.*, 138–46.   [49] *Ibid.*, 138ff.

would have found it very much more difficult – indeed, 'too hard' to demonstrate morality in 'all its parts'. In saying that revelation helped to direct men's attention to the content of morality, however, Locke did not deny that with this help men of ability should attempt to demonstrate morality in all of its parts. The 'great business' of reason was still explicitly declared to be the establishment of morality; it was in that great task that 'unassisted reason' had failed, but it was in that great task that 'christian philosophers' had made their great strides with the help of Revelation.[50]

Locke's remaining 'great advantage' brought by Christ suggested an equally serious diminution of the historical generation of knowledge of natural law by the light of reason alone, and raised further theoretical problems about gaining such knowledge without revelation. He argued that 'another great advantage received by our Saviour', was 'the great encouragement he brought to a virtuous and pious life' by his testimony about rewards and punishments attached to virtue and vice, and the evidence from his resurrection that there was an afterlife. As we have seen, in the *Essay* Locke had not managed to *show* how men could *know* that God was just in arguing that an afterlife with punishment and reward was necessary to reward the virtuous who had suffered in this life, and he had removed the proof of an afterlife offered by the natural proof of the immortality of the soul.

In the *Reasonableness* Locke argued that 'The portion of the righteous has been in all ages taken notice of, to be pretty scanty in this world. Virtue and prosperity do not often accompany one another; and therefore virtue seldom had many followers.' This was a passage apparently far more bleak about the terrestrial rewards of virtue than the *Essay*'s declaration that the vicious had 'little odds' to brag about, although Locke had not here explicitly declared that in contrast to virtue vice was actually accompanied by prosperity. Locke's wager argument is less effective in a situation where vice is much better rewarded than virtue. According to Locke, 'Mankind' had to be 'allowed to pursue their happiness, nay, cannot be hindered'. Locke declared that as a consequence of this fact, before Christ men 'could not but think themselves excused from a strict observation of rules, which *appeared* so little to consist of their chief end, happiness; whilst they kept them from the enjoyments of this life; and they had *little evidence and security* of another'.[51]

Christ had taught men about the afterlife and had brought miracles to testify that his teaching was from God. The resurrection of Christ had further testified to the existence of the afterlife, and had therefore aided virtue because it 'Put into the scales on her side, "an exceeding and immor-

[50] *Ibid.*, 138ff. [51] *Ibid.*, 149 (my emphases).

tal weight of glory"'". 'Interest' came to support virtue and 'virtue now is visibly the most enriching purchase, and by much the best bargain'. Locke declared that if men's eyes were opened 'upon the endless, unspeakable joys of another life' then men's 'hearts' would 'find something solid and powerful to move them'. Indeed, it was 'Upon this foundation, and upon this only' that morality stood firm, and could 'defy all competition'.[52]

Again, Locke's argument was overtly historical and not theoretical, declaring that most men had not known of the afterlife and had therefore needed Christ's testimony, but suggesting that some men could have known and that a few had known of this afterlife – although, apparently, 'unclearly' – without such a revelation. Locke argued explicitly that men could have established the existence of the other life precisely on the basis of the lack of reward for the virtuous in this life, but indicated that they had not done so. Argument from God's justice to an afterlife on the basis of the need for reward of virtue was thus very briefly indeed implied to be valid; it was suggested that it had simply not been the method that had been adopted historically before Christ. The chief argument of philosophers had instead been 'from the excellency of virtue; and the highest they generally went, was the exalting of human nature, whose perfection lay in virtue'. Using the word which we have seen was then becoming fashionable among free-thinkers in England to assault the panoply of religious doctrines maintained only to support clerical power, Locke declared that the priests' discussion of an afterlife had been suspected to be merely 'priestcraft', and had not been used to support virtue. The result was that 'Before our Saviour's time, the doctrine of a future state, though it were not wholly hid, yet it was not clearly known in the world.' Again, then, Locke's fideism was practical rather than theoretical; nonetheless, that practical orientation of his argument significantly provided a convenient way for Locke to shelve problems in his epistemology about knowledge of reward and punishment that he had not yet solved.[53]

The same combination of practical fideism and theoretical commitment to the remote possibility of moral knowledge for the few, the able and the leisured who had had the principles of natural law suggested to them by revelation was maintained in a series of writings in the late 1690s: in Locke's continued publications of the *Treatises*, and the *Essay*, in the *Vindications*, in two manuscripts – the 'Conduct of the Understanding' and 'Error' – and in Locke's continued correspondence with Molyneux.

In the *Second Vindication*, published in 1697, nearly two years after the *Reasonableness*, but almost certainly before the composition of the 'Conduct of the Understanding', Locke made it clear that Christians were

52 *Ibid.*, 147–50.   53 *Ibid.*, 147–50.

still obliged to study the law of nature. He wrote that 'as men, we have God
for our King, and are under the law of reason: as Christians, we have Jesus
the Messiah for our King, and are under the law revealed by him in the
Gospel. And . . . every Christian, both as a deist and a christian, be obliged
to study both the law of nature and the revealed law, that in them he may
know the will of God and of Jesus Christ, whom he hath sent.' He declared
that he had shown that morality was 'now, with divine authority, established into a legible law, so far surpassing all that philosophy and human
reason had attained to, or could possibly make effectual to all degrees of
mankind'. He described this argument as having been designed to persuade
deists, who had thought that there was no need of revelation, to accept
Christianity.[54]

Locke voiced a similar description of men's continued ability to know
the law of nature, but combined it with a stress upon the value of revelation
increased still further, in a letter to William Molyneux in April 1696.
Molyneux had again pressed Locke to publish a 'Book of Offices or Moral
Philosophy' in March 1696. He was apparently aware of Locke's authorship of the *Reasonableness*; he seems to have seen that work as raising no
new theoretical problems about a book of offices. Having been ill for most
of the winter, and describing himself as having been 'near to death', Locke
replied to Molyneux's request that he had not 'wholly laid by the thoughts
of it. Nay I so far incline to comply with your desires, that I ever now and
then lay by some materials for it, as they occasionally occur in the rovings
of my mind.'[55]

There are no surviving manuscripts to confirm this declaration, but this
is not surprising since Locke continued that 'when I consider, that a book of
Offices, as you call it, ought not to be slightly done, especially by me, after
what I have said of that science in my *Essay* . . . I am in doubt whether it
would be prudent in one of my age and health, not to mention other disabi-
lities in me, to set about it'. In the light of assaults upon the *Essay* for not
providing a certain basis for morality, having removed its basis in innatism
and not shown how men could know of the rewards and punishments of
natural law, Locke's comment here on the problem of expectations raised
by his comments in the *Essay* suggests clearly that by 1696 Locke had come
to have an additional reason for not composing a work on the content of
morality: fear that if he did it would be used to assault the *Essay* itself.[56]

Locke continued that

Did the world want a rule, I confess there could be no work so necessary, nor so
commendable. But the Gospel contains so perfect a body of Ethicks, that reason
may be excused from that enquiry, since she may find man's duty clearer and easier

[54] *Ibid.*, 218–29; 265; 385–6; 187–8.   [55] *Correspondence*, VI, 2038; 2059.
[56] *Correspondence*, VI, 2038; 2059.

in revelation than in herself. Think not this the excuse of a lazy man, though it be, perhaps, of one, who having a sufficient rule for his actions, is content therewith, and thinks he may, perhaps, with more profit to himself, employ the little time and strength he has in other re-searches where he finds himself more in the dark.[57]

Taken at face value, Locke's very general comment that reason might be 'excused that enquiry' is startling, and seems to mark a retreat beyond even the *Reasonableness*'s argument that most men would believe and not know morality. However, since the passage from the *Second Vindication* reiterating the need for study of the law of nature cited above was published after this declaration, it would be unwise to take this as Locke's final word on the role of reason. It is important to underline that in this letter Locke was responding not merely to Molyneux's repeated requests for a work on morality, but also to his description of this as a duty Locke owed to mankind, as Locke's references to no more 'necessary' or 'commendable' work indicate. Locke's comment was special pleading, particularly since Molyneux's apparent knowledge of Locke's authorship of the *Reasonableness* would have suggested to Locke that Molyneux realised that he had not, as promised, bestowed his 'first leisure' upon such a work. It would be unwise to place too broad an interpretation or too much weight upon Locke's comment that reason could be excused the task of generating a complete ethics. Perhaps more importantly, Locke's letter also confirms that he apparently still did not accept that there was any theoretical impossibility in the generation of ethics by reason in 1696, after publishing the *Reasonableness* and its first *Vindication*.

In 1698 Locke composed a lengthy note in his commonplace book, 'Error', which identified Scripture, advice from experts on the Scripture, a natural light of reason able to know a very narrow range of duties, and the very limited range of duties necessary to be known by the poor, as the ways for the illiterate to gain knowledge of the duties that were required of them. The 'first step to orthodoxy' once men believed in Jesus Christ was 'a sincere obedience to his law'. Locke argued that 'a ploughman that cannot read, is not so ignorant but he has a conscience, and knows in those few cases which can concern his own actions, what is right and what is wrong'. If he 'sincerely' obeyed 'this light of nature' which was 'the transcript of the moral law in the Gospel' then a ploughman would be led 'into all the truths in the Gospel that are necessary for him to know'. A man did his duty who

in earnest believes Jesus Christ to be sent from God, to be his Lord and ruler, and does sincerely and unfeignedly set upon a good life as far as he knows his duty; and where he is in doubt in any matter that concerns himself . . . inquire[s] of those

---

[57] *Correspondence*, VI, 2038; 2059.

better skilled in Christ's law, to tell him what his Lord and Master has commanded in the case, and desires to have his law read to him concerning that duty which he finds himself concerned in, for the regulation of his own actions.

'Other men's actions' were not his concern: 'his business is to live well with himself, and do what is his particular duty'. According to Locke, this was 'knowledge and orthodoxy enough for him, which will bring him to salvation' and was 'an orthodoxy which nobody can miss, who in earnest resolves to lead a good life; and therefore I lay it down as a principle of Christianity, that the right and only way to a saving orthodoxy, is the sincere and steady purpose of a good life'.[58]

All men were ignorant of 'many things contained in the Holy Scriptures' and held 'Errors concerning doctrines delivered in the Scriptures', but this indicated only that 'these . . . cannot be damnable, if any shall be saved'. 'A good life in obedience to the law of Christ' was men's 'indispensable business, and if they inform themselves concerning that, as far as their particular duties lead them to enquire, and oblige them to know, they have orthodoxy enough, and will not be condemned for ignorance in those speculations which they have neither parts, opportunity, nor leisure to know'.[59]

Locke expressed similar views upon the restricted extent of knowledge necessary for the poor and illiterate in the 'Conduct of the Understanding'. This made clear that all men were to gain knowledge of parts of morality, but reiterated the theme of 'Error' in arguing that 'Nobody is under an obligation to know every thing.' Men with 'particular callings ought to understand them', and should 'think and reason right about . . . their daily employment', but beyond this limited knowledge they needed to know little. He argued that 'The one day of seven, besides other days of rest' allowed 'in the christian world time enough' for study of necessary parts of religion, 'if they would but make use of these vacancies from their daily labour, and apply themselves to an improvement of knowledge with as much diligence as they often do to a great many things that are useless'. The peasantry of France were under a 'much heavier pressure of want and poverty, than the day-labourers in England' but those of the reformed religion in France understood their religion better 'than those of a higher condition' in England.[60]

Arguing that all men thus had time to study religion, Locke declared that there was 'indeed, one science . . . incomparably above all the rest, where it is not by corruption narrowed into a trade or faction, for mean or ill ends, and secular interests'. This was 'theology' which contained 'the knowledge

[58] *Life and Letters*, ed. P. King (1884), 282ff.
[59] *Life and Letters*, ed. P. King (1884), 282ff.
[60] 'Of the Conduct of the Understanding', *Works*, III, 202–7; 218; 224; 258ff.

of God and his creatures, our duty to him and our fellow-creatures, and a view of our present and future state' and so was 'the comprehension of all other knowledge directed to its true end; ie the honour and veneration of the Creator, and the happiness of mankind'. Locke made clear that this was the 'noble study which is every man's duty, and every one that can be called a rational creature is capable of'. Locke suggested that if men had 'time and industry' they could then 'go [in]to the more abstruse parts of it', but was quite clear that the 'works of nature and the words of revelation', displayed to mankind 'in characters so large and visible' that any who were 'not quite blind' could 'in them read and see the first principles and most necessary parts of it'. Theology was 'that science which would truly enlarge men's minds, were it studied, or permitted to be studied, every where, with that freedom, love of truth and charity which it teaches, and were not made, contrary to its nature, the occasion of strife, faction, malignity, and narrow impositions'. According to Locke, for a man 'to understand fully the business of his particular calling in the commonwealth, and of religion, which is his calling as he is a man in the world' was 'usually enough to take up his whole time'. There were few men who informed themselves in this 'as they should'.

The 'Conduct' declared that it was particularly shameful for any man 'furnished with time' if that was not properly used. Those who by 'the industry and parts of their ancestors, have been set free from a constant drudgery to their backs and their bellies' ought to 'bestow some of their spare time on their heads'. For Locke, gentlemen, at least, were still to become rational studiers of the entire law of nature. The 'Conduct' offered a method for such study, arguing that 'in all sorts of reasoning, every single argument should be managed as a mathematical demonstration; the connexion of ideas should be followed, till the mind is brought to the source on which it bottoms, and observes the coherence all along'. He contended that there were 'fundamental truths that lie at the bottom, the basis upon which a great many others rest, and in which they have their consistency'. These were 'teeming truths, rich in store, with which they furnish the mind, and, like the lights of heaven, are not only beautiful and entertaining in themselves, but give light and evidence to other things, that without them could not be seen or known'. It was here that Locke cited as bottoming principles Newton's discovery that all bodies gravitate to one another, the basis of natural philosophy, and 'do unto others', the basis of social morality, a scriptural injunction that Locke did not demonstrate, but which he said should found demonstrations in social morality.[61]

Locke did, however, give as his third example of a bottoming principle

[61] 'Of the Conduct of the Understanding', *Works*, III, 202–7; 218; 224; 258ff.

one depicted in more clearly naturalistic terms, the appropriate response to the question of whether 'the grand seignour', the archetypal absolute monarch, could 'lawfully take what he will from any of his people'. This question could not be resolved, Locke argued, 'without coming to a certainty, whether all men are naturally equal; for upon that it turns, and that truth well settled in the understanding, and carried in the mind through the various debates concerning the rights of men in society, will go a great way to putting an end to them, and showing on which side truth is'.[62]

The 'Conduct' does thus suggest that in denying that all of morality could be known with ease by reason alone in the *Reasonableness*, Locke had not thereby denied that the part of morality surveyed in the *Treatises* could be known without much difficulty if men studied rationally. Locke did not revise his argument that the law of nature was 'plain' to 'rational studiers' of it in his continued editions of the *Two Treatises* in the late 1690s and early 1700s. As late as 1704 Locke was recommending the *Two Treatises* as the best work written on property. Locke's confidence in recommending the *Treatises* on property in 1704 and his confidence that the natural equality of man provided a plain evident principle from which to infer men's rights to property in the 'Conduct' suggest that he still thought that he had demonstrated that part of morality, and that it would still have been the central axiom of any moral philosophy that he would have written. It appears likely that the 'Conduct''s appeal to revelation instead of reason on the principle of loving others, while pointing to natural equality as the basis for questions of political obligation, indicated a recognition by Locke of his personal failure to see how to generate by reason alone a social morality considerably more extensive than the political morality set out at length in the *Treatises*.

Even though Locke still thought of the *Treatises* as accurately demonstrating from reason the duties of political obligation and property, however, their reception surely also fostered his awareness that for him to be able to 'demonstrate' a significant part of morality to his own satisfaction and for others to be convinced by a demonstration, however 'plain' to him as a 'rational studier' of the law, were two very different matters. He was faced by stony indifference to the arguments of the *Treatises* from most of his contemporaries. He also cannot have forgotten how he himself had unequivocally denied them on grounds of the reasoned need for security throughout his life until (about) 1681–2. An exacerbated sense of the difficulty of demonstrating his conception of property persuasively to others in the mid-1690s was probably also indicated in an amendment to the third edition of *Some Thoughts* in 1695, which suggested that justice

[62] 'Of the Conduct of the Understanding', *Works*, III, 202–7; 218; 224; 258ff.

was difficult to explain to children since justice was dependent upon understanding that men came by property through labour, and children did not labour. Even those who ought to have been the most rational – the children of the gentlemen who had been educated by the precepts of Locke's own educational theory – would therefore have difficulty generating the principles of property until they were older. Locke did not make explicit that such children would not themselves have to labour to receive the vast majority of property that would come to them through inheritance, nor did he recognise that most children of the poor did indeed labour.

VII

Locke argued in the *Paraphrase*, as throughout his earlier works, that men could know God through the works of his creation. He described the gentiles as failing to recognise him through weakness: 'Though God made himself known to them by legible characters of his being and power visible in the works of the creation yet they glorified him not.' Men had not lived up 'to the light that god has given them'. Locke was similarly absolutely clear that men could know their duties by the light of nature and that the law of nature or 'rule of rectitude' was given to them in giving them their natures. He spoke of 'the rule of rectitude which god has given to mankind in giving them reason'. He argued that the gentiles had acknowledged 'a natural and eternal rule of rectitude which is made known to men by the light of reason'. He contended that mankind 'without the positive law of God knew by the light of nature that they transgressed the rule of their nature, Reason, which dictated to them what they ought to doe'.[63]

Locke was characteristically adamant that the law of Moses and the Gospel had republished 'the eternal immutable rule of right'. Reiterating the argument of the *Reasonableness* that Christ had provided a fuller and clearer exposition of morality than had existed before his coming, in his notes to Eph. 2:15 Locke declared that Jesus was 'so far from abrogating' that 'unmoveable Rule of Right which is of perpetual Obligation' that he had 'promulgated it a new under the Gospel fuller and clearer than it was in the Mosaical Constitution, or any where else; and by adding to its Precepts the Sanction of his own Divine Authority, has made the Knowledge of that Law more easy and certain than it was before'. According to Locke, subjects of Christ's kingdom could be 'at no doubt or loss about their duty, if they will but read and consider the Rules of Morality, which our Saviour and his Apostles have deliver'd in very plain words in the holy

---

[63] *Ibid.*, 258–9; *Paraphrase*, Romans synopsis; cf. 1 Cor. 1:21 and explanatory note; *Paraphrase*, Rom. 1:32 note; Rom. 2:14–15; Rom. 2:26n.

Scriptures of the New Testament'. Christ had come to 'establish' the law. Christ's law had reinforced the law of nature and the law of Moses 'with penaltyes attached to the breach of it'.[64]

Locke argued, however, that while the gentiles before Christ had recognised, even if they had not obeyed, this law of nature, they had not then known that the price of sin was death. His discussion of this theme at various points seemed to suggest that this was because in fact there had been no punishments at all for failure to keep natural law until these had been declared in revelation. He argued that only one transgression had death annexed to it, and that that was the transgression of Adam. He spoke of Mosaic law as failing to procure men justification but instead rendering them 'liable to punishment' by God 'who by the law has made known to them what is sin, and what punishment he has annexed to it. For there is noe incurring wrath or punishment where there is noe law that says any thing of it.' The 'law alone' was said to expose men to 'punishment by force and sanction of a law', and Locke declared that it was the 'law alone that exposes us to wrath'.[65]

The law 'annexed' death to transgression. Sin without the law had been 'as good as dead' because it was 'not able to have its will and bring death upon me', whereas 'under law' men were 'exposed to certain death'. The law came and sin recovered again 'a power to kil[l]'. This theme reached its zenith in Locke's interpretation of Rom. 5:13, 'For until the law sin was in the world, but sin is not imputed when there is no law.' Locke paraphrased this as saying that 'Tis true indeed sin was universally committed in the world by all men all the time before the positive law of god delivered by Moses, but tis as true that there is no certain determined punishment affixed to sin without a positive law declareing it.' His notes expanded upon the theme: 'without a positive declaration of god their Soverain they could not tell at what rate god taxed their trespasses against this rule. Till he pronounced that life should be the price of sin, that could not be ascertained, and consequently sin could not be brought to account.' The notes continued by describing Paul's declaration in Rom. 4:15, 'For where there is no law there is noe transgression' as meaning that 'There is noe transgression with a penalty attached to it without a positive law.'[66]

There are two distinct possible meanings of this tissue of arguments. The most obvious is that Locke had come to believe as a result of his interpretation of Paul's epistles that there was in fact no punishment for sin under natural law alone, that before Christ all men had been made mortal by Adam's sin without any possibility of their gaining eternal life even if they

---

[64] *Ibid.*, Rom. 3:31; Eph. 2:15n. (p).   [65] *Ibid.*, Rom. 5:20; Rom. 4:1–25.
[66] *Ibid.*, Rom. 7:8; Rom. 5:13.

had acted (*per impossibile*) completely righteously. There was no punishment for sin under natural law alone because there had been no offer of eternal life to men under natural law alone, and all men after Adam were naturally mortal. The Jews had then been offered the opportunity of eternal life through obedience to Moses' law, but none had managed to keep that law and all men had died terrestrially and had lost eternal life until Christ had come. Christ had then restored the possibility of eternal life to those men who believed in him, not merely the Jews, and had thus reinstituted the punishment of loss of eternal life for all of those who did not.

This interpretation of Locke's thought certainly makes sense of the passages of the *Paraphrase* on punishment just quoted, interpreting sin being brought to 'account' or 'imputed' as speaking of God's reckoning of sin against men and punishing them with loss of eternal life and other punishments in Mosaic and Christian times when he had not punished them before his declarations of positive law but simply allowed them to die from their natural mortality. This implicitly contradicts what Locke had said in the *Reasonableness* about the fate of those who had had the light of reason alone by which to discern their duty, that they could attempt to obey him and repent for their sins and could gain eternal life. It also contradicts the argument of the *Reasonableness* that all men were restored to the possibility of eternal life by Christ. We have already seen that Locke changed his mind on a number of important interpretations of the Bible between composing the *Reasonableness* and the *Paraphrase*; it is possible that this was another such change.

It is difficult on this interpretation to see how Locke could have continued without inconsistency to imply in his editions of the *Essay* that men could have known that there were punishments and rewards and an afterlife by the light of nature alone, but we have seen that Locke's argument in the *Essay* on men's capacity to know of these rewards had always been plagued by serious problems in showing how men could demonstrate the existence of an afterlife and of rewards and punishments for sin, and that he may well have been trying to obscure or circumvent these problems by speaking of 'divine law' and by trying to provide another basis for morality by argument on the basis of wagering on the possibility of an afterlife. The *Paraphrase* was to be issued anonymously, and it was only published posthumously; Locke may simply have felt himself unable to retract the suggestion of the later editions of the *Essay* that men could know of reward and punishment and an afterlife by the light of reason alone.[67]

It is very difficult, however, to see on this interpretation of Locke's argu-

---

[67] *Reasonableness*, 109ff.; *Works*, V, 489.

ments how Locke could claim not merely in the *Essay* but also in the *Paraphrase* itself that there was a natural law that men should have obeyed before Moses and Christ that was the same as that 'promulgated . . . a new' by Christ. Locke continued his arguments of the *Essay* about the resurrection changing the measures of virtue and vice from what they would have been without an afterlife by contending in the *Paraphrase* – as, for instance, in interpreting 1 Cor. 15:32 – that 'If there be noe resurrection 'tis wiser a great deale to preserve our selves as long as we can in a free injoyment of all the pleasures of this life, for when death comes as it shortly will there is an end of us forever.'[68]

This suggests the second possible interpretation of Locke's arguments in the *Paraphrase*. There is potentially a significant distance between Locke's statement that 'There is no certain determined punishment affixed to sin without a positive law declareing it', and an argument that there is no punishment at all for failure to obey natural law, a distance marked by the words 'certain' 'determined' and 'affixed'. Locke's other notes cited above spoke of men not having been able to 'tell' at what rate God taxed their trespasses against the law of nature, or to know 'yet' or to 'ascertain' (gain certainty) that death was a punishment for sin, and of the historical result that 'men did not look on death as the wages or retribution for their sin'. It was by the positive law of God that he declared that men 'knew' that 'death was certainly annexed to sin as its certain and unavoidable punishment'.[69]

Locke's point in the *Paraphrase could* thus have been that men did not know and could not have known that the *specific* punishment of eternal death followed disobedience to the law of nature until this was declared in revelation, but that it did indeed follow such disobedience without it being punishment by the 'force' and 'sanction' of 'the law', or as a 'declared judgement', or as 'wrath'. Locke's point could alternatively have been that such a specific punishment did not certainly follow disobedience, but that other forms of punishment always did follow such disobedience, and that loss of eternal life followed in some cases. In this interpretation, Locke's discussion of sin not being brought 'to account' describes the inability of men to place that *specific* punishment in the balance of expected rewards and punishments for virtue and vice inferred by reason alone, not God's inability to publish them by bringing their sins to account.

This interpretation would suggest that Locke thought of all men until Moses as dying on account of Adam's sin. Then Moses had made the Jews alive again in the sense of giving them the possibility of eternal life after death upon the conditions of a covenant of works. Men had, however,

[68] *Ibid.*, 1 Cor. 15:32; cf. *Essay*, II.xxi.60.   [69] *Ibid.*, Rom. 5:13.

proven unable to live up to this covenant and thus had been killed eternally by their sins as well as terrestrially by their natural mortality after Adam; it was in this sense that sin had recovered its power to kill. After Moses, Christ had come and had restored to *all men* the possibility of eternal life lost by Adam, apparently including all of those men born after Adam and before Christ (presumably, that is, other than the Jews who had been given the Mosaic law and had already failed in obedience and died, but including all Jews contemporary to Christ). All men were then to be judged by their own righteousness (and perhaps, God being merciful, by their repentance) or by their faith in Christ and attempts to be righteous. There are points in the *Paraphrase* where Locke did seem to suggest, as he had very clearly suggested in the *Reasonableness*, that men could have made a claim of right to eternal life by righteousness under the natural law alone if they had obeyed this natural law; what he explicitly denied was that any man before Christ, or since, had been thus righteous, thus 'perfect' by being without any sin.[70]

In this interpretation of his arguments, Locke would have maintained room for the implication of the *Essay* that men *could* have known before Moses and Christ that there was an afterlife and that they would have rewarded and punished for their virtue or vice, and combined with this view one of two beliefs. He could have thought that men could not have known by unassisted reason alone that the specific punishment for vice would be loss of eternal life and hell fire, but that in fact those were its punishments. Or he could have thought that loss of eternal life and hell fire were not in fact necessarily the punishments for sin until they were declared to be the certain and unavoidable punishment of sin by positive law, but that there was nonetheless some form of punishment for vice that had made the same forms of virtuous behaviour as under Christianity the best prudential and obligatory course. This had enabled Christ to be the republisher of natural law with a divine authority that had made its knowledge more easy and certain than it had formerly been, but not the instituter of a different law.

---

[70] *Ibid.*, Rom. 5:13; Rom. 5:18; introduction, i, 49; Rom. 5:15; Rom. 2:26; Romans 'synopsis'; Rom. 1:32; Rom. 1:12; Rom. 1:26; Rom. 2:12.

CONCLUSION

By the time of his death, Locke was justifiably proud of his accomplishments in epistemology, political philosophy, educational theory and religious enquiry, but also had good reason for concern because many of his deepest convictions were not accepted by the vast majority of his contemporaries, several of his works were under fire, and significant issues in his thought remained unresolved. He was able to declare that he knew of no work which had explained property better than the *Two Treatises*. Yet they had been largely ignored, and their understanding of the principles of the Revolution of 1688–9 had been rejected by almost all of his contemporaries.[1] They were to receive only very limited support before the end of the eighteenth century, and the support that they did receive came largely from the critics of the establishment among the theologically heterodox and republican.[2] He had come to be fêted for his epistemology by many in France, England and Holland. The *Essay* was already influential, and it was to become profoundly influential in the eighteenth century in ways that are still being charted.[3] Yet it was under significant attack for fostering heresy, and in 1703 it was suppressed by his own university, Oxford. The grounds for the demonstrability of ethics, arguably to Locke the most significant claim of the *Essay*, were being questioned in Locke's own lifetime in ways that at the very least he could not see how to answer adequately by

---

[1] J. G. A. Pocock, *Virtue, Commerce and History*, Cambridge (1985), passim; Clark, *English Society*, passim; M. Thompson, 'The Reception of Locke's *Two Treatises*'; J. Dunn, 'The Politics of Locke in England and America in the Eighteenth Century' in J. Yolton (ed.), *John Locke: Problems and Perspectives in the Eighteenth Century*, Cambridge (1969); M. A. Goldie, 'The Roots of True Whiggism, 1688–94', *History of Political Thought* 1 (1980), 195–236; K. Wilson, 'A Dissident Legacy: Eighteenth Century Popular Politics and the Glorious Revolution' in J. R. Jones (ed.), *Liberty Secured? Britain before and after 1688*, Stanford (1992), 299–334; M. Jacob, *The Radical Enlightenment* (1981) 84–5; 118; 152; 236–7.

[2] M. Jacob, *The Radical Enlightenment* (1981) 84–5; 118; 152; 236–7; idem, *Living the Enlightenment* (1991), 63–4; 110–19; Clark, *English Society*, passim.

[3] There are of course many works on the influence of the *Essay* in the eighteenth century; we stand in need of many studies of the calibre of J. Yolton, *Locke and French Materialism*, Oxford (1991) before we will understand the full dimensions and complexities of the influence of the *Essay*.

demonstrating an afterlife and punishments for sin by the light of reason alone, given his agnosticism about substance and God's attributes. That argument of the *Essay* may even have been partially undercut for Locke himself by religious enquiries at the very end of his life that had made him believe that there had been no punishments for transgression of natural law alone, since all men after Adam were naturally and inescapably mortal; even if he had not actually come to such views, that part of his argument was very heavily dependent in practice in his last years upon the information about reward and punishment provided by revelation.[4]

Locke had not managed to demonstrate the full content of ethics, and had come to depict even the prospect of a full demonstration by others in increasingly bleak terms; by making such a demonstration analogous to Newton's work in science Locke made it the work of a genius. Locke had never thought that all men would be able to search into their own and others' moral duties, not even when arguing in the *Essay* that men had the intellectual capacity at birth by possession of reason to do so, because of his acute sense both of the practical depravity of most men and of the pressures of economic necessity upon most men. In that sense the shift in his perspective to the arguments of the *Reasonableness* did not involve a substantial diminution in his expectations about the results of men's great duty of search into morality. However, in his failure to 'bottom' the principles of social morality in the way that he remained convinced that he had 'bottomed' those of political morality, and in his recognition of the problems attached to demonstrating even such an understanding of political morality to the sons of properly educated gentlemen – leisured, intellectually able, and habituated into the desire of virtue and virtuous enquiry – the late 1690s do seem to have involved a more consciously pessimistic recognition by Locke of the extent of the difficulties faced by even the very few with the potential to enquire into their own and others' duties. Such men included himself.

In this situation, Locke's theological enquiries and his reliance on Christ for a saving faith and for information about virtue, about its rewards and about the very existence of an afterlife, did clearly become more important. These theological enquiries generated two major works, the *Reasonableness* and the *Paraphrase*, that set out many views that Locke's contemporaries considered heretical. His theological unorthodoxy must have made him extremely anxious at a time when he was collecting information about the execution in Scotland of Thomas Aikenhead for antitrinitarianism, and when a Blasphemy Act against antitrinitarianism was passed in England in 1697. Until he was in middle age burning was a potential

---

[4] Cf. Wootton, 'Locke and Socinianism'.

punishment for public expression of the views that he apparently held in private at the end of his life; even after that punishment was abolished in England imprisonment could have followed two public expressions of these views. The toleration established in 1689 in England was not established on the principles of the *Letter Concerning Toleration* but only by limited exemptions from the penalties of the law and then only for orthodox Protestants and not for antitrinitarians. Locke still had good reason in the last decade of his life to fear the power of clerics of all religions, including the majority of Anglicans. Although he upheld a minimal creed in the *Reasonableness* against Deism, he shared much ground with Deists in his opposition to 'priestcraft' and his works, especially the *Essay*, gave Deists much inspiration in ways that he was unwilling to repudiate. He became close friends in his final years with deistically inclined thinkers such as Matthew Tindall and expecially Anthony Collins. He even declared that he numbered his days by Collins' friendship. Locke's dying views were close to many of the major strands of Enlightenment thought, whose theology and arguments for toleration were unitarian as well as Deist. In the eighteenth century, Locke was to have at least as significant an influence upon dissent as upon Anglicanism; dissent had by then become in significant part unitarian rational dissent.[5]

Locke's theology had travelled a long way from the years of his Calvinist youth and Oxford Anglican orthodoxy, and by the late 1690s it stood at a considerable distance from the views of most of his contemporaries. It is not surprising that the further he travelled along this eccentrically independent path the stronger became his assertions of the importance of the enquiry itself rather than the truth realised by the enquiry. In 1698 in 'Error' this culminated in the declaration that a man who examined 'and upon a fair examination embraces an error for a truth, has done this duty, more than he who embraces the profession . . . of the truth without having examined whether it be true or no'.[6] There was no point in Locke's life where he showed the slightest sign of the conviction and confidence that nonconformists claimed to have experienced as the result of the 'Gales of God's grace', not even when he came in his final work to recognise the need for a faith that prominently included 'trust'. The convictions that sustained him were instead that God was good and merciful and that God had given men reason to enquire into their duties, to interpret Scripture, and to establish a secure society with a significant degree of liberty. Thus God would

---

[5] R. K. Webb, 'From Toleration to Religious Liberty' in J. R. Jones (ed.), *Liberty Secured?*, Stanford (1992), 158–98; R. B. Barlow, *Citizenship and Conscience*, Philadelphia (1962); J. G. A. Pocock, Review of I. Kranmick, *Republicanism and Bourgeois Radicalism*, *Eighteenth Century Studies* 25 (1991–2), 219–27 at 224–5.

[6] *Life and Letters*, ed. P. King (1884), 282ff.

then reward with 'rivers of pleasure' in heaven those men who had sincerely attempted to obey him and to understand his word. No particular doctrinal belief that Locke set out in his theological treatises of the 1690s and 1700s was as important to him as the belief that he expressed in the *Paraphrase* that God would 'accept of his good intention'.[7]

Locke wrote his own epitaph. It enunciated very clearly several of his central concerns at the end of his life. He declared that he had been contented with his 'modest lot'. He emphasised his mortality, pointedly hoping that the reader of his tombstone might 'learn from it'. For an example of virtue, he supposed that the reader should turn 'to the Gospels'. He declared that he had 'devoted his studies wholly to the pursuit of truth. Such you may learn from his writings, which will also tell you whatever else there is to be said about him more faithfully than the dubious eulogies of an epitaph.' Locke lived and died a gentleman, convinced that his was only a 'modest lot', that it was vital to encourage others to a life of virtue, and that it was most important to influence others of similar status: his epitaph was written in Latin. He expressed many of the values of a gentleman over the course of his life. The truth that he sought was conditioned in many different ways by his own experiences and status. It is nonetheless the extent to which he does indeed seem to have been pursuing truth in ways that challenged many of the cherished views of the vast majority of his contemporaries that is most remarkable. It is in this daring to know and to enquire that Locke most clearly deserves his place in the pantheon of the Enlightenment.[8]

---

[7] *Paraphrase*, preface, i, 103ff. Cf. Dunn, *Political Thought*, 243.
[8] Cranston, *Locke*, 481–2; cf. Parry, *Locke*, 160.

BIBLIOGRAPHY

Place of publication is London unless otherwise stated.

(a) PRIMARY SOURCES BY LOCKE

All manuscripts by Locke that are described as 'MS Locke' are in the Locke Room, Bodleian Library, Oxford. All books cited as being his personal copies are also in the Locke Room, the Bodleian Library, Oxford. Manuscripts which start 'BM' are in the British Library, London. Manuscripts which start 'PRO' are in the Public Record Office, Chancery Lane, London.

(I) MANUSCRIPTS

MS Locke b2.
MS Locke b3.
MS Locke b7.
MS Locke c27.
MS Locke c28.
MS Locke c30.
MS Locke c31.
MS Locke c32.
MS Locke c33.
MS Locke c34.
MS Locke c41.
MS Locke c42.
MS Locke c43.
MS Locke c44.
MS Locke c47.
MS Locke d1.
MS Locke d2.
MS Locke d3.
MS Locke d10.
MS Locke e3.
MS Locke e6.
MS Locke e10.
MS Locke e17.
MS Locke f1.
MS Locke f2.
MS Locke f3.

MS Locke f4.
MS Locke f5.
MS Locke f6.
MS Locke f7.
MS Locke f8.
MS Locke f9.
MS Locke f10.
MS Locke f11.
MS Locke f14.
MS Locke f15.
MS Locke f16.
MS Locke f17.
MS Locke f27.
MS Locke f28.
MS Locke f29.
MS Locke f30.
MS Locke f32.
MS (Locke) Film. 77.
MS (Locke) Film. 79.
Bm Add. MS 15642.
Bm Add. MS 28227.
Bm Add. MS 28273.
PRO 30/24/5pt.3/276–8.
PRO 30/24/6A/347.
PRO 30/24/6B/427–31.
PRO 30/24/47/3.
PRO 30/24/47/30.
MA 998; MA 232 Pierpont Morgan Library, New York.

(2) LOCKE'S ANNOTATED COPIES OF BOOKS EXAMINED:

Bibles, Testaments:

Le Nouveau Testament, Mons (1673).
Holy Bible (1648).
Holy Bible (1654).
Testamentum Graecorum (missing title page; *Library*, 2862; Locke Room, shelved
    under 9.40).

Other Works:

Anon. *Irenicum Magnum* (1700).
Baxter, R. *Church History of the Government of Bishops* (1681).
Blount, Sir Thomas Pope, *Censura Celebriorum Authorum* (1690).
Calamy, E. *An Abridgement of Mr Baxter's History of his Life and Times* (1702).
Cicero, M. T. *Epistolae, quae Familiares vocantur* (1596).
Clerc, J. le *Ars Critica*, Amsterdam (1697).
Episcopius, S. *Opera Theologica* (1678).
Hales, J. *Several Tracts* (1677).
S. N[ewman]. *A Concordance to the Holy Scriptures* (1698).

Nye, P. *A Declaration of the Faith and Order owned and Practised in the Congregational Churches in England* (1688).
Patrick, S. *Jesus and the Resurrection* (1677).
Smith, J. *Select Discourses* (1660).
Stillingfleet, E. *Defence of the Discourse concerning the Idolatry Practised in the Church of Rome* (1676).
The Confession of Faith: Together with the Larger and Lesser Catechisms Composed by the Reverend Assembly of Divines Then Sitting at Westminster (1688).

(b) PUBLISHED WORKS BY LOCKE

The Correspondence of John Locke, ed. E. S. De Beer, Oxford (1978–), 8 vols.
Discourses Translated From Nicole's Essais, ed. T. Hancock (1828).
An Early Draft of Locke's Essay, ed. R. Aaron and J. Gibb, Oxford (1936); Draft B, ed. B. Rand (1931).
An Essay Concerning Human Understanding, ed. P. Nidditch, Oxford (1978).
John Locke, An Essay Concerning Toleration and Toleratio, ed. K. Inoue, Nara Women's University, Nara, Japan (1974).
'John Locke's "Essay on Infallibility": Introduction, Text, and Translation', ed. J. C. Biddle *Journal of Church and State* 19 (1977), 301–27.
A Letter Concerning Toleration, ed. J. Tully, Indianapolis (1983).
A Letter Concerning Toleration, ed. R. Klibansky and J. Gough, Oxford (1968).
The Library Catalogue of John Locke, ed. P. Laslett and J. Harrison, Oxford (1965).
The Life and Letters of John Locke, ed. P. King (1884), vol. II.
Of the Conduct of the Understanding, ed. F. Garforth, New York (1966).
A Paraphrase and Notes Upon the Epistles of St Paul, ed. A. Wainwright, Oxford (1989), 2 vols.
Some Thoughts Concerning Education, ed. J. Axtell, Cambridge (1969).
Some Thoughts Concerning Education, ed. J. and J. Yolton, Oxford (1989).
Two Tracts Upon Government, ed. P. Abrams, Cambridge (1969).
Two Treatises of Government, ed. P. Laslett, Cambridge (1963; 1987).
The Works of John Locke (1794), 9 vols.
The Works of John Locke (1801), 10 vols.

(c) PRIMARY SOURCES BY AUTHORS OTHER THAN LOCKE

(1) MANUSCRIPTS

MS Aubrey 10, Bodleian Library, Oxford.
PRO SP 104/177 (Minutes of the Committee for Trade and Plantations).
PRO 30/24 (Shaftesbury papers).

(2) PRINTED WORKS

Allestree, R. *The Whole Duty of Man* (1659).
Alsop, V. *Antisozzo: or Sherlocismus Enervatus* (1675).
Anon. *An Account of the Life and Writings of Jean Le Clerc* (1712).
Anon. *An Argument for Self-Defense* (1710).

Anon. *The Complete Statesman* (1683).
Anon. *The Faith of One God* (1691).
Anon. [A. Sidney et al.?] *A Just and Modest Vindication of The Two Last Parliaments* (1682).
Anon. *The Last Speech and Behaviour of William late Lord Russell* (1683).
Anon. [Shaftesbury, Earl of?] *A Letter From A Parliament-Man*, n.p.p. (1675).
Anon. *Liberty of Conscience in its order to Universal Peace* (1681).
Anon. ['A Person of Quality'] *Moral Essays* (1677).
Anon. *The Presentment and Humble Petition of the Grand Jury for the County of Middlesex, May 18, 1681* (1681).
Anon. *The Trinitarian Scheme* (1692).
Bagshawe, E. *The Great Question Concerning Things Indifferent In Religious Worship* (1660).
Barbeyrac, J. 'An Historical and Critical Account of the Science of Morality' in S. Pufendorf, *The Law of Nature and Nations* (1729).
Barlow, T. 'The Case of a Toleration in Matters of Religion' in idem, *Several Miscellaneous and Weighty Cases of Conscience* (1692).
Barne, M. *The Authority of Church Guides Asserted* (4th edn. 1685).
Barrow, I. *Theological Works*, ed. A. Napier, Cambridge (1859), 2 vols.
Works (1687), vols. II and IV.
Baxter, R. *Church History of the Government of Bishops* (1681).
The Cure of Church Divisions (1670).
Holy Commonwealth (1659).
Reliquiae Baxterianae (1696).
Richard Baxter's Answer to Dr Edward Stillingfleet's Charge of Separation (1680).
A Search For the English Schismatick (1681).
The Second Part of the Nonconformists' Plea for Peace (1680).
A Treatise of Episcopacy (1681).
Biddle, J. *The Apostolical and True Opinion Concerning the Holy Trinity* (1653).
Bodenham, J. *Politeuphia* (1598).
Boyle, R. *Some Considerations Touching the Usefulness of Experimental Natural Philosophy*, Oxford (1663; 1665).
Buchanan, G. *De Jure Regni Apud Scotos*, transl. D. MacNeill as *The Art and Science of Government among the Scots* (1964).
Bull, G. *Harmonia Apostolica* (1669–70).
Burnet, G. *An Apology for the Church of England* (1688) in *A Collection of Scarce and valuable tracts . . . particularly . . . of the late Lord Somers*, ed. Sir W. Scott (2nd edn. 1809–15), IX.
An Exposition of the 39 Articles of the Church of England (1819).
Four Discourses (1694).
History of My Own Time, Oxford (1823).
A Relation of the Death of the Primitive Persecutors, Amsterdam (1687).
A Sermon Preached at the Funeral of . . . John . . . Archbishop of Canterbury (1695).
A Supplement to Burnet's History of My Own Time, ed. H. Foxcroft, Oxford (1902).
[Bury, A.] *The Naked Gospel* (1690).
Calvin, J. *Commentaries on the Epistles of St Paul to the Romans*, transl. J. Owen, Edinburgh (1849).

Institutes of the Christian Religion, ed. J. T. McNeill (1960).
Cary, L. (2nd Viscount Falkland) *Discourse on Infallibility* (1659).
Chillingworth, W. *The Religion of Protestants* (1638).
Cicero, M. T. *De Officiis*, Loeb Classics, (25), Cambridge, Mass. and London (1913).
Clerc, J. le *An Account of the Life and Writings of Mr John Locke* (1706; 1713).
    Five Letters Concerning the Inspiration of the Holy Scriptures (1690).
Clerc, J. le (ed.), *Bibliothèque Universelle et Historique de l'année 1686–93*.
Cockham, T. *Tully's Offices in Three Books* (1699).
Coleman, T. *Hopes Deferred and Dashed* (1645).
Coles, E. *English Dictionary* (1676).
[Croft, H.] *The Naked Truth* (1674).
Cromwell, O. *The Writings and Speeches of Oliver Cromwell*, ed. W. C. Abbott,
    Cambridge, Mass. (1937–47).
Cudworth, R. *The True Intellectual System of the Universe* (1678).
Cumberland, R. *A Treatise of the Laws of Nature*, transl. J. Maxwell (1727).
Dallington, R. *Aphorismes Civil and Militarie* (1st edn. 1613).
Denton, W. *Jus Regiminis* (1689).
Dodwell, H. *An Admonitory Discourse Concerning the Late English Schism* (1714).
    *A Discourse of the one Altar and the One Priesthood insisted on by the Ancients
    in their Disputes against Schism* (1683).
    Dissertationes Cyprianicae (1682).
    Dissertationes Irenaeii (1689).
    *Separation of Churches from Episcopal Government as practiced by the Present
    nonconformists, proved Schismatical* (1679).
    S. Caecilii Cypriani Opera, Amsterdam (1700).
Dryden, J. *Absalom and Achitophel* (1681).
    *A Vindication: or the Parallel of the French Holy League and the English League
    and Covenant* (1683).
Edwards, J. *The Socinian Creed* (1697).
    Socinianism Unmask'd (1696).
    Some Thoughts Concerning the Several Causes of Atheism (1695).
L'Estrange, R. *Observator*: 18 December 1682; 1 October 1683.
    Seneca's Morals by Way of Abstract (1678).
    Tully's Offices (2nd edn. 1681).
Fenton, G. *The History of Guiccardini* (1st edn. 1579).
Ferguson, R. *An Impartial Enquiry into the Administration of Affairs in England*
    (1684)
    The Interest of Reason in Religion (1675).
    Justification Onely Upon a Satisfaction (1668).
    No Protestant Plot (1681).
    A Representation of the Threatening Dangers (1688).
    The Second Part of No Protestant Plot (1682).
Filmer, R. *Patriarcha and Other Political Works*, ed. P. Laslett, Oxford (1949).
Ford, Lord Grey *The Secret History of The Rye House Plot* (2nd edn. 1754).
Fowler, E. *Certain Propositions* (1694).
    The Design of Christianity (1671).
    The Principles and Practices of Certain Moderate Divines (1670).
[Furly, B.] *Bibliothèque Furliana*, Rotterdam (1714).
Glanvill, J. 'Antifanatical Religion and Free Philosophy' in idem, *Essays on Several
    Important Subjects* (1676).

Philosophia Pia (1671).
Goodwin, J. *Obstructours* (1649).
Goodwin, T. *Patience and its Perfect Work, under Sudden and Sore Tryals* (1666).
Grotius, H. *De Jure Belli ac Pacis* (1625); transl. and ed. F. Kelsey, Oxford (1925).
  De Jure Belli ac Pacis, transl. B. Kennett with notes by J. Barbeyrac (1738) as
  The Rights of War and Peace.
  De Veritate Religionis Christianae, transl. S. Patrick (1680).
[Gunning, P?] *Lex Talionis* (1676).
Hammond, H. *Dissertationes Quatuor* (1651).
  The Miscellaneous Theological Works of Henry Hammond (1850) vols. I & III.
  Of the Power of the Keyes (1647).
  A Pacifick Discourse of God's Grace and Decrees (1660).
Helvyn, P. *Cyprianus Anglicus* (1668).
  History of Episcopacy in idem, *Historical and Miscellaneous Tracts* (1681).
[Howard, R.] *A Twofold Vindication* (1696).
Howe, J. *Memoirs of John Howe,* ed. E. Calamy (1724).
Hunt, T. *A Defence of the Charter and Municipal Rights of the City of London*
  (1683).
Johnson, S. *Julian the Apostate* (1682).
Laney, B. *A Sermon Preached Before the King at Whitehall* (1675).
Lawson, G. *Politica Sacra et Civilis* (1660).
[Leslie, C.] *The Change of Socinianism,* Edinburgh (1695).
Limborch, P. van *Theologia Christiana,* Amsterdam (1686).
Lodge, T. (transl. and ed.) *The Works of Seneca* (1614).
Luther, M. *Lectures on Romans,* Library of Christian Classics, XV, ed. W. Pauck,
  Philadelphia (1961).
Luttrell, N. *Luttrell's Brief Historical Relations of State Affairs, 1678–1714,*
  Oxford (1857).
[Marvell, A.] *An Account of the Growth of Popery and Arbitrary Government*
  (1677).
Milner, J. *An Account of Mr Lock's Religion* (1700).
Milton, J. *The Tenure of Kings and Magistrates* (1649).
Naninni, R. *Civil Considerations* (1601).
Nye, P. *The King's Authority in Dispensing with Ecclesiastical Laws, Asserted and
  Vindicated,* ed. H. Nye (1687).
[Nye, S.] *A Brief History of the Unitarians* (1687).
[Nye, S.] *Considerations on the Explication of the Doctrine of the Trinity* (1694).
[Nye, S.] *A Discourse Concerning Natural and Revealed Religion* (1695).
Overton, R. 'An Arrow Against all Tyrants' (1646?), printed most accessibly in G.
  Aylmer, *The Levellers in the English Revolution,* Cornell (1975).
Owen, J. *Works,* ed. W. Goold (1967), 15 vols.
Parker, S. *A Defence and Continuation of the Discourse of Ecclesiastical Polity*
  (1671).
  A Demonstration of the Divine Authority of the Law of Nature (1681).
  A Discourse of Ecclesiastical Policy (1670).
  A Free and Impartial Censure of the Platonick Philosophie (1666).
  History of His Own Time (1727).
Parry, J. *A Resolution of a Seasonable Case of Conscience,* Oxford (1660).
S. P[atrick]. *A Brief Account of the New Sect of Latitude-Men* (1662).
Patrick, S. *Jesus and the Resurrection* (1677).

A Sermon Preached at the Funeral of Thomas Grigg (1670).
Works (Oxford 1858).
Pearson, J. *An Exposition of the Creed* (1659).
Promiscuous Ordinations (1668).
Vindiciae Epistolarum S. Ignatii (1672).
Pepys, S. *The Diary of Samuel Pepys*, ed. R. Latham and W. Matthews, 11 vols. (1970–83), vols. V and IX.
Pett, P. [R. T.] *A Discourse Concerning Liberty of Conscience* (1661).
Phillips, E. *New World of English Words* (1671; 1678; 1706).
Philodemius, *The Original and End of Civil Power* (1649).
Proast, J. *The Argument of the Letter concerning Toleration Briefly Considered and Answered*, Oxford (1690).
Pufendorf, S. *De Jure Naturae et Gentium*, Lund (1672); transl. and ed. C. H. & W. Oldfather, Oxford (1934).
De Officio Hominis et Civis, Amsterdam (1673).
Of the Law of Nature and Nations, transl. B. Kennett, with notes by J. Barbeyrac (1729).
Purfoote, T. *A brief collection of all the notable and material things contained in the Historie of Guicciardini* (1591).
Reynolds, E. *A Sermon Preached before the Peers in The Abbey Church at Westminster, November 7 1666* (1666).
Rutherford, S. *Lex Rex* (1644).
Sanderson, R. *Bishop Sanderson's Lectures on Conscience and Human Law*, ed. and transl. C. Wordsworth, Oxford and Cambridge (1877).
Seneca, L. A. *De Beneficiis*, Loeb Classics, Cambridge, Mass. and London (1935).
Settle, E. *Remarks Upon Algernon Sidney's Paper, Delivered to the Sheriffs at his Execution* (1683).
Shakespeare, W. *Coriolanus* (1608?).
King Lear (1606?).
Timon of Athens (1607?).
Sherlock, W. *A Defence of Dr Sherlock's Notion of a Trinity* (1694).
A Discourse About Church Unity (1681).
A Discourse Concerning the Knowledge of Jesus Christ and our Union and Communion with him (1674).
A Vindication of the doctrines of the Holy and ever blessed Trinity and the Incarnation of the Son of God (1692).
Shower, B. *The Magistracy and Government of England Vindicated* (1689).
Sidney, A. *Discourses Concerning Government* (1704).
Smith, *Select Discourses* (1660).
Smythies, W. *A Reply to a Letter sent by William Newbery and William Edmunds to Dr Fowler*, n.p., n.d. [1685?].
[Somers, J.?] *A Discourse Concerning Generosity* (1693).
South, R. *Animadversions on Dr Sherlock's book entituled a Vindication of the Trinity* (1693).
Sprat, T. *A True Account of the Horrid Conspiracy to Assassinate the Late King Charles II at the Rye House*, ed. E. Goldsmid (1685; 1886 reprint).
Stillingfleet, E. *The Bishop of Worcester's Answer to Mr Locke's Letter* (1697).
The Bishop of Worcester's Answer to Mr Locke's Second Letter (1698).
A Discourse in Vindication of the Trinity (1696).
Irenicum (1662).

The Mischief of Separation (1680).
Origines Sacrae (1662).
The Unreasonableness of Separation (1681).
Works (1710).
Stubbe, H. *An Essay in Defence of the Good Old Cause* (1659).
Tate, N. *The History of King Lear* (1681).
The Ingratitude of a Commonwealth (1682).
Thorndike, H. *Theological Works*, Oxford (1844–56), 9 vols.
Tillotson, J. *A Letter Written to My Lord Russell in Newgate*, 20 July 1683 (1683).
The Protestant Religion Vindicated (1680).
Sermons of the Divinity and Incarnation of our blessed Saviour (1694).
Works (1704).
Works, Edinburgh (1748).
Works, ed. T. Birch (1752).
Works (1757).
Works (1820).
Tindall, M. *Letter to the Reverend Clergy* (1694).
The Rights of The Christian Church Asserted (1706).
Towerson, G. *An Explication of the Catechism of the Church of England* (1678).
An Explication of the Decalogue (1676).
Turner, F. *Animadversions upon a Late Pamphlet entituled the Naked Truth* (1676).
Tyrrell, J. *Patriarcha Non Monarcha* (1681).
Volkel, J. *De Vera Religione libri v. Quibus praefixus est J. Crelli Liber de Deo et eius attributis et nunc demum adjuncti eiusdem De Uno Deo Patre libri ii*, Amsterdam? (1642?).
Walton, I. *The Life of Dr Robert Sanderson* (1678).
Walwyn, W. *Toleration Justified* (1646).
Whichcote, B. *Moral and Religious Aphorisms* (1753).
The Select Sermons of Benjamin Whichcote (1698).
Wilkins, J. *Ecclesiastes, or a Discourse concerning the Gift of Preaching* (1646).
Of the Principles and Duties of Natural Religion (1674).
Williams, R. *The Bloody Tenent of Persecution* (1644).

(d) SECONDARY SOURCES

Abercrombie, N. *The Origins of Jansenism*, Oxford (1936).
Abernathy, G. R. 'Clarendon and the Declaration of Indulgence', *Journal of Ecclesiastical History* 11 (1960), 59–64.
Allison, C. F. *The Rise of Moralism* (1966).
Ashcraft, R. 'Latitudinarianism and Toleration: Historical Myth versus Political History' in R. Kroll, R. Ashcraft and P. Zagorin (eds.), *Philosophy, Science and Religion in England 1640–1700*, Cambridge (1992), 151–77.
Locke's Two Treatises of Government (1987).
'Political Theory and Political Reform: John Locke's Essay on Virginia', *The Western Political Quarterly* 22: 4 (1969), 742–58.
Revolutionary Politics and Locke's Two Treatises of Government, Princeton (1986).
'Simple Objections and Complex Reality: Theorizing Political Radicalism in Seventeenth Century England', *Political Studies*, xl, 1, (1992), 99–115.

Ashcraft, R., Kroll, R. and Zagorin, P. (eds.), *Philosophy, Science and Religion in England 1640–1700*, Cambridge (1992).
Ashton, R. 'From Cavalier to Roundhead Tyranny' in J. Morrill, (ed.), *Reactions to the English Civil War* (1982).
Ayers, M. R. 'The Ideas of Power and Substance in Locke's Philosophy', *The Philosophical Quarterly* 25: 1 (1978), 1–27.
   'Mechanism, Superaddition and the Proofs of God's Existence in Locke's Essay', *Philosophical Review* 90: 2 (1981), 211–51.
Bahlman, D. *The Moral Revolution of 1688*, New Haven (1957).
Barker, G. F. R. *Memoir of Busby* (1895).
Barlow, R. B. *Citizenship and Conscience*, Philadelphia (1962).
Bate, F. *The Declaration of Indulgence 1672* (1908).
Beddard, R. A. 'The Commission for Ecclesiastical Promotions, 1681–4: An Instrument of Tory Reaction', *Historical Journal* 10: 1 (1967), 11–40.
   'The Privileges of Christchurch, Canterbury: Archbishop Sheldon's Enquiries of 1671', *Archaeologia Cantiana* 87 (1972), 81–100.
   'The Restoration Church' in J. R. Jones (ed.), *The Restored Monarchy* (1979).
   'Sheldon and Anglican Recovery', *Historical Journal* 19: 4 (1976), 1005–17.
   'Vincent Alsop and the Emancipation of Restoration Dissent', *Journal of Ecclesiastical History* 24 (1973), 173–84.
Bennett, G. V. 'Conflict in the Church' in G. S. Holmes (ed.), *Britain After the Glorious Revolution, 1688–1714* (1969).
   The Tory Crisis in Church and State, Oxford (1975).
Bennett, H. *English Books and Readers 1603–40*, Cambridge (1970).
Berlin, I. 'Two Concepts of Liberty' in idem, *Four Essays on Liberty*, Oxford (1969).
Biddle, J. 'Locke's Critique of Innate Principles and Toland's Deism', *Journal of the History of Ideas* 37 (1976), 410–22.
Birch, T. *The Life of Robert Boyle* (1744).
Bolam, C. G. et al. *The English Presbyterians*, Boston (1968).
Bosher, R. S. *The Making of the Restoration Settlement* (1951).
Brown, L. F. *The First Earl of Shaftesbury*, New York (1933).
Burtt, S. *Virtue Transformed*, Cambridge (1992).
Carroll, R. *The Commonsense Philosophy of Religion of Bishop Edward Stillingfleet*, The Hague (1975).
Cargill Thompson, W. D. J. 'The Philosopher of the "Politic Society": Richard Hooker as a Political Thinker', in W. Speed Hill (ed.), *Studies in Richard Hooker* (1972), 3–76.
Chadwick, H. *Augustine*, Oxford (1986).
   The Early Church (1967).
Champion, J. A. I. *The Pillars of Priestcraft Shaken*, Cambridge (1992).
Christie, W. D. *The First Earl of Shaftesbury* (1871).
Clark, J. C. D. *English Society 1688–1832*, Cambridge (1985).
Colie, R. 'John Locke in the Republic of Letters' in J. Bromley and E. Kossman (eds.), *Britain and the Netherlands* (1960), 111–29.
Colman, J. *John Locke's Moral Philosophy*, Edinburgh (1983).
Condren, C. *George Lawson's 'Politica' and the English Revolution*, Cambridge (1989).
   'Resistance and Sovereignty in Lawson's *Politica*: An Examination of a Part of Professor Franklin, His Chimera', *Historical Journal* 24: 3 (1981), 673–81.

Costello, W. *The Scholastic Curriculum at Early Seventeenth Century Cambridge*, Cambridge, Mass. (1958).

Cragg, G. *From Puritanism to the Age Of Reason*, Cambridge (1950).

Cranston, M. *John Locke*, Oxford (1957, 2nd edn. 1985).

Daly, J. *Sir Robert Filmer and English Political Thought*, Toronto (1979).

Davis, J. C. 'Religion and the Struggle for Freedom in the English Revolution', *Historical Journal* 35: 3 (1992), 507–30.

Dewhurst, K. 'Locke and Sydenham on the Teaching of Anatomy', *Medical History* 2 (1958), 1–12.

John Locke, Physician and Philosopher (1963).

Dickinson, H. T. *Liberty and Property* (1977).

Dodge, G. H. *The Political Theory of the Huguenots of the Dispersion*, Columbia (1947).

Driscoll, E. A. 'The Influence of Gassendi on Locke's Hedonism', *International Philosophical Quarterly* 12 (1972), 87–110.

Dunn, E. C. *The Concept of Ingratitude in Renaissance English Moral Philosophy*, Washington (1946).

Dunn, J. 'Consent in the Political Theory of John Locke' in G. Schochet (ed.), *Life, Liberty and Property*, California (1971), 129–61.

'Individuality, Clientage and the Formation of Locke's Social Identity' in idem, *Rethinking Modern Political Theory*, Cambridge (1985).

John Locke, Oxford (1984).

'Justice and the Interpretation of Locke's Political Ideas', *Political Studies* 16 (1968), 68–87.

The Political Thought of John Locke, Cambridge (1969).

Elton, G. R. *The Tudor Constitution*, Cambridge (1960).

Every, G. *The High Church Party* (1956).

Farr, J. and Roberts, C. 'John Locke on the Glorious Revolution: A Rediscovered Document', *Historical Journal* 28: 2 (1985), 385–98.

Ferguson, J. *Robert Ferguson the Plotter*, Edinburgh (1887).

Firpo, M. 'John Locke e il Socinianismo', *Rivista Storica Italiana* 92 (1980), 35–124.

Forbes, D. *Hume's Philosophical Politics*, Cambridge (1975).

Force, J. *William Whiston, Honest Newtonian*, Cambridge (1985).

Fox Bourne, H. R. *The Life of John Locke* (1876), 2 vols.

Franklin, J. *John Locke and the Theory of Sovereignty*, Cambridge (1978).

Furley, O. W. 'The Whig Exclusionists: Pamphlet Literature in the Exclusion Crisis', *The Cambridge Historical Journal*, 1st series, 13 (1957), 19–36.

Furnivall, J. (ed.) *Harrison's Description of England* (1877).

Gascoigne, J. 'The Holy Alliance', unpublished Ph.D thesis, Cambridge University (1981).

Gawlick, G. 'Cicero and the Enlightenment', *Studies on Voltaire in the Eighteenth Century* 25 (1963), 657–82.

Golden, S. A. *Jean Le Clerc*, New York (1972).

Goldie, M. A. 'John Locke and Anglican Royalism', *Political Studies* 31: 1 (1983), 61–85.

'John Locke's Circle and James II', *Historical Journal* 35: 3 (1992), 557–86.

'Locke and Proast'; 'Priestcraft and Politics', unpublished typescripts.

'The Roots of True Whiggism, 1688–95', *History of Political Thought* 1 (1980), 195–236.

'Sir Peter Pett, Sceptical Toryism and the Science of Toleration in the 1680s' in W. Sheils (ed.), *Persecution and Toleration* (Studies in Church History, vol. 21), Oxford (1984), 247–73.

'Tory Political Thought 1689–1714', unpublished Ph.D thesis, Cambridge University (1978).

Gough, J. 'James Tyrrell, Whig Historian and Friend of John Locke', *Historical Journal* 19 (1976), 541–60.

John Locke's Political Philosophy: Eight Studies, Oxford (2nd edn. 1973).

Grant, R. *John Locke's Liberalism*, Chicago (1987).

Green, I. M. *The Re-establishment of the Church of England 1660–3*, Oxford (1978).

Grell, O. et al. (eds.) *From Persecution to Toleration*, Oxford (1991).

Gunn, J. *Politics and the Public Interest in the Seventeenth Century* (1969).

Haley, K. H. D. *The First Earl of Shaftesbury*, Oxford (1978).

Hampsher-Monk, I. 'Tacit Concept of Consent in Locke's *Two Treatises of Government*: A Note on Citizens, Travellers, and Patriarchalism', *Journal of the History of Ideas* 40 (1979), 135–9.

Hardacre, P. 'Sir Edward Hyde and the Idea of Liberty to Tender Conscience 1641–56', *Journal of Church and State* 13 (1971), 23–42.

'The Genesis of the Declaration of Breda 1657–60', *Journal of Church and State* 15 (1973), 65–82.

Harris, T. *London Crowds in the Reign of Charles II*, Cambridge (1987).

Harris, T. et al. *The Politics of Religion in Restoration England*, Oxford (1990).

Harrison, P. *'Religion' and the Religions in the English Enlightenment*, Cambridge (1990).

Higginbotham, J. (transl. and ed.) *Cicero, On Moral Obligation*, Berkeley (1967).

Hill, C. *The World Turned Upside Down* (1972).

Holt, J. C. *Magna Carta*, Cambridge (1965).

Hont, I. and Ignatieff, M. *Wealth and Virtue*, Cambridge (1983).

Hooker, R. *Of the Laws of Ecclesiastical Polity*, ed. A. S. McGrade and B. Vickers (1975).

Horwitz, H. 'Protestant Reconciliation during the Exclusion Crisis', *Journal of Ecclesiastical History* 15 (1964), 201–17.

Revolution Politics: The Career of Daniel Finch, Second Earl of Nottingham (1968).

Hume, D. *Essays Moral, Political and Literary*, Indianapolis (1987).

Jacob, J. *Henry Stubbe: Radical Protestantism and the Early Enlightenment*, Cambridge (1983).

Jacob, M. *Living the Enlightenment*, Oxford (1991).

The Newtonians and the English Revolution, Suffolk (1976).

The Radical Enlightenment (1981).

James, E. D. *Pierre Nicole, Jansenist and Humanist*, The Hague (1972).

Johnson, M. S. *Locke on Freedom*, Texas (1978).

Jolley, N. *Leibniz and Locke*, Oxford (1984).

Jones, J. R. *The First Whigs: The Politics of the Exclusion Crisis* (1961).

Jordy, A. de 'A Library for Younger Schollers', *University of Illinois Studies in Language and Literature*, Illinois (1961), vol. 48.

Keeble, N. *The Literary Culture of Nonconformity*, Leicester (1987).

Kelly, P. 'Locke and Filmer: Was Laslett so Wrong After All?', *Locke Newsletter* 8 (1977), 77–86.

Kelso, R. *The Doctrine of the English Gentleman in the Sixteenth Century*, Urbana (1929).

Kenyon, J. P. *The Stuart Constitution*, Cambridge (1966).

Keohane, N. *Philosophy and the State in France*, Princeton (1980).

Kirby, E. W. 'The Naked Truth: A Plea for Church Unity', *Church History* 7 (1938), 45–61.

Klaaren, E. M. *The Religious Origins of Modern Science*, Grand Rapids, Michigan (1979).

Knights, M. 'Petitioning and the Political Theorists: John Locke, Algernon Sidney and London's "Monster" Petition of 1680', *Past and Present* 138 (1993), 94–111.

Kroll, R. 'The Question of Locke's Relation to Gassendi', *Journal of the History of Ideas* 45: 3 (1984), 339–61.

Lacey, D. *Dissent and Parliamentary Politics in England 1661–89*, Rutgers (1969).

Lacey, F. A. *Herbert Thorndike* (1929).

Lamont, W. *Baxter and the Millennium* (1979).

Godly Rule (1969).

Laslett, P. 'John Locke, the Great Recoinage and the Board of Trade 1695–8' in J. Yolton (ed.), *John Locke: Problems and Perspectives*, Cambridge (1969).

The World We Have Lost, Cambridge (1965).

Leeuwen, H. G. van *The Pursuit of Certainty in English Thought 1630–40*, The Hague (1963).

Letwin, W. *The Origins of Scientific Economics* (1963).

Leyden, W. von 'Locke and Nicole', *Sophia* 16: 1 (1971), 41–55.

Locke, L. 'Tillotson: A Study in Seventeenth Century Literature' in *Anglistica* (1954).

Lough, J. *Locke's Travels in France 1675–9*, Cambridge (1953).

McAdoo, H. R. *The Spirit of Anglicanism* (1965).

McGee, J. Sears *The Godly Man in Stuart England*, New Haven (1976).

MacIntyre, A. *After Virtue* (1981).

McLachlan, H. *The Religious Opinions of Milton, Locke and Newton*, Manchester (1941).

Socinianism in Seventeenth Century England, Oxford (1951).

McNally, D. 'Locke, Levellers and Liberty: Property and Democracy in the Thought of the First Whigs', *History of Political Thought* 10: 1 (1989), 17–40.

Macpherson, C. B. *The Political Theory of Possessive Individualism*, Oxford (1962).

Marshall, J. W. 'The Ecclesiology of the Latitude-Men 1660–89: Stillingfleet, Tillotson and "Hobbism"', *Journal of Ecclesiastical History* 26 (1985), 407–27.

'John Locke in Context: Religion, Ethics and Politics', Ph.D diss., The Johns Hopkins University (1990).

'John Locke and Latitudinarianism' in R. Kroll et al. (eds.), *Philosophy, Science and Religion in England 1640–1700*, Cambridge (1992), 253–82.

'John Locke and Socinianism' forthcoming in M. A. Stewart (ed.) *Seventeenth Century Philosophy in Historical Context*, Oxford.

'John Locke's Religious, Educational and Moral Thought', *Historical Journal* 33: 2 (1990), 997–1007.

Miller, J. *Popery and Politics in England 1660–88*, Cambridge (1973).

Montuouri, M. *John Locke on Toleration and the Unity of God*, Amsterdam (1983).

More, L. T. *The Life and Works of The Honourable Robert Boyle*, Oxford (1944).

Morrill, J. 'The Church of England 1642–9' in idem (ed.), *Reactions to the English Civil War* (1982), 89–114.

Notes and Queries (1851).

Nuttall, G. *Visible Saints: The Congregational Way 1640–60*, Oxford (1957).

Ogg, D. *England in the Reign of Charles II*, Oxford (1934).

Orr, R. R. *Reason and Authority*, Oxford (1967).

Packer, J. W. *The Transformation of Anglicanism* (1969).

Pangle, T. *The Spirit of Modern Republicanism*, Chicago (1988).

Parker, T. M. 'Arminianism and Laudianism in Seventeenth Century England' in C. W. Dugmore and C. Duggan (eds.), *Studies in Church History* (1964), I, 20–34.

Parry, G. *John Locke*, Manchester (1978).

Peck, L. Levy *Northampton: Patronage and Policy at the Court of James I* (1982).

Pocock, J. G. A. *The Ancient Constitution and the Feudal Law*, Cambridge (1987).
   The Machiavellian Moment, Princeton (1975).
   Review of I. Kranmick, *Republicanism and Bourgeois Radicalism*, *Eighteenth Century Studies* 25 (1991–2), 219–27.
   Virtue, Commerce and History, Cambridge (1985).

Popkin, R. *The History of Scepticism From Erasmus to Spinoza*, Berkeley (1979).

Prideaux, H. *The Letters of Humphrey Prideaux to John Ellis*, ed. E. M. Thompson, Camden Society (1875).

Rahe, P. 'John Locke's Philosophical Partisanship', *The Political Science Reviewer* 20:1 (1991), 1–43.

Redwood, J. *Reason, Ridicule and Religion* (1976).

Reedy, G. *The Bible and Reason*, Pennsylvania (1985).

Rees, T. (ed.) *The Racovian Catechism* (1818).

Robinson, H. W. and Adams, W. (eds.) *The Diary of Robert Hooke* (1935).

Russell, C. *The Crisis of Parliaments*, Oxford (1971).

Russell, C. (ed.) *The Origins of the English Civil War* (1973).

Salmon, J. *Renaissance and Revolt*, Cambridge (1987).

Sargentlich, T. (ed.) 'Locke and Ethical Theory: Two MS Pieces' in *Locke Newsletter* 5 (1974), 26–8.

Schochet, G. 'Ashcraft on Locke', *Journal of the History of Ideas* (1989), 491–510.
   Patriarchalism in Political Thought, Oxford (1975).

Scott, J. *Algernon Sidney and the English Republic 1623–1677*, Cambridge (1988).
   Algernon Sidney and the Restoration Crisis, Cambridge (1991).

Seaward, P. *The Cavalier Parliament and the Reconstruction of the Old Regime*, Cambridge (1989).

Shapiro, B. *Probability and Certainty in Seventeenth Century England*, Princeton (1983).
   John Wilkins, Berkeley (1969).

Shaw, W. A. *The History of the English Church during the Civil War*, 2 vols. (1900), II.

Simon, W. 'Comprehension in the Age of Charles II', *Church History*, 31 (1962), 442.

Skinner, Q. *The Foundations of Modern Political Thought*, Cambridge (1978), 2 vols.

Sommerville, J. *Politics and Ideology in England 1603–40* (1986).

Sommerville, M. 'Independent Thought 1603–49', unpublished Ph.D thesis, Cambridge University (1981).

Spellman, W. *John Locke and the Problem of Depravity*, Oxford (1988).
Spurr, J. '"Latitudinarianism" and the Restoration Church', *Historical Journal* 31: 1 (1988), 61–82.
The Restoration Church, Yale (1991).
Stephenson, H. 'Thomas Firmin', DPhil. thesis, Oxford University (1949).
Sullivan, R. *John Toland and the Deist Controversy*, Harvard (1982).
Sykes, N. 'The Sermons of Archbishop Tillotson', *Theology* 58 (1955).
From Sheldon to Secker, Cambridge (1959).
Sutch, V. *Gilbert Sheldon*, The Hague (1973).
Tarcov, N. *Locke's Education for Liberty*, Chicago (1984).
Thomas, R. 'Comprehension and Indulgence' in G. Nuttall and O. Chadwick (eds.), *From Uniformity to Unity 1662–1962* (1962), 191–253.
Thompson, E. P. *Customs in Common* (1992).
Thompson, M. 'Hume's Critique of Locke and the Original Contract', *Il Pensiero Politico* 10 (1977), 189–201.
'The Reception of Locke's *Two Treatises of* Government', *Political Studies* 24: 2 (1976), 184–91.
Toon, P. *God's Statesman: The Life and Work of John Owen*, Exeter (1971).
Trevor-Roper, H. R. *George Buchanan and the Ancient Scottish Constitution*, *English Historical Review*, Supplement 3 (1966).
Tuck, R. *Hobbes*, Oxford (1989).
Natural Rights Theories, Cambridge (1979).
Tucker, S. *Enthusiasm* (1972).
Tully, J. *A Discourse on Property*, Cambridge (1980).
'Governing Conduct' in E. Leites (ed.), *Conscience and Casuistry in Early Modern Europe*, Cambridge (1988).
'Locke' in J. Burns and M. A. Goldie (eds.), *The Cambridge History of Political Thought 1450–1700*, Cambridge (1991), 616–52.
Tyacke, N. *Anti-Calvinists – The Rise of English Arminianism c. 1590–1640*, Oxford (1987).
Underdown, D. *Revel, Riot and Rebellion*, Oxford (1985).
Venn, J. A. (ed.) *Alumni Cantabrigienses*, Cambridge (1922).
Waldron, J. 'Locke: Toleration and the Rationality of Persecution' in S. Mendus (ed.), *Justifying Toleration*, Cambridge (1988), 61–86.
The Right to Private Property, Oxford (1988).
Wallace, D. D. *Puritans and Predestination*, Chapel Hill (1982).
'Socinianism, Justification by Faith, and the Sources of John Locke's *Reasonableness of Christianity*', *Journal of the History of Ideas*, 45 (1984), 49–66.
Wallace, J. 'John Dryden and the Conception of an Heroic Society' in P. Zagorin (ed.), *Culture and Society from Puritanism to the Enlightenment*, Berkeley (1980).
Wallace, R. *Antitrinitarian Biography* (1850), 3 vols.
Walzer, M. *The Revolution of the Saints*, Cambridge, Mass. (1965).
Waszek, N. 'Two Concepts of Morality: A Distinction of Adam Smith's Ethics and its Stoic Origins', *Journal of the History of Ideas* 45: 4 (1984), 591–606.
Webb, R. K. 'From Toleration to Religious Liberty' in J. R. Jones (ed.), *Liberty Secured? Britain before and after 1688*, Stanford (1992), 158–98.
Western, J. R. *Monarchy and Revolution* (1972).
Westfall, R. *Never at Rest*, Cambridge (1980).
Whiteman, A. O. (ed.) *The Compton Census of 1676: A Critical Edition* (1986).

Bibliography

Willey, B. *The Eighteenth Century Background* (1967).
Williams, G. H. 'The Confessio Fidei of *Jonas Schlichting*' in L. Szczucki (ed.), *Socinianism*, Warsaw (1983).
The Polish Brethren, Montana (1980), 2 vols.
Wilson, K. 'A Dissident Legacy: Eighteenth Century Popular Politics and the Glorious Revolution' in J. R. Jones (ed.), *Liberty Secured? Britain before and after 1688*, Stanford (1992), 299–334.
Wood, N. *John Locke and Agrarian Capitalism*, Berkeley (1984).
The Politics of Locke's Philosophy, Berkeley (1983).
Woodhouse, A. S. P. *Puritanism and Liberty* (1938).
Woolrych, A. *Commonwealth to Protectorate*, Oxford (1982).
Wootton, D. 'John Locke: Socinian or Natural Law Theorist?' in J. Crimmins (ed.), *Religion, Secularization and Political Thought: Thomas Hobbes to J. S. Mill* (1989), 39–67.
'John Locke and Richard Ashcraft's *Revolutionary Politics*', *Political Studies* 40: 1 (1992), 79–98.
John Locke: Political Writings, Harmondsworth, Middlesex (1993).
'Leveller Democracy and the Puritan Revolution' in J. Burns (ed.), *The Cambridge History of Political Thought, 1450–1750*, Cambridge (1991), 412–42.
Worden, B. *The Rump Parliament*, Cambridge (1972).
'Toleration and the Cromwellian Protectorate' in W. Sheils (ed.), *Persecution and Toleration* (Studies in Church History, vol. 21), Oxford (1984), 199–233.
Wordsworth, C. *Scholae Academicae*, Cambridge (1877).
Wormald, B. H. G. *Clarendon*, Chicago (1967).
Wrightson, K. *English Society* (1982).
'The Social Order of Early Modern England: Three Approaches' in L. Bonfield et al. (eds.), *The World We Have Gained*, Oxford (1986).
Yolton, J. *Locke*, Oxford (1985).
Locke and the Compass of the Understanding, Cambridge (1970).
Locke and French Materialism, Oxford (1991).
John Locke: Problems and Perspectives, Cambridge (1969).
John Locke and the Way of Ideas, Oxford (1957).

INDEX

471

Cambridge Studies in Early Modern British History

Titles in the series

*The Common Peace: Participation and the Criminal Law in Seventeenth-Century England**
CYNTHIA B. HERRUP

Politics, Society and Civil War in Warwickshire, 1620–1660
ANN HUGHES

*London Crowds in the Reign of Charles II: Propaganda and Politics from the Restoration to the Exclusion Crisis**
TIM HARRIS

*Criticism and Compliment: The Politics of Literature in the England of Charles I**
KEVIN SHARPE

Central Government and the Localites: Hampshire, 1649–1689
ANDREW COLEBY

John Skelton and the Politics of the 1520s
GREG WALKER

Algernon Sidney and the English Republic, 1623–1677
JONATHAN SCOTT

Thomas Starkey and the Commonwealth: Humanist Politics and Religion in the Reign of Henry VIII
THOMAS F. MAYER

*The Blind Devotion of the People: Popular Religion and the English Reformation**
ROBERT WHITING

The Cavalier Parliament and the Reconstruction of the Old Regime, 1661–1667
PAUL SEAWARD

The Blessed Revolution: English Politics and the Coming of War, 1621–1624
THOMAS COGSWELL

Charles I and the Road to Personal Rule
L. J. REEVE

George Lawson's 'Politica' and the English Revolution
CONAL CONDREN

Puritans and Roundheads: The Harleys of Brampton Bryan and the Outbreak of the English Civil War
JACQUELINE EALES

An Uncounselled King: Charles I and the Scottish Troubles, 1637–1641
PETER DONALD

*Cheap Print and Popular Piety, 1550–1640**
TESSA WATT

The Pursuit of Stability: Social Relations in Elizabethan London
IAN W. ARCHER